LAW IN PERSPECTIVE

DR MICHAEL HEAD is an associate professor of law at the University of Western Sydney. He has taught law previously at Columbia, LaTrobe, Adelaide and ANU. He is author of *Administrative Law: Context and Critique* and *Evgeny Pashukanis: A Critical Reappraisal*.

DR SCOTT MANN has taught philosophy, psychology and critical social theory in the universities of Sussex, Sydney and New South Wales. He now teaches in the School of Law and in the Social Science degree at the University of Western Sydney. He is author of *Psychoanalysis and Society*; *The Heart of a Heartless World: Religion as Ideology*; and *Economics, Business Ethics and Law*.

LAW

IN PERSPECTIVE

ETHICS, SOCIETY and CRITICAL THINKING

SECOND EDITION

Michael Head and Scott Mann

A UNSW Press book

Published by
University of New South Wales Press Ltd
University of New South Wales
Sydney NSW 2052
AUSTRALIA
www.unswpress.com.au

© Michael Head and Scott Mann 2005, 2009
First published 2005
Reprinted 2007
Second edition 2009

National Library of Australia
Cataloguing-in-Publication entry
Author: Mann, Scott.
Title: Law in perspective: ethics, society and critical thinking/Scott Mann and Michael
Head.
Edition: 2nd ed.
Publisher: Sydney: UNSW Press, 2009.
ISBN: 978 1 921410 80 2 (pbk.)
Notes: Includes index.
Subjects: Sociological jurisprudence.
        Law and ethics.
        Law.
Other Authors/Contributors: Head, Michael, 1952–
Dewey Number: 340.115

Design Josephine Pajor-Markus
Cover istock
Printer Ligare Press

This book is printed on paper using fibre supplied from plantation or sustainably
managed forests.

CONTENTS

SECTION ONE

Law, Logic and Science

SECTION TWO

Law, ethics and social theory

SECTION THREE

LAW AND CONTEMPORARY SOCIAL PROBLEMS

PREFACE

The four years since the first edition have been eventful, not least in the fields covered by the third section of this volume, *Law and Contemporary Social Problems*. Accordingly, the chapters on terrorism and refugees have been substantially updated and reworked and a new chapter added on war.

In the first two sections of the book we have made the order of presentation more coherent, tightened up the material and sought to make it more accessible to new readers.

Once again, for their unique role in inspiring and assisting us to prepare what is becoming a pioneering text, our first thanks go to the students we have taught over the years in Law Foundation at the University of Western Sydney. Their questions, comments and criticisms of our efforts to place law in perspective have been invaluable.

Every year, we set out to prove to our students that our course is the most important they will do in studying law-related subjects. All too often, through no fault of their own, students have been initially unfamiliar with many of the historical and theoretical issues posed. But they have enthusiastically taken up the task of acquainting themselves with the contributions made over centuries by great thinkers in logic, science, ethics, legal theory and social sciences. For us, every year has been a rewarding experience as we have developed and enriched the subject, and we trust that this is reflected in the book.

Thanks must also go to our colleagues at UWS, notably Carolyn Sappideen and Razeen Sappideen, for their support and encouragement. We are indebted to reviewers of the first edition and all our academic colleagues who have made comments and suggestions. We are also grateful to everyone at UNSW Press for their fine work in bringing this volume to fruition.

Michael Head owes a particular debt to his partner, Mary, and children, Tom, Daniel and Kathleen, for their love and patience throughout the long hours and labours devoted to this work. Scott Mann would like to thank Kay, Jocelyn and Claire for lots of moral support.

INTRODUCTION

The principal aim of this book is to encourage critical, responsible and creative thinking about law as a system of ideas and as a social institution. It aims also to encourage exploration of the interrelations between legal methods, ideas and practices and those of other disciplines and institutions with which law continuously interacts.

To this end, the book focuses on a range of powerful critical thinking tools, in the form of ideas and techniques drawn from logic, science, ethics and political and social theory. Effective application of these tools allows for an appreciation of law in its historical, philosophical, economic, political and social context. It provides a foundation for critical assessment of the value and significance of particular legal principles and practices, and for principled proposals for future legal development and reform.

In later chapters, the book demonstrates such tools in action, developing critical analyses of the role of law in relation to a range of contemporary social issues. Problems with existing legal interventions are highlighted and possible alternative approaches are explored.

The book has been designed, first and foremost, as an introductory textbook, following on from a basic introduction to the common law system. But no detailed or specialised knowledge of the legal system is required in order to understand and benefit from it.

At the same time, we believe that this material will be of broad interest, not only to law students but also to legal academics and practitioners, social policy and welfare academics, students and practitioners, professional and business people and all active and concerned citizens.

It is all too easy for starting law students to be overwhelmed by the sheer mass of data they are expected to master in a relatively short time. Some law teachers and practitioners argue that this leaves no time for critical analysis. And some maintain that 'the basics' have to be mastered before meaningful critical analysis is possible.

The fact that some teachers have equated a 'critical and interdisciplinary approach' with woolly ramblings or faddish post-modern deconstructions lacking in all substantive content has appeared to provide further support for a strongly disciplinary and black-letter approach.

But the dangers of such positivism are substantial. To discourage critical thinking from the start is to encourage an uncritical acceptance of what are, in some cases, logically and morally unacceptable ideas, practices and consequences. To discourage interdisciplinarity is to encourage a view of law as a self-subsistent system of ideas and values closed off from all broader social significance, impact and responsibility – and shut off from effective comprehension, participation and critical assessment by all but qualified legal specialists.

In contrast to such a positivist perspective, we believe that it is crucially important for students to master basic tools of critical thinking and analysis at the earliest possible stage of their studies. This helps them to clarify, develop and apply their own values and priorities. Through empowering students, as active participants in the learning process, it makes the whole process a great deal more exciting and enjoyable.

Through challenging and questioning, rather than merely accepting, through exploring the interrelations of law with other disciplines, ideas and social practices, students acquire an altogether deeper, more grounded, more responsible and multidimensional understanding of legal ideas, methods, practices and institutions. They are in a better position to understand, anticipate and evaluate new legal developments and trends in an epoch of far-reaching change on a global scale.

Over recent years, courses on law and its social context have become cornerstones of undergraduate law school degrees. The Pearce Report, an assessment of legal education released in 1987, criticised Australian law schools for neglecting the critical and theoretical dimensions of law required for a flourishing intellectual academic legal culture and an understanding of what role law and lawyers should play in society.[1]

Most university law schools now insist that aspiring lawyers and others seeking law-related careers have at least some exposure to the sorts of questions canvassed in this book. A 1994 review of the impact of the Pearce Report found that most law schools attached 'considerable importance' to the critical examination of legal issues in their social context, while noting that the expression and emphasis of such issues varied.[2]

Almost all students now do their law degree as a joint degree or as a second degree, rather than as a purely professional training course. However, the benefits of this paradigm shift in legal education have been diminished by the tendency of many students, acting under increasing economic pressure, to make their other degree a relatively narrowly focused business or commerce degree. These combinations can mean that students have little exposure to the methodologies and critiques of the social – or natural – sciences.

The need to counteract this tendency is amplified by the apprehension that, through no fault of their own, few students come to law school with any adequate grounding in intellectual history, let alone legal and constitutional history. The study of history in secondary schools has often been neglected in favour of more vocationally oriented subjects. To take just one example, in our several years of experience in teaching Law Foundation, the introductory law, theory and society course at the University of Western Sydney, we have yet to find a new school-leaver student acquainted with the name John Locke. Locke's writings are central to understanding two pivotal features of the legal system: the separation of powers doctrine and the inviolability of private property.

Without an historical and theoretical background, it is difficult to recognise that law is an instrument of social regulation that has been fashioned, and continues to be shaped, by deep-rooted economic and political factors. The existing socio-economic structure of society and its corresponding legal framework can therefore appear to have a permanence, inevitability and even naturalness that belie the historical record of convulsive changes (such as the fall of the Roman Empire, the English, American and French revolutions of the 17th and 18th centuries and the emergence of communism and fascism in the 20th century).

Even within the realm of the existing western legal system, it is impossible to grasp the content and significance of pervasive doctrines such as the separation of powers, natural justice, habeas corpus and the presumption of innocence without some knowledge of the historical battles that produced them.

On one level, this book seeks to fill a yawning gap – the current lack of a text or published set of readings for introductory (and compulsory) Australian university and TAFE courses on law and society (for example, Law Foundation at UWS). Until now, these subjects have rested on internally produced volumes of reproduced materials and have lacked a core or synthesising volume. We hope that the present work will remedy the situation, perhaps augmented by other selected materials.

More broadly, by providing substantial critiques of existing works on law and its relationship to logic, science, social theory and contemporary social issues, we seek to make a contribution to scholarly and civic debate. Our approaches to the subject matter are not purely pedagogical. We believe it is necessary to combine logical, scientific and intellectual rigour with a humane, ethical and progressive approach.

In a number of chapters we advance alternative perspectives that challenge the general adherence to market-driven and nation-state-based viewpoints. Whether or not our readers – they may be students or people working at the legal and social coalfaces – agree with our analyses, we are confident that our research and insights will provoke thought, discussion and debate.

Method of approach

The book is divided into three main sections. The first section, *Law, Logic and Science*, explores the relations between these three disciplines. It shows how a range of key ideas, insights and techniques drawn from logic and the philosophy of science can be of significant practical benefit to law students and legal practitioners, as well as those in other disciplines and other professions. A basic understanding of such principles can help in the organisation and analysis of complex information, in more effective reasoning and argument and particularly in interdisciplinary research and communication.

Chapters 1 and 2 provide a concise introduction to logical reasoning, including the role of conditional statements, processes of deductive and inductive reasoning and argument, explanation and analysis

of extended logical arguments. They explore the central role of logical reasoning in the historical development and day-to-day operation
of the common law.

Chapters 3 and 4 provide a systematic examination of common
errors of reasoning – or fallacies – including formal fallacies, fallacies
of relevance, inductive fallacies and others. They focus particularly
on fallacies most common in legal contexts, including the prosecutors' fallacy, and misinterpretations of DNA evidence. They explore
some of the dire social consequences of fallacious reasoning in law.

Chapters 5, 6 and 7 provide an introduction to general features
of scientific method, focusing particularly on the means for establishing the existence of causal relationships. The reader is introduced to
simple but powerful statistical techniques, of increasing importance
in many different areas, and of particular significance in establishing
causal relationships in populations. Also considered are the precautionary principle and fallacies of hypothesis testing.

The second section of the book, *Law, Ethics and Social Theory*,
explores some of the principal theoretical approaches to the nature
and social role of law. It explains and critically analyses a range of
ideas and models of the social and ethical foundations and consequences of current legal institutions and practices.

Chapters 8 and 9 provide an introduction to ethical ideas and ethical reasoning, including basic principles of meta-ethics and normative
ethics and their application to law. Chapter 8 explores the strengths
and weaknesses of utilitarian theory, and of the ethical theories of
Kant and Ross, as well as considering religiously based ethical ideas.
Other topics covered include ethics and free will, rights and freedoms
and equality and justice. Chapter 9 looks more deeply into the nature
and evolution of ideas of human nature and human rights, and the
role of human rights as a foundation of public international law. It
also explores the relations between rights and justice.

Chapter 10 sketches the two most prominent philosophical theories of law – natural law and legal positivism - putting them in their
historical perspective. It outlines the contradictory evolution of natural
law, noting its classical, revolutionary, reactionary, conservative and
human rights phases, as well as the dominant positivist backlash in
the 19th and 20th centuries. It critically appraises the post-World War
II debates provoked by the crimes of fascism and Stalinism, followed
by the revival of natural law under the rubric of human rights.

Chapter 11 outlines key ideas and institutions of contemporary liberal democracy. Topics covered include separation of powers and voting rights, democracy, money and markets. Social democracy is compared and contrasted with neo-liberalism, and ways are considered for increasing democratic participation in contemporary politics.

Chapter 12, on Marxism and law, outlines the classical Marxist propositions on law and the state and tackles some common misconceptions. The collapse of the Soviet Union and its satellite states has led many to conclude that Marxism is dead and communism is no longer an alternative worth considering. In our view, this confuses Stalinism with communism. In any case, no study of law can ignore the considerable historical influence of Marxism over the past 150 years. Some of the issues canvassed are revolution, participatory democracy, the possibility of law 'withering away' and the rich experiences of the early (pre-Stalinist) years of the Russian Revolution. Basic issues of Marxist economic analysis are also canvassed.

Chapters 13 and 14, on law and economics, consider and question the economic assumptions of neo-liberalism, particularly ideas of the superior efficiency of market relations compared to other systems of organisation of production and distribution, and the need for law to support and/or mimic such market efficiency.

Chapter 15 focuses on questions of distributive justice – of what would constitute a fair and just system of distribution of property. Here again the major focus is on capitalist market relations, with critical consideration of the claim that markets deliver effective equality of reward and that individuals are rewarded in proportion to their valuable social contribution. Topics covered include fair wages, inheritance and unearned income.

The final section of the book, *Law and Contemporary Social Problems*, asks what role law plays in alleviating or exacerbating some modern social conflicts. It also draws attention to the need to consider the social impact of the legal system, and the stark reality of some of its institutions, such as prisons.

Chapter 16 looks into issues of free will and criminal culpability. It focuses on the defence of duress, and considers the class basis of the criminal justice system. Logical and practical problems of the current system are identified and explained. Chapter 17, on crime and punishment, considers the nature, rationales and objectives of punishment in the criminal law. Prison theory and practice are questioned and compared, with a view to possible alternatives.

Among the most contentious and far-reaching issues of the opening years of the 21st century are terrorism, refugees and war. These are the subjects of the final three chapters.

Chapter 18, on refugees and the nation-state, documents the growing global refugee crisis, outlines the curtailing of refugee rights and the need for a new global perspective. Among the topics are the *Tampa* case, the banishing of asylum seekers, indefinite detention and the underlying flaws of the Refugee Convention.

Chapter 19, on terrorism and democratic rights, examines how the so-called war on terrorism has been utilised as a pretext for the dismantling of basic democratic rights. It questions the introduction of sweeping definitions of terrorism, detention without trial, powers to ban political groups and measures to allow the armed forces to be mobilised to put down domestic unrest. The chapter reviews the military call-out legislation of 2000 and 2006 and the anti-terrorism laws of 2002–05 in some detail and examines the case of Mohammed Haneef.

The concluding chapter 20, on just wars and criminal law, probes some of the moral and legal issues behind war and violence and the concept of self-defence, with comparisons to domestic law enforcement and references to international law.

Each chapter includes some questions for discussion, along with some extra readings which complement or extend the discussion in the text.

While this volume has been a collaborative effort, Scott Mann has been primarily responsible for chapters 1–9, 11, 13–17 and 20, and Michael Head for chapters 10, 12, 18 and 19. Chapter 16 was a joint project between Scott Mann and Mouaid Al-Qudah. We welcome any comments or suggestions.

Law, logic and science

Chapter 1

BASIC CONCEPTS
OF LOGICAL REASONING*

Logic

Logic concerns the study and assessment of arguments.[1] Arguments are sequences of statements, one of which is presented as a conclusion, while the others, known as the premises, are presented as providing evidence or support for the conclusion.[2] A statement is a representation that is either true or false. Typically, this will be a declarative sentence, but statements can be made in many different ways, including using pictures and gestures.

When someone presents someone else with a logical argument they are engaging in a series of illocutionary, or communicative, acts – spoken or written.[3] The speaker is saying to the listener that if they accept the truth of particular statements, the premises, then they should accept the truth of another statement, the conclusion. Quite likely they are asserting the truth of the premises, and of the conclusion as implication of the premises, as corresponding to or representing relevant facts of the world or of human convention or agreement[4]. For example:

> P1 If you have broken the law then you will be punished.
>
> P2 You have broken the law.
>
> C Therefore you will be punished.

Often the premises come first in public presentations of arguments. Likewise, conclusions are commonly preceded by *indicator words* such as 'therefore', 'hence', 'so' and 'it follows that'. Premises are identified by indicators such as 'given that', 'inasmuch as', 'for the reason that', 'since' and 'because'. But sometimes there are no indi-cator words. And to decide whether or not they are dealing with a logical argument, the reader or listener must ask themselves such questions as: Is the writer or speaker trying to get me to believe some-thing by giving me reasons for doing so? What are they trying to get me to believe? What reasons are they giving me?

Closely related to the concepts of *argument* and *statement* are those of *inference* and *proposition*. A proposition is the idea or meaning expressed by a statement on a particular occasion of its use. Different statements or sentences can be used to express the same essential meaning, as for example in the case of 'Peter closed the door' and 'The door was closed by Peter'. Inference is the actual process of reasoning by a particular reasoner.[5] In making an inference we move from one or more pieces of information – A, B, C – to another piece of information, D. We see that A, B and C together 'point to' or 'imply' D. Logical implication is a relation between statements or ideas. A implies B where it really is the case that B follows from A. But it is humans or other intelligent agents who infer B from A, who make the psychological step of drawing B from A, or seeing that or how B follows from A.

Many animal species show evidence of elementary logical reason-ing. Our own reasoning abilities are presumably grounded in deep structures of thought and perception that are products of our evolu-tionary and social history. But it is important that we all seek to sharpen up and improve our logical reasoning powers so that our beliefs and actions are solidly based in facts and evidence, rather than in prejudice, illusion and misconception.

Truth

We can think of the propositional content of an illocutionary (commu-nicative) act as 'picturing' a particular possible event, happening or state of affairs. We understand the meaning of the proposition if we understand what it would be for it to be true – how the world would have to be for it to be true. When we engage in the illocutionary act of making a statement, as a claim to truth about the world, the truth or falsity of our claim depends upon how things actually are or were in the world. Our statement is true if it corresponds to the facts of the world.[6]

The truth – or falsity – of an 'empirical claim' does indeed depend upon the facts – of nature or society or history. But complex processes of scientific investigation might be needed to establish such truth, rather than merely checking out the relevant facts. And there are other sorts of ways in which statements can be true or false. It might be necessary to make certain assumptions in order to be able to make sense of our experience of the world. So-called 'axioms' – or basic assumptions – of mathematics or logic are taken to be self-evident truths, or truths in all possible worlds, rather than truths deriving from specific facts of this world. Euclid begins his treatise on geometry with ten such axioms, including the ideas that 'given two points, there is one and only one [straight] line passing through them: given a point and a line, one and only one [straight] line may be drawn that passes through the given point and is parallel to the given line'.[7]

Definitions – as statements which assign meanings to specific words or phrases – are taken to be true by virtue of human convention or agreement, rather than by virtue of corresponding to specific empirical facts. Stipulative definitions create new terms to apply to specific – typically newly observed – phenomena. Lexical definitions report the meanings that words already have in the language. Precising definitions aim to reduce the vagueness of particular terms – for purposes of legislation, for example. Theoretical definitions provide a way of viewing or conceiving entities or processes which gives deeper insight into the nature and explanation of such entities or processes (for example, f = ma).

Definitions can be extensional – identifying members of the class of things a term denotes or refers to; or intensional – indicating the particular qualities or attributes of the entities referred to. And there are a number of different sorts of intensional definitions. A synonymous definition provides a word or expression which picks out the same attributes as the word or expression to be defined; a definition by genus and difference identifies some relatively larger class of entities to which a particular entity belongs and a relatively smaller subclass of the genus. While great white sharks share a range of features in common with other sharks – a range of features which make them sharks rather than other fish – so are they distinguished by specific features of their own, including their size, their preference for eating seals, their warm blood, their mode of attack, etc.[8]

Definitions are clearly of importance in law. Statutes often include lists of definitions of terms referred to in the legislation. And much legal debate and discussion, including the particular interpretation of statutes, revolves around consideration of the meaning given to particular terms. Indeed, all statutes and legal principles can be thought of as extended definitions along the lines of 'certain sorts of empirical facts X count as legal category Y in context Z'. As Sir Edward Coke said:

> When a man of sound memory, and of age of discretion, unlawfully killeth within any country of the realm any reasonable creature in rerum natura under the kings peace, with malice aforethought, either expressed by the party or implied by law, so as the party wounded or hurt, etc, die of the wound or hurt, etc, within a year and a day after the same ... [9]

then this counts as 'murder' and attracts a particular penalty in English law. The law thus provides a definition of murder. But this is more than just a definition, insofar as this definition sustains and supports processes of criminal investigation and prosecution.

Logic in law

It should by now be clear that logic is relevant to law. Prior to their submission to parliament, proposals for particular bills are discussed and debated within government circles. Relevant evidence and arguments are considered. Interested outside bodies are often consulted. Law reform commissions and other bodies pursue research aiming to produce solid arguments in favour of particular changes to legislation and case law.

Proposals for Acts of Parliament have to pass through lower and upper houses and become statutes only through the assent of both houses. Arguments for and against such proposed legislation are constructed, debated, modified and developed throughout the process.

Logical argument is equally relevant to ideas and practices of 'due process' in the day-to-day operation of the common law system. In civil proceedings plaintiffs have to assert their right to legal redress and call for the issue of court orders against defendants. These arguments are set out in documents issued by court officers and are met by counter-arguments (in similar documents) issued by defendants.

In criminal cases, the onus is on the arresting (or summonsing) authority to provide the accused with justification of the charge in question. If the accused is charged with an indictable offence, a preliminary hearing may be held before a magistrate. The Crown produces its evidence in order to establish that it has a plausible ('prima facie') case against the accused. The magistrate is called upon to provide a logical assessment of the strength of the Crown case, to decide whether the evidence is sufficient and the argument strong enough to warrant putting the accused to trial.

In civil cases, the onus is on the plaintiff – or their representative – to persuade the court – judge or jury – through logical argument that the facts they allege are true on a balance of probabilities, and together with relevant legal principles and precedents support and justify the issuing of a particular order of the court, typically requiring that they receive some sort of compensation from the defendant. Meanwhile, the defendant tries to refute such claims with logical arguments of their own. In criminal cases, the prosecution must prove the accused's guilt beyond reasonable doubt. A particularly strong logical argument is, or should be, required to establish such guilt.

The role of magistrate, judge or jury is that of assessing the strength of the competing arguments, for and against defendant or accused. This is sometimes said to be a largely passive role. But it involves active construction of arguments to justify a particular verdict. Jurors will discuss and debate among themselves before arriving at some agreed structure of argument, though they are not required to provide public justification for their final conclusion. Judges are expected to provide written outlines of the processes of logical reasoning leading to and justifying their conclusions. In particular, they are expected to clearly identify established general rules or principles applied, and the justification for such application in the case in question. Starting law students learn to look for the 'ratio decidendi': the 'rule of law expressly or impliedly treated by the judge as a necessary step in reaching his/her conclusion, having regard to the line of reasoning adopted by him/her'.[10]

Such written judgments, and transcripts of court proceedings, can, in turn, become the basis for appeals, involving logical criticisms of the arguments in question.

In all of these cases it would seem to be vitally important that good arguments prevail over bad. This depends on the parties concerned being able to clearly and consistently distinguish good arguments from bad, to identify and criticise the bad and develop and defend good arguments of their own.

If a lawyer sees their role as that of 'winning at all costs' and they have little in the way of valid or strong logical argument with which to do so, or believe that bad argument will be more effective than good in convincing judge or jury, then they could come to believe that they have a responsibility to utilise such bad reasoning. Such logically bad reasoning could be instrumentally or functionally good reasoning from their perspective, or that of their clients.

And if bad argument nonetheless serves to protect the innocent from wrongful punishment or ensure that the guilty get what they deserve, then it might appear difficult to say that it is not morally justified.

But in a reasonably run legal system, we should expect that bad argument, not recognised as such, is more likely to protect the guilty than the innocent. And lawyers' primary duty is supposed to be to the court, rather than to their clients. As Lord Denning MR said in *Rondel v Worsley*:

> The barrister must accept the brief and do all he honourably can on behalf of his client. I say honourably can because his duty is not only to his client. He has a duty to the court which is paramount. It is a mistake to suppose that he is the mouthpiece of his client to say what he wants or his tool to do as he directs. He is none of these things. He owes allegiance to a higher cause. It is the cause of truth and justice. He must not consciously misstate the facts. He must not knowingly conceal the truth. He must not unjustly make a charge of fraud, that is, without evidence to support it. He must produce all the relevant authorities, even those that are against him. He must see that his client discloses, if ordered, the relevant documents, even those that are fatal to his case. He must disregard the most specific instructions of his client if they conflict with his duty to the court.[11]

Particular defenders and prosecutors have achieved great fame and fortune effectively manipulating judges and juries through clever use of fallacious arguments (that is, bad arguments that look good), sometimes freeing the guilty and sending the innocent to punishment. On the one hand, this is testimony to failure of relevant law societies to police the ethical codes of the profession. On the other, it demonstrates the failure of logical education of all parties concerned.

In an adversarial system the opposing counsel should be able to highlight, explain and refute such fallacious argument so as to prevent the judge or jury being taken in by it. And in the absence of such refutation the judges should intervene to disallow misleading argument.

Legislation or judge-made law introduced on the basis of poor justification and bad reasoning might, nonetheless, turn out to be good in its application. It may have good consequences for individuals or for society as a whole. But this would at best largely be a matter of chance. At worst, such unjustified law making would involve disastrous unforseen consequences or conspiracy by the legislators to favour particular groups at the expense of others without appearing to be doing so. Certainly, such unsupported or 'covert' law making has nothing to do with genuine democratic choices of effective means to generally agreed ends.

Logic has undergone continuous development and evolution for more than 2000 years so that today there are well-established principles for differentiating good and bad reasoning of all kinds. Yet contemporary Australian law texts seldom make any reference to such developments. Nor are law students in Australia generally expected or required to have any training in logic prior to graduation.

Where law textbooks do discuss logical reasoning their references are often outdated, confused or just plain wrong. We shall see some examples of this in what follows. Even the best-regarded introductory treatments of logic in law – for example Waller's chapter on 'The Reasoning of Lawyers' in his *Introduction to Law* – are less than entirely clear in some areas.[12]

Lawyers sometimes speak of there being a special kind of logic called 'legal logic', different from logic per se, or from logic as applied in other areas. It is true, as we will see, that there are many different kinds of logical arguments, with different criteria of strength or adequacy. And some sorts of arguments are more common or more significant than others in particular areas of human endeavour like science or maths or law. As we will see, analogical arguments are particularly important in law.

But there are no special, discipline-specific logics with their own unique rules. There is good logical reasoning and there is bad – illogical – reasoning. The criteria for distinguishing good from bad analogical reasoning are, in general terms, the same inside law as outside it. So if legal logic is not 'ordinary' good logic then it is simply bad reasoning masquerading as good. And, unfortunately, as we will see, there is far too much of such bad reasoning in law.

Some rules of evidence – for example the general non-admissibility of prior convictions in a criminal trial – are specifically designed to reduce the likelihood of bad reasoning and fallacy in particular areas. But they are far from foolproof and are offset by what might be called the institutionalisation of bad reasoning and fallacy in other areas of the legal system.

It is all the more important, therefore, that starting law students do have a basic understanding of the nature of logical reasoning to guide them through this logical minefield. And a first crucial step here is to be able to actually distinguish logical arguments from the many other sorts of things people do with language and symbols.

Identifying arguments

Once we recognise that logical arguments involve the offering of reasons or evidence claiming to provide support of particular conclusions, we recognise that not all written or spoken communication involves logical argument. Such communication can involve alleged descriptions of people, things or situations, statements of belief or opinion, explanations or value judgments without any reasons or evidence offered in support of such descriptions, statements, explanations or judgments.

The reader or the listener will frequently respond to such statements and judgments by considering possible evidence relevant to their truth or falsity. But for an argument to be present in the particular passage of discourse itself it must include 'a group of statements that can be analysed into premises and a conclusion, where an inferential claim is made that the conclusion, although controversial, should be accepted because of the evidence offered in the premises'.[13]

On first attempting to identify and analyse logical arguments – in textbooks, newspaper articles or legal judgments – it is easy to be misled by certain sorts of constructions that at first appear to be such logical arguments, but in fact are not. Here we consider two sorts of things frequently misidentified as logical arguments – conditional statements and explanations. We see how, while not themselves being logical arguments, they nonetheless play a central role in such logical argument.[14]

Conditional statements

So-called conditional or hypothetical statements, 'if x then y', create particular problems insofar as they look like pairs of statements connected by indicator words. They do indeed include component statements, that following the 'if' being called the *antecedent*, and that following the 'then', the *consequent*. But they are not logical arguments because there is no claim that either of these statements is true, or that one follows logically from the other.

As we have seen, in a logical argument purportedly true (or probable) statements are presented as evidence or reasons to believe the truth (or probable truth) of another statement. 'In a conditional statement, there is no claim that either the antecedent or the consequent presents evidence … no assertion that either is true. Rather, there is only the assertion that if the antecedent is true, then so is the consequent.'[15]

But although conditional statements are not in themselves arguments, they play a very important part in logical reasoning and argument insofar as they express what are called *necessary and sufficient conditions*. A is said to be a sufficient condition for B whenever the occurrence of A is all that is needed for the occurrence of B, or the truth of A guarantees or necessitates the truth of B. B is said to be a necessary condition for A whenever A cannot occur without the occurrence of B, or A cannot be true unless B is true. In conditional statements antecedents identify sufficient conditions as in:

- If a body is subjected to a net gravitational force (and in the absence of countervailing forces) then it will accelerate.

- If it doesn't accelerate then it hasn't been subjected to a net gravitational force.

The force of gravity is sufficient to accelerate a body, but not necessary; some other force could achieve the same result (for example, an electrical force).

Consequents identify necessary conditions as in:

- If you gained your LLB then you obtained a Pass mark (or higher) in your core law subjects.

Passing the core subjects is a necessary but not a sufficient condition for getting your degree. You also need to have passed your electives, paid your library fines and student fees, completed necessary paper-work and so on.

Another way of expressing a conditional statement is to identify the antecedent (the necessary condition) by the phrase 'only if'.

• You will gain an LLB degree only if ... etc.

And particular conditions can be both necessary and sufficient for other conditions:

• A solution is an acid if and only if litmus paper turns red when dipped in it.

Conditional statements often assert a causal connection between antecedent and consequent:

• If a metal is heated then it expands.

• If the money supply is increased when all productive resources are fully utilised then inflation will result.

The term 'cause' can apply to either necessary or sufficient conditions, and to conditions that are both necessary and sufficient. Most often each of a number of necessary and jointly sufficient conditions are called *causal factors*.

When all other necessary conditions are present, a single necessary factor becomes sufficient to produce a particular result. Where other necessary conditions are relatively constant (the presence of oxygen, the availability of combustible materials), we are prone to identify a new development (the striking of a match), which together with such constant or background conditions is sufficient to bring about a particular effect or change (the fire), as 'the' cause. Where such a 'final' necessary condition involves some sort of human action, or something like human action, we are even more likely to identify it as 'the' cause.

Absences can be necessary conditions also. Just as the presence of oxygen and combustible materials are necessary conditions for fire, so are the absence of heavy rain or fire-retardant materials.

Lawyers are familiar with necessary conditions (and absences) treated as causes via the so-called 'but for' test. As Fleming says:

> The formula postulates that the defendant's fault is the cause of the plaintiff's harm if such harm would not have occurred without [but for] it. Thus a bather would not have drowned if a lifeguard had

been present; the customer would not have fallen down the stairs if there had been a handrail; nor would he have suffered the brain haemorrhage if he had not received a blow on the forehead [the blow was a necessary condition of the haemorrhage]. Conversely, it is not a cause if the harm would have happened just the same, fault or no fault.[16]

But not all conditional statements express causal relationships. Another important role of conditional statements is to formulate *definitions*. For example, operational definitions involve specification of experimental procedures providing necessary and sufficient conditions for application of particular terms. We already encountered such a definition of the term 'acid' above. Here is another such definition:

• One substance is harder than another if and only if it scratches the other when the two are rubbed together.

Statements containing the expression 'if and only if' are called *bi-conditionals*. As Pine points out, such an expression is rare in every-day communication.

> However, such statements are found in logic, science, law, diplomacy, and any field where precise communication is very important. In 1979, the government of Iran told the US government: 'The US hostages will be freed *only if* the United States returns the Shah of Iran and his assets to the Iranian government.' It was important for US leaders to know the difference between this offer and: 'The US hostages will be freed *if and only if* the Shah and his assets are returned.' The Iranian statement implied no guarantee that the hostages would be released, even if the Shah and his assets were returned. On the other hand, the use of 'if and only if' would have been an implied guarantee.[17]

Many basic principles of law can be expressed in terms of a range of necessary conditions, jointly sufficient for a particular legal result – for example, forming a contract or establishing liability in negligence, or establishing various kinds of criminal liability.

• If it is established that (sufficient condition) (a) there is complete concordance between the parties as to the terms of an agreement and (b) the parties intend to be legally bound by their agreement and (c) the promises which constitute the agreement are supported by consideration and (d) various other conditions are fulfilled, then (necessary condition) the courts will enforce the agreement as a contract.

- If a plaintiff is to be able to make a successful claim in negligence then (necessary condition) they must be able to prove that the defendant owed them a duty of care, that the defendant breached that duty (by their act or omission) by failing to exercise the necessary level of care, and that they (the plaintiff) suffered injury or loss (physical or financial harm, usually called 'damage') caused by the defendant's breach of duty, and that the injury or loss was a foreseeable result of the defendant's breach.

- If the plaintiff is to establish that the defendant owed them a duty of care then (necessary condition) they need to establish reasonable foreseeability of (probable) harm to themselves as a consequence of the particular act or omission of the defendant.

- If (sufficient condition) a person dishonestly appropriates property belonging to another with the intention of permanently depriving the other of it then (necessary condition) they have committed an act of theft.

These are definitions (or partial definitions) of particular legal terms (contract, negligence, theft). But they also express particular sorts of causal relations. In this case the agency of causation is the legal system itself, instituting 'appropriate' action if and only if it is established that particular social facts fulfil all of the necessary requirements for particular legal classifications.

Explanations

Another area that can create confusion is that of explanations. Like arguments, explanations involve two distinct components, in this case, the *explanans* and the *explanandum*. The former are the statements that do the explaining, the latter describe the thing to be explained.[18]

Whereas a logical argument provides reasons for believing some otherwise doubtful claim, an explanandum, the thing to be explained, is typically some established fact. And rather than providing a reason for belief, the explanans aims to shed light on the fact in question, typically by reference to the mechanism of its causation.

We noted earlier how causal relationships can be expressed through conditional statements. We can now see how such conditional statements can figure in explanations of particular observations or facts. We might, for example, want to know why railway lines buckled.

Explanans

- If a metal is heated then it expands (all metals expand in proportion to heating).

- These metal railway lines were heated by extreme temperatures (and insufficiently large spaces were left between rails to allow for expansion beyond x centimetres).

Explanandum

- Therefore they expanded (beyond x centimetres and buckled).

Much explanation involves such general principles or 'laws of nature' along with specific conditions of instantiation of such 'laws'. And it is general principles of causation that typically provide the most useful explanations. But there are many different ideas about the appropriate nature and scope of explanation. As Burbidge notes:

> ... many people equate explanation with cause. If you give a cause and show how something was brought about, you have explained it ... But there are other kinds of explanations as well ... Another kind of explanation attempts to fit a number of different facts into a single, coherent picture. In Conan Doyle's classic detective story, 'The Speckled Band', we are told that Sherlock Holmes notices a number of details: the second half of a return ticket in the palm of his visitor's left glove, the left arm of her jacket spattered with fresh mud in no less than seven places. He puts these facts together to reach the explanation that Miss Stoner had started early to catch the train, and had a good drive in a dog cart along heavy roads before reaching the station. He has explained why a set of curious facts are just the way they are.[19]

Although explanations themselves are not arguments, we are certainly arguing when we provide reasons why others should believe that particular explanations are the correct ones. Lawyers in criminal and civil cases are often involved in arguing in favour of particular explanations of crucial facts. And expert witnesses are called upon to justify their (technical) explanations of particular relevant facts.

Another possible source of confusion here is that the same logical machinery involved in explanation, including appeals to natural laws and causal powers, can be used for purposes of prediction. There is always some doubt about what will happen in the future. And prediction is typically a form of argument, seeking to persuade the listener or reader that some specific thing will happen in the future.

This, of course, raises the question of what constitute good reasons for accepting particular explanations rather than others. Burbidge suggests that the fact that a particular explanation combines all the relevant facts into a single, integrated pattern provides good reason for accepting it. But we must be wary not to accept particular explanatory stories merely because they show how relevant facts can be coherently fitted together. As demonstrated in numerous legal proceedings, there will typically be many different stories that can be told around the same pieces of evidence (mud stains, tickets, etc). Lawyers are skilled at weaving isolated facts into suitably coherent and appealing stories.

Here again, it is important to focus our attention on the causal claims involved in the explanation and the means for supporting such claims. We have already considered an elementary understanding of causation in terms of necessary and sufficient conditions, and in chapters 5, 6 and 7 we will consider ways of discovering and establishing such conditions.

A deeper understanding of causation typically centres on identifying and explaining the characteristic powers and tendencies possessed by particular sorts (or 'natural kinds') of things by virtue of their particular structures. We must then also consider the way in which particular powers are released or triggered to bring about particular sorts of results in particular sorts of situations. For example, by virtue of their cellular structure, seeds have the capacity to germinate and grow into plants – but such a power is released only in the presence of (such necessary conditions as) water, appropriate substrate and nutrients, including carbon dioxide and oxygen, appropriate temperature, and sunlight or an appropriate substitute, and the absence of growth-restricting toxins or obstacles.

Metals have a power or propensity to expand when heated because of the movement of free electrons inside the metal behaving in similar fashion to the molecules of gas in a balloon. The attraction between the negatively charged electrons and positive ions in the metal hold the electrons trapped and create the effect of an impermeable but elastic sheath all over the surface of the piece of metal.

The electrons are confined within this surface, with which they are continually colliding and recoiling. There is a resulting pressure on the surface of the metal. The average speed of the electrons increases as the temperature rises, thus causing the pressure to increase and the metal to expand.

Scientific experiment and observation provide logical support for general laws or principles relating to such powers and necessary conditions. The nature of the scientific reasoning involved in establishing such basic principles of causation is considered in some detail in later chapters.

In law, the principal causal agents are humans. We have already referred to the 'but for' test in the law of negligence. Here, a crucial issue is whether the defendant's negligent action (or inaction) really did cause the plaintiff's detriment. A defendant's action is judged to be negligent by reference to objective criteria of 'reasonable behaviour'. So the crucial causal question is typically whether a particular action really did produce a particular result. (Did lack of maintenance cause the gas storage tank to explode? Did the explosion kill the workers?)

In criminal law, a crucial issue is whether the accused's 'guilty mind' – or *mens rea* – has caused a particular criminal action – or *actus reus*. Here the law generally has to consider the subjective state of mind of the individual concerned: did they really intend to perform the action in question and did their intention really cause them to perform that action? Legal issues of 'mind as cause' are considered in detail in chapter 18.

Arguments

Arguments can be divided into two main groups: *deductive* and *inductive* arguments. In claiming to present a deductive argument, the arguer is claiming that if the premises were true, then this would ensure the truth of the conclusion. If the premises are true, the conclusion cannot be false, and follows necessarily. In claiming to present an inductive argument, by contrast, the arguer is claiming that the truth of the premises provides support only for the probable truth of the conclusion.[20]

It is often said that 'deductive reasoning moves from the general to the particular while inductive reasoning goes from the particular to the general'.[21] And it is certainly true – as we will see – that some important forms of deduction do move from the general to the particular and some important forms of induction move in the opposite direction. But this is far from always being the case.

The distinction between inductive and deductive arguments lies in the strength of the argument's inferential claim; in how strongly the conclusion is claimed to follow from the premises. Sometimes people are explicit in identifying the strength of the claims they are making. In this case, they use indicator words: prefacing the conclusion with 'necessarily' to indicate deduction or 'probably' to indicate induction.

Deduction

P1 A square piece of land has sides 100 feet in length.

C   Therefore, necessarily, it has an area of 10 000 square feet.

Induction

P1 In a random sample of 1000 voters, 60% said they would vote Labour.

C   Therefore, probably, around 60% of all voters will vote Labour.

On other occasions, the interpreter has to rely on the character or form of the argument and the actual strength of the inferential link between premises and conclusion to decide the strength of the claim being made. The majority of mathematical arguments, like the one above involving an area, typically involve deductive claims. But in the area of inferential statistics, where claims are made about the properties of populations (parameters) on the basis of the properties of samples (statistics), conclusions always follow with a certain probability, rather than with absolute necessity.

Every argument makes two basic claims: a factual claim, that the premises are true or probably true, and an inferential claim, that the conclusion follows probably or necessarily from the premises. If the premises fail to support the conclusion, it does not matter whether or not the premises are true: the argument is worthless. So logical argument analysis starts with consideration of the inferential claim.[22]

Deduction

As noted above, arguments presented as *deductive arguments* are those in which it is claimed that the conclusion follows necessarily from the premises (that it is impossible for the conclusion to be false if the premises are true). If the premises do in fact support the conclusion in this way, the argument is said to be valid.[23]

Arguments are often said to be valid by virtue of their (most specific)[24] form or structure. As Fisher says:

> The idea behind the notion of logical form is that one can distinguish between the 'structure' of an argument and its subject matter – or between its form and content. The content of an argument is what it is about (animals, atoms or whatever) and its form is expressed by means of those words which occur in reasoning about any subject whatever. If we call these the 'logical' words they include such examples as 'every', 'all', 'some', ... 'no', 'if ... then', 'implies', 'entails', 'follows from', 'because', 'so', 'therefore', 'and', 'but', 'or', 'not', 'is a' and many others. One can easily imagine a collection of arguments about very different subjects ... which exhibit the same form when the words which are peculiar to each subject matter are replaced by neutral, schematic letters, A, B, C, etc and one is left only with logical words.[25]

'An argument is said to be valid if it has a valid logical form, and a logical form is valid if there is no argument of that form which has true premises and a false conclusion.'[26] Certain structures of argument are always valid, whatever particular content we feed into them. Some basic valid forms of argument are as follows:

Modus ponens (MP)

P1 If A, then B. (If you dishonestly appropriated another's property then you are guilty of theft.)

P2 A. (You did.)

C Therefore, B. (So you are.)

Modus tollens (MT)

P1 If A, then B. (If you are to be found guilty then you must have intended to permanently deprive the other of their property.)

P2 Not B. (You did not intend this.)

C Therefore, not A. (So you are not guilty.)

Hypothetical syllogism (HS)

P1 If A, then B. (If you dishonestly appropriated then you are guilty of theft.)

P2   If B, then C. (If guilty of theft then penal servitude will apply.)

C   Therefore, if A then C. (If dishonest appropriation occurred then penal servitude will apply.)

Notice that in each of these cases the first premise is a conditional or hypothetical statement of the kind considered earlier. For this reason they are called conditional or hypothetical arguments. But there are also other sorts of valid arguments:

Disjunctive syllogism (DS)

P1   Either A or B.

P2   Not A.

C   Therefore, B.

A problem here is that we use 'or' to say two different things; at least one or the other and possibly both, or either one or the other but not both. But in either case, this argument form remains valid.

By comparison, here is an example of a clearly invalid argument form:

P1   If A then B. (If you are human then you are warm blooded.)

P2   If C then B. (If you are a duck then you are warm blooded.)

C   Therefore, if A then C. (So if you are human, then you are a duck.)

This conclusion clearly does not necessarily follow from these premises. It is quite possible for the premises to be true and the conclusion false – as in the example given here.[27]

There is no middle ground between validity and invalidity. Either an argument is valid or it is invalid. And there is only an indirect relationship between validity and truth. It is quite possible for an argument to have false premises and still be valid. Furthermore, a valid argument with false premises can have a true conclusion:

P1   All dogs are fish.

P2   All fish are mammals.

C   Therefore all dogs are mammals.

The point is that if all dogs were fish and all fish were mammals then it would necessarily follow that all dogs were mammals.

This highlights the fact that validity is a necessary but not a sufficient condition of a good deductive argument. Not only must the argument be valid, but its premises must be true (or well-supported) also. Where the premises (used to support the conclusion) are true, and the argument is valid, it is called a *sound argument*. Otherwise it is unsound.

If the argument is sound then the validity of its structure transmits the truth of the premises to the conclusion: it too must be true. In the unsound argument above, the falsity of the premises means that the conclusion is unsupported: we are given no good reason to believe it, even though the argument is valid and the conclusion happens to be true.

Induction

In a valid deductive argument, if the premises are true it is impossible for the conclusion to be false. If someone puts forward an argument as deductive, they are committed to the claim that this relationship holds – that the conclusion follows necessarily from the premises. But this same relationship is not claimed to hold true for inductive arguments.

> P1 All swans we have observed are black.
>
> (This might be an observation by Indigenous Australians prior to the arrival of the Europeans.)
>
> C Therefore all swans are black.

Here an inductive inference has been made from the characteristics of swans we have observed (a sample) to the characteristics of all swans, most of which we haven't seen. The reasoners realise that the premise of this argument could be true yet the conclusion turn out to be false. They state the premise as offering strong support for the conclusion; they do not claim that it necessitates the truth of the conclusion.

In a sense, valid deductive arguments say nothing more in the conclusion than is already said in the premises. But the conclusion of an inductive argument always goes beyond the information content of the premises; it always has a greater information content and therefore opens itself to the possibility of being wrong – despite the truth of the premises.

If the premises do in fact provide such strong support for the conclusion, the argument is said to be – inductively – strong. A strong inductive argument is an inductive argument where the truth of the premises implies the probable truth of the conclusion.[28] Unlike validity, inductive strength is a matter of degree. And whereas a valid argument remains valid as we add further premises, strong inductive arguments do not necessarily remain strong with the addition of further information. If I add premises to the swan argument above to the effect that other competent witnesses report seeing numerous white and off-white swans, the earlier argument suddenly becomes much weaker.

An inductive argument that is strong and also has all true (or well-supported) premises is sometimes said to be a *cogent argument*.[29] Sometimes the term 'strong' is used to cover this sort of case also.

Just as there are different forms of deductive arguments, so there are different forms of inductive arguments. Two of the most common are *analogical arguments* and *simple inductive generalisations*. The former depend on analogies or similarities between two or more things or situations. On the basis of such a similarity, a particular 'condition that affects the better known thing or situation is concluded to affect the similar, but lesser known thing or situation.'[30] The latter proceed from knowledge of a selected sample to some claim about the whole group of things of which the sample things are members.[31] Because all (or a percentage) of the sample things have a particular attribute, it is argued that all (or the same percentage) of the members of the group have the same attributes.

Simple arguments from analogy have the following structure:

P1   Entity A has attributes a, b, c, and z.

P2   Entity B has attributes a, b, c.

C   Therefore, entity B probably has attribute z also. [32]

What matters in analogical argument is ensuring that the similarities between the things are appropriate to sustain the inference in question. Most important, the similarities must be relevant in the sense that a, b, c and z are somehow closely bound together in A, such that a, b and c cause z, or z causes a, b and c, or a, b, c and z are all produced by some common cause, or a, b, c and z are necessary structural features of a particular 'natural kind' of thing. So must we take account of the nature and degree of relevant disanalogy, or dissimilarity between the entities concerned.

Burbidge provides a nice example of what happens without such a close connection:

> P1 We can add, subtract, multiply and divide and we can write poetry as well.
>
> P2 Calculators can add, subtract, multiply and divide.
>
> C   So calculators can [probably] write poetry.[33]

As Burbidge says:

> Our ability to write poetry is more closely related to our imagination, our feelings, and our ability to sympathise with other people than to our ability to do arithmetical operations. And calculators are different from us in that they do not have imagination, feelings or sympathy.[34]

Analogical argument is itself very closely related to what we call creativity and imagination, once we include references to dissimilarities as well as similarities:

> P1 A's are like B's in attributes a, b, and c, but different in attributes d, e and f.
>
> P2 B's also have attribute g.
>
> C   So possibly A's have something like attribute g, suitably modified to take account of the differences, d, e and f.

> P1 Mountains are like molehills in shape, location and material content, but radically different in size (that is, much bigger).
>
> P2 Molehills are made by moles.
>
> C   So possibly mountains are made by something like moles, but radically different in size (that is, much bigger).

Through the simple (mechanical) process of juxtaposing similarities and dissimilarities we have generated a strange new idea, seemingly out of nowhere – that of a giant, mountain-generating mole. It is easy to apply this process in other cases, though with no guarantee of useful results.

We have already encountered an example of simple inductive generalisation in the earlier argument about swans. Such simple generalisation becomes increasingly organised and reliable in the science of statistics. The crucial issue here is ensuring that the sample is representative of the population. Samples that are not representative are said to be *biased*. And inferences from biased samples are not at all reliable. Samples are likely to be biased if they are too small and/or not randomly selected.[35]

Lawyers in the modern world need to know a little bit about statistics in order to be able to make sense of scientific research and expert testimony. We will return to this point in later chapters.

As might by now be clear, there is a close relationship between reasoning based on generalisation and reasoning by analogy. While the former moves from the particular to the general by simple induction and then back to the particular by deduction, the latter moves directly from particular to particular. In the former sort of case we infer that all metals expand on heating by generalisation from a sample of different metals and then deduce that some other metal will behave in the same fashion. In the latter case we move from observation of one or more particular metals directly to a prediction about another similar metal.[36]

Probability

As we have seen, good inductive arguments are distinguished by the fact that their premises, if true, render their conclusions probably, rather than definitively, true. The term 'probability' has various different meanings but all concern situations where intrinsic uncertainty, or our lack of 'perfect' or complete information about the situation, means that we do not know with certainty whether a particular statement is true or whether a particular event will happen. And all include the idea of a quantitative measure of the likelihood that a given event will happen or has happened or that a given statement is or will be true, in light of relevant evidence.[37]

More specifically, probabilities are always measured from zero to one, where zero means it's not true or won't happen, one means it definitely is true or will happen, and 0.5 means it's as likely as not that it is true or will happen.[38]

Wherever we have a situation of equal likelihood outcomes, the probability of any particular outcome is the ratio of the total number of outcomes corresponding to that event to the total number of outcomes. For example, the probability of achieving an even number with one dice throw is $\frac{3}{6} = \frac{1}{2}$.[39]

The probability of at least one of two events occurring is the sum of the probabilities of the two events, minus the probability that both events will occur. For example, the chance of getting either a spade or a jack in picking a card from a deck is the probability of getting a spade ($^{13}/_{52}$) plus the probability of getting a jack ($^{4}/_{52}$) minus the probability of getting a jack of spades ($^{1}/_{52}$) – to avoid double counting – = $^{16}/_{52}$.[40]

Dice throws are independent of each other. For independent events, the probability of joint occurrence is equal to the product of the probabilities of the separate events. In other words, we multiply the separate probabilities together to get the probability that both will occur. For example, the probability of two threes in two dice throws is $^{1}/_{6} \times ^{1}/_{6} = ^{1}/_{36}$. [41] (This is called the multiplication law.)

For dependent events, we need to multiply the probability of one event by the conditional probability of the second event, given the first event has occurred. The probability that two marbles picked from an urn containing 10 blue and 10 red marbles will both be red is $^{9}/_{38}$. The probability that the first is red is $^{10}/_{20} = ^{1}/_{2}$. This leaves 10 blue and 9 red, so the probability that the second is red is $^{9}/_{19}$. We have $^{1}/_{2} \times ^{9}/_{19} = ^{9}/_{38}$ probability that both are red.[42]

Probabilities of all events within a given space of possibility must add up to 1.00 or 100%. Where we are considering the probability of any specific event A happening, then P (A) + P (not A) = 1.0 = 100%. And P (not A) = 1.0 – P (A). Considering two independent events, A and B, if one event or the other or both occurred then it's not the case that both complements of the events A and B (that is, not A and not B) happened. So P (A or B) = 1 – P (not A and not B). So the chance of getting at least one head on three throws of a fair coin is 1 – the chance of three tails in a row = 1 – ($^{1}/_{2} \times ^{1}/_{2} \times ^{1}/_{2}$) = $^{7}/_{8}$.[43]

In many cases there is no clear-cut space of equally likely possibilities. This is typically the situation in law. In this sort of case we are concerned with what has been called 'subjective probability' as an individual's subjective intuition or estimate of likelihood. However, such an intuition can be given a numerical value by reference to the odds that a person would accept on a bet or by reference to what has been called an 'equivalence lottery'.[44] And, as we will see, there are actually quite a few sorts of legal situations in which objective probability values can be obtained and do (or should) have a significant bearing on legal consequences.

Standard of proof

In criminal law, the prosecution is supposed to prove their case beyond a reasonable doubt in order to secure a conviction. This does not mean they must prove their case with deductive (mathematical) certainty. Even if the relevant principle of law is clear (if A then B), the facts (A) have still to be established. And this will always involve some form of inductive, and hence probabilistic, argument. Even if the criminal is (apparently) clearly identified on the surveillance video, there is still some doubt: it could be someone wearing a mask designed to look like someone else.

This raises the question of what degree of probability (likelihood) counts as 'beyond a reasonable doubt'. In some scientific applications 95% is regarded as good enough to 'refute the null hypothesis' – equivalent to refuting the presumption of innocence. In others, 99% probability is required.

In civil law, the required standard of proof is considerably weaker. The plaintiff succeeds in establishing the defendant's liability if their case is stronger 'on the balance of probabilities' (or balance 'of the evidence'). This presumably means that even a tiny advantage in terms of probability wins the decision. This has its own problems, especially considering how much could hang on the decision. Fifty-one per cent likelihood hardly seems much better than forty-nine per cent. And what if neither case looks particularly convincing?

Extended arguments

All of the arguments considered so far have been *simple arguments*, which is to say, single sets of premises offered in support of single conclusions. In day-to-day social life, and certainly in legal proceedings, real arguments are often complex or *extended arguments*. Extended arguments are interconnected systems of simple arguments where the conclusions of one or more such arguments become inputs – as premises – into other such simple arguments. Such conclusions, which are also premises, are called *intermediate conclusions* – stages on the way to a *final conclusion*. In this way, complex chains and trees of argument are developed, with different branches or tributaries feeding into or converging upon a single final conclusion.

As we will see, legal procedures typically involve such interconnected chains of argument. Factual statements established as true conclusions of inductive arguments become premises in legal arguments about the correct legal decisions and responses.

It is often difficult to sort out the structure of complex and lengthy extended arguments. It is useful to number all of the relevant statements and then draw diagrams to show the logical relations between the relevant numbers. Premises go at the top, either on their own or linked to other premises (depending on whether they are taken to imply conclusions alone or in combination), with downward pointing arrows to their conclusions. Different sorts of arrows can be used to distinguish deductive from inductive steps.

The situation is further complicated because not all logical arguments – outside the pages of logic textbooks – are presented in fully explicit form. Intended conclusions and/or one or more of the premises might not actually be stated. Such arguments, with components only implicitly suggested, are called *enthymemes*. Typically conclusions are left out because they are presumed to be obvious from the context. Premises are left out because the arguer assumes their audience is already aware of, and accepts, the facts in question.

As a general rule, in reconstructing and assessing arguments, we can apply what has been called a *principle of charity*, giving the arguer the benefit of the doubt in supplying whatever missing statements are needed to make the argument as strong as possible. Consider the following argument:

Argument A

(1) If God can create a stone too heavy for Him to lift, there is something He cannot do; (2) and if He cannot create a stone too heavy for Him to lift, there is something He cannot create. (3) If there is something God cannot do then He is not omnipotent, (4) and if there is something He cannot create He is not omnipotent. (5) Therefore God is not omnipotent.

From statements (1) and (3) it follows that if God can create a stone too heavy for Him to lift, then He is not omnipotent. From statements (2) and (4) it follows that if He cannot create such a stone He is not omnipotent. These are unstated intermediate conclusions. And it therefore follows (as another unstated intermediate conclusion) that if He can or cannot create such a stone He is not omnipotent. An unstated – but obviously true – premise here is that it is true that

He either can or cannot do so– there is no third possibility. So the stated conclusion does indeed follow, by *modus ponens*.

In analysing any complex extended argument it is often helpful to start out looking for the beginning and the end of the argument. What is being assumed to be known or accepted here (where does the argument start)? And what is the final conclusion (where does it end)? Then we look for intermediate conclusions and the evidence offered to support them. Here is a simpler example:

Argument B

(1) When parents become old and destitute, the obligation of caring for them should be imposed on their children. (2) Clearly, children owe a debt to their parents. (3) Their parents brought them into the world and cared for them when they were unable to care for themselves. (4) This debt could be appropriately discharged by having grown children care for their parents.[45]

In this case, we see that the final conclusion is stated first: the arguer is trying to convince their audience that children should be the ones to take responsibility for care of their aged parents. Then we ask: are there any statements presented merely as matters of fact without further justification or reference to other parts of the argument? And we see that there is one such statement, statement (3), to the effect that parents cared for their children when such children couldn't care for themselves. This is therefore a premise, offered as ground or reason for believing statement (2), that such children, therefore, owe a debt to their parents. Statement (2) is therefore an intermediate conclusion on the way to the final conclusion.

Statement (4) is also presented as fact, and is also only a premise, but in this case it makes reference to the debt which has (supposedly) been established to exist in the sub-argument 3 → 2. This tells us that it is 4 and 2 together that are presented as justification for the final conclusion, 1. The overall structure of the argument is this:

$$
\begin{array}{c}
3 \\
\downarrow \\
2 + 4 \\
\downarrow \\
1
\end{array}
$$

Here is another (mathematical) example:

Argument C

(1) The whole number series is infinite. (2) If it weren't infinite then there would be a last or highest number. (3) But by the laws of arithmetic, you can perform the operation of addition on any arbitrarily large number; call it n to obtain $n + 1$. (4) $n + 1$ always exceeds n, (5) so there is no last or highest number (6) and the series of integers [whole numbers] is infinite.[46]

Here, the final conclusion appears at both the beginning and the end. Statements (3) and (4) stand together to support statement (5), and statements (2) and (5) together support the final conclusion, statement (1).

$$\frac{3 + 4}{\downarrow}$$
$$\frac{5 + 2}{\downarrow}$$
$$1$$

Here we see that the second sub-argument, $2 + 5 \rightarrow 1$, has the form of *modus tollens*:

P1   If not I then H.

P2   Not H.

C   So not not I (that is, I).

Here is a slightly more complex example:

Argument D

(1) Mrs Compton is old and frail. And (2) it's unlikely that anyone in her physical condition could have delivered the blows that killed Mr Smith. Moreover, (3) two reasonably reliable witnesses who saw the murderer say that she was not Mrs Compton. And finally, (4) Mrs Compton had no motive to kill Mr Smith and (5) she could hardly have killed him without a motive. Thus (6) she is innocent of Mr Smith's murder.[47]

And a final example:

Argument E

When a lawyer suspects a client of being guilty, is it ethical for the lawyer to conduct a vigorous defense? Yes it is ethical. Look here; being ethical as a lawyer involves playing by the rules of our adversary system. According to our system, every defendant has a right to a fair trial. It follows that even a defendant everyone thinks is guilty has that right. Now, you can't have a fair trial without a vigorous defense. So even if everyone thinks a defendant is guilty, under our system the defendant still has to be given a vigorous defense. This couldn't be done if no ethical lawyer would take the case and defend it vigorously. So you see it can be ethically all right for lawyers to defend vigorously clients whom they suspect of being guilty.[48]

In these two cases readers are encouraged to work out their own structure diagrams.

Discussion topics

1. What is it for a statement to be true or false?
2. What are definitions?
3. What is logical reasoning? Explain arguments, premises and conclusions. What is the role of logical reasoning in law?
4. Discuss some major problems in recognising arguments. Explain conditional statements, explanations and arguments.
5. Explain deduction and induction. Include reference to validity, truth, soundness, inductive strength, modus ponens, analogical and generalisation.
6. What are extended arguments? Include examples. Refer to textbooks, newspaper editorials and leader articles and judgments.
7. What is analogical reasoning? Why is it important?
8. What is probability?

For preliminary consideration of legal reasoning see Lord Keith's judgment in *Hill v Chief Constable of West Yorkshire* (1989) 1 AC 53 (House of Lords) from J. Swanton, B. McDonald, R. Anderson, *Cases on Torts*, Federation Press, Sydney, 1992, pp 135–7. What kinds of argument are involved here? Are they strong?

See also Panelli J's judgment in *Moore v Regents of the University of California* (1990) 793 P 2d 479 (Cal Sup Ct), along with Mosk J's dissent from I. Kennedy and A. Grubb, *Medical Law: Text and Materials*, 2nd edition, Butterworths, London, 1994, pp 1112–24. What are the key arguments? Who is correct?

Chapter 2

LEGAL REASONING

Law reform

All the sorts of arguments considered so far, deductive and inductive, occur in legal contexts. But different sorts of arguments predominate depending upon whether we consider the creation of law or its application.

The traditional view is that laws exist to fulfil particular social functions. So at the law-making stage the central questions are: What issues that we might reasonably expect law to be able to address are most urgently in need of addressing? What sorts of laws are capable of effectively addressing such issues?

Thus, in government departments, in parliaments and in organisations involved in lobbying and law reform, logical arguments are developed to demonstrate how and why particular social issues or problems need to be given priority. And other arguments are developed to demonstrate how particular changes or additions to the body of established law can be expected to effectively address such issues or problems, without creating greater problems of their own. Often, such arguments give rise to counter-arguments and counter-proposals of various kinds.

In broad terms, issues of social needs and priorities are moral issues. Why are some rights or interests in more urgent need of protection than others? Why are some duties in more urgent need of enforcement? Why and how should we aim to achieve the greatest good for the greatest number? Why and how best should we protect those rights and interests are threatened?

Clearly, there are also economic issues involved here. Particular rights and interests cannot be prioritised, protected or enforced without the material wherewithal to do so. There will always be questions of how such reforms are financed and who pays. We will look in greater detail at the nature of such moral and economic issues and arguments in later chapters.

Issues of the practical efficacy of proposed legislation in effectively addressing such social problems are basically scientific issues. They depend upon an understanding of the causes of the problems in question, and of the likely consequences of particular sorts of legal interventions. We will look in greater detail at these sorts of issues and arguments also in later chapters.

A stark example of the interaction and interdependence of ethical and scientific issues in possible law reform is provided by ongoing debate about the continued application of the death penalty for first degree murder in 38 of the 50 US states (along with the military and the US federal jurisdiction). On the one side are straightforwardly factual issues of determining the causal efficacy of capital punishment in reducing homicide rates (through effective deterrence) or increasing these rates (through legitimating violence or other considerations). Here too are factual issues of discriminatory application of capital punishment (through racist and class-ist attitudes on the part of police, lawyers, judges and juries and inadequate access to legal resources on the part of black or poor Americans) and numbers of innocent people wrongfully convicted and executed.[1]

On the other side are ethical issues, with some ethical approaches finding the death penalty intrinsically unacceptable, others finding it intrinsically appropriate and just retribution for first-degree murder, and others again – specifically utilitarians – seeking to assess it in terms of the overall balance of pain and happiness (or social welfare) achieved through retention or abolition.

The significance of factual data for the utilitarian position is immediately apparent. Utilitarians cannot make judgments about the quantitative balance of overall pleasure and pain – or social benefit and detriment – without reliable evidence of the quantitative consequences of capital punishment. They need to know about the extent of effective reduction (or increase) in homicide rates, of inequality of application of the death penalty and miscarriages of justice.

We might not think that factual issues would be so relevant for the other two sorts of ethical perspective. But, here again, factual data can be of crucial significance. Those who find the death penalty intrinsically unacceptable have a great interest in determining the real causes of homicide, so as to be able to take effective action – other than capital punishment – to reduce it. And even those who believe in retribution need to seriously consider issues of radical inequality of application of capital punishment (with a 40-times greater chance of a death penalty being sought against someone convicted of killing a white person than a black person) and of executions of the innocent. It is, after all, quite possible that they put a significant value upon fairness and protection of the innocent as well – possibly a higher value than they put on retribution.

In Australia, the death penalty is – supposedly – no longer an issue. But precisely similar considerations apply to incarceration within the prison system as the most serious criminal penalty, especially given the high levels of homicide and fatal disease in Australia's prisons.

It is all too easy in our current system for serious moral deliberations to be subverted by powerful minorities, concerned only with their own interests in expanded wealth and power. In a capitalist society certain groups – particularly business leaders – are in a position to effectively influence law-making in their own favour – and at the expense of other groups – through their organised political lobbying,[2] their contributions to political parties, their threats and promises in relation to job creation, and their control of the mass media. But in a supposedly open and democratic society such powerful minorities (or their political representatives) will typically try to disguise such pursuit of narrow self-interest with a veneer of moral concern for the 'general will', for the good of the majority, or for the good of oppressed and suffering minorities. We examine these issues further in the second and third sections of the book, dealing with Law, Ethics and Social Theory and Contemporary Social Problems.

Nor do the deliberations of law-makers necessarily centre upon real scientific understanding of the issues in practice. Cynical politicians may push through repressive laws in order to win easy votes, knowing full-well that such laws will not achieve their stated aims and/or will create further serious social problems. Or else the science is covert, with laws enacted to supposedly address matters of general concern, when in fact they have been carefully constructed to serve the narrow interests of powerful minorities.

All this applies first and foremost to legislation, rather than to judge-made law, although courts can be subject to similar economic and political pressures, at least indirectly. In practice, judges make law (cannot help making law) in the course of application of existing law. And it is to such application that we now turn.

Arguments in court

As noted earlier, general legal principles (expressed in statutes or judgments of common law), in the form of conditional statements, play a central role in assigning particular sorts of facts to particular legal concepts or categories, and identifying appropriate (accepted) legal responses to the facts in question when so assigned. The prosecution or the plaintiff is claiming that certain things happened and that those things have a certain legal significance, calling for a particular legal response. The accused or the defendant will be contesting these claims.

Much legal discussion and argument therefore revolves around issues of what actually happened in the circumstances identified by prosecution or plaintiff, and involves inductive-logical arguments supporting or refuting particular factual claims. This will include arguments relating to eyewitness testimony and expert testimony.

If an eyewitness claims to have seen certain things, then evidence that they are a truthful and competent witness, that they have no reason to lie in this case, that they were indeed in a position to witness the events in question and were unlikely to have misunderstood the significance of what they saw, counts in favour of the likelihood that the events in question did indeed take place. This is, of course, inductive reasoning, since we can never be absolutely certain of what really happened.

Experts will typically be called in to testify about the sorts of events likely to have produced particular items of evidence including such material evidence as bloodstains, tracks, and DNA, as well as the nature and causation of injuries or illnesses (including mental illnesses) on the part of accused persons, their victims and plaintiffs. They will typically be called upon to explain the evidence in question, by reference to some mechanism of causation. They might, for example, explain the behaviour of the accused in terms of a particular psychopathology, or the disease symptoms of the plaintiff in terms of exposure to a particular toxin or pathogen.

Here, the mere fact that such witnesses are accredited experts in a relevant area carries some weight in supporting their assertions.

> P1 Most accredited experts can be relied upon most of the time to form true or probable opinions in the areas of their special knowledge and expertise.
>
> P2 This is an accredited expert.
>
> P3 They are testifying in an area where they have special knowledge.
>
> C So, probably, we can assume that what they say is true.

But experts are (or should also be) called upon to justify their explanations by appropriate logical argument. Typically this means justifying the general principles involved in such explanations by reference to the scientific evidence in support of such general principles.

They might refer to clinical, epidemiological or laboratory evidence providing support for their causal claims. This might include experiments in which a certain percentage of rats or dogs subjected to a particular toxin in certain amounts for certain periods developed some form of cancer, and so-called prospective studies of particular human populations exposed to high levels of the toxin in question (and compared with control groups, not so exposed).

There is also legal argument about whether – agreed – facts are really the kinds of facts that figure as necessary (or sufficient) conditions in general principles of law (statutes, by-laws or principles of common law).

The doctrine of stare decisis, to the effect that cases involving the same essential or material facts must be decided in the same way, ensures that analogical argument plays a central role in the common law. For no two cases are exactly alike, and all cases are alike in some way or another. So, even with agreement as to the facts of the present case, there are always questions of which previous cases are relevantly similar to the present case and therefore define the appropriate response in the present case also.

In an adversarial context, each side will typically seek to assimilate the present case to past cases with an outcome that would be favourable to them if applied in the present case. This means competing analogical arguments. Muragason and McNamara describe the circumstances in *R v Easom* [1971] 2 QB 315:

D had taken V's handbag while sitting in a cinema and had examined it to see if there was anything worth stealing. D decided there was nothing worth stealing and replaced the handbag. D was arrested and charged with theft. But the Court of Appeal stated that in every case of theft the appropriation must be accompanied with an intention of permanently depriving the owner of the property; 'conditional appropriation will not suffice'. Lord Edmund-Davies LJ, delivering the judgment of the court, held (at 319), 'if the appropriator has it in mind merely to deprive the owner of such of his property as, on examination, proves worth taking and then, finding that the booty is valueless to the appropriator, leaves it ready to hand to be re-possessed by the owner, the appropriator has not stolen'.[3]

In the later case of *Sharp v McCormick* (1986) VR 869, D was caught by the police in possession of a motor car coil that he admitted having taken from his employer dishonestly and without permission. D claimed that he was intending to fit it to his car. If it worked D intended to keep it. However, if it did not work he planned to return it. He argued that he had only a conditional intention and that the decision in *Easom* governed the case.

> P1   This case is like *Easom* in that there was a merely conditional appropriation of the property of another.
>
> P2   In *Easom* the accused was found not guilty of theft (it was not a case of theft).
>
> C   So the accused should be found not guilty in this case as well (this also is not a case of theft).

The prosecutor, by contrast, sought to assimilate the facts of this case to those of others where the actions in question had been deemed to constitute theft. And this was supported by the decision of the Supreme Court of Victoria. The judges distinguished the case from *Easom* by reference to D's intentions at the time of appropriation, arguing that at that time he was 'clearly treating the coil as his own to dispose of as he saw fit', unlike the accused in Easom, who did not so treat the contents of the handbag. 'He may or may not have' returned the coil if it didn't fit, whereas the accused in *Easom* had returned the contents of the handbag.

In other words, they appealed to (what they claimed to be) a significant disanalogy between the two cases: sufficiently significant to support a guilty verdict in this case. They argued that the 'essence' or true nature of theft is such that *Easom* falls outside of the concept while *Sharp* falls inside. And all of this can be seen as modifying, developing or clarifying the definition of theft; the necessary conditions for determining what particular sort of material facts count as theft.

In many cases, issues revolve around questions of *statutory interpretation*. As Hall notes, 'It is suggested that courts are required to rule upon the meaning of legislation in approximately 50% of all cases.'[4]

One side might argue that the word 'false' in a particular Act dealing with false statements about the importation of goods means any statement that is found not to have been true. The other side might argue that the Act in fact refers only to the making of purposefully untrue statements by the person concerned, not to simple errors of fact.

The fundamental issue here is the ambiguity of the words used in legislation (the precise scope of their reference), and the different possible techniques available to resolve such ambiguity.

> While the starting point for the court is still the ordinary meaning of the words used in legislation, the courts are more willing [than once they were] to consider the outcome that results from a particular interpretation in deciding whether ambiguity exists.[5]

And they increasingly look to the purpose underlying legislation in order to resolve such ambiguity.

Section 15AB of the *Acts Interpretation Act 1901* (Cth) allows consideration of such 'extrinsic' evidence as records of parliamentary debates and speeches, explanatory memoranda, executive documents, reports by parliamentary committees and commissions, and international agreements in order to clarify the purposes underlying the legislation where a provision is ambiguous or obscure, or where the 'ordinary meaning' leads to a result that is manifestly absurd or unreasonable.

Various common law guidelines and presumptions are available for resolving problems of statutory interpretation, but as Hall says, these are not now seen as overriding the purposive approach, based upon clarifying the intentions or purposes of the legislators.

The concluding statement of a prosecutor or counsel for the plaintiff is likely to take the form of a deductive, *modus ponens*-type argument: Given that X and Y are the kinds of facts referred to in a particular principle of law, as necessary and jointly sufficient conditions for a particular legal state of affairs, and for a particular legal response, and given that X and Y have been found to pertain in this case, then it necessarily follows that judge or jury should draw the appropriate legal conclusion and take the appropriate action.

> P1   If A and B (particular types of fact are found to pertain), then C (a certain type of legal situation is established to pertain) and D (certain types of legal response must follow).
>
> P2   A and B (the sorts of facts in question have been established to pertain in this case).
>
> C   Therefore C and D (the relevant legal response must follow).

The first premise may be true as a matter of law, and the argument might be valid, but the crucial question is whether it is sound: in other words, whether the second premise is also true (or well supported). This is where the jury is called upon to make a judgment of fact.

The concluding statement of counsel for the accused or the defendant is likely to take the form of a deductive, *modus tollens*-type argument: Given that facts of type X are necessary conditions for guilt or liability in this sort of case, and that it has not been established – beyond reasonable doubt or on the balance of probabilities – that a type X fact is involved in this case, then it necessarily follows that judge and jury should reject the claim of the other side and dismiss their case.

> P1   If C and D (if particular legal consequences are to follow), then A (a particular type of fact needs to be proved to pertain).
>
> P2   Not A (this type of fact has not been proved to pertain in this case).
>
> C   Therefore (not C and D).

Judgments

Finally, there are written judgments delivered by presiding judges. And it is here, particularly in appeals to higher courts, that we most clearly see the judges in the process of making law, through inductive generalisation and analogy.

Such judgments typically start with identification of what are taken to be the relevant facts, followed by identification of what is taken to be the relevant category of law. The issues in dispute within that area are identified, and relevant cases and/or legislation cited. Some relevant general principles are derived – by inductive generalisation from past cases, or by direct reference to statements of such common law principles in previous cases or to legislation. Such general principles are sometimes analysed – and justified – in terms of broadly ethical or social considerations. Qualifications to such general principles are then considered, including issues of 'policy' leading to the formulation – and application – of a more specific rule, dealing with the application of the general principle to the particular sort of case at issue.

A straightforward example of identification and application of an existing rule is provided by *Hirachand Punamchand v Temple* (1911) 2 KB 330. The rule in question does not allow a creditor to sue a debtor for the remainder of a debt if that creditor has agreed to accept a lesser amount from some third party. In this case, moneylenders Hirachand sued Temple, to whom they had lent a sum of money after cashing a cheque from the debtor's father who had stipulated that said cheque was in full settlement of the debt. In the Court of Appeal, Fletcher Moulton LJ argued as follows:

> If a third person steps in and gives a consideration for the discharge of the debtor, it does not matter whether he does it in meal or in malt, or what proportion the amount given bears to the amount of the debt. Here the money was paid by a third person, and I have no doubt that upon the acceptance of the money by the plaintiffs with full knowledge of the terms on which it was offered, the debt was absolutely extinguished (at 340).[6]

It is easy to see the basic *modus ponens* form of argument employed here:

P1 If a third party offers some amount in full discharge of a debt and the creditor accepts this amount then the debt is absolutely extinguished.

P2 In this case both of these conditions were fulfilled (in cashing the cheque the creditor 'accepted' the money in question as discharge of the debt).

C   Therefore in this case the debt was absolutely extinguished.

Classic examples of formulation of new principles through inductive generalisation are *Heaven v Pender* (1883) 11 QBD 503 and *Fletcher v Rylands* (1866) LR Exch 265. In the former case, 'the plaintiff, a painter, had been injured when some defective scaffolding, supplied by the defendant to the plaintiff's employer, collapsed'.[7]

Brett MR reasoned that there were many separate classes of cases in which persons owe a duty of care not to injure others. Specifically he mentioned four such classes of cases: 'when two drivers [of carriages] or two ships are approaching one another', the case of a railway company carrying a passenger, and cases 'with regard to the condition in which an owner or occupier leaves his house or property'.[8] From such cases he drew out the following general principle:

> Whenever one person is by circumstances placed in such a position with regard to another that every one of ordinary sense who did think would at once recognise that if he did not use ordinary care and skill in his own conduct with regard to those circumstances he would cause danger of injury to the person or property of another, a duty arises to use ordinary care and skill to avoid such danger.[9]

In the latter case:

> Rylands and his partner had built a water-storage dam, which happened to be over some old, filled mine workings. Water from the dam broke through the old shafts and flowed through Fletcher's mine, still lower down. Blackburn J on behalf of the whole court reasoned that as there were separate rules imposing strict liability for cattle trespass, the escape of filth from privies, and the escape of noxious gases and smells, there was a general rule that whoever brought onto his or her land something which by its nature was liable to escape and cause damage was strictly liable when it did so. He then applied this rule to the escape of water in this case.[10]

The decision in *Fletcher v Rylands* was confirmed on appeal by the House of Lords, but Brett MR's argument was rejected by the other trial judges who saw his general principle as in conflict with an already established principle that attributed a duty of care to a seller of a good only to the extent that such a duty had been established through a contract of sale with the purchaser of the good in question.

Privity of contract provided that someone not a party to a contract could not sue for breach of that contract, even if they had suffered harm through the defective character of the goods in question.

The only exception (following the 1851 decision of *Longmeid v Holliday* 6 Ex 761; 155 ER 752) was articles said to be 'inherently dangerous'. But this situation changed profoundly with Lord Atkin's famous speech in *Donoghue v Stevenson* (1932) AC 562, which defended Brett MR's reasoning as basically correct, once his 'too wide' principle was narrowed down to produce the famous 'neighbour principle' as the 'general conception of relations giving rise to a duty of care, of which the particular cases found in the books are but instances' and the 'common element' upon which all liability in negligence was 'based':

> The rule that you are to love your neighbour becomes in law, you must not injure your neighbour, and the lawyers' question, Who is my neighbour? receives a restricted reply. You must take reasonable care to avoid acts or omissions which you can reasonably foresee would be likely to injure your neighbour. Who, then, in law is my neighbour? The answer seems to be – persons who are so closely and directly affected by my act that I ought reasonably to have them in contemplation as being so affected when I am directing my mind to the acts or omissions which are called in question.[11]

From this general principle, along with the facts of the case, is then derived a more specific rule determining the outcome in this case:

> By Scots and English law alike a manufacturer of products, which he sells in such a form as to show that he intends them to reach the ultimate destination in the form in which they left him with no reasonable possibility of intermediate examination, and with the knowledge that the absence of reasonable care in the preparation or putting up of the products will result in an injury to the consumer's life or property, owes a duty to the consumer to take that reasonable care.[12]

From this point, and along with the facts of the case taken to be established, the decision becomes a straightforward matter of deduction.

It is also important to note, with MacAdam and Pyke, that 'in the cases where judges announce a new principle or a broad rule' including all the cases just considered, 'they characteristically appeal both to a number of precedents and to moral notions or popular thought, as evidence of the existence of the principle'.[13]

In *Fletcher v Rylands*, Blackburn J speaks of his general rule as 'reasonable and just'. In *Heaven v Pender*, Brett MR appeals 'not only to 'the logic of inductive reasoning' but to 'the universally recognised rules of right and wrong'.[14] And in *Donoghue v Stevenson*, Lord Atkin appeals not only to 'logic' but also to 'a general public sentiment of wrongdoing' to 'sound common sense' and to the biblical injunction to 'love your neighbour as yourself' (Leviticus 19; 18). The moral principles themselves are not justified but are rather seen as offering independent support for the new legal principles.

Logic, law and history

There is a long tradition of thought arguing that the common law is grounded in, and logically derived from, a handful of general principles, handed down from the remote past. According to the 'declaratory' doctrine of the common law, judges do not make law, but merely transmit, interpret and apply it. As Blackstone said, they are 'the depositories of the laws, the living oracles, who must decide all cases in doubt'.

Such interpretation and application involves the application of deductive and inductive reasoning. But it does not involve any sort of principled or creative response to changing historical circumstances in the light of personal moral or political commitments.

Yet the extension of established precedent and principle through analogy depends, as we have seen, on principles of relevance that themselves change and develop through time. With changing social and political consciousness, new principles of relevance come to the fore. As we have seen, inductive generalisations like the neighbour principle always go beyond specific cases – and groups of cases; differently selected cases or the same cases can sustain a range of different generalisations.

The historical forces underlying the logical development of the law of negligence, just considered, are complex and cannot be properly explored at this stage. There is general agreement that the increasing pace of the industrial revolution throughout the 19th century played a central role, increasing the range and frequency of serious accidents involving strangers, with victims (increasingly isolated from traditional social support systems) turning to the legal system for redress. The second half of the century also saw an increasing ideological shift away from the extreme libertarian individualism of the early industrial revolution to more social-liberal thinking, including utilitarian ideas of pursuit of general social welfare as an intrinsic good, legislation dealing with health and safety at work, legalisation of trade union activity, and the extension of the franchise, with universal male suffrage in Britain by 1867.

These changes were arguably bound up with substantial political movements affecting broad layers of the population – Chartism, the growth of trade unionism, socialism. Commentators have also pointed to the influence upon jurisprudential thinking of the rapid pace of scientific advance in the later 19th and early 20th centuries, supposedly achieved through application of inductive generalisation.[15]

All of these processes brought pressure to bear for the application of inductive reasoning to 'a residual category-less number of non-contractual, non-criminal wrongs encompassing the torts of trespass and case' in order to produce 'a comprehensive theory of universal applicability' recognising the rights of individuals to the due care of their fellows over and above the purchase of such care through contractual arrangements.[16]

As we have seen, Brett MR sought to achieve this goal in 1883, but failed to win the support of fellow judges. It is likely that at this stage, in Britain, such a principle was seen as too much of a threat to 'national economic development', threatening the profits of industrial entrepreneurs through actions by injured workers and consumers. Indeed, from the mid-1800s the law of negligence seems to have been an effective means through which the legal profession ensured the active subsidisation of industry by 'shifting the costs of entrepreneurial activity from industrialists and on to workers, consumers and bystanders'[17], through such common law doctrines as contributory negligence, voluntary assumption of risk and common employment.

However, in the course of the later 19th century, all of these restrictive principles were significantly relaxed or abolished. And by 1932, the time of *Donoghue v Stevenson*, much more social-liberal ideas were in the ascendant, following further massive extension and consolidation of the power of the industrial middle class, and the Great Depression, indicating the clear need for greater regulation and accountability on the part of industrial capitalists.

We will return to consider some of these issues and ideas in greater depth in later chapters. For present purposes, the important point is that they in no way detract from the importance of logic in the common law, or of students' understanding of logic in understanding the historical development of the common law.

Logic is the means through which legal practitioners respond to the historical forces constantly impinging upon them. And we must be able to follow the threads of such logical reasoning to understand precisely how this is happening, to see where their true priorities lie and whose interests they are really trying to serve. In particular, we must be able to see how bad legal reasoning frequently serves to mask a hidden political and social agenda, a covert system of political and social priorities and reasoning based upon such priorities, beneath the surface of the public justifications and rationalisations.

Discussion topics

1. What is the role of logical reasoning in law reform?
   ...in court proceedings?
   ...in judgments?
2. What is the relationship between logic, law and history?
3. Demonstrate the use of deductive reasoning in application of a statute and/or the use of inductive reasoning in a judgment of case law.

Additional resources

For examples of derivation of a general principle through inductive generalisation, see Brett MR's judgment in *Heaven v Pender* (1883) 11 QBD 503; Lord Atkin's judgment in *Donoghue v Stevenson*; Blackburn J's judgment in *Fletcher v Rylands* (1866) LR 1 Exch 265; Lord Denning's judgment in *Lloyd's Bank v Bundy* (1975) QB 326.

In relation to analogical reasoning, see Goddard LJ's judgment (and Clauson LJ's dissent) in *Haseldine v Daw* (1941) 22 KB 343; for an example of distinguishing a precedent on grounds of relevant disanalogy, see Lord Denning's judgment in *Thornton v Shoe Lane Parking Ltd* (1971) 2 QB 163.

Chapter 3

FORMAL FALLACIES AND FALLACIES OF RELEVANCE

Fallacies

Logic is just as much concerned with bad reasoning as with good. In particular, logicians have identified a range of common errors in reasoning, which go beyond mere falsity of premises. Specifically, they have identified a range of argument forms that have the appearance of being deductively sound or inductively strong (or cogent), when, in fact, they are not. Such arguments, which mislead people into thinking that they are good when they are not, are called *fallacies*.

Fallacies can be the results of simple errors in reasoning. And here it seems that humans are particularly prone to particular sorts of errors, perhaps by virtue of deep structures of their brains, or deep structural features of their social situation.

But fallacies can also be constructed for the express purpose of producing particular results. On the one hand, individuals can construct fallacious arguments (while unaware that they are fallacious) for the purpose of convincing themselves of the truth of appealing (but unsupported) ideas and the falsity of unappealing (but strongly supported) ones.

On the other hand, individuals can quite consciously produce and disseminate fallacies with a view to fooling and manipulating other people seeking to establish in them beliefs that support the interests of the ideas producers or their patrons, but that have no solid basis in fact or moral principle.

Advertisers, political parties and corporate-sponsored 'think tanks' such as 'Consumer Alert', 'The National Wetlands Coalition' and the 'Tobacco Industry Research Council' in the United States and similar organisations in Australia have devoted vast time and resources to such systematic manipulation through construction and propagation of fallacious arguments. As noted earlier, lawyers have all too often been guilty in this regard also.

The richest and most powerful lawyers are rich and powerful because they represent the richest and most powerful organisations and individuals, which, in capitalist society, are mainly major corporations, their managers and leading shareholders (but also include politicians, entertainers and sports stars). Many such lawyers work in the inhouse legal departments of the corporations themselves as employees. Others work in huge law firms specialising in corporate clientele. Vast sums of money are involved here with the largest grossing law firms in the United States producing billions of dollars of revenue each year, and leading corporate lawyers, particularly corporate employees, earning multimillion dollar salaries. Even beginning lawyers hired by big corporate law firms earn far in excess of average wages and gain numerous special benefits.[1]

Such lawyers are involved in vigorous competition among themselves for partnership positions 'where the real influence and money awaits'.[2] And as Nader and Smith argue, 'in this intensely competitive atmosphere, idealism and rigorous adherence to professional ethics can easily take a backseat to simply getting the job done'.[3] They quote Michael Josephson, a lawyer running a California-based ethics institute, to the effect that

> Lawyers are competitors. They tend to look at what they do as a sport. The way law is practised today is to get away with what you can. Why? Because money is the only way to judge ... The big firms are doing the bad things because the big firms have the big cases.[4]

Attorney Steve France, editor of *Bank Lawyer Liability*, notes that business executives

> want lawyers with guts of steel and no morals. Under this theory lawyers are machines – you just point them in the direction you want and away they go. This stick-it-to-the-other-guy approach to law, especially if the other guy is weaker and perceived to have fewer resources, creates an attitude that often condones misbehaviour

and thereby extracts a terrible price, often in the lies of ordinary people made unjustly miserable by the blitzkrieg methods of power lawyers.[5]

Nader and Smith conclude:

> This is cause for alarm. Unless tempered by adherence to the higher calling of professional honour and restraint, unquestioning client loyalty can cause profoundly adverse consequences. The lawyer devolves into the proverbial hired gun, where, as in the old Westerns, an ethic of might makes right prevails. Reputations are made, not by doing right, not by avoiding wrongdoing, not by wise counsel, but by winning. The system descends into legal Darwinism, as natural selection increasingly favours those clients with the most money to spend on lawyers willing to do whatever it takes to please the patron.[6]

For present purposes, the crucial point is that such 'guns for hire' are unlikely to feel any compunction in setting out to mislead and manipulate judge and jury through active use of fallacious argument. As suggested earlier, judges intent upon realising particular political agendas, without acknowledging that this is what they are doing, can also utilise fallacious reasoning to mask their actions. They can offer logical justifications that are really rationalisations for their manipulation of the law in one direction or another.

Fallacies of all kinds can be extremely dangerous, whether individuals fool themselves or allow others to fool them. And it is crucial that individuals sharpen up their abilities to detect and refute fallacies, if they are not to be regularly misled, manipulated and exploited. If law students are genuinely interested in justice, then it is crucial that they are ready and able to identify and unmask the fallacies of less scrupulous practitioners and lawmakers.

Formal fallacies

Formal fallacies can be identified through consideration of the structure of the argument. In particular, people seem to be prone to confuse necessary and sufficient conditions in conditional statements leading to the fallacy of *affirming the consequent*. Here, the truth of the consequent is taken as sufficient for the truth of the antecedent, when it is really only necessary.

> **P1** If it rains, the car will get wet at that time.
>
> **P2** The car is wet now.
>
> **C** Therefore, it is raining now.

The truth of the first two statements might provide some inductive evidence for the truth of the third. But if this is presented as a valid deductive argument, where the conclusion follows necessarily from the premises, as it appears to be, then it is clearly a fallacy. There are lots of other ways the car could have got wet. Rain is sufficient to make the car wet, but not necessary.

A closely related fallacy is that of *denying the antecedent*:

> **P1** If someone drives in the park then they break a rule.
>
> **P2** Andrea didn't drive in the park.
>
> **C** Therefore, Andrea didn't break a rule.

Again, the premises might provide some (very weak) inductive support for the conclusion. But the conclusion certainly does not follow with deductive necessity. Andrea might not have broken the rule about driving in the park. But she has just murdered her employer and has his body in the boot of her car along with boxes of heroin and unlicensed guns. She has broken a number of other rules. It is sufficient to drive in the park to break a rule. But it is not necessary. There are lots of other ways to break rules.[7]

There is a well-known psychological test in which subjects are presented with four cards, one displaying a vowel, one a consonant, one an even number and one an odd number (for example, A R 2 7). Subjects are told that each card has a letter on one side and a number on the other. They are asked which cards they need to turn over to test the hypothesis that if a card has a vowel on one side then it has an even number on the other. Most subjects turn over the vowel card and the even number card. Very few turn over the odd number card. These results are commonly taken to show a 'confirmation bias': that is, a tendency to look for confirming rather than refuting evidence. If the vowel card does have an even number on the other side, the hypothesis is confirmed, similarly if the even number has a vowel on the other side.

Certainly, these results suggest a general failure to grasp the relations of necessary and sufficient conditions underlying the deductive

arguments of *modus ponens* and *modus tollens*. To see this we identify vowel = p, consonant = not p, even number = q, and odd number
= not q. As we know, the hypothetical statement 'if p then q' says that
p is sufficient for q, q is necessary for p. As we also know, 'if p then
q' is quite a different statement from 'if q then p'. Finding a vowel
behind the even number does provide some inductive support for 'if p
then q', but finding a non-vowel does not refute the hypothesis.

If it were costly to turn over the cards we should probably ignore
the even number card. On the other hand, because q is necessary for
p in 'if p then q', then 'if p then q' is logically equivalent to 'if not
q then not p'. So we should turn over the odd number (not q). If we
find a vowel behind it we have refuted the hypothesis. Similarly, we
should turn over the vowel card, not primarily because of the opportunity of providing some inductive support for the hypothesis, but
rather because of the possibility of definitive refutation – if there is
an odd number on the other side.

Fallacies of relevance

Informal fallacies are those that can be detected only through analysis of the content of the argument. There are many sorts of informal
fallacies, which can be classified in different ways. Some particularly
important types have been called fallacies of relevance, weak induction, presumption, ambiguity, and grammatical analogy. But such
categories cannot be rigidly demarcated and inevitably overlap at
various points.

Fallacies of relevance substitute psychologically or emotionally
appealing connections between premises and conclusions for logically relevant connections, so that the conclusion can seem to follow
when really it does not.

Appeals to force suggest that listeners should accept certain conclusions to avoid some harm that will come to them if they do not.
Appeals to pity aim to get listeners to accept particular conclusions
out of pity for some individual or group. *Appeals to the people* (or
ad populum arguments) play upon an individual's need to be loved,
esteemed, admired and accepted by others.[8]

We might imagine all of these fallacies intruding into protracted
jury deliberations, particularly where one juror holds out in face of
unanimity among the rest.

> P1 You want to get out of here before the weekend and see your family/
> you want to be appreciated and approved by the rest of us jurors
> and all right thinking people/you want to be kind to the family of the
> victim.
>
> P2 You can do these things by agreeing with the rest of us that the
> accused is guilty.
>
> C Therefore you should agree that they are guilty.

The *straw man fallacy* is committed when the arguer distorts an opponent's argument for the purpose of more easily attacking it, refutes
the distorted argument, and then concludes that the opponent's original argument has been refuted.[9] This sort of fallacy is particularly
common in political debate, and particularly in relation to proposals for reform of current institutions and practices. Defenders of the
status quo are typically reluctant to seriously engage with any such
proposals and tend, instead, to fall back upon the creation of straw
men. For example, a critic of 'anti-terrorism' legislation might be
accused of supporting terrorism.

The adversarial format of the common law also provides strong
temptations to misrepresent an opponent's argument in such a way
as to make it easier to attack it. We are all familiar with such a process in a legal context from numerous fictional portrayals of lawyers
'summing up' their cases, even if we have no experience of real court
cases. Judges and juries have to be on their logical toes to recognise
that this is, indeed, happening.

Ad hominem arguments direct attention to the (alleged) bad character of a person involved in presenting their own logical argument,
and away from the real structure and content of that person's argument. The arguer themselves is criticised or denigrated, with the aim
of getting some third party to see the limitations of the arguer as
limitations of their argument.

> P1 Smith says heroin should be legalised.
>
> P2 Smith is a communist/drug addict/prostitute.
>
> C Therefore her argument is no good and we should reject it.

This fallacy also is common in political debate, particularly in relation to radical critique.

> P1 Karl Marx lived off the profits of Frederick Engels' cotton mills.

P2 He failed to acknowledge paternity of an illegitimate son.

C Therefore we cannot take seriously any of his critical ideas about capitalist society.

In a criminal legal context we can see how jurors might be deflected from serious consideration of the facts of the current case by evidence of the previous 'bad character' of the accused, particularly any record of previous criminal acts. The courts have taken steps to try to avoid this.

> In the case of *R v Perrier* (No 1) [1991] 1 VR 697, the Supreme Court of Victoria made it clear that normally the prosecution cannot lead evidence of an accused's bad character. It is only if the accused has attempted to establish her or his own good character [and hence put that character at issue] that the evidence of the accused's bad character will be admissible. The court also stressed that it is the conduct of the accused in raising the issue of his or her own character that makes the evidence of bad character admissible.[10]

This 'character shield' is formalised in *Evidence Act 1995* (NSW), ss 110 and 104. Section 104 states:

> Leave must not be given for cross-examination by the prosecutor about any matter that is relevant only because it is relevant to the defendant's credibility unless (a) evidence has been adduced by the defendant that tends to prove that the defendant is, either generally or in a particular respect, a person of good character, or (b) evidence adduced by the defendant has been admitted that tends to prove that a witness called by the prosecutor has a tendency to be untruthful, and that is relevant solely or mainly to the witness's credibility.

It is good that the accused cannot, as a matter of course, be forced to reveal facts about themselves that might prejudice the jury against proper consideration of the facts of the present case. But it is unfortunate if defendants, in attacking the reliability of the prosecution witnesses, thereby open themselves to what may prove to be far more damaging revelations about themselves, which do indeed encourage fallacious reasoning on the part of judge or jury.

The fallacies of *missing the point (ignoratio elenchi)* and *red herring* (distracting the hunting dogs with its smell) are often difficult to clearly distinguish in practice. In the former case, the premises support one conclusion, but the arguer, instead, draws a different one, only vaguely related to the correct one. In the latter, the arguer diverts the attention of the reader or listener by changing the subject to some totally different issue. He or she then finishes by either drawing a conclusion about this different issue or by merely presuming that some conclusion has been established.[11]

Gigerenzer identifies a particularly insidious example of a red herring in the OJ Simpson criminal case. As he says:

Alan Dershowitz, a renowned Harvard law professor, advised the Simpson defence team. In his best-selling book *Reasonable Doubts: The Criminal Justice System and the OJ Simpson case*, Dershowitz explained the team's success in quashing the prosecution's argument that spousal abuse and battering should not be admissible in a murder trial: 'The reality is that a majority of women who are killed are killed by men with whom they have a relationship, regardless of whether their men previously battered them. Battery, as such, is not a good independent predictor of murder.'

The defence told the court that some studies estimated that as many as 4 million women are battered annually by husbands and boyfriends [in the United States].Yet in 1992, a total of 913 women were killed by their husbands, and 519 ... by their boyfriends ... From these figures Dershowitz calculated that there is less than 1 homicide per 2500 incidents of abuse ... [W]e were convinced from the very beginning that the prosecutors' emphasis on what they called 'domestic violence' was a show of weakness. We knew that we could prove ... that an infinitesimal percentage ... of men who slap or beat their domestic partners go on to murder them.' Dershowitz concluded 'there is never any justification for domestic violence. But neither is there any scientifically accepted evidence that domestic abuse ... is a prelude to murder'.[12]

As Gigerenzer points out, the figure of one homicide per 2500 incidents of abuse is largely irrelevant in determining the likely guilt of OJ Simpson, or any abuser accused of murdering their abused partner. As he says, the relevant percentage is not how many men who slap or beat their domestic partners go on to murder them, [rather] the relevant probability is that of a man murdering his domestic partner given that he battered her and that she was murdered.'[13]

Using figures from the *Uniform Crime Reports for the United States and its Possessions* (1993) Gigerenzer shows that around 40 out of every 45 murdered and battered women are killed by their batterers every year in the United States. 'That is, in only 1 out of 9 cases is the murderer someone other than the batterer.'[14] Far from being irrelevant to the issue of his guilt, as Dershowitz argues, the fact that OJ Simpson battered his wife was profoundly relevant to the question of his guilt in relation to her murder. Gigerenzer concludes:

> This probability [the 8 out of 9] must not be confused with the probability that OJ Simpson is guilty; a jury must take into account much more evidence than battery to convict him beyond a reasonable doubt. But this probability shows that battering is a fairly good predictor of guilt of murder, contrary to Dershowitz's assertions. Evidence of battery is probative not prejudicial.[15]

The prosecutor's fallacy

The best-known example of systematic fallacious reasoning (in the red herring category) in a legal context is that of the *prosecutor's fallacy*. This has become particularly significant with the advent of DNA fingerprinting, and has been responsible for major miscarriages of justice.

> The term seems first to have been used by attorney and social psychologist William Thompson and his student Edward Schumann in relation to a deputy district attorney's argument that if a defendant and perpetrator match on a blood type found in 10% of the population, there is a 10% probability that the defendant would have the blood type if innocent and therefore a 90% probability that they are guilty.[16]

The 10% figure is called a *random match probability*: in other words, the chance that a randomly selected individual will exhibit the property in question. There is no way a probability of guilt can be derived from any such figure. On its own it is indeed a red herring in relation to any attempt to establish likelihood of guilt.

We need, at a minimum, to have also information about the pool of possible perpetrators – about those who could, possibly, have committed the crime. Assuming that anyone in a population of 100 000 people could have done it, then the matching blood types narrow the figure down to the 10% of that number with the blood type in question – 10 000 people. The match indicates a 1-in-10 000 chance of guilt, rather than 90%.

The prosecutor's fallacy confuses the probability of innocence given a match (the figure of interest to judge and jury) with that of a match given innocence (the random match probability). That these are far from being the same thing is shown by examples such as the following: The probability of being a head of state or CEO of a major corporation given that you are a man is virtually zero. The probability that you are a man given that you are a head of state or CEO is virtually 100%.

If you are innocent, the probability that your blood type matches that at the scene of the crime is the random match probability (in this case, 10%). But, as noted earlier, (a rational assessment of) the probability of innocence given a match depends also upon the population of possible perpetrators and upon any other relevant evidence that might be available.

In fact, in all cases where bodily tissues at the scene of the crime are an issue, there are a number of things to consider:

> First, a reported match [in tissue types] may not be a true match because of laboratory errors ... that produce false positives.[17]

So we need to consider the 'error rate' of the laboratory concerned.

> Second, a defendant who provides a true match may not be the source of the trace if the match is co-incidental; even rare tissue types can occur in more than one person, particularly in biological relatives.[18]

> Third, a defendant who is truly the source of the trace may not have been present at the crime scene, if ... someone else deliberately, or unintentionally ... transferred the defendant's biological material to the scene ... [And] finally, a defendant who had been present at the crime scene may not be guilty – they may have left the trace before or after the crime was committed, or been an innocent bystander.[19]

Bayes' theorem and prior probabilities

Another variation of the prosecutor's fallacy, or of the broader category of ignoring prior or unconditional probabilities, is nicely illustrated by reference to a test problem used by psychologists David Kahneman and Amos Tversky:[20]

> A cab was involved in a hit and run accident at night. Two cab companies, the Green and the Blue, operate in the city. The following facts are known:
>
> 85% of the cabs in the city are green and 15% are blue,

A witness identified the cab as blue. The court tested the reliability of the witness under the same circumstances that existed on the night of the accident and concluded that the witness correctly identified each one of the two colours 80% of the time and failed 20% of the time.

What is the probability that the cab involved in the accident was actually blue?[21]

The typical answer, from subjects in all walks of life, including lawyers, was around 80%. People think 'it does not matter what percentage of cabs in the city are blue. What matters is the eyewitness testimony. The eyewitness is right 80% of the time and they say it is blue. So it probably is blue'. The 'prior' or unconditional probability of its being blue is ignored. But it shouldn't be.

To find the correct answer we can employ a mathematical formula called Bayes' theorem to the effect that $Pr(A/B) = Pr(B/A) \times Pr(A)/Pr(B)$. $Pr(A/B)$ is the probability of A given B; the cab is blue given that the witness says it is. This is what the court needs to know. $Pr(B/A)$ is the probability of B given A: the witness says it is blue, given that it is blue. This probability is 80%; if the cab is blue the witness will correctly identify it as blue 80% of the time. This is analogous to the random match probability shown in the earlier prosecutor's fallacy example. And, as in that case, the subjects of the test have confused this figure – on its own irrelevant to issues of guilt and innocence – with the figure of real significance to judge and jury, the probability that the cab really was blue, given the witness says it was.

Bayes' theorem enables us to find the probability it is blue, given the witness says it is (the figure the court should be interested in) by considering the probability of the witness saying it is blue, given that it is blue. But to do so, we need to also consider $Pr(A)$ and $Pr(B)$. $Pr(A)$ is the unconditional or prior probability that the cab is blue, which is 15% (0.15). $Pr(B)$ is the unconditional probability that the witness says it is blue. This is the tricky bit.

> Because the witness is not infallible, they will on some occasions correctly identify a blue cab and on others incorrectly identify a green cab as blue. [And because there are a lot of green cabs they will call quite a few green cabs blue]. Consequently the required unconditional probability is given by the sum of the probabilities of these two events:
>
> Cab is blue and witness correctly identifies it as blue [0.15 x 0.80].
>
> Cab is green and witness incorrectly identifies it as blue [0.85 x 0.20].

Therefore the required unconditional probability of the witness saying the
cab is blue is [0.15 x 0.80] + [0.85 x 0.20] = 0.29.[22]

We now have all that is necessary to apply Bayes' theorem, which
yields: Pr(A/B) = 0.80 x 0.15/0.29 = 0.41 (approximately).

Most people, including lawyers, thought the cab was most probably blue. But in fact, there is less than a 50% chance that it was blue;
it was probably green. This is certainly an artificial example. But it
is not a million miles from the sort of consideration with which real
judges and juries are confronted every day.

A somewhat bizarre finding in the Court of Appeal in the United
Kingdom in 1997 stated that 'introducing Bayes' theorem … into a
criminal trial … plunges the jury into inappropriate and unnecessary
realms of confusion' and Bayes should therefore be excluded from
future criminal proceedings. Nonetheless, informed members of the
legal profession now recognise that DNA evidence, in particular, has
to be understood in terms of Bayes' theorem in order to yield any
genuinely legally significant results.[23]

Although the Court of Appeal was mistaken in arguing that Bayes
should be kept out of the courtroom, it is true that the mathematics remains intimidating to many people. But Gigerenzer has shown
how the same information can be much more accessibly presented in
diagram form in terms of 'natural frequencies'.

If we take the cab case and consider 1000 cabs in the city, 150 of
them are blue (15%) and 850 are green (85%). The witness sees 120
of the blue cabs as blue (80%). Thirty are seen as green (20%). She
sees 680 of the green cabs as green (80%) and 170 as blue (20%).
So the total number seen as blue = (120 + 170) = 290. So Pr(actually
blue/identified as blue) = 120/(120 + 170) = 120/290 = 12/29 =
0.414%.[24]

Discussion topics

1   What is a fallacy? Include reference to formal fallacies and
    fallacies of relevance.
2   What is the prosecutor's fallacy? Include reference to Bayes'
    theorem and forensic DNA testing.
3   Find and explain some examples of fallacious reasoning from
    textbooks, newspapers and judgments.

Additional resources

B. Atchison, 'Criminal Law: DNA Statistics May Be Misleading', *Law Society Journal*, February 2003, p 68.

Chapter 4

WEAK INDUCTION AND PRESUMPTION

In the previous chapter we considered formal fallacies and fallacies of relevance. There is a wider range of informal fallacies. Among the most important are those relating to weak induction. These include weak analogies and hasty inductive generalisations.

Weak analogy

As Hurley says:

> The fallacy of *weak analogy* is committed when the analogy is not strong enough to support the conclusion that is drawn. The basic structure of an argument from analogy is as follows:
>
> P1 Entity A has attributes a, b, c, and z.
>
> P2 Entity B has attributes a, b, c.
>
> C Therefore, entity B probably has attribute z also.[1]

If there is some 'causal or systematic relation' between z and a, b, and c, and this is not 'offset' by strong disanalogy, the argument is strong. But if there is not then it is weak.

It is less than immediately obvious what sorts of connections are likely to be relevant in a legal context. Different sorts of connections seem to be relevant in different legal situations. But it is certainly possible to detect weak analogies in legal reasoning.

It is easy to see how stare decisis might lend itself to weak analogising as a rationalisation for politically motivated decisions that might be difficult to defend as such (claiming relevant similarities with a prior case where the 'desired' result was achieved, where no such relevant similarities actually exist, or where they are more than offset by relevant dissimilarities).

One example is found in *Hill v Chief Constable of West Yorkshire* (1989) AC 53. The case arose out of a series of horrific murders, in Leeds, Bradford, Halifax, Huddersfield, Farsley and Manchester in northern England. Over a five-year period from October 1975 to November 1980, Peter Sutcliffe, the Yorkshire Ripper, killed 13 women in northern England. He bashed their heads with a hammer and mutilated their bodies.

The mother of Sutcliffe's last victim sued the Chief Constable of West Yorkshire for negligence on behalf of her daughter's estate. It was claimed that during the police investigation of the series of crimes a number of mistakes were made such as the failure to compare and evaluate properly information in possession of the police pointing to the perpetrator. It had to be assumed that he would have been arrested before the murder of the plaintiff's daughter if the police had exercised reasonable care and skill.

The case followed two others in which the plaintiff attempted to sue the Chief Constable of West Yorkshire as vicariously liable for the torts of police officers under his direction, under the *Police Act 1964* (UK). In both earlier trials the statement of claim was struck out as 'disclosing no reasonable cause of action'. But the plaintiff pursued the matter in the House of Lords.

In the leading judgment (with which the other judges agreed), Lord Keith focused mainly upon the prior case of *Dorset Yacht Co Ltd v Home Office* (1970) AC 1004, as establishing an appropriate precedent, insofar as it involved 'reasonable foreseeability of likely harm arising from failure to control another man to prevent his doing harm to a third'.[2]

In *Dorset Yacht*, owners of yachts damaged by Borstal escapees under the care of prison officers successfully sued the Home Office for compensation. The Home Office argued that Borstal officers owed a duty only to the Crown, not to the public, with no previous precedents for such Home Office employees or employees of other statutory authorities owing any such duties to the public. But the Appeal Court rejected this argument, referring instead to the neighbour principle to find that such officers did indeed owe a duty of care to certain members of the public under certain circumstances. The neighbour principle should be generally applied, 'unless there were some good reasons to the contrary'.

The court spent some time in considering issues of 'remoteness' in limiting (or clearly defining) the application of the principle in 'this sort of case.' Lord Diplock compared the specific circumstances of *Dorset Yacht*, involving criminal damage by known offenders inflicted upon property very close to their area of confinement in the course of their escape with a hypothetical alternative case. In *Hill*, Lord Keith summarised what he took to be Lord Diplock's position, to the effect that

> no liability would rest upon a prison authority which carelessly allowed the escape of a habitual criminal, for damage which he subsequently caused, not in the course of attempting to make good his getaway to persons at special risk [as with the boat-owners in this case] but in further pursuance of his general criminal career to a person or property of members of the general public.[3]

Lord Keith interpreted this judgment to have established that a specific sort of 'proximity', determined by the 'category of case', was now a necessary condition of liability in negligence. In *Dorset Yacht*, the warders knew of the identity and criminal proclivities of the escapees prior to their escape, they should also have seen that the yachts were at special risk from such escapees, by virtue of their location, and they could have taken speedy action to prevent the damage without radical disruption of their 'normal' responsibilities, by virtue of their close physical proximity to the yachts in question.

The suggestion is that others would be liable in negligence to third party victims only if those others were (similarly) aware of the identity and criminal habits of relevant second parties, and only if the relevant victims could reasonably have been identified (by those others) as at special risk prior to the crimes in question.

This seems reasonable enough – at least at first sight – in relation to prison warders. Once an escaped criminal has passed out of physical proximity to the institutional base of the warders – with no particular 'person' (or property) any longer identifiable as at special risk – such escapees should be taken as having passed beyond such warders' legal responsibility of recapture or protection of potential victims. Warders lack resources and training to go chasing around the country after escaped prisoners or protecting the general public from the criminal actions of such ex-prisoners. Certainly they lack resources to determine the identities of unknown criminals. On the contrary, this would seriously interfere with their primary responsibilities of care in relation to fixed prison sites if they abandoned such sites in favour of hunting down escaped career criminals.

But then Lord Keith proceeded to apply these principles in the *Hill* case. As he said, the police lacked the appropriate relationship of proximity to both killer and victim. They did not know the killer's identity or habits prior to the murder, and they could not reasonably have identified the victim as someone at special risk.

> Sutcliffe was never in the custody of the police force. Miss Hill was one of a vast number of the female general public who might be at risk from his activities but was at no special distinctive risk in relation to them.[4]

Several problems arise here. The whole point of Mrs Hill's argument was, of course, that the facts show that the police should have known the identity of the killer and/or victim prior to the murder, had they done their job properly. But the Law Lords did not consider these facts and therefore entirely 'begged the question' really at issue.

Lord Keith defended his claim of no special risk to Miss Hill simply by saying 'all householders are potential victims of an habitual burglar'.[5] From this we are presumably supposed to infer that all women are potential victims of an habitual woman-killer.

Lord Keith's premise is simply false. Particular burglars are only able, or likely, to target particular households. Greater knowledge of relevant criminological data and the empirical details of particular cases could be expected to significantly narrow the focus of relevant investigation. And the same applies in relation to the much less common crime of serial murder.[6]

Most important, it is not reasonable to apply principles derived from consideration of the responsibilities and practical capacities of prison warders to the police force. There are significant disanalogies between police and prison officers. The very things which it is unreasonable to expect prison warders to do are precisely the things that police are employed – and amply funded – to do, due to a clear division of labour between agencies of criminal law enforcement. Prison warders (supposedly) protect the public through keeping known criminals in jail (perhaps even trying to rehabilitate them); police protect the public by identifying and apprehending previously unknown criminals. And proper investigations (of previous crimes) might, in some cases, at least, be expected to allow for identification and protection of likely future victims. Certainly, we should expect the police to make reasonable efforts in these areas – and hold them responsible where their negligence leads to disastrous results.

It seems, indeed, as if the Law Lords, led by Lord Keith, were determined to radically limit police liability in negligence, and were prepared to use the weakest of arguments – particularly the 'weak analogy' comparing the police with prison officers – to achieve this.

Hasty generalisations and false causes

> Inductive generalisation involves the drawing of a conclusion about all members of a group from evidence that pertains to a selected sample. The fallacy [of hasty generalisation] occurs when there is a reasonable likelihood that the sample is not representative of the group. Such a likelihood may arise if the sample is either too small or not randomly selected.[7]

Hasty generalisations in this sense are very common and form the basis for much stereotyping and prejudice. On the basis of limited experience of particular ethnic or cultural groups (or on the basis of a very biased selection of people or events), some people are ready to make sweeping general statements about the nature of all members of such groups – unsupported by the facts available to them. People see only the crimes committed by particular members of such groups and leap to the conclusion that all members of such groups are criminals, often due to systematic scapegoating by mass media outlets.

Such prejudices can be particularly dangerous when established within agencies of law enforcement, where they can motivate and legitimate persecution and victimisation of particular groups by armed, intimidating and dangerous police officers. And, unfortunately, there is substantial empirical evidence of just such prejudices firmly established amongst such agencies around the world.[8]

We earlier noted Lord Atkin's argument that Brett MR's inductive generalisation in relation to duty of care in negligence was too hasty in this sense. Others, including the dissenters at the time, have seen Lord Atkin's own inductive leap to the neighbour principle as similarly unjustified.

A number of different fallacies involve causation. Hurley identifies the best-known:

> The fallacy of *false cause* occurs whenever the link between premises and conclusion depends upon some imagined causal connection that probably does not exist.[9]

> The fallacy of *slippery slope* is a variety of the false cause fallacy. It occurs when the conclusion of an argument rests upon an alleged chain reaction and there is not sufficient reason to think that the chain reaction will actually take place.[10]

We earlier referred to the institutionalisation of fallacious argument in the common law. It was the slippery slope fallacy, in particular, that we had in mind. This sort of argument crops up again and again, both in relation to law reform and, particularly, in so-called policy arguments by judges in the higher courts.

Proposals for, or practices of, legalisation of active, voluntary euthanasia often provoke comparison with the Nazi Holocaust, in which euthanasia of the mentally and physically damaged ultimately extended into mass genocide. It is suggested that active euthanasia contributes to a disrespect for the value of human life that leads, ultimately, to mass murder. Here, faulty analogy jostles with false cause and slippery slope. More temperate critics argue that even attempts to clearly confine euthanasia and/or assisted suicide to fully informed and voluntary decisions of terminally ill people will inevitably fail, leading to less than fully voluntary or informed termination of those not necessarily terminally ill.

A similar situation exists in relation to the duty of rescue. Unlike continental civil law, the common law recognises no general duty to rescue others in distress, even when this can be accomplished with ease and little threat to the rescuer: that is, where great benefit can be achieved, great harm can be avoided, at little cost. A frequent argument is that once we start down the path of liability for omissions in this area, there will be no turning back, with those who fail to give alms to a beggar held responsible for the beggar's subsequent illness or death, perhaps years later.

One obvious counter-argument in relation to rescue is that the line should be drawn at clear cases of opportunity to rescue others from serious and immediate distress, with no unreasonable risk, cost or inconvenience, with the definition of reasonableness left to prosecutors, judges, juries and legislators, as in other areas of law. Another would refer to the operation of the principle in civil law jurisdictions.

Slippery slopes have also been prominent in the increasingly prevalent policy arguments of presiding judges, pushing the law in particular directions. Cook et al note:

> In judicial decision-making at the appellate level, principle and policy play an increasingly important – some would say a dominant – part, in addition to legal authority or the doctrine of stare decisis.[11]

A large number of so-called policy decisions revolve around what has been called the 'floodgates' argument. Such arguments assert a narrowly circumscribed formulation of a principle seen to underlie a group of previously decided cases and then argue that any broadening of such a principle will inevitably create the grounds for a vast increase in new actions, lacking in real moral foundation and/or threatening to completely overwhelm the legal system itself, and/or leading to other highly socially undesirable consequences (of collapse of civilisation as we know it).

It is true, as MacAdam and Pike point out, that in many milestone torts cases since *Donoghue v Stevenson*, 'the floodgates argument has received pretty short shrift'.[12] But arguments of this form have still been influential in shaping the recent development of law in a number of crucial areas. And as MacAdam and Pike admit, 'the main function of policy arguments in negligence cases is as a factor limiting the breadth of application of the neighbour principle'.[13]

Looking back to the *Hill* case, already considered in relation to faulty analogy, we see such a policy argument aiming to justify the radical restriction of police liability in negligence by reference to a (problematic) slippery slope. Thus, at the end of his judgment, Lord Keith says:

> Potential existence of liability [in negligence] may in many instances be in the general public interest, as tending towards the observance of a higher standard of care in the carrying out of various different types of activities. I do not however consider that this can be said of police activities. The general sense of public duty which motivates police forces is unlikely to be appreciably reinforced by the imposition of such liability so far as concerns their function in the investigation and suppression of crime. From time to time they make mistakes in the exercise of that function, but it is not to be doubted

that they apply their best endeavours to the performance of it. In some instances the imposition of liability may lead to the exercise of that function being carried out in detrimentally defensive frame of mind.[14]

Furthermore, 'preparation of the defence' of such actions would result in a

> significant diversion of police manpower and attention from their most important function; that of the suppression of crime ... Closed investigations would require to be re-opened and re-traversed, not with the object of bringing any criminal to justice but to ascertain whether or not they have been competently conducted.[15]

The problems here are by no means confined to the slippery slope. What is perhaps most striking is the way in which the judge seems to take for granted that he can present sweeping empirical generalisations with absolutely no empirical evidence presented to support them. And this is especially so given the substantial body of data that clearly refutes his assertions, including numerous police royal commissions and similar investigations around the world that consistently show the police to be no more free from corruption and incompetence than other professions.[16]

In answer to the final slippery slope suggestion, that is, that liability in negligence will radically undermine police effectiveness in 'investigation and suppression of crime' through increasing 'defensive' tactics and greater and greater time taken up in 'preparing defences', we can refer to the case of other professions where this has not happened and, more relevantly, to other jurisdictions that have held the police responsible in negligence in similar circumstances (for example, Canada and Germany)[17] without any such consequences.

The 'other side' of the false cause fallacy (identifying a non-cause as a cause) is the fallacy of denying that a real cause actually is a cause or *cause as non-cause*. It is easy to see the importance of this in negligence cases where a great deal can hang upon the issue of causation and the relevant (scientific) evidence can be quite complex.

Thus, the plaintiff might advance scientific evidence to demonstrate the likelihood that their illness or injury (their lung cancer, for example) has been produced by the defendant's product or by-product (cigarettes or asbestos or benzene or diesel fumes), and that the defendant had or should have had knowledge of the likelihood of such an eventuality (relevant evidence was readily available in the public domain prior to the exposure in question) and has therefore been negligent in producing and selling the product in question (with inevitable exposure of workers or consumers).

Counsel for the defendant might reply that the evidence cited by the plaintiff does not actually establish causation at all, but merely demonstrates a 'statistical' relationship, or a correlation between the product and the injury or illness in question. The mere fact that significantly more smokers than non-smokers develop lung cancer proves nothing about causation: perhaps (a very early stage of development of) lung cancer causes smoking, perhaps some third (possibly genetic) factor causes both. This line is all too familiar from decades of arguments about tobacco products.

Correlation is indeed not the same as causation. But correlation can provide (indirect but strong) evidence of causation. If we can precisely map the incidence of an extremely rare cancer to sales of a particular drug 20 years previously, for example, then we have a correlation strongly suggestive of causation.[18]

Evidence of causation can be 'statistical' in the sense that we know only what percentage of cases of particular illnesses are caused by exposure to particular toxins or carcinogens, without knowing which particular cases are so caused. But with use of appropriate control and experimental groups and statistically significant results it can be strong evidence of causation nonetheless.

The law has been slow to come to terms with modern scientific understanding of the nature of causation. This issue is considered in detail in the next two chapters.

Argument from authority

The 'other side' of *ad hominem argument is argument from authority (ad Verecundiam)*. In this case, the argument is uncritically accepted on the basis of the authority of the arguer, without serious consideration of its real, logical strength.

The situation here is complicated by the fact that appropriately qualified authorities generally can be – and sometimes have to be – trusted to have good reasons for considered pronouncements within their area of special expertise. As Fogelin and Sinnot-Armstrong note:

> An authority is a person or institution with a privileged position concerning certain information ... [A]n appeal to experts and authorities is essential if we are to make up our minds on subjects outside our own range of competence.[19]

Thus, the *ad Verecundiam* is sometimes equated only with 'Appeal to Unqualified Authority'. Certainly, we can see the danger in trusting an expert in area A (for example, medicine) to make reliable judgments in a quite different area B (for example, nuclear physics).

Here again, rules of evidence are supposed to guard against this sort of thing. As Dawson J noted (in *Murphy v R* (1989) 167 CLR at 131):

> [E]ven though most juries are not prone to pay undue deference to expert opinion, there is at least a danger that the manner of its presentation may, if it is wrongly admitted, give to it an authority which is not warranted.

Thus, in Australia:

> There must be a correlation between the field of knowledge about which a witness is to testify and that witness' qualifications and experience. A trial judge must ascertain this correlation by identifying the issue about which the witness is to testify and comparing this issue with the witness' qualifications and experience.[20]

But even if we are concerned with judgments within the area of the expert's special skill and knowledge, it is still dangerous for jurors or anyone else to merely 'accept' the truth of such pronouncements without critical consideration of the underlying evidence and argument. If the alleged expert really is an expert in the area concerned they should be able to clearly explain the reasoning involved.
Again, rules of evidence require that

> In order to admit expert opinion, it is necessary for the expert to demonstrate the assumptions, or the facts, upon which his or her opinion is based ...[21] The failure of an expert witness to state the assumptions upon which her or his opinion is based is likely to render the evidence of the expert inadmissible.[22]

Nonetheless, the special position of the expert – or alleged expert[23] – still gives them special opportunity to mislead judge and jury. And it is important not to neglect the forces militating towards such a development in the modern world. In particular, we must remember that many scientists are now employees of big private corporations, or are themselves corporate entrepreneurs, in both cases committed to maximisation of short-term profits, rather than to any idea of the public good.

This does not, of course, necessitate lying and cheating on the part of these employees (in the service of corporate profits) in their research publications or their public statements. But it can mean this in some cases. And we must not underestimate the power of the employment contract or research funding, in a time of widespread unemployment and increasing reduction in public research funding, to even unconsciously influence the behaviour of a scientific expert witness in a court room situation, or out of it.

Fallacies of presumption

In some arguments the premises presume what they purport to prove. As Hurley says:

> *Begging the question* occurs when the arguer uses some form of phraseology that tends to conceal the questionably true character of a key premise. If the reader or listener is deceived into thinking that the key premise is true, he or she will accept the argument as sound, when in fact it may not be.[24]

We have already seen an example of begging the question in the *Hill* case. As noted, Lord Keith simply stated that the police did not know the identity of the killer at the time of the murder of Mrs Hill's daughter. This was then used, by reference to *Dorset Yacht* as precedent, to exempt the police from negligence in relation to that murder. But the point of Mrs Hill's argument was that the facts showed that the police should have known the identity of the killer and/or victim prior to the murder, if they had done their job properly.

There was ample evidence of police negligence in the investigation, with Sutcliffe a serious suspect as early as October 1977. Sutcliffe had been interviewed nine times over three years before his arrest. But the massive backlog of unprocessed actions allowed Sutcliffe's file to be hopelessly outdated and inadequate for police officers intending to interview him. Many times they did not know what had happened in previous interviews, or that any previous interviews had taken place. One policeman later revealed that on four occasions officers mistakenly believed it was the first time Sutcliffe had been questioned.

As Smith points out, Sutcliffe's boots left clear impressions at two crime scenes and were in his garage when he was interviewed. His alibis were given only by close relatives, including his wife.

> He had a previous conviction ... as a result of being found in a woman's garden with a knife and a hammer – the weapons used by the Ripper. His appearance closely ... matched photofit pictures created by two surviving victims. His various cars, which had left tyre prints at the scene of some ... murders, were frequently logged by police in red light districts of Bradford, Leeds and Manchester [where the police expected to find the killer].[25]

Police failed to link the cases of his first three victims who survived with later murders, despite obvious similarities. Having decided they were dealing with a prostitute killer the police excluded genuine Sutcliffe victims and included a murder he didn't commit as a Ripper victim by reference to the 'character and habits' of the women involved, rather than relevant forensic evidence. Apparently the police expected the Ripper to be some kind of obvious monster and 'spent millions of pounds fruitlessly searching for an outsider when the culprit was just an ordinary bloke, a local man who shared their background and attitudes to a remarkable degree'.[26]

Sutcliffe was finally arrested and identified as the killer by chance, by police from a different force, not the West Yorkshire police who were conducting the investigation.

By refusing to allow any of these issues to be considered in court, the Law Lords completely 'begged the question' of police negligence, which was really, or should really have been, the central question at issue.[27]

The closely related fallacy of *complex question*

> is committed when a single question that is really two or more questions is asked and a single answer is then applied to both questions. Every complex question presumes the existence of a certain condition. When the respondent's answer is added to the complex question, an argument emerges that establishes the presumed condition.[28]

In law, complex questions are called *leading questions* (or double-barrelled questions) and rules of evidence exist to prohibit the use of such questions at certain times. Counsel is not permitted to 'lead' her or his own witness by using questions that suggest an answer or that assume unestablished facts in dispute: see, for example, *Evidence Act 1995* (NSW), s 37.[29]

On the other hand, as McNicol and Mortimer acknowledge, 'the witness must ... confine themselves to the questions asked and presumably a well-thought out question will produce an answer favourable to that party's case'.[30] Most important, 'Unlike examination in chief, the general prohibitions on asking leading questions and attacking the witness's credit do not apply in cross examination'.[31]

It is easy to see the dangers here, with witnesses browbeaten and confused into incriminating themselves. Genuinely complex (double-barrelled) questions are objectionable – open to objection by the other side. But if the other side is asleep, judges can assume that they have consented to such questions.

In the past police interrogation has been notorious for use of complex questions. McConville et al set out four kinds of questions frequently encountered in police interrogations, through which 'facts' are created:

1 *Leading questions*. These seek to persuade the suspect to give a particular answer and to foreclose other possible answers. 'You intended to injure him, didn't you?', 'You set fire to the house deliberately, isn't that so?' are typical such questions.

2 *Statement questions*. These are statements which masquerade as questions; the suspect is confronted with a 'statement of fact' which the suspect is defied to contradict or invited to confirm. 'You took the money after displaying a knife and threatening the victim, didn't you?'

3 *Legal-closure questions*. These purport to invite the suspect to provide information but in reality force information into a legally significant category in the hope that the suspect will 'adopt' it. This may involve introducing some matter not previously mentioned or it may reshape what has been said so that it now 'fits' into an appropriate legal category. Thus, for example, where a suspect states that she took goods from a shelf in a shop and was apprehended outside the shop and had not paid but has not admitted that his was an intentionally dishonest act, the interrogation might continue 'So you stole the goods?' apparently re-stating what is already disclosed but in fact by supplying the conclusory concept 'stole', by-passing the need to establish the legal elements of 'intention to permanently deprive' and 'dishonestly' which are the basis of the offence of theft.

4 *Imperfect syllogistic questions*. The method involves persuading the suspect to accept the truth of a disputable or erroneous prop-

osition by inducing the suspect to accept that it logically follows from acceptance of other (unarguable) propositions which have already been agreed. This will occur, for example, where the suspect agrees that an act was done which led to a particular consequence, and is persuaded to accept that guilt follows from these concessions (it often will not, without further findings relating, for example, to the suspects state of mind).[32]

The current requirement for videotaping interviews yielding admissions used in court only overcomes the problems of such complex questions if the court is fully aware of the issues involved here.

False dichotomy is another familiar fallacy of presumption.

The fallacy of false dichotomy is committed when one premise of an argument is an 'either ... or ... ' [that is, disjunctive] statement that presents two alternatives as if they were jointly exhaustive [as if no third alternative were possible]. One of the alternatives is usually preferred by the arguer. When the arguer then proceeds to eliminate the undesirable alternative, the desirable one is left as the conclusion. Such an argument is clearly valid; but since the disjunctive premise is usually false, the argument is almost always unsound.[33]

Let us imagine that a bunch of white police have been caught on video engaged in an unprovoked attack upon an unresisting black motorist. The videotape creates major problems for the police defence counsel in a subsequent criminal trial. But false dichotomy comes to the rescue:

Ladies and gentlemen of the jury, there is one simple question that you must address. Is it true that my clients are really the ruthless and inhuman criminal psychopaths they have been painted to be by the prosecutor, or are they merely ordinary decent people trying to do their best for the public in a difficult and dangerous situation?

There will probably be elements of the straw man here also. The prosecutor probably did not actually paint such a purely negative picture. But the crucial point is to get the jury to accept that these are the only two possibilities. It has to be one or the other. So if they reject the first, as they are likely to do if it is obviously exaggerated, false and unfair, they have to accept the second.

A basically similar argument was presented by defence counsel in the criminal trial following the police beating of Rodney King in Los Angeles. Whether or to what extent it influenced the jury is unclear because of the lack of any requirement for written justifications or explanations of jury verdicts.

Arguably, while it is important to shield juries from external pressures, the inscrutability of jury decisions is a major anomaly in a supposedly rational common law system. If jurors have made some serious error in reasoning then it should be open to challenge and a possible basis for appeal.

Discussion topics

1   What are fallacies of weak analogy? Explain with reference to the *Hill* case.
2   What are fallacies of hasty generalisation, causality and presumption? Include reference to police interrogation.
3   Seek out and analyse inductive fallacies and fallacies of causality and presumption in textbooks, newspapers and judgments.

Additional resources

R. Graycar and J. Morgan, *The Hidden Gender of Law*, Federation Press, Sydney, 2003 (on police negligence cases in different jurisdictions).

M. McConville et al, 'The Case for the Prosecution' (1991), in D. Brown et al, *Criminal Laws*, 2nd edition, Federation Press, Sydney, 1996, pp 204–7.

For interesting parallels between police and advocates' immunity, see *Swinfen v Lord Chelmsford* (1860) 5 H&N 890; *Rondel v Worsley* (1969) 1 AC 191; *Giannarelli v Wraith* (1988) 165 CLR 543: FC 88/047; *Boland v Yates Property Corporation Pty Ltd* (1999) HCA 64 (particularly Callinan J's observations on *Giannarelli*); *Arthur JS Hall & Co v Simons* (2000) UKHL 38 (20 July 2000); *D'Orta-Ekenaike v Victorian Legal Aid* (1997) 2 SLR 729 (comparing the comments of Kirby J with those of Callinan J).

Chapter 5

SCIENCE AND STATISTICS*

Science and law

It is more difficult to provide any sort of simple and concise definition of science parallel to the definition of logic provided in chapter
1. Clearly, this chapter cannot consider all the different disciplines,
ideas, theories and research practices of modern natural and social
sciences. Its aim is the more modest one of focusing upon key elements
of *scientific method*. These include methods of producing and reliably
testing scientific theories (or producing reliable scientific knowledge)
and applying such theories in explaining otherwise inexplicable facts
and observations.

There are problems here too, insofar as many people have argued
that there is no such thing as scientific method, rather a host of different sorts of methods employed by different sciences, with no single
set of ideas or practices common to them all. But we will be focusing upon what are widely argued to be central structural features of
methods employed across a range of different scientific disciplines.
We have, in fact, already taken some significant steps in that direction
in earlier chapters, insofar as *deductive and inductive logical reasoning* processes are integral to all scientific method. The next step is to
consider the precise role of such logical reasoning in scientific experiment, scientific theory testing, and scientific explanation.

Here, in particular, we will consider the formulation, testing and
explanatory application of what have been called *theoretical hypotheses* (such as Newton's theory of gravity and Darwin's theory of

evolution) and *causal hypotheses* (such as the claim that high intensity magnetic fields cause cancer, or free trade agreements increase the
gross domestic product (GDP) of all parties). We will see why a basic
knowledge of *statistics* is necessary to understand causal hypotheses
and why it is increasingly important for lawyers to be able to make
sense of such hypotheses.

We will see that it is not necessary to understand the specific
details of individual theories in order to able to critically assess and
respond to scientific evidence of all kinds by reference to basic ideas
of scientific method and scientific reasoning. And where it is necessary to gain a deeper understanding of such specific details, previous
acquaintance with such basic issues of method and reasoning can be
extremely helpful.

The previous two chapters identified a number of areas where
science impinges upon the theory and practice of law. Four of these
areas will be considered in greater depth in this chapter and subsequent chapters. They are:

1   the influence of ideas of scientific method upon legal methods;
2   problems of scientific evidence in the courtroom;
3   the role of scientific evidence in establishing causation, in civil
     and criminal law;
4   the role of social scientific research in law reform.

Many crucial issues of the relation between science and law are not
covered here, most notably issues of effective control and legal ownership of scientific knowledge and tools of scientific research.

Science and anti-science

Some people say that science, like religion, rests upon certain articles of faith or fundamental (unquestioned) assumptions, to the effect
that the world has a determinate structure that is discoverable by,
and comprehensible to, human beings, using appropriate methods.
The methods that are most effective in this regard are the methods
of science, involving the use of human faculties of perception, intro-
spection, memory and reason, in ways that are, in theory, open to
everyone. In fact, the progress of modern science provides 'rational'
empirical support for such claims, making them more than mere
'assumptions' or articles of faith.

Many people today associate science with a mechanistic, materialistic and atomistic world view, which encourages and sustains the manipulation and destruction of the natural world in pursuit of private profit. They argue for the adoption of more organic, holistic and ecologically responsible perspectives.

But as Theodore Schick and Lewis Vaughn point out, while particular world views are dominant in particular scientific communities at particular times, 'it would be a mistake to identify science with any particular worldview'.[1] For science, or at least the part of science that concerns us here, is nothing more than a 'method of discerning the truth', along with the body of, at least provisionally, established truths produced by application of that method. It is, in fact, the best or only method for discovering the deeper structures or mechanisms that lie behind the world of immediate, day-to-day experience, which generate and shape that world, and reference to which therefore explains such experience.

> Those who believe that we should adopt a more organic and holistic worldview do so on the grounds that it offers a more accurate description of reality than does a mechanistic and atomistic one. That may well be the case, but the only way to find out is to determine whether there is any evidence to that effect, and the best way to make such a determination is to use the scientific method.[2]

It may be the case that this powerful method is currently employed primarily in the service of private profit. Current political-economic arrangements may render some results a source of greater harm than good. But both the method and the results can, and should, be used for the benefit of all people, of society and of the natural world.

Naive inductivism

For a long time scientific method was assumed, by many, to be a simple four-stage process. First of all we observe the world, and accumulate a mass of singular observation statements such as:

> At time A on date B, the planet Venus appeared in position X, Y, in the sky above Sydney.

> This A-centimetre long bar of iron was seen to increase its length by B centimetres when heated from Y to Z degrees Celsius.

Providing certain conditions are satisfied, we then generalise from a finite list of singular observation statements to a *universal hypothesis*. From a list of observation statements referring to the expansion of specific heated metals, for example, we generalise to the universal hypothesis that

All metals expand when heated.

The conditions that must be satisfied for legitimate generalisation include the following:

The number of observation statements forming the basis of a generalisation must be large.

The observations must be repeated under a wide variety of conditions.

No accepted observation statement should conflict with the derived universal law.[3]

We can then deduce specific things that must be true if our hypothesis is true:

This newly discovered metal will expand when heated.

Railway lines will buckle on hot days if inadequate space is left between them.

And we can verify, or refute, the hypothesis by experimental testing of such deduced implications. If it survives such testing it comes to be regarded as a universal 'law' of nature.

Such universal generalisations are valuable resources to the extent that they enable us to make reliable predictions about the future and provide reliable explanations of current observations – the kind of explanations considered in chapter 1. The rail buckled because the temperature exceeded X degrees. Similarly laid tracks will buckle in similar fashion when the temperature exceeds X degrees in the future.

We suggested in chapter 1 that such a model of inductive generalisation probably influenced judicial thinking in the later 19th and earlier 20th centuries. Because it appeared to have been so successful in the natural sciences, it was thought that it should therefore be adapted and applied in law. Hence the search for universal principles underlying specific judgments in particular areas, culminating in the neighbour principle and the *Fletcher v Rylands* principle. Such general principles could then be applied, not in prediction and explanation, but in the simplification and ethical rationalisation of legal reasoning processes, now reduced to a simple matter of deduction (of application of *modus ponens*), rather than complex and uncertain reasoning by analogy. Instead of having to balance lots of difficult similarities and dissimilarities (in analogical reasoning) it now becomes a matter of checking off a list of necessary conditions.

As we will see below, there are good grounds for regarding analogical reasoning, rather than simple inductive generalisation, as a major mechanism of theory construction in science. But we also saw in chapter 1 that inductive generalisation and analogy are closely related. And we should not be too quick to completely reject the significance of inductive generalisation in science, as some have tried to do. Newton's 'discovery' of universal gravitation seems to have involved analogies between a falling apple, a cannon ball and the moon, but so did it involve a sweeping generalisation drawing out essential and by no means obvious features common to falling apples, flying cannon balls, the orbiting moon and a host of other earthly and celestial motions.

Lord Atkin's derivation of the neighbour principle looks more like Newton's derivation of the gravity principle through abstraction of deep structural principle from diverse cases rather than the simplistic 'all metals expand on heating' type of inductive generalisation. He has seen beyond the concrete details of dogs biting neighbours, surgeons chopping off the wrong limbs and manufacturers selling drinks full of snails to abstract structural-ethical features shared by all such disparate fact situations.

Scientific theories

There are still many problems with the simple inductive/deductive model as a paradigm of scientific method, highlighted by philosophers of science since the mid-20th century. It is frequently argued that scientific enquiry typically starts with some sort of question or problem, considering why something occurred (Why did the dinosaurs become extinct?), why some thing has the particular properties it does have (Why do metals expand when heated? Why do the continents fit together like a jigsaw puzzle?), or how particular things are related (for example, mammals and reptiles, electricity and magnetism), rather than engaging in undirected observation. Observations are needed to recognise that such problems exist, but it is the attempt to solve the problem or answer the question that stimulates the production of (explanatory) hypotheses of some kind, along with subsequent testing of such hypotheses.

There are also serious problems with the naive inductivist assumption that theories are straightforwardly verified or refuted by new observations, consistent with, or contradictory to, the theory. As Schick and Vaughn note, 'when new hypotheses are first proposed, there is often a good deal of evidence against them'.[4] This is because both the theory itself and the background of other theory upon which it depends have not yet been adequately developed to address such counter-evidence.

Other serious problems revolve around the simplistic empiricist *epistemology*, or *theory of knowledge*, built into the model, which suggests that scientific knowledge of the world can be gained through purely passive observation and generalisation without the need for any kind of directed and active intervention in theory or in material practice.

As noted in chapter 1, science involves the search for general causal principles, in terms that we can use to explain and predict the world as perceived. We have already briefly considered the nature of causes and causal explanation. But to better understand science and scientific method we need to look at bit more deeply into what is involved.

Both science and everyday observation tell us that the world is made up of relatively enduring and qualitatively distinguishable types of things: gases, liquids and solids; bacteria and fungi; plants and animals; and stars, galaxies and clusters of galaxies. They also tell us that that each different 'natural kind' of thing possesses particular 'causal powers' or capacities or tendencies to exert sorts of force, able to influence other things – as well as themselves – in characteristic ways. And they possess such powers by virtue of particular internal and external structural relations that make them the kind of things they are.

Material bodies exert powers of mutual gravitational attraction (directly proportional to the product of their masses and inversely proportional to the distance between their centres of mass) or powers to respond to the local curvature of space. Once in motion, they move themselves along with a constant velocity in a straight line unless acted upon by an external force, and resist the action of such a force in proportion to their mass. They respond to such an external force by accelerating in proportion to, and in the direction of, that force. Liquids have the power to flow downhill, dissolve various sorts of solid, freeze at low temperatures and turn to gases at higher temperatures. Chemical elements can combine with other elements in particular proportions to create new sorts of substances with different properties from the elements in question. Plants and animals can grow and develop and reproduce. Animals and humans can move, and sense and think. Such powers are released or blocked depending upon the particular configuration of types of things involved. Certain conditions are 'necessary' for release of the powers in question.

Some such intrinsic powers do reveal themselves to the sort of passive observation considered in the simple inductive/deductive model (of scientific method) insofar as they are triggered into action without the need for human intervention to produce directly observable effects. Metal rails expand as a result of heating by the sun and by friction with train wheels, iron turns to rust through interaction with air and water, animals mate and produce offspring. But in many cases, to gain a deeper understanding of the true nature of the powers in question, substantial active intervention by people is required. This is nicely illustrated by the classical physical ideas of gravity and inertia.

Everyday observations tell us that unsupported bodies generally do fall, though not if they are very light or the wind is very strong. But to observe – and measure – the effects of gravity uninfluenced by friction of earth and atmosphere requires the isolation of a gravitational system from other such – predominantly electromagnetic – influences. Such isolation can, initially, be achieved in the imagination, in a 'thought experiment'. And particular 'real world' experiments can help with such mental extrapolations. Galileo achieved this (viz-a-viz gravity) by extrapolation from observations of bodies falling in media of decreasing density and rolling down slopes of increasing inclination. But beyond this point, countervailing forces must be effectively excluded or balanced against each other to approach a 'pure' gravitational interaction, as when a feather is dropped in a vacuum chamber or on the surface of the moon or when we look out into the vacuum of space.

The same is true of inertia. Everyday observation tells us that heavy objects are more difficult to redirect once they get moving at a reasonable pace. But on the earth we never directly perceive the tendency of masses to continue in uniform motion in a straight line so long as no forces act upon them, because forces always do act upon them. Again we can extrapolate from movement over surfaces of decreasing friction. And again, countervailing forces must be excluded or balanced to get close actually seeing inertial motion. An orbiting spacecraft is still affected by the gravitational force of the earth. But in the frame of reference of objects within such a craft, this gravitational force is counterbalanced by an equal and opposite centrifugal force, leaving no net force upon such objects and rendering them weightless. So they do, indeed, exhibit uniform inertial motion.

In many cases we discover the causal powers of things only by creating special 'artificial' situations that trigger or release powers which normally lie dormant by virtue of the ubiquitous presence of countervailing or blocking forces in our immediate environment. We release such powers by blocking off the blocking forces. The technologies of internal combustion engines and atomic reactors, for example, are based upon the creation of special environments that release the (generally dormant) heat energy-producing powers of petrol and uranium (dormant on the surface of the earth at least).

In many other cases, we observe correlations (or concomitant variations) of various kinds, or situations of contiguity (where A-type events are regularly found together with B-type events) without knowing whether, or what sort of, a causal relationship is involved. More smokers than non-smokers are observed to develop lung cancer. Lung cancer rates appear to be directly proportional to quantities of cigarettes smoked, richer people on average live significantly longer than poorer people, inflation seems to rise in inverse relation to unemployment. Chinese herbs appear to produce good results in some cases. But does smoking cause cancer? Are Chinese herbs effective medicines? Again, the answers to these sorts of questions cannot generally be found by simply – passively – accumulating more observations of the same kind. Active intervention is required to decide such questions, through application of appropriate procedures of controlled experimentation, or complex analysis of existing data from a variety of different sources.

In all of these cases we are indeed concerned with the production of a particular theory or hypothesis on the basis of particular sorts of observations, as suggested in the simple inductivist model. The theories in question, dealing with entities and causal powers and tendencies of such entities that are – more or less – directly observable, have been called *Type 1 theories* (to distinguish them from *Type 2 theories*, dealt with in chapter 7).[5] They include theories about the biological, chemical, gravitational, electrical and magnetic properties of observable things (moving electric charge gives rise to magnetism, changing magnetism gives rise to electricity), about the pressure, temperature and volume of gases (pV = nRT), about the physiology, development, behaviour and circumstances of animals and people, including the role of particular substances or experiences or life circumstances in causing or curing illness (Chinese herbs cure illness, smoking causes lung cancer) and about the interaction of such observable and measurable social variables as GDP, inflation, inequality, morbidity, mortality and violent crime.

Rather than further passive observation, the subsequent testing of such theories typically involves a range of different sorts of experimental investigation, actively seeking relevant data through surveying and sampling, and subjecting selected phenomena to isolation and controlled manipulation.[6]

Testing Type 1 theories: proportions

Here we concentrate upon a particular subset of Type 1 theories that raises special problems (qualitatively different from those considered in relation to Type 2 theories,) by virtue of the necessary involvement of statistics. Many law students and lawyers recoil in horror at the prospect of mathematical complexities. But the sorts of hypotheses considered here, *simple statistical hypotheses*, *correlations* and *causal hypotheses*, are, as Giere points out, 'the stock in trade of psychology and the social sciences, and of science related fields such as bio-medicine, public health and education'.[7] They are, therefore, precisely the kind of ideas with which lawyers are increasingly likely to come in contact, both in relation to issues of factually based law reform, and expert testimony in the court room. And, luckily, the basic principles of theory testing in this area can be grasped with minimum statistical detail.

Considering first simple statistical hypotheses, we see that all such hypotheses identify 'a population, a property that each member of the population may or may not exhibit, and a percentage'. As Giere says:

> Each of these statements could therefore be expressed in a statement with the following structure:
>
> X per cent of (Population) are (Property).
>
> The percentage tells us the relative number or *proportion* of the members of the population that exhibit the property in question.[8]

Here are some examples:

- 12% of sentenced prisoners in gaol in Australia on 30 June 2000 had been convicted of sexual offences.[9]
- 4% of male prisoners serving a sentence of 12 months or more in the NSW prison system in 1973 had completed the HSC.[10]
- 80% of female prisoners in NSW prisons in 1996 had been in at least one violent relationship.[11]

Simple statistical hypotheses can be seen as answers to specific sorts of questions:

- How many (what proportion of) apples in this consignment are rotten?
- How many (what proportion of) Australians are now HIV-positive?
- How many (what proportion of) Australian teenagers are cigarette smokers?
- Are more people in prison for violent than non-violent offences (that is, more than 50 per cent)?
- How many (what percentage of) men in Australian prisons are raped each day?

There are three (fundamental) scientific, issues that arise in relation to these sorts of questions:

1   *Providing appropriate – operational – definitions for the properties in question, as observable and measurable properties.* What counts as a rotten apple? How precisely do we distinguish the rotten from the non-rotten? What counts as a violent

relationship? How many cigarettes make you a smoker? What if you don't inhale?

2   *Identifying and accessing the relevant population.* Who counts as a teenager? Who counts as a male prisoner?

3   *Selecting an appropriate sample.* Do we test the whole population? If not, how big a sample do we choose and how do we select the sample?

Special problems are involved in questioning people in order to elicit the relevant information, questioning them about their beliefs, habits, past experience, present emotional/physical condition or future plans (as opposed to counting apples). People may misremember facts, they may be mistaken about their own future actions or unwilling to tell the interviewer the truth, for one reason or another. Special efforts may be required to try to avoid or overcome these problems.

Sometimes we can check a whole population. For example, beginning in 1982, a national prison census has been conducted each year in Australia on 30 June. The census was administered by the Australian Bureau of Criminology until 1993 and thereafter by the Australian Bureau of Statistics.[12]

Our first example of a simple statistical hypothesis came from the year 2000 census, which involved all prisoners in Australia. This sort of thing is informative but also costly and difficult to organise. Very often we cannot check the whole population of interest, and must instead take and check a *sample*. On this basis, we make an *inductive generalisation* about the whole population.

For a statistical induction to be successful, the sample must adequately represent the population. It is not enough that the sampled individuals be of the same category (apples, prisoners, teenagers); they must also have the same mix of sub-categories (or 'secondary properties' – male, female, old, young) which may be relevant in determining the 'primary properties' of interest to us. Such a mix can best be achieved through ensuring that our selection is made randomly, with each member of the population (who might exhibit the property of interest) having an equal chance of being selected (and no correlation between the outcome of one selection and another).

How we achieve such random sampling depends upon the particular population we are sampling. It might involve an appropriate mixing of the entities in question or it might involve assigning numbers to each of them and using random number tables to select some. The latter sort of approach was adopted in two other prison surveys that yielded data referred to above. The NSW Bureau of Crime Statistics survey of 1973 involved a random sample of 1000 male prisoners serving a sentence of 12 months or more. The 1996 NSW Corrections Health Service Inmate Health Survey involved a randomly selected sample of 789 prisoners from NSW gaols.

> P1   A random sample of 789 prisoners was collected from NSW gaols.
>
> P2   One-quarter of the women prisoners sampled reported having used heroin in prison.
>
> C   So probably close to a quarter of women prisoners in NSW gaols have used heroin while in gaol.

Even with a random sample, probability theory tells us that the sample probably will not directly or precisely reflect the distribution of the property of interest in the population as a whole. Suppose that 50% of a population of people have at some time been victims of property crime. So the probability of being such a victim in the population is said to be 0.50.[13] But the chance that our sample will precisely mirror the proportions in the population is actually rather slim. One sample of 100 might yield 55 victims, another 47. Even if we are careful to choose a representative sample, this in no way guarantees the proportion of such victims will be exactly 0.50.

Such 'sampling error' cannot be eliminated. But it can be reduced by taking sufficiently large samples. Furthermore, a major statistical result, called the *central limit theorem*, says that the (probability) distribution of all possible sample proportions (or sample means) – indi-cating the different probabilities of each possible proportion – is normal, as long as the sample sizes are large enough, that is, over about 30.

In the bell-shaped normal distribution, the mean or average value is the central high point of the curve, which also corresponds with the median or central value. In a normal distribution of all possible sample proportions (47/53, 48/52, 49/51, 50/50, 51/49, etc) this mean value corresponds to the actual population proportion (or mean). Furthermore, the variability of the sample proportions, that is, the spread around the mean value, decreases as sample sizes increase.

Here, we need to briefly consider the key statistical concept of standard deviation, as a kind of average of individual deviations from the mean of a distribution, or measure of how widely dispersed the values are (with big standard deviation = big dispersion). To calculate the *standard deviation* of a variable in a population or a sample, we add the squared deviations from the population or sample mean, divide by the size of the population or sample and then take the square root of the result.

The so-called *empirical rule* states that in a normal distribution, approximately 68% of values lie within one standard deviation of the mean, or between the mean minus one standard deviation and the mean plus one standard deviation. Approximately 95% of values lie within two standard deviations (either side) of the mean, and 99.7% within three standard deviations (either side) of the mean.

Population values deviate from each other due to natural phenomena. Sample values vary because of the errors that occur because the whole population has not been considered. The variability of the latter is therefore referred to as *standard error* (SE) rather than standard deviation. But the empirical rule applies also in relation to such SE in sample distributions. SEs are calculated by reference to the value of the population variable in question (in this case proportion – p = 0.50 victims of property crime) and the size of the samples involved, n (in this case 100). Thus, SE of the distribution of sample proportions is square root of $[p(1-p)/n]$. We see that the SE decreases as n, the sample size, increases.

Because the sampling distribution of sample proportions (or means) is normal, we can use the empirical rule to determine how much a given sample proportion is expected to vary from the true population proportion. Applied to the normal distribution of all sample proportions (for any given size of sample over 30) the empirical rule says that we can expect about 68% of sample proportions to lie within one SE of the population proportion, about 95% to lie within two SEs, and about 99.7% to lie within three SEs of the population proportion.

Generally, we want to discover the population proportion by reference to a single sample proportion. We know that 95% of all sample proportions lie within two SEs of the population proportion. So if our estimate is actually a range including the sample proportion plus or minus two SEs, our estimate should be correct about 95% of the time. The number of SEs added or subtracted is called the *margin of error* (ME). Thus, the ME is supposed to measure the maximum amount by which the sample proportion (or other statistic) is expected to differ from that of the population. By combining our sample proportion, as estimate of the population proportion, with the margin or error, we come up with a confidence interval. One SE either side of our sample estimate gives a confidence interval of 68%: we can be 68% confident that the actual population proportion is within an interval of one SE either side of the sample proportion. Generally, statisticians go for a 95% confidence level, which means an interval two SEs either side of the sample proportion.

The problem is that SE depends upon population data that will generally not be available: in this case, the actual population proportion. This is what we are probably trying to discover, on the basis of sample data. As it happens, on the assumption that our sample is, indeed, representative of the population, we can estimate the SE proportion by reference to the observed proportion (or 'frequency') in our single random sample. Estimated SE proportion = square root $[(f)(1 - f)/n]$, where f = observed sample frequency and n = sample size.

For example:

> For a sample size of 200, and observed frequency of 0.4:
>
> SE proportion is the square root of $[0.4 \times 0.6]/200 = 0.035$;
>
> $0.035 = 1$ SE = confidence level of 67% = 80 plus or minus 7;
>
> $0.07 = 2$ SEs = confidence level of 95% = 80 plus or minus 14.

By assuming the sample frequency to be 0.50, we can produce tables of approximate MEs at the 95% confidence level for different sample sizes. Such tables give over-simplified results, but they can be extremely handy for purposes of rough calculation, and speedy assessment of relevant data.

Sample size	Margin of error
25	+/- 0.25
100	+/- 0.10
500	+/- 0.05
2000	+/- 0.02
10 000	+/- 0.01[14]

Larger sample sizes give better information. A larger sample with the same ME gives a higher confidence level. A smaller sample with the same confidence level gives a larger ME. Higher confidence requires better information.

Correlations (1)

So far, we have considered only single variable properties of members of particular populations, and how to generalise from the observed properties of a sample to a whole population. The next step is to consider the relationships between two or more variable properties of individuals. Consideration of the strength of relationships between variable properties brings us into the study of correlations.

Correlations are concerned with the strength of the relationships between the values of two variables. A high positive correlation means close to direct proportionality: one value increases at the same rate as the other. A high negative correlation means close to inverse proportionality: one value decreases as the other increases. The nature and extent of such associations are measured in terms of what are called *correlation coefficients* (CC). A perfect positive correlation corresponds to a CC of plus 1, a perfect negative correlation to a CC of minus 1.

Although a relationship of correlation is not the same thing as a relation of causation, correlations are generally indicative of causal relationships of some kind. Depending upon how we define causation, correlation could be a necessary feature of a causal relation, though not, in itself, sufficient to demonstrate causation.

To establish the existence of a correlation is often to take a first step towards establishing a causal relationship, though the correlation itself does not necessarily indicate the nature of the causal relationship involved. As Philips points out, when variable X and variable Y are substantially correlated, it might be that X is causing Y; it might be that Y is causing X; it might be that both are caused by a third variable or set of variables or that each is a single aspect of a 'multifaceted but indivisible whole', as with the similar speeds of the two front wheels of a car.[15]

An example here would be a sample of circles of different radii. As Rowntree notes, 'the circumference increases in length when the radius increases. Big values of one variable are associated with big values of the other, and small with small'.[16] If we plot circumference in centimetres on the y axis against radius in centimetres on the x axis, we get a straight line (rising from left to right), indicating a very strong correlation. But it is misleading to say that either variable causes the other. Rather, the formula $C = 2\pi r$ describes a fundamental structural feature of all circles.

Another example involves the variables of acceleration and force in relation to a population of objects of similar mass (or indeed, the same object subjected to different degrees of force). Here, following appropriate experimental procedures to generate the results in question, we plot force (f), increasing from one to five (arbitrary) units, on the x axis, against acceleration (A), in m/sec2, on the y axis. And again, we get a straight line rising from the left to right that would, in this case, pass through the origin.

Acc (m/sec^2)	Force
0.20	1.0
0.40	2.0
0.60	3.0
0.80	4.0
1.00	5.0[17]

This suggests a direct relationship between force and acceleration. A is proportional to f, when the mass of the object is held constant.

Next we consider objects of differing mass, with the force kept constant (at one unit). We again plot acceleration on the y axis, with mass on the x axis:

Acc (m/sec^2)	Mass
0.8	1
0.4	2
0.210	3
0.200	4
0.160	5[18]

This time, we get a concave curve falling from right to left. This suggests an inverse relationship between mass and acceleration (with force held constant). It seems that A is proportional to 1/m.

The next stage is to plot f/A (on the y axis) against m (on the x axis). Again we get a straight line rising from left to right (intersecting the origin) and suggesting direct proportionality – f/A proportional to m. In fact, f = kma, and we can choose units that make k = 1, to give Newton's second law, f = mA. And in this case, the correlation does point to a causal relationship, with applied force causing acceleration (and mass resisting such acceleration).

Another straightforward example involves increasing volume (V) of a gas, plotted on the y axis, against the pressure (p) exerted by that gas, plotted on the x axis, with the temperature and amount of gas particles held constant. Here again appropriate experimentation yields results that give a concave curve falling from left to right (basically similar to the mass/acceleration graph) suggesting that V is proportional to 1/p. And this is confirmed when we plot A against 1/p to get a straight line graph. This is known as Boyle's Law, and is again indicative of a causal relationship, in this case involving the impacts of gas particles on the walls of the vessel containing the gas.

Finally, to see that correlations are significant in the social, as well as the natural sciences, we consider the quantitative studies of Lars Schoultz, Michael Stohl, David Carleton and Steven Johnson,[19] examining the relationship between US foreign aid and observance or non-observance of human rights by receiving governments between 1962 and 1983. As Gareau points out:

> The human rights [violations] tested for in the first study [covering the years 1962 to 1977] were torture and other forms of cruel, inhuman, and degrading treatment, including prolonged detention without trial ... The problem of determining the level of observance or non-observance of human rights was left in this study to the composite judgment of 38 experts from Western non-communist countries who had published widely on the subject or who had occupied key positions in non-governmental human rights organisations. The experts' mean evaluation of human rights violations for the 23 Latin American countries serve as the dependent variable ... The independent variable was aid from Washington ... The correlations between the level of human rights violations and aid in the first study were found to be 'uniformly positive', indicating that aid had tended to flow disproportionately to Latin American governments that torture their citizens. In addition, the correlations are relatively strong ... The seven countries that received little aid ... maintained a relatively high level of support for human rights, while the 16 that received comparatively large amounts of aid had a low level of respect for these rights.[20]

The second study found a direct relationship between foreign assistance and human rights violations during the Nixon and Ford administrations. 'The more violations, the more aid received.'[21] And the third study, covering 59 countries over the period 1978–83, found 'that no matter what scale was used for human rights violations no significant negative correlations with aid from Washington could be found for any year tested'.[22] In some cases, 'the more violations that occurred, the more aid was forthcoming. This was found to be the case both for economic and for military aid'.[23]

Correlations (2)

Here we concentrate upon a more restricted version of the idea of correlation that allows us to carry over the ideas of sampling and margin and error considered earlier. In a population whose members have properties P (and not P) and Q (and not Q), P is positively correlated with Q when the proportion of Q's amongst the P's is greater than the proportion of Q's amongst the non-P's.

As far as sampling is concerned, exactly the same principles apply as with simple proportions. We need to aim for a random sample, and to take account of appropriate margins of error. Sticking with our example of crime victims, we might consider two variables: victimisation status in respect of crimes of violence and employment status. We assume that each has two possible values: victim or non-victim, and employed or unemployed.

When the percentage of victims is the same among both employed and unemployed people, we can say that the two variables – victimisation and employment status – are not correlated. If the percentage of victims amongst the unemployed is greater than the percentage amongst the employed, we can say that for this population, being a victim of violent crime is positively correlated with being unemployed.

Here again, Giere provides a concise analysis of precisely what is involved. Let's say, in a sample of 600 people from a particular region 500 turn out to be unemployed and 100 employed. Amongst the unemployed, 325 turn out to be crime victims. In other words, f(V/U) = 65% (frequency of victims amongst the unemployed). Amongst the employed people in the sample, 35 out of 100 are victims, so f(V/not U) = 35% (frequency of victims amongst the employed).

There is a clear difference in the sample between these two values, f(V/U) and f(V/not U). The question is whether this difference in sample frequencies constitutes good evidence for the existence of a correlation in the population. To find out it is necessary to construct the relevant interval estimates (the relevant ME's)

By our rules of thumb (established earlier in relation to distributions), ME for a sample of 500 (unemployed people) = 0.05. So we estimate P(V/U) = f(V/U) +/– ME = (65 +/– 5)%. Similarly for n = 100, ME = 0.10. So we estimate P(V/not U) = f(V/not U) = (35 +/– 10)%.

If we check the lowest possible value for P(V/U), that is, 60%, against the highest possible value for P(V/not U), that is, 45%, we see that there is no overlap between these two distributions (or sets of values). That is good evidence for concluding that P(V/U) really is larger than P (V/not U) in the population. Being a victim really is positively correlated with being unemployed. You are more likely to be a victim of violence if you are unemployed, and more likely to be unemployed if you are a victim of violent crime in this imaginary population.

If we knew precisely how many unemployed people were victims, and how many were not, we could use the difference between these two figures as a measure of the strength of the correlation between being unemployed and being a victim. For example, if 75% of unemployed people were victims and 25% of employed people were victims, then we could measure the strength of the correlation as 0.75 – 0.25 = 0.50, which is a fairly strong correlation. Measured in this fashion, correlations would range from 1.00, where all the unemployed were victims and none of the employed were, through to 0.00 for non-correlation, and to –1.00, where none of the unemployed are victims and all the employed are.

Where we do not know the exact proportions, but only the end points of 95 per cent confidence intervals, then we can use the end points of the two intervals to determine both the maximum and the minimum difference allowed by the two intervals. The maximum allowed difference is between the top of the higher interval and the bottom of the lower interval. The minimum allowed difference is between the bottom of the higher interval and the top of the lower interval.

In the example above, the maximum allowed difference in proportions is 0.70 – 0.25 = 0.45. The minimum allowed difference is 0.60

– 0.45 = 0.15. So the estimated strength of the correlation is the interval (0.15, 0.45). This does not include zero, and therefore non-correlation is excluded.

As noted earlier, this is a rather restricted idea of correlation. A broader version of correlation is a relation between sets of variables, for example, numbers of police per 10 000 population in different countries, compared to violent crimes per 10 000 population in these countries. There are a number of statistical procedures that can be applied to calculate the extent of the correlations in question, with direct proportionality measured as plus one, inverse proportionality as minus one and no apparent relationship as zero. Perfect positive correlations correspond to straight lines rising left to right when the variables are plotted on x and y axes, falling left to right for perfect negative correlation.

Discussion topics

1. What is science? How is it related to law? Include reference to anti-science, junk science, naive inductivism and scientific theory.
2. What are Type 1 theories? Include reference to proportions, correlations and causation.
3. Find and discuss some references to theories you now know to be Type 1 theories from textbooks, newspapers and cases.
4. What is statistics? Include reference to random sampling, normal distributions, standard deviation, margin of error and significance testing.

Chapter 6

CAUSATION AND THE PRECAUTIONARY PRINCIPLE

Causal hypotheses

Quite a lot has already been said about causation. Scientific research-ers generally act as though everything has a cause, and they aim to find the causes in their chosen area of research. At the same time, they distinguish between strictly deterministic causes, where A is sufficient for B, and stochastic causes, where the occurrence of A merely increases the likelihood of the occurrence of B.

As noted earlier, we typically identify a range of different condi-tions as individually necessary and jointly sufficient to bring about particular effects. An individual's ankle pain is the result of overexer-tion in the tennis game just completed, the hardness of the court, the length of the game, a genetic weakness in the ankle and a fall.

To take another example, it seems that cancers typically develop only through a number of different mutations in an individual's genome. Some such mutations might be inherited, but others will result from exposure to a range of different environmental carcino-gens. Only with all of the sequence established will the cell become cancerous, and only an immune system weakened by other environ-mental stresses will allow the cancer cells to proliferate.

It is causation in this sense, in which every event is recognised as 'the result of many conditions that are jointly sufficient to produce it',[1] that is the typical object of legal consideration. As Fleming states:

> in legal enquiries it does not matter if we are unable to identify all, or even most, of the individual elements which constitute the complex

set of conditions jointly sufficient to produce the given consequence. The reason is that we are usually interested only to investigate whether one, two or perhaps three specific conditions [for example, identified acts or omissions by the defendant or other participants in the accident] were causally relevant ... Whether a particular condition qualifies as a causally relevant factor will depend on whether it was necessary to complete a set of conditions jointly sufficient to account for the given occurrence.[2]

We also recognise the existence of long chains of causation, as, for example, where the better tennis court was closed for repairs, so the tennis player had to go to a different (harder) court, where they had to make greater than usual efforts to compete with a better player, leading to a fall, leading to greater stress on the leg, etc.

Such chains of causation are frequently objects of legal consideration. As Fleming points out:

the defendant's default must be accounted a *'proximate' cause* of the [plaintiff's] harm, the consequence must not be too 'remote' [if legal liability is to be recognised]. And what is meant by 'proximate' [is] that because of convenience, of public policy, or a rough sense of justice, the law arbitrarily declines to trace a series of events beyond a certain point.[3]

We have also seen how we tend to pick out certain factors (from clusters of necessary conditions) as 'the causes' of particular events, typically changes shortly before the events in question, as opposed to standing conditions, which are constant for longer periods. Assumptions and beliefs of people looking for explanations are clearly relevant here. We know there is oxygen around, we are looking for some other reason for the fire. But the unknown conditions of interest are not necessarily the most recent changes. We might want to know why the tennis player was playing upon a different court from their usual one.

Reproductive disorders in seal species in the Baltic Sea in the 1970s might turn out to be the results of the production and sale of longlasting toxins (for example, DDT and PCBs) in US chemical plants years or decades earlier. The death of a particular person from mesothelioma cancer in one country could be traced back to a brief workplace exposure to asbestos decades earlier in another country. A violent act of abuse by an adult today might be, in part, a consequence of abuse that they suffered in childhood.

Causes can also be connected in positive and negative feedback loops, the former leading to accelerated change (as where, as Robert Martin suggests, plant death causes soil erosion, which causes more plant death and more soil erosion), the latter to stable equilibria (as where a nation's trade deficit leads to devaluation of its currency through sales in international money markets, which in turn leads to cheaper exports and the removal of the deficit – supposedly). Positive feedbacks are particularly implicated in global warming, with melting ice reducing the reflection of sunlight from the ocean and land surface. This leads to further heating of the water and land and melting of the ice, melting permafrost releasing methane, which accelerates global warming, leading to further melting. Further melting leads to increased CO2 accelerating plant growth in peat bogs, which in turn leads to break down of the peat and further release of CO_2.

As noted above, correlation is typically a sign of causation. This is clear in the example of force, mass and acceleration in the previous chapter. There we considered experimental 'application' of different forces to a fixed mass to produce different accelerations.

But there are many possible complications here, as nicely outlined by philosopher Robert Martin. We might find a positive correlation between measles spots and bodily aches and pains, not because either is the cause of the other, but because both are the effects of the progress of the infection. We might find a negative correlation between sunburn and mosquito bites, not because mosquitos don't like burned skin, but because hot dry summer weather reduces the water available for mosquito development and causes sunburn. We might find a negative correlation between eating lots of vitamin C and catching colds, not because vitamin C protects against colds but because the same people who take vitamin C also tend to do other things that reduce their chance of catching colds.[4]

It is possible for A to be negatively correlated with B even though A, by itself, might be a positive causal factor for B. Here Martin considers the case of a negative correlation between arteriosclerosis and consumption of birth control pills. Although birth control pills are a positive causal factor for arteriosclerosis, pregnancy is a much stronger causal factor, and by massively reducing the chances of pregnancy, consumption of birth control pills reduces the chances of arteriosclerosis.[5]

A particularly notorious example here is that of the long-noted positive correlation between cigarette consumption and lung cancer. Early suggestions, particularly supported by the tobacco industry, included the idea that bodily precursors to cancer (at an early age) cause people to take up smoking, or that some people had a genetic predisposition to both taking up smoking and developing lung cancer. In this case, of course, neither seems likely, and there are serious questions about why precautionary action was not taken as soon as the correlation was established.

All these examples demonstrate the need for *reliable testing procedures* for definitively establishing the existence (or non-existence) of causal relations, given the existence of some suggestive correlation. And such procedures do exist, though there can be serious difficulties in applying them in some cases.

Controlled experiments

As Martin points out, a typical pattern of scientific investigation from correlation to causation is nicely illustrated by reference to gastritis and bacteria. In 1979, workers in an Australian pathology laboratory discovered what they believed to be a correlation between inflammation of the gut and the presence of a particular bacterium: every tissue with the bacterium was found to be inflamed. A strong correlation was definitively established in 1983.[6]

The question then arose of whether the presence of the bacteria was causing the gastritis (hypothesis one), the gastritis was causing the presence of the bacteria (creating an environment favourable to them – hypothesis two), or some third factor causing both the gastritis and the presence of the bacteria (hypothesis three).

In 1985 one pioneer researcher consumed a mass of the bacteria and subsequently developed gastritis. But as Martin points out, this was a rather small sample (of only one). And even if 1000 people had consumed bacteria and subsequently developed gastritis this would not have definitively ruled out hypothesis two and hypothesis three. They could still have been exposed to the cause of the gastritis before consuming the bacteria. And this other factor could either cause gastritis, which, in turn, causes the presence of bacteria (Factor C) or it could cause both gastritis and bacterial presence (Factor D). The results would be compatible with all three hypotheses.[7]

The next step in this sort of situation is to try to select a study group randomly from the population of interest. This could be rats or other animals or it could be humans. The experimenters then randomly divide the study group (50/50) into an experimental group and a control group. They give all of the experimental group the bacterium and none of the control group. And they aim to treat both groups in otherwise identical fashion throughout the course of the experiment. In the case of humans they would give the control group a suitable placebo, so subjects do not know they are not receiving the bacterium. This is called *blind testing*.

It is also important that those organising the experiment and assessing the result, in this case determining the percentage of gastritis in the two groups, don't know who got the bacteria and who got the placebo. Otherwise they may treat the groups differently or they may appraise the results differently. The possibility of fraud also arises without such *double blind* procedures.

Now it does not matter if there is a Factor C or D. With reasonably large control and experimental groups, we can expect that C and D in both groups match those in the general population. Then, if all of the EX (experimental) group developed gastritis and only 5% of the K (control) group did, this suggests that (at least) 95% of the gastritis in the EX group was caused by the bacterium.

It does not matter whether we exclude pre-existing gastritis and/or bacteria. If 5% of the general population has both, so will 5% of each of our groups. We should still see a difference between the two groups when the other 95% of the EX group get the bacterium.

Suppose all were initially free of infection and the results were 49% gastritis (EX) and 28% gastritis (K). It then seems that bacterial infection raises the chances of gastritis from 28% to 49%. But we need to calculate the relevant margins of error, assuming a confidence level, and to check for overlap. With a confidence level of 0.95 and a sample size of 100 (EX) and 100 (K), we apply standard error (SE) for a proportion; -1 SE proportion = square root $[(f)(1 - f)]n]$; for EX = square root $(0.5 \times 0.5/100)$ = SR $0.25/100$ = SR $1/400$ = $1/20 = 0.05$. 2 SE [95% confidence level] = 0.10. For K = SR$(0.28 \times 0.72/100)$ = 0.045; 2 SE = 0.9

So we're looking at 49% plus or minus 10% = 39–59%; and 28% plus or minus 9% = 19–37%; There is no overlap, and the strength of the causal factor is 59% – 19% = 40%; 39% – 37% = 2%. A positive causal factor with 2% strength is very weak. A positive causal factor with 40% strength is quite strong. A small sample size makes it difficult to assess strength. Nonetheless, the absence of overlap in this case demonstrates a statistically significant result and quite good evidence for the existence of a causal relationship between bacteria and gastritis.

The actual experiment, involving human volunteers, provided good evidence for bacteria as a strong positive causal factor for gastritis, and led to new cheap and efficient drug treatments for what was previously believed to be a stress-related condition.[8]

This example highlights the problems of using human subjects in unpleasant or potentially dangerous experiments. Fully informed and free consent is obviously crucial.[9] If we are looking at ill people involved in clinical trials of possible treatments, it will probably be crucial to run the new treatment against the best available existing treatment, rather than allowing some to go untreated. (Of course, those receiving the new drug could then be untreated or worse.)

Typically, rats (or other animals) will be used before humans, or instead of humans (where the experiment is expected to lead to serious harm or death). But this too raises serious ethical and technical issues. Are we justified in damaging or killing rats to test the toxicity of possibly quite unnecessary products? How do we ensure that they don't suffer needlessly? Are we justified in extrapolating from humans to rats and back again?

In many cases tests for toxicity or carcinogenicity involve estimation of (possible) lifetime doses for humans exposed to such agents (chemical compounds, electromagnetic fields or whatever): for example, 100 grams of compound X. Rats have one-hundredth of human body weight so we should feed them one gram of the compound. But if we anticipate relatively low levels of the effect (low levels of causal efficacy of the agent), this would involve using large numbers of rats in order to achieve a statistically significant effect, so in practice the dose is increased to 10 grams. We can infer results of normal patterns of exposure from such tests providing the cause–effect relationship is more or less linear. Problems arise where there is a threshold effect: where normal amounts of the agent have no effect but higher ones have a big effect. A possible example here, cited by Martin, is foetal alcohol syndrome. One study suggests that more than three drinks a day are necessary for any of 16 problems associated with the syndrome, but above three drinks such problems proliferate.[10]

A more general possibility is that the cause–effect relation is non-linear, with more cause leading to more effect at all levels. But it could also be that above a particular level a small increase produces an increasing effect. If there is a substantial increase in cases of the effect – in the experimental animal population – with large doses and if we have some reason to expect linearity, then we can conclude that a small dose increases the risk to humans. The crucial question is the extent of the increased risk as against the possible benefits of use of the agent in question.

Prospective and retrospective tests

There are many types of cases where controlled experiments are not possible. Planes cannot be crashed or cars with people in them, large earthquakes cannot be triggered in urban areas. In these sorts of cases scale models can be built, including models of human bodies and such models tested to destruction. Computer models can be built and tested in virtual reality.

In other sorts of cases involving threats to human life and health, including the crucial case of cigarettes and human illness, obser-vational alternatives to experimental methods can be used. These are called prospective and retrospective studies. The basic idea of *a prospective design* is to find two groups of subjects, on average, similar in every feature except for the fact that all members of one group exhibit the suspected causal factor (for example, smoking) and all members of the other do not. Both groups are then followed into the future, and at some point they are compared for the effect vari-ables under investigation (presumably no encouragement is offered to continued smoking, and hopefully strong discouragement).

There are a number of issues here. There are practical problems in finding appropriately homogenous populations or in matching groups for all possibly relevant variables. The major potential cause under investigation may be correlated with other potential causal factors. The 24-year long US National Institute of Health Framington study on the causes of heart disease and other illnesses (looking at 5127 individuals over the period 1950–74), for example, found smoking, a likely causal factor for coronary heart disease, positively correlated with another possible causal factor, coffee drinking. Investigation of the effects of smoking therefore required comparison of non-smoking coffee drinkers with non-smoking non-coffee drinkers. This showed no significant differences between the groups. Investigators could also have looked at smoking coffee drinkers and smoking non-coffee drinkers, but this would have raised problems of possible toxic inter-action of smoking and coffee drinking as cause of coronary heart disease (CHD).

Ideally, the study should have aimed to match the incidence of the suspected third factor in the control group with that in the experi-mental group at the beginning.

> Having obtained randomly selected samples of coffee drinkers and those not drinking coffee, the Framington investigators could have examined both samples for smokers. Then, by randomly eliminating some smokers from the sample of coffee drinkers, they could have ensured that there would be the same number of smokers in both groups. Thus, the effect, if any, of smoking would be equalised in the two groups.[11]

But as Giere also observes:

> a drawback of matching samples for suspected third factors is that this strategy does not protect against interactive effects. If coffee drinking contributes to CHD only for smokers ... then the EX group would tend to exhibit more cases of CHD than the control group with an equal number of smokers. Investigators could be misled into thinking that coffee by itself is a positive causal factor.[12]

Things get increasingly complicated when we consider greater numbers of potential third-factor correlations, and interactive protec-tive effects.

So the basic principles of a prospective study are:

1   find a homogenous population or collect masses of data in a non-homogenous population relating to possibly relevant variables;
2   distinguish those with and without the supposed cause and match groups;
3   follow both groups long enough for the effect to appear;
4   compare percentage of effects amongst possible cause group with percentage of effects amongst non-cause group.

Such prospective studies can be done either in *real time*, as with the Framington study, or *after the fact*. In the first case we find a group with the cause before they show the effect and follow them possibly for many years. This can be costly and difficult. In the second, we find a group with the cause and then check for the effect. In this case no follow up is required. But if we choose groups with and without the cause only after the effects have shown up, it is less likely those groups will be representative of the population as a whole. Some smokers will have died of heart disease already, so the smokers will look as if they have less heart disease than they really do.

Giere cites this particularly compelling real-time prospective study relevant to the issue of smoking and disease:

> In the mid-1960s the [US] National Cancer Institute sponsored a prospective study that enrolled more than 400 000 men between the ages of 40 and 80 ... the investigators matched 37 000 smokers with an equal number of non-smokers [in terms of] age, race, height, nativity, residence, occupational exposure to potential carcinogens, religion, education, marital status, alcohol consumption, amount of sleep, exercise, stress, use of drugs, current state of health and history of illness. Every pair of men exhibits the same values of all these different variables, but in each case, one was a smoker and one a non-smoker. After three years and 2000 deaths, the rate of death from all causes was twice as great for the smokers as for the non-smokers. Nearly half of all the deaths were due to heart disease, with the rate for smokers being double that for non-smokers ... the death rate from lung cancer for smokers was nine times that for non-smokers.[13]

Another possibility is a *retrospective study*. In this case, we begin with a sample of subjects that already have the effect and look back in time to isolate a suspected causal factor. An example here, cited by Giere, is a British study (by the UK National Case Control Study Group) which looked at all women (younger than 36) diagnosed as having breast cancer between 1 January 1982 and 31 December 1985, in 11 different areas of England, Scotland and Wales: a total of 1049 women. 'For each case in the [final] sample of 755, the researchers selected, at random, one woman as a control from amongst the list of patients of the same physician as the corresponding case. The control subjects [were matched with the experimental subjects], except, of course, they had to be free of any symptoms of breast cancer.'[14] Both groups were then compared for use of oral contraceptives. 'Amongst those with breast cancer, 470 of 755 or 62% had used oral contraceptives for more than four years. Amongst the controls, 390 of 755

or 52% have used oral contraceptives for more than four years.'[15]
We see here the basic principles of retrospective study:

1   collect a sample of those with the effect and match them with a
     similar sample without it;
2   look into the past of the two groups to see whether the group
     with the suspected effect had more exposure to the suspected
     cause;
3   compare percentage of causes amongst effect group with
     percentage of causes amongst non-effect group.

Retrospective studies have the same sorts of problems as after-the-
fact prospectives, as well as special problems of their own. As Giere
says:

> the data they yield allow no estimate of the effectiveness of a causal
> factor. Effectiveness is defined in terms of the percentage of the popu-
> lation that would experience the effect depending on whether all or
> none had the cause. The frequencies of the effect in two samples,
> as in a prospective study, may thus be used directly to estimate
> the effectiveness of the causal factor in the population [how many
> people are dying as a result of smoking, for example]. Retrospective
> studies, however, give you the frequency of the cause in groups with
> and without the effect. There is no way to use these frequencies to
> estimate the effectiveness of the causal factor. Knowing that 62% of
> women younger than 36 diagnosed for breast cancer had used oral
> contraceptives for more than 4 years tells you nothing about the
> percentage of women using oral contraceptives for more than four
> years who will get breast cancer.[16]

Also:

> any observed statistically significant difference between the two
> sample groups may all too easily be merely a refection of bias in
> the selection process that produced the samples. There is also the
> possibility of correlations existing in the population that, even with
> random sampling, could lead to a statistically significant difference
> in the sample groups even if here were no causal connection between
> the variables being studied.[17]

Fallacies of statistical reasoning

Having thus briefly considered the statistical reasoning involved in
testing simple statistical claims (relating to proportions), claims relat-

ing to correlations and simple causal hypotheses, we can now see various potential areas of confusion and fallacy.

1   First of all, we need to consider the way in which the concepts used in the relevant percentages and proportions have been operationalised. We are regularly bombarded with statistical claims involving terms that are so imprecisely defined that the use of some precise figure in such a claim is meaningless. Just as often we are presented with statistical claims requiring evidence that is practically or logically impossible to obtain.

2   Second, there are problems in ensuring samples are representative of populations. As Hurley points out, it is no good a quality controller for a manufacturing firm checking every tenth component on a conveyor belt if the components are not randomly arranged on the belt. 'As a result of some malfunction in the manufacturing process it's quite possible that every tenth component turned out perfect and the rest imperfect.'[18]

3   The randomness requirement presents particular problems where the population consists of people, with phone polls, for example, effected by different patterns of work at different times of day. Not everyone has a phone or an address appearing in a city directory. And, as noted earlier, people's answers will not necessarily be error-free or truthful.

There are opportunities for error or fraud in proper application of the procedures for collecting and interpreting the data (considered above). Particularly insidious is the case of corporations carrying out numerous trials of the causal efficacy – or safety – of new products, but publishing only results favourable to their own economic interests. As should be clear, even if a product is useless or dangerous, enough trials will, by chance, eventually yield results that make it appear useful or safe.

As Chalmers notes, the new generation of antidepressants were originally billed as

> effective, safe and non-addictive ... Now [after billions of dollars worth of sales worldwide] ... some patients and doctors claim they are of questionable efficacy and can induce suicidal thoughts ... It would be easier to judge which side was right if all the relevant information about the drugs were publicly available. But ... the law

does not oblige companies to disclose the findings of their research on licensed medicines and scientists, doctors, patients and ... public organisations have no legal right to inspect the evidence that led regulators to licence drugs [let alone other results not made available to regulators].[19]

Another consideration here is the use of *surrogate endpoints* in clinical trials. A new drug is tested for a comparatively short time and is found to produce some apparently desirable result, for example, reduction of high blood pressure. On this basis, it is approved by relevant government bodies and widely prescribed. As Moynihan points out:

> the trouble is, high blood pressure itself is not a disease that needs treating; it is ... only a risk factor for stroke or heart disease. Preventing these diseases is the real aim of drug therapy. In order to measure the really important effects of the drug it is necessary to conduct long-term studies which will measure the number of strokes or heart attacks which the drugs prevent in patients, rather than whether they simply lower their blood pressure.[20]

He cites the case of the drug flecainide, found in brief clinical trials to reduce irregular heartbeats in people at risk of cardiac arrest. It was assumed that if the drug reduced irregular heartbeats then it would prevent heart attacks, and it was widely prescribed. A belated large-scale trial showed that in fact the drug was causing cardiac arrest in those with less serious symptoms of irregular heartbeat. Health policy researcher Moore estimated that 50 000 patients had died from taking flecainide and the related encainide before they were withdrawn. As Chalmers says, 'by 1990, more than a decade after these drugs were introduced, it has been estimated that they were killing more American every year than died in action in the Vietnam war'.[21]

Gigerenzer highlights a further problem area concerning the way in which the results of clinical trials are presented. He cites the case of a press release from the West of Scotland Coronary Prevention Study of the effect that 'People with high cholesterol can rapidly reduce ... their risk of death by 22% by taking a widely prescribed drug called prevastatin sodium. This is the conclusion of a landmark study presented today at the annual meeting of the American Heart Association.'[22]

This information presents a potentially misleading picture of the efficacy of the new drug to the statistically naive. As Gigerenzer says, 'studies indicate that a majority of people think that [this means that] out of 1000 people with high cholesterol 220 of these people can be prevented from becoming heart attack victims [through the use of this drug]'.[23] The clinical trial actually showed that out of 1000 people taking prevastatin over five years, 32 died compared to 41 in a placebo control group.

The relative risk reduction was indeed 22% and the drug manufacturers were happy to use this figure in promoting their product. However, the absolute risk reduction, probably of more interest to both potential users and governments subsidising public medicine, is 0.9%. 'Prevastatin reduces the number of people who die from 41 to 32 in 1000. That is, the absolute risk reduction is 9 in 1000.'[24]

Furthermore, the number of people who must participate in the treatment to save one life is 111, because 9 in 1000 deaths – which is 1 in 111 – are prevented by the drug. This could be a substantial cost to a public health system, with the money better spent elsewhere. Most obviously, there is the possibility of much cheaper, less dangerous non-drug-based means of reducing high cholesterol.

Recognising that good clinical trials are expensive and difficult undertakings, we must recognise also that the wealthy private companies that can afford to fund such trials are highly unlikely to fund trials of already available – non-patentable – alternative (including non-drug-based) treatments from which they can derive no profit. Nor are they likely to develop drugs to treat the illnesses of the poor (however widespread and serious) because the poor cannot afford to pay inflated prices for patented drugs.

Legal issues and the precautionary principle

There are many legal issues arising out of consideration of Type 1 theory testing. Here we focus upon two particularly important and closely related issues concerning correlation and causation. The first concerns the centrality of the requirement of proof of causation as the basis for culpability in criminal law and liability in the law of negligence. Even 'regulatory' laws, setting permissible standards in relation to workplace safety, food safety and pollution, and aiming to thereby avoid possible damage to people or the environment in the future, have generally only been enacted as a result of proof of the damage-generating potential of particular practices in the past.

We have seen some of problems in definitively establishing causation; it can be extremely difficult, costly and time consuming, taking
decades rather than months. By the time such definitive proof of
causation is available, terrible damage can have been inflicted upon
people and the environment, on a vast scale. It is of little benefit to
the victims that their deaths contribute to eventual legal action years
down the track. At the same time, we have also seen that evidence
of correlation, along with other circumstantial evidence, can point
very strongly towards particular patterns of causation long before
any such 'definitive' evidence becomes available.

There are many well-known examples. Awareness of the dangers
of asbestos, for example, goes back to ancient times, at least in areas
of large accessible asbestos deposits. In the West, in 1898, a woman
factory inspector reported 'injury to bronchial tubes and lungs' of
workers 'medically attributable' to asbestos in the workplace.[25] This
was followed by a succession of similar observations of lung disease
amongst asbestos workers by doctors and factory inspectors. But it
was only in 1931, following a British government inquiry, that the
first asbestos dust control regulations were introduced, along with
medical surveillance of workers and compensation arrangements.

In the 1930s and 40s reports of lung cancers being associated with
asbestos appeared in the US, UK and German medical literature. A
British report of 1953 found a rate of lung cancer 10 times greater in
asbestos workers than in the general population. And a South African
report of 1960 found all but 2 of 47 cases of the rare cancer mesothelioma involved prior asbestos exposure, in some cases involving only
very short periods of exposure.

Yet as Gee and Greenberg point out, the UK asbestos regulations of 1931 'were only partially enforced', with only two prosecutions between 1931 and 1968. Updated regulations in 1969 failed
to consider the cancer hazards. And only in 1998 following a World
Health Organisation report of 1986, finding all types of asbestos to
be carcinogenic, with no known safe level of exposure, did the British
government adopt a ban on all forms asbestos. A ban in the European
Union allowed continued use of asbestos till 2005. 'Meanwhile, the
annual UK cancer death rate from mesothelioma, a lung cancer from
asbestos, is estimated by the Health and Safety Commission to be
around 3000 deaths per year and rising.'[26]

It was only in the early 1980s that asbestos was banned for most uses in Australia, once the authorities had 'strong epidemiological evidence' of the dangers. As Deville and Harding note:

a consequence of the lack of precautionary action is that many people have died from asbestos related disease, there have been large claims against corporations involved with asbestos mining and manufacture and Australia has the highest rate of mesothelioma in the world.[27]

We can see how early reports, although perhaps less than 'definitive' – insofar as they involved small samples, retrospective studies and after-the-fact prospective studies – were nonetheless highly suggestive of causation. The first of the modern reports (that of factory inspector Lucy Deane in 1898) even pointed to the precise nature of the mechanism involved, identifying the 'sharp, glass-like jagged nature of the particles'[28] revealed by microscopic examination.

Most important was the nature of the damage involved here: a serious threat to life and health for vast numbers of people. Given this sort of combination, of possible or likely causation with intensity and scale of possible or likely damage, it seems clear that radical legal action should have been taken decades earlier.

There are many similar stories of failure to take action in time to save health, life and the natural environment. It has become increasingly clear that waiting for definite proof of causation can be the height of social irresponsibility in many cases and that it is vitally necessary to apply some sort of strong *precautionary principle* to avoid such disasters in the future.

The basic idea here is clearly explained by Deville and Harding:

Where there are threats of serious or irreversible damage [to people or to the environment] lack of full scientific certainty should not be used as a reason for postponing moves to prevent [such damage][29] ... Under the precautionary principle it is the [potential victims] rather than those whose actions may impact upon [them] that [are] given the benefit of the doubt.[30]

And only with strong evidence of a big balance of real social benefits over costs are new projects allowed to proceed.

It is crucial here to put the onus of proof of safety (or social benefit significantly outweighing safety risks) onto any organisations or individuals preparing to institute such new projects, market some new product or introduce some new technology. Potentially safer alternatives must always be seriously considered before any such project is allowed to proceed. And those in a position to approve such new developments should try to apply the most precautious project management in the early stages. Ongoing and effective monitoring of all potentially dangerous consequences of projects of all kinds is an integral part of the program, with strong action taken at the first signs of trouble.

> Many case studies indicate the value of thorough, long-term monitoring. While for asbestos, benzene and PCBs evidence was accumulating of the adverse health effects ... no role was then played by systematic monitoring.[31]

Deville and Harding argue for legislation leading to the establishment of environmental regulators to require all such bodies to apply the precautionary principle in decision-making. They call for the banning of any – potentially – seriously dangerous activities before scientific proof of damage, for 'reverse' lists of safe substances to replace lists of known hazardous substances banned from particular uses. All substances should be assumed to be harmful until there is good evidence that they are not. 'The long-term effect of this listing is that the onus is then on the developers, users and disposers of particular substances to prove that they should be on the list. Reverse lists should be linked to [extended principles of strict and absolute liability].'[32]

Harremoes et al emphasise the importance of extending regulatory appraisal beyond the most 'straightforward and direct impacts', to 'as wide a range of conditions and effects as can reasonably be anticipated'.[33] They also argue that we need to take 'account of the potential irreversibility of actions, even if the consequences might not be known'.[34] And they cite the examples of halocarbons (dissolving the ozone layer), PCBs (accumulating in the food chain) and methyl tert-butyl ether (as a potential serious-illness causing petrol additive) as artificial chemicals whose 'very novelty' should have been taken as a warning sign long ago.

> Enough was known at the outset regarding their persistence in the environment to serve as another warning. They would also readily disperse to become ubiquitous throughout the physical environment ... it could have been reduced from the outset that if these substances were released into the environment and if a problem subsequently developed, it would take many years for both them and the problem to 'go away'.[35]

They emphasise also the need for regulators and others to search out and address 'blind spots' and gaps in scientific knowledge relevant to issues of potential serious and irreversible harm. 'For halocarbons the chemical mechanism for depletion of stratospheric ozone was identified in the prestigious journal *Nature* in 1974. Nevertheless, this did not prevent regulatory neglect until first empirical evidence of causal effects became available.'[36] They focus upon the need for interdisciplinary risk assessment (including use of lay and local knowledge as well as specialist expertise), for taking account of 'real world conditions', for proper systematic scrutiny of claimed pros and cons, and, above all, for regulators effective independence from economic and political special interests.

Developers of all kinds will (and do) argue that further moves towards precautionary policies will radically slow the pace of technological innovation. And it is true that we must always consider the costs of failing to develop new technologies, as well as the potential costs of the technologies themselves. In particular, some risks are justified in the interest of saving human life and restoring the health of the environment. But genuine technological progress, as distinct from profit-driven innovation, should be predicated upon ensuring safety. The disasters cited in this chapter are enough to demonstrate the need for truly responsible scientific caution.

Social science

Before leaving the issue of the precautionary principle, it is important to briefly note its significance in relation to other areas of law reform. In particular, the work of Wilkinson and other researchers has focused attention upon an increasing body of empirical evidence relating to the social causes of crime, accidents and ill health. Amongst other evidence, Wilkinson refers to a strong correlation (above 0.72, P = 0.01) between homicide rates (0–20 per 100 000 population) and the share of total household income received by the least well off 50% of the population (17–23%) across 46 US states for which data is available. And he refers to data from more than 30 other countries establishing a strong correlation between inequality and violent crime.

It turns out that greater income disparities, around the world, are correlated with reduced life expectancy, particularly for those at the lower end of the income scale, and greater incidence of death from illnesses, alcohol-related conditions, traffic accidents and injuries. And an older study of 192 metropolitan areas in the United States between 1967 and 1973 found 'clear relationships between most of the major categories of crime and the size of the "income gap" between the incomes of the poorest 20% of the population and average incomes in each area'.[37]

These (largely correlational) studies do not provide definitive proof that inequality causes violent crime (and serious illnesses and accidents). It could be suggested that the causal arrow goes the other way. Or that some third factor is causing inequality, accidents and crimes. Undoubtedly, there are multiple complex interactions of different variables in this area. However, there is a mass of other relevant evidence, nicely explored by Wilkinson, to support the hypotheses of inequality as a major causal factor in all of these areas. In particular, evidence from many different sources suggests that stress in the family and at work, associated with feelings of general powerlessness (destruction of immune systems, frustration and anger), is the key *result* of income inequality, which, in turn, becomes the *cause* of accident, illness and crime.

As Wilkinson notes, the fact that

> links between crime and income inequality to some extent parallel those between health and inequality, is highly indicative of the channels through which health is affected. It not only provides independent confirmation that income distribution has important psychosocial effects on society, but shows that the effects are consistent with the view that wider income differences are socially divisive. Indeed, there are suggestions that they undermine the legitimacy of the society's institutions more widely.[38]

Coupled with substantial empirical evidence of the radical failure of criminal law to effectively reduce crime (through traditional policing and punishments – see chapters 18 and 19) and of tort law to effectively reduce 'accidents' or properly compensate victims, this data provides a very strong 'precautionary' foundation for a radically different approach.

Causation in populations

While major social-structural reforms could radically reduce accidents and injuries (through reducing social inequality and applying a strong precautionary principle to release of potentially dangerous products), it is important also for the law to catch up with the sort of understanding of causation achieved through the experimental studies considered so far.

A basic principle of the tort of negligence is the requirement of the plaintiff to establish, among other things, that the negligence of the defendant caused them injury or other detriment. Tort textbooks still suggest that 'common sense' is all that is required to establish whether or not a particular act or omission has caused damage to the plaintiff in any particular case. However, we have already seen good reasons for doubting any such idea.

Causation might indeed have been a relatively simple matter in earlier periods of development of the common law when it was merely a matter of establishing whether or not A really did hit B hard enough to produce the relevant injuries, or whether or not A's pig escaped and ate B's cabbages. But as we have seen, establishing the causation of lung cancer and heart disease in years gone by has been a rather more complex issue. And establishing the health effects of the use of mobile phones or of mass consumption of genetically modified foods or new drugs controlling blood pressure will similarly depend upon large-scale epidemiological investigations and complex controlled experiments.

Where relevant research has already been carried out, and relevant data already exists, lawyers need a basic knowledge of scientific research methods (such as that provided in this chapter) to begin to make sense of the material. But there are serious problems of the courts previous inability to properly understand and apply such knowledge.

The fundamental problem concerns the difference between causation in individuals and in populations. The law's basic model of causation is one involving direct perception of the causal activity (the exercise of the causal powers of) individuals. But the sorts of tests we have considered yield results in terms of increased percentages of particular effects in particular populations as a result of exposure to particular causal factors.

In many cases the harm inflicted by the pursuit of corporate profit registers in just such an increasing percentage of cases of some illness in a large population: more cases of heart disease, or lung cancer or asthma, or whatever. It is quite possible, in some such cases, to establish the percentage involved, without being able to trace the actual pathway of (mechanical) causation in particular individuals. That is to say, we might have solid evidence (from observational studies) to prove that, for example, 60% of the lung cancer cases in this group of workers have been caused by their exposure to asbestos in a particular workplace. But we cannot 'prove' the causation in any particular case. The other 40% of cases in this population will have different causes and we can't show which is which.

The standard of proof in tort cases makes direct reference to the 'balance of probabilities', which means a more than 50% chance of causation. In this case, this requirement would seem to be satisfied; in any individual case the chance is more than 50% asbestos causation. But it is quite possible that, while causing a significant percentage of cases of a particular illness, a defendant's negligence actually causes less than 50% of all such cases, meaning that there will be a less than 50% chance of causation in any particular case. But then it seems that in law the defendant in question gets off completely, even though they might have knowingly (or negligently) killed thousands of people.

The idea that a defendant corporation (or its controllers) should escape liability for increasing the prevalence of a particular cancer in a population simply because they remain responsible for less than 50% of cases overall is absurd.

If 15% (3000 people) of population A, exposed to chemical X, succumb to cancer Y while only 10% of population B, not exposed to X, but in all other ways identical, succumb, then it is true there is a less than 50% chance that the cancer of any particular sufferer in A was caused by chemical X. Reference to appropriate observations of the two matched populations (even with properly statistically significant results) fails to prove causation 'on the balance of probabilities'. But if executives of chemical company C were responsible for such exposure, despite their having prior access to information from earlier studies showing the cancer-causing powers of X, then they are knowingly or negligently responsible for killing or seriously damaging 1000 people.

It is easy enough to see 'logical' ways in which the law could deal with such a situation (which never should have been allowed to develop in the first place). While there is a greater than 50% chance that any individual victim considered in isolation contracted their cancer from something other than chemical X, if we consider two victims together, there is only 2/3 x 2/3 = 4/9 chance that both got it from something else, or a greater than 50% (5/9) chance that one got it from chemical X.

We could say that for any pair of two victims there is a greater than 50% chance that one of them got their cancer from chemical X; therefore, the company should pay each victim half of what they would have paid with direct 'individual' proof of causation. Or we could say that the company caused a third of all cases in population A so they should pay each victim a third of what they would have paid with such direct proof.

The development of 'market share liability' in the case of *Sindall v Abbott Laboratories* 26 Cal 3d 588; 607 P2d 924; 163 Cal Rptr 132 (1980) in the United States represents significant progress in this area. This case involved the widespread damage caused by the synthetic hormone diethylstilbestrol (DES), marketed worldwide to pregnant women between 1940 and 1971 to prevent miscarriage. There was no doubt about the negligence of the manufacturers who had failed to carry out basic tests of the material and ignored the damning results of other tests (which showed that it actually caused miscarriages as well as cancers). The problem for the plaintiffs lay not in proving their injuries were caused by DES but in establishing which of the around 200 manufacturers had made the DES they had consumed.

The Supreme Court of California held that each manufacturer 'be held liable for the proportion of the judgment represented by its share of the market unless it [demonstrated] that it could not have made the product that caused [the] plaintiffs injuries'.39 They therefore dispensed with the requirement for a necessary mechanical linkage in every individual case. It is only a small logical step from such market share liability to a general principle of liability in proportion to increased percentage effect produced in relevant populations. Hopefully, developing awareness amongst responsible lawyers of the true nature of causal relations, and the scientific means for establishing their existence, will accelerate the process.

Discussion topics

1. What are causal hypotheses? How are they tested? Include reference to prospective and retrospective experimental designs.
2. What are fallacies of statistical reasoning? Include examples (not just from this chapter).
3. Explain the precautionary principle and causation in populations.

Debate topics

1. Ideas of causation in common law should be guided by science, not 'common sense'.
2. Serious application of the precautionary principle would put an end to scientific and economic progress.

Additional resources

S. Beder, 'Scientific Controversy: Dioxin', in *Global Spin*, Scribe Publications, Carlton North, 1997, pp 141–60.

A. Chetley, *Problem Drugs*, Stirling Books, Australia, 1995, ch 19 on DES.

R. Graycar and J. Morgan, *The Hidden Gender of Law*, Federation Press, Sydney, 2003, pp 334–6 (section on dangerous products and dangerous drugs).

E. Handsley, 'Market Share Liability and the Nature of Causation in Tort' (1994) *Torts Law Journal* 24 at 24–44.

S. Mann, *Economics, Business Ethics and Law*, Lawbook Co, Sydney, 2003, chs 17 and 18.

D. Weatherburn, 'What Causes Crime? (section on poverty and unemployment), <http://www.lawlink.nsw.gov.au/bocsar1.nsf/pages/cjb54text>.

R. Wilkinson, *Unhealthy Societies*, Routledge, London, 1996.

Chapter 7

THEORETICAL HYPOTHESES

What are theoretical hypotheses?

In chapter 5, references were made to Type 2 theories, but no details of the nature of such theories were provided. This chapter provides a concise introduction to such Type 2 theories.

To understand Type 2 theories, we must first recognise that the further progress of our understanding of the nature, properties, powers and behaviours of things requires us to go beyond directly observable and measurable phenomena. In many cases, there is, anyway, nothing in the world as directly perceived that offers any kind of explanation for observed properties of things. If we want to find out why and how particular observable things have the properties they do have (why metals expand when heated, why rich people live longer), why and how they are able to exercise the particular observable causal powers they do exercise (how salt dissolves in water, how asbestos causes cancer), or why and how particular events – perhaps events in the remote past – came about (how the earth came into being, how mountains were formed), we typically have to consider internal structures and external relations of such things that are either too small, too quick, too big, too slow, too long ago, too far away, too complex or too deeply buried for any kind of direct observation. In this sort of case, we are completely dependent – in the first instance – upon *imagination* to construct hypothetical models of such unperceivable structures and mechanisms. Later, under the guidance of such models, we can sometimes construct instruments, extensions to our sensory systems, capable of rendering such structures and mechanisms more or less directly perceptible.

We can see how *analogy* plays a central role in the construction of such higher-order Type 2 theories. More specifically, we can see the importance of the sort of 'creative' analogising considered in chapter 1, which takes account of differences as well as similarities, in extending human understanding beyond the limits of what is directly perceptible and controllable.

The key idea here is that we find something similar to the phenomenon in need of explanation, but whose causation has already been established, typically through direct observation. We then reason back to similar, hypothetical causes for the phenomenon of unknown causation, allowing for the likely difference of scale involved.

P1   We know that object d (the mountain) resembles object x (the molehill) in respects e, f and g (it is made of similar earthy materials, has a similar location, rising up from the surface of the earth and a similar – conical – shape). It also differs from object x in respects h and j (it is much bigger and older).

P2   We know that object x (or objects of type x) is a product (or are products) of the action of causal agent y (or agents of type y) acting upon some pre-given material z in circumstances a, b, c (this molehill has been brought into being by a mole piling up earth and stones from its underground tunnelling last night).

C   We therefore formulate the hypothesis that the object d is (possibly) the product of the action of a causal agent j, similar to y, but differing from it in ways related to h and j (the mountain has been brought into being by a giant mole tunnelling under the earth long ago in the dreamtime).

Here we have constructed a sort of *model*, a model of an unknown mechanism (the giant mole). Our model is also a theory, a theory to explain an otherwise inexplicable phenomenon by reference to a particular sort of mechanism (giant moles created the mountains). In this case, the reader's first response is to say that this is not science but rather a pre-scientific animistic speculation. And such thinking is indeed characteristic of pre-scientific cultures. But it is important to see that a precisely similar form of reasoning has played a central role in the development of modern science, providing the first insights into the (unobservable) causal mechanisms operative in many different areas.

Consider the following cases:

- Democritus and Leucippus' atomic theory and its modern development as the kinetic theory of matter;

- Harvey's theory of the circulation of the blood;

- Darwin's theory of natural selection and Mendel's theory of genetics;

- Wegener's theory of continental drift and the modern theory of plate tectonics;

- Van Helmont and Pasteur's bacterial theory of disease;

- Einstein's general theory of relativity (his gravity theory).

In every case we are concerned with theories at the heart of specific disciplines of modern science (including the modern explanation of mountain formation). And in all of these cases it is easy to see the central role of analogical reasoning in the development of the theories in question, extending human thinking into areas too small, too big, too slow, too complex or too distant in time and space for direct perception.

What distinguishes the science from the pre-science has to do with the nature of the assessment procedures applied to such theories, rather than the mechanism of creation or the basic structure of the ideas.

- In the first instance, such hypotheses must be *internally consistent, possible* and *plausible*. In the case of the mole theory, we should ask such things as: Does what we know of a small mole's physiology present any problems for our hypothetical large mole? Can the design be effectively scaled-up? Would such a scaled up version be strong enough to shift the sorts of weights of material involved? Could any living creature do so? How would these moles have lived? What would they have eaten?

- Second, we need to consider the consistency of the new theory with other theories we already accept as true. Does the theory generally fit in with what we know of biology and geology? Could the moles have lived in the sorts of environments we believe existed in the remote past? A theory that does not conflict with our background beliefs is said to have the virtue of *conservatism*.

- But most important as far as science is concerned is that the theory be *testable* and *capable of generating significant new knowledge* of matters of empirical fact, over and above providing a convincing *explanation* of the (problematic) facts that originally motivated its formulation. These two considerations, of testability and of new knowledge generation, are closely related.

As far as testability is concerned the issue is straightforward. As Schick and Vaughn observe:

> Since science is the search for knowledge, it's interested only in those hypotheses that can be tested – if a hypothesis can't be tested, there is no way to determine whether it's true or false.[1]

And a theory's capacity to generate new knowledge refers to the ability of the theory to generate new and unexpected predictions of observable facts (deduced from the theory, along with specific initial conditions – that is, states of the world), which turn out to be *confirmed by observation*. Thus, although the theory itself refers to entities or processes that are not, at the time, directly observable, it can still generate predictions relating to things that are so observable.

Atoms were not directly observable at the start of the 20th century. But the atomic theory turned out to be testable by reference to the (observable) Brownian motion of pollen grains immersed in water. Einstein developed a model of molecular motion, based upon consideration of the behaviour of solute molecules in a solvent, which yielded quite precise predictions as to the behaviour of such particles.

To be suitably unexpected and 'independently' testable such predictions must relate to types of things different from those the theory was originally formulated to try to explain. It would be no good to derive a prediction from the mole theory to the effect the more mole-created mountains will be found on hitherto unexplored continents. We would expect to find more mountains whether or not they were created by moles.

Such predictions must be different from predictions that can be generated by other theories, either already accepted as true or competing with the new theory for our allegiance. If we already have a theory that predicts the existence of giant moles in the past, then a prediction derived from our theory to the effect that we might hope to find the fossilised remains of such moles does not provide a suitable test of the theory. Were we to discover such remains, such evidence would fail to favour one theory against the other (though it could be said to offer some support to both).

Another, possibly more suitable, prediction might be the existence of huge tunnels beneath mountain ranges. If mountains were indeed the products of the tunnelling activities of giant moles, then we might reasonably expect to find such further traces of their activities, perhaps including fossil mole bones or coprolites inside the tunnels. And, of course, if we did find such tunnels, this would be a substantial addition to our knowledge of the world; the theory would have demonstrated its value as a knowledge-generating tool and in the process it would have received substantial empirical confirmation.

If the theory were sufficiently rich to suggest other explanations and tests (in other areas) this would be a further point in its favour. Perhaps the moles are implicated in the creation of other geological phenomena, or other things altogether.

This example also demonstrates some of the problems involved in testing Type 2 scientific theories. For it shows how the progress of science is dependent upon the development of increasingly sophisticated *technology* – in this case, of drilling equipment or seismic or radar systems capable of detecting and mapping underground passages. Real scientific theory testing has been crucially dependent upon telescopes, microscopes, particle accelerators and a host of other sorts of apparatus.

The example also shows that while it is possible to provide strong verification for a new theory, it is difficult to provide any such strong refutation. Failure to confirm the prediction, even after long and detailed investigations with powerful technology, does not necessarily show the theory to be false. It is quite possible that the fault lies not in the theory itself but rather in the background assumptions we have had to make in order to render it testable. The tunnels might not have been strong enough to persist down through the millennia, but could rather have been crushed by the weight of material above, or they could have filled up with silt and rocks from underground streams.

Usually, some of our assumptions will indeed be wrong, even with the best theories, leading to failures to confirm some predictions. But as long as some new predictions are confirmed, this tells us we are on the right track. It means that our theory is successfully generating new knowledge in the form of new (observable) facts about the world, and we can continue to work on our background assumptions to try to find out where the other predictions went wrong.

Broadly speaking, as long as verifications keep ahead of refutations, we have what philosopher of science Imre Lakatos calls a 'progressive research programme' and it is rational to push ahead with the theory in question. But once refutations get the upper hand, once the theory ceases to lead the way to substantial new knowledge and rather seems to follow after empirical studies, with continuous modifications to the theory 'after the event', then we have a 'degenerating' research tradition.

If our theory fails to deliver any such substantial new knowledge despite our best efforts, then, at some point, it's time to think again about the theory itself and start looking for alternative possible causal mechanisms to explain the original inexplicable facts, along with the accumulating anomalous observations.

Of course, we can't just abandon theories that have demonstrated some real explanatory content (through a good record of confirmation) in the past without having something better to replace them. Nor should we necessarily reject theories (like some interpretations of quantum theory) which are currently untestable. As suggested above, the crucial technology for proper testing might not yet be available. Some theories display virtues of 'simplicity', ' scope' and 'fruitfulness' in predicting hitherto unknown phenomena well before the possibility of effective testing of novel predictions.

Scientists originally accepted Copernicus' heliocentric cosmology, despite empirical refutation (and no confirmation) because it was simpler than the preceding Ptolemaic theory. And, ultimately, their support was justified as new technology and advances in other areas of sciences came to provide solid empirical confirmation.

As noted earlier, the theory itself, along with its novel predictions, often functions as a guide for the construction of new scientific instruments. And, ultimately, via such instruments, the originally unobservable underlying entities and mechanisms identified by the theory can actually become (more or less) directly observable, as a particularly powerful *verification of the theory*. But even if they do not become so observable, the theory can still be *strongly supported* via a developing tradition of confirmation of far-reaching novel predictions manifesting the causal consequences of the operation of such underlying entities and mechanisms.

Deductive reasoning in scientific theory testing

So far we have concentrated largely upon non-deductive patterns of reasoning: specifically, the inductive-analogical reasoning involved in Type 2 theory creation or construction. But a deeper understanding of the nature of theory testing involves reference also to some basic patterns of deductive reasoning.

Three basic forms of valid deductive argument are particularly relevant here. Two we are already familiar with, *modus ponens* and *modus tollens*.[2] The third, DeMorgan's Law, is equally straightforward.

P Not (A and B).

C So not A or not B (and vice versa).

These two statements are logically equivalent, so each necessarily implies the other. If it's not the case that A and B are both true (together) then at least one of the propositions, A or B (or both), must be false. And if at least one is false, they cannot both be true.

We have seen how analogical reasoning allows us to construct 'models' of underlying causal mechanisms or structures, responsible for producing particular observed appearances (events, processes, situations). Such models include reference to specific causal agents (electrons, quasars, tectonic plates), to specific causal powers or abilities of such agents (to repel negative charges, radiate galaxies of energy from star-sized volumes of space, change the patterns of the earth's crust), and to the particular circumstances in which such powers are actually exercised or realised to produce some (observable) effect or consequence (the flow of a current, creation of an image on a photographic plate, the formation of a mountain range).

Such causal mechanisms are 'triggered' or become operative in producing observable consequences in particular sorts of situations only. In other situations, their powers remain dormant, are blocked by countervailing forces or produce effects that cannot be distinguished by human observers, leading to no such observable consequences or effects. (Current only flows with a potential difference in a circuit).

In some cases, we will be concerned with mechanisms or processes that might no longer be operative, or no longer be able to be triggered into operation (or operating so slowly in the present as to be invisible). This is often the case where we seek to explain specific occur-

rences in the past – unique individual events such as the extinction of
the dinosaurs or the origin of the universe – rather than specific types
of occurrence continuing in the present like the periodic orbits of the
planets, the heating of the earth's core, the appearance of antibiotic-
resistant bacteria, or earthquakes in California.

In the latter sort of cases, we will be concerned with mechanisms
that are presumed to be operative still, such as radioactive decay,
biological evolution and plate tectonics. But in both sorts of cases, we
need to be able to deduce predictions of possible observable consequences other than those that originally motivated the production of
the theory. And to do this, we must take account of the specific conditions surrounding the mechanism in question: the interaction of the
mechanism in question with its ambient environment of other such
mechanisms and processes.

In the simplest sort of case, of a mechanism still thought to be
operative in the world, and capable of being triggered (or 'liberated')
by direct human intervention, we can create the conditions ourselves.
For example, in 1919 physicist Ernest Rutherford used a naturally
radioactive material as a source of a beam of alpha waves in a
vacuum. He focused the beam into a sample of nitrogen gas, thereby
transforming some of the nitrogen into oxygen, and demonstrating
the power of such particles to transmute one physical element into
another. Later investigators used electric and magnetic fields to artifi-
cially accelerate such beams of charged particles, to create many new
isotopes.

In other cases we will have no such direct control of proceedings.
But we can still, hopefully, generate testable predictions by reference
to the generative mechanism and its surrounding conditions.

To take a simple and well-known example, suppose that we have
formulated the theory that the impact of a substantial asteroid or
comet, of 10 kilometres or so across, was responsible for the extinction of the dinosaurs (and half the other species then alive through
massive climatic disruption) at the end of the Cretaceous period,
about 66 million years ago.

This theory was originally motivated by discovery of a thin layer
of the heavy metal iridium – apparently of extraterrestrial origin – in
rock deposits of this period. But in order to further test the theory,
we must look for some further observable evidence, other than that
which suggested the theory in the first place. And we do not have far

to look. Once we begin to consider other aspects of the environment of the impact, and other likely consequences of such an impact within such an environment, other possibilities immediately suggest themselves. Most obviously there is the hope that we might find an impact crater of the appropriate size and date, still observable today. (Other consequences might include evidence of particular sorts of climatic disruption at the relevant time.)

In this sort of case, where we cannot actually control the system concerned to exclude interfering or counteracting forces, we have to assume that such forces are absent. In this case, we assume (or hope) that the impact was on land, rather than in the sea, and that the land in question is still available for observation, rather than having been completely eroded away, covered by deep ocean sediments or 'subducted' beneath a continental plate.

In the following, M is our model or theory, C our initial conditions and P is our prediction.

> M = Comet of type x strikes land at time y (and the land it struck is still visible).
>
> C = A comprehensive search of all land areas is carried out (of a type suitable for detecting comet craters).
>
> P = A crater – of appropriate type – is found.

We now have a definite prediction: M and C together imply P. And if our reasoning is sound, we can then take a second deductive step. We now know the truth of the conditional statement

> If (M and C) then P.

The truth of 'M and C' is sufficient for the truth of P, since 'M and C' implies P.

As we have seen, we want to produce predictions that are quite novel and unexpected. In particular, we do not want to duplicate predictions than can already be derived from other known or accepted theories. For then, confirmation of such predictions would provide support for both theories, in no way favouring our (new) theory. Nor would it provide any genuinely new knowledge about the world.

As Ronald Giere suggests, we can capture this requirement in the idea that

> If (not M and C) then very probably not P.

If the theory (M) is false (but we are otherwise correct about the conditions at the time of our test (C)) then very probably the prediction will not eventuate; we do not expect it to be confirmed under the circumstances in question (C).

One obvious way to satisfy this criterion is to *make the prediction as precise as possible*. The more precise, the more unlikely. Notice that the crater prediction from the cometary impact theory seems to satisfy this criterion quite well, providing that size and date are precisely specified and checked.

Producing such a novel prediction, and establishing that it really is novel, will often be a far from straightforward process. Interesting theories or models will often be complex, and their relations to perceived (or measurable) reality by no means direct. A great deal of cognitive work can therefore be required to produce such a testable prediction.

Consider the search for dark matter or for black holes in the universe. By definition, we are concerned with types of things that cannot be (or can only with great difficulty be) observed directly; similarly with Freudian psychology and its postulation of unconscious mental processes and agencies. Even a theory of such antiquity and power as atomic theory was still rejected by some authorities at the beginning of the 20th century on grounds that no definitive empirical evidence was available.

But this has not prevented committed researchers from devising ingenious tests, and unexpected predictions that really do follow from the theories in question – along with consideration of appropriate (initial) test conditions(as in the examples above).

Once we have such a prediction, we can carry out our experiment or test of the theory. As noted above, in some cases this will actually involve creating condition C capable of triggering mechanism M into producing observable effects. And this will typically involve isolating the mechanism in question as much as possible from the influence of others that might block or obscure its operation.

In other cases, as with mechanisms no longer operative, or large-scale geological, astronomical or cosmological processes, on a scale beyond the reach of human intervention, we have no such direct control. But the principle remains the same. We must take account of the relevant causal mechanism and the (presumed) specific conditions of its operation to guide our search for relevant evidence.

On the one hand our prediction can be refuted: wide-ranging searches fail to reveal any crater of the right size and age. The logic of *modus tollens* (MT) and DeMorgan (DeM) then tells us that we are wrong about our proposed model or about the prevailing conditions, or we have simply failed to carry out our experiment properly.

P1 If (M and C) then P.

P2 Not P.

C1 So not (M and C). (MT)

C2 So not M or not C. (DeM)

Certainly this does not necessarily mean we are on completely the wrong track. We could be right about the basic mechanism involved; we just need to refine our understanding of the conditions. Perhaps conditions are not actually such as to allow the mechanism to operate as predicted; some other forces were operating to counteract it or block it after all. Perhaps the comet landed in the sea and could not therefore produce a crater. Perhaps the crater has indeed disappeared beneath ocean sediment or below continental rocks. Perhaps we have simply failed to search long and hard enough.

On the other hand, our predictions could be confirmed. There is the crater in all its glory, at the tip of the Yucatan peninsula; there is the measurement, precisely as predicted. In this case, *modus tollens* and DeMorgan give us good grounds for taking the theory seriously and continuing to develop it further.

P1 If not M and C then very probably not P.

P2 But P.

C1 That is, not not P (double negation).

C2 So, very probably, not (not M and C). (MT)

C3 So, very probably, M or not C. (DeM)

P3 And assuming we're right about C,

C4 Very probably M, or something close to it.

Here we clearly see how confirmation of such an unexpected prediction increases our state of knowledge of the objects and processes of the perceived world, as well as providing strong evidence for the existence of particular 'underlying' mechanisms and structures. Now we know about the crater (about the existence of the planet Neptune, about the holes in the ozone layer or whatever); about many things that were once no more than predictions. In this way, deductive logical reasoning makes a central contribution to the generation of new knowledge of the world. But notice also that it is not the reasoning alone that has increased our knowledge, it is the test: the physical contact with the new 'situation', entity or process, interpreted in the light of such reasoning, that is crucial.

Fallacies of Type 2 theory testing

Here we can follow Giere, once again, in identifying a number of fallacies of Type 2 scientific theory testing, that is, a number of 'recognisable patterns' of reasoning that 'seem superficially to be alright, but do not in fact provide adequate support for the stated conclusion'.[3] As Giere says, 'the general mistake in these fallacious patterns is the failure to satisfy the second condition of a good test (a prediction not likely to be fulfilled if the theory is false). But the failure gets disguised in various ways'.[4]

We first consider probably the most familiar of such fallacies, those of *vague predictions* and *multiple predictions*. They apply particularly to claims for special future-predicting powers of psychics and astrologers. In the first case, the prediction might at first appear improbable if the psychic or astrologer lacks special powers, but in fact is sufficiently vague to stand a good chance of being fulfilled whether or not the theoretical hypothesis (that they do indeed have such special powers) is actually true. 'You will have some money problems, but things will work out alright. A new relationship is a serious possibility.'

With multiple predictions, the oracle makes quite specific and unlikely predictions, but makes so many of them (and/or repeats them for such long periods) that at least one is likely to be fulfilled. At least one of their selected famous people will (eventually) marry, die, be murdered or arrested in the course of one year, two years, three years. Then, of course, the oracle makes a great deal of the one or two predictions that are confirmed and keeps quiet about all the others that weren't. It looks as if an unexpected prediction has been confirmed. But this is not so. If we treat all their predictions on a given occasion as a single – conjunct – super-prediction it is clearly refuted. If we treat it as a disjunct – x or y or z or a or b, then it not unlikely that one of the disjuncts will be fulfilled and condition two is not satisfied.

Giere also identifies a fallacy of *no predictions*, and a version of *false dichotomy*, common in relation to theory testing. In the former sort of case, the theory proponent focuses upon some apparently inexplicable events – typically in the remote past – and then proposes a possible explanation. In fact, no new predictions can be derived from the theory, but it looks as if it satisfies condition two by virtue of the (alleged) mystery surrounding the past events in question; they could not have happened if the theory were not true. For example:

P1 The pyramids could exist only if aliens built them.

P2 The pyramids do exist.

C   So aliens built them.

But P1 is simply false; there are other possible (and much more plausible, independently testable) explanations. So really they give us the fallacy of *affirming the consequent*.

P1 If aliens (of our favoured kind) had come to Earth in the past, then pyramids would exist, because they had built them.

P2 Pyramids do exist.

C   So aliens came to Earth in the past, and built the pyramids.

In the latter sort of case, of false dichotomy, a theory proponent seeks to convince us of some radical explanation for a particular observation, for example, strange lights observed in the sky. They set up a series of possible explanations, including more 'straightforward' ones (weather balloons, clouds, aircraft, artificial satellites), dismiss all of the other ones and claim the truth must lie in their favoured 'non-straightforward' explanation (an alien spacecraft). Quite apart from the likely difficulty of any such definitive refutation of all straightforward possibilities, the problem is that there will always be further possibilities (in particular, some little known but still terrestrial phenomenon) which have not been considered. Independent verification of the theory is required.

Finally, there is the *ad hoc rescue*. The prediction is refuted and a new theory is concocted to explain why this happened, despite the (supposed) truth of the original theory. As we have seen, this, in itself, is not a fallacy, but rather an important part of scientific advance.

But if the new theory is not independently testable, worse still, if the observations that refuted the original prediction are then presented as evidence confirming the modified theory, then a fallacy is involved. Again, this is an example of affirming the consequent.

> **P1** If the new (modified) hypothesis is true, then it follows that there will be observations that refute the original hypothesis.
>
> **P2** We have made an observation that refutes the original hypothesis.
>
> **C** Therefore, the new (modified) hypothesis is true.

Creationism versus Darwinian theory

Many of the issues discussed so far in relation to Type 2 theory can be illustrated by reference to the contrasting models of Darwinian evolutionary theory and creationism, both aiming to explain the complexity, diversity, interdependence and functional specialisation of living things and their constituent organs and structures. As Richard Norman says:

> Creationism is the view that the creation story in the first chapter of the Bible is literally true, that the whole universe, including our own earth with its species of plants and animals and the first human beings, was created by the direct agency of God in a period of six days, a few thousand years ago.[5]

According to this conception, God has created humans as creatures quite different from animals. Whereas animals are mere bodies (or perhaps bodies with feelings), humans are also, and essentially, immaterial souls, capable of intelligence, free will, moral judgment and a life after the death of the body.

So do creationists generally assume a fixity of the 'essential natures' or 'forms' of animal and plant species: fixed limits within which the descendents from common parents always remain. And they assume that everything in the world, including individual animals and species (as well as the organs of individual animals), has some aim or purpose within the grand scheme of things, typically the purpose of satisfying some human or divine requirement.[6]

The analogical basis of this theory is nicely brought out by Norman's succinct formulation of the design argument of the creationists:

P1 Living things [and their component parts] and other features of the natural world are organised in such a way that they serve a purpose [eyes for seeing, feet for walking, trees for providing oxygen].

P2 Where [the components of] human artefacts are organised in such a way that they serve a purpose, this is because they have been created by an intelligent designer.

C   Therefore those features of the natural world that are organised to serve a purpose must have been created by an intelligent designer.[7]

As Norman says, the analogy does have some appeal. But so too does it have major weaknesses.

> The trouble is that we have no idea how to fill in the details of the explanation. We cannot specify any of the physical processes, comparable to the carpenter's cutting and shaping of the wood, or the builder's assembling of the bricks and mortar. However powerful we may suppose the divine creator to be, we have no idea what physical techniques he might have used.[8]

According to the Darwinian model, by contrast, the world and the first life forms were created by purely 'material' or 'natural' processes in the very remote past, and have, since then, been slowly changing in various ways (through similarly material processes). Every group of organisms is descended from a common ancestor, including humans who share a (recent but now extinct) ancestor with the great apes. Rather than being 'fixed', species multiply, give birth to new species by splitting into daughter species, by budding, or simply by changing sufficiently through time.

This process is illustrated in the first of Darwin's two major analogical arguments, which compares species to branches of a single 'tree of life'. As Mayr notes:

> already in the summer of 1837 Darwin clearly stated that 'organised beings represent an irregularly branched tree' (Notebook B.21) and he drew several tree diagrams in which he distinguished living and extinct species by different symbols.[9]

Darwin's tree starts out as a single trunk some time in the remote past, thereafter generating many new branches. Some such branches continue to grow with little change for thousands or millions of years, some divide into two or more new branches, some change their form gradually over the millennia, and some make it through to the present day while others terminated long ago. Each branch is an individual species, or breeding population, at least until it splits or becomes so transformed in the course of time that descendents could no longer interbreed with their own (long dead) ancestors (the latter now being called 'speciation by anagenesis', or the accumulation of small changes). And a major cause of such splitting is geographic separation, leading to an eventual lack of compatibility between the populations concerned (called 'speciation through cladogenesis').

But most important was Darwin's account of the (underlying) mechanism that makes such species formation possible: the process of 'natural selection'. Again, Norman provides a succinct analysis of the analogical reasoning involved in this case.

> P1   We know that artificial selection of domesticated plants and animals can produce new varieties [with favoured random variations chosen for breeding].
>
> P2   We know that an analogous process of natural selection takes place in nature to produce new varieties better adapted to their environment.
>
> P3   There is no reason why the process of natural selection that produces new varieties may not, over sufficiently long periods of time, also produce varieties so different as to constitute new species.
>
> C   The mechanism of natural selection can therefore explain how new species have come into existence with features adapted to their environment.[10]

Self-replicating systems tend to expand their populations at an exponential rate. But in practice, such growth is self-limiting as population pressure upon scarce resources produces intense competition, famine and disease. Darwin was well aware of the high fertility of animal and plant species and limitation of resources throughout the natural world, leading to fierce competitive struggle for existence within and between species.

Organisms in a population differ in their abilities to survive and reproduce (in the given circumstances). Given such intense competition for limited resources, even small differences can determine survival to reproductive age, or failure to do so. So are such differences, to some degree, passed on across the generations. And natural selection leads to increasing adaptation of populations to the demands of their environments. Such populations come to consist of individuals with properties that help them to survive and reproduce. And it is process of adaptation that gives the appearance of 'design'.

In stark contrast to the creationist model, which leaves the details of the creation process completely mysterious, the Darwinian model

> works because it invokes familiar processes, of biological reproduction and inheritance, natural variation, and the struggle for survival, and it shows how, given a sufficient time span, these mechanisms can account for the emergence of species adapted to their environment and possessing physical organs adapted to their functions. And the experimental biosciences, including modern genetics, can fill out, in immense detail, the picture of how these mechanisms work.[11]

Most important, Darwinian evolutionary theory has sustained a substantial record of generation of new knowledge through verification of clear, precise and otherwise unexpected predictions. The broad idea of generation of increasing complexity and diversity from greater simplicity and homogeneity has been amply confirmed by the fossil record going back billions of years. Many specific predictions of the nature of intermediate forms to fill earlier gaps in that record have been spectacularly verified. And more recent genetic studies have provided a solid biochemical foundation for the theory.

To take some obvious examples, given fossil evidence of fish preceding amphibians, amphibians preceding reptiles, reptiles preceding mammals and birds, and apes preceding humans, evolutionary theory clearly implied the existence of a succession of intermediate forms in each case, their character more or less predictable on the basis of structural similarities and differences between previously known forms. And indeed, since Darwin's day, examples of such intermediate forms have been discovered, in increasing numbers, refuting the creationist idea of fixed, 'essential natures' of species, and confirming the evolutionary idea of the emergence of new species through natural variation and selection.

Some of the most spectacular recent cases here include 3.5–2.8 million-year-old hominid fossils of Australopithecus afarensis from Africa (a creature with a bipedal skeleton similar to that of modern humans, but a brain little larger than that of a modern chimpanzee) and the increasing numbers of feathered dinosaurs and dino-birds, clearly showing the dinosaurian ancestry of modern birds.

By contrast, creationist theory has provided no predictions, and hence no confirmed predictions. Certainly, the fossil record yields no radical and unexpected evidence of divine intervention. Instead creationists have responded to the increasing mass of new knowledge generated by the evolutionary model with the fallacy of 'ad hoc' rescue, claiming that the divine creator did, in fact, also put all these strange fossils into the ground as well, for mysterious reasons, with no possibility of independent testing of any such claims (or no empirical support for them whatsoever).

Theories in court

Until relatively recently, the criterion used to evaluate and determine the admissibility of expert scientific testimony in US courts was the so-called Frye Rule. This required that the 'major premise' (the scientific technique or theory used) must have 'gained general acceptance' and not be merely 'experimental' in nature. In *Frye v United States* (1923), the Court of Appeals for the District of Columbia noted:

> Just when a scientific principle or discovery crosses the line between the experimental and demonstrable stages is difficult to define. Somewhere in this twilight zone the evidential force of the principle must be recognised, and while the courts will go a long way in admitting expert testimony deduced from a well-recognised scientific principle or discovery, the thing from which the deduction is made must be sufficiently established to have gained general acceptance in the particular field in which it belongs.[12]

As Walton points out, this principle was applied for more than 50 years, until the late seventies when 'courts began to repudiate or seriously question it and loosen the requirements for expert opinion testimony'.[13] And in 1975 new Federal Rules of Evidence were introduced that some saw as rejecting the Frye Rule. They mainly focused upon three requirements: appropriate specialised knowledge based upon 'experience, training or education' allowing an expert to 'assist the trier of fact'; this expert's obligation to disclose the reasoning behind their factual opinions on cross examination; the requirement for juries, rather than experts, to decide 'ultimate issues' in criminal cases.

> In the case of *Daubert v Merrill Dow Pharmaceuticals Inc* (1993) the US Supreme Court definitively rejected the Frye Rule, instead advocating as the criterion of admissibility of scientific testimony that it be 'not only relevant but reliable. According to the majority opinion, 'reliable' means 'derived by the scientific method' and 'supported by appropriate validation' ... The Court made it clear that the intent

of this ruling was to make the judge the gatekeeper to determine the admissibility of scientific testimony in a case. Amongst the criteria given [to define appropriate validation] were (1) 'testability' of the theory or scientific technique, (2) peer review and publication, (3) known or potential rate of error, and (4) general acceptance, not as the exclusive criterion [as in the Frye Rule] but as part of the court's assessment of reliability.[14]

Among other things, this decision is interesting because it seems to require that judges apply precisely the sort of criteria of the 'reliability' of scientific theories considered in this chapter, specifically their record of successful experimental verification (balanced against their record of refutation).

It seems to be true that the Frye Rule was dangerously restrictive – given the fundamental theoretical disagreements found in many areas of science, the subsequent rejection or substantial modification of virtually all theories deemed thoroughly reliable in the past, and the fact that even the best new ideas will take time to be understood, accepted and properly developed amongst particular communities of researchers.

On the other hand, the new rule places the judge in a position of great responsibility as far as these considerations are concerned. And it is interesting that evidence that Merrill Dow tried to exclude because of an alleged failure to meet the requirements of the Frye Rule, evidence that proved decisive in finding Merrill Dow liable, ultimately turned out to be unreliable. Given that this centred upon a single paper describing a single animal test, showing 2 out of 8 rabbits receiving high doses of a chemical similar to the one under consideration in the case with foetal abnormalities, while a large body of published data described many properly constructed experiments showing no significant relation between the actual chemical and birth defects claimed by the plaintiff to be caused by it, the question arises of how well the Supreme Court judges understood their own principle.

In Australia, the Uniform Evidence Act (s 79) allows opinion based on specialised knowledge deriving from a person's training, study or experience, leaving 'specialised knowledge' undefined. Under the common law it is accepted that expert opinion must derive from a 'field of expertise' but as Odgers points out, 'Australian law has never clearly resolved the test for a "field of expertise" ... There are authorities which appear to adopt a test of "general acceptance" in the relevant scientific discipline, authorities which require a court to make an assessment of "reliability" and authorities which adopt both tests.'[15] The Australian Law Reform Commission considered that such matters should be left to the discretion of the court, but some recent High Court decisions show the influence of *Daubert* in interpreting s 79 of the Act in terms of expert testimony meeting a standard of 'evidentiary reliability and relevance' to be admissible. In particular, the recent cases of *HG v The Queen* (1999) 197 CLR 414 and *Velevski v The Queen* (2002) 76 ALJR 402 involve the High Court applying a test of reliability closer to the *Daubert* approach.

Discussion topics

1   What are Type 2 theories? Find some examples and clearly explain the analogies involved.

2   How are Type 2 theories tested? Include reference to deductive reasoning in scientific theory testing.

3   What are fallacies of Type 2 theory testing? Find some examples of your own.

4   Was the Frye Rule dangerously restrictive? Were the new US evidence rules an improvement? Find some relevant examples.

5   In what ways do *HG v The Queen* and *Velevski v The Queen* show Australian courts moving towards a *Daubert* approach? See Odgers et al below.

Additional resources

S. Odgers, E. Pedern and M. Kumar, *Companion to the Uniform Evidence Act*, Lawbook Co, Sydney, 2004, ch 8.

R. Freckelton, *The Trial of the Expert: A Study of Expert Evidence and Forensic Experts*, Oxford University Press, Melbourne, 1987, pp 152–65.

Law, ethics and social theory

Chapter 8

ETHICS AND LAW

We all have elaborate world views or belief systems as structured systems of ideas which guide our perceptions, thoughts and actions. The factual side of our belief systems concerns ideas of what is happening in the world today, what has happened in the past, and what could happen in the future, including what it's possible for humans to achieve. Our factual beliefs are more or less strongly and comprehensively informed by scientific research, going beyond description into explanations and predictions grounded in research and experimentation.

But there is also a moral or ethical side to our belief systems, concerning our ideas of what should happen, what sorts of things are intrinsically worth striving for, what sorts of characteristics make a good person and what sorts of duties or commitments we think should be taken most seriously – by ourselves and by others.

Social ethics is concerned with how society should be organised, what policies should be pursued, what laws should be passed and enforced. Personal and professional ethics is concerned with how we should act in relation to others with whom we have more or less direct contact – family members, clients, work colleagues.

Many people think only of the latter sorts of personal relations when they think of moral decision-making. But this is misguided. There are always important moral issues involved in political decision-making and law reform. This is not just of concern to politicians and High Court judges. Because we live in a democratic society, we all have some input into wider social decision-making. We can all lobby and campaign and educate others if we are not happy with the moral decisions of our leaders or fellow citizens. We can all vote for change, in some areas at least. And democracy only works to the extent that we all recognise a responsibility to involve ourselves in such processes.

We get our *moral ideas* from our family, from society, from formal education and from our human nature and our own critical thinking. But *ethics* is about serious consideration and rational justification of moral decision-making. Ethical thinking allows us to clarify, critically assess and possibly revise and improve our moral decision-making.

Most people would agree that morality is about empathising with other people: putting ourselves into their shoes, and trying to treat them with consideration and respect. A lot of people see the 'Golden Rule' as central to ethics: 'try to treat other people as you would want them to treat you if you were in their situation'. But empathising with others allows us to see that sometimes they might not want to be treated as we would want to be treated in their situation. They want us to treat them as they want to be treated.

Philosophical consideration of moral decision-making has focused on ideas of what have been called 'deontology' and 'utilitarianism'. Deontology centres on the idea of moral duty or obligation. This includes (1) general duties to respect and further the autonomy, dignity and human rights of all people and (2) particular duties to respect and honour the promises and commitments we make to (specific) others.

Although human rights are regularly invoked in popular discourse, the concept of a 'right' is actually quite a difficult one to come to grips with. When we talk about rights we are considering legitimate entitlements of individuals to particular goods and to the free exercise of particular abilities and powers. Rights for some individuals imply responsibilities of others: not to infringe particular individuals' rights, and to respect or facilitate the effective realisation of the rights in question.

Legislation and judge-made law create legal rights, as entitlements given the force of legal sanction. Contract law, for example, is designed to enforce the rights of someone who has accepted the promise of another to provide some good or service, and has themselves contributed some consideration to the promiser, without receiving the good or service in question. It orders a promiser who is failing to deliver to do so or to compensate the promisee if they fail to deliver. But legal rights don't have to be moral rights. In the past the law has upheld rights of slave ownership and punished those who sought to help slaves to escape their servitude.

Moral or human rights are rights that all people have by virtue of being human. If such rights are not respected then people cannot live properly human lives. Health care is a good example here. If seriously ill people are denied access to health care then they cannot live a good life and quite likely they cannot live any life at all.

Laws can be enacted and enforced that aim to ensure that human rights are respected by making them legal rights. The United Nations' Universal Declaration of Human Rights sets out a range of basic human rights, which should be seen to be equally available to all people at birth, 'without discrimination', and subsequent human rights treaties oblige their signatories to ensure the protection of all such rights through their own national legal systems.

The nature of human rights and their role in international law is considered in detail in chapter 9. In this chapter the major focus is on other issues in deontology and utilitarianism.

Utilitarianism centres on the idea of human wellbeing or welfare. The basic idea of utilitarianism is to try to maximise the happiness or wellbeing of all of those affected by our actions. In any situation we need to consider all the actions available to us and all the people who will be affected by our actions. We then have to pick the action with the greatest balance of utility or social welfare over disutility (or the smallest balance of disutility over utility) for all concerned. No-one's welfare should be prioritised over anyone else's, but a minority might have to lose out in order to further the wellbeing of a majority.

The decisions of High Court judges, Cabinet ministers and army generals can profoundly affect millions of others. But even if our social power is limited, our actions can still affect many other people. Each individual's actions are an example for others and society continues to exist only through a mass of such individual actions. In democratic voting, for example, small individual decisions can have profound cumulative effects. And individual decisions to campaign against, or refuse to obey, what are seen as unjust laws or policies can go far in combating institutionalised prejudice and injustice.

We owe respect and support for human rights and for overall social welfare just because we are humans ourselves. But we are born into complex networks of social relationships and we can choose to create or maintain social relationships with others, which carry with them specific moral responsibilities. Through making various sorts of commitments or promises to other people, thereby raising legitimate expectations on the part of such people, we incur specific moral responsibilities towards those people.

This includes commitments to assist and care for others, not to harm them, to be truthful with them, to prioritise their interests and their welfare over those of others and to try to compensate them for wrongs we inevitably do them.

As highlighted by Christine Parker and Adrian Evans in their study *Inside Lawyers Ethics*, a lot of teaching called 'professional ethics', including 'lawyers ethics', is really teaching about rules and regulations of professional conduct set out in practice or profession statutes or in the codes of professional associations, or about the ways in which the general law applies to professionals in their relationships with clients.[1]

More genuinely 'ethical' consideration of professional practice centres on differing ideas of what constitutes a responsible role for particular sorts of professional practitioners in contemporary society. Parker and Evans consider a range of influential ideas of the role of legal practitioners in the common law world, including what have been called 'adversarial advocacy, responsible lawyering and moral activism'.[2]

Adversarial advocacy argues that a lawyer's primary moral responsibility is to advance their client's particular interests with the maximum commitment allowed by law. There are obviously ethical problems with this, particularly where the rich can buy more and better legal services.

Responsible lawyering is the idea of the lawyer as officer of the court, attempting to make the law work as fairly and justly as possible. In this case duties to the client are tempered by duties to ensure integrity of and compliance with the spirit of the law, to ensure that issues are decided on their substantive merits, rather than on procedural or formal grounds. Neither of these approaches allows much scope for critique of the law in accordance with ethical standards and, in particular, standards of social justice external to it.

Moral activism is based on the idea that 'it is not appropriate for lawyers to have a special ethics' defined by their particular social role.

Rather they should try to apply the principles of deontology and utilitarianism to legal practice. In particular, lawyers have a responsibility to 'involve themselves in public interest and law reform activities to improve access to justice and change the law and legal institutions to make the law itself more just'.[3]

As Parker and Evans observe, 'unlike the responsible lawyer approach, moral activism is not confined to the idea of justice set out in the legal system'; instead it contemplates that the legal system may need to be changed to become more just and that lawyers have a responsibility 'to contribute to such change'.[4]

Morality is difficult because of conflicts within and between these different sorts of values and commitments, as well as between our own selfishness and our concerns for others. Our personal commitments tell us to put our own family and friends first. But considerations of equal respect for the rights of all people and of support for the social good appear to conflict with this. Who do we save from the burning building – our own child or five of someone else's?

We might believe that everyone should have a right of equal access to high-quality education. But if we find that private schools with high fees produce better results than public schools, if we can afford it, don't we owe it to our kids to give them the best education money can buy? But through paying the high fees, we are keeping such schools in operation, maintaining inequality and unfairness that denies such high-quality education to children of poorer families. Perhaps this is an area where government has the responsibility to create a situation where individuals don't have to make such choices by ensuring that everyone has access to the highest quality education.

Another area of difficulty is the potentially complex relationship between ethical and factual or empirical issues. This can be illustrated by reference to the issue of abortion. Killing people is wrong. But is a first-trimester foetus a person? This is a scientific question rather than an ethical one. What appear at first to be ethical questions often turn out to actually be questions about empirical facts. We need to be clear about relevant empirical facts in order to make good moral judgments.

Our ideas about human rights and social welfare are deeply influenced by our factual beliefs about people and society. As noted earlier, such beliefs exist in structured systems. We see the world and make sense of our experience through such systems. When we consider such systems from the point of view of their assumptions about the nature of people and society, they are typically called *ideologies*. In particular societies, particular ideologies are dominant in the sense of being actively promoted by dominant social groups and of being deeply embedded in education, law and political decision-making.

The dominant ideology of the English-speaking world and other western cultures (for example France and Italy), which shapes all of our beliefs and perceptions, is (small 'l') liberalism. All liberals believe in democracy and the rule of law. But different groups have different ideas about the nature of people and of society, justice and fairness.

In particular, more right-wing, or 'free market', liberals, see justice – both in distribution of social benefits and in retribution for criminal acts – essentially in terms of 'just deserts'. It is morally right, fair and just that you should receive good things: goods, money, power and reputation in proportion to your positive social contribution, particularly your contribution to social wealth creation. Similarly, you should expect to be punished in proportion to the extent of harm you have caused to others.

Left-wingers, on the other hand, see a close relationship between justice and equality. They look to the state to try to achieve a basic equality of access to the means for protection and realisation of human rights, including rights to work, fair pay, social security, democratic participation, health care, education and legal access and to provide compensation for undeserved suffering.

Again, these differing ideas of justice are explained in detail in the next and subsequent chapters. Here, we look a bit more deeply into the nature, origin and rational justification of other moral ideas.

Metaethics

Philosophers have traditionally distinguished three major divisions within the study of ethics: *metaethics, normative ethics* and *applied ethics*. Metaethics is closely bound up with those areas of philosophy called metaphysics and epistemology. Metaphysics or ontology enquires into the fundamental nature of things, and epistemology into the possible or appropriate techniques available for producing or establishing reliable knowledge of the world. Metaethics enquires into the fundamental nature of moral beliefs, judgments and actions, and into the appropriate means available for discovering or establishing the truth or appropriateness of moral ideas, rules and values.

We will return to look at normative and applied ethics shortly, but here we consider metaethics, starting out with the fundamental nature of moral judgments, beliefs or ideas. As noted earlier, specifically *moral judgments* are distinguished by their reference to obligation (what we ought to do, or have a duty to do), to value (what is good or valuable) and to virtue (to the kind of person we ought to be). Moral judgments are not the only sorts of judgments that make reference to duties and obligations and values. Science tells us what we ought to do to achieve particular sorts of ends. But generally science says nothing, or appears to say nothing, about precisely what sorts of (ultimate or final) ends we should pursue.

Judgments of what is right and wrong in law – of what we 'ought' to do in order to uphold the law – depend on established legal principles. But as noted earlier, legal principles are not necessarily ethical principles. Some particular action or inaction (for example, not helping your terminally ill friend to end their life) might be the 'right' or 'correct' thing to do if you want to obey the law. But you might feel no moral obligation to obey the law because you judge it to be an immoral law.

Moral values are things of intrinsic worth, rather than things that derive value as a means to achieving other things. So-called *teleological* or *consequentialist* ethical theories see specifically moral or ethical obligation as derived from such ultimate values, considered as goals of action. Because some consequence of action is intrinsically good, perhaps the happiness, freedom or equality of all people, then we should necessarily and without qualification pursue it: we have a moral duty to do so. We must aim to maximise good consequences of action and minimise bad.

Other so-called *deontological* theorists argue that some actions are, by their nature, intrinsically morally right or good, so that we ought (necessarily) to perform them independent of consideration of consequences. In particular, they argue that we have ethically fundamental duties – particularly duties to respect the rights and autonomy of others. Or they argue that it is the intention with which the act is carried out or the way in which consequences are brought about that is most important from an ethical perspective.

Some argue that there is only one thing of intrinsic value: classical utilitarians argue that the only such intrinsically valuable thing is happiness, or pleasure and the absence of pain. Therefore all moral obligations concern individual responsibilities to try to maximise such happiness (for all creatures capable of experiencing it). Others recognise a range of different sorts of things as having intrinsic value – health, knowledge, empowerment, equality, loyalty, respect, fidelity, kindness – which we are morally obliged to try to achieve.[5]

Virtually all ethicists agree that specifically ethical obligations integrally involve other people. Such obligations always go beyond merely or essentially self-interested considerations of our own wellbeing. It might be true that individual A ought to get more exercise in order to stay healthy. And good health might indeed be a moral value – something of intrinsic worth. But for a judgment about health to be a moral or ethical, rather than a merely prudential, judgment, it must take account also of the health of others, or of the role of the health of the person concerned in realising other values that integrally involve the wellbeing, rights or autonomy of other people.

Many would go further and say that a condition called *universalisability* is also characteristic of all specifically moral obligations and judgments. This means that any moral obligation we attribute to ourselves or any other in any particular situation we must also attribute to any and all other people in the same type of situation. This is basically the same as the Golden Rule: do unto others as we would have then do unto us.[6]

Ethics and free will

As the eighteenth century philosopher Immanuel Kant argued, ethics is closely bound up with human *free will*: the capacity of people, not merely to respond directly to external and internal stimuli as causes with particular decisions and actions as effects, but rather to be able to deliberate about such stimuli as reasons for actions, in the light of numerous different possibilities of decision and action; to adjudicate between competing or conflicting reasons for action (and the different actions they suggest) and formulate particular decisions or intentions prior to engaging in action, on the basis of such deliberation.

Desires arise spontaneously in people as a result of particular perceptual stimuli. We feel hungry and desire food. We might also believe that we can get food, easily and quickly, without other problems, by doing X. But the gap between reason and decision allows us to consider moral obligations or commitments that might conflict with or override the performance of X. They might more urgently command the resources necessary for accomplishing X – resources of time, effort, money or whatever.

This 'gap', as contemporary philosopher John Searle calls it, provides a space not just for adjudicating between conflicting reasons for action, but for rethinking the nature of moral obligation and commitment in the light of new information and experience. And such rethinking is not just a matter of internal thought processes, but also of discussion and debate with other people.

Just as the gap between desire and decision allows for the possibility of moral decision and action, so does the gap between decision and action (and gaps within ongoing sequences of actions) allow for failure of moral will or resolve, traditionally called *weakness of will*. Here, 'we judge unconditionally it would be better to do (the morally correct thing) y than x, believe that we are able to do either, and yet intentionally do x instead of y'.[7]

As Searle says:

> ... making up your mind is not enough: you still have to do it. It is in this gap between intention and action that we find the possibility, indeed the inevitability of at least some cases of weakness of will ... As a result of deliberation we form an intention. But since at all times we have an indefinite range of choices open to us, when the moment comes to act on the intention several of the other choices may be attractive, or motivated on other grounds.[8]

Guilt and conscience

Ideas of morality are closely bound up in many people's minds with ideas of guilt and of conscience. The conscience is usually thought of as a particular internal mental agency or faculty with the power to monitor an individual's feelings, thoughts and actions. Such an agency 'assesses' the moral status of such thoughts and actions, punishing wickedness with feelings of anxiety, guilt and self-loathing, and rewarding goodness and the renunciation of evil with feelings of pride and elevated self-worth. Supporters of conscience in this sense see it as a necessary counterweight to weakness of will, providing the moral strength to carry through moral intentions in action.

Some see such an agency as the voice of God, some as a biological product of evolution and some as a social creation, a policeman in the head, enforcing social norms and laws. Indeed, some identify the conscience-less individual with the psychopath or sociopath, ruthlessly exploiting and using others as means to their own immediate gratification, without reference to moral, social or legal rules.

Sociological theorists have highlighted the role of socio-economic factors in shaping dominant ideologies or belief systems within particular societies. Some have emphasised the importance of social anxiety – of concern about the approval or disapproval of others (and avoiding experiences of shame) – as a major element of conscience, motivating individual conformity to the dictates of such ideologies. Others have highlighted the power of dominant elites to shape and influence the conscience, and hence the behaviour, of the majority.

Sigmund Freud identified conscience with what he called the *social superego*, a young child's image of parental values and parental discipline, 'introjected' or internalised as a way to try to come to terms with oedipal conflicts. Fearing parental retribution for their own jealous aggression and incestuous desires, the young child fantasises taking parental authority into their own mind to monitor and control their thoughts in such a way as to keep them safe from parental retribution in the external world.

Freud was highly ambivalent about the moral and social status of such an agency. On the one hand, he agreed that those with weak or absent superegos were likely to be prey to selfish instincts and highly anti-social. On the other hand, he saw too strong a superego as too recalcitrant to advance beyond infantile moral beliefs and tending to overwhelm (or preclude) free action, initiative and fulfilling personal relationships with feelings of anxiety, guilt and depression.[9]

Other psychoanalytic traditions have been clearer in condemning the social superego as an agency just as likely to support immorality as morality. There is no guarantee that the values of parents or the dominant social values of the environment of the young child will be genuine moral values, as opposed to destructive and corrupt values of racism, sexism or fascism. A corrupt superego will leave individuals feeling guilty about thinking or doing the right (morally correct) thing, and feeling good about thinking or doing the wrong (immoral) thing. To the extent that they identify the voice of conscience with the voice of God, so will they see God as demanding support for such corrupt social practices and institutions.

At the same time, so have such traditions focused on a minimal core of early parental love and care necessary for the infant's survival. The child's identification with the loving parent provides a – transhistorical and transcultural – basis for ethical feelings and actions, prior to any such social 'distortion'. It provides a foundation for further development of genuinely ethical ideas and actions. And no matter how deeply it might be repressed (or shut away from conscious awareness) as a consequence of disappointment, mistreatment and abuse, it can still be accessed under appropriate circumstances.

The nature of moral ideas

Ethical judgments and beliefs are distinguished by their reference to intrinsic values, obligations and virtues, rights and duties, equality and justice. But there are other important questions we can ask about *the nature of ethical judgments and beliefs*. Are they claims to truth? Are they expressions of feelings or attitudes, rather than truth claims? Are they prescriptions or imperatives or calls for others to think or act in particular ways?

Cognitivists generally see moral judgments as truth claims – supposedly true propositions – whose truth can be determined through the use of our cognitive faculties of reason and perception. *Non-cognitivists*, on the other hand, see moral judgments as expressions of emotion, of our (positive or negative) *feelings* about particular issues, expressions of our attitudes, choices or decisions, seeking to evoke similar attitudes, choices or decisions in others, or universal *prescriptions*, through which we prescribe or require particular courses of conduct of specific others and of anyone else in similar circumstances.[10]

There are problems with all these ideas. To see moral judgments as mere expressions of individual feeling seems to undermine all possibility of serious moral deliberation, debate, decision-making or progress. But to see moral judgments as truth claims also raises difficulties. Most philosophers today see factual statements as referring to objects, events or situations in a world that exists independently of our language and judgment, and what we say about such objects, events or situations as true or false depending on whether it *corresponds* to how things are in the world. But then the issue arises of what particular things or states of affairs in the world render moral statements true or false. What states of affairs do true moral statements correspond to? And if such moral facts are out there to be perceived or understood then why is there not greater consensus among people about moral truths?

Plato argued that the facts in question are not to be found in this earthly world, but rather in a heavenly world properly seen only after death. In this other world, such things as goodness, justice and beauty exist in their pure forms. Or rather, such pure forms, unlike physical objects, have a non-spatio-temporal existence, and are accessible only through the exercise of pure reason rather than perception. Such reason can show us the truth or falsity of moral clams, by reference to such pure forms. A particular earthly thing or action is good to the extent that it partakes of, reflects or approximates to the pure form of goodness.[11]

If we reject this two-worlds approach then we have to find the truth of moral statements in the ordinary physical world. And there are numerous different suggestions about how we might do so.

Moral psychology

As well as inquiring into the nature of moral judgments, metaethics considers issues of the origin, rational justification and truth conditions of such judgments. Clearly, origin, rational justification and truth conditions are closely related. If we assume that moral judgments are rendered true by virtue of their corresponding to moral facts, then the question becomes one of how we gain access to such moral facts.

There are three sorts of answers which have been offered to the question: *God* reveals such facts to us, our own *human nature* does so through inbuilt faculties of feeling, intuition and/or logical reasoning, or *society* does so either through some universal process of socialisation or through some specific social-historical dynamic of development, creating the right social circumstances to allow recognition of fundamental moral truths.

These different forces need not be mutually exclusive. It is possible, for example, that our evolutionary history has equipped us with capacities or tendencies to recognise fundamental moral truths, but only certain sorts of social situation allow such faculties to properly develop, while others thwart or restrict their development in some or all people.

As we will see, a number of different approaches tend to emphasise either feelings or rational thought as fundamental sources of moral insight. But it is quite possible to see that both feeling and logical reasoning are equally necessary and interdependent in this regard. As Hume, among others, argues, our ethical ideas could have their origins in particular sorts of feelings – perhaps feelings of sympathy for others or humanity or fellow feeling, as intrinsic parts of our human nature:

> Through sympathy we identify with and are moved by the happiness and suffering, joy and sorrow, pleasures and pains of others. Under the force of this feeling we tend to express our approval of those actions which promote the happiness ... of others and our disapproval of actions which have the opposite effect.[12]

But then:

> ... our judgment can, Hume acknowledges, 'correct' our emotions, so that we recognise a person or an action to be admirable or deplorable, whatever the feelings we may happen to have ... Our judgments can transcend our feelings and can have an impersonal character.[13]

Richard Norman argues that, in fact, 'there is a great range of such 'primitive responses (in addition to sympathy or empathy) ... which underlie our shared vocabulary of evaluation', including respect for other people:

> Whereas sympathy is primarily a response to others as passive experiencers, as beings who are affected by a world in various ways and who enjoy or suffer accordingly, respect is a response to others as active beings, as agents. So, whereas sympathy involves a spontaneous inclination to respond to other people's needs and interests as our own, respect may in contrast involve distancing oneself and recognising that others' projects are theirs, not mine. It is the inclination, not to live others' lives for them, but to stand aside and let them live their own life in their own way.[14]

Others have traced what they believe are fixed psychological stages of moral development corresponding to different stages of cognitive development, through which all children and adolescents are supposed to pass. The most influential scheme is that of Lawrence Kohlberg. According to Kohlberg, for very young children, 'bad' means 'what incurs punishment'; 'good' means obedience to parental rules. Later, 'good' comes to mean 'what gets you what you want' in the form of reward. Then it comes to mean 'what parents approve of', and then 'what is approved of in the wider society'. Finally, in adolescence, the individual moves on to rule utilitarianism and Golden Rule consistency.

There are problems with any such mechanistic models. In particular, it is far from obvious that children's moral awareness necessarily develops in tandem with their cognitive abilities. Very bright, knowledgeable people can be selfish, ruthless and cruel.

Divine commands

For divine command theorists, moral standards are simply the commands of God which instruct humans as to how they should behave. And to test the truth of moral claims we have merely to consult the relevant religious authorities or sacred texts.

As Waluchow shows, there are, in fact, two different versions of divine command theory:

> The *moral ground* version ... says that the grounds for our moral claims lie in God's will or commandments. If X is morally right, this is because God has commanded that we do X ...

The *divine index* theory, by contrast, says that while God does indeed always command us to do the morally right thing, this is because that thing is independently morally correct:

> Being a supremely perfect being with unlimited knowledge and benevolence, God knows the true standards of morality and lets us know what they are.[15]

There are major problems with both theories. The moral ground theory seems to render moral values completely arbitrary. God could command us to torture and kill. And we cannot say that he would never do such things because according to this theory there are no independent moral standards with which to make such judgments. 'Good' just means 'what God commands' so if God commands torture then torture is good by definition.

As Waluchow points out, it would be good if we were sure, as in the divine index theory, that God always commanded us to the morally correct thing, even if we did not know why it was good. But how could we be sure that God commands the good if we had no independent means for assessing goodness? And how do we know anyway what God commands?

> Where are we to discover the commands of God? In the Bible? In the Koran? How about the various sacred Hindu texts, or the disputed gospels of St Peter? Perhaps God's word is found in the pronouncements of divinely inspired prophets and religious leaders? But which prophets? Which religious leaders?[16]

Even if we – somehow – identify the true word of God, such a true word has still to be interpreted and applied in practice. The New Testament in the Bible tells us not to kill. But what about self-defence? And state-sponsored execution? What about 'just wars'?

> [We] cannot entertain such questions without engaging in moral reflection, that is, some form of moral reasoning which is grounded in something other than the commands of God whose meaning is in question. So even if we believe that God's word is a guide to the requirements of morality, it cannot be a sufficient guide.[17]

It is easy to see the dangers of grounding moral belief – or legislation – in (supposed) divine commands. Whatever religious authority claims privileged access to such commands has no requirement to provide rational justification for whatever it claims to be the 'true' content of such commands. To the extent that others accept such an idea, they require no such justification and, in effect, hand over total and arbitrary power to the group in question. And any who challenge such alleged commands, instead of being answered with logical argument, are likely to be answered with repression and persecution.

Moral relativism

Moral relativists argue that moral principles and rules are basically sets of conventions, assumptions and practices accepted as right and appropriate within particular societies or communities at particular times. 'Correct' moral precepts can therefore be discovered by empirical observation of behaviour of the members of any society we happen to be in. Within that society it's right to do what the majority think it's right to do.

Some relativists see moral standards as *cultural conventions* internalised (to some extent) by all or most individuals growing up in a particular community. Such values are (typically) handed down to the new generation by parents and other authority figures. Others see such standards as *personal choices or commitments* of particular individuals selected from an available stock of cultural options. Once chosen, such values are 'right' for the person doing the choosing.[18]

On first consideration, relativism has a lot going for it. The great diversity of different values found across different cultures suggests the absence of any sort of culture-independent 'objective' rational foundation for morality. Moral relativism appears to be the only alternative to moral imperialism: judging our own values to be correct and all others wrong, perhaps asserting our right and responsibility to impose our correct values on others by force. Certainly, it is difficult to see how the values of one society can be demonstrated to be true to members of a different society, given the absence of agreed criteria for assessing moral values. And as existentialists say, if God is the source of objective moral values, the end of belief in God is also the end of belief in such objective standards.[19]

On the other hand, to see moral values as no more than cultural conventions seems to undermine the possibility of moral criticism within and across cultures. What the people over there, or the majority of the people over here, do or believe (or at least what they think of as moral values in which they should believe) can never be 'wrong', no matter how cruel or apparently irrational. It is morally correct by definition. And reference to 'the majority' highlights the fact that no society is actually homogenous in moral beliefs and actions – though there can be considerable homogeneity within particular social classes of class-divided societies (such as workers, peasants and capitalists). In complex and large-scale societies in particular there are hundreds of different subgroups, social strata and sub-communities within and between which people move, with quite different sets of beliefs, values and priorities. Which are supposed to be the values 'of society'? And what about all those who claim to support particular values but fail to do so in practice?

If morals are just personal choices of cultural possibilities, there can be no real moral disagreements. On this view, apparently contradictory moral beliefs are not really contradictory: what is right for some may not be right for others. But this really does not make sense. As long as we assume that all people share a common reality, and at least sometimes refer to the same entities and processes in the course of making moral judgments, then contradiction seems unavoidable.

It is crucially important here to distinguish the ways in which people acquire particular moral values from the truth of such values, although there will be close connections between the two. It is quite possible to see values as social products – with different values produced and transmitted in different social situations – without accepting that all such values are equally valid or that every society's 'dominant' values are 'true for that society'– as relativists contend.

Some see moral values as influenced by particular social-historical circumstances, by an individual's position within the social division of labour, and by historical forces of conflict, change and development. Marxists, in particular, see individuals' moral values as profoundly shaped and directed by social class positions, by ongoing inequalities and conflicts between different class groups, by changing economic circumstances and by new technological developments. In a class-divided society, those enjoying the benefits of economic and political power and privilege will seek to justify and rationalise such power, both to themselves and to the exploited and powerless majority. Their economic power will enable them to propagate such ideas as 'ruling ideologies'.

Many would agree with relativists that parents and other authority figures can significantly influence the values of the growing child. And many would agree that at later stages of moral development individuals can free themselves to some extent from such influences to choose or develop systems of values of their own (or at least appropriate and develop available ideas in their own way).

But most theorists (including most Marxists) would still distinguish between the origin of moral beliefs and the truth status of such beliefs – with the latter having to do with what such beliefs say rather than where they come from; or distinguish between rational processes of construction of moral beliefs (perhaps building on a foundation of empathy as suggested by Hume and some psychoanalytic theorists) – making it more likely that they are in fact true – and less rational processes based on prejudice, fear or ignorance.

Some sorts of social situations will make it easier for individuals to perceive, discover or accept such objective moral truths; some will make it difficult or impossible. So both true and false moral values are indeed social products, but nonetheless true or false for that.

Just because there are differences between the values of different culture groups this does not mean that there are no correct answers. Some groups can be right and others wrong. And it is possible to stand up for what we believe to be right without necessarily being a cultural imperialist. Ideas can be changed through example, through education and through rational argument and dialogue.

And perhaps there is actually less disagreement in some areas than cultural relativists claim. A lot of supposedly moral disagreement turns out in practice to be factual disagreement, with different factual beliefs in different societies – or between different individuals – leading to different moral prescriptions and values. Referring again to an earlier example, A and B both believe in the sanctity of human life but A opposes abortion altogether, believing that human life begins at conception, while B believes that the foetus is not truly a person in the first three months of its existence and therefore does not necessarily oppose abortion during this period.

It is also possible that much apparent diversity in moral beliefs is really rather a sign of the necessity to adapt and apply the same basic moral principles to radically different natural and social circumstances – of war and peace, poverty and plenty, town and country, agrarian and industrial societies.

Utilitarianism

As noted earlier, normative ethics is about the fundamental rules, principles and values underlying and justifying moral judgments. One of the most influential normative ethical theories is *utilitarianism*, originally developed in the eighteenth and nineteenth centuries through the work of Jeremy Bentham and John Stuart Mill.

Utilitarianism decisively rejects divine command theory, natural law and moral relativism in favour of establishing what is seen as a straightforwardly empirical foundation for moral decision-making. This is the principle of *utility* as universal objective standard for rational determination of moral rights, obligations and duties.[20]

Classical utilitarianism involves a monistic consequentialist theory of obligation, resting upon a particular theory of value. For classical utilitarians, the only intrinsic value is that of happiness or pleasure and the absence of pain and suffering. For Jeremy Bentham it is only the quantity of such happiness that matters, while John Stuart Mill considers also its quality, with 'higher' mental forms of happiness counting for more than 'lower' bodily forms.

Some later utilitarian theorists have argued rather for *pluralistic* theories, which see a range of human experiences in addition to pleasure as also of intrinsic worth, including knowledge and aesthetic experience. Others see the satisfaction of rationally chosen and socially responsible individual preferences of all kinds as the basic goal of moral action. Others emphasise objective human wellbeing, in the form of health, longevity, welfare, empowerment and fulfilment as such ultimate goals.

Act utilitarianism identifies an act as right and good 'if and only if there is no other action we could have done instead which either (a) would have produced a greater balance of utility over disutility or (b) would have produced a smaller balance of disutility over utility'.[21] The second condition deals with situations where we cannot help but do some harm and we are trying to minimise such harm.

For *rule utilitarians*, by contrast, it is not consequences of individual actions that matter: it is the consequences of everyone adopting a general rule under which the action falls. If not everyone could do what we propose to do now without great disutility resulting, then it's wrong for anyone to do it. For rule utilitarianism an act is morally right 'if and only if it conforms with a set of rules whose general observance would maximise utility'.[22]

All utilitarians agree that the wellbeing of each and every sentient being affected by our actions should count equally in our decision-making. We should consider each and every person as equally deserving of happiness or fulfilment or wellbeing, and act accordingly.

In theory, both act and rule utilitarianism offer clear means for establishing moral priorities and resolving moral disputes. If we are a classical act utilitarian, we simply compare the overall happiness levels likely to result from each of the actions open to us and then perform the one which generates the greatest happiness.

The first and most obvious problem with this idea is the problem of measuring, quantifying and comparing happiness levels of different experiences and different individuals. It is far from clear that this is possible. Even if it were, trying to calculate the precise long-term happiness consequences of numerous different possible actions could be fantastically difficult and time consuming. How could any decisions ever be made? And is setting out to maximise happiness really the best way to actually maximise happiness? Individuals typically achieve happiness not by setting out to do so but rather by doing specific sorts of useful things well. Why should things be any different for an individual trying to maximise the happiness of others?

Even if we could both quantify happiness and successfully plan to achieve it, the utilitarian emphasis on maximisation could come into conflict with pursuit of equal shares of happiness for all. If action A produces one unit of happiness for Bill and six units for Ted, while action B produces three units for each of them, then action A should be chosen over action B on strict principles of maximisation, but action B should be chosen on grounds of equal rights to happiness.

Things are actually worse than this, since the act utilitarian maximisation principle would also seem to allow total sacrifice of the happiness – or objective wellbeing or interests – of the few, to increase the happiness of the many. A hypothetical example frequently cited here is that of police authorities framing an innocent black man for murder of a white man to prevent violent race riots in a town in the southern USA. Another example is Lord Denning's infamous statement about the need to preserve public confidence in the police even at the expense of allowing the wrongful conviction of the Guildford Four through fabricated police evidence.

Norman observes:

> What utilitarianism fails to take on board ... is that though some people's interests sometimes have to be sacrificed for the interests of others, there are limits. There are some things which, morally, you cannot do to people for the sake of the greater good.[23]

As Norman points out, this idea of 'the moral limits to the permissible treatment of human beings' can be articulated in the language of human rights, as legitimate entitlements of all people by virtue of their common humanity.

> One significant use of the language of rights ... is to set limits to utilitarian calculations. So to talk of each individual's right to life is to recognise that human beings are not just items to be weighed against one another in a utilitarian calculation of total net benefit. If I have a right to life, that means that other people may not deprive me of that right; my life is mine, not just a component of the general happiness, and it is for me to decide what is to be done with it. Likewise the rights to certain basic freedoms establish the constraints on the ways

in which human beings may be treated, and to violate those rights is to begin to rob them of their humanity.[24]

We will return to consider the role of rights in moderating utilitarian decision-making in chapter 9.

Act utilitarians fail to take account of special responsibilities created by past actions – of promising, for example – and by established relationships with family, friends or colleagues. An example here is that of the parent who has promised to buy their child a particular birthday present but gives the money to a homeless person on the street instead. Another example might be that of saving a family member rather than a leading heart surgeon or wealthy philanthropist from a burning building. Perhaps the surgeon or philanthropist will save lives and produce masses of happiness or wellbeing, but your family members may legitimately expect you to rescue them first.

Another problem is that of free riders or law-breakers. An individual can reason that their theft of an item from a big store will greatly increase their happiness while contributing little or no sadness to any particular others, and is therefore not only legitimate but mandatory from a utilitarian perspective. Similarly, it would seem that utilitarians should steal from the rich to give to the poor if the rich cannot be persuaded to voluntarily redistribute their wealth to those in greatest need.

An act utilitarian response in these cases would be to refer to long-term consequences. By betraying the trust of family and friends through helping beggars, by colluding in framing the innocent or by stealing from stores or rich folk we may well do more harm than good in the longer term. But such act utilitarians generally do accept the rightness of sacrificing some happiness – including some lives – to produce greater happiness (through saving more lives, for example). Military intervention in genocide situations could involve some loss of life among the intervention force to save many more lives on the ground. Shooting down the hijacked airliner could save many more lives in the urban centre for which it is headed.

As far as inequality is concerned, act utilitarians would remind us of the declining marginal utility of wealth – the fact that extra wealth for those who already have plenty will increase their happiness less than the same resources given to those in poverty and need. Similarly, they can refer to the epidemiological research of Wilkinson and others that shows greater inequality of income leads to increasing disparities of health, with those at the lower end dying 5, 10 or 15 years earlier than those at the top, and significantly earlier than the poor in a more egalitarian system. So that far from increasing inequality, utilitarian judgments as guides to social policy will generally support redistribution in favour of material equality.

Rule utilitarianism appears to provide another possible response to some of the problems. We cannot condone general principles of robbery and 'fitting up' and betrayal; if everyone did these things this would lead to great social unhappiness. Rather, rule utilitarianism requires us to respect individual rights to life, property and justice.

Here we recognise also the impossibility of being able to predict precise long-term consequences of every act. Instead we settle for general rules that will generally, or in aggregate and in the long term, be more likely to do a bit more good than harm.

But rule utilitarianism has its own problems. By supporting some rights it inevitably overrides others and loses the benefits of principled resolution of conflicts of rights. If we insist on sticking with the rules no matter what special circumstances arise then we would seem to be following the rules for their own sake rather than for utility maximisation. But if we allow for deviation then we are back with act utilitarianism.

And we cannot follow ideal rules, which would create the happiest society if everyone followed them, given that not everyone is following them now. If private property were equally distributed, it might make sense to respect the property of others. Given that it is radically unequally distributed, taking from the rich to give to the poor might make moral sense.

We can see why many have recognised a close relationship between rule utilitarianism and law. In fact, some would say that the laws of the land are simply rules whose general observance and/or consistent legal enforcement maximises utility in the long term. Breaking particular laws on particular occasions or failing to enforce such laws may lead to an increase in happiness levels. But in the longer term, happiness will be maximised if all or most laws are obeyed by all or most people and/or consistently applied by the legal system.

Such claims – about the common good – have the benefit, at least in theory, of being open to empirical confirmation or refutation. As suggested earlier, this may be difficult in practice if we stick with the classical utilitarian emphasis on happiness levels. But if we focus instead on objective means of social welfare, it may not be so difficult after all.

When judges say they are making decisions on grounds of 'public policy', the most obvious ethical interpretation would be that they are aiming to establish general legal principles whose consistent application by other judges will maximise overall social welfare. When legislators recognise and support certain rights in law it could be that they believe that such rights are intrinsically valuable, or it could be that they believe that consistent legal recognition and support of such rights will maximise overall utility in the long term, even if ignoring such rights could increase utility in individual cases. Alternatively, legislators might support general legal principles that explicitly override particular individual rights in pursuit of the common good.

In theory, judges and legislators do not have the problem of failure of other legal practitioners to follow such principles because of the institutionalisation of consistent application (through *stare decisis*, etc). But there still remain difficult issues of discretion and interpretation which undermine such consistent application in practice. Most importantly, it cannot be assumed that simply outlawing particular harmful behaviours or enforcing particular significant rights will necessarily maximise social welfare. The real social costs of such legal intervention could simply outweigh the social benefits – for many possible reasons.[25] This has been recognised in recent years particularly in relation to criminalisation of drug use, with an increasing – utilitarian – emphasis on genuine harm minimisation.

Kant and Ross

Kant's deontological theory presents a radical alternative to utilitarianism. Whereas utilitarians accept no absolute and unconditional moral rules (apart from happiness maximisation), Kant supports absolute and exception-less principles of action; lying and committing suicide, for example, are never morally justified under any circumstances. Whereas only consequences matter for utilitarians, consequences are irrelevant for Kant. It is principles of action that matter: the way things are done. More specifically, actions have moral value by virtue of conforming to 'maxims' – general principles which specify (a) what we see ourselves doing and (b) our reasons for doing it.

Rationally based maxims must conform to what Kant calls *the Categorical Imperative* – a monistic theory of obligation. This requires universality and respect for the autonomy of other people. As Kant says: 'Act only on that maxim [that general rule or principle of action, including the reasons for that action] whereby you can at the same time will that it should become a universal law'.[26] Kant thinks that we can discover moral rules through application of the purely rational, logical requirement of avoiding contradiction. When I think about lying in a particular sort of situation, I must think of the consequences of such an action becoming a 'universal law'; of everyone else lying in such a situation. And I will then find that in some sense I would contradict myself by lying. Lying presupposes people trusting each other to tell the truth. But with lying as a universal law there can be no such trust. I am relying on an institution I am simultaneously destroying.

The Categorical Imperative requires us never to treat people as mere ends to our own objectives. What makes them people is the fact that they have their own rational faculties to determine their own moral and practical ends. So, again, there is a kind of contradiction involved in treating people as mere means to our own ends. Instead, we must always respect their goals and purposes. To respect others as persons is to respect their worth and dignity as rational beings – beings able to rationally choose their own goals and purposes. We must respect their autonomy – or power of rational self-governance.

There is general agreement among ethicists that universalisability is a necessary condition of valid moral judgment. We cannot morally act for a reason unless we accept that everyone else in the same situation should act in the same way. There are problems with this idea, nonetheless. In fact, it seems to come into conflict with respect for others' autonomy. The way we might want others to treat us might not be the way others want others to treat them. Perhaps we should rather treat others as they would want us to treat them.

Ethicists also generally agree about the central moral value of respect for autonomy. But different theorists have emphasised different senses of autonomy. Some focus primarily on an absence of external coercion, allowing the individual to freely act as they choose to do. Others emphasise the provision of facilities that allow individuals to exercise a genuine freedom to choose between viable alternatives. And others again focus on an absence of internal constraints that obstruct effective deliberation and selection of both the best means to chosen ends and of those ends themselves. We have already considered such possible 'internal' constraint in the form of an oppressive and infantile superego. Others would include stresses that interfere with the effective operation of our mental deliberative faculties – like drugs, trauma or mental illness. Where other people, in a position to do so, fail to provide us with appropriate information, where they lie to us or otherwise deceive us, this too limits the effective exercise of the abilities required for rational deliberation.

The value of autonomy is recognised in law. In particular, requirements of informed consent to medical procedures, and consumer protection law which requires reliable information to be provided to purchasers of goods, focus on this last consideration of removing obvious obstacles to rational deliberation. Contract law now recognises that contractual arrangements entered into on the basis of a radical imbalance of power or knowledge may be unconscionable, and therefore unenforceable in law. Criminal law has recognised duress as a justification or excuse for otherwise illegal actions, insofar as the individual concerned is not seen as acting autonomously where their 'will is overborne by another'.

On the other hand, the law fails to adequately consider the way in which lack of autonomy – in terms of how the 'duress' of social situation or radical restriction of available options – may contribute to 'criminal' behaviour in a radically unequal and class-divided society. With its black-and-white picture of absolute 'free will' on the one hand, or complete absence of such free will on the other (in situations of duress or insanity), the criminal law radically fails to consider the ways in which real life options are more or less narrowly restricted for individuals and groups by virtue of their class positions.

At the other end of the social scale, so does the system fail to address the encouragement to law-breaking offered by the effectively unrestricted scope of 'free' and autonomous action available to the rich and the powerful. They can come to take it for granted that they can 'do whatever they want'.

For William D Ross, both consequences and intentions are important in moral decision-making. But Ross's theory is particularly distinguished by its emphasis on the centrality of special relationships in creating particular moral rights and duties.

Utilitarianism treats everyone as equally a beneficiary or victim of the action of everyone else. But in fact every person stands in different and specific moral relations to different people (and to the same ones). Particular sorts of relationships – of friend to friend, doctor to patient, teacher to student, colleague to colleague, child to parent, husband to wife, promisor to promisee – carry with them different and specific moral values, commitments and responsibilities. And such values and commitments can be important enough to override utilitarian calculations of maximisation of overall happiness – or objective social welfare.

Ross identifies six so-called prima facie duties, deeply grounded in our past actions and social relationships. These are duties of fidelity (telling the truth, keeping promises, honouring commitments), reparation (compensating for our wrongdoing), fair distribution of goods, beneficence (improving the condition of others), self-improvement and non-maleficence (not harming others). They are all things we should generally try to do. But different duties will be more significant, depending upon the nature of the situation. We should generally try to tell the truth and keep promises, for example, but where doing so will produce great harm to others we should prioritise non-maleficence.

Ross sees such duties, and the dominant duties in particular situations, as generally evident to our faculties of moral intuition. Others are not so sure and suggest that, while these might be good rules of thumb, something like a utilitarian calculation is still necessary to decide what to do in difficult cases of conflict.

Aristotle and feminist ethics of care

Whereas Kant, Ross and the utilitarians all consider the question of what moral rules or principles should govern our choice of actions, Aristotle focused rather on virtues or qualities of character which determine what kind of person we are. Rather than rules or principles to follow, he considered virtuous habits of life to develop or achieve and vices to try to avoid.

For Aristotle virtue is essentially a disposition or tendency acquired through practice and reason to choose well. We can relate this idea to Searle's identification of the crucial gap in human conscious experience between desire and decision, noted earlier. Virtuous actions are not simply acts which conform to particular principles of value.

By its nature moral action presupposes rational deliberation: serious consideration of available alternatives. For Aristotle such deliberation is as important as the action itself. But all such deliberation is essentially concerned with choice of means to the end of a particular sort of wellbeing to which all people are directed by their inherent human nature.

Aristotle's 'doctrine of the mean' sees virtue as consisting in observing the mean between excess and deficiency in our emotional responses to others and to the world. Some have understood this essentially as a doctrine of 'moderation in all things'. And Aristotle encourages such an interpretation by identifying a number of virtues as the mid-points between specific vices. One such virtue is temperance, which concerns appetites for food, drink and sexual activity, standing midway between the excess of gluttony and the deficiency of starvation and frustration. However, Aristotle also says that observing the mean does not necessarily involve always choosing a midpoint, and that sometimes the right way to feel anger or fear or other emotions is to feel them very strongly.

Norman seeks to reconcile these ideas by arguing that what Aristotle was really doing was rejecting Plato's earlier idea of reason and emotion as essentially antagonistic, with the requirement for reason to dominate and control emotion.

> For Aristotle feelings can themselves be the embodiment of reason. It is not just a matter of reason controlling and guiding the feelings. Rather, the feelings can themselves be more or less rational. Reason can be present in them ... Essentially it is a matter of their being more or less appropriate to the situation. Take the case of anger. Suppose I become furious because someone fails to say hello to me ... Here my anger is irrational. Suppose, in another case, that I become furious because I see a gang of children heartlessly taunting and bullying a younger child. Here my anger may be quite appropriate; the cause may be genuinely appalling.[27]

In other words, the doctrine of the mean commands that we avoid what would on the occasion in question be an excess or a deficiency – of tolerance, courage, benevolence, friendliness, generosity or loyalty. Our feelings are rational 'in the sense that they are sensitive to the real nature of the situation, not distorted by extraneous considerations'.[28]

Discovering the mean, and responding accordingly, is a matter of what Aristotle calls 'practical wisdom' rather than theoretical knowledge. Whereas the latter is about discovering universal principles, the former is rather about sensitivity to the particularity of the situation. Such practical wisdom is a product of life experience.

> The knowledge which enables us to understand [the doctrine of the mean] is acquired not by learning theoretical principles, but by moral training, by being properly brought up in a morally civilised community.[29]

In such a civilised community, the virtuous life, in this sense, is also the fulfilled and happy life.

The Aristotelian account has been criticised for failing to provide clear guidance in difficult situations of moral conflict and requiring supplementation with a theory of right action and obligation. But others have seen it as a strength of the theory that it recognises no clear or simple answers, since there are no such answers.

A number of feminist theorists have been sympathetic to Aristotle's rejection of abstract, universal principles and rules in favour of emotional responses as central features of ethical life. But in contrast to Aristotle's emphasis on manly virtues of courage on the battlefield and temperance off it, they have tended to emphasise actions and values of 'communication, compromise, caring, special attention to concrete details and the various personal relationships and emotional bonds involved in particular situations'.[30]

Carol Gilligan critically re-examined Kohlberg's ideas of ethical developmental stages considered earlier. In particular, she compared the different responses of boys and girls to moral problem situations, including one involving a man who cannot afford to buy an expensive drug from a pharmacist to save his wife's life. She found that whereas boys in the later stages of moral development 'looked for answers in abstract principles governing property and the value of human lives' – in this case calling for the man to steal the drug – girls of a similar age looked for solutions through 'mediation, communication, compromise and the personal relationship' between the man and the pharmacist.[31]

> Under Kohlberg's model, [the girls] had not ascended to the more advanced stage of moral reasoning [attained by the boys]. According to Gilligan, [the girls] response is in no way inferior or less advanced than [the boys]. [They] appealed to what many feminists now call an 'ethics of care'.[32]

The boys' appeal to abstract, impartial and universal principles:

> ... misses out on a good deal of what actually concerns people in their everyday moral lives. [It] ignores the roles played by special relationships, emotional bonds, discussion and compromise in our everyday moral lives. It misses out on an important fact well recognised by most women, and now by many advocates of feminist ethics generally; that a good deal of our moral lives is concerned with the particular personal relationships we share with others. Personal, caring relationships, with all their individuality, subtlety and complexity, are the cornerstones of our moral lives.[33]

In her *In a Different Voice: Psychological Theory and Women's Development*, Gilligan seeks to show that women's moral values tend to emphasise responsibility, whereas men stress rights. In Gilligan's view, women look to context, while men appeal to neutral, abstract notions of justice. She speaks of a female 'ethic of care', deriving this from nurturing.[34]

Applied ethics

As noted earlier, applied or practical ethics is about finding ways to apply such general principles and ideas of ethical decision-making and ethical living to the concrete contexts of particular professional activity: of medicine, business, scientific research, education or law. And this includes practical systems of education, dispute adjudication and regulation aiming to encourage, develop or apply appropriate values in the disciplines in question.

Traditional legal education includes some final-year study in professional ethics. As noted at the beginning of this chapter, often what is called 'professional ethics' isn't really ethics at all, but rather is simply a survey of the limits of legally permissible behaviour on the part of lawyers in their dealings with their clients and with the courts. The great danger here is that students then equate such legal limits with moral limits, or fail to question the law involved here.

Even when such studies do have some genuinely ethical content, there are good grounds for seeing this as, all too often, too little and too late. As Nader and Smith note:

> Robert Granfield, a sociologist who teaches at the University of Denver wrote a book published in 1992 titled *Making Elite Lawyers* about what happens to Harvard Law School students between their

acceptance and the time they graduate. Granfield says that legal education often turns idealists into amoral pragmatists: 'A lot of people who go into law school have a strong sense of right and wrong and a belief in moral truths. Those values are destroyed in law school, where students are taught that there is no right and no wrong and where such idealistic, big-picture concepts get usurped. The way the majority of students deal with this is to become cynical. They actually come to disdain right versus wrong thinking as unprofessional and naïve.

Professor H Richard Uviller teaches legal ethics at Columbia University School of Law. He says: 'Professors try to keep the ideals of the students high. But when they learn that their highest obligation is to the client, students begin to think of the rest of it [duty to society and the justice system] as wimpy and soft and not what clients respect. One reason they get that message is because it is true.' And many professors do not attempt to instil idealism in their students. They come from corporate law backgrounds and, indeed, some law professors maintain lucrative corporate law practices on the side. Others, even critics of corporate power, are simply cynics who see little chance of reforming the legal profession. Such cynicism is infectious and convinces many students, often burdened with large tuition debts in the tens of thousands of dollars, to avoid idealistic pursuits and simply maximise income.[35]

To the extent that this sort of situation still prevails, many different things can and should be done to more effectively address it. But one small step is to encourage students' consideration of broad ethical issues, ideas, theories and possibilities from the start of their legal education, moving from general metaethical and normative ethical ideas on to issues of social and applied ethics, rather than merely tacking some applied ethical considerations on at the end.

Much of the rest of this book is about social and applied ethics. In particular, it concerns the ethics of legal decision-making at all levels – from the formulation and enactment of legislation, to the creation of law by judges and the day-to-day operation of the legal system, including the behaviour of legal professionals.

Discussion topics

1 What is ethics and how does it relate to law? Include reference to metaethics, free will, guilt and conscience.
2 What kinds of things are 'moral ideas'? Include reference to

moral psychology, divine commands and moral relativism.

3. What is *utilitarianism*? Include reference to 'act' and 'rule' versions. What are their strengths and weaknesses? How are they related to law?

4. Briefly explain the ethical ideas of Kant, Ross and Aristotle.

5. What is *feminist ethics*?

6. What is *applied ethics*? What are lawyers' ethical responsibilities?

Additional resources

C. Parker and A.Evans, *Inside Lawyers' Ethics*, Cambridge University Press, Melbourne.

R. Nader and W. J. Smith, *No Contest*, Random House, New York, 1996

S. Mann, *Economics, Business Ethics and Law*, Lawbook Co, Sydney, 2003, chapter 3.

Chapter 9

HUMAN NATURE, HUMAN RIGHTS AND LAW

In the last chapter we considered a number of important ethical concepts and principles, and introduced the idea of an objective foundation for ethical ideas and principles, rather than seeing such ideas and principles as merely subjective constructions or accidents of historical development.

In this chapter we look more deeply into the possibility of such an objective foundation for ethical principles, as well as introducing other ethical ideas and principles of particular significance for politics and for law. In particular, we focus on the idea of human rights as objective ethical foundation for law-making and law enforcement. This includes consideration of the central role of human rights in public international law, primarily concerned with relations between states, rather than with private, commercial transactions across national boundaries. So too we briefly touch on ideas of justice and equality.

We see how two different currents of political, social and legal thought, of right-wing liberal atomism on the one side and left-wing liberal structuralism on the other, have developed significantly different ideas of human nature and its relationship with society, which, in turn, lead to significantly different ideas of human rights, justice, politics and law. This provides a foundation for later considerations of major contemporary political and legal conflicts and possibilities in the following chapters.

Rights

Whatever we might think about human rights as moral rights, or about the ethical foundations of law, it is clear that rights more generally understood play a central role in law, and in the common law system in particular. Rights in this general sense can be defined as legitimate entitlements of individuals or groups to access to or effective control of particular goods or services or the free exercise of particular abilities or powers. As rights theorist James Nickel says, 'rights have right-holders ... [as] ... parties that possess and exercise the right'; and 'a right is to some freedom, power, immunity, protection or benefit, which is its scope or object'.[1]

Rights imply responsibilities or obligations: the responsibilities of the rights holder to exercise their rights in an appropriate fashion, not infringing the rights of others, and the responsibilities of others to respect and facilitate the effective realisation of the rights in question. Such responsibilities or obligations of others towards the rights holder might be of limited scope – merely not to interfere in various ways; or of greater scope – to actively provide the material means for realisation of the rights in question. They might be the responsibilities of particular individuals or groups or institutions or of everyone.

To quote Nickel again:

> ... almost all ... rights are or include claim-rights, and such rights identify a party or parties [the addressees or duty-bearers] who must act to make available the freedom or benefit identified by the right's scope ... Rights are commonly classified as positive or negative, according to whether the right requires the addressees merely to refrain from doing something or instead to take some positive action they might not otherwise take.'[2]

Reference to 'legitimate' entitlement raises the question of the nature of the legitimation process. As considered in detail in chapter 10, for legal positivists such legitimation is understood in terms of the actions of legitimate authority in endorsing and enforcing such rights. Here, we can distinguish *acquired* rights – those gained through the exercise of some sort of social power, authority, agreement or decision-making – from rights which individuals might be thought to possess by virtue of their common humanity.

In the modern world there are a range of different sorts of acquired rights which receive the support of the legal system, or of the authority structure of a particular social organisation other than the state. Individuals acquire such rights by reaching a particular age, by becoming a citizen of a particular state, by entering into contractual or quasi-contractual arrangements of one sort or another, including acquisition of private property through market transactions or through gift, and by entry into particular jobs or offices.

In a capitalist world, legitimate acquisition of property through contract or gift is of particular significance, insofar as property ownership, understood as a range of different, but related, rights – to possess, sell, use, bequeath, consume, waste, manage, derive income from particular goods or resources – occupies a central role in civil and criminal law.

Influenced particularly by the separation of ownership and control in the modern corporation, the common law system has developed an elaborate systematisation of different sorts or components of property rights. These include a right to possess (as a right to exclusive physical control of an object), a right to use (as opposed to managing and reaping income from an object), a right to manage (as a right to determine who may use an object and how they do so), a right to the income (a right to any profits that may be generated through use of an object by that individual or another), a right to the capital (a right to alienate, consume or waste an object), a right to security (as immunity from expropriation of the object) and a right of transmissibility (as the power to devise or bequeath an object). Some such rights are associated with occupation of specific social roles. Workers have some rights to use the tools of their trade. But full or complete ownership rights to particular goods, including all of these different dimensions of right, are acquired through receipt of such goods via market exchange or by gift from previous owners.[3]

Individuals acquire rights by being selected for a job or an office. Because of their association with particular jobs or offices, these might be called *positional* rights to engage in particular sorts of activities without interference, including rights of access to the means to engage in the activities in question. On joining the Australian police force, an individual is given a gun and the rights to carry and use it (under certain circumstances). On being elected to the legislature, an individual acquires the right to propose legislation and have their proposals debated. These sorts of positional rights are typically seen as functionally necessary for effective fulfilment of the requirements of the social roles in question. In a capitalist society, access to positional rights of jobs or professions is mediated through the job market, where individuals trade their time, effort, strength and skills for wages. Such income then becomes the means of access to property rights in goods and services purchased in the market.

The role of law includes the articulation and endorsement of rights (in statutes and legal principles), along with provision of means, including police, courts and prisons, for realisation of rights and removal of obstacles to such realisation. Much of the common law system is about facilitating acquisition of property rights through ensuring the effective operation of free-market relations. This includes contract law, labour law, competition policy and some anti-discrimination law. Much of tort law and criminal law is about protecting private property rights through preventing or compensating unauthorised interference with such rights. Anti-discrimination law is essentially concerned with ensuring effective access to the granting of positional rights associated with particular jobs, professions and offices.

The state via the system of civil law provides individuals with means for enforcing their rights against others who have infringed such rights, through negligence, trespass, slander or theft, or by failing to deliver upon a legitimate contract. The system provides monetary compensation paid to victims of such transgression by the perpetrators. Through the criminal legal system the executive authority of the state intervenes directly to arrest and punish those who undermine others' rights to safety and property.

Moral rights

A crucial jurisprudential question is that of whether such legal and 'practical' recognition and enforcement of rights is itself ultimately justified by fundamental human or ethical rights which exist in their own right; whether, in particular, core legal rights, at least, require justification in terms of objective moral rights in order to have genuine legitimacy as law – over and above the legitimacy of the law-making authority and the law-making process.

Ideas on this subject have changed and developed through the centuries. In Roman times the concept of rights as entitlements associated with duty-claims addressed to others had predominantly legal rather than moral significance. 'Individuals had rights and corresponding duties in consequence of the laws under which they lived.'[4] In mediaeval times, law defined the inherited rights and privileges of the ruling class of lords and church officials, as rights of control over the working population of peasant-serfs.

According to Thomas Aquinas, leading thirteenth century theorist of feudal society, 'God had created a world ordered and organised according to degrees of rationality and perfection, and society, too, was created as a hierarchy ordered according to degrees of rationality. ... [While] the eternal law of God went far beyond human understanding ... Aquinas called the part of God's eternal law which human reason was capable of understanding and proving 'natural law' or 'natural right'. These rules laid down duties and goals for all human beings in accordance with their place in the social hierarchy.'[5]

Later feudal monarchs typically claimed a divine right to rule as the source of all authority and all law, with the rest of the population subject to such absolute authority. In this context, and for most people, obligation was mainly about the duty of the subject to obey and conform to the dictates of such divine authority.

At the time of the English Revolution in the mid-seventeenth century, the first of the great social revolutions of the modern age that overthrew royal absolutism and ultimately shifted political power to representative parliamentary bodies, the concept of rights was extended beyond institutional legal support for the interests of particular social groups to embrace the entire political community. The revolutionaries developed the idea of universal human rights to articulate their demands for change. Such rights were seen as possessed by all individuals simply by virtue of their common humanity, and as conferring duties of respect of such rights upon all people by virtue of the moral status of such rights.[6]

A number of new currents of political and social thought developed in and through this and subsequent revolutionary challenges to feudal hierarchy. Historically most significant was the tradition of classical liberalism, developed through the work of Thomas Hobbes, John Locke and Adam Smith.[7]

Classical liberalism

Ideas of human rights among the classical liberal thinkers of the seventeenth and eighteenth centuries are very closely bound up with their particular ideas about the relations between human individuals on the one side and social structures and relations on the other. Classical liberals tended to be what are today called 'methodological individualists', seeing social structures and social relations as effects, products, creations or consequences (sometimes unintended consequences) of intentional action and interaction of human individuals – or, indeed, as nothing more than the totality of such actions and interactions. Insofar as such actions are themselves seen as driven by individual psychological instincts or tendencies, predating social structure and common to all human beings, such 'human nature' clearly has huge significance in this theory in creating and hence explaining social structures, processes and developments seen as manifestations or products of human decision, co-operation and conflict.

In the classical liberal tradition of thinking, such psychological instincts, responses and tendencies are understood as centred on rational pursuit of individual self-interest. All human beings, unrestricted by central power, are by nature selfish, lazy, greedy creatures seeking the gratification of their ultimately insatiable desires through appropriation of relevant goods and services. They are intrinsically competitive, power-seeking and domineering, at least when they are able to be. At the same time, in the right circumstances, so too can they be creative, dynamic, innovatory and productive. They engage in continual calculation of the balance of cost and benefit to themselves in the different actions available to them and choose the optimally beneficial action. And they are strongly naturally motivated to barter, trade and accumulate wealth and respond badly if not allowed to do so.

Reflecting the aspirations of the new capitalist middle class of merchants and manufacturers in their struggle against feudal absolutism, classical liberal theory centres on ideas of the positive potential of individual nature and the need to free such potential from unnecessary restriction and distortion by state power and established hierarchy in order to allow for individual fulfilment and social progress. All individuals should be maximally free to choose to do what they want without impinging on others' freedom to do the same.

We see this central focus on freeing and protecting the individual from arbitrary state power reflected in an emphasis on what are now called 'due process rights': to a fair trial and to freedom from arbitrary arrest, torture and cruel punishments. But we cannot properly understand the classical liberal ideology of rights without also recognising the centrality of free markets and capitalist pursuit of profit through such free markets in this way of thinking.

Here, in particular, the apparently conflicting tendencies of human nature – towards selfishness and greed on the one hand and potentially socially useful creativity and effort on the other – are seen as reconciled and constructively directed through the operation of free markets, as both 'natural' expressions or consequences of the free activity of such human nature and as mechanisms uniquely suited to harnessing selfishness, competitiveness, power-seeking and greed and turning them into the driving forces of creativity, innovation and effort serving the common good of all, through effective wealth creation and distribution.

From this perspective, market relations are seen as 'natural' and the requirements for ongoing operation of such relations, in the form of respect for life and property, are therefore also seen as 'natural' rights or entitlements of all humans. And the right of liberty or freedom is equated with freedom to engage in market relations – to buy and sell whatever you can – without political restriction.

But since markets require constructive effort in production of goods in demand, their orderly operation is always threatened by human self-interest and by competition for scarce resources. According to classical liberal theory this threat motivated rationally self-interested humans to contract together to grant coercive power to a sovereign – political authority – to formulate and enforce such rights to life and property as laws, to render the lives of all more ordered and secure.

The possibility of coercive sanction for law-breaking shifts individual cost benefit analysis away from robbery and murder and towards respect for life and property and constructive effort. Such an authority retains its legitimacy only insofar as it effectively safeguards such basic human rights to life and property through effective exercise of a monopoly of armed force. To this end it is legitimate for the state to levy taxes upon its citizens to finance such protection. Beyond this point, classical liberals were generally hostile to what they saw as any further government 'interference' in individual decision-making and action or imposition of financial imposts on its citizenry. The individual should be free from any further government control, regulation or restriction. And citizens retain a political right to remove or replace it if the sovereign fails to protect life and property, or goes beyond this point to try to oppress or control its citizens.

As CB Macpherson observed:

> What was needed was the kinds of laws and regulations and tax structure that would make the market society work, or allow it to work, and the kind of state services – defence, and even military expansion ... and various sorts of assistance to industry, such as tariffs and grants ... that were thought necessary to make the system run efficiently and profitably. These were the kinds of political goods that were wanted. But how was the demand to call forth the supply? How to make the government responsive to the choices of those it was expected to cater for? The way was ... to put governmental power in the hands of men who were made subject to periodic elections at which there was a choice of candidates and parties. The electorate did not need to be a democratic one, and as a general rule was not; all that was needed was an electorate consisting of men of substance, so that the government could be responsive to their choices.[8]

Early on, then, political rights came to be associated with ideas of representative government, with rules for the orderly replacement of political authority failing to effectively maintain such security, through periodic electoral decision processes. But initially, voting rights were severely restricted. Classical liberal thinkers were not originally democrats, or they supported a very limited franchise, extending only to those with significant property qualifications.

Nonetheless, to the extent that social order is subsequently maintained, individual members of the society in question who continue to enjoy the benefits of such order without breaking the laws are taken to have tacitly or implicitly agreed to abide by the terms or rules which make such order possible, including basic criminal and civil laws. Indeed, such institutions are maintained through their actions. Individuals who are not prepared to abide by such rules are threatening such order. They should consider finding or creating some other society more suited to their values or wants, or expect to suffer the consequences in terms of punitive sanction.

Classical liberalism and justice

Ever since Aristotle introduced the distinction, philosophers and social theorists have divided questions of justice into those concerned with criminal punishment – retributive justice, where the punishment is in some sense proportional or appropriate to the crime – and those concerned with the distribution of social benefits and burdens – distributive justice. In keeping with its central focus on free will as a product of biology rather than society, and free individual action as creator rather than product of social relations, the classical liberal view of both legal and economic justice centres on ideas of just deserts. People should, and generally do, reap the benefits or suffer the consequences of their own free choices of action.

In the economic sphere, this inevitably produces inequality of outcome, with some acquiring more material rewards as they work better, harder and longer than others. But this is, in itself, a good thing. Inequalities of wealth and power are seen as necessary incentives to productive effort, initiative, innovation and best use of available resources to maximise efficiency and output. Here too are ideas of the role of inequalities in fuelling aspirations for more consumption goods that in turn fuel economic growth. At one end of the scale, substantial rewards are thought to be necessary to ensure that the most talented people use their talents to the best advantage of all, or that someone is willing to make the effort and take on the massively onerous responsibilities involved in positions of power in society. At the other end, the miseries of poverty and privation are necessary to overcome the inherent sloth, laziness and inertia of some or all human beings.

As it happens. free market forces, left to themselves without government intervention, are seen to provide precisely such positive and negative incentives, ideally suited to ensuring optimum social contribution and social welfare. For such market forces ensure that individuals are rewarded in direct proportion to the value of their real productive social contribution, and therefore also punished through lack of any such reward if they fail to make any such valuable contribution.

Classical liberal ethics tends to follow classical liberal psychology. In line with what are seen as the psychological facts of selfish human nature, an individual's first (moral) responsibility is to themselves: to take charge of their own life and make the best of it, without any legitimate expectations of help or support from others. Nor do individuals have any general responsibility to look after or support others, though they may freely choose to do so and commit themselves accordingly through family relationships in particular, and through market-based contractual arrangements.

Selfish individuals can be expected to enter into and maintain particular social relations only insofar as they see such relations as optimally rewarding to themselves (compared to other possible actions or relations). At the same time, the effective operation of free market forces depends on recognition of the private property rights of individuals and corporations. Ways must therefore be found to ensure that such rights are respected, rather than undermined through theft, fraud, robbery, factory occupations or pickets. And here, the criminal justice system is seen as a necessary complement to the free market. Because the market requires some degree of effort and sacrifice in order to achieve legitimate rewards, some selfish individuals will inevitably freely choose to ignore the basic property rights of others in pursuit of their own gratification. The threat of effective punishment is necessary to deter some such potential criminal wrongdoers. Serious infringements of others' basic life and property rights require equally serious responses from the forces of law and order in terms of negative consequences for the wrong-doers, both to deter them from future wrongdoing and to deter others from such criminal choices. And those that cannot be effectively deterred need to be effectively restrained or incapacitated, in the public interest.

In reaction to the arbitrary and hierarchical justice system of feudal society, which quite literally operated one law for lords and another for merchants or peasants, classical liberals demanded a formal or procedural equality in formulation and application of legal principles. All should be subject to the same laws and all should expect to be treated in similar fashion by the justice system, with the punishment fitting the crime rather than the perpetrator.

In respect of both distributive and retributive justice we see an underlying principle of equality and proportionality of deserts. An individual can legitimately expect reward in direct proportion to their social contribution of value creation and punishment in direct proportion to the extent of harm they have inflicted.

Early bills of rights

Historical documents such as the English Bill of Rights of 1689, the French Declaration of the Rights of Man and the Citizen of 1789, and the American Declarations of 1776–1789 clearly reflect the economic, civil and political preoccupations and priorities of classical liberal thinking. The English Bill of Rights, as 'the first document to use the language of 'rights' and which introduced the system of free elections, was merely intended to ensure that royal absolutism was firmly dissolved in favour of the monarch's accountability to Parliament ... thus, the rights it gave were to Parliament, not the people.'[9] However, the Parliament 'upheld the existence of inalienable rights (of individuals) as an absolute truth', drawing on the philosophies of John Locke and others. And O'Byrne quotes Cassese to the effect that:

> ... 'for those Declarations, man ... is worthy of being called 'man' only if he fulfils these conditions: to be free, equal, or have undisturbed enjoyment of his property, not to be oppressed by a tyrannous government and to be able freely to realise himself.' They are based ... on a model of society comprised of 'free individuals equal to one another ... and subject only to the law, which in turn is and must be an expression of the general will; political institutions should exist only as a means of realizing the freedom of the individuals and their common good.'[10]

The American Declaration of Independence of 1776 famously proclaimed a 'self-evident human equality and inalienable rights to life, liberty and the pursuit of happiness' as well as government power derived from the consent of the governed. The French Declaration of 1789 equally famously asserted the 'liberty, fraternity and equality' of all citizens, as well as rights of property, liberty of conscience, freedom of the press and freedom from arbitrary imprisonment.

It is important to emphasise that 'equality' here refers to formal or procedural political and legal equality. These early declarations concern rights of equal protection of all citizens' life and property, due process in legal proceedings, and political participation for all, without discrimination, and perhaps some idea of equal economic opportunity, rather than actual economic equality of outcome. As noted above, classical liberal thought generally offers little support for equality of distributive outcome.

Following the work of French jurist Karel Vasak, these civil and political rights have been called 'first generation' rights, to distinguish them from second generation rights, which later came to the fore as rights of guaranteed access to the means of material need satisfaction. It remains to be seen whether first generation rights are actually compatible with such second generation rights, as is assumed by later bills of rights, or whether unrestricted rights of property acquisition and ownership might function to preclude fair and equal satisfaction of need.[11]

Social liberalism

Social liberalism developed originally as a reaction to issues and problems of the classical liberalism of the seventeenth and eighteenth centuries and as a response to radical socialist and historical materialist ideas in the later nineteenth century. By this time, the downside of the operation of free market relations, driven by individual initiative and individual greed, were becoming increasingly apparent in terms of increasing polarisation of wealth and poverty, the distortion of democratic politics by such increasing inequality (including the economic underpinnings of imperialism) and the pollution and destruction of the natural environment.

A key figure here was JS Mill, whose ideas combined a traditional liberal individualism and faith in progressive power of the market with a recognition of the need for significant state intervention to protect the political rights and promote the free development of individuals. Mill was increasingly critical of what he came to see as radical inequality supported by free market relations, with the excess wealth of the rich minority obstructing the liberty of the less well off. And he advocated a heavy inheritance tax and guaranteed basic income, as well as state provision of educational services for all.

Later social liberals such as TH Green, JA Hobson and LT Hobhouse emphasised the value of positive freedom to allow for the full development of individual capacities, and the need for appropriate social support to make this possible for all. As Self observes:

> ... to enjoy positive freedom, it was necessary to have an adequate minimum of resources and opportunities, particularly of an educational kind. If the opportunities were there, individuals would respond by developing their skills and interests in a positive and beneficial way.[12]

Later still, social liberal ideas came to be associated with the economic ideas of JM Keynes, aiming to ensure full employment through government demand management, and political programmes of European Social Democratic and British Labour and Australian Labor parties,

and more recently Greens parties (around the world), focusing particularly on the expansion of the welfare state, with 'social security
provisions, comprehensive health service, and large public housing
programmes' seen as providing the 'basic material security' necessary
for positive freedom of all.[13]

Social liberals followed classical liberals in seeing human nature
as a creative potential which needed to be liberated from excessive restriction and restraint, and could contribute to overall social
welfare through profit-seeking initiatives. But so too did they recognise the side of human nature involving human need, the integral
role of need satisfaction in human life and human fulfilment, and
the necessity for social intervention in free market operations that
fail to ensure basic need satisfaction for all. In a world of limited
resources, unconditional protection of the ownership rights of a few
can deny many more the basic means of survival. And without appropriate protection, many will inevitably fail to acquire such necessary
means through no fault or failing of their own. Like classical liberals,
social liberals sought legal support for a right to life, but whereas
the former interpreted this primarily in terms of criminal legal sanctions and civil compensation for trespass to the person in the form of
assault or homicide, the latter rather focused on the collective social
protection and preservation of human life through active provision of
the objects of human need.

While classical liberals tended to see political rights merely as a
means to the end of efficient governance, social liberals have understood political rights as means to a goal of genuine mass participation and involvement in political life. And for social liberals, good
government is itself allotted a much more active role and responsibility to ensure the satisfaction of the basic needs of all citizens – and
others who need help.

From this perspective human rights are seen as ethically grounded
insofar as they are rights to objects of need, to the things that all
humans must have in order to be able to survive and live a fulfilled
life. By definition, if people are denied access to the things they need,
they will suffer in more or less serious ways. And such human rights
were seen to imply a universal responsibility of all to respect and
facilitate the rights in question.

Human needs

It is a fact of human biology that deprivation of certain things 'regularly results in reduction of the ability to move or to feel or to think'.[14] In extreme cases, 'deprivation of air for a short time, or food or water over a longer time,' results in the end of all movement or feeling or thought. But 'deprivation of shelter, affection or variety of activity over differing periods of time also regularly results in morbidity or disablement of the human so deprived'.[15]

There is substantial empirical evidence to support the idea that significant inequality and powerlessness contribute to high levels of insecurity and stress in the lower reaches of the social hierarchy, which in turn contribute to morbidity and premature mortality. If and when humans do get sick, deprivation of access to health care can result in worsening illness and avoidable death. Deprivation of education radically diminishes the quality of life and threatens the continued survival both of the individual concerned and of their offspring. So – along with clean air, clean water, healthy food, adequate shelter, affection and constructive social contribution – the provision of greater equality, security and empowerment (as protections against stress) and of adequate health care and education can also be seen as significant human needs.

Philosopher John McMurtry develops these ideas by reference to 'three planes of being: (1) organic movement, (2) sensation and feeling and (3) conceptual and imag[istic] thought' as the 'ground of all life value'. As he says:

> ... there is no value of life that exists which is not such in virtue of bearing or contributing to one or more, at best all, of these planes of life participation and enjoyment .... Overall, each of the three parameters of life and value always admits of ranges of function. These ranges of function or capability, in turn, grow or diminish with the nature of [relevant] economic conditions.[16]

McMurtry refers to 'means of life' as 'whatever enables life to be preserved, or to extend its vital range on these planes of being alive'. And he identifies 'basic means of life' as goods without which 'human life is known to be reduced in its range of vital capabilities by precise degrees of loss which the practices of the health sciences, educators and social scientists variously investigate and report'.[17]

In this context, 'a need for something exists if and only if, and to the extent that, deprivation of it regularly results in an absolute reduction of its owner's life-range capability ... [and] we can prove what is or is not needed by the simple device of observing what happens to a human life without it'.[18] Without it, people die before their time, suffer avoidable and unnecessary mental or physical illness or other forms of ongoing misery and restriction.

We can see how reference to such human needs can provide an objective foundation for the idea of moral rights, or at least for the creation of legal rights to the objects of such needs. And depending on social and natural context, access to the objects of such biological need necessarily depends on access to particular means for their achievement. In a capitalist society, access to the 'need requirements of life which cannot be synthesised by the body itself or by independent production' can be assured only through income security: through guaranteed continuity of income (or private wealth) adequate for the purchase of relevant objects of need, or of political or legal measures necessary to secure such objects in the market. So it makes sense to regard such necessary means to the ends of need satisfaction as 'human rights' also.[19]

Against methodological individualism

In line with socialist and materialist ideas, social liberals came increasingly to reject the reductive atomism of earlier classical liberal ideology. They came to recognise the reality of society as an ensemble of structures and relations with their own autonomy, identities, dynamics and causal powers to influence each other and to shape, direct and constrain human decisions and actions. The causal power of such structures and relations is mediated by the perceptions, intentions, decisions and actions of individual human beings. But social structure provides the context and limits to individual human action: people make decisions and act in reference to the social circumstances in which they find themselves.

In contrast to classical liberal ideas of society as created and ongoingly maintained by human decisions and actions, in particular decisions to contract together and action of ongoing co-operation and competition, social liberals recognise that society pre-exists both the human species and individual human life, with pre-existing social structures shaping and directing human personality, perception, thought and action. Social structures and relations only continue to exist in and through the action of people. But such structures maintain themselves through their causal power to direct such actions in particular ways, so that such actions do continue to maintain the structures in question.

Insofar as humans are essentially social creatures, so are their individual identities and their priorities to a significant extent constituted through their social relations. People define themselves, fulfil themselves and realise their specifically human potentialities through their relations with others, particularly personal, familial and work relations, but also a great range of other sorts of relations and activities associated with art, politics, sport, research and many other things.

The classical liberal idea of individuals as fundamentally self-serving, seeing others in essentially instrumental terms as means or obstacles to their own gratification, needs to be radically modified insofar as relations with others are seen as integral to individual identity. Integral to the identity of parent, for example, are ideas of love and protection of children. Integral to the identity of many professional practitioners are ideas and practices of commitment and service to particular groups of people (eg patients, students, clients), to other living creatures, to the environment and to the growth of knowledge.

In line with their focus on the necessity of need satisfaction, and the recognition of the limitations of unregulated capitalist market relations in ensuring such need satisfaction, social liberals came to see the crucial importance of equality of access to material means of need satisfaction, rather than mere absence of legal restriction upon individuals' rights to pursue the satisfaction of their needs and wants. So did they come to recognise that the effective exercise or realisation of 'higher' civil and political rights depends on the material foundation of satisfaction of basic biological and psychological needs.

Social liberals have therefore increasingly come to recognise a broader range of basic human rights than those identified by classical liberals calling for legal support. These include workers' (positive) rights to be able to work, to decent pay and healthy working conditions (with corresponding duties of employers to provide such things), workers' (active) right to form unions, participate in collective bargaining and engage in strikes and pickets, consumers' rights to be properly informed of the nature of goods or services available to them and to be protected from harm attributable to such goods and services (with corresponding duties on the part of producers and marketers), parents' rights to paid maternity and paternity leave from work, citizens' rights of access to public health, education and welfare services and to proper legal representation and freedom from racial discrimination and vilification. Some have supported animals' rights to decent and respectful treatment.

For these rights to be effectively realised, those benefiting disproportionately from private property rights and market forces have to accept responsibilities towards those not doing so well. Thus, social liberals recognise the necessity for progressive taxation and regulation of markets in order to provide the public funding and economic stability to allow for enforcement of universal rights to employment and social services for those in need.

Social liberal ideas of justice

Whereas classical liberals tend to hold the individual wholly or largely responsible for all of the consequences of their actions, both good and bad, social liberals recognise such decisions and actions as facilitated and constrained by social situations. And where classical liberals seek to influence such action through rewarding, punishing or physically constraining the individual, social liberals recognise the need for changing social situations in order to achieve any significant change in social actions. They are hostile to what they see as the generally futile and gratuitously cruel punishments which classical liberals sought to enforce as their only, or primary, answer to criminal activities. On the one hand, such punishments are typically inflicted on the downtrodden and the weak who have already suffered as victims of an unfair social system. Indeed, if they have actually broken the law it is in part a consequence of such earlier victimisation. On the other hand, there is substantial evidence (including very high recidivism rates in prison populations) of failure of deterrence through highly punitive (retributive) means. And this is what we would expect if working-class crime is largely a product of social restriction of choice, rather than a free and rational choice to break the law.

Once we see individual decisions and actions as facilitated and constrained by social circumstances, so do we see that some people, through no fault or virtue of their own, are in circumstances that promote and expand meaningful free choice of action while others are in situations that restrict and contract such freedom of choice. Here, in particular, we need to see issues of individual social responsibility in the context of pre-established social inequality of power, wealth and income. It is quite legitimate to hold the privileged to a higher standard of individual accountability in view of their much greater scope of free decision and action.

It is a fact of basic social causation that individuals growing up in an environment of wealth and privilege will generally find it easier than others to acquire valuable professional skills and qualifications and make much more money. But this doesn't mean there is any moral or practical justification for preferential reward of such privileged individuals. Individuals growing up in an environment of poverty, disrespect, violence and crime will generally be more likely than others to suffer deprivation, or to become involved in domestic and street crime in later life. But this does not justify the state subjecting them to further cruel punishment, especially given the empirical evidence indicating the failure of such punishment to achieve any significant deterrent or socially protective consequences. Rather, the emphasis needs to be on constructive rehabilitation of the individuals concerned and on addressing the social causes of such crime so as to reduce it in the future.[20]

It's true that the same social circumstances bearing on different individuals will produce different results. But this is not because of some free moral choice by the individuals concerned. It is rather because, in the first instance, such social forces are bearing upon a different biological substrate. Relevant biological variations are probably normally distributed in human populations. And under the impact of social forces, such biological variation gives rise to individual psycho-social variation, which explains subsequent differential responses.

Insofar as humans can satisfy their specifically human needs and realise their specifically human potentials only in and through appropriate pre-existing social structures and relations, there is a crucial ethical imperative for those with social power to do whatever they can to ensure provision of such social structures and relations. On the one hand, this means social provision for protection from poverty, ill health, inequality, ignorance and prejudice. On the other it means provision of opportunities for optimum realisation of human potential through challenging, useful and rewarding labour, art, science, music, literature, exploration, sport and political participation.

In this context, social liberals look beyond the purely formal or procedural legal equality of classical liberal theory. They recognise that the same procedures applied to people in very different social situations can produce thoroughly unjust or unfair outcomes. It is unfair, for example, to impose equally onerous punishments on the wealthy and powerful individual who steals through greed than on the poor and powerless individual who steals the same (or a lesser) amount through need. It is unfair to apply the same standard of proof – beyond a reasonable doubt – in the criminal prosecution of a powerful corporation whose officers can call on huge resources of legal and scientific expertise in their defence, as it is in respect of an ordinary individual lacking access to any such resources. It is far from fair and just to impose the same fine or the same driving ban for the same driving offence where, in the case of the poor worker it could mean severe hardship or loss of a job, while for the rich executive (who can be driven around by someone else) it means nothing at all.

Similarly, in the area of distributive justice, it is unfair that an individual whose privileged social position has allowed them to acquire special professional skills should receive substantially greater reward for a particular number of hours of productive utilisation of such skills than someone whose position denied them the opportunity to acquire such skills and who makes a similar contribution of socially useful time and effort. It is radically unfair that an individual who is unable – by virtue of their social, psychological or biological situation – to make any such contribution of their time and effort should thereby receive nothing at all, or should be reliant on private charity for their survival.

Here we see an underlying focus on attempting to provide equality of reward for socially useful effort and sacrifice, rather than value creation; upon equality of outcome in terms of equal fulfilment of need and equal realisation of the human potential of all; and of equality of opportunity for social contribution and need satisfaction through equality of access to necessary social and material means – of health, education and welfare.

The UN and the UDHR

Contemporary public international law, particularly as developed in and through the United Nations Organisation, is strongly influenced by social liberal ideas. A substantial part of such international law revolves around ideas and codifications of universal human rights, thought of as grounded in universal human needs, or the requirements for a healthy and fulfilled human life.

Article 1 of the Charter of the United Nations, signed in June 1945, identifies the purposes of the organisation as:

1   the maintenance of international peace and security, including taking effective collective measures for the prevention and removal of threats to the peace, and for suppression of acts of aggression or other breaches of the peace, and to bring about by physical means, and in conformity with the principles of justice and international law, adjustment or settlement of international disputes or situations which might lead to a breach of the peace

2   developing friendly relations among nations based on respect for the principle of equal rights and self-determination of peoples, and to take other appropriate measures to strengthen universal peace

3   achieving international co-operation in solving international problems of an economic, social, cultural or humanitarian character, and in promoting and encouraging respect for human rights and for fundamental freedoms for all without distinction as to race, sex, language or religion

4   being a centre for harmonising the actions of nations in the attainment of these common ends.[21]

The UN Charter is a treaty, which means a legally binding agreement between states. In theory, states are not supposed to ratify (sign) a treaty until after the state authority has taken steps to bring their domestic law in line with the treaty provisions through appropriate legislation. The Charter provides a 'constitutional framework for the governance of the organisation through organs, including the Office of the Secretary General, the Security Council, the General Assembly and a number of other councils'.[22] In particular, the Charter makes Security Council (SC) resolutions binding on member states and Chapter VII provides a framework of allowable enforcement procedures, including the use of sanctions and military intervention by the SC, in relation to acts of aggression and war.

After the approval of the Charter, a UN committee was charged with producing an international bill of rights, which emerged in 1948 as the Universal Declaration of Human Rights (UDHR). As Piotrowicz and Kaye point out: 'the universal application of the declaration is reinforced in its title, its preamble and its first and second articles which provide that the rights set out in the declaration are to be [equally] available to all people at birth, without discrimination'.[23] From a social liberal perspective, such rights can be seen as ethically grounded, in considerations of human need, to serve as a basis for national legislation to recognise and protect such entitlements around the world, to allow healthy, fulfilled and empowered lives for all.

Civil and political – first generation, classical liberal – rights in the Declaration include rights to life, liberty and security of person, equality before the law, a fair trial, presumption of innocence, political asylum, freedom from arbitrary deprivation of property, freedom of opinion, expression, assembly and association and freedom from arbitrary arrest, detention or exile. Economic, social and cultural – second generation, social liberal – rights include rights to social security, to work with equal pay for equal work, to join trade unions, to a satisfactory living standard, to rest and leisure, to education (free at elementary stages) and to participation in the cultural life of the community.

As Nickel points out: 'this was a set of proposed standards, rather than a treaty'. In other words, it was not a legally binding agreement between the parties. 'It recommended promotion of human rights through teaching and education and measures, national and international, to secure ... universal and effective recognition and observance of such rights.'[24]

But it was intended to serve as the basis for such a legally binding treaty, supervised by relevant UN committees, promoting and monitoring compliance, which was, in turn, supposed to direct appropriate national legislation on the part of member states to ensure effective protection and enforcement of the rights in question. And, indeed, it was eventually followed by a succession of such legally binding treaties, or covenants, including the Civil and Political Covenant and Social Covenant of 1966, which together constitute an international bill of rights based on the UDHR.

As Nickel points out, differences between the Covenants and the

UDHR in part reflect the influence of new member states, recently freed from colonial rule, with the Covenants 'asserting the rights of peoples to self-determination and to control their natural resources' giving a prominent place to 'rights against discrimination' and omitting 'the UDHR's rights to property and to remuneration for property taken by the state'.[25] Reforming governments in the developing world were typically committed to radical redistribution of land stolen by the colonising powers and their supporters among significant sections of their populations, without necessarily supplying compensation acceptable to the 'owners' in question.

As Nickel notes: 'the Universal Declaration has been amazingly successful in establishing a fixed worldwide meaning for the idea of human rights … … the list of human rights that it proposed still sets the pattern for the numerous human rights treaties that have gone into operation since 1948'.[26] Such widespread acceptance provides a powerful practical refutation of ethical subjectivism and relativism considered in chapter 8.

However, as Shutt points out:

> In spite of the fact that the most important of these treaties, the International Covenant on Civil and Political Rights, formally commits the vast majority of UN members who have ratified it to apply its principles since its adoption by the General Assembly in 1966, there has manifestly been continued violation by most signatories of the principles they are pledged to uphold. [And] the failure of the United Nations to take any action to enforce conformity with its own principles, in clear contravention of the spirit of the rule of law, is obviously a reflection of the interests and attitudes of the key member states, particularly the permanent members of the Security Council.[27]

Those hoping to see an end to large-scale violence with the end of the Cold War have been sadly disappointed, with continuous and increasing low-level conflict on virtually every continent, periodically erupting into mass slaughter. And the United Nations has notoriously failed to intervene, even in the latter situations, where member states have totally failed to maintain order within their boundaries, or have themselves engaged in massive human rights abuses. Where the UN has intervened, such intervention has been too little or too late.

As noted earlier, the major covenants are supposed to be legally binding, with the Human Rights Committee (HRC) of 18 international experts receiving, studying and critically commenting on periodic reports from states which have ratified the Civil and Political Covenant. At the end of the process, which includes participation of non-governmental organisations, the Committee publishes its evaluation of the compliance of the states in question, aiming to put pressure on those failing in their responsibilities. It can also 'receive, investigate and mediate complaints from individuals alleging they are victims of rights violations. But as Nickel says:

> The reporting system has few teeth to deal with countries that stonewall or fail to report, and the HRC's conclusions often receive little attention ... Overall this system for implementing human rights is limited. It does not give the HRC the power to order states to change their practices or compensate a victim. Its tools are limited to persuasion, mediation, and exposure of violations to public scrutiny.[28]

As also noted, the Security Council has the power to impose binding resolutions on other member states insofar as it has the power to authorise economic sanctions and military intervention. But from the late 1940s to the late 1980s cold war rivalries among the permanent members precluded effective decision and action. Article 2(7) of the Charter, which explicitly rejects any right of the UN 'to intervene in matters which are essentially within the domestic jurisdiction of any state', along with a 1970 Declaration on Friendly Relations and Co-operation which elaborates upon 2(7) to identify 'armed intervention and all other forms of interference against the personality of a state or against its political, economic and cultural elements', as violations of international law, were taken to preclude any sort of 'humanitarian' military intervention by the UN in response to human rights abuses.

The end of the Cold War and the shift towards capitalist private property in Russia and China did open up the possibility for effective SC action. And this has allowed for humanitarian military intervention in Somalia, Rwanda and the former Yugoslavia. Although, as Clarke points out, the relevant SC mandate in most such cases has 'not identified humanitarian intervention to end human rights abuses' as the primary reason for such intervention, there does nonetheless seem to be increasing recognition that the SC's major role in maintaining international peace and security (under Article 24 of the Charter) is actually closely bound up with considerations of serious human rights abuses.[29] Not only does war typically encourage and involve gross violations of fundamental rights, but major rights violations can also produce frustration, anger and desperation which lead to conflict and warfare.

At the same time, as Singer observes, so does there seem to be increasing recognition that 'the rights of domestic jurisdiction retained by the states in Article 2(7) do not extend to committing crimes against humanity, nor to allowing them to be committed within [their] domestic jurisdiction'.[30] He refers, in particular, to that body of international law that, 'as suggested by the Eichmann case, holds that there is universal jurisdiction over those who commit genocide or other crimes against humanity'.[31] And he suggests that 'the United Nations Charter cannot have intended, in granting domestic jurisdiction to the states, to set aside this important doctrine of customary international law'.[32]

The SC's role in setting up ad hoc tribunals to prosecute perpetrators of genocide in Rwanda and war crimes in the former Yugoslavia clearly acknowledged the serious breaches of international criminal law in these situations and the SC's responsibility to take action to try to address them.

However, the SC is radically lacking in democratic legitimacy, dominated as it is by the five permanent members, the US, UK, France, Russia and China, each of which has the power to veto any proposed resolution, with the other ten temporary positions distributed in terms of regional quotas. As has frequently been pointed out, this structure seems fundamentally incompatible with Article 2, Paragraph 1 of the UN Charter, which maintains the sovereign equality of all member states as the basis of the United Nations.

There have been numerous proposals for democratic reform of the SC, including getting rid of permanent members and veto powers, increasing permanent members, and/or effectively subordinating the SC to the more democratic General Assembly (GA). But no particular proposals have found widespread acceptance. Poorer southern hemisphere states (sometimes called 'the South') have been anxious to avoid an increase in the number of wealthy northern (industrially developed) permanent member states. And as Clarke says, 'it is unlikely that the powers of the SC will ever be altered during the lifetime of the UN Organisation, as any amendment to the UN Charter requires support of two-thirds of the General Assembly and all members of the Security Council'.[33]

Many have seen the establishment of the International Criminal Court (ICC) following the Rome Statute's entering into force in 2002 as a significant step forward in relation to legitimate and effective prosecution of major human rights violations. The court has jurisdiction over crimes against humanity, war crimes, genocide and crimes of aggression. It has 18 elected judges from the states that have ratified the statute, and recognises the presumption of innocence, the rights to silence and to legal representation and the right not to be subject to arbitrary arrest and detention.

However, there are numerous problems associated with the court, including the limits placed on its jurisdiction by the Rome Statute. In particular, it has jurisdiction only if relevant states fail to investigate alleged crimes, and it can do nothing if such states go through the motions of serious investigation but take no action. The SC retains the right to intervene in its operations and indefinitely postpone any prosecutions. And the ICC remains dependent on the SC and other states within the UN for the enforcement of court orders. US President George W Bush withdrew US support for the statute and has brought pressure to bear upon other states to not ratify and to commit themselves to protecting US citizens from prosecution by the Court.[34]

While the GA is definitely much more democratically organised and run than the SC on the principle of *one nation one vote*, and it would make democratic sense to give it greater powers within the UN system, there are major problems here also. As Singer notes:

> Its appearance of egalitarianism is misleading. It is an assembly of the world's states, not the world's people. Some of the states themselves are not democratic, but even if we overlook this, there is the problem that the government of India has the same voting power as the government of Iceland. In fact, if the 95 states with the smallest populations were to line up against the 94 states with the largest populations, it is possible that a GA resolution could be supported by a majority of states that represented a combined total of only 198.5 million people while on the other side, the outvoted 94 largest states would represent 5.7 billion. States representing less than 4% of the total UN member state population could carry the day in the General Assembly.[35]

In this case, reform proposals have included exclusion of undemocratic governments from membership and turning the GA into 'a democratically elected World Assembly' like the European Parliament, possibly including 'delegates allocated to its member states in proportion to their population' as forum for debate and review and possibly also giving it real legislative power.

There are again many issues and problems arising here, including the need for two-thirds support of the GA members and support from all the permanent SC members for necessary changes to the UN Charter, noted earlier. A major issue here is the lack of real national sovereignty on the part of many member states, particularly ex-colonial, developing states, by virtue of their economic weakness and subordination by economically more powerful states, by the international organisations controlled by such powerful states (particularly the International Monetary Fund (IMF), World Bank and World Trade Organisation (WTO)), and by large transnational corporations.

Neo-liberalism

As considered in detail in later chapters, recent decades have seen a major reaction against social liberalism and in favour of a return to something closer to classical liberal ideology by key world leaders and opinion formers, particularly in the English-speaking countries. This new ideology is most commonly called 'neo-liberalism', 'economic rationalism' or the 'Washington Consensus'.

It is questionable whether neo-liberalism deserves to be identified as a single, coherent political-economic perspective attempting to elucidate the true nature of social reality, rather than a mere pragmatic cobbling together of discordant and in many cases incompatible ideas, aiming, first and foremost, to support the power and privilege of particular elite groups. But its profound importance in shaping world opinion and world events in recent decades makes it crucial to come to grips with the ideas in question.

Contemporary neo-liberals go along with the common law tradition in allotting a special status to private property rights – of exclusive possession and control of legitimately acquired resources, including rights to freely buy and sell items of such property – as well as rights to life and bodily integrity. These are in the first instance *negative* rights, to preclude others from unauthorised access to their bodies or their property.

Neo-liberals recognise the particular significance of private property rights in major productive forces of land and technology insofar as such productive forces are the means of social wealth creation. While they might expect the police to spend some time investigating theft of consumer goods from a private house, they would expect and require the forces of law and order to come out into the streets in force for as long as necessary to protect factories or offices from occupation, picketing or attack by striking or locked-out workers.

Neo-liberals are distinguished by their firm rejection of any idea of special social responsibilities or duties on the part of those who derive special benefits by virtue of protection of such property rights, associated with or arising out of such special benefits (over and above general responsibilities of non-interference in the basic rights of others). For them, ownership of substantial private property carries no necessary responsibility to support public services available to others with much less. The extensive rights of free speech available to a newspaper publisher carry no responsibilities to ensure fair and balanced treatment of the issues of the day, with a diverse range of perspectives represented. Those occupying positions of political power owe no necessary duties to the powerless, to reduce inequality and poverty, expand social services and safeguard the natural environment. From a neo-liberal perspective, beyond a basic respect for others' life and property, individuals can only expect others to act responsibly towards them if they pay for the privilege, through contractual arrangements of some kind.

Neo-liberals recognise the foundation of liberal democracy in citizens' basic political rights: to free speech and political activity, including campaigning and voting. Such political rights and freedoms are seen to complement and support basic rights of equality before the law and economic rights of ownership and free trade. But neo-liberals also believe that the state can legitimately deprive citizens of some or all of these rights if they are judged to have committed criminal offences of greater or lesser severity. If individuals freely choose to break the law, so do they freely choose such loss of rights as a consequence.

Beyond such core rights to life and property and to political participation, neo-liberals are generally sceptical of or hostile to the sort of broad extension of human rights found in the social liberal-inspired UDHR. Many of the things identified as rights in the Declaration, to be assured by government to all citizens, are rather seen by neo-liberals as privileges to be earned by individuals. Universal (Declaration) rights to jobs, to education, to health care and to legal access are seen as best supported in and through legal support for free market operations, insofar as these things are seen as most efficiently and most fairly acquired through free market transactions.

In respect of both the acquired rights of social position and 'universal' human rights of access to education, health, legal resources and employment, the role of the state is therefore seen as an indirect or negative one, ensuring no direct discrimination in promotion to the positions in question or impediment to free market exchange of relevant goods or services. Anti-discrimination legislation aims to preclude exclusion of potential candidates for particular social positions on grounds not relevant to successful fulfilment of the requirements of the positions in question. So too does it aim to prevent individuals or institutions preventing others from gaining market access to particular goods on grounds of the others' appearance, ethnicity, gender or age.

However, neo-liberals generally do not support any such direct state intervention to address indirect economic discrimination or impediment to individual participation or effective exercise or enjoyment of the rights in question in the form of poverty or joblessness, or failure to acquire relevant qualifications or experience by virtue of such poverty or joblessness. The onus is on individuals to acquire the material resources to be able to pay for such things in a free market through their own market contributions: making available their strengths, skills and material assets, at reasonable cost, for useful, productive work.

A neo-liberal government will facilitate individual employment through policies of microeconomic reform, motivating employers to take on workers by increasing such employers' rights and powers in relation to such workers and offering such industry support as tax breaks, subsidies and research grants. The central bank will contribute through interest rate manipulations to encourage growth without inflation. But if the government were to guarantee work for all, as employer of last resort, this would undermine free market competition and efficiency. Those not employed by the market lack skills in demand, or demand too much for the use of the skills they have. They should seek to acquire skills in demand, and moderate their unreasonable wage demands.

In terms of distributive and retributive justice, the neo-liberal ideology runs closely parallel to the classical liberal perspective, with a strong emphasis on just deserts and reward in proportion to social value creation, rather than the social liberal rehabilitation, harm minimisation and reward in proportion to useful effort and sacrifice.

Neo-liberalism and international law

As might be expected, neo-liberal regimes in power in the United States since the early 1980s have not been sympathetic to the social liberal principles of the UDHR and subsequent human rights treaties. Nor indeed have they been prepared to support first-generation civil and political rights where these have been seen to conflict with the economic interests of US corporations and the US state. The US Congress Kassebaum amendment of 1985, requiring the US to pay no more than 20% of the annual budgets of any part of the UN system without weighted voting on budgetary matters, aimed to give the US government power to steer the UN organisation along a more acceptably neo-liberal path.[36]

As Patomaki and Teivainen point out, a proposal for the US to reduce its contribution of 25% of the UN budget was rejected in the interest of continued US control of the UN agenda through ongoing threat of withholding this substantial contribution. As they note, 'financial blackmail by the US has changed many UN practices', with huge 'over-representation of US and UK citizens in top UN jobs'. And 'agenda-setting powers and decision-making criteria have been, in practice, changed towards the one dollar/one vote principle'.[37]

Despite his initial support for this policy, the US expelled Secretary General Boutros-Ghali for his subsequent failure to sufficiently conform to US wishes.[38] And the office of the Secretary General has subsequently remained under US control. 'Half of Kofi Annan's speech writers [were] from the US, and in effect the speech writers act[ed] as the Secretary-General's censors.'[39] And US-inspired talk of making the UN more 'efficient' and financially accountable is essentially about reducing democracy in the interests of complete US domination.

Critics have called for the creation of new sources of income to free the UN from financial blackmail by current major contributors, 'including international levies and taxation'.[40] But such schemes would be opposed by the US and other powerful economies. And there are other channels for the exercise of US power.

To the extent that they have not been able to exercise total control over the UN:

> there has ... been a tendency [for the US] to marginalise the UN or to sidestep it when [this has been seen by the US leadership to be] necessary. In effect the US – either as the hegemonic sovereign state of the 'free world' or as the leader of NATO – has assumed many of the powers that were originally granted or meant to be granted to the UN system.[41]

As noted by Amnesty International, the extreme neo-liberal regime of George W Bush has increasingly acted to undermine international co-operation and the rule of international law.

> It has pulled out of the Kyoto Protocol on climate change, failed to ratify the Comprehensive Test Ban Treaty despite clear prom- ises made under the NPT (Non Proliferation Treaty), pulled out of the ABM (Anti-Ballistic Missile) Treaty, refused to submit the treaty on the International Criminal Court to the Senate for its consent and refused to sign the Biological Weapons Protocol. At the World Summit on Sustainable Development in 2002, US delegations to international negotiations worked hard to weaken treaty language, and then failed to ratify them anyway. All of these unilateral actions by the United States are undermining the power and authority of the UN, discouraging international co-operation and breaking down the rule of international law.[42]

But most important in undermining UN democracy has been the role of the US in redirecting the operations of the IMF and the World Bank, and shaping the development of the WTO as governing body of international trade. Since the 1980s in the case of the IMF and the World Bank, and since its formation in 1995 in the case of the WTO, these organisations can be seen to have exploited developing nations' poverty and debt in order to radically undermine the economic and political autonomy of the world's poorer nations in the interests of domination by US-based multinational corporations. This and all of the other issues raised in this chapter are explored in greater depth in subsequent chapters.

Discussion topics

1. What are *rights*? What are *human rights*?
2. How do classical liberal ideas on rights and justice differ from those of social liberals?
3. What are *human needs*? How do we measure need satisfaction?
4. How much progress has been achieved in the development of public international law?

Chapter 10

NATURAL LAW
AND
POSITIVISM

This chapter considers some major jurisprudential themes, issues, schools and debates. Natural law and legal positivism are the most commonly referred to schools of jurisprudence, so it is important to have a basic grasp of their origins, scope and rationales. But it must be emphasised that these are far from being the only two strands of legal theory. Many others exist, including sociological, psychological, Marxism, Critical Realist, postmodernist and feminist.

Several other preliminary points must be made. First, as will become clear later in the chapter, when discussing the post-World War II debates between legal positivists and naturalists, the two approaches are not opposites, as they are often portrayed, but can find substantial agreement. Second, it is better to begin with natural law, as the older theory, and to examine the positivist reaction (backlash) to the evolution of naturalism. Third, natural law has taken on many different legal and political hues over the centuries.

In particular, during the great capitalist revolutions (the English, American and French) of the 17th and 18th centuries, natural law produced a revolutionary emphasis on basic rights and human equality. The reaction that this provoked led to the positivist response of Jeremy Bentham and John Austin in the 19th century. The legal positivists insisted that law had to be defined as the commands of the legitimate or effective government in power, freed of all other considerations such as morality, social justice, politics and economics.

Natural law

Natural law theorists argue that society's laws are derived from, or must be derived from, a higher source than the promulgations of governments. The definition given by Freeman in *Lloyd's Introduction to Jurisprudence* is a good starting point: 'the essence of natural law may be said to lie in the constant assertion that there are objective moral principles which depend upon the nature of the universe and which can be discovered by reason'.[1]

Natural law can be defined in terms of:

a) nature
b) ethical or moral considerations
c) religious precepts
d) social contract
e) human reason.

These approaches embody various lines of reasoning, including:

- proceeding from what 'is' to what 'ought' to be, that is, deriving principles from observed human nature or society

- viewing nature and humanity teleologically, that is, as tending toward predetermined ends (for example, acorns grow into oaks). The teleological view sees humanity as having ends that can be ascertained by reflecting on its nature and its needs.

- asserting that propositions of natural law are self-evident, either given by God or derived from the common features of human societies, or having been determined by economic and political struggle. Hence the American Declaration of Independence in 1776 proclaimed: 'every man is endowed by his Creator with inalienable rights, and that among these are life, liberty and the pursuit of happiness'. These were described as 'self-evident' but in reality arose out of the struggle of the aspiring American capitalist class against British colonial domination.

- conceiving natural law as having a variable content, according to time, place and circumstance. This is an attempt to overcome the fact that natural law theory is capable of embracing varied social orders. Thus, in their time, natural law thinkers tended to see both slavery and feudalism as moral and natural.

These strands are not exhaustive and also overlap. But they share some immediate implications. One is that bad laws may be assessed as defective and perhaps not laws at all. Another is that there are limits on the obligation to obey official authority.

This is precisely why Bentham, in his *Anarchical Fallacies* and *A Fragment on Government* railed against Blackstone's *Commentaries* for suggesting that the common law embodied natural rights. Bentham wrote: '[T]he natural tendency of such doctrine is to impel a man, by the force of conscience, to rise up in arms against any law whatever that he happens not to like.'[2] This was written in 1776, the year of the American Revolution, which claimed a right to overthrow British rule.

Broadly speaking, there are four epochs of natural law, the:

1   Ancient Graeco-Roman theory
2   Judaeo-Christian tradition
3   Age of Reason
4   post-World War II revival.

The Ancient Greeks and Romans

The two most important figures were Plato (427–347 BC) and his student Aristotle (384–322 BC). Plato also referred to the thought of Socrates, who had been his teacher.

They wrote and taught in a city-state system that rested on slavery, which created the economic conditions for reflective thought by a privileged layer. They were generally rationalist in their approach. The ultimate source of concepts of good or evil, whether divine or natural, was not important to their legal theory.

Plato's 'ideal' means of conducting society were open to suitably trained human reason – hence his 'model' of a 'philosopher king' with little role for a legal code. But he contended that laws should not only compel, they should also persuade and educate in virtue.

On the obligation to obey, there is an apparent contradiction between the *Apology* and the *Crito*. In the *Apology*, Plato drew on the experience of Socrates' trial for impiety, corruption of youth and, in effect, sedition. He asserted that the state has no right to demand that a person commit evil, with the only honourable course being refusal.

However, in the *Crito*, he said an individual has an obligation to obey a law that wrongs him or her, as distinct from requiring wrong to be committed by the individual. In other words, individuals cannot validly be compelled to wrong others, but must submit to the injustice of the state themselves.

Plato gave three reasons to obey, all of which feature throughout the history of jurisprudence and each of which is dubious:

1   The *parent-child analogy* – this is much over-stretched, not least because societies are historically forged and contain conflicting interests, pursued by adults, whereas children are largely dependent on their parents.
2   *Social contract*, that is, those who disagree can leave. The right to leave society is often unrealistic, as it is today for many refugees.
3   *Unrest will destroy the social fabric.* The social fabric may be the cause of intolerable injustice and hence discontent.

Aristotle took a teleological approach: human beings have an inherent potential for good, the achievement of which it is the proper function of the state to facilitate. He regarded humans as 'political animals' combining for mutual life in societies. He postulated the existence of universal justice higher than that expressed in 'good' laws. Aristotle said little on obligation to obey, seemingly agreeing with Plato.

Aristotle tutored Alexander the Great, who undertook military expansion of the ancient Hellenistic world. This was reflected in the rise of Stoic philosophy, which taught that there is a rationally observable higher order, a cosmic reason, which may be appreciated by all peoples, not just a 'civilised few'.

This universalism held attractions for the theorists of the Roman Empire, with its vast and diverse territories. This can be seen in the work of Cicero (106–43 BC), the most important pre-Christian Roman legal theorist. He defined natural law as 'right reason in agreement with nature'. He also postulated the striking down of positive laws that contravened natural law.

He drew a distinction between positive law, *lex vulgus* – essentially an exercise of political power that might or might not be appropriate – and the divine law, *lex caelestis*. The latter was accessible to rational insight and inquiry, which would produce natural law, the *lex naturae* – the proper model for making laws.

In Roman practice, this notion of natural law found expression in the concept of *jus gentium*, a body of legal principles common to all peoples of the world, as compared to the *jus civile*, the particular law of a given state. Conquest and trade necessitated the development of law that could be applied to foreigners, hence the assertion of universal law.

The Judaeo-Christian tradition

The final phase of Graeco-Roman jurisprudence was readily adaptable to the adoption of Christianity as the official religion of the Roman Empire by Emperor Constantine in 312 AD. This required a fusion of the Hellenistic and Judaeo-Christian traditions, which continues to influence jurisprudence today.

This tradition is based on an unequivocal and more absolute assertion of a higher, divine authority, with a detailed legal code, as set out, for example, in Exodus 20:1 to 22:17. Like natural law theory as a whole, this can be used to either sanctify an existing order as 'the will of God' or justify disobedience by appeal to a higher authority.

Certainly, Christ was crucified by the Roman state for encouraging revolt against slavery, but after 312 the Church became incorporated into the Roman order, wherein it was used to legitimise the Empire. This also happened with the emergence of the feudal order after the Dark Ages that followed the fall of the Roman Empire.

Christian theory tends to have particular problems with change, since the written scripture is meant to be the eternal law of God, expressed in very concrete prescriptions. As we shall see, Aquinas had difficulties in enunciating a theory to allow for changing economic requirements.

The first early theorist was St Augustine of Hippo (345–430) who himself converted to Christianity and wrote shortly after Constantine's adoption of Christian doctrine. His best-known assertion is that 'an unjust law is no law'. Citing Cicero, he equated unjust governments with criminal gangs or pirates – able to have their way only through force. This did not necessarily mean a right to rebel. An unjust law could be coercively enforced, but would not have any moral force. Anything just in positive law (*lex temporalis*) would derive from eternal law (*lex aeterna*).

Augustine had a minimalist view of positive law, limiting it to the coercive discouragement of sin. By the 13th century St Thomas Aquinas had radically altered this latter view. He was writing nearly

900 years later as part of the consolidation of feudalism after the Dark Ages. By then the works of Aristotle had been rediscovered. Like Aristotle, Aquinas considered that positive law plays a proper and 'natural' role in political and social life. In the words of one writer, he afforded the law a greater dignity than suppressing sin. By this stage, the Church was thoroughly institutionalised as part of the state. Arguably, this was a greater influence than the rediscovery of Aristotle.

Aquinas postulated four types of law:

1   *lex aeterna* (eternal Will of God)
2   *lex divine* (divine law, as revealed by scripture)
3   *lex naturalis* (natural law, the fruit of rational human observation)
4   *lex humana* (positive law, 'good' as far as it rests on these foundations).

According to this view, known as the Thomist view of law, human law forbids and punishes transgressions of natural (moral) law, and aims to encourage and support adherence to such moral law. However, any human law that radically departs from natural law is not a true law at all.

In those circumstances, the moral obligation to obey fails, unless greater scandal would result from disobedience. That is, some degree of unjust government should be tolerated for fear of bringing worse things by rebellion or disobedience, but there are limits. Tarquinius, the last king of ancient Rome, was cited as an example of a properly deposed tyrant.

In the battle against the rising capitalist class, this doctrine became more openly reactionary. In the Counter-Reformation, later Thomist thinkers insisted that to challenge positive law was to sin against the eternal law of God.[5] Thus, before they were ousted by Cromwell, the Stuarts claimed 'the Divine Right of Kings'.

The Age of Reason

The Age of Reason, which culminated in the Enlightenment of the 18th century, was bound up with the expansion of human geographic, cultural and intellectual horizons over the two previous centuries. Some of the factors involved included great scientific advances, the discovery of the New World, the expansion of world trade and the emergence of nation-states (first in Britain then in the Netherlands, the USA and France).

We cannot here review these developments and their impact in detail. Suffice to say that the unchallengeable authority of the Church had been slowly eroding since Copernicus (followed by Galileo) proved that the earth was not the centre of the universe but revolved around the sun. Giordano Bruno went further and postulated many suns and an infinite universe. For this he was burnt at the stake in Rome in 1600.

The great advances in science were reflected in philosophy, for example, in Locke's (1632–1704) *Essay Concerning Human Understanding*, which repudiated the concept of innate ideas, given by God, and established the objective source of thought in sensations derived from the external world.

Human thinking, and therefore moral character, was, in the final analysis, a reflexive product of the material environment in which they lived. Contained within this conception was a profoundly subversive notion: the nature of humanity could be changed and improved by changing and improving the social environment. Humanity was no longer cursed forever by original sin.

How was life to be improved? Through the invincible power of human reason. The motto of the Enlightenment, as Kant (1724–1804) wrote, was: 'Dare to know!'

Legal theory likewise sought to locate the state's authority and legitimacy in human, rather than divine, sources. This led to a recasting of the naturalist analysis in revived forms of the social contract, in some ways reminiscent of Plato. This is common to the three principal jurisprudential figures of the 17th and 18th centuries, Hobbes, Locke and Rousseau. However, their theories were very different, reflecting different historic and political circumstances.

Thomas Hobbes (1588–1679) wrote his principal work, *Leviathan* in 1651, in reaction to the Cromwellian revolution in Britain, which had seen a civil war, a king lose his head, the establishment of a parliamentary dictatorship and the emergence of radical egalitarian tendencies such as the Levellers.

He argued that the proper purpose of government and law was primarily to guarantee peace and order. In a time of war, he wrote, 'the life of man is solitary, poor, nasty, brutish and short'.[6] He set out two basic principles:

1 All should strive for peace but may resort to self-defence when the endeavour proves impossible.
2 The people should be satisfied with as much liberty as they are willing to allow to others.

For Hobbes, the obligation to obey only ceased when the sovereign fails to maintain the order that is the fundamental term of the social contract. Then the individual right of self-defence will abrogate the duty of obedience owed to the ruler.

Whereas Hobbes was the theorist of the post-Cromwell Restoration, John Locke (1632–1704) provided the theoretical underpinning for the 1688 'Glorious Revolution' in which the parliament and the emergent capitalist class re-established their supremacy by overthrowing James II and replacing him with Protestants, William II and Mary II of Orange.

Locke is a seminal figure in political and legal philosophy, with two principal, interlinked influences. He provided initial rationales for the concepts of liberty and private property, while leaving the underlying tensions between the two unresolved.

His rationale for the Settlement between the monarchy and the parliament had two key planks:

1 the rejection of any 'absolute' power in favour of a limited sovereign
2 all individuals had 'natural rights' to life, health, liberty and property.

If these principles were transgressed, 'the people have the right to resume their original liberty'. Thus, he proclaimed a right of revolution, although he was not an enemy of political authority. He postulated the existence of 'tacit and scarce consent' as well as express consent.[7] Merely by remaining within a state, people tacitly consented to obey its laws because they benefited from the actions of its sovereign. He declared that to disturb government was also to breach the law of nature – it could only be justified when the sovereign had betrayed this trust.

Locke helped forge the necessary ideological weapons for the emergence of a new capitalist society. One of the most important battles in the development of capitalism was the establishment of *exclusive* property rights, above all in land, over the common property rights which had played such a central role in the lives of the peasantry under feudalism.

This new form of property had to establish itself against the conception that land should be held in common and its fruits available to all. The forms of property, based on exclusion, which are considered as emanating from human nature today, were once regarded as so 'unnatural' that they had to be argued for. Locke wrote:

> But this [that the earth was given to mankind in common] being supposed, it seems to some a very great difficulty, how any one should ever come to have a *Property* in any thing ... I shall endeavour to show, how Men might come to have *property* in several parts of that which God gave to Mankind in common, and that without any express Compact of the Commoners.[8]

Locke could be characterised as the advocate of propertied revolution. By insisting on the inviolability of property against tyranny, his was the classic bourgeois outlook. This notion found its way into judicial judgments. Take, for example, the remark of Pratt CJ in *Entinck v Carrington* that: 'The great end for which men entered into society was to secure their property.'[9]

However, Locke's conception of property was more complex than simply privately held assets. It included the right to the fruits of one's own labour. He deplored the growth of inequality and espoused a right to physical subsistence, even where it cut across property rights. Locke argued that if a man insisted on the market price for food for a man dying of hunger, he was guilty of murder.[10]

In many respects, the social contract approach to natural law culminated in Jean-Jacques Rousseau (1712–78) who wrote in the lead up to the French Revolution. Unlike Locke, he postulated rights to life and liberty, but not property. In fact, private property was at the centre of his famous observation, uttered at the outset of *The Social Contract*, that 'human beings are born free but are everywhere in chains'.[11] The revolutionary implications of this insight found expression in his *Discourse on the Origin and Foundation of Inequality Among Men*, published in 1755. Property, he explained, was not a natural attribute of human existence. In his natural state, man did not have property. It is the product of the growth of civilisation which, once having come into existence, destroys man's humanity and enslaves him:

> The first man who, having fenced off a plot of land, thought of saying, 'This is mine,' and found people simple enough to believe him was the real founder of civil society. How many crimes, wars, murders, how many miseries and horrors might the human race have been spared by the one who, upon pulling up the stakes or filling in the ditch, had shouted to his fellow men, 'Beware of listening to this impostor; you are lost, if you forget that the fruits of the earth belong to all and that the earth belongs to no one.'[12]

As there was once no property, so was there once no inequality. Like property out of which it develops, inequality is a product of civilisation. The poor are oppressed by the power of property. Those who possess property are morally and intellectually disfigured by the struggle to obtain, keep and augment it.

The background to the positivist reaction

Writing before the French Revolution, David Hume (1711–76) was among the Enlightenment figures whose rationalism and secularism came into conflict with the idea of a universal natural law common to all mankind.

He declared it was a leap of logic to deduce 'ought' from 'is', that is to derive the normative prescriptions of natural law from descriptive observations of humanity and society as it is.[13] In addition, Hume asserted that governments and laws were the creation of men and reflected 'human interests' and 'conventions', not the laws of nature.

Nonetheless, Hume developed an empirical view of the principles of justice, describing them as 'natural laws' because 'they are as old and universal as society and the human species, but prior to government and positive law'. He said observation of the rules of justice was 'palpable and evident, even to the most rude and uncultivated of the human race'. So perhaps the separation of man and nature is not so simple?[14]

In response to the American and French Revolutions, western jurisprudence took a sharp turn, particularly in England. This took two forms, one personified by Burke and Blackstone and the other by Bentham and Austin.

Edmund Burke appealed to natural law to attack French egalitarianism and to support the wage system. He was a conservative whose heritage is often claimed today by Tory parties.

He appealed to 'the eternal principles of truth and justice' to denounce arbitrary rule and interference with the rights of property and employers. He railed against the Speenhamland system of paying labourers a supplement related to the cost of bread and the size of their families. This was because the wage relation was part of a natural 'chain of subordination'. He equated the capitalist market with the divine and natural order and asserted that capitalism 'had in fact been the traditional order in England for a whole century'.[15]

Similarly, in his *Commentaries*, William Blackstone appealed to natural law to sanctify the English common law. For this, as mentioned earlier, Bentham denounced Blackstone because the natural law doctrine tends to impel people, by force of conscience, to rise up against laws they do not like. Natural law was 'nonsense on stilts'.[16]

Classical positivism

The founder of classical legal positivism is Jeremy Bentham (1748–1832), whose ideas were developed, arguably to their detriment, by John Austin (1790–1859). Positivist theories describe law as it is in a given time and place, by reference to formal, rather than to moral or ethical, criteria of identification.

This has been the dominant school since the early 19th century. It also accords with the demand for a 'practical' definition of law. But as we shall see, that quest is fraught with difficulties.

Bentham was far from indifferent to the quality of law. He actively sought to correct laws that he regarded as offending against principles of utility. However, he made a distinction between expositorial jurisprudence (what the law is) and censorial jurisprudence (what it ought to be). For the latter, he sought to develop a 'science of legislation'.

Classical positivism had two main features: (1) a separation of law from morality and other factors, such as economics and (2) an attempt to define law by a command theory.

The command theory as suggested by Bentham and developed by Austin was simplistic and divorced from the underlying forces giving rise to a legal system. It postulated three requirements: (1) a command, (2) a sovereign and (3) a sanction.

Bentham defined a law as 'an assemblage of signs declarative of a volition conceived or adopted by the sovereign in a state, concerning the conduct to be observed by persons, who are or are supposed to be subject to his power: such volition trusting for its accomplishment to the expectation of certain events'.[17]

But not all laws are simply orders, even from a positivist view. For example, laws facilitate the making of contracts and wills. Another obvious difficulty was that by the early 19th century, the sovereign power, at least in England, was limited and somewhat dispersed. There was a separation of powers, and also of local government.

Bentham was anxious to avoid the assertion of a right to rule; hence he focused on the so-called 'fact of rulership'. He defined a sovereign as 'any person or assemblage of persons to whose will a whole political community are (*no matter on what account*) supposed to be in a disposition to pay obedience' (our italics).

Thus, the basis of authority was an actual or supposed habit of obedience, no matter why. This view not only leaves room for tyrants and dictators, it cannot account for revolutions, military coups, acts of secession and so on which erupt when people are no longer disposed to be obedient.

Bentham depicted sanctions in terms of pain and pleasure. Fear of pain was a coercive sanction; expectation of pleasure was an alluring sanction. He admitted other motivations for compliance with law, including physical, political, moral and religious sanctions, but argued that a sanction imposed by a sovereign was a definitive characteristic of law.

Among other things, the command theory cannot explain legitimacy. Can obedience be reduced to habit? Do not reason and agreement play a role? Is mere coercion sufficient to retain stability? In the words of McCoubrey and White: 'Laws are much more complex than simple orders, and a sovereign body is not just a glorified sergeant-major.'[18]

Modern positivism and the revival of natural law

Now we turn to the 20th century debate between modified positivism and revived natural law, notably the so-called 'Hart-Fuller debate', augmented by Finnis, a contemporary naturalist. These theorists emerged in the context of the post-World War II restabilisation after the victory of the US and Britain over Germany and the beginning of the Cold War. Their discussion on the nature of law was also motivated by the experiences under the Nazis.

The perceived abuses of legal process inherent in the Nazi and Stalinist regimes led to a questioning of the validity of formalist legal theories. Positivism's exclusion of questions of morals, ethics, human rights and political considerations from the realm of jurisprudence – even if they were to be examined in other spheres or disciplines – seemed to ignore matters that should be central to the nature of law in the 20th century.

On one side of the debate, HLA Hart sought to develop a more sophisticated form of positivism, avoiding the rigidity and narrowness of the Austin-Bentham command theory by outlining a less precise notion of the concept of law.[19] One of Hart's main contributions is said to be his enunciation of a scheme of primary and secondary rules. He suggested three categories of secondary rules: (1) rules of recognition, (2) rules of change and (3) rules of adjudication.

Hart's rules of recognition were ultimate rules underpinning a legal system. However, he did not provide a clear definition of the rule or rules of recognition, instead suggesting that common acceptance by officials was sufficient.[20] He illustrated his conception by the simplistic, mythical example of a tyrant Rex I – in effect, a crowned gunman – whose son Rex II succeeds him and is accepted as legitimate on the basis of the rule of succession by the eldest son. In Hart's view, this was adequate to constitute a formal right to rule. This seems a poor example in the 20th century, divorced as it is from any conception of popular support or acceptance.

Later, Hart enunciated what he called a 'minimum content of natural law'. Despite his formalistic legal positivism, he asserted that there was a minimal, or perhaps essential, moral content to law. He claimed there were 'truisms concerning human nature' that do form a common element in the law of all societies. His five truisms – approximate equality, human vulnerability, limited altruism, limited resources, limited understanding and strength of will – are highly debatable. For example, what is 'approximate equality'? It is certainly not genuine social equality, nor a right of any kind. Perhaps it is based on a rough political assessment of what will be tolerated without social unrest.

The Hart versus Fuller debate took place on the question of the validity of some or all of Nazi laws and judicial decisions. Hart's argument was broadly that the Nazi laws, however oppressive or immoral, were in accord with the rule of recognition and must be considered to be law.

If Nazi informers were to be punished, it would be preferable to openly state that as a matter of policy, and to enact retrospective legislation to do so, rather than infringe on the distinction between law and morality. Thus, to preserve his positivist conception, Hart was prepared to embrace backdated criminal laws, despite a centuries-old principle abhorring such retroactive measures as permitting arbitrary rule.

Lon Fuller was professor of general jurisprudence at Harvard from 1948 to 1972. He sought to answer the issues raised by the belatedly recognised totalitarianism of the 1930s by advancing a theory that he labelled 'procedural naturalism' in an effort to define the minimal requirements for a recognisable legal system.

There is debate whether the Nazi regime was a 'rule of law' and some commentators have observed that Hitler's administration would have passed nearly all the requirements specified by Fuller. He insisted that his was a natural law theory, but arguably, Fuller's scheme is not correctly termed 'naturalist' in that it is primarily concerned with the minimal procedural prerequisites for a legal system, not the substantive content of a legal system.

In the *Morality of Law*, he explains the narrower task that he assigned himself, although he saw it as a larger issue: 'There is little recognition ... of a much larger problem, that of clarifying the directions of human effort essential to maintain any system of law, even one whose ultimate objectives may be regarded as mistaken or evil.'[21]

Fuller rejected the Christian doctrines of natural law and sought to apply human reason to discover 'principles of social order which will enable men to attain a satisfactory life in common'. His 'morality of duty' sought to lay down eight 'basic rules without which ordered society is impossible, or without which an ordered society directed toward certain specific goals must fail of its mark'.[22] Laws had to be (1) general, (2) publicly promulgated, (3) sufficiently prospective, (4) clear and intelligible, (5) free of contradictions, (6) sufficiently constant, (7) possible to obey and (8) administered congruently with their wording.

This raises many questions. What is an 'ordered society'? Whose order? Are the procedural means, even in this minimal sense, so easily separated from the ends of society? Fuller himself argued that the procedural requirements will 'affect and limit the substantive aims that can be achieved through law'. He wrote of their 'reciprocal influence'.

Fuller asserted one 'imperious' tenet of substantive naturalism in the maintenance of 'channels of communication' between people and peoples.[23] This attempt to define, perhaps, a minimalist content of natural law sits as incongruously with Fuller's proceduralism as does Hart's rather different 'minimum content' with Hart's separation of law and morality.

There is no doubt about John Finnis' credentials as a natural law scholar. He set the classical natural law concerns of Aristotle and St Thomas Aquinas in the contemporary language of 'natural rights'.

He took issue with David Hume's 'is' and 'ought' deductive fallacy by denying that natural lawyers have ever sought to derive ethical norms from facts, that is, from simple observation of human conduct. He argued that people have an 'internal' perspective of their aspirations and nature and from this it is possible to extrapolate an understanding of the 'good life' for humanity in general.

He claimed to derive 'seven basic forms of human good' from a survey of anthropological investigations: life, knowledge, play, aesthetic experience, sociability or friendship, practical reasonableness and religion.[24] Obvious questions arise. Are these exhaustive? Essentially, Finnis argued that they are. He said there are countless objectives and forms of good but on analysis they are always found to be one or a combination of the seven basic forms of good.

The list has some troublesome omissions. What about political freedom? Equality? Freedom from exploitation? Indeed, the list seems culturally specific to contemporary free market capitalism.

For example, what is 'practical reasonableness'? Finnis wrote of 'a measure of effective freedom' and 'genuine realisation of one's own freely ordered evaluations, preferences, hopes and self-determination'. This is quite relative and individualist. There are none of the inalienable rights of liberty, fraternity and equality invoked by the leaders of the French Revolution. There is no right to 'happiness', let alone insurrection proclaimed by the American Revolution.

And how can such conceptions, even as vaguely phrased, be realised outside economic welfare and freedom from material want? There is no mention of this under the heading of 'life', only references to famine relief and keeping children alive until they can fend for themselves. This is not only an extremely minimalist notion, it is tied to family responsibility and not social responsibility.

Notably, Finnis defended private property. He argued that 'the good of personal autonomy in community' suggests private property as a requirement of justice. A socialist, following the observation first articulated by Rousseau, would suggest the opposite: that private ownership of the means of production, resting on wage slavery, is incompatible with genuine personal autonomy.

Finnis, like Aquinas, greatly qualified the right to defy an unjust law. In effect, he argued that in disobeying a law, even a bad law, a person places at risk the whole legal system and that therefore there may be a 'collateral' moral obligation to obey such a law.[25]

Notwithstanding these and other problems, which are arguably inherent in contemporary natural law theory, conceptions of natural law have been broadly influential since the middle of the 20th century, notably in international law. This can be seen in the development of international conventions and treaties, such as the Geneva Conventions on the conduct of war (1949), the Universal Declaration of Human Rights (1948), the Refugee Convention (1951), the International Covenant on Civil and Political Rights (1966), the International Convention on the Elimination of All Forms of Racial Discrimination (1966) and the International Covenant on Economic, Social and Cultural Rights (1966).

Natural law and science

It is important to see that, while natural law theory underwent significant development in a feudal and Catholic Christian context, it is quite possible to develop secular natural law theories based on objective scientific truths about what is good for all human beings. In particular, a number of contemporary theorists have followed Plato in focusing on medical considerations of physical and mental health as crucially bridging the gap between fact and value and thus providing a solid foundation for a modernised, secular natural law theory.

The crucial point about natural law theory is the idea that rational faculties of logic, observation, experiment and calculation can allow us to identify – and perhaps quantify – *objective facts about what is good for human beings*. And given that biological, psychological and social science show that all humans have a range of basic needs which have to be satisfied in order for them to remain healthy and to fully realise their human potentials of mental and physical growth and development, this would seem to be a logical starting point for contemporary natural law theory. That which promotes such healthy development is good and that which obstructs it is bad.

Here is a possible rational foundation for particular, legally supported, rights and duties. With basic needs recognised as rights of all, crucial social and legal questions revolve upon effective means of achieving or realising such rights, equally and for all.

Discussion topics

1. What is *natural law theory*? What are its strengths and weaknesses?
2. What is *legal positivism*? What are its strengths and weaknesses?

Additional resources

M. Davies, *Asking the Law Question*, Law Book Co, Sydney, 1994, Ch. 3.

M. Freeman, *Lloyd's Introduction to Jurisprudence*, 6th edition, Sweet & Maxwell, London, 1994, Chapters 3, 4 & 6.

H. McCoubrey and N. White, *Textbook on Jurisprudence*, 3rd edition, Blackstone Press, London, 1999, Chapters 2, 3, 4 & 5.

Chapter 11

LIBERAL DEMOCRACY

A political system is a system by which a particular group of people is governed, 'that is, made to do things they would not otherwise do, and made to refrain from doing things they otherwise might do'.[1] Government exists:

> to uphold and enforce a certain kind of society, a certain set of relations between individuals, a certain set of rights and claims that people have on each other, both directly and indirectly through their rights to property. These relations themselves are relations of power, they give different people in different capacities, power over others.[2]

Politics is about overall integration, organisation and regulation of social activity through development and application of public policy and law, adjudication, and dispute resolution, including the application of punitive sanctions in pursuit of social order. It is about the organisation of collective response to problems and threats, including defence against external attack and the provision of necessary infrastructure. In different times and places, such functions have been fulfilled by different sorts of social structures, institutions and practices. In the modern world we associate politics with the nation-state where a central law-making authority exercises an effective monopoly of coercive power to enforce such laws within a territory.

In this chapter we concentrate on the liberal representative democratic nation-state as the dominant form of political organisation in the modern world, particularly the western world, including the USA and Australia. According to the western powers this is the ideal towards which the rest of the world should be moving and towards which it inevitably is moving as a result of increasing freedom of trade and free flow of information and ideas around the world.

Separation of powers

Contemporary liberal representative democracy is generally understood to involve a division and sharing of power between different agencies and different social groups at the national and international levels, with all citizens accorded equal rights of participation in the political process. Rights of universal suffrage, of participation in (legitimate) political organisation, lobbying and campaigning, and free speech to allow for communication of competing political programmes, have been seen as crucial to the effective operation of a representative democratic system.

A written constitution, defining the nature and scope of the basic political institutions of the country and the rights of its citizenry, is typically seen as central to modern liberal democracy. But so too can such basic ideas, including ideas of legitimate processes of change of political institutions and of the limits of the power of government, be embodied in conventions, as generally accepted rules, not directly enshrined in law.

At the national – and, in federal systems, also the state – level, power-sharing is taken to imply a separation of powers between *executive* (of government leaders and civil servants who advise them) engaged in policy-making and law-enforcement, *legislature* engaged in law making, and *judiciary* engaged in interpretation of the law and adjudication of disputes. Powers of legislation and government are considered best exercised through representative democratic forms of political organisation. Membership of a legislative assembly – or law-making body – is chosen by popular vote in a secret ballot. Geographically based electorates each select one or more candidates to represent the people of that area, on the basis of their achieving a majority of the votes. In some cases such voting is compulsory, in others not. In some cases a preference system is in operation.

Such elections are typically dominated by political parties as organised groups seeking to 'take power for their leading members' as government of the country, united by commitment to a particular political programme associated with the interests of a particular social group.[3] Rank and file members support the party through paying subscriptions; activists and party employees can formulate policy, run local party groups and organise election campaigns. But nationally elected politicians generally exercise overall power within the organisation.[4]

Elected representatives can introduce bills into parliament, which are proposals for new laws. Such bills are debated under parliamentary privilege. Sometimes they are then examined by parliamentary committees with amendments proposed and incorporated, prior to another reading and a vote. In some cases, such bills are then handed on to an upper house of review. Such an upper house, representing the states in a federal system, can introduce its own amendments, handing the amended bill back to the lower house for a final decision. With agreement, the bill becomes law. If the two houses cannot agree, the bill may be passed anyway or it is set aside or put to a referendum, or may be a trigger for an election. The legislature has to approve the use of tax funds to finance executive operations on a yearly basis. But executive authority does have its own law-making powers of 'delegated legislation'.

Executive government members – cabinet and ministers – may belong to the legislature. In the Westminster System, governments are derived from the party that receives a majority in the lower house. And the party with the second highest representation has special privileges as recognised opposition. In a presidential system, the head of government is directly elected by a popular vote, separate from voting for the legislature. Senior public servants are chosen on merit by peers with more or less input from the political leadership. In the USA federal judges are appointed only after Senate endorsement and hearing of its Judicial Committee, and are supported by constitutional guarantees of independence. In the UK and Australia senior judges are appointed in secrecy by executive authority, typically from the ranks of Queen's Counsel. Some positions of judicial authority may be subject to direct election from a pool of suitably qualified candidates, as in 33 states of the USA, with popular election of judges for limited terms.[5]

National government retains control of security and foreign affairs, but in federal systems, states typically have substantial legislative powers. In Australia the Commonwealth alone has the power to control defence, interstate and overseas trade and commerce, external affairs, and customs and excise, and commonwealth legislation in other areas overrides any state legislation with which it conflicts. But the Commonwealth Constitution gives the states a general power to make laws dealing with issues within their own boundaries.

In Australia, as White and Perrone point out:

> ... public policing activities are predominantly the responsibility of the police agencies of state and territory governments, with the Australian Federal Police providing a community policing service in the Australian Capital Territory on behalf of the ACT Government. Funding for these services comes almost exclusively from state and territory government budgets ... Police services represent the largest component of the justice system, accounting for approximately 66% of the total justice-related expenditure, while corrective services account for a further 23%, and court administration the remaining 11% ... In 2002 there were over 45 000 sworn police officers and over 12 000 civilians employed by police services around Australia.[6]

This compares with 50 000 full-time military personnel in the army, air force and navy, with a further 19 000 in the reserves and 17 000 civilians employed by the Defence Department (in 2006), and 3324 employed by intelligence agencies (for example, ASIO (Australian Security Intelligence Organisation) (in 2005).[7]

At the same time, around the liberal democratic world, government services involving public space, welfare, local environment, local policing, health, housing and education are the responsibilities of regional, municipal and local government. Such local government is also supposed to be organised in terms of representative democracy, with local elections of town council members, for example. But:

> ... these lower order structures typically have no constitutional existence of their own, ... owing their legal arrangements to the decisions of national or state governments. And national or state governments retain the right to intervene to change electoral arrangements, eliminate mayors, redraw municipal boundaries and even eliminate whole layers of government.[8]

Citizens' interest groups, seeking to influence particular aspects of government policy and legislation by persuasion and provision of information, are generally seen as integral to the operation of liberal democracy. Professional and business groups can offer the benefit of specialised knowledge, skills and experience, and are frequently represented on advisory committees associated with particular government departments.[9]

The rule of law has historically been taken to involve limitation of government power by law, as well as legal protection of core rights of citizens, as enshrined in a constitution, including protection from indefinite detention without trial and the power to challenge executive decisions in court. Separation of powers implies a real independence of legislative, executive and judicial authority, to avoid too great a concentration of power, with each branch kept in check by the others. In particular, judges should have the power to review executive actions and statutes, to ensure that they are constitutionally valid. As noted, the legislature has the power to approve – or refuse – executive funding requests on an annual basis. And the armed forces remain under the control of the elected government, at arms length from domestic politics.

The constitution of the United States enshrines such separation of powers, with the two houses of Congress – the Senate (Upper House) and House of Representatives (Lower House) as legislature, the President as head of government, and judicial power in the Supreme Court, with no-one allowed to be both legislator and government member, or legislator and judge or government member and judge. The President can veto legislation passed by Congress, while the Congress can then overrule the President with a two-thirds majority. President and Supreme Court judges can be charged by the Senate with various crimes and removed from office if found culpable. Supreme Court judges are chosen by the President but have to be confirmed by the Senate and have the power to declare laws passed by the Congress as unconstitutional, and therefore not valid law.[10]

In the United Kingdom and in Australia, the executive government of cabinet and ministers belong to the legislature. The government must resign if it loses the confidence of the lower house. The lower house:

> ... also depends upon the government, because if the government decides that the time has come for a general election the members of the House will have to face re-election and may lose their seats ... ... the judges in Britain are more independent, since a judge of the higher courts cannot be dismissed except if the legislature asks the Queen to dismiss [them] for misbehaviour. Even so, the highest judges are members of the House of Lords, which is part of the

legislature. And their independence is less important than in the USA, since they cannot declare that a law made by the legislature is against the constitution and so invalid.[11]

However, they can now assess legislation in terms of the UK Bill of Rights based on a European model. In Australia, both houses of parliament can agree to dismiss judges, at federal and state level, for misbehaviour or incapacity. Judges interpret the constitution, dealing mainly with the boundaries of state and federal jurisdictions. But there is no Bill of Citizens Rights in terms of which judges can assess legislation.

It remains true that however independent and objective the processes of legislation and adjudication, they will always have to prioritise certain basic rights over others as conflicts arise. It is the role of the constitution to provide appropriate guidance in this process. As noted earlier, rights to life and legitimately acquired property (where such legitimate acquisition is understood to include inheritance, as well as income from labour and assets) have historically been allotted a special status, with state intervention via courts, police and prisons to prevent, compensate and punish trespass to person or to property. Similarly, military forces are deployed to protect citizens' life and property from large-scale external or internal threat.

Voting rights

Liberalism as a political ideology has always supported individual rights of ownership and inheritance of property, of choosing one's own occupation and profiting from one's own abilities through the operation of free market forces, seen as fair and efficient principles of social organisation. In the late seventeenth century political philosophy of John Locke, human beings were seen to possess 'natural rights' to life and property. People were conceived as rightfully owning their own bodies and the products of their own labour and free to dispose of such possessions as they chose. Such property rights were taken to include rights to take necessary steps to protect individual life and property. The state and legal system were originally seen to exist in order to protect individual rights to life and property from a minority of stupid or wicked people who failed to recognise such natural rights.

In order to have an efficient defence against such people, it was necessary for peace-loving respecters of property to organize a state apparatus which would legislate in accordance with natural rights, and enforce this legislation. The power of the state, therefore, was based on a contract between the members of society who transferred their natural right to punish violations of natural rights to authorities specially created for the purpose. These authorities were to be elected for a fixed term by a simple majority vote, and everyone participating was expected to agree in advance to accept whatever the majority might decide. Those who were elected were themselves parties to the contract, and were not above the law; they held power by courtesy of the electors, who were sovereign.[12]

But Locke didn't think that everyone was entitled to participate in such elections. Because the state existed essentially to protect private property rights, it made sense that those without property should not be entitled to interfere in the operations of government. And this meant the great majority of the population didn't get to vote, including all women and all men who did not actually own productive property and were forced to work on the land of those who did.

Locke's ideas corresponded closely to the actual political arrangements of England at the end of the seventeenth century, where fewer than 250 000 adult males out of a population of about 5 500 000 had a vote. This denial of voting rights to working-class men and to all women became a major focus of political struggle, particularly with the formation of trade and labour unions in the course of the Industrial Revolution. In England, the trade unions led the Chartist movement as a campaign for a radical extension of the franchise, which even after significant reforms in 1832 still excluded most industrial workers and all women. It was not until the late nineteenth and early twentieth centuries, more than two hundred years after the birth of liberal society in the English Revolution, that the fight to extend the democratic franchise to all adults was gradually achieved. But these struggles continued even in the industrial heartlands of liberal democracy right through the 1960s – with the US civil rights movement striving to enfranchise black people in the southern US. And they continue around the world today, with many different groups including immigrants, poor people, prisoners and former prisoners still denied effective voting rights even in nominally democratic polities.[13]

Social democracy and after

Following the increasing development of the trade union movement and the contribution of JS Mill in the later nineteenth century, a trend of liberal thought and action committed to active state intervention in promoting the free development of individuals increasingly challenged earlier 'laissez faire' liberal ideas.

> 'Positive' liberals came to argue that individuals could be formally free and yet, caught in the toils of the market system, have little or no opportunity to develop their capacities or lead worthwhile lives ... To enjoy positive freedom, it was necessary to have an adequate minimum of resources and opportunities, particularly of an educational kind.[14]

It came to be recognised that unregulated market forces could challenge basic freedoms of thought and of speech, thereby also threatening democracy, and provided no guarantee of even the most basic education, health care, housing or work for all citizens.

> In the early years of the twentieth century, pushed along [first] by reforming Liberal governments [and then by Labour or Social Democratic governments], the positive liberals saw their aims being achieved by the growth of public education, the beginnings of social security and unemployment relief, and a strengthening of the role of trade unions.[15]

Given the power of unregulated markets to create increasing inequality, a particularly significant development in Australia was the creation by federal and state parliaments of a national system of industrial courts, arbitrators and conciliators, operating independently of government, and determining and enforcing 'fair and reasonable' wages and conditions for all workers. 'Much of the system's business [was] done by registering and enforcing agreements negotiated by the employers and unions.'[16] Only where these two disagreed would there be a court case and a judgment, with the judges taking account of workers' cost of living expenses and productivity, as well as bosses' ability to pay. And for a long time such ability to pay was protected and supported by substantial tariffs and restrictions on imported manufactures.

In Sweden, following the political victory of Social Democrats in 1932, leaders of business and organised labour negotiated an agreement under which wages rates were decided by periodic national negotiations between them. With unions and government generally agreeing on economic policies and more than 90% of workers in trade unions, organised labour had considerable power in determining the outcome of such negotiations. There was general agreement that wages should be as equal and as high as possible, with government providing high-quality health, housing, education, child care, retraining, jobs or unemployment benefits for the unemployed. On their side, workers should be prepared to respond flexibly and constructively to necessary technical and economic changes.[17]

The post-World War II boom period saw the acceleration and extension of positive or social liberal reforms, sustained by active government intervention in job creation through fiscal and monetary policy, and progressive taxation. In Britain for example, on the basis of demand management and economic regulation, as Self points out, the post-1945 welfare state:

> ... represented the logical culmination of the reforms initiated by the Liberals early in the century. Through its social security provisions, its comprehensive health service and its large public housing programme, it offered in principle ... the basic material security for all that the positive liberals had long wanted.[18]

Along with such comprehensive social welfare and government commitment to achieving and maintaining full employment by means of demand management there was substantial extension of legislation and state regulation in areas of consumer protection, environmental impact, occupational health and safety, unfair dismissal, monopoly pricing, indigenous voting rights and land rights, and in many other areas.

All of the major political parties, and the electors, came increasingly to see these developments as 'naturally' complementing, advancing or moderating the basic ideas and practices of liberal politics, as considered earlier. Liberal democracy was thought to have developed into social democracy.

However, a minority of right-wing or 'negative' liberals always saw these developments as a distortion of 'true' liberal ideas and values, and an increasing threat to the effective operation of free and efficient markets as the foundation for social wealth and individual freedom. They sought to strip away what they saw as indefensible over-extensions of state power to return to earlier 'core' values and institutions of liberal politics and economics. This included substantial reduction in any rules and regulations which could be seen as hampering or restricting the operation of free market forces.

Key figures here, in paving the way for later 'neo-liberal' politics, were the Austrian political philosopher, Friederich von Hayek (founder of the Mont Pelerin Society) and Chicago School economist Milton Friedman. In his book, *Capitalism and Freedom*, published in 1962, Friedman advocates:

> ... the elimination of (1) taxes on corporations, (2) the graduated income tax, (3) free public education, (4) social security, (5) government regulations of the purity of food and drugs, (6) the licensing and qualifying of doctors and dentists, (7) the post office monopoly, (8) government relief from natural disasters, (9) minimum wage laws, (10) ceilings on interest rates charged by usurious lenders, (11) laws prohibiting heroin sales, and nearly every other form of government intervention that goes beyond the enforcement of property rights and contract laws and the provision of national defence.[19]

While receiving financial and political support from 'wealthy individuals and corporate leaders opposed to all forms of state intervention'[20], the movement 'remained on the margins of both policy and academic influence' until a period of major economic crisis in the 1970s, with increasing inflation and economic stagnation. Such developments suggested that key economic ideas and policies underlying social liberalism were no longer working. As Harvey says:

> At this point [neo-liberal ideas] began to move centre stage, particularly in the US and Britain, nurtured in various well-financed think tanks (offshoots of the Mont Pelerin Society, such as the Institute of Economic Affairs in London and the Heritage Foundation in Washington), as well as through its growing influence within the academy, particularly at the University of Chicago, where Milton Friedman dominated ... Neo-liberal theory gained in academic respectability by the award of the Nobel Prize in economics to Hayek in 1974 and Friedman in 1976.[21]

From here, neo-liberal theory, particularly as developed by Friedman, exerted an increasing influence on political decision-making. Key developments here were the election of Margaret Thatcher as British Prime Minister in 1979, with 'a mandate to curb union power' and to put an end to stagflation[22], the takeover of the US Federal Reserve by Paul Volker later that same year, with full employment policies sacrificed to the 'fight against inflation'[23], and the election of Ronald Reagan as US President in 1980, similarly committed to deregulation of markets and destruction of the power of organised labour.[24]

The subsequent period of neo-liberal political consensus, across all major parties, particularly in the English-speaking world has not seen the full realisation of Friedman's programme of privatisation and deregulation. But neo-liberal governments have moved in this direction, with significant winding back of the welfare state in favour of private provision of health, eduction and infrastructure, on a user-pays basis, reduced availability and level of unemployment benefits, reduced trade-union rights and powers, including the substitution of individual contractual arrangements for collective and centralised wage fixing, and reduced levels of protection for workers and for the environment in face of increasingly unscrupulous corporate operations.

In the neo-liberal world view, increasing privatisation and deregulation, along with decreasing taxation of corporate profits, of capital gains, high incomes and private wealth, such as has been instituted by governments throughout the western world since 1980, are associated with both increasing individual freedom and increasing efficiency of market-based production and distribution. And such market efficiency is seen as both intrinsically desirable and as strongly supporting political democracy. Efficiency drives growth, which creates more social wealth which provides more incentives for further growth through free individual initiatives. Markets effectively distribute such wealth to those that deserve it by virtue of their contribution to its creation and to those that can make best use of it.

Neo-liberalism and democracy

Neo-liberals tend to see such democracy in functional terms, as a means for preserving and promoting economic rights and economic efficiency and for ensuring that appropriately qualified experts are empowered to achieve such goals. Without an appropriate level of capitalist development (or intervention by the IMF and World Bank, as explained in the next chapter) majority rule can undermine rather than promote such rights and such efficiency. And non-democratic forms of government – by particular elite groups – might be more effective.[25]

Given the economic 'neo-liberalisation' of China, following Deng Xiaoping's economic reforms in 1978, with the opening up of the economy to foreign trade and foreign investment, and the increasing privatisation of previously state-controlled enterprise, western neo-liberals have been muted in their criticism of the Chinese leadership's failure to support reforms in the areas of human, civil and democratic rights.

More generally, neo-liberals claim to see free markets as complemented by liberal democratic political forms which allow freedom of speech and of political activity, and freedom of voters to choose their political representatives and law-makers. Neo-liberals counterpose the individual freedom made possible by unregulated market relations and liberal democracy to the absence of individual freedom in a planned or command economy, where production and distribution are directed by central state power. They highlight the totalitarianism and absence of political rights and freedoms that went along with such central planning in the old Soviet Union, to argue for a necessary interdependence of economic and political freedom.

Neo-liberals argue that the recent historical record provides empirical evidence for the interdependence of democracy, private property and free competitive markets. With increasing freeing up of world trade and cutbacks in government ownership and regulation of business operations around the globe over the last thirty years, so has there been an extension of liberal democracy. According to Freedom House in New York, 119 nations or 62% of UN members are now democracies, three times more than thirty years ago.[26]

Neo-liberals counterpose liberal representative democracy – seen as viable, efficient and desirable, in an appropriately developed capitalist society – to more radical ideas of participatory or direct democracy, with ongoing involvement of all in day-to-day political debate, negotiation and decision-making. While such direct democracy might have been possible in the tiny city-states of past ages it is no longer viable in a large and complex industrial society, both because of the numbers involved and the complexity of the issues, which can only really be dealt with by appropriately qualified experts. Liberal representative democracy gives all people who are interested a meaningful input into the political process, without requiring non-experts to waste time and resources in detailed deliberations they are ill-equipped to effectively pursue.

In fact, as CB Macpherson pointed out, right-wing liberals see the political system as, essentially, an extension of the market system. Parties of experts offer their different political programmes to the electorate, and the electors freely choose which one they want. In particular, politicians are required to be good economic managers, not in the sense of actually planning production and distribution, but rather in the sense of effectively ensuring that markets operate as freely and efficiently as possible. Voters then decide who will be the more efficient managers and thereby most effectively serve their own economic interests.[27]

Insofar as the primary goal of politics is to ensure such effective economic management, it makes sense that politicians should regularly consult with business representatives in the formulation of legislation. And neo-liberal parties in power have frequently installed business representatives on influential advisory committees and appointed them to cabinet positions. Professional associations of doctors, lawyers and others can also be recognised as valuable contributors in respect of relevant issues of legislation. But neo-liberals are not generally so sympathetic to trade unions or to interest groups associated with issues of environmental protection and human rights insofar as such groups are seen to threaten, rather than enhance, economic efficiency.

While neo-liberals generally defend basic democratic rights of freedom of speech and association, of habeas corpus and jury trial for indictable offences, neo-liberals in power have argued for a need to restrict such democratic rights in order to protect life and property threatened by global terrorism and uncontrolled migration.[28] In particular, they have enacted legislation to support indefinite detention of terror suspects for interrogation prior to trial and of illegal migrants prior to deportation, and tightened sedition laws to facilitate prosecution of those challenging state power and authority. Right-wing liberals have traditionally sought to restrict the rights of offenders in various ways, including preventing prisoners from voting or engaging in civil litigation. Some of them have endorsed torture as a legitimate tool in the war on terror.

From a neo-liberal perspective, government spending is seen as, ideally, financed through some balance of personal income taxes, corporations taxes and flat-rate consumption taxes, with income and corporation taxes minimised to encourage productive work and investment[29], and perhaps also dividend imputation (as in Australia) to avoid 'double taxing' of corporate income. Similarly, neo-liberals do not favour any kind of wealth taxes (including death taxes), also seen as 'double taxing', or environmental taxes (seen as threatening economic expansion and progress through increased costs).

Neo-liberals are strongly supportive of the idea of politically independent central banks, regulating the money supply in line with the 'natural growth rate' of the economy, rather than seeking to appease any particular social interests. Private banks are allowed to create money through offering loans not covered by deposits. But the central bank still supervises the process, cutting back the money supply and bank lending to reduce investment to stave off inflationary overheating and making money cheaper and more readily available to encourage spending to avoid recession.

Such central monetary authorities generally seek to control the national money supply through manipulation of private banks' reserve assets. Such manipulation is achieved through changing reserve requirements, for example reducing the minimum asset ratio, allowing more bank loans to increase consumer spending to avoid a recession, through open market operations, buying bonds from or selling them to banks to put more or less cash into the system for lending, and through changing the discount rate as the interest rate on their own loans. This contrasts with a position which would see money creation and interest rates as within the ambit of democratic political control and decision-making.[30]

Democratic markets and corporations

There are grounds for scepticism about the neo-liberal idea that the deregulated market operations and big business corporations of contemporary capitalism necessarily complement, support or encourage political democracy. On the face of it these institutions seem, in themselves, to be profoundly anti-democratic.

Consumer sovereignty, as the power of consumers' purchasing decisions to influence the production process, is sometimes identified by neo-liberals as popular, democratic control of production through expression of the common will. But this neglects the radical imbalance of 'voting' power in the market. Even if there is a real basis to the idea of consumer sovereignty, there is little democracy in 'one dollar one vote' when a minority have vast wealth and most others have comparatively little – or more debt than equity. The reality of inheritance, in particular, strongly supported by neo-liberals, radically undermines any such idea of market democracy, and is impossible to reconcile with 'just deserts'. Some enter the market with billions, even though they have contributed nothing to it. Many more enter with nothing and struggle all their lives just to survive.

In a past age of social liberalism, it was assumed that progressive taxation and social welfare would periodically redistribute wealth to 're-set' the system on a basis of relative equality (of bargaining power), with longer-term trends to radical inequality and poverty arrested. Individuals would thus confront each other in the market-place on relatively equal terms, genuinely able to exercise meaning-ful choices and to see such choices reflected in investment decisions. But neo-liberalism is generally hostile to such redistribution through welfare and progressive taxation as antithetical to fairness (as just deserts) and efficiency, as noted earlier.

The concept of consumer sovereignty is, anyway, highly problem-atic in face of the power of big oligopoly and monopoly corpora-tions to control and restrict supply of goods and manipulate demand through advertising and public relations. Superficially different prod-ucts often turn out to be essentially similar products of the same monopolies. So too is such 'sovereignty' undermined by the very restricted purchasing power of the majority of the population. They buy what they can afford to buy, which often dramatically reduces their capacity for meaningful choice.

Neo-liberals highlight the legal freedom and legal right of all indi-viduals in a free society to improve their situation and to increase their purchasing power – without limit. But it is impossible for all work-ers to become CEOs of major multinational corporations, no matter how hard they might try. Available positions decline in direct propor-tion to height up the pyramid of social power, income and wealth. And empirical evidence shows that while some can progress from the working class into the middle class through loans to start small busi-nesses or university degrees to get them into the lower professional ranks, few such new small businesses started in the upturn of a busi-ness cycle survive the next downturn and very few members of the professional middle class get anywhere near the social power elite.

Corporate board selection by votes of shareholders is sometimes presented by neo-liberals as 'democratic' control of corporate power. But again, even if shareholder voting rights were genuinely significant in determining the composition and policies of corporate boards, there is little democracy in 'one share one vote' when a minority have thousands of shares and most others have comparatively few. Strategic blocks of shares in the hands of wealthy individuals (including CEOs and company directors), families, groups and powerful fund managers can give these people effective control of board selection, given the dispersal of other shares and lack of co-ordinated action by other shareholders.

Except in cases of corporate takeover, boards of directors are generally hand picked by the CEO of the previous board, and 'rubber-stamped' by shareholders quite happy to maintain the status quo so long as the profits keep rolling in. But, as Glasbeek says, the low level of relevant knowledge of most shareholders makes it difficult for them to make meaningful judgments about the competence or social responsibility of managers. Here, indeed, the separation of ownership and control within the corporation offers huge possibilities for directors and controllers to pursue their own interests at the expense of the shareholders (as well as of workers and the environment).[31] Some commentators have equated the increase in the proportion of corporate equity owned by financial institutions in the English-speaking world (now around 40% in the UK and USA) with increasing democratisation of share markets, insofar as all members of the working population are now shareholders via private pension or superannuation funds. But again, this situation gives power to fund managers – to monitor and control company performance – rather than to the actual membership of such funds, who have little control over either the fund managers or the companies concerned.

Just as neo-liberals highlight the (legal) freedom of consumers to increase their purchasing power, so do they emphasise the freedom of smaller shareholders to organise together so as to influence board selection, and, indeed, of all shareholders, as legal owners of the corporation, to take legal action to ensure that managers are properly safeguarding their interests. This raises major problems of so-called transaction costs – the costs of actually developing such effective organisation. Add to this the costs of effective legal representation and expert financial advice and it looks increasingly less cost effective to most of those concerned.

Free world trade and democracy

There are also grounds for scepticism in relation to the claim that free world trade necessarily functions to promote democracy around the world. The idea seems to be that exposure to western culture and values through trade, along with the increased wealth supposedly generated by such trade, will motivate the citizens of less-developed nations to reject totalitarian rule in favour of liberal democracy. But history suggests otherwise.

Throughout the post-World War II boom period, the same pattern was played out around Latin America and other less-developed territories. A reign of free trade and free investment led to increasing inequality, poverty and concentrated wealth and power, in the hands of local elites working closely with foreign (mainly US) investors. Following the development of popular reform movements, reforming governments were democratically elected on platforms of increasing intervention and government economic control, including nationalisation of major productive resources which had fallen into foreign hands, significant land reform to return land to the dispossessed peasantry, and protection of local industries in the face of global competition, to challenge such increasing inequality and poverty.

The USA or other western powers then engineered violent military coups, and following significant loss of life, they oversaw the replacement of democracy with ruthless police-state totalitarianism and a return to 'unrestricted' freedom of trade and investment, as the western powers understood these ideas.

It seems clear that democracy is a potential threat to free trade and investment insofar as it allows the people to vote against such things. And it is notable that the USA has become an active supporter and proponent of third world democracy only since burgeoning third world debt has provided the basis for effective political-economic takeover of the countries concerned by the IMF and World Bank (see below) . Such takeover is associated with enforcement of a US model of freedom of trade and investment, completely undermining any meaningful representative democratic choice for the many countries concerned.

Brown highlights the willingness of the US to enter into free-trade deals with 'countries that demonstrably lack political freedom'. These deals are supposedly justified on the ground that they will promote democratic reforms in the countries concerned. In fact, as Sherrod Brown points out:

> ... by constructively engaging with totalitarian and authoritarian governments, the US is offering the elites of these countries financial incentives to continue repressive regimes, to limit freedom, and to crack down on workers and independent labour unions.[32]

The WTO free-trade rules actually forbid any economic action aimed at weakening police-state totalitarianism. As Brown observes, when the Massachusetts state legislature:

> ... passed a law prohibiting state agencies from doing business with companies that have business interests in Burma (renamed Myanmar), now a nation with one of the world's worst records of human rights abuses ... the EU prepared an action at the WTO against [that state] arguing that the state violated the rules of free trade which the US had ... forcefully argued during GATT adoption. The National Foreign Trade Council, an organisation of US exporters that had joined the EU [in this action] convinced a federal judge to invalidate the Massachusetts law ... and the state lost its appeal before the US Supreme Court.[33]

Democracy and the power of money

Representative democracy, separation of powers and the rule of law at the level of the individual nation-state are very significant improvements on fascist and other totalitarian systems and on earlier feudal absolutist and fundamentalist religious states. Even radical socialist critics have argued for a strengthening rather than abolition of key elements of liberal democracy. As Norman Geras, for example, says:

> Any real socialist society would need to incorporate ... a national representative assembly elected by direct universal suffrage, some separation of powers [in particular] the independence of judicial from political processes, the protection of individual rights, [and] a constitutionally guaranteed pluralism.[34]

Similarly, Ralph Miliband argues that just because the advances that have been achieved 'under capitalist conditions are constrained and corrupted by the context in which democratic forms function and by the determination of conservative forces not to endanger existing structures of power and privilege', they remain significant gains on earlier political forms nonetheless, and need to be vigorously defended.[35]

At the same time, we have to recognise that the effective operation of any political system, and the possibility of achieving any kind of progressive reforms, depend on 'a high degree of ideological congruence' between the three branches, with 'the power of government ... constrained but not subverted' by judicial review.[36] And, as noted earlier, which particular rights are prioritised by the constitution and by the judiciary are clearly crucial in this regard. As Miliband says, 'the age-long struggle for the extension of democratic rights has largely been a struggle against the rights of property owners ... to do what they will with their own'. And the judiciary have 'traditionally used their power to impede legislation which offended their conservative prejudices'.[37]

Support for private property rights of a wealthy minority inevitably undermines basic democratic rights to freedom of speech, organisation and campaigning. This is because democracy depends on genuinely equal access to such rights by all citizens. But it is obviously the case that a minority monopoly of private wealth can be turned into a minority monopoly control of the political process through control of the media, and funding of campaigning and of government. Such effective disempowerment of the majority leads to increasing disillusion and alienation from the political process for increasing numbers of ordinary people – which only serves to further increase the effective political power of private wealth.

Once concentrated private wealth has been allowed to subvert and control the democratic political process, there is nothing to prevent it from further reducing or eliminating whatever basic economic and democratic rights are still available to the majority of citizens. General political disillusionment and alienation from the political process can assist in this process, insofar as ordinary citizens believe they have nothing further to lose, or simply fail to realise what is happening until it is too late.

Social liberals point to recent developments in the western heartlands of democratic ideas and institutions undermining and restricting what have long been recognised as basic democratic rights. In Australia, recent changes in the areas of anti-terrorism legislation, including military call-out legislation and changes to sedition laws, as well as denial of legal rights to asylum seekers and radical restrictions of workers' rights in relation to union activities, collective bargaining and protection from unfair dismissal are all very significant steps backwards from the sorts of values and practices prevailing and the gains achieved in the previous era of regulation.

Such erosion of democratic rights and public alienation from politics point to fundamental structural problems and weaknesses in basic ideas and institutions of political democracy as currently understood and practised in the western world. Along with the very limited breadth of penetration of democratic forms into the social structure and social relations of late capitalism (including a total lack of democracy in corporate governance), social liberals highlight also the inbuilt obstacles to any real depth of meaningful participation on the part of the mass of the population – even within formally democratic political institutions and processes.

In particular, they point to the weakness of contemporary democratic institutions in face of subversion by the power of big corporations and private wealth. The vast power of big corporations and super-rich individuals to acquire media monopolies to shape public opinion, to finance multi-million-dollar election campaigns of their chosen parties and candidates, and to blackmail incumbent regimes through threats of capital flight and disinvestment, radically undermine meaningful political choice for the majority of the population.

Social liberals point to the even greater limitations of much of the new democracy in the developing world (and in parts of Asia and Eastern Europe) where many such governments have appalling records of repression and abuse of basic human rights of their own citizens. Elections in some such nations involve high levels of bribery, corruption and intimidation, and restriction of opposition parties campaigning in some or all areas. Many citizens fail to participate because they see real power over the nation as residing with foreign corporations and international agencies, particularly the World Bank and the IMF. And there are grounds for arguing that such political problems can – again – be traced back, to a great extent, to the economic weaknesses and disadvantages of such nations, oppressed, victimised and manipulated by more powerful nations in the global marketplace.

Lack of democratic depth

This raises deeper questions of the democratic foundations of the separation of powers, of the extent and nature of meaningful popular participation in shaping the exercise of executive, legislative and judicial power. There are grounds for believing that recent attacks on democratic rights and the rule of law (particularly in Australia and other common-law jurisdictions), including the erosion of free speech and freedom of association by strengthened sedition, anti-terror and anti-trade union laws, as well as the use of delegated legislation and bypassing of judicial review by administrative fiat, ultimately derive from deeper problems, intrinsic to fundamental ideas and institutions of liberal democracy itself. In particular, that it is the lack of institutional support for any real breadth or depth of political involvement on the part of the mass of the population that has paved the way for such developments.

Lack of breadth here refers particularly to the absence of democratic control of market forces and corporate structures and activities. Lack of depth refers to the absence of popular participation in, and democratic control of, the activities of political parties, governments and public services. Depth and breadth are closely related. Most obviously, a person's working life significantly determines the level of emotional, physical and financial resources available to them for participation in political activity.

Considering first the lack of democratic depth, we have already noted that contemporary political theory recognises a wide range of different forms of political activity open to the citizens of a democratic polity. 'These include working in electoral campaigns, contacting government officials, attending protests, working informally with others to solve a community problem, serving without pay on local elected and appointed boards, and contributing money to political causes.'[38] And we can add to this list participation in various forms of trade union activity, lobbying and political education and research.

But for the majority, such involvement has long been confined to ticking a ballot paper every four or five years. And since ruling parties can and do routinely break major election pledges without legal penalty, even ticks for the winning party can count for very little in practice. This means that political power is actually very unequally distributed throughout the population, with the great majority effectively powerless or politically disempowered.

At the same time the economic rationalist ideology of all major parties preaches that the real decision-making power of government is very limited, apparently unable to directly determine such vital issues as investment, jobs, working conditions, and wages. Parliamentary politics is widely thought of as corrupt and corrupting, with professional politicians seen as dishonest and untrustworthy. Elections are seen, at best, as a choice of the lesser of two evils. In this context, it is unsurprising that feelings of frustration, anger, apathy and powerlessness lead large numbers of people to abstain from voting.

Deregulated corporate operations contribute to increasing social inequality which, in turn, promotes frustration, mistrust and envy, which obstruct effective collaboration and participation in political activity. Generally, the lower the levels of social affiliation, including participation in voluntary associations, the 'poorer the voter turn out at election time'.[39]

Only one in five British citizens trusted politicians to tell the truth in surveys between 1983 and 2004, compared to greater trust in the 1950s and 1960s.[40] And numbers in all political parties have 'shown a substantial decline since the 1960s'.[41] US evidence shows a 'sharp decline in confidence in government since 1964 when three-quarters expressed confidence in the federal government. By the late 1990s the level had reduced to a quarter, with a similar pattern of decline being replicated at state levels of government.'[42] Robert Putnam presents clear evidence of 'declining voter turnout, social disengagement and a weakening of civic institutions' in the last quarter of the twentieth century.[43] In Australia, recent survey materials showed respondents 'mistrustful of politicians, the federal parliament, the legal system and the public service'.[44]

With governments no longer committed to the maintenance of full employment through fiscal policy, and the availability of cheap overseas labour, with government banning of strike action and of collective bargaining and repeal of protections from unfair dismissal, as well as reduced and inadequate welfare for the unemployed, fear of job loss keeps people working longer hours in a state of increased anxiety, which leaves little time or energy for political participation. This makes them more vulnerable to the politically and culturally paralysing effects of television, alcohol and drugs outside of work time, and to a media-driven consumer culture that substitutes possessions for participation and empowerment.

Such processes contribute to a positive feedback: the more disempowered and disillusioned people feel, the less they participate. The less they participate, the more disillusioned and disempowered they feel. At the same time, disempowerment renders people liable to regression to child-like perceptions of, and responses to, threat and trauma. Such regression encourages acceptance of simple solutions, couched in black-and-white terms, to complex problems. In particular, it encourages a passive, dependent relationship to established external authority, looking to such authority – as caring parent figure – to solve the problems in question, and prepared to be completely obedient to such authority in order to be thus cared for and saved. Or in the face of the radical failure of such established authority to provide such care and protection (to particular groups), it encourages a search for alternative counter-cultural family-like support in criminal gangs, cult groupings, dissident political factions and terrorist cells.[45]

Neo-liberal politicians have actively contributed to these processes of disempowerment. In addition to their failure to rein in corporate power and reduce inequality, they have sought to create fearsome bogies through demonisation of particular individuals and groups inside and outside the societies concerned, with a view to producing a climate of fear, mistrust and hatred. On the home front this facilitates divide-and-rule tactics. The disempowered and dispossessed fight among themselves rather than challenge central power. Fear and hostility towards foreigners serves to justify attacks on foreign nations to steal their resources. And such engineered threats and conflicts then serve to 'justify' suspension of democratic rights and the increase of unaccountable power at home.

Executive authorities have repeatedly tried to remove voting rights from individuals and groups unlikely to support them. This has included disenfranchising those in prison for more than a certain period and even those with any sort of criminal record or those refusing to pay poll-tax. In Australia, the Howard government not only tried to remove the voting rights of all prisoners, but also attempted to impose stringent evidentiary requirements on those trying to get their names on the electoral roll and to stop all new enrolments immediately the writs are issued for an election.[46] As Swift points out, 'migrant workers are excluded [from voting] almost everywhere, and this is particularly unfair ... in parts of Europe [where] they form a significant percentage of the working class'.[47] Voters regularly find 'their preferences frustrated' through constituency boundary arrangements manipulated by ruling parties to favour themselves. Such 'gerrymandering' frequently favours more conservative rural voters over city dwellers.[48]

The lack of constitutional support for political structures at the regional, municipal and local levels has already been touched upon, allowing national or state governments to intervene in local electoral arrangements – sacking local politicians and eliminating whole layers of elected government. Neo-liberal theorists present this as a desirable safeguard in face of local corruption and inefficiency. But such ideas are actually used to try to legitimate politically based attacks on the local democratic process, as with Margaret Thatcher's abolition of the socialist Greater London Council in 1986.

Political parties

Lack of democratic participation within the major parties means that if an ordinary person joins one of them they will have little input into the policy making of the leadership. Such parties are typically characterised by radical divisions between self-selecting and self-perpetuating ruling elites with effective control of policy and rank and file memberships denied any real involvement in policy making. And while the minor parties might offer higher levels of internal participation and empowerment for rank and file party members, this is counterbalanced by such parties' lack of real political power within the nation.

When in power, prime ministers and presidents typically exercise total control over selection of cabinet members and other senior officials, including High Court judges. As judges retire, this can produce courts stacked with political appointees all following the ruling party line (as has happened in Australia). But so too has this allowed for increasing politicisation of the public service. As Peter Self explains, by 1975, western bureaucracies had:

> ... acquired a reputation for integrity and impartiality, due to their
> Weberian features of appointment on merit, security and detach-
> ment from ... political patronage [and] any financial interest in their
> advice or decision ... Bureaucrats had a collective duty to assist

and co-ordinate government decisions, usually through numerous committees; to process and submit essential information; to convey faithfully the viewpoints of affected interests; and to apply laws without fear or favour.[49]

Under subsequent neo-liberal regimes, 'reduction of security, ... increasing appointments of outsiders, often businessmen, to senior public service jobs ... with much more freedom over appointments, pay and conditions [down the line], ... extensive use of outside consultants ... [and] introduction of financial incentives' have produced a situation where 'senior public servants have become much less willing to give independent advice to ministers' and there are serious threats of 'loss of bureaucratic integrity over such matters as due process, and administering the law without fear or favour'.[50]

In some cases, particularly in Australia and the UK, political leaders also exercise near-dictatorial power over the legislative process. Backbench parliamentarians of the ruling party may be bullied into following the leadership line in supporting all legislative initiatives from the top, on pain of loss of party membership and support. And where the same party acquires a majority in both houses of the two-house system, as in Australia recently, this radically undermines the capacity for upper-house review and encourages such ruling parties to pursue ideological objectives going far beyond any mandate they might claim on the basis of earlier election campaigns.

The Westminster first-past-the-post system means that the first candidate to achieve enough of the vote not to be overtaken by any other wins the seat and becomes the single representative for the constituency in question. As Swift points out, such a system tends to revolve around a couple of well-funded parties with similar ideologies, with other perspectives and political groupings pushed into the sidelines as 'extreme' and 'irrelevant'. Indeed smaller parties are unlikely to have any legislative representation under this system. As a result, votes for such parties are effectively wasted. As highlighted by JS Mill:

> A system of majority voting makes it possible for the majority to dominate the minority as tyrannically as any autocrat. This will be particularly so if certain people are permanently or regularly in the minority. Though formally they have the same share of power as everyone else, they have no real control over what is decided, and their votes thus count for nothing.[51]

Preferential voting systems, such as exist in Australia at the state and federal levels, could be said to give the minor parties themselves and/ or those whose first preferences are minor parties with no hope of election, some participation in the 'real game', by virtue of 'transfer' of their votes to the majors. But this is a pretty low level of meaningful involvement.

In theory, and in their own propaganda, all of the mainstream parties represent the interests of the majority or 'the nation as a whole'. This is not logically possible in societies where class divisions create diametrically opposed interests in different sections of the population (high wages versus low, full employment versus a reserve army of unemployed, welfare versus user pays, wealth taxes and progressive income taxes versus flat consumption taxes, etc). In fact, domination of the political process by the elite leadership of a couple of such well-funded parties, particularly in the English-speaking world, has become the means for the exercise of real power by and in the interests of the principal financial backers of such major parties, which means corporate business and the lobbies associated with it.

As Miliband notes, 'institutional independence masks the very real dependence of legislatures on the 'special interests' represented by business'.[52] So that even where the legislature appears genuinely independent from executive authority and free from 'party discipline', as with the US Congress, such senators and representatives remain crucially dependent 'for election purposes' on, and therefore beholden to, the support of the same corporate business interests and lobbies that fund campaigns for such executive authority.

This situation is a consequence of the very significant concentration of financial and material resources now under the control of 'a relatively small number of large private sector corporations which are accountable to nobody but themselves. This wealth is translated into political power by means of the huge and ever expanding contributions made by these organisations to the financing of the major political parties.'[53] In the USA in particular, such funding is 'estimated to have reached around US$3 billion in the federal election of 2000'.[54]

As Shutt continues, 'the stranglehold which big business has gained over the political process and the agenda of mainstream parties in all industrialised countries is ... further re-enforced by its effective control of the press and other mass media'.[55] Centralised monopoly control of what most people read in their papers and see on TV every day offers huge power of social control, by no means offset by the broader range of ideas available over the Internet. Such power is supplemented by increasing corporate control of education and research, and by the power of big business to corrupt the political process through promises of lucrative sinecures for retiring politicians and the threat of financial sabotage through disinvestment, capital flight and job loss, as well as politicians' and their families' corporate shareholdings.

A situation in which all of the major parties have thus been effectively 'bought off' by big business is reflected in a lack of any real policy differences between them. All now subscribe to basic elements of the neo-liberal consensus with no substantial disagreements in fundamental policy areas. To the extent that any real alternative ideas are ever allowed to enter the public domain, they are presented as 'divisive', 'extremist', un-Australian, un-American or whatever, or hopelessly 'utopian' and impractical.

As Swift points out, 'where real policy differences are absent, politics tends to revolve around personality'[56] with a substantial proportion of campaign funding going to vicious, ad hominem attacks on individual candidates, rather than rational assessments of policy. The personalities in question are typically those who have 'already accumulated a high level of economic and social power' prior to their involvement in parliamentary politics, or those who aspire to do so.[57] They are, in other words, already members of, or close to, the corporate elite, and already inclined to associate their own interests – and those of the nation – with the interests of that group.

Increasing democratisation

Political parties could easily be democratised, with leaders chosen by all of the membership. Parliamentary candidates could be chosen by the party as a whole or by the branches associated with the relevant electorates, rather than by the leadership or by factional power groups.

Proportional representation, in which political groups are represented in legislative and executive bodies in proportion to the votes cast for them by the electorate as a whole (at the national or state level), goes some way to addressing the issue of big party domination, as vehicle of corporate political control. Here all votes end up counting towards the final result and are not wasted. 'This allows people to vote more with their conscience and according to their desires rather than being put in a position of having to choose the lesser of two evils to ensure their votes will count.'[58] Here effective action depends more on negotiated consensus, co-operation and multiparty coalition, reconciling the differing views of different sections of the electorate, rather than the bully-boy tactics of individual 'strong leaders'.

Standard neo-liberal criticisms of such a system focus on the possibilities for lack of agreement and paralysis of effective political action without concentration of political power, and the likely gap between constituents and their representatives. They also highlight the possibility of minor parties exercising power out of all proportion to their public support in holding together fragile coalitions, or sabotaging the political programmes of major parties with majority support. While there is some truth to such claims, advantages can generally be expected to outweigh disadvantages, with proportional representation being a very significant advance for democracy. However, it is also true that proportional representation – on its own – in no way guarantees the protection of the political process from corporate subversion.

There are other fairly obvious steps which could be taken to reduce such corporate subversion of the political agenda and of voters' ideas. In the first place, any private contributions to the funds of political organisations other than flat-rate subscriptions from members would have to be outlawed.[59] At the same time, ways must be found to prevent parties in power from using public funds to preferentially finance their own campaigning. Extra funds for political campaigning could be supplied by the state equally to all parties or other organisations or in proportion to members' contributions. The public costs of such a system could undoubtedly be more than recouped by the higher levels of taxation of corporate profits, wealth and unearned income possible under such a system.[60]

All such political organisations would also need genuinely equal access to newspapers and mass media to communicate their ideas and arguments. This would seem to require either an end to current concentration of media ownership and/or some very strong legal requirement for balance and fairness in reporting and comment – not just at election times. In addition to some form of proportional repre-

sentation, powers of selection of cabinet and other senior appointments could be shifted to the legislature, and ways could be found for
smaller parties and groups to draft constitutional amendments and
other legislation for submission to popular ballot.[61]

Ways would also need to be found to hold public officials to
account once they have been appointed. As Shutt says:

> This would involve measures to ensure both that commitments
> and obligations were adhered to, and that no conflict of interest or
> opportunity for personal gain had been introduced or sought. This
> would mean requiring officials and their departments to submit to
> regular scrutiny by elected representatives of the public, who would
> have the power to censure the officials or even remove them from
> office. [It would require such officials] to abstain from any other
> gainful employment or receipt of gifts while in office and to decline
> any offers of employment after leaving office with bodies affected by
> [their] decisions or actions while still in office.[62]

These latter considerations, including absolute transparency and
public access to information on all government activities, could and
should be given strong legal sanction.

These considerations apply to the public service as well as to
government ministers. While recognising the subordination of the
former to the latter, it is crucial to get away from political patrimony
and back to more traditional ideas of bureaucratic objectivity and
impartiality. Election of higher public servants by all of those within
the particular ministry concerned, best placed to recognise the 'merit'
of the candidates, with possible input from the wider public also,
could contribute to this process. And the specialised knowledge of
such public experts needs to be accessible and available to all.

Deeper democracy

The current status quo – of rule by alleged political experts – is
typically justified by reference to the practical impossibilities (of
size and time) for any deeper involvement of the majority, to their
lack of interest and to their lack of specialised political-managerial
knowledge or ability appropriate to any further involvement. The
party system ensures that those with the interest and the ability also
have the time to be able to best use such ability in the interests of
the majority, while freeing the uninterested from the need to partici-

pate and preventing those without the ability from making a mess of things.

It is true, as Norman points out, that completely 'direct' democracy, with all participating in all decision-making, 'would seem to be unworkable on anything other than the smallest scale'.[63] It might work at the level of a single small business, for example, but certainly not at the level of a large city or nation-state. And 'even at a small-scale level, the constraints of time would militate against equal participation in decision-making. Most people do not have enough time to be constantly involved in running the affairs of their community.'[64] And it is certainly true that meaningful political decision-making in a complex society requires access to specialised knowledge in a variety of different areas.

However, there is nothing democratic about depriving people of input into – or even representation in – decision-making in situations where their immediate or major interests or concerns are most directly affected. It is perfectly possible, as Norman emphasises, for ordinary people to get advice from experts. It is only through participation that individuals' capacities for meaningful political contribution can be developed – including their capacities to make the best use of expert advice. And any justification for the present system disappears if it turns out that the 'expert' political leaders are not really experts, or do not really represent the interests of those they claim to represent.

As Norman points out, there have been a number of proposals over the years as to how to address the issue of mass participation, while avoiding or minimising such problems of size and time, of human limitations and of the earlier noted tyranny of the majority. These include increased participation through decentralisation, through referendum democracy, through pyramidal democracy or through statistical democracy.

Devolving decision-making as much as possible to periodic mass meetings at the local level of the workplace, the town or the neighbourhood could allow participation, but in itself does not address the larger scale issues inevitably bearing on such units. Referendum democracy can allow mass involvement in decision-making but it is more difficult to apply to the discussion and agenda setting preceding the voting process, and it can create 'tyranny of the majority' problems.[65] Nonetheless, as Shutt argues, 'greater resort to referenda' could ensure some consultation of the public before 'major legislative changes are enacted'.[66]

Pyramidal democracy goes a long way towards meeting some of the problems of devolution of power. The idea here is that of a number of tiers or layers, operating at different social levels, for example, the level of the neighbourhood, the city, the region, the nation and beyond. As Norman says:

> Issues are discussed at the local level in some kind of ... mass meeting. Some of them can be dealt with entirely at that level. Those that require wider consideration will be forwarded to a meeting at the next level, where the presentation of them will be entrusted to an elected delegate. All such delegates are mandated, accountable and recallable ... ... Similarly, matters which are initiated at one of the higher levels will be passed down to the local level for the local delegate to be mandated, the local delegates will vote at the city meeting to mandate their delegate to the region, and so on, back up the pyramid.[67]

Regular council meetings are 'deliberative and public'. Legislation, appropriate to the level in question, is formulated and enacted at such meetings.

Comparatively few levels are needed to cope with substantial populations. In this connection, Michael Albert considers Stephen Shalom's model of 'nested councils' where 'the primary level councils – of 25–50 people – would include every adult in the society'. These councils would elect delegates to second-level councils of similar size and so on up to 'one single top level council for the entire society'.

> A council size of 25, with 5 layers [and a half-adult population] can accommodate a society of 19 million people; a council size of 40 ... would need 5 layers to accommodate 200 million people ... With a sixth level, 25-person councils could accommodate a society of half a billion people.[68]

A major problem with this system concerns the process of mandating. Without it, the democratic input of lower level councils is undermined. But with it, there would be little meaningful planning, debate and discussion beyond the lowest level councils. The obvious answer is to give delegates some leeway, at least in some areas, 'to reflect the actual views of the council they came from' without telling them precisely how they have to vote.[69] Such leeway is, in fact, crucial to the running of the system. As Norman argues, 'the decisions made by the higher levels' have to add up to a coherent policy for the society as a whole, and this can't be achieved by a 'mere adding together of decisions produced by mandated votes of delegates'.[70]

As Norman points out, the danger 'is then that the mandating would tend to become more and more nominal. Real power would gravitate away from local meetings to the delegates, who would simply have to report back to their electors periodically' and 'this very quickly begins to look like the system of representational democracy with which we are familiar'.[71]

The idea of statistical democracy is to select individuals for higher co-ordinating bodies in proportion to the size of the particular social groups or interests most directly and significantly affected by such bodies' decisions. And this could be achieved by random selections from the groups in question. Such representatives would serve for a limited period before making way for others. Such replacements would be lagged so that new appointees could be assisted by others who have had time to acquire relevant knowledge and skills on the job. And representatives would be able to call on 'external' expert advice (from public servants and others).

The aim here is to avoid the intrinsic problems associated with voting: problems of support acquired by bribery, threats and misinformation, of monopolisation of decision-making by power seekers and of the corruption associated with entrenched power. As with the jury system, such statistical representation aims to ensure that those in power are truly representative of their constituents rather than being – or becoming – any kind of race apart from them. They remain ordinary people in touch with the needs, problems and priorities of such people – or with the specific needs and problems of their particular social groups. Thus, a hospital could be run by a board with proportional representation of nurses, patients, doctors, social workers, suppliers of medical equipment and drugs, admin personnel, cleaners, ambulance drivers, local community members, etc – chosen by lot, rather than election. Existing organisations of local, regional and national government could, fairly easily, be transformed into such statistical representative bodies – including current national legislative assemblies. Or elements of statistical democracy could be combined with some of the other reform proposals considered here.[72]

There are obviously problems with all of these proposals for reform, both in terms of the extent of opposition (from current power holders) that would inevitably be encountered by any moves to try to achieve them and in terms of their effective institutional implementation. No moves towards increasing democratic depth are likely to be successful without parallel increases in democratic breadth – bringing the exercise of economic power into the ambit of democratic decision-making and control. In chapter 15 we will briefly return to consider some possible first steps in that direction.

However, the problems should not deter us from considering such proposals for political reform. In particular, we can see how implementation issues could be addressed through creative development and integration of the different ideas considered here, with the possibility of incremental movement towards greater democratic participation. And there are grounds for seeing any and all of them as offering very significant improvements on current arrangements.

Discussion topics

1. What is meant by separation of powers?
2. How do neo-liberal ideas of democracy differ from those of social liberals?
3. Does free trade promote democracy?
4. How democratic is liberal democracy?

Chapter 12

MARXISM AND LAW
(AND ECONOMICS)

This chapter provides an introduction to the Marxist analysis of the basic contradictions of capitalism and the Marxist conceptions of the state and law. As we shall see, Marxist ideas are radically different from those of both neo-liberals and social liberals.

What is Marxism?

Marxism is an internationalist outlook and method of analysis developed by Karl Marx and Frederick Engels from the 1840s, in the wake of the emergence of industrial capitalism and its creation of a world economy. Marxism found in these convulsive socio-economic developments, and their inherent contradictions, the material basis for socialism, that is, a higher and egalitarian form of society. From the outset, Marxism was based on a global perspective. In the words of the *Communist Manifesto*, first published in 1848:

> The need of a constantly expanding market for its products chases the bourgeoisie over the entire surface of the globe. It must nestle everywhere, settle everywhere, establish connections everywhere. The bourgeoisie has, through its exploitation of the world market, given a cosmopolitan character to production and consumption in every country. To the great chagrin of reactionaries, it has drawn from under the feet of industry the national ground on which it stood.[1]

This was the basis for the famous concluding words of the *Manifesto*: 'Workers of all countries, unite!' The full text of the *Manifesto* can be read on the Marxists Internet Archive site at: <http://www.marx-ists.org/archive/marx/works/1848/communist-manifesto/index.htm> (This site can be used to read all the basic Marxist works, including those referred to in this chapter).

Marx and Engels concluded that the driving force of all history is the development of the productivity of labour and that each stage in that historical development, such as primitive communism, slavery, feudalism and capitalism, produces definite social relations. These social relations then become barriers to the further development of the productive forces, ultimately giving rise to periods of revolution. They found that two fundamental interrelated contradictions wrack the capitalist mode of production. The first contradiction is between the global development of production and the division of the world into rival nation-states, inevitably giving rise to wars for economic and strategic supremacy. The second is that between the socialised character of production, based on the combined labours of millions of people, and the appropriation of production for private profit, giving rise to economic anarchy, continual destruction of productive capacity and social polarisation.

By way of introduction, perhaps the best brief summary of Marxism's basic concepts came from Engels in his graveside oration for his life-long collaborator Marx in 1883:

> Just as Darwin discovered the law of development of organic nature, so Marx discovered the law of development of human history: the simple fact, hitherto concealed by an overgrowth of ideology, that mankind must first of all eat, drink, have shelter and clothing, before it can pursue politics, science, art, religion, etc; that therefore the production of the immediate material means, and consequently the degree of economic development attained by a given people or during a given epoch, form the foundation upon which the state institutions, the legal conceptions, art, and even the ideas on religion, of the people concerned have been evolved, and in the light of which they must, therefore, be explained, instead of vice versa, as had hitherto been the case.

> But that is not all. Marx also discovered the special law of motion governing the present-day capitalist mode of production, and the bourgeois society that this mode of production has created. The discovery of surplus value suddenly threw light on the problem, in trying to solve which all previous investigations, of both bourgeois economists and socialist critics, had been groping in the dark.[2]

In his oration, Engels summed up the three central features of Marxism:

1   historical materialism – or the development and application to human society of dialectical materialist philosophy
2   political economy – the discovery of the secret of surplus value
3   the revolutionary role of the working class – the arrival onto the scene of history of the class capable of overthrowing previous class society and establishing a higher, classless society.

Briefly, these three concepts raise the following issues:

•   materialism versus idealism: these terms are not used in the crude, everyday sense. These are the two great schools of philosophy: is the world determined by ideas (ultimately God) or does the world (matter) determine ideas? Or to put it another way, does social being determine social consciousness, or vice-versa, and how do the two interact? Which is primary? Marx and Engels concluded that the development of humanity's productive capacity, from primitive times onward, shaped the social relations between members of society and ultimately determined the prevailing ideas and morality of each historical epoch.

•   free market versus surplus value: the extraction of surplus value from wage labour is hidden under capitalism, unlike in slavery and feudalism. On the surface, all is exchanged for equal value: the employee is 'free' not to work and he gets 'a fair day's pay for a fair day's work' in the 'labour market'. In reality, capitalism gives the vast majority of producers no choice but to become wage labourers, and it is the purchase of labour-power as a commodity that provides the only underlying source of surplus value.

•   utopianism versus science: utopian communists had been around for centuries, producing visions of an equal society: for example, the Anabaptists in the German Reformation, the Levellers in the English Revolution, Babeuf in the French Revolution. Marx and Engels analysed capitalism's creation of the working class as a property-less class, with nothing to lose but its chains. Capitalism created its own 'grave-digger' – a class with the self-interest and material force to overturn class society. (The working class consisted of all those with nothing to sell but their labour power, that is, with no ownership of the means of production.)

- dialectics: this is the understanding that everything in nature and society is in interconnected motion. Nothing is static or fixed, but always part of a process, driven by opposing tendencies. Dialectics did not begin with Marxism; it can be found in natural science and philosophy dating back at least to the ancient Greeks. Modern science confirms that even the tiniest atoms consist of opposing particles. Every phenomenon is a unity of opposites, continually changing. For example, each of us is both living and dying. Marxists developed the analysis of human society as dialectical, both in its historical development, from primitive communism to slavery, feudalism, capitalism and socialism, and in the interrelationship between economic and ideological factors.

One of the most brilliant summaries of dialectics was provided by Leon Trotsky:

> The dialectic is neither fiction nor mysticism, but a science of the forms of our thinking insofar as it is not limited to the daily problems of life but attempts to arrive at an understanding of more complicated and drawn-out processes.

> Dialectical thinking is related to vulgar thinking in the same way that a motion picture is related to a still photograph. The motion picture does not outlaw the still photograph but combines a series of them according to the laws of motion. Dialectics does not deny the syllogism, but teaches us to combine syllogisms in such a way as to bring our understanding closer to the eternally changing reality. Hegel in his *Logic* established a series of laws: change of quantity into quality, development through contradictions, conflict of content and form, interruption of continuity, change of possibility into inevitability, etc, which are just as important for theoretical thought as is the simple syllogism for more elementary tasks.[3]

Three sources of Marxism

Like Engels, Vladimir Lenin, the leader of the 1917 Soviet Revolution in Russia, identified philosophical and historical materialism, political economy and the theory of surplus value, and the doctrine of the class struggle as the three sources and component parts of Marxism in his 1913 article of that name: 'The Three Sources and Three Component Parts of Marxism'.[4] He described Marxism as a world outlook, which arose from the previous conquests of human thought, combined with the emergence of industrial capitalism and the working class, or proletariat. It was not simply the product of Marx and Engels' heads but (a) part of the whole Enlightenment and (b) the product of a definite development of world economy and society, the new stage of global capitalist growth augured in by the English, American and French revolutions. In Lenin's analysis:

- *German philosophy* gave rise to dialectical and historical materialism

- *English political economy* and the *labour theory of value* gave rise to the doctrine of surplus value

- *French socialism*, or *utopian socialism,* gave rise to scientific socialism based on the class struggle and the working class.

Let's briefly examine the origins and essential content of each of these propositions.

Dialectical and historical materialism

Marx and Engels began, as did most young German students at the time, as left Hegelians. Hegel had studied the history of human thought, including that on law and the state, in an encyclopaedic manner. The conclusion he drew was that human knowledge was an historical progression or spiral – not a straight-line development but a dialectical interaction of ideas and society. However, Hegel presented this as the working out of the Absolute Idea – ultimately a religious notion. As Engels once remarked, the only thing absolute about the Absolute Idea was that Hegel said absolutely nothing about it. The Absolute Idea was in fact a contradiction because once realised, all motion would end. Marx grasped that although in Hegel the dialectic took an idealist form: it was essentially correct when understood materialistically. That is, nothing in nature and society was static – it was constantly changing, driven on by the struggle of opposing forces. But the source of this development was not the Idea: it was the material world itself. As Marx put it in 1873, Hegel's dialectic had to be stood on its feet in the material world to 'discover the rational kernel within the mystical shell'.[5]

At the same time French materialism had reached an impasse. It was mechanical or contemplative, with man as a receptor and reflector and essentially passive. The materialists grasped that to change humanity one had to improve the conditions of life, but this was to make men like machines or mirrors and to be incapable of explaining the role of thought. Marx and Engels rejected this in their 'Theses on Feuerbach', a German left Hegelian, whom they initially followed. Theirs was an active conception, in which men changed the world through their (increasingly theoretically guided) practice. In the words of the first thesis:

> The chief defect of all hitherto existing materialism – that of Feuerbach included – is that the thing, reality, sensuousness, is conceived only in the form of the *object or of contemplation*, but not as *sensuous human activity, practice*, not subjectively. Hence, in contradistinction to materialism, the *active* side was developed abstractly by idealism – which, of course, does not know real, sensuous activity as such.[6]

Marxism is not a technological theory of history, nor mechanical economic determinism, but sees the development of the productivity of labour as the ultimate driving force of history, upon which all other aspects of society, including political, ideological and legal conceptions rest. This was seen as a dialectical interplay, in which opposing class forces 'fought matters out'. The political and legal superstructure could impact back on the development of the productive forces. Ideas play a crucial role, but their true power is rooted in their capacity to more and more accurately and completely reflect the complexities of the objective world.

The theory of surplus value

Marx and Engels did not discover the labour theory of value. Marx, rather, toiled away on *Capital* in order to solve the riddle that the best minds of English political economy – such as Adam Smith and David Ricardo – could not. That is: how can surplus value be produced if all commodities are exchanged for their value, measured in terms of the labour time contained within them?

This was mystified further by 'freedom of contract' and the

exchange of equivalents on the market. Yet, only one commodity produced more than its value – labour power. Herein also lay the reason for the historical tendency for the rate of profit to decline as production became ever more capitalised at the expense of human labour.

The revolutionary role of the working class

Capitalism had to create its own gravedigger – the mass of the population had to be stripped of independent means of support and drawn into the factories and workplaces. This also inevitably produced ever-greater social inequality and polarisation.

The working class had not existed in 1789 when the French Revolution erupted, but did by 1848 when revolutions again swept across Europe. From the failure of these revolutions, because the bourgeoisie proved more fearful of the proletariat than the aristocracy and autocracy, Marx and Engels drew the necessity for the political independence of the working class if society were to be reorganised along classless lines. From the defeat of the Paris Commune in 1871, Marx and Engels drew the conclusion that the working class had to take power in no uncertain terms in order to do so. This was the origin of the much-misunderstood theory of the dictatorship of the proletariat, to which we will return when we consider the question of the state withering away under communism.

Marx and Engels saw the development of the working class itself as a revolutionary force within society, as an objective process. Its world-historical role was determined, in the most fundamental sense, not by its consciousness but rather by its unique position in the capitalist mode of production. They said in *The Holy Family*:

> It is not a question of what this or that proletarian, or even the whole proletariat, at the moment *regards* as its aim. It is a question of what the proletariat is, and what, in accordance with this being, it will historically be compelled to do. Its aim and historical action is visibly and irrevocably foreshadowed in its own life situation as well as in the whole organisation of bourgeois society today.[7]

Who are the Marxists?

This chapter refers to the works of the most recognised classical Marxists – Marx and Engels themselves, George Plekhanov (the founder of the Marxist movement in Russia), Lenin and Leon Trotsky (who led the struggle against Stalin's betrayal of Marxism after Lenin's death in 1924). Each of these figures insisted that socialism, and eventually communism, could only arise on an international basis, through the revolutionary overturning of capitalism worldwide. Marx and Engels participated in the founding of the First International – the first international working-class party – in 1864, which preceded the Paris Commune of 1871, the first attempt to establish a workers' government. Following the defeat of the Paris Commune and the demise of the First International (and Marx's death in 1883), Engels was involved in the establishment of the Second International in 1889.

That International, however, collapsed at the outbreak of World War I, with each of the major parties supporting their 'own' national states. Following the 1917 Soviet Revolution in Russia, Lenin led the founding of the Third International in 1919, on the understanding that the fate of the Russian Revolution depended entirely on a worldwide victory over capitalism. The Third International underwent its own nationalist and bureaucratic degeneration under Stalin, who eventually dissolved it during World War II. Trotsky, a co-leader of the Russian Revolution, formed the Left Opposition in 1923 to fight Stalinism, and led the 1938 establishment of the Fourth International, which continues today.

Who are the Marxists?

Karl Marx	*The Communist Manifesto 1848*
Frederick Engels	*The First and Second Internationals, 1864 and 1889*
Vladimir Lenin	*The Russian Revolution October 1917*
	The Third International 1919
Leon Trotsky	*The Left Opposition 1923*
	The Fourth International 1938

Marxist economic analysis

As mentioned earlier, Marxists identified two fundamental interrelated contradictions that wrack the capitalist mode of production: between world economy and the nation-state system, and between socialised production and private appropriation. Marx and Engels also pointed to the inevitably unsustainable social polarisation generated by capitalism – the division between rich and poor.

In *Capital*, Marx analysed the 'law of the tendency of the rate of profit to fall' underlying both shorter-term crises in profitability and longer-term stagnation and deepening crisis in the world capitalist system. The pursuit of productivity gains constantly impels capitalist innovators to introduce new technology into the production process. Such innovators' surplus profits last only until others catch up in accessing the new technology, at which time average prices are driven back down towards the new, reduced production costs.

Marx argues that the process contains the seeds of an inescapable contradiction. He argues that only 'living labour' – the productive life of the working class – is actually capable of generating new value, over and above the cost of its own production, whereas 'dead labour' or means of production – tools, machinery, infrastructure – merely transfers its own, embodied labour-time value to the products it contributes to producing in the course of its productive life.

The cost of production of labour power – of the productive capacity of the working class – is simply the cost of subsistence and reproduction of that class, as people ready and able to work – that cost including food, housing, practical education, transport costs, etc. The cost of production of things, including both means of consumption and means of production, is ultimately reducible to the quantity of human labour-time necessary on average to produce them.

The pursuit of productivity gains, followed by catch-up on the part of the rest of the industry, inevitably increases the ratio of 'dead' to 'living' labour. In the course of time, each worker comes to use more and more means of production. As Harman points out, 'for the capitalist ... spending on the means and materials of production grows much faster than spending on employing workers. So the very process of capital accumulation involves an increase in the ratio between the two, between (what Marx calls) *constant capital* and *variable capital*.'[8]

As Nick Beams explains, Marx did not maintain that the rate of profit everywhere and always continues to fall. But, like all laws of capitalist production, the law of the falling rate of profit operated as a tendency which continually exerted itself. He described this tendency as the 'most important law of political economy' above all from 'an historical point of view'. This is because the tendency of the rate of profit to fall is the driving force behind the constant revolutionising of technology and other productive forces, the chief means by which capital attempts to overcome its effects.[9]

Marx acknowledged significant 'countervailing tendencies' opposing pressures towards capitalist crisis. Most obviously, the increased productivity achieved through use of new and more productive technology will continuously reduce the labour-time cost of both labour power and technology itself, thereby counteracting the tendency of the rate of profit to fall. And the rate of exploitation of labour can also be increased through increasing the duration or intensity of work and cutting real wages.

Marx allows that these and other factors can indeed temporarily slow down or even reverse the falling rate of profit in the short term. But there are limits to these factors, so that the tendency will still assert itself in the longer term. Summarising this result, Marx wrote:

> The larger the surplus value of capital *before the increase of the productive force*, the larger the amount of presupposed surplus labour or surplus value of capital; or, the smaller the fractional part of the working day which forms the equivalent of the worker, which expresses necessary labour, the smaller is the increase in surplus value which capital obtains from the increase of productive force. Its surplus value rises, but in an ever smaller relation to the development of the productive force. Thus the more developed capital already is, the more surplus labour it has created, the more terribly it must develop the productive force in order to realise itself in only smaller proportion ... The self-realisation of capital becomes more difficult to the extent that it has already been realised.[10]

Many economists contend that there are problems with the Marxist account. They contest Marx's conclusion that living labour is the only source of new value. And they say that Marx has trouble explaining precisely how labour-time values 'determine' the actual market prices of commodities. It is impossible to review and evaluate this debate here.

But Marx's analysis does seem to have been borne out by the economic problems that have dogged world capitalism since the 1970s. Beams reviews the changes that followed World War II.[11] In the final analysis, the period of global expansion from 1945 to 1971 rested on the increase in the mass of surplus value made possible by the extension of the more productive assembly-line methods of mass production, first developed by American capitalism, to Europe and Japan. This brought an enormous increase in the productivity of labour and, consequently, an increase in the average rate of profit – benefiting the more efficient and less efficient firms alike – leading to further investment, expansion of industry and employment. Out of the growing mass of surplus value, capitalist governments were able to finance social welfare spending and other concessions to the working class.

However, empirical data points to the re-emergence of the tendency of the rate of profit to fall by the end of the 1960s. By 1974–75, this produced the deepest recession since the 1930s. Big business has responded to the re-emergence of falling profit rates in two intercon-nected ways: it has undertaken a continuous drive against the living standards and social position of the working class, and it has initiated a global reorganisation of production based on new computerised technologies. Nevertheless, no upturn occurred in global capitalism until about 1990, when it acquired new markets and sources of cheap labour through the dismantling of nationalised property relations in the Soviet bloc and China. By 2008, there were signs, in the financial turmoil gripping global share markets, that the period of upswing had ended.

In the post-World War II period, economic expansion brought an increase of secure, relatively well-paid jobs. Today the situation is the reverse as major corporations maintain their profits not through expansion of production, sales and employment but through downsiz-ing and cost-cutting, combined with financial speculation. A Marxist analysis suggests that these differences are rooted in the underlying crisis of surplus value accumulation, produced by the tendency of the rate of profit to decline.

Marxism and the role of law

Marxism challenges basic assumptions about law and its role in society.

- Where western law asserts the sanctity of private property, freedom of contract and the 'rule of law' itself, as supposed guarantors of liberty and formal equality, Marxists argue that these doctrines inherently produce economic and social inequality.

- While western law enforces the stability of the nuclear family as an economic unit, Marxists call for genuine freedom of choice in undertaking and leaving marriage and gender equality in family and social relations.

- Whereas western law declares miscreants punishable because of their alleged personality defects, Marxists regard 'crime' primarily as a product of social inequity and, accordingly, seek to replace 'punishment' with social improvement, education and other remedial measures.

- Western jurists insist that law is an organic and indispensable method of governing society, essential to combat or curb the alleged deficiencies and aggressive tendencies of human nature. Marxist jurisprudence regards humanity as capable of rising to a higher social and moral level, given the right conditions. It views the state and law as legacies of exploitative, class society and seeks to create the social conditions for them to be supplanted by more participatory and democratic forms of administration.

The Soviet experience

But what is the relevance of this today? Has not communism failed? In the early 1990s, certain writers asserted that the demise of the Soviet Union and the Eastern European Stalinist regimes signalled the irrevocable triumph of the market over socialism and even the 'end of history', to use Francis Fukuyama's phrase.[12] It is necessary to review the historical record in order to assess these claims.

The early years after the 1917 Russian Revolution produced groundbreaking achievements in legal policy. In several spheres, Soviet approaches were the most progressive in the world. They included the transformation of family and sexual relations – the recognition of the rights to divorce, de facto marriage and abortion – and the decriminalisation of the official response to anti-social behaviour. Underpinning these initiatives were the broader abolition of private ownership of basic production and finance, as well as efforts to de-formalise and provide for popular participation in social administration.

However, these experiments were cut short by the severe difficulties of the civil war and the New Economic Policy (NEP), followed by the Stalinist degeneration.

The adoption of the NEP in 1921 caused a shift back to legalism, particularly with regard to the protection of private property rights. After late 1923, with the ascendancy of Stalin and the doctrine of 'socialism in one country', a new atmosphere of 'corrections' and diatribes set in, accompanied by a strengthening of the repressive state apparatus. The classical Marxist perspective of the withering away of the state and law was ditched in favour of the entrenchment of a legal edifice, erected in the name of 'socialist legality'. In this sphere, as in others, Stalinism was a repudiation of Marxism, not a continuation of it.

These implications can be seen in the fate of Eugene Pashukanis, the best-known early Soviet jurist.[13] Pashukanis' 1924 commodity theory of law initially became part of the regime's official doctrine. It helped reconcile the needs of the NEP, including the legal protection of private property rights, with the Marxist understanding of the withering away of the state. By the late 1920s, Pashukanis was under attack within the Soviet Union because he maintained, in keeping with authentic Marxism, that the law and indeed the state apparatus of the Soviet Union would ultimately disappear with the construction of a genuinely communist society. He initially resisted the Stalinist notion that the law and the state itself had become organically 'socialist' and therefore occupied a permanent place in social organisation. By 1935, his views were incompatible with the Kremlin line, which was based on the wholly self-contradictory claim that socialism had been built; yet the 'dictatorship of the proletariat' had been simultaneously strengthened.

Marxist jurisprudence

None of the leading Marxists – Marx, Engels, Plekhanov, Lenin, Trotsky – attempted to set out a comprehensive model of society under socialism. They regarded such ventures as overly prescriptive, as well as premature and utopian. For them, socialism consisted of human self-emancipation and would be shaped by the actions and ideas of millions of working people, tempered by the concrete historical and international circumstances that prevailed. The classical Marxists were even less inclined to provide a detailed blueprint for the role of law and the state machinery in the transition from the overthrow of capitalism to socialism and then communism. They regarded law's role as being fundamentally bound up with and, in the final analysis, dependent on the development of humanity's economic capacities and social wellbeing.

Nevertheless, while Marx and Engels did not write systematic expositions on legal theory, many of their works examined the role of law in society. They provided a definite framework of analysis and orientation, as well as basic principles, which initially guided the early leadership of the Soviet Union but were later betrayed under Stalinism.

The two fundamental, underlying Marxist conceptions are that, in general, all forms of law and the state were in the end derived from the development of the productive and hence cultural level of human society, and that law and the state would wither away in the process of arriving at a genuinely communist society. That is, the need for formal, bureaucratic and repressive instruments of rule would disappear with the creation of a bountiful, egalitarian and democratic world.

The starting point for understanding this historical materialist view is Marx's 1859 Preface to *A Contribution to the Critique of Political Economy*, where he tentatively described the following propositions, derived from years of research and experience, as 'a guiding thread for my studies':

> In the social production of their life, men enter into definite relations that are indispensable and independent of their will, relations of production which correspond to a definite stage of development of their material productive forces. The sum total of these relations of production constitutes the economic structure of society, the real foundation, on which rises a legal and political superstructure and to which correspond definite forms of social consciousness. The mode of production of material life conditions the social, political and intellectual life process in general. It is not the consciousness of men that determines their being, but, on the contrary, their social being that determines their social consciousness.

> At a certain stage of their development, the material productive forces of society come in conflict with the existing relations of production, or – what is but a legal expression for the same thing – with the property relations within which they have been at work hitherto.

From forms of development of the productive forces these relations turn into their fetters. Then begins an epoch of social revolution. With the change of the economic foundation, the entire immense superstructure is more or less rapidly transformed.

In considering such transformations, a distinction should always be made between the material transformation of the economic conditions of production, which can be determined with the precision of natural science, and the legal, political, religious, aesthetic or philosophical – in short, ideological forms in which men become conscious of this conflict and fight it out.[14]

Three themes can be discerned in this seminal passage. The first is that law, like other aspects of the political superstructure, arises from definite relations of production and the forms of social consciousness forged by those relations. The second is that those relations are not static but are inevitably shattered by the further development of technology and production itself, ultimately leading to social revolution. The third is that law is one of the ideological forms in which humanity becomes conscious of the underlying conflicts and 'fights them out'.

Essential propositions

Properly understood, the Marxist view of law includes a number of pivotal propositions. First, that socialism means democracy and the withering away of the state, not the bureaucratic 'command economy' that subsequently emerged in Soviet Russia under Stalin.

Second, that socialism cannot be achieved by seeking to reform the state machine of the old order. It requires a thoroughgoing popular revolution to establish a new kind of state, a genuinely democratic state (the dictatorship of the proletariat), as a transitional regime to create the ultimate conditions for a classless, stateless communist society.

Third, that law is not inherent or organic to society; rather it arises out of conflicting interests in society and primarily reflects the interests of the ruling layers. Therefore, in a classless society, the legal form of social regulation will become redundant. This withering away of the state and law can and must begin as soon as the socialist revolution has successfully wrested power from the old ruling class.

Fourth, that the relationship between law and socio-economic power is dialectical. Against crude materialism and class reduction-ism, Marxists explain that legal definitions and measures can, in some circumstances, exert a sharp influence on economic and social developments. In part, this arises from the mystified, ideological form in which law and legal theory present themselves.

Finally, the Marxist view of law rejects the notion that capitalism, based on private ownership of the means of production, is some-how natural while socialism is alien to human nature. Under capital-ism, law also plays an ideological role in disguising social inequality, dulling consciousness of class divisions and reinforcing 'commodity fetishism'.

Socialism, democracy and the state

Marx argued that the development of a socialist society will not take place according to a series of prescriptions and rules laid down by an individual, a political party or a governmental authority. Rather, it will develop on the basis of the activity of the members of society who, for the first time in history, consciously regulate and control their own social organisation as part of their daily lives, free from the domination and prescriptions of either the 'free market' or a bureau-cratic authority standing over them.

In Marx's view, the precondition for such a society is the devel-opment of the social productivity of labour to such a point that the vast bulk of humanity does not have to spend the greater portion of the day merely trying to obtain the resources to live. The over-turn of capitalist rule would not see the overnight abolition of the market. The price mechanism would still be needed for a period as a guide in the provision of information regarding the relative costs of alternative production methods. But increasingly it would be made subordinate to and eventually be replaced by the conscious regula-tion of the economy according to a plan, decided on, checked and altered to meet changing circumstances through the involvement of workers and the population as a whole in process of economic deci-sion-making.

The emergence of the Stalinist bureaucracy in the early 1920s, and its complete usurpation, by 1927, of political power meant that genu-ine socialist, that is democratic, planning, could never be carried out in the Soviet Union. Such democratic input would have immediately threatened the privileged social position of the bureaucracy and its monopoly of political power.

Democratic participation was an essential prerequisite and ongoing requirement for the harmonious development of a genuinely socialist economy and the all-round growth of productive output, as well as social emancipation. This imperative has enormous implications for law, being a central component of the need to de-legalise social life as far as possible and facilitate the withering away of the state.

The transition to communism

The dictatorship of the proletariat, in the writings of Marx and Engels, means the temporary and emergency political rule of the working class, as the first stage in the transition to a classless, stateless society. This political rule must include the control by the associated produc-ers – the working class which constitutes the overwhelming majority of society – of the productive forces they themselves have created. In other words, the dictatorship of the proletariat means from the outset the establishment of genuine democracy, with the majority of the population exercising economic power.

The term 'dictatorship of the proletariat' as used by Marx and Engels does not mean tyranny or absolutism or rule by a single indi-vidual, a minority or even a single party but political rule exercised by the majority of the population. This is clear from their analysis of the Paris Commune of 1871, which ruled Paris for a period of 72 days before being militarily crushed. In his 1891 introduction to the re-issue of Marx's analysis of the Commune in *The Civil War in France*, Engels explained that the Commune, which was the first attempt at establishing the dictatorship of the proletariat, began with the 'shattering of the former state power and its replacement by a new and truly democratic one'.[15]

In the *Critique of the Gotha Program*, Marx distinguished between the two stages of socialism. In the first, it would be impossible, given the economic, intellectual and moral birthmarks of the old capitalist order from whose womb socialist society emerged, to go beyond the 'narrow horizon of bourgeois right' – by which he meant the formal legal equality that invariably masks social inequality. 'Law can never stand higher than the economic order and the cultural development of society conditioned by it', Marx wrote.[16] That is, the law would

inherently reflect the fact that society could not provide a plentiful and satisfying life for all. Only after individuals were no longer
enslaved by others, labour had become a meaningful and enjoyable
pursuit rather than a burden, and the productive forces had increased
abundantly would the communist ideal be realised.

Trotsky defended this underlying conception in *The Revolution
Betrayed*, his analysis of the degeneration of the Soviet Union:

> The material premise of communism should be so high a develop-
> ment of the productive forces that productive labour, having ceased
> to be a burden, will not require any goad, and the distribution of
> life's goods, existing in continual abundance, will not demand – as
> it does not now in any well-off family or 'decent' boarding-house
> – any control except that of education, habit and social opinion.[17]

Central to this view, as first expounded by Marx and Engels in the
Communist Manifesto and later by Lenin in *The State and Revolution*,
was that the state and law must begin to fade away as soon as the
dictatorship of the proletariat was established. That is, inherent in
the seizure of political power and the establishment of a workers'
state was the creation of a unique kind of government that would
immediately begin to transfer society's administration into the hands
of the population at large.

Engels returned to this theme in his 1891 Introduction to Marx's
The Civil War in France, which described the formation and suppression of the Paris Commune. Engels contrasted the Commune to all
previous revolutions, which had replaced one oppressive state by
another.

> From the very outset, the Commune was compelled to recognise that
> the working class, once come to power, could not go on managing
> with the old state machine; that in order not to lose again its only just
> conquered supremacy, this working class must, on the one hand, do
> away with all the old repressive machinery previously used against
> itself, and, on the other, safeguard itself against its own deputies and
> officials, by declaring them all, without exception, subject to recall
> at any time.[18]

Apart from the right of recall, Engels reviewed three other measures
taken to prevent 'careerism': election to all posts – administrative,
judicial and educational; restriction of the wages of all officials, high
and low, to those paid to workers; and binding mandates for delegates to representative bodies.

Interaction between law and social structure

In many western academic writings, Marx and Engels are presented as mechanical economic determinists. This somewhat simplifies their analysis. They were determinists in the following sense. For them, the driving forces of all economic, political and social life are the contradictions in material and economic life. Essentially, these contradictions arise from the conflict between the social forces of production and the relations of production – the class and property relations of society – within which those productive forces have hitherto developed.

More specifically, the development of capitalist economic relations shaped the content and structure of law in many ways. The most fundamental relate to the core concepts of private property and contract. Both required an essential break with feudal relations, based on communal and feudal property, fixed status and personal allegiance. Capitalism, as an expansionary economic system, demanded the unfettered accumulation of capital based on the private ownership of the means of production.

Marx and Engels concluded that the ultimate driving forces of all economic, political and social life are the contradictions in material and economic life. This analysis is far from passive, lifeless and mechanical. While the decisive factors shaping law are economic relations, the legal system remains one of the arenas within which the class struggle is fought out. As Engels pointed out in his 1890 letter to Conrad Schmidt, Marx's section on the working day in *Capital* shows that legislation can have a 'drastic effect' on social conditions and the class struggle.[19]

This conflict is not automatically reflected in legal doctrines but is refracted through the need to elaborate legal principles that have the appearance of internal coherence and universality and to continually adjust those doctrines to meet changing economic circumstances. On law, as on other social phenomena, Marx and Engels demonstrated the dialectical interaction between the economic base of society and the ideological superstructure.

In a letter to J Bloch, Engels emphasised that the economic situation is the 'ultimately determining factor in history' but:

> ... the various elements of the superstructure – political forms of the class struggle and its results, such as constitutions established

by the victorious class after a successful battle, etc, juridical forms, and especially the reflections of all these real struggles in the brains of the participants, political, legal, philosophical theories, religious views and their further development into systems of dogmas – also exercise their influence upon the course of the historical struggles and in many cases determine their *form* in particular [italics in original].[20]

This analysis was also dynamic in relation to the continual contradictions produced by the further development of the productive forces and new forms of property rights. Further contradictions arose constantly from the ideological role of law – from the need of any modern ruling class in the epoch of mass politics to present its political order as just and impartial. In his letter to Conrad Schmidt, Engels stated:

> In a modern state, law must not only correspond to the general economic condition and be its expression, but must also be an *internally coherent* expression which does not, owing to internal conflicts, contradict itself. And in order to achieve this, the faithful reflection of economic conditions suffers increasingly. All the more, so the more rarely it happens that a code of law is the blunt, unmitigated, unadulterated expression of the domination of a class – this in itself would offend the 'conception of right'.[21]

Law and ideology

While Marx and Engels recognised that under capitalism, ideological factors could determine the form of legal development, the resulting process produced a mystification, by presenting economic interests as philosophical principles. In his 1890 letter to Schmidt, Engels wrote:

> The reflection of economic relations as legal principles is necessarily also a topsy-turvy one: it happens without the person who is acting being conscious of it; the jurist imagines that he is operating from *a priori* principles, whereas they are really only economic reflexes; so everything is upside down. And it seems to me obvious that this inversion, which, so long as it remains unrecognised, forms what we call ideological conception, reacts in its turn upon the economic basis and may, within certain limits, modify it.[22]

Precisely because law was a distorted reflection of economic reality, the distortion could, to the extent that the deformation went unrecognised, impact on the underlying economic relations. This view has a number of implications. In the first place, the mystified distortion served to legitimise exploitation. By reproducing in legal form the commodification of all relations, law presented these relations in an 'inverted' way, camouflaging their real content. This was not simply a conspiracy or confidence trick perpetrated by the ruling class, aided by legal theorists and lawyers. Because law was shaped by the objective requirements of the capitalist mode of production, it was organically shrouded in a distorted view of social relations. Bourgeois legal theorists were themselves trapped in an ideological inversion, mistakenly regarding their ideas as the source of jurisprudential development.

Law and human nature

The proponents of the free market and capitalist ownership of the means of production argue that socialism is unnatural and therefore doomed to failure because it violates the inherent drive in every human being towards the exclusive ownership of property. This conception is filled with unstated assumptions.

In the first chapter of *Capital*, in his analysis of commodity fetishism, Marx explained that one of the great difficulties in coming to an understanding of society is that it has already undergone a considerable development:

> Man's reflections on the forms of social life and consequently, also, his scientific analysis of those forms, take a course directly opposite to that of their actual historical development. He begins, post festum, with the results of the process of development ready to hand before him.[24]

In other words, analysis begins with categories and forms of thought already at hand, under conditions where the historical processes that gave rise to these forms is obscured from view. Hence these forms of thought are not understood as the product of historical processes, but seem to spring from the 'inner nature' of man himself. Take, for example, the question of interest. Nothing may seem more natural than that there should be a payment or interest charged on the use of money. Under capitalism, economic life would quickly grind to a halt if lending for profit ceased. Yet for hundreds of years there were denunciations of usury and severe punishments inflicted for its practice. Moneylending was depicted as sinful, essentially because it threatened to undermine feudal relations, which were based on status, not money.

In capitalist society, the extraction of surplus labour does not take place through political means, but economically. That is, while there were a myriad of laws in feudal society, which spelt out the obligations of the peasant, there are no such laws under capitalism. There is no statute that compels the worker to sell his or her labour power to the owner of capital. He or she is forced to do so by the pressure of economic necessity. And that compulsion arises from the fact that, unlike the peasant or small producer in feudal society, the worker in capitalist society has been separated from the ownership of the means of production.

Therefore, the crucial question to be examined in the transition from feudalism to capitalism is how this transformation took place. That is, how it was that a class of free wage labourers emerged – free both from feudal obligations and from the means of production – with nothing to sell but their labour power. History shows that this transformation did not result from some innate human nature, but was the outcome of new forms of social organisation based on the market. Those who maintain that the emergence of capitalism is the result of some inherent drive to own private property can never answer the question as to why the transition to capitalism took place between the 16th and 18th centuries, rather than earlier. Capitalism could only emerge once society's technology and productive capacity – for example, steam power – had developed to the point where large-scale manufacturing could arise.

One of the most important battles in the development of capitalism was the establishment of *exclusive* property rights, above all in land, over the common property rights that had played such a central role in the lives of the peasantry under feudalism. Far from expressing some inherent human characteristic, manifesting itself at a young age, this new form of property had to establish itself against the conception that land should be held in common and its fruits be available to all. Locke, in particular, had to argue strenuously for the right to individual property, against the conception of common property and custodianship. Locke identified certain inalienable rights – the right to life, liberty and property. According to Locke, every man was the sole proprietor of his own person and capacities. His right to property derived from his right to enjoy the fruits of his own labour.

The theory that identifies freedom with private ownership is based on the claim that each individual has the natural right to the fruits of their own labour and that private property is the means through which this right is secured. But concentration of ownership and the separation of the mass of the population from the means of production with nothing to sell but their labour power to the owners of capital means that private property itself has long ago undergone a transformation. No longer is it a social mechanism through which individuals secure the fruits of their *own labour*, it is rather the mechanism through which capital secures the fruits of *other people's labour* in the form of profit.

Leon Trotsky's observations

Leon Trotsky was one of the foremost leaders of the October 1917 Revolution and of the fight against Stalin's bureaucratisation of Soviet society. Trotsky defended the October 1917 Revolution and the initial actions of the Bolsheviks, including the seizure of power, the dissolution of the Constituent Assembly, the banning of parties that took up arms against the revolution and other measures taken during the civil war of 1919–21. In *Terrorism and Communism: A reply to Karl Kautsky*, Trotsky responded to Kautsky, previously a major figure in the Marxist movement, who accused the Bolsheviks of proceeding undemocratically. Members of the Austro-Marxism school, who, in some instances, claimed to be Marxist legal theorists, joined Kautsky's denunciation of the revolution. They included Karl Renner, Otto Bauer, Max Adler, Rudolf Hilferding and Friedrich Adler.

Trotsky insisted that the Soviet revolution was far more democratic than the parliamentary apparatus defended by Kautsky. He pointed to the innate fraud of capitalist democracy, which leaves the economic power and control over the state apparatus in the grip of a ruling elite, arguing that it gives the working masses no other way but revolution to take charge of society.

Trotsky also examined democracy from a theoretical and historical standpoint. He pointed to the degeneration of the democratic conception in the hands of the capitalist class and its jurisprudential theorists.

As a battle cry against feudalism, the demand for democracy had a progressive character. As time went on, however, the metaphysics of natural law (the theory of formal democracy) began to show its reactionary side – the establishment of an ideal standard to control the real demands of the labouring masses and the revolutionary parties ... Natural law, which developed into the theory of democracy, said to the worker: 'all men are equal before the law, independently of their origin, their property, and their position; every man has an equal right in determining the fate of the people.' This ideal criterion revolutionised the consciousness of the masses in so far as it was a condemnation of absolutism, aristocratic privilege, and the property qualification. But the longer it went on, the more it sent the consciousness to sleep, legalising poverty, slavery and degradation: for how could one revolt against slavery when every man has an equal right in determining the fate of the nation? ... In the real conditions of life, in the economic process, in social relations, in their way of life, people became more and more unequal; dazzling luxury was accumulated at one pole, poverty and hopelessness at the other. But in the sphere of the legal edifice of the state, these glaring contradictions disappeared, and there penetrated only unsubstantial legal shadows.[25]

Trotsky related the need for the dictatorship of the proletariat in the transition to communism to the political and economic tasks involved in overthrowing capitalism. He argued that genuine socialism and communism were impossible to achieve without the free and creative involvement of all people. The bureaucratic police state erected by Stalin was not only an affront to socialist democracy but also a suffocating barrier to the development of the productive and cultural capacities of society.

The socialistic economy must be directed to ensuring the satisfaction of every possible human need. Such a problem it is impossible to solve by way of commands only. The greater the scale of the productive forces, the more involved the technique; the more complex the needs, then the more indispensable is a wide and free creative initiative of the organised producers and consumers. The socialist culture implies the utmost development of the human personality. Progress along this path is made possible not through a standardised cringing before irresponsible 'leaders', but only through a fully conscious and critical participation by all in a socialistic creative activity.[26]

In line with Marx and Engels, Trotsky's emphasis was on the self-liberation of the entire population. This was the essence of communism. Therefore, the task of the Soviet state was to encourage, not stifle, the maximum degree of conscious, well-informed and independent participation in political and administrative affairs.

In *The Revolution Betrayed*, published in 1937, Trotsky restated the warnings that the Left Opposition had sounded since 1923 about the dangers at the heart of the Soviet state.

> The state assumes directly and from the very beginning a dual character: socialistic, insofar as it defends social property in the means of production; bourgeois, insofar as the distribution of life's goods is carried out with a capitalistic measure of value and all the consequences ensuing therefrom. Such a contradictory characterisation may horrify the dogmatists and scholastics; we can only offer them our condolences.

> The final physiognomy of the workers' state ought to be determined by the changing relations between its bourgeois and socialist tendencies. The triumph of the latter ought ipso facto to signify the final liquidation of the gendarme – that is, the dissolving of the state in a self-governing society. From this alone it is sufficiently clear how immeasurably significant is the problem of Soviet bureaucratism, both in itself and as a symptom![27]

Trotsky also made a frank assessment of the Bolshevik leadership's lack of preparedness for the economic and class pressures produced by the failure of the Soviet revolution to spread to the more advanced countries of Europe. He stated that Lenin had not fully anticipated the depth of the difficulties that would beset the Soviet state, because Lenin had not envisaged the Russian Revolution standing for any length of time isolated in a capitalist world.

> Basing himself wholly upon the Marxian theory of the dictatorship of the proletariat, Lenin did not succeed, as we have said, either in his chief work dedicated to this question (*The State and Revolution*), or in the program of the party, in drawing all the necessary conclusions as to the character of the state from the economic backwardness and isolatedness of the country. Explaining the revival of bureaucratism by the unfamiliarity of the masses with administration and by the special difficulties resulting from the war, the program prescribes merely political measures for the overcoming of 'bureaucratic distortions': elections and recall at any time of all plenipotentiaries, abolition of material privileges, active control by the masses, etc.[28]

In other words, Lenin and the Bolsheviks had seriously underestimated the difficulties presented by the primitivism of the economy they had inherited from Tsarism and the implications of the revolution failing to spread to the more advanced countries of Western Europe. This meant that the measures Lenin had prescribed in *The State and Revolution* for checking the rise of bureaucratic tendencies were inadequate. Organisational safeguards alone could not combat bureaucratism because the root causes lay deeper. These could only be overcome through a difficult combination of mass political participation, rapid industrial development and the completion of the revolution internationally. Trotsky continued:

> This obvious underestimation of impending difficulties is explained by the fact that the program was based wholly upon an international perspective. 'The October revolution in Russia has realised the dictatorship of the proletariat ... The era of world proletarian communist revolution has begun.' These were the introductory lines of the program. Their authors not only did not set themselves the aim of constructing 'socialism in a single country' – this idea had not entered anybody's head then, and least of all Stalin's – but they also did not touch the question as to what character the Soviet state would assume, if compelled for as long as two decades to solve in isolation those economic and cultural problems which advanced capitalism had solved so long ago.[29]

Trotsky's analysis highlighted the doctrinal and political problems that beset the early Soviet legal debates. The unanticipated international isolation of the Soviet state created immense difficulties that could not be remedied in the legal sphere alone. These problems were compounded by Stalin's insistence that socialism could be built in a single country. Regrettably, there are no indications that the Opposition's insights were permitted to inform the legal discussion. Instead, the discourse degenerated into name-calling and scapegoating after 1927, as the grip of Stalin's group tightened.

The prognosis of the Left Opposition was confirmed in the most malignant fashion. Despite subsequent industrial growth, the stranglehold of Stalin's henchmen meant that the capitalist tendencies continued to strengthen at the expense of the socialist tendencies. Stalin's increasingly bureaucratic and repressive regime exterminated its communist opposition in the 1930s. Even before then, genuine Marxist discussion was strangled and replaced by slavish adherence to an official line, falsely presented as Marxism. In the legal sphere this meant ascribing a permanence and sanctity to the 'dictatorship of the proletariat' and 'Soviet law' and the reversal of all the progressive achievements in democratic involvement, family relations and criminal law. Despite often recanting their previous writings, some of the leading figures in the early legal debates were among the victims of Stalin's purges. This brutality laid the basis for a protracted economic and social putrefaction that ultimately culminated in Stalin's heirs, Gorbachev and Yeltsin, dissolving the Soviet state, paving the way for the complete restoration of capitalism after 1991.[30] Over the following decade, this led to a social catastrophe of widespread impoverishment, mass unemployment, gross inequality, collapsing public facilities and a dramatic decline in life expectancy.[31]

Contemporary relevance

The Stalinist degeneration of the Bolshevik Party and the Soviet state was, in the final analysis, the product of unfavourable objective conditions – principally, the historic backwardness of Russia, the economic devastation produced by seven uninterrupted years of world war, revolution and civil war, and, finally, the protracted isolation of the Soviet state that resulted from the defeats suffered by the European, and especially the German, working class after World War I. Under these powerful adverse pressures, the Stalinist regime arose on the basis of a Russian nationalist reaction against the internationalism that was embodied in the Bolshevik government under the leadership of Lenin and Trotsky. The program of 'socialism in one country' provided a banner for all those elements within the bureaucracy who identified their own material interests with the development of the USSR as a powerful national state. The bureaucracy obtained its privileges through the mechanism of state ownership of the means of production. The more it became conscious of the national-state foundations of its privileges, the less willing was the bureaucracy to place these at risk in the interest of world revolution.

However, the objective material foundations of Stalinism did not dictate that there could only be one political outcome – the irreversible bureaucratic degeneration of the USSR and its ultimate collapse in 1991. Any such conception ignores the role of politics, of program, of the struggle of tendencies, of consciousness – the significance of the decisions made by individuals, motivated by a greater or lesser degree of political insight into the historical process, about what they intended to do. The growth of the bureaucracy and its usurpation of political power were consciously and systematically opposed from within the Bolshevik Party. The most significant opposition was that which arose in 1923 under the leadership of Leon Trotsky. Trotsky and the Left Opposition were subjected to a degree of repression that was as brutal as it was relentless. Always conscious of the dubious character of his own claim to the continuity of Bolshevism, Stalin himself believed that Trotsky represented the most dangerous political opposition to his regime.[32] In the end, Stalin could not defeat the opposition without recourse to police-state measures.[33] Thus, there was an alternative to the Stalinist variant of Soviet development, and the Stalinist terror was the means by which it was annihilated. What was destroyed in the cellars of the Lyubianka and countless other execution chambers throughout the Soviet Union were hundreds of thousands of revolutionary socialists who had contributed to the October 1917 Revolution.

Partly as a result of that bitter experience, which severely damaged the reputation of Marxism, capitalist market relations currently dominate the globe, even in the major countries that claim to adhere to some form of Marxism, namely China and Vietnam. No-one would suggest a mechanical or simple application of Pashukanis' ideas.

Nevertheless, it would be premature and short-sighted to conclude that the present state of world affairs will last indefinitely. Just as powerful economic processes and contradictions produced the 1917 Russian Revolution, and the French, American and English Revolutions of the seventeenth and eighteenth centuries, there will undoubtedly be profound social, economic and political convulsions in the century ahead. Seen in this light, Marxism remains acutely relevant to contemporary society, particularly in view of several underlying trends.

One of these trends is the overturning of traditional civil liberties and the growth of executive power, most apparent since the United States government's declaration of the 'war on terrorism' in 2001. Many of the previous legal and democratic norms identified with the capitalist state – such as free speech, habeas corpus, freedom of association and the presumption of innocence – have been eroded.

Another disturbing development is the rise of 'law and order' politics and legal measures. In many countries, most notably the United States, arguably the most powerful nation-state and also a model of 'free market' policy, the growth of police powers and institution of tougher approaches to punishment have seen imprisonment rates rise dramatically since the 1970s. This phenomenon suggests that the supposed triumph of the market has not produced social harmony and contentedness. On the contrary, it seems to have intensified economic inequality and exacerbated the resulting social and class tensions.

Discussion topics

1. What is Marxist theory? How does it relate to law?
2. What is the role of law in a socialist society?
3. Can law 'wither away'?
4. Is law, in the final analysis, an instrument of class rule?

Additional resources

Marxists Internet Archive site at <http://www.marxists.org>

M. Cain and A. Hunt, *Marx and Engels on Law*, Academic Press, London, 1979.

F. Engels, *The Origin of the Family, Private Property and the State*, International Publishers, New York, 1942.

F. Engels, *Ludwig Feuerbach and the End of German Classical Philosophy*, Progress Publishers, Moscow, 1978.

M. Head, *Evgeny Pashukanis: A Critical Reappraisal*, Routledge-Cavendish, London, 2007.

V. Lenin, *The State and Revolution*, Progress Publishers, Moscow, 1970.

K. Marx, *A Contribution to the Critique of Political Economy*, Progress Publishers, Moscow, 1977.

K. Marx, *The Civil War in France*, Progress Publishers, Moscow, 1948.

K. Marx, *Critique of the Gotha Program*, International Publishers, New York, 1970.

P. Phillips, *Marx and Engels on Law and Laws*, Martin Robertson, Oxford, 1980.

L. Trotsky, *Terrorism and Communism*, New Park Publications, London, 1975.

L. Trotsky, *The Revolution Betrayed. What is the Soviet Union and Where is it Going?*, Pathfinder Press, New York, 1972.

Chapter 13

ECONOMIC EFFICIENCY AND LAW

All human societies have some kind of economic foundation, meaning some organised system for the production and distribution of the goods necessary to sustain human material life. In a communist or socialist society productive resources are owned collectively or by state authority, and production and distribution are organised through a plan. In a capitalist society, by contrast, major social productive forces are privately owned, with goods produced by such private owners for sale in a market, in response to consumer demand, with a view to generating a profit. Capitalists acquire factors of production – land, labour, technology and raw materials – through the market and put them to work to generate goods which can be sold for more money than it cost to acquire such factors.

Economists frequently speak of the market itself organising production and distribution, without the need for a plan or for the exercise of central authority. But the continued operation of 'market forces' depends on government protection and facilitation of such market operations through enforcement of civil, criminal and corporations and industrial law, through appropriate infrastructure and welfare provision, and through regulation of the money supply and interest rates.

There are many different models and explanations of the operation of contemporary economic institutions and practices. But one particular approach dominates contemporary economic education and policy-making: the neoclassical 'micro' economic theory originally developed by William Jevons, Carl Menger, Leon Walras and Alfred Marshall in the later 1800s. Such 'orthodox' theory focuses particularly on the operation of market exchange processes and it is this approach which is the major focus of consideration in this chapter.

Neoclassical economics

From this perspective, as Stillwell explains, the economy is seen as 'a set of interconnected and self-regulating markets in which buyers and sellers freely interact without the need for substantial government regulation'.[1] Left to their own devices, without coercion or intervention, such markets ensure 'mutually advantageous exchanges' and the efficient allocation of economic resources. Markets allow consumers to choose what they want to buy, in line with their own preferences, at a price they can afford to pay. Producers' success – and economic survival – depends on giving such consumers what they want at such affordable prices. They too are rewarded for doing so, in terms of profit, and are punished for failing.

In a free market, the same sorts of goods tend to sell at the same price, no matter who is buying or selling them. Different prices for the same goods would intensify competition for lower priced goods, as purchasers try to resell them for higher prices elsewhere, thereby pushing up prices towards a uniform level. And the uniform market price itself adjusts until the number of units buyers want to buy (or are prepared to buy at a price they can afford) is equal to the number of units sellers are willing to sell (to make a minimally acceptable profit).[2]

Consumers are motivated to consume that combination of goods and services which, given their income, gives the greatest utility or satisfaction.[3] Because of diminishing marginal utility, with the satisfaction derived from additional units increasingly reduced, a consumer with a fixed income requires a fall in price of a particular commodity in order to motivate increased consumption of that good. 'Given a price fall for a given product, an individual will increase consumption until [their] marginal utility diminishes to just equal its price, that is, the value of the cash that could be spent on other goods.'[4] And the lower the cost of a particular good, the more the poorer people can afford to buy it.

Aggregating the demand decisions of all consumers in a particular market, we can construct a demand curve for a particular product.

With diminishing marginal utility and poorer consumers unable to choose to pay higher prices, it will typically show the quantity of the good demanded decreasing with increasing price. The slope of the demand curve depends on responsiveness or elasticity of demand resulting from a change in price. Sales of some goods are much more price sensitive than others.

A change in demand caused by an increase or decrease in price is illustrated by a movement along the demand curve. A fall or rise in demand caused by any other 'exogenous' change, such as a successful advertising campaign or a scare about product safety, is illustrated by a shift in the whole curve, to the left for reduced demand at any particular price point, or to the right for increased demand.[5]

Increasing the supply of any good requires the relevant producers to employ more resources or find a way to get more output through better use of the same input (that is, increase productivity). As a firm grows in size it typically benefits from cost advantages called 'economies of scale': buying, utilising and storing materials in bulk, employing technologies of mass production and increased division of labour. The ideal mix of resources to enable the most efficient level of output depends on the particular industry concerned.

But in all industries, short to medium term increase in output, produced by the addition of labour and raw material inputs, while other factors of production (capital and land) are kept fixed in quantity, leads, beyond a certain point, to steady erosion in production gains. Output increases with additional inputs, but in steadily decreasing amounts. Firms therefore require increased sale prices for their goods in the short to medium term in order to motivate increased production. At the same time, rising prices will tempt higher cost, less efficient producers to enter the market.

Aggregating the production decisions of all producers in a particular industry, this leads to an upward-sloping supply curve, with an increased quantity of any particular good supplied in response to an increased unit price for the good in question.

A change in supply caused by an increase or decrease in price is illustrated by a movement along the supply curve. And here again, a fall or rise in supply caused by 'exogenous' change, such as a sudden change in production costs due to technological innovation, or a change in government taxation or regulation, will cause the whole supply curve to shift to the left or the right.

In the longer term, when all inputs to the production process can be increased together, to counteract diminishing returns, the curve flattens out. While most businesses benefit from economies of scale as size increases, for some businesses there are constant returns to scale over certain ranges of output, and for most, diseconomies of scale beyond a certain point.

Any particular rational profit-maximising producer continues to expand output as long as each additional unit produced adds more to revenue earned than it does to costs. Production can continue so long as selling prices are maintained above costs. But, due to diminishing returns, costs (per unit of output) continue to rise up to this point. The point of profit maximisation is described as that at which marginal revenue = marginal cost, that is, the point where the revenue earned from the sale of one extra unit of the good equals the cost incurred in the production of that unit.[6]

Neoclassical theory also says that in a free market, competition among producers for sales pushes prices and therefore also profits down to the lowest level compatible with continued business operation. The only way for a particular business to increase profits is to come up with some innovation that reduces production costs. But then other businesses rush to catch up and competition brings prices down again to the minimum profit level, in line with lowered production costs.

Putting together upward-sloping supply curves and downward-sloping demand curves for particular products, we can see how the point of intersection indicates a stable equilibrium, where supply equals demand and the market clears. Producers are selling all of the goods they are making for an acceptable price and profit level, while consumers are buying all the goods they can afford at a price they are prepared to pay.

This neat model of supply and demand is taken to apply to all goods and services, including the 'factors of production': capital and labour.

> For each factor there is a demand that normally varies inversely with price and a supply that responds positively to price increases. For each product or factor of production there is just one market clearing price at which demand equals supply.[7]

> People will be employed only so long as they are productive. Employment is not a right. In a market society, any resource will only

find it is in demand if it can help produce something that consumers are willing to buy. And the scarcer the resource, the higher the price it will command.[8]

Left alone, without government interference, individual markets will tend towards a stable equilibrium, which is also a situation of optimal efficiency. If someone wants something badly enough that they are prepared to pay its production costs (including minimum profit) then someone will be motivated to produce it. If they want it badly enough they will be motivated to offer something sufficiently valuable in the market to get the money to pay for the thing they want – including offering the use of their own strengths and skills in productive labour.[9]

If demand for a particular product increases, for some reason other than a fall in price, this pushes its price – and the producer's profits – up as buyers compete for restricted supplies and calls forth increased production. But as others take up production of the good in question, in pursuit of higher profits, increased competition among greater numbers of producers pushes the price to consumers, and profits, down again to the lowest level compatible with continued supply. If demand falls for reasons other than a price decrease, sellers compete for restricted demand, and higher-cost producers are forced out of the market by falling prices.

It is frequently said that consumers thus exercise 'sovereignty' or rule over the market. Through their purchasing decisions they tell producers what to produce, in the form of greater or lesser amounts of particular goods: more coffee, less tea; more cars, less bicycles.

Market prices above equilibrium prices create excess supply (unsold goods) which motivates sellers to cut their prices, bringing the market price back to equilibrium and eliminating the excess supply (as supply decreases with falling prices). Market prices below equilibrium price create excess demand which motivates buyers to offer higher prices, again bringing the market price back to equilibrium and eliminating the excess demand (as demand decreases with rising prices). In this way markets are supposed to respond flexibly, quickly and effectively to changing conditions of demand, to keep societies functioning and developing without the need for any central plan, central co-ordination or coercion. The prevailing prices respond to changes in the conditions of demand or the conditions of supply in such a way as to shift to a new equilibrium position. A 'systemic stability' prevails, beneath the day-to-day price oscillations of a competitive market economy.

'General equilibrium' is said to exist when a set of prices for goods and factors of production equates supply and demand in all markets simultaneously. And while there are always forces causing disequilibrium in particular markets, leading to consequences in others, according to neoclassical theory, market adjustments operate inevitably in the direction of restoration of equilibrium. And this means the direction of optimal efficiency – with no 'excess' supply or demand.[10]

Efficiency

Neoclassical 'welfare' economics defines 'efficiency' as 'Pareto optimality', after an Italian economist Vilfredo Pareto.

> A Pareto optimal outcome is one where it is impossible to make anyone better off without making someone else worse off. The idea is simply that it would be inefficient or wasteful not to implement a change that made someone better off and nobody worse off. Such a change is called a Pareto improvement, and another way to define a Pareto optimal; or efficient outcome is an outcome where there are no further Pareto improvements possible.[11]

Free and rational people will not engage in market exchange unless both benefit from such arrangements, so all such free market exchanges will be Pareto improvements. And as Hunt notes:

> On the basis of the conditions of utility maximisation and profit maximisation, neoclassical economists have built an elaborate, symmetrical, aesthetically pleasing deductive and mathematical edifice [which] proves that, given competitive conditions, utility maximising exchanging consumers and profit maximising exchanging entrepreneurs will automatically act and interact so as to maximise the social welfare ... Given the initial 'endowment' of ownership of productive factors – or the initial distribution of wealth – utility [is] increased through production and exchange to the maximum possible level consistent with the original distribution of wealth.[12]

Most theorists have acknowledged that non-Pareto optimal outcomes can be desirable insofar as the benefits to some can significantly outweigh the losses to others – and allow for compensation for such losses. They emphasise a broader idea of efficiency based on cost benefit analysis. On this basis, if the overall benefits of doing something outweigh the overall costs, then it's efficient to do the thing in question. Here neoclassical theorists plot marginal social cost curves for production of particular goods which closely resemble the upward-sloping supply curves of standard (micro) economic analysis insofar as it is assumed that increased output takes scarce resources away from other uses ('opportunity cost') and contributes to increased pollution. The latter are now identified as private marginal cost curves of the producers. So too do they plot marginal social benefit curves for such goods which closely resemble the standard downward-sloping demand curves on account of declining marginal utility considerations. The efficiency of particular markets can then be determined by how closely marginal private cost and benefit curves match marginal social cost and benefit curves.

On a more practical level, as Stillwell shows, cost benefit analysis takes the form of evaluating all the outcomes of a possible action in monetary terms, 'estimating the net present value of the future costs and benefits, comparing the net present value of the costs and the net present value of the benefits', and 'selecting the policy alternatives where the cost benefit ratio is less than 1; or, in the case of mutually exclusive alternatives, selecting the policy alternative with the lowest cost benefit ratio'.[13]

Neo-liberalism and neoclassical theory

These key ideas of neoclassical economic theory are also central pillars of neo-liberal ideology. Neo-liberals draw upon neoclassical economic ideas to justify their rejection of any state responsibility for actively ensuring provision of resources to allow the fulfilment of human rights – to health, education, employment, income, housing and other necessities – beyond the 'core' rights to protection of life and property. They favour leaving it to individuals to make their own contractual arrangements in these areas, purchasing the services of private providers. This includes private insurance against the possibility of accident, illness and job loss, rather than state-based welfare systems. The role of the state is merely to ensure that such individuals are not denied market access to such things on the basis of racial or other discrimination, and enforcing valid contracts or appropriate compensation for broken contracts.

Market exchange, as an exercise of free will and choice, is identified as superior to central allocation of resources, insofar as the latter is seen as intrinsically authoritarian and inefficient. Markets reward those who make a valuable social contribution by offering goods or services others want to buy. People have to contribute to the social good through producing things of value in order to participate in market exchange – rather than merely being allocated the fruits of others' labours. And since individuals will only enter into market exchange together if both see themselves as benefiting from such exchange, market relations produce continuous improvements in human wellbeing achieved without any external exercise of authority.

Considerations of 'efficiency' are supposed to determine the balance of public and private provision of goods and services, the latter through the mediation of competitive 'free' market processes and forces, supported by civil laws of contract and tort. Since free competitive markets are generally taken to be more efficient than non-market systems by definition, the theory favours an increasing shift towards privatisation and user-pays in areas of health, education, legal representation (in an adversarial system), infrastructure, welfare and even some areas of criminal law enforcement.

Neo-liberals favour competition at all levels of society, on grounds of threat of failure and promise of rewards of success bringing out the best in all participants. In freely competitive markets, those who contribute to the production of what people want to buy, most cheaply and effectively, are rewarded with the biggest wages and profits. This, in turn, provides more resources to those with a track record of success, to expand production and improve their performance in the future.

Similarly, neo-liberals utilise neoclassical theory to support their opposition to trade unions as agents of collective bargaining on workers' behalf, of state supervision of such bargaining and centralised wage fixing, including determination of national minimal wages and industry-wide awards, based on need, by a 'neutral umpire' in the form of a court or arbitration tribunal. They support private contractual negotiations between individual workers and employers on wages and conditions which facilitates remuneration in proportion to the value of individual contribution to production. So too are they opposed to government 'intervention' to try to maintain full employment through deficit-financed demand management or direct job creation. All of these are seen as reducing market efficiency and economic growth.

Macroeconomics

Whereas microeconomics concerns the interaction of producers and consumers in individual markets, macroeconomics considers the national and international economy at the aggregate level, with particular reference to aggregate demand, production, employment and inflation. Following the experience of the Great Depression and the contribution of John Maynard Keynes, it has been recognised that the state has a key role to play in overseeing national economic performance through appropriate macroeconomic policies. Particularly important in this context are *fiscal policies* of adjustment of government expenditure and taxation and *monetary policies* of control of the money supply and the costs of borrowing money.

Neo-liberals argue that expansionary government fiscal policies (of infrastructure spending), such as those pursued in the post-war period, to reduce the intensity of cyclical recession and maintain employment, actually 'crowd out' private sector investment, insofar as government deficits put significant demand pressure into credit markets and compete with business investment for such loanable funds, thereby forcing up interest rates and reducing business investment. So, at best, they fail to boost the national economy, while more likely causing national income to fall due to government inefficiency and failure of private investment.

From a neo-liberal perspective macroeconomic policy essentially concerns the role of an independent central bank – in Australia the Reserve Bank – in manipulating interest rates in such a way as to facilitate the 'natural' progress of the national economy along a path of steady and continuous growth. Most of the time this means ensuring relatively low interest rates in order to encourage consumer spending and business investment. But if, for some reason, the economy grows too quickly, threatening inflation and recession, it is the job of the central bank to slow it down, through judicious rate increases. Ideally the bank will not let growth get out of hand in the first place and therefore won't be required to brake too sharply, threatening an interest-driven recession. But such interest-driven recessions can sometimes be necessary to shake out endemic inflation from the system.

Neo-liberals believe in a 'natural rate of unemployment', some-times equated with 'frictional unemployment' or the number of people in process of moving from one job to another. They argue that social liberals confuse such 'temporary' unemployment with 'real' unemployment and create serious economic problems by pumping extra demand into the economy to try to reduce it. More often, such a natural rate is identified as a level of unemployment necessary to avoid inflation produced by rising wage costs. Once unemployment becomes so reduced as to produce serious labour shortages, busi-nesses then have to offer higher and higher wages to keep their staff or attract new staff. At the same time, higher wages lead to higher demand (for consumption goods) and such increased wage costs and increased demand threaten increased inflation. This, in turn, threat-ens economic growth and erodes real incomes.

Such a 'natural' level of unemployment maintains competitive labour markets (with workers competing among themselves for jobs) which allow businesses to choose the best available person for the job. At the same time neo-liberals emphasise the need for higher wages and salaries for those with special qualifications – over and above the need to pay for private provision of the relevant training – as a necessary incentive for acquisition of such qualifications and for retaining skilled labour within a particular nation-state.

They rely on automatic market adjustments of wages, the natural growth rate of the economy and individual initiatives in retraining and relocation to ensure high levels of employment, rather than govern-ment spending. At most, they sometimes support some degree of government intervention in such reskilling and relocation to deal with 'excess demand' for labour in particular industries and regions (slow-ing growth and pushing up production costs) and ameliorate 'struc-tural' unemployment (due to a mismatch between available jobs and labour skills). Increased money supply in line with the natural growth rate of the economy is provided by private banks offering loans in excess of their deposits to finance investment and consumption.

Market failure and externalities

The neo-classical economic theory favoured by neo-liberals under-stands inefficiency in terms of 'market failure' and 'externalities'. The former is particularly associated with the idea of free markets inability to guarantee provision of 'public goods'. Public goods, in this sense, include things like provision of basic infrastructure (roads, ports, power and water distribution systems), military protection and large-scale pollution reduction, from which whole populations (necessarily) benefit. Any particular individual or group has a very limited incentive to buy such things in a free market, because of the limited benefits they will derive compared to the huge costs they will incur; they will be paying largely for others' benefit, rather than their own. They have a strong incentive to wait for others to pay for things, from which they then benefit at no cost. So such things are never provided.[14]

Externalities are the positive and negative consequences of market transactions for third parties. On the negative side, this includes the effects of pollution generated through the production process and through consumption of particular commodities. Thus car production in big cities produces acid rain that destroys surrounding forests and lakes, including those in neighbouring countries. Use of the cars contributes to respiratory disease and global warming. But the costs of such pollution are not considered in decision-making about how many cars to produce or whether to buy a car – because car producers and users don't pay for these costs.[15]

Neo-liberal defenders of free markets generally seek to show how market forces and procedures can themselves address such issues without government involvement – beyond the operation of the civil law. In the former case, the emphasis is generally on motivating private contractors to provide such infrastructure or services through allowing them to charge the public for use of the facilities in question – a user-pays principle – rather than the government providing such facilities through use of tax money. In some cases, it is acknowledged that public provision may be necessary, but then ways need to be found to ensure market-like efficiencies in the public sector.

In the latter case, it is suggested that negative externalities can be effectively addressed through modifications and clarifications of property rights, rather than through direct regulation of business operations. On the assumption that pollution continues because of lack of effective property rights and economic interests in the land, water and air where pollutants are dumped, the suggestion is that assigning such property rights (including exclusivity and transferability), ideally to those who can make best use of them, as evidenced by their ability and willingness to pay for them, and encouraging such economic interests, will empower and encourage owners to resist such dumping.[16]

When and where they are prepared to recognise a need to reduce toxic and climate-changing emissions, neo-liberals are typically advocates of emission trading schemes, which assign quotas and allow trading of such quotas, to provide incentives for emission reduction – rather than direct regulation of the operation of individual businesses. Following a successful US drive to reduce sulphur dioxide pollution by allowing companies to buy and sell emission credits from each other under a federally imposed cap on total emissions, the US lobbied for carbon emission trading in the early Kyoto negotiations. The idea was subsequently taken up by the EU with its emission trading scheme (ETS) launched in 2005.[17]

Economic analysis of law

Neoclassical ideas have influenced legal theory and practice in many ways, but perhaps most directly in the influential 'economic analysis of law'. The basic idea of the economic analysis of law is that law should function to facilitate social wealth creation through the operation of efficient market relations as understood by neoclassical theory. And that such efficiency will generally be maximised where direct legal intervention and regulation is minimised.

Proponents of this approach question the understanding of negative externalities as products of the cost-minimising actions of particular culpable agents inflicted on innocent and powerless victims. And they are generally hostile to the idea of legally enforced internalisation of such costs as the best solution to the problem, through taxing or fining pollution (or other damage) in order to reduce it to an acceptable level. They highlight the complex interrelation of action and inaction by all concerned in producing any particular economically significant outcome. As Whitman says:

> Cost benefit analysis treats the inputs into the production of damage symmetrically – both the injurer and the injured can reduce harm. The issue is which person can reduce the harm at the lowest cost [that is, with minimal disruption of wealth-generating activity] and whether the cost of reducing harm is less than the benefit.[18]

Rather than treating the upstream steel producer or mine operator as wholly responsible for the death of a farmer's fish downstream through discharge of toxic pollution into the river, they highlight the culpability of the farmer also, for siting their fish farm at this location, for failing to take appropriate protective measures of filtering the water, growing pollution-resistant fish or moving away.[19]

Following the work of Ronald Coase, they argue that as long as transaction costs (as the costs of organising and successfully achieving a negotiated agreement) are low, the economically optimum solution in such situations can typically be achieved through free negotiation between the parties concerned, supported only by basic laws of contract and tort, with the possibility of civil action to recover for financial loss. Coase argued that, with low transaction costs, whatever the assignment of relevant rights to those involved, as long as they are free to negotiate mutually beneficial solutions, the outcomes will be economically efficient, or optimal.

This is typically illustrated by reference to examples of ranchers' cattle trampling farmers' fields. If transaction costs are low it makes no difference whether ranchers have the right to trample or farmers have the right to be protected from trampling – and will be legally compensated for the costs of damage done. In either case, free and rational negotiations between the parties concerned will lead to the same, economically optimal result in terms of the amount of damage done and the steps taken to avoid it.

Using a numerical example from Whitman, we can see how, if it costs $30 000 to build a wall which will prevent $40 000 damage to the farmer's crops, then a rancher would rather build the wall than compensate a farmer with rights (providing they can still produce enough profit to stay in business), and a farmer without rights would rather build the wall themselves than suffer the extra $10 000 loss (assuming they too can afford to do so). If the wall costs $50 000 then it's not worthwhile for either party to build the wall. The 'most efficient outcome is for the rancher's cows to trample the crops'.[20] Typically, as most probably in the steel and fish case, there will be some intermediate solution with an economically optimum level of pollution or other damage.

Law and economics theorists acknowledge that where transaction costs are high, legal regulation, restricting pollution through taxes or fines, can sometimes be the best solution. Whereas it is comparatively straightforward for a single victim of pollution to negotiate with a single polluter (especially if they are both businesses), the situation is much more complicated with a large number of victims spread over a large area.

But, at the same time, they argue that the law has a crucial role to play in many high transaction cost situations in assigning rights or entitlements in such a way as to ensure optimally efficient solutions in potential conflicts of interest. As Whitman says:

> The law should in general try ... to allocate entitlements to the party that [probably would] end up with [them] if there were zero transaction costs of exchange. In this way an unnecessary and costly transaction is ... avoided and misallocation will not occur ...[21]

Here Whitman considers the example of whether airlines should have the right of use of the airspace 10 000 feet above homes to fly planes, or whether landowners should have rights of ownership (and prevention of trespass) to the sky above their properties (as was apparently the case in Roman times). He argues that negotiation wouldn't work with rights assigned to landowners, because 'each landowner along a flight path would try to [be] the monopoly holdout since unanimous agreement is required'.[22] Neither would negotiation work with rights assigned to the airlines since high transaction costs and free-rider problems would preclude collective action by the homeowners even if they 'valued airplane-free air more than airlines profited' from using such air.[23]

Whitman suggests that the 'wealth maximising' solution is clearly to give the right to the airlines, rather than the homeowners. 'The value of the aesthetic loss [if any] from having airplanes flying 10 000 feet overhead is considerably less than the amount the airlines would be willing to pay for the privilege of having flights.'[24]

Proponents of the economic analysis of law see it as a logical application, complement or extension to neoclassical economic theory. As Whitman says:

> The only difference between the neoclassical analysis of the firm [with efficiency maximised through rational cost minimisation relative to demand] and the analysis of efficient legal rules is that according to neoclassical economic theory, the owner of the firm has control over the inputs into the production process, while in the cases of interest in the law, different people have control over different inputs. The objective of the law should be to design a system that encourages optimal behaviour by these unrelated people.[25]

Corporations

Neoclassical theory centres on the idea of perfect competition, where there are a large number of medium-sized business enterprises, with none big enough to gain any special advantages. In particular, each business accounts for only a small proportion of total output for the industry, their outputs are homogenous and substitutable, and there is no restriction to the entry of new producers. Businesses have no significant power to determine the prices of goods; they can only make decisions about the quantity of goods they will produce; they are 'price takers' rather than 'price makers'. These are preconditions for 'efficiency' in the neoclassical sense of the term.[26]

Despite this, neo-liberals generally see large-scale corporate bureaucracies as appropriate organisations of control of major productive forces, with ownership of corporate assets vested (in the final instance) in private shareholders. Such bureaucracies are identified as efficient structures of organisation by virtue of their effective, large-scale mobilisation and integration of the work of professional experts, directed by a central authority, in pursuit of profit maximisation. CEOs, board members and higher managers as economic planning experts work together with, and direct the activities of, other such experts – scientists, accountants, lawyers, marketers, etc – to maximise output, productivity and profit.[27]

The professional and hierarchical structure of the modern corporation allows general policy to be translated into specific directives by experts. The hierarchy allows for permanent monitoring of policy and action and masses of information from the base can be centralised for policy review. Large size allows for accumulation and cross-referencing of information and for economies of scale and concentration of resources for otherwise impossible large-scale projects, which themselves sustain further scale economies. In particular it allows for substantial research budgets, for increased division of labour, specialisation and automation of production, along with bulk purchase, storage and application of inputs to bring down costs.[28]

Equality of opportunity, promotion through the hierarchy based on merit, and reward (in salaries, bonuses and decision-making powers) in proportion to social contribution, ensure efficiency and fairness. Substantially greater material rewards to those higher up the pyramid provide the motivation for others to strive to join them by developing and conscientiously applying socially valuable abilities. Higher profits are both the consequence of effective management and the means to ensure the rewards which drive such effective management.

Unlike state-owned enterprises, which are frequently run as monopolies and whose managers are mere 'hired hands' with little incentive to efficiency, the performance of private-sector management is directed by the exigencies of competition and monitored by shareholders. Since these managers face the sack if share prices fall, and are often themselves major shareholders in the companies they run, they are strongly motivated to efficient performance to keep such share prices high.

Offerings of shares allow for flexible funding of productive undertakings, independent of control by banks. Purchasers' ability to acquire diversified portfolios of shares in different corporations and exit from corporations as they choose in face of negative assessments of such corporations' future potential makes share buying more attractive. Along with shareholders' liability for corporate debts only to the extent of the value of their shareholding in that company, these considerations have facilitated the sale of vast blocks of shares which have provided the capital to take advantage of new large-scale (mass) productive technologies and economies of scale not otherwise possible.[29]

Shareholders who sacrifice immediate consumption and risk exposure in the stock market to supply the physical capital for such corporations are therefore legally empowered to select board members to manage such assets, and to receive a return which reflects both the extent of their sacrifice – and risk – and the social utility of their investment.[30] Managers who successfully maximise the return to such shareholders continue to receive their support and a share of the profits. And neo-liberals have long argued for rewards in the form of stock options for such managers to further ensure their ongoing diligence in maximising share values through maximising corporate wealth.[31]

Regulating corporations

Neo-liberal ideology is somewhat ambivalent in relation to the application of this model – of corporate managerialism – to the government and public sector. On the one hand there is a requirement for professional managerial skill and efficient organisation in the state sector as in the private sector. On the other hand there is also the idea that managerial bureaucracies easily degenerate into inefficiency and corruption without the discipline of competitive market forces. The answer is, again, to aim to cut back the public sector as far as possible, and where this is not possible, to try to model the organisation of the public sector as closely as possible on the private.

There is also some degree of ambivalence in relation to the size of the bigger private sector organisations as a possible obstacle to effective operation of free competitive markets. On the one hand, large size allows for economies of scale and for substantial research budgets to develop new and more productive technologies. It allows national corporations to expand overseas, gaining access to cheap labour, resources and markets and to compete successfully with the corporations of other nations on a world scale. And such large and successful national corporations can contribute significantly to the funding of state operations through their tax payments.

On the other hand, there is legitimate concern that large transnationals, sometimes working together in oligopolistic market-sharing and price-fixing arrangements, can undermine free market efficiency through monopoly pricing. Other smaller businesses and consumers pay the costs of monopoly super-profits in higher input prices and lower than average profitability. At the same time, an increasing number of international transactions involving subsidiaries of the same corporations threaten to undermine effective corporate taxation through transfer pricing arrangements, with costs of imports into higher tax regions exaggerated and of exports to lower tax regions undervalued.

In a large and complex corporation it is more difficult for shareholders to monitor and control the actions of the boards they appoint to manage their investment. And the bigger the corporations, the greater the losses in corporate collapses brought about by managerial incompetence and criminality. In Australia, the recent HIH collapse is said to have cost $5.3 billion in losses to shareholders, creditors and others.[32]

In opposition to those who have argued that an increasing gap between ownership (by shareholders) and control (by CEO and board members) offers problems for the 'efficient' operation of free competitive markets (through misuse of resources by managers, looking after their own interests rather than pursuing profit maximisation through cost-cutting, and therefore requiring substantial specialised regulatory legal intervention), law and economics theorists argue that 'there is no loss of control by the owners of capital who invest in publicly traded corporations'.[33]

As Glasbeek says, such theorists argue that what really happens when a corporation is formed:

> ... is that the investors/owners of capital contractually agree with other investors/owners of capital to give their combined capitals to others to manage. As a group of contracting owners they also contract with these managers, and therefore it is up to them, as contracting owners, to determine the terms of the contract for the management of the aggregated capitals; that is, they do, or could control what these managers are to do. Even though it is the norm for the board of directors and the management team to have their duties on how to manage the corporation spelled out by law, rather than by any actual contract between the owners and managers, that is said not to be the point. While owners/shareholders could be (and sometimes are) specific about the objectives they want the corporation to pursue and how those goals should be pursued, inasmuch as they do not do this it is to be assumed that the statutory provisions covering these matters accurately reflect what these investors/owners would have put into any contract with the other investors/owners if it had been practical for them to do so. Inasmuch as they do not, the statutes should be changed.[34]

This does allow for appropriate regulatory statutes, over and above the operation of the standard civil law of contracts, providing they aim to protect shareholders' interests through enforcing appropriate behaviour on the part of managers. And, indeed, around the world, particularly the English-speaking world, so-called 'corporations law' consists of rules aiming essentially to protect shareholders' financial interests through enforcing due diligence on directors in the efficient pursuit of profit.

Neo-liberals are typically committed to some degree of legal regulation of corporations in the areas of transparency and competition policy, the former centred on informing and protecting shareholders through the issue of audited financial reports by the CEO and board as a basis for maintaining confidence, the latter on breaking up or preventing monopoly power concentrations that radically undermine competitive market forces. Some libertarian free marketeers also acknowledge a place for consumer protection legislation.

In Australia, the Australian Securities and Investments Commission (ASIC) is charged with investigating and prosecuting suspected contraventions of the laws governing the operation of corporations, including company or financial services fraud or dishonesty. It is concerned with consumer protection in relation to financial services, the regulation of insurance and superannuation, and monitoring and promoting market integrity and consumer protection in relation to the Australian financial system.

ASIC has powers to examine persons believed to be able to provide relevant information, to inspect corporate books and records, and to quickly obtain information about financial products. So can it initiate prosecutions for criminal offences where its investigations reveal contraventions of the law, and civil proceedings in the name of a company, where it is in the public interest to do so – for the recovery of damages for fraud, negligence, default, breach of duty or other misconduct. In its annual report for 2004–05 it listed two criminals jailed, 121 civil orders handed down to people and companies, a 94% success rate in civil litigation, 161 additional disclosures from directors, $123 million worth of financial penalties, cost recoveries and assets frozen.

The work of ASIC is complemented by that of APRA, the Australian Prudential Regulation Authority, aiming to ensure a minimum level of financial soundness in financial entities. It oversees banks, building societies, credit unions, insurance companies and superannuation providers, seeking to ensure the financial health of these institutions in the interests of depositors and policyholders.

The Australian Competition and Consumer Commission (ACCC) is supposed to play a central role in enforcing anti-monopoly and consumer protection legislation. Part IV of the *Trade Practices Act* (TPA) covers anti-competitive practices that limit or stop competition. It aims to:

> ... foster the competitive environment necessary to give consumers a choice in price, quality and service. It prohibits commercial conduct that substantially lessens competition in a market, as a lack of competition might allow some traders to push prices up and lower the quality of the goods and services they offer to consumers. Some anti-competitive conduct is prohibited outright (for example, price fixing), while other types are prohibited only if they substantially lessen competition. A substantial lessening of competition is appar-

ent when the ability of buyers to shop around for a deal that suits them is significantly diminished.[35]

There are some circumstances in which a refusal to supply is unlawful under the Act. These include a misuse of market power, third line forcing, boycotts, resale price maintenance and placing limitations on resellers.[36]

Section 51AC deals with 'unconscionable conduct', including bullying of smaller firms by larger ones. Other sections deal with consumer protection, including misleading or deceptive advertising, failure to provide necessary safety information with products and sale of dangerous products. And the ACCC is supposed to take action in relation to mergers and acquisitions which threaten to reduce competition, as well as ensuring the competitiveness of key infrastructural industries such as providers of electricity, telecommunications and communications.

Like ASIC, the ACCC has substantial powers of investigation and prosecution. It can pursue both criminal and civil penalties for breaches of the TPA. Substantial jail sentences and big fines can be imposed for breaches of the TPA. A recent case involved the use of whistleblower evidence to mount prosecutions of power transformer and distribution transformer cartels, leading to record $35 million penalties against companies and senior executives. And in 2005–06 it concluded 23 cases of 53 matters before the court, including the imposition of penalties of $8.9 million for Australian Safeway stores for price-fixing offences, accepted 54 public undertakings, commenced 14 new cases, assessed 87 trade practices compliance programmes, and finalised 18 compliance programme matters. However, as Solomon points out, the number of cases pursued by the ACCC under the chairmanship of Graeme Samuel has decreased compared with the previous regime of Allan Fels. As he says, 'under Samuel, the ACCC ... has lost ground for abuse of dominance and willingness to litigate or conclude anti-trust cases'. It has also lagged in the area of abuse of market power.[37]

Insider trading

Neo-liberal ambivalence in relation to regulation of corporations extends to the area of insider trading, where corporate officers – or others acting for them – buy or sell stock on the basis of undisclosed inside information available to them. Generally neo-liberals support laws which forbid insiders of corporation A buying stock in corporation B where A intends to make a tender offer for B, or buying land that corporation A plans to buy later.

In Australia, insider trading is prohibited under the *Corporations Act*, which is administered by ASIC. As Lipton and Herzberg point out, 'the insider trading provisions cover a wider range of financial products than shares. They also include derivatives, superannuation products and other financial products able to be traded on a financial market.'[38] And these laws are complemented by the continuous disclosure provisions of the *Corporations Act*, which reduce the opportunities for insider trading by requiring listed companies and other entities 'to disclose price-sensitive information that is not generally available.'[39]

However, neo-liberals have also used neoclassical economic ideas to argue for decriminalisation of insider trading. In this connection, Donald Whitman argues that insider trading 'may be desirable' in some circumstances. As he says:

> ... the more informative the price of the stock, the less the risk and the greater the return to the original stockholders. If the price is not fully informative (some information does not get translated into price) then buyers of stock need a higher expected return either to overcome the greater risk or to compensate for obtaining information about the stock. This means a lower purchase price of the stock. Managers can make an announcement or put their money where their mouth is ... ... With continuous insider trading, the stock price is more informative. In turn, the more informative the stock, the less the fluctuation in the price of the stock.[40]

At the same time:

> Insider information is cheaper than outsider information. If the managers do not provide inside information, others such as stock analysts can spend time obtaining special information, thereby making an 'unlevel' playing field. Clearly this is much more costly, and, more important, the average stockholder is hurt even more by outsiders information than insiders information. This is because managers will be paid less if managers can accrue additional income from inside trading. Outsiders do not benefit the firm in this way.[41]

The international level

At the international level, neo-liberals argue for the universal benefits of maximum freedom of trade, investment and lending. As Hahnel points out, 'mainstream theory teaches that as long as international trade and investment is consensual and countries do not mistake what the effects will be, no country can end up worse off, and all countries should end up better off'.[42] Neo-liberal policy therefore favours removal of barriers to free trade and investment in the form of tariffs, quotas and capital controls.

In relation to trade, the theory of comparative advantage rules.[43] Even if one country is more productive than another in respect of two particular sorts of goods, both can benefit from trade in the goods in question if each concentrates relevant resources on the production only of the good in respect of which it is relatively more productive. This will allow for a higher combined output of the two countries (using the same inputs) compared to what could be achieved with each country pursuing self-sufficiency through production of both goods. Such increased output can then be shared between the two countries through an appropriate exchange rate for the goods in question.

In relation to investment, the assumption is that in a free market, it will flow to where it can be used most efficiently, so that such free flow of investment increases global efficiency. Big corporations will only shift technology and skilled labour offshore – in direct foreign investment (DFI) – if such resources will increase productivity more offshore than if utilised in the home country. Big banks, wealthy individuals and mutual funds will not loan money or buy stocks or bonds abroad – in international financial investment (IFI) – unless higher productivity is yielding higher returns from the foreign countries in question.

As Hahnel says:

> Mainstream theory assumes that if profits are higher from FDI than domestic investment this is because the investment raises productivity more abroad than at home ... [and] if foreign borrowers are willing to pay higher interest rates than domestic borrowers this is because the loan raises foreign productivity more than it would domestic productivity.[44]

Neo-liberals generally favour floating exchange rates and 'free' inter-

national currency markets as a means to achieving balanced international trade. The key consideration here is the state of a country's
balance of payments account – made up of its trade account (the
balance of exports and imports) and its short- and long-run capital accounts (the balance of investment funds and repatriated profits flowing in and out). Countries running up overall balance of
payments deficits find the value of their currencies falling in international currency markets. This makes their exports cheaper while
increasing the cost of imports and so does it reduce the cost of others
investing in their economies, allowing their economies to grow and
the deficit to be reduced. Countries running up surpluses find the
value of their currencies increasing, thereby increasing the cost of
their exports and reducing their surpluses.

International governance

To understand the neo-liberal ideology of international governance
we can consider the transformation of the Bretton Woods institutions in the years since they were originally established. As Patomaki
and Teivainen point out: 'The Anglo-American agreements of 1944
... established rules for a relatively open multilateral system of trade
and payments, reconciling 'openness and trade expansion with fixed
yet changeable exchange rates, strict capital controls and the commitment of national governments to full employment and economic and
political stabilisation'.[45]

The International Monetary Fund was originally established to
stabilise the international monetary system through administering a
system of monetary regulation, built around fixed exchange rates,
helping out member states with short-term balance of payment problems, to preclude their dropping out of the world trading system.
This included loans offered to overcome such deficits and improve
export performance to avoid their recurrence in the future. JM
Keynes, as British treasury representative at Bretton Woods, wanted
to completely reorganise world trade, channelling it all through a
central bank that would have the power to tax trade surpluses as
partial causes of deficits, motivating trade surplus nations to help the
debtors by quickly putting such surplus funds back into circulation.
But the United States rejected any such taxing of surplus.

The International Bank for Reconstruction and Development

(which now forms the core of the World Bank Group) was originally set up to assist in post-war reconstruction, and to provide loans for specific, post-colonial development projects.

As Susan George says: 'Neither institution was [originally] supposed to function as an arbiter of internal national policies nor make their loans conditional upon following certain policy prescriptions.'[46] Keynes wanted to see the IMF staffed by 'professional independent international civil servants' to avoid superpower domination.

But the US insisted on 'politically appointed executive directors operating full-time'.[47] With voting power in both the IMF and World Bank distributed among executive directors 'according to each government's financial contributions to the institutions'[48], and the US as major contributor to IMF funding, US government policies and priorities increasingly dominated the operation of the fund. And with an increasing shift in US ruling ideology away from social liberal reformism and towards neo-liberal reaction from the later 1970s, so did such neo-liberal ideology come to increasingly direct IMF and World Bank policy.

Under the presidency of Robert McNamara from 1968, the World Bank offered bank bonds on international capital markets to make more funds available for loans, with personnel rewarded in proportion to the quantity of loans to developing nations they could establish. Such countries were encouraged to borrow for big capital works projects (typically centred on large-scale electricity generation) to jump-start their industrial development (while also benefiting first-world exporters). Following the oil crisis of 1973, with oil prices quadrupling, western banks were choked with deposits from OPEC members, and they too began to offer loans to the developing nations, in an effort to pay the interest on the new deposits.

Lots of the projects financed by such loans failed to deliver the hoped-for benefits. Much money was spent on importation of military technology used by dictators of developing nations to oppress their own populations. Corrupt officials simply appropriated substantial amounts of loan money, with nothing left to pay the debts. And in 1981, in the interests of inflation control, the US Treasury Department massively pushed up interest rates, provoking a debt crisis in developing nations.

By 1952 the IMF executive board had already adopted a principle of 'conditionalities', putting the burden of proof on recipients of IMF funds to show 'whether the policies the member will pursue will be adequate to overcome the problem'. Following the debt crisis, neo-liberal ideology came to define the sorts of policies increasingly demanded of developing nation governments, as conditions for rene-gotiation of such debts and access to further loans to service such debt.

So-called 'structural adjustment programmes' included key features of neo-liberal policy such as encouragement to competition at all levels, inflation minimisation, concentration on exports and increased trade volume – typically achieved through devaluation of the local currency, to increase exports to provide foreign currency for debt service, removal of any restrictions on foreign capital flow into the countries in question, reduced taxation of corporations and rich individuals to encourage such investment, privatisation of any government-owned resources and introduction of cost recovery or user-pays for any previously free or subsidised goods or services, and the introduction of 'flexible' labour markets – through removal of workers' rights to job security, health insurance, maternity leave or minimum wages.[49] Supposedly such 'Washington Consensus' poli-cies, if pursued actively enough, would encourage growth and elimi-nate debt.

These have been rightly called 'austerity' programmes insofar as they inevitably produce some short- to medium-term pain and diffi-culty to significant numbers of people in the countries concerned. But the argument is that this will be temporary, and is necessary, both to protect the creditors from default and to pull the countries concerned back from debt and underdevelopment. And as Patomaki and Teivainen point out, by the early 1980s 'the Bank began to follow the Fund's example in applying programmes of economic austerity as conditions for some of its loans'.[50]

Neo-liberals have also been actively involved in shaping the poli-cies of the World Trade Organisation, developing out of a series of international negotiations (the GATT round) aiming at reducing tariffs and increasing world trade. As Susan George says: 'The WTO is not the same kind of organisation as the Bank or the Fund, but rather an umbrella secretariat overseeing the implementation of a number of different agreements signed in Marrakech' in 1994 after eight years of the 'Uruguay Round' of negotiations.[51] 'These agree-ments cover not just [trade in] industrial goods, but agriculture, services, intellectual property [including patents on life forms], technical standards and a Dispute Resolution Body whose decisions are binding.'[52] What are conspicuously absent are any enforceable standards of worker and environmental protection.

The General Agreement on Trade in Services (GATS) defines services very broadly and provides for a further series of negotiations aiming to 'achieve a progressively higher level of liberalisation … [and] as a means of providing effective market access'. Only the central bank, the army, the police and the justice system are defined as 'public' services, so that the aim is to open all other sectors up to foreign commercial competition.

WTO rules oblige countries to treat all other WTO members in exactly the same way – the 'most favoured nation' rule. So there can be no preferential treatment, in terms of exports or imports, given to countries because they are poor or democratic or ethically or environmentally responsible. Members are not allowed to judge products, or discriminate between them, on the basis of 'processes and methods of production'.[53] Goods cannot be banned because they are products of child labour, because they are produced in unsustainable ways, or because genetically engineered (GE) hormones are used in their production.

It's interesting to note that the International Labour Organisation (ILO), created as the first specialised UN agency in 1946, has presided over a number of global agreements on labour standards and workers' rights, forbidding child labour and prison labour and requiring decent wages and conditions. But the same nations that have signed these treaties support WTO rules in blatant contradiction to their ILO commitments.

A major argument here is that ('ethical') discrimination would be unfair, and disastrous, to the less-developed world, where economies need to grow further in order to be able to afford protection of labour and the environment. And it can do so only through freer international trading conditions, allowing poorer countries to take advantage of their currently low wages and poor working conditions to acquire foreign currency to finance such growth.

To enforce these and other rules the WTO can intervene in a government's internal affairs through dispute resolution, potentially overruling democratically decided issues of foreign and domestic policy. Fines and sanctions can be imposed. And it is the unelected 'expert' Dispute Resolution Body that deals with any complaints, not elected representatives of the countries concerned.

It is difficult to present the neo-liberal line on international governance without highlighting some of the obvious problems associated with it. Even World Bank leaders have recently acknowledged that structural adjustment programmes based on neo-liberal principles have exacerbated poverty, inequality, environmental destruction and economic instability around the less developed world without providing any kind of real economic benefits. But they still have little to offer by way of new policy directions to address the issues.

What is offered, by more 'liberal' theorists, is 'a new reform agenda' or 'augmented Washington Consensus' based on 'institutional reform', poverty elimination, debt relief and Millennium Development Goals, as championed by rock stars Bono and Bob Geldof as well as by some orthodox neo-liberal economists. The basic argument is that the Washington Consensus has failed to assist the poorest peoples because of their initial lack of capital and infrastructure. These things therefore need to be provided as aid from the developed world – to the tune of around US $135 billion a year in assistance. In particular, the health and education level of workers in developing nations needs to be increased through provision of more aid, in order to make them more employable.

But in order to receive increased aid and debt relief:

> ... poor countries have to agree to [further] open their markets to foreign competition, privatise public enterprises, withdraw the state from service provision, reduce state budget deficits, redirect their economies in an export orientation, flexibilise their labour markets, and so on down the Washington Consensus list drawn up in the belief that markets and free competition can guide an economy into the magic realm of growth ... if only the workers are made more employable.[54]

In other words, these are more of the same policies which have created the problems in the first place.

Discussion topics

1. What are the basic principles of neoclassical economic theory?
2. What are strong and weak points of neoclassical ideas of efficiency?

3   What is the economic analysis of law?

4   What are corporations and how should their activities be regulated?

5   Comment on the roles of the World Bank and IMF in international governance.

Chapter 14

PROBLEMS OF THE MARKET

Economic efficiency, in the sense of avoidance of wastage of resources, including human time and effort (and skill and health), is not only desirable but necessary for a good society and for effective democracy. The satisfaction of human needs depends on the expenditure of limited resources. Wastage of such resources can threaten the most basic need satisfaction. Wastage includes depletion and ultimately exhaustion of non-renewable resources, as well as the accumulation of toxic pollutants throughout the ecosphere. Effective recycling allows for transformation of dangerous waste into useful materials.[1]

But there are also a number of fundamental questions raised by the 'orthodox' analysis of market efficiency developed in earlier chapters. Are the neoclassical ideas of efficiency (of Pareto optimality and the 'efficiency criterion') the best ways of understanding efficiency for significant social policy decision-making, or could we apply more socially or ethically acceptable ones? Is the market really as efficient, in these terms, as the orthodox analysis suggests? And, even if we accept orthodox ideas of the nature and value of efficiency, could there not still be good grounds for downgrading the pursuit of such efficiency in favour of other social and economic goals?

The first and third of these questions are dealt with in greater depth in later chapters. In this chapter we focus mainly on the second question, and on its implications for economics and law.

Inefficient markets

As noted earlier, the neoclassical economic theory favoured by neo-liberals centres on an idea of harmonious equilibrium of supply and demand. A free market system is supposed to embody negative feed-back mechanisms that automatically reproduce such an equilibrium following the (temporary) disruption of changing conditions of supply and demand, including the introduction of new technology, changing patterns of consumption and changing numbers of people seeking work. This is the foundation for neo-liberal policies of deregulation and laissez-faire. Competition is supposed to encourage technology-driven productivity gains – and price reductions – from which all ultimately benefit. At the same time, such negative feedback maintains the overall stability of the system.

For capitalism to continue to exist there must be systematic and ongoing exchange between different sectors of production. In each cycle of production each sector must produce what it needs in order to continue to function, plus what is needed by all the other sectors, with all sectors together producing a surplus, divided between them as profit. Producer-goods sectors must produce enough replacement technology for all sectors; similarly the consumer-goods sector must continue to feed, clothe, house and transport workers and capitalists from day to day. Prices for all goods must be such as to allow such systematic exchange ratios while delivering approximately equal profit rates to all sectors.

Economists have long emphasised the way in which the pursuit of profit can function to stabilise and maintain such systematic exchange. A producer or sector with output in excess of demand (in their own and other sectors) will see their profits falling (below average profits) as their goods remain unsold and prices fall, and they will reduce their output to avoid such wastage. A producer failing to generate sufficient output to satisfy demand will increase output to take advantage of demand-driven price increases (they will thus derive super-profits up to the point where such super-profits are competed away with increased supply).

On the other hand, it is easy to see how capitalist competition can also undermine any such equilibrium of exchange and profitability. Competition encourages increasing productivity to bring down the production costs of individual producers. The first to innovate, through introducing new, more productive technology, can gain super-profits – selling at a price determined by the general level of productive efficiency in the industry. But as others within the industry take up the innovation in question, the sector as a whole requires reduced input of factors of production from other sectors. This means that the other sectors have reduced funds for the purchase of the output of the sector in question. So technical progress threatens crises of overproduction or under-consumption disrupting the harmonious reproduction and expansion of the system.[2]

Competition-driven price reduction in the innovating sector can reduce the costs of their output to other sectors. So those other sectors need to sell less in order to purchase necessary inputs from the sector in question. But competition drives similar unplanned and unsynchronised pursuit of increased productivity and reduced costs in those other sectors themselves, increasing the likelihood of over-productive crisis for the system. Only rapid and continuous growth of the system as a whole can counteract such tendencies, with the expansion of the scale of production in innovating sectors compensating for the reduction in inputs produced by innovation. But such growth has its own problems, which only intensify the longer the period of growth in question.

The business cycle

As businesses hurry to acquire new and more productive technology, the producer-goods sector acquires more workers and raw materials to satisfy the demand. More employment means more demand for consumer goods, more employment in the consumer-goods sector and so on, as a positive multiplier of growth drives the economy. Competition for resources, including labour and raw materials, forces up their prices, eating into profits. And as all businesses become equipped with the new technology, demand for such producer goods falls sharply; workers are laid off in the sector producing such goods and so on in a negative multiplier of economic contraction.

Throughout most of its history the capitalist world economy has been subject to a succession of business cycles, reflecting the turnover time of significant items of fixed capital, only ever approaching anything close to full employment at the height of the boom. The rest of the cycle, particularly the depths of the downturn, has been

characterised by high levels of unemployment. Disruption of reproduction and expansion of the system of production has created problems for owners and controllers of capital, as some businesses have
collapsed and others struggled to stay afloat. But the great majority
of real victims have been working people without any property or
savings to cushion them. And without adequate welfare provision,
unemployed workers have been threatened with destitution, starvation and disease.

The worse the bargaining position (due to excess labour supplies
competing for limited jobs) of those who still do have work, the
greater the social class inequality produced, as employers and owners
appropriate an increasing share of social surplus (produced by greater
labour time and effort). And with social wealth increasingly concentrated in the hands of a few, the greater the demand for expensive
luxuries, at the expense of basic necessities for all. More and more
resources go into mansions, private hospitals and petrol-guzzling
sports cars. Fewer and fewer resources go into basic subsistence,
health and education for the majority.

Limited purchasing power means that the majority can only
choose cheap goods. In a competitive market this typically means
goods produced with little consideration for the pay and conditions
of workers, of the long-term sustainability of the production process,
or durability or safety of the products. Workers simply cannot afford
to pay for such 'luxuries'.

Concessions in the form of increased political-legal rights and
powers achieved by workers in the boom are withdrawn in the slump.
And increasing poverty and inequality foster political tension and
instability, and encourage increasing repression of the 'have-nots'
by ruling classes fearful of revolt. This means the steady erosion or
complete abolition of democratic rights and practices.

Orthodox theory emphasises the supposedly self-correcting character of the business cycle, with the downturn itself paving the way
for a new upturn, without 'external' political intervention. Scientific
progress ensures the availability of new and more productive technology. And at some point wages and interest rates fall sufficiently
to motivate new investment, to realise the possibilities of the new
technologies in a new period of economic growth. But this radically
neglects the suffering of working people in the downturn. And, as
Keynes showed, the theory provides no real basis for expecting any

such inevitable recovery. Without appropriate political intervention, the crisis can merely deepen.

Limits to growth

Nor is it only declining demand for producer goods (and limits to workers' consumption) that creates an inbuilt limit to growth. Other markets can also become saturated, with the satisfaction of short- to medium-term demand. There are limits to how many consumer durables (how many cars, washing machines, vacuum cleaners, computers, etc), how much food or electricity each household can be persuaded to purchase, and how much built-in obsolescence companies can get away with. Industries thus reach a steady state, as 'mature' industries with fixed levels of consumption of their products and comparatively low profit rates – unless monopoly pricing and supply restrictions can keep prices and profits up. Here, indeed, is a major motivation for the formation of monopoly pricing agreements.

Growth requires increased inputs to the production process and not all such input costs can be continuously kept in check by productivity gains. At some point increased pressure on non-renewable natural resources registers in massive cost increases. This consideration is particularly relevant today, at a time of increasing environmental overload and depletion of resources. Soil, usable land surface, accessible fresh water and fishing stocks are all running out, along with oil and mineral supplies.

It's also true that near-full employment produced by the long-term expansion of the system increases the bargaining power of workers with bosses competing for scarce labour and workers demanding ongoing wage increases. Only continuous productivity gains can prevent real wage increases eating into profits. And there are always limits to such innovation.[3]

Here again we can foresee political intervention – on behalf of the employing and owning class as a whole – to end such full employment and recreate a reserve army of unemployed people – through increased interest rates, for example, in order to reduce the power, wages and conditions of the working population and restore profitability. As in a 'normal' business cycle downturn, lots of smaller, weaker businesses collapse. But the more powerful can survive and prosper, on the basis of renewed subservience of the workforce, forced into longer hours, worse conditions and lower wages. Such recessions, whether natural or induced, accelerate the concentration and centralisation of capital, promoting monopoly and oligopoly.

Monopoly and oligopoly

As Adam Smith emphasised, the trend towards competitive price and profit reduction drives a corresponding tendency towards collusion and monopoly price fixing between different producers within a sector. Business leaders from competing firms secretly negotiate together to agree on a profit-maximising price and output level of their product, dividing the market between them. The creation of such monopoly power allows producers to regulate output so as to maximise profits. This will typically mean restriction of output (and increase in prices), meaning wastage of increasing quantities of resources, including human labour power. And such wastage is exacerbated by individual corporations' ongoing investment in new, unutilised technology as protection in face of resurgent competition.

Restriction of output leaves workers without employment which intensifies the radical power imbalance in wage negotiations between workers and big monopsony corporations. Monopoly profits are still restricted by the total amount of surplus product. And bigger profits for the monopoly sector mean smaller profits for the non-monopoly sectors that have to pay monopoly prices for their inputs.

Periodic economic downturns, exacerbated by debt and multiplier effects, as well as policy-induced recessions, can be expected to accelerate tendencies towards concentration and centralisation of capital, as typically larger enterprises, with higher profit margins due to scale economies, are able to 'weather the storm' and acquire the resources and markets of smaller competitors driven out of business by the profit squeeze. To the extent that some level of consumption is maintained through the use of savings and credit, even as wages and profits are squeezed, falling costs, including labour costs, and new innovations can pave the way for such survivors to preside over a new period of growth, on the basis of further concentrated monopoly power.

New businesses, perhaps with new ideas and technologies, find it increasingly difficult to enter particular industries. As Stilwell points out, this is because of 'the inherent difficulties of establishing sufficiently large productive capacity or because the collusive practices of existing firms (sometimes involving government co-operation) impose substantial barriers to entry'.[4] And new businesses perceived as a threat can be destroyed by temporary price reductions on the part of the established players, or simply be bought out by them, with their new technologies suppressed. Thus, productive resources, including human skills and ideas, are further wasted and demand and output is further restricted. Increasing stagnation takes the place of growth and development.

In practice, with the top 200 multinationals producing one-third of total world output of commodities and conducting two-thirds of international 'trade'[5], markets are far from the sort of freely competitive markets of neoclassical theory.[6] Neoclassical theorists themselves bemoan a situation where 'a small minority of giant firms dominate the market place such that small producers feel relatively powerless'[7], where oligopolists 'generally prefer to collude than compete on prices, keep prices high and stable as long as conditions allow, drive out or vigorously resist entry of new competitors' and 'manage the media, public opinion and government contacts to resist any restriction on their operations'.[8]

Powerful monopolistic and oligopolistic corporations operate in ways completely at odds with the orthodox model of free markets sustaining consumer sovereignty, competitive productivity increases and cost minimisation to consumers. Such monopolies and oligopolies 'use their power over economic resources to suppress socially beneficial innovation' (to protect established investments), to control consumption through extensive advertising and marketing, 'to limit the freedom of entry of new firms' (temporarily dropping their prices to put newer, weaker entrants out of business, before raising prices again to recoup their losses once the newcomers are eliminated), and 'to influence government policy to serve their interests at the expense of other community concerns'.[9]

Behind the protective barriers of such monopoly pricing arrangements, forms of organisation far removed from traditional ideas of entrepreneurial and managerial efficiency develop and flourish. Empirical investigation shows that large corporate bureaucracies in the English-speaking world are actually 'patrimonial' rather than 'pure' bureaucracies, the latter being built upon competence and integrity. Rather than legalistic objectivity, impartiality and separation of offices from persons, they are actually built upon those lower down the line currying favour with powerful officials up the line, and those at the top being insulated from day-to-day stress and from the consequences of their own decisions.

As big corporations utilise their surplus profits to diversify into other industries and other territories, their own planning increasingly undermines free-market relations. And as their investment flows to wherever costs can be minimised through access to cheap labour and raw materials and maximum cost externalisation, they drive an 'international race to the bottom' in terms of wages, conditions and government revenue (as corporate tax rates are forced down and corporate welfare forced up), which itself threatens renewed crises of under-consumption as the effective demand of working people and of governments declines. Inequality within and between countries intensifies as a result of such corporate globalisation.

Natural monopolies

Under certain conditions, a free competitive market is not actually the most efficient, even in neoclassical terms. Shutt explains:

> This applies in particular to those sectors of the economy requiring substantial investment in infrastructure networks – such as trunk roads, railways, water supplies, energy distribution and telecommunications. For in such cases the creation of competing networks has generally been shown to be uneconomic because of the need to undertake double or treble the amount of capital expenditure to provide a service which can quite easily be supplied from a single network – a consideration which until the 1980s was reflected in the general acceptance that such public services were *natural monopolies*. Likewise in the case of industries, such as manufacture of defence equipment, serving a very limited market (often comprising only their own national governments) but requiring massive investment in research and development as well as fixed capital, it is clearly highly inefficient to require competitive bids.[10]

As long as such monopolies are government controlled, cost-saving can be passed on to the public with limited monopoly profits available to subsidise public services. But with the neo-liberal demand for privatisation in the name of 'market choice' and 'efficiency', such monopolies are handed over to direct increasing monopoly profits to a minority of super-wealthy shareholders and executives (with little effort to develop future services), or attempts are made to introduce 'competition' through wasteful duplication of infrastructure that similarly pushes up costs to the public.

In the past, company use of such resources as telephone lines has subsidised public access. This created an incentive for major private users to take control of such resources and force the public to subsidise corporate use of them. As Stillwell points out, application of 'competition policy' to public utilities has led to the 'relinquishment of community service obligations that previously guided the behaviour of the public enterprises'.[11] Dividends and executive salaries are maximised at the expense of updating infrastructure, leading to shortages and breakdowns such as have been experienced since the 1990s in various places, including California and New Zealand.[12]

We need to be cynical about the real reasons for such privatisation, considering the incredible political and economic power associated with control of such crucial elements of infrastructure, especially considering the inevitable pressure on state provision of public health and education with the removal of direct subsidies from such state monopolies. This is all the more important given the ongoing pressure for further reductions of company taxation in a world of internationally mobile big capital.[13]

Keynes analysis

Neoclassical theory assumed that the costs incurred in the production of goods provide the funds for purchase of such goods; supply creates its own demand. Through paying their costs of production, including wages, salaries, rent, supplies and raw materials and interest on loaned funds, along with profit as income to the owners of the firm, businesses put into circulation the funds for purchase of their products. And such purchase then gives them back the funds to continue the next cycle of production – with a similar level of output. So if a particular national economy starts from a position of full employment, it will tend to remain in such a situation as workers are kept on or rehired from one cycle to another. At the same time, it was assumed that the system could accommodate increased demand for employment, providing workers were prepared to accept wage reductions in line with the declining marginal productivity of labour.

But for the cycle of production and consumption to continue, people must spend, in the aggregate, all of their income. And this cycle is therefore threatened by leakages in the form of savings, imports and taxes. Imports can be offset by exports (we earlier noted reasons to expect such a balance), and the government uses its tax income to pay for goods and services. It was also assumed that the rate of interest would always balance savings and investment.

People prefer present to future consumption so they need interest to motivate savings. The higher the interest rate the more people will be prepared to save. The lower the interest rate, the cheaper would be investment, and the more investment entrepreneurs would be prepared to undertake. If savers couldn't find sufficient investment to absorb all the funds they want to save, they will bid the interest rate down. If investors can't find sufficient savings to finance the investment they want to make, they will bid up the interest rate. So competition equalises saving and investment.

Keynes decisively rejected the idea that supply automatically creates its own demand. Instead, he argued that demand creates supply in the sense that 'supply will follow aggregate demand if it can'.[14] If goods remain unsold in warehouses and shops, indicating production above demand, producers will cut back supply to follow demand downwards. If the rate of sales is higher than the rate of production, producers will increase supply to follow demand upwards. But if the productive resources of a society are already 'fully and efficiently' employed, aggregate demand above such 'full employment GDP' will create 'demand-pull inflation' as prices are pushed up by employers competing for limited productive resources and consumers compete for limited goods and services.

If, as a result of private productive initiatives, aggregate demand is insufficient to ensure full employment, with people able and willing to work but unable to find jobs, then government has the ability and the responsibility to use its spending and taxation powers to increase aggregate demand to allow such people to be employed. If demand-pull inflation is causing social problems then the government can use such power to reduce aggregate demand.

Keynes rejected the idea that if a capitalist economy started from a situation of full employment then the rate of interest would automatically equate saving and investment to keep aggregate demand equal to aggregate supply. He argued that the level of aggregate income was more important in determining the amount of saving than the rate of interest. And the interest rate was the price that equalised supply of and demand for money, rather than the product of interaction of saving and investment.[15]

He saw the trend of consumption and saving as determined by levels of income with high and increased income leading to more saving. And the rate of interest was determined by the demand for, and supply of, money. Demand for money was determined by what Keynes called (a) the transaction motive – the need for cash to buy things; (b) the precautionary motive – the need for cash to be available in face of unforeseen emergency; and (c) the speculative motive. The speculative demand is crucially dependent on expectations of what will happen to the interest rate in the future. High interest rates generally discourage cash holding because few expect rates to increase in the future. But lower interest rates can encourage cash holdings, in the expectation of such rate rises in the future. This can lead to failure of businesses to sell their products, leading to reduced production and employment, further reduced consumption and deepening crisis.[16]

Further increased money supply, by the central bank or other lending authorities, could motivate more investment to stop a slide into recession. But Keynes highlighted the possibility that income could be so unevenly distributed, with the wealthy saving so much, and the full employment level of output and income so high, that saving and investment couldn't be equated no matter how low the interest rate sank. And pushing interest rates down very low could lead to further hoarding of cash in the expectation of future increases in interest rates.[17]

In this sort of situation, Keynes argued that depression or permanent high unemployment could be countered by the government borrowing the excess savings and spending the money on socially useful projects like schools, hospitals, parks and infrastructure, thereby bringing into use unutilised resources and maintaining full employment without increasing the capital stock to create consumption problems in the future.[18]

As Stillwell points out, far from 'crowding out' private initiatives, as neo-liberals argue, such government spending (in a recession) generally 'opens up further opportunities for private sector profits and capital accumulation'.[19] In the modern world, governments borrow on international money markets, where such borrowing typically makes little impact on the available funds. And, of course, governments and central banks typically aim to ensure low interest rates to try to reduce the impact of significant recession.

Military Keynesianism

The Great Depression of the 1930s appeared to provide massive confirmation of Keynes' ideas. In the USA, 85 000 businesses failed between 1929 and 1932, 5000 banks collapsed, stock values fell by US$68 billion, output of manufactured goods fell by nearly 50% with 12 million workers unemployed and a quarter of the population left without income. And with the crisis spreading around the world, orthodox economic responses – cutting back on corporate taxation, wages and government spending, including welfare spending – only worsened the situation.

Only massive government expenditure on war pulled the United States, Britain and Germany out of the depression, and subsequent government (counter-cyclical) demand management played a part in maintaining low rates of unemployment throughout the post-war boom period.

But other forces also contributed to this unprecedented period of growth from the 1940s to the 1970s. Substantial productivity gains were achieved through civil applications of military technology rapidly developed in World War II, and the war itself generated massive reconstruction demand to rebuild and repair the damage it had caused.

Keynesians argued that government could pay back the money it borrowed in the slump through increased taxation in the boom. But, in practice, with powerful resistance to increased company taxation, Keynesian policies tended to lead to ever-increasing government debt (at federal, state and local level). And all too much of government spending to maintain aggregate demand has remained military spending, particularly in the USA. As Hunt points out, such military spending suits rich and powerful corporate interests because it stimulates aggregate demand without redistributing income from rich to poor.

As noted earlier, the capital goods sector is the most volatile and crisis prone, and military spending keeps it operating without increasing its productive capacity (and creating future demand problems).

Military spending provides a solid core of demand for the output of big corporations effectively outside of market competition and sale. Military technology sustains imperialism, providing cheap labour and raw materials and monopoly markets for corporations overseas. Arms exports bring further wealth to the developed economies while reducing the economic development of potential overseas competitors – whose resources go into destruction rather than production. And an ideology of militarism – with ongoing external threat – generally keeps workers at home in docile support of big business.[20]

Such militarism, particularly in the US, keeps the world on the brink of, or actually involved in, warfare. And increasing debt as the basis of economic development creates the possibility of economic collapse more serious than the Great Depression that generated Keynesian ideas and policies. History shows just how disastrous militarism combined with depression is likely to be for civilisation.

The end of the post-war boom

All of the long-term limits to growth considered so far seem to have played a part in the end of the boom from the later 1960s. Post-war reconstruction of the developed world was completed, with infrastructure renewed, and markets for a range of new consumer durables were saturated. The new war-time productive and distributive technologies had permeated the system with nothing radically new to replace them. And with full employment, an end to significant productivity gains and continuous, albeit relatively low, inflation, workers' pay demands and accelerating raw material input costs seriously threatened the continued profitability of capitalist enterprise.

Full employment and welfare protection in the boom had strengthened the organisations of the working class and stimulated workers' expectations of further political economic gains. In this connection, Andrew Glyn notes that in the 1970s:

> ... budget discipline was breaking down as demands for rising public spending ran well ahead of political capacity to levy high taxes and the inflation resulting from conflict between workers and employers was accommodated with lavish doses of money and credit. Employers were under pressure to accede to more stringent limits on their ability to hire and fire whilst the growth of the welfare state tempered the impact on workers of market forces; further incursions

into management prerogatives to allocate capital where and when they liked were threatened.[21]

This was the environment that nurtured the neo-liberal reaction, starting with big interest rate hikes by Margaret Thatcher's conservative government in the UK and Paul Volker's Federal Reserve in the US, supposedly to protect currency values and squeeze out inflation. With fiscal policies of government budget deficit reduction, such increased interest rates actually functioned to produce recession and unemployment, with official unemployment levels around the western world up from less than 5% in the late 1970s to over 10% by the mid-80s. The sacrifice of whole strata of typically smaller business operations was taken to be a price worth paying in order to recreate a 'reserve army' of unemployed workers to weaken working-class organisation and power and keep up continuous pressure on the wages and conditions of those still employed.

Simplistic attacks on Keynes' ideas argued that the 'stagflation' of the mid-1970s to mid-80s refuted his basic theory. The argument was that the observed coexistence of stagnation and unemployment with high levels of inflation refuted Keynes' claim of an inverse relationship between the two. But Keynes had actually identified such a relationship only between cyclical unemployment – due to inadequate aggregate demand – and demand-pull inflation, due to excess demand. As Robin Hahnel points out, this still allows for the possibility of demand-pull inflation coexisting with structural unemployment – 'where the skills and training of people in the labour forces don't match the jobs available'. And cost-push inflation, due to rising wage and/or profit demands driving increasing sale prices for goods, can coexist with significant unemployment.[22]

Milton Friedman and others argued that Keynes' ideas motivated governments to pump money into the economy in excess of its 'natural' growth capacity. This inevitably produced inflation (with more funds chasing the same limited supply of goods) eating into the real value of workers' wages. This, in turn, motivated increased wage demands, leading to runaway cost-push inflation. This feedback had to be stopped by radical cutbacks in the money supply. Such was the ideological justification for interest rate-induced recession and mass unemployment.

Keynes was declared to be well and truly dead, with inflation

– rather than unemployment – identified as the major enemy of civilisation, and, indeed, the cause of all economic problems, including unemployment. Government deficit spending was identified as first cause of such inflation and was outlawed in favour of budget balancing. Here privatisation of valuable government-controlled productive assets simultaneously contributed to short-term debt reduction and to the (supposed) extension of free market forces.

Friedman argued that the cause of the Great Depression was actually a sudden and severe collapse in money supplies due to a chain reaction of commercial bank failures. Money supply failed to keep pace with the growth of the economy. The moral was taken to be the need to keep money supplies growing in tandem with the 'natural' growth rate of the economy. Of course, there remain the questions of why such banks collapsed and why governments allowed such collapses to proliferate and impact so disastrously on production.

Since the 1980s, following neo-liberal demands for balanced budgets, governments have, to some extent, reduced their indebtedness in the short term by selling off profitable state enterprises (developed with taxpayers' money) to private ownership and cutting back on social welfare spending. Quite apart from the intrinsically bad social consequences of such actions – in terms of worsening conditions for poorer people, forced to pay more for basic services – this has also led to accelerated private borrowing to sustain consumption, while loss of income from the profits of government instrumentalities threatens higher government debt and further reduced welfare – or higher taxes – in the future.

Neo-liberal regimes have continued to rely on interest rate manipulations to try to achieve growth without inflation. This means cutting back on investment whenever the economy threatens to get near to (genuine) full employment of labour and other resources. And deregulated bank lending can still threaten demand-pull inflation. A major problem here is that when the interest rate is increased to cut back inflation, so does this cut back on income and profits needed to service expanding private debt. Homes are lost and businesses collapse. This problem is exacerbated in that all the new money created to sustain economic growth is created as debt by private banks, rather than through direct government action. Repayment of such debt eats into wages and profits – and future capacity for continued expansion.

Deepening debt crisis

Recent history suggests that neo-liberal policies which increase inequality, with stagnant wages and limited productive innovation, can maintain sales and profits, growth and jobs only by provision of easy credit, to sustain high enough levels of consumption, leading to increasing levels of debt. Deregulation of banking operations has opened the way to such easy credit, with banks creating ever more new money in the form of loans.

With house prices in particular increasing due to increased debt-driven demand, and heavy marketing of credit cards with high interest rates, there is a trend towards exponential growth of such debt. Default on a large scale becomes increasingly likely, and governments and central banks are in a serious dilemma. If they try to reduce borrowing by pushing up interest rates and curbing lending, they produce large-scale default, triggering economic crisis through rapidly declining consumption, investment, jobs, wages, profits and so on. If they keep interest rates low or further reduce them, borrowing and asset prices continue to inflate, making the eventual collapse all the more profound. So far they have – generally – followed the latter course of continued credit provision.

Just as national economies are increasingly driven by the accumulation of unpayable consumer debt, it is unpayable US private and government debt which is driving the continued growth of the world economy – such as it is. Ever since the US dollar replaced gold as the global reserve currency, the US has increasingly paid for its imports by printing treasury bills as bank money rather than actually selling exports of its own. The phenomenal growth of the Chinese economy – the only country achieving significant growth in recent years – has centred largely on sales to the US, which now imports half as much again as it exports, producing a trade deficit of 7% of national output. China and Japan finance their own exports to the USA out of their own trade surpluses to the tune of US$321 billion and US$640 billion of US treasury bonds held by these nations in 2006.

As Ann Pettifor points out, the US can, in theory, reduce or cancel its debts by printing more money and lowering the value of the dollar as reserve currency, or by threatening to do so, and thereby lowering the value of the dollar in international currency markets. In 2003–04

US authorities allowed the dollar to devalue to a limited extent to try to reduce debt and improve export performance. This devalued the treasury bills held by foreigners. At the same time it reduced the cost of US assets to overseas purchasers, accelerating such foreign takeover, with an increasing proportion of profits generated by such assets moving overseas.[23]

The powerful foreign creditor nations' relationship to the United States debt is similar, in crucial respects, to national governments' relationships to their own citizens' personal debt. If such creditor nations allow significant devaluation of the US dollar, their own (massive) dollar holdings are correspondingly devalued, with their own currencies increased in value relative to the dollar, and the US can no longer afford to import from them. But if they resist it, then US deficits continue to increase, creating still greater problems in the future. Here again, as with national governments, such creditors have adopted the course of continued cheap credit provision. As fearful private investors have pulled out of US bond markets, overseas central banks have stepped in, buying hundreds of billions of dollars worth of US treasury bills with their own taxpayers' money, to prop up the value of the US dollar. Thus, as Pettifor points out, money flows from where it is scarce to where it is plentiful, from poor to rich.

Inequality and efficiency

Free marketeers tend to emphasise the importance of short-term wealth creation per se, in terms of increased output of commodities, without reference to the nature of the goods produced (whether they are land mines, medical equipment or GE foods), to the distribution of such goods (whether they are distributed equally to all or concentrated in the hands of a few) or to the long-term sustainability of such production processes. As long as buyers are found for an increasing output of commodities, the economy is considered to be 'healthy'.

There are grounds for believing that capitalist market relations, and capitalist corporations, left to themselves, tend to produce dangerous, shoddy and unnecessary output, including wasteful luxuries (like SUVs and spa baths), weaponry and massive pollution. They tend to concentrate wealth in the hands of a few to maintain demand for such luxuries while leaving the majority with only subsistence or below-subsistence income, able to buy only cheap and shoddy goods.

And they encourage the rapid depletion rather than conservation of non-renewable resources. Certainly, recent decades of relatively unfettered capitalist market operations provide ample verification of these ideas.

A major consideration here is the need to maintain share values and dividends to share owners. Improving workers' wages and conditions or developing long-term sustainable technologies are likely to absorb available surplus in the medium term, leading to reduced dividends, falling share prices and the threat of takeover and asset stripping. So while it is true that big corporations are in a position to engage in effective long-term planning, so is it true that if they are publicly listed, they have to maintain high levels of profit in order to remain in operation. The market simply doesn't allow substantial wage increases and sustainable technologies without government intervention.

Inefficient share markets

Efficient share markets are supposed to respond to the real profit potential of productive enterprises. The collective expectations of stock market investors are supposed to be 'accurate predictions of the future prospects of companies', with share prices 'fully reflecting all information relevant to the future prospects of traded companies' and changes in share prices therefore 'entirely due' to changes in such relevant information.[24] And neo-liberal orthodoxy sees attempted external 'regulation' – putting restrictions on share sales – as undermining such efficient operation.

Good corporate prospects are therefore reflected in increased demand for shares which pushes such share prices up. Thus, accurate asset values are maintained, and managers can be motivated to still greater heights of performance through offers of stock options. Booming share values inspire confidence, making it easier for 'successful' corporations to raise capital through loans or further share offerings. Sales and falling values of shares in a poorly managed enterprise allow new owners to sack inefficient boards and start afresh. Falls in share values below the company's asset values provide a strong motivation for asset stripping takeover, allowing such resources to be put to better use elsewhere.

However, there are good grounds for arguing that, in reality, share markets never have and never could actually operate in this fashion; that Keynes 'beauty contest' model actually provides a much more accurate picture of the essential irrationality of all such markets. As Eatwell and Taylor explain, the contest he had in mind was one run by British newspapers in the 1930s where:

> ... readers were asked to rank pictures of young women in the order they believed would correspond to the average preferences of the other respondents as a whole. So, in order to win, the player should not express his or her own preference, nor even try to estimate the genuine preferences of average opinion. Instead, the successful player should anticipate 'what average opinion expects average opinion to be'. In the same way, the key to success in the financial markets [including money and foreign exchange markets, as well as markets for stocks and bonds] is not what the individual investor considers to be the virtues or otherwise of any particular financial asset, nor even what the mass of investors actually believe are virtues of that financial asset. The successful investor is concerned to establish what everyone else in the market will believe everyone believes.[25]

This can mean paying attention to what are conventionally taken to be 'fundamental' forces shaping company performance, rather than the actual forces. As Eatwell and Taylor explain, 'so long as the market follows what average opinion believes average opinion to be, then anyone who bucks the trend will lose money'.[26] This is because conventional or average opinion is self-fulfilling. Stocks the majority believe will increase in value will do so, as the majority rush to acquire them. Stocks they believe will fall will do so as they rush to unload them.

Convention is vulnerable to 'fashions' which can themselves change rapidly, leading to wild fluctuations in asset values, with incompetently run and criminal operations rising and falling along with the competent. Even where such 'herd behaviour' keeps markets stable for long periods, such stability still contains the seeds of its own destruction. Where the stock markets are rising rapidly it becomes the convention that they will continue to rise. The longer such a process continues, the bigger the inevitable 'correction', as all ultimately rush to unload their overvalued stocks. And the social consequences of mass business collapse and rationalisation (or mass devaluation of workers' pension funds) resulting from such falling share prices can be terrible indeed. All of these considerations apply equally to 'free' unregulated international currency markets, as determinants of floating exchange rates. In this case, the threat is sudden and massive devaluation of particular currencies as a result of speculative fashions, fads, prejudices and bubbles.

Insider trading

Separation of ownership and control in big public corporations creates a situation where large numbers of owners with relatively small shareholdings are without either any clear idea of how efficiently such corporations are being run, and/or without effective means of doing anything to improve a situation of inefficiency – or criminality in corporate management.

This inherent 'asymmetry of information' between the majority of shareholders (investors in mutual funds, bondholders, pensioners) on the one side and managerial 'insiders' on the other provides the basis for substantial gains through 'insider trading'. Here, the insiders cash in on the fact that they are privy to information which, when more widely available, will significantly change share prices, but which is not currently reflected in such prices. With prior knowledge of impending share price increases due to takeovers or technological breakthroughs, they acquire big blocs of the shares in question, selling them later at the new, increased price. With prior knowledge that particular share values will fall in the future, the insiders can sell at current higher values, handing on the future losses to others.

As noted in previous chapters, some neo-liberals and neoclassical welfare economists have tried to defend insider trading or argue for market regulation of such activity rather than legal intervention on grounds that (a) there are no real victims, and/or (b) 'it tends to make stock less volatile, and therefore, on average, higher priced'[27] and (c) 'the cost of information acquisition by stockholders is reduced and therefore stockholders are better off'.[28]

In fact, the shareholders who sell their shares to the insider who knows of an immanent increase in value of such shares clearly lose out on such increased value, as do other possible purchasers. If party A informs party B in confidence that they intend to take over another corporation, and party B (or an agent for party B) then acquires substantial stock in the target corporation, then party A could end up paying more for the company in question as a result of B's purchases

pushing up the share price. B has betrayed A's confidence, and profited through such betrayal.

The information acquisition argument is based on the idea that
some can read the signs of insider trading and get out before disaster
strikes or get in while there are still some gains to be made from future
price increases without having to pay for specialist advice. But others
will, inevitably, not be able to read the signs or take action until the
'horse has well and truly bolted'. After all, insider traders often try
to cover their tracks by buying and selling through other people. And
it's far from clear why the lion's share of gains should be appropriated by such privileged insiders and the bulk of losses handed on to
others, especially where these people already enjoy great wealth and
privilege.

The volatility argument recognises some of the earlier points
about herd behaviour, convention and contagion, and therefore is an
implicit criticism of the whole institution. At the same time, so does
it contradict the 'free information' argument, since it recognises that
some will inevitably be slower to respond to the signs (of insider trading) and will therefore miss out.[29]

Economic analysis of law again

It should by now be clear why we need to be sceptical of neoclassical ideas of the efficiency of private negotiation, supported only by
standard civil and criminal law, in dealing with externality issues.
Currently it is big corporations and their major shareholders and
officers who are the principal perpetrators and beneficiaries of toxic
pollution and environmental destruction, and large numbers of
poorer people who are its major victims. The transaction costs of
effective action (including prohibitively expensive legal fees) on the
part of the individuals concerned to protect themselves are potentially
very significant. It's difficult to imagine neo-liberal governments ever
giving such poor people genuinely effective property rights to clean
air, water, earth and food. And as EK Hunt points out, to give any
such pollution rights to polluters to continue to pollute, while forcing victims to negotiate for lower levels of pollution, is to encourage
pollution and harm maximisation by those with the rights in order to
maximise their returns from pollution reduction.[30]

The assumption of the economic analysis of law is that victims will only be able and willing to bribe polluters to reduce their pollution if such pollution impinges upon their own wealth-generating activities. If they can afford to compensate the polluters with an amount equal to or greater than profits lost by pollution reduction, while themselves still managing to make enough profit to stay in business after such payment (or make a profit greater than the reduced level of profit with the pollution), then such bribery creates an 'efficient' solution. But this effectively leaves everyone other than profit-making businesses, and every consequence of pollution other than easily measurable loss of revenue in the short term, completely out of consideration.[31]

Quite apart from the issue of transaction costs for numerous (typically poor and isolated) victims of pollution – spread out over potentially huge reaches of time and space – there are also issues of difficulty of tracking such pollution to its source, of interaction of different pollutants, of proving causation in law and of the futility of compensation for death, untreatable cancers and birth defects. Any responsible polity will act to stop such pollution at source before the (irreversible) damage is done. And it is perfectly obvious that the threat of civil litigation has radically failed to protect people in the past.

The inadequacies of the Pareto principle as an efficiency measure have frequently been pointed out. As Hahnel says, 'most policy choices will make some people better off but others worse off, and in these situations, the Pareto criterion has nothing to tell us'.[32] What it does tell us is that a development which makes a handful of people massively better off in monetary terms while bringing no change for the majority will be an efficiency gain for orthodox theory. But, in fact, such increased inequality will actually have a host of disastrous consequences for the majority in terms of increased mortality, morbidity, violent crime, mistrust and loss of social cohesion.

Serious consideration of the 'efficiency criterion' only goes to show the significant divergence of marginal private and social costs and benefit curves in many industries, with higher social costs and lower social benefits showing the ubiquity of externalities, and the requirement for significantly lower levels of output to achieve socially optimal levels of output and consumption. And Whitman highlights the ethically compromised 'subjectivist' foundation of his position when he says, in respect of compensation for the 'losers', that in 'a large society ... it is impossible to identify and compensate all the losers ... ... it is costly, if not impossible, to discover people's true preferences'.[33]

Cost benefit analysis

In the real world of capitalist market relations – as opposed to the models of law and economics theorists – corporations (or rather directors and managers, sheltering behind the 'corporate veil') perform cost benefit analyses all the time. As Joel Bakan points out, such analyses 'are at the heart of corporate decision-making'.[34] But far from utilitarian concerns for 'the common good', the issue is solely that of the financial good of the corporation itself, understood first and foremost as the interest of corporate shareholders (or of the managers).

> The corporation's institutional makeup, its [legal and practical] compulsion to serve its own financial interests above everything else, requires executives to make only those decisions that create greater benefits than costs for their corporations.[35]

Harm to others, 'workers, consumers, communities, the environment'[36], figure in the equation in terms of expected monetary costs incurred through application of existing criminal and civil law: penalties for breaches of health and safety or pollution-control regulations, and compensation payouts to victims resulting from civil litigation. This includes the cost accorded by the legal system to such externalities as lost human lives, horrific injuries and significant environmental degradation. Over the years, such cost benefit analyses have had terrible consequences. Bakan considers the 'General Motors (GM) fuel tanks' case in 1993, involving horrific burns to a woman (Patricia Anderson) and her children due to dangerous placement of the fuel tank in her Chevrolet Malibu.

> The evidence in the trial showed that General Motors had been aware of the possibility of fuel-fed fires when it had designed the Malibu and some ... other models. Six fuel-fed fire suits had been filed against the company in the 1960s, twenty-five more in the early 70s, and in May 1972, a GM analyst predicted that there would be another 60 by the mid 70s. On June 6 1973, around the time GM began planning the ... Malibu that Patricia Anderson was driving, GM management asked a [company] engineer to analyse [such] fires in GM vehicles ... In his report, [he] multiplied the 500 fuel-fed fire

fatalities that occurred each year in GM vehicles by $200 000, his estimate of the cost to GM in legal damages for each potential fatality, and then divided that figure by 41 million, the number of GM vehicles ... on US highways. He concluded that each [such] fatality cost GM $2.40 per automobile ... The cost of [safer] fuel tanks [$8.59 per car] meant that the company could save $6.19 per [car] if it allowed people to die ... rather than alter the design ...[37]

The Los Angeles Supreme Court found that GM had dangerously positioned the fuel tanks to save costs and the jury awarded compensatory damages of $107 million and punitive damages of $4.8 billion. GM appealed to the California Court of Appeals, where the US Chamber of Commerce, 'a leading voice of big business'[38], described the previous jury decision as 'illegitimate' and argued that the kind of cost benefit analysis applied by GM was 'the hallmark of corporate good behaviour'.[39]

Even substantial legal payouts to victims and regulators appear to have failed to deter ongoing corporate wrongdoing – and social harm – on a huge scale. According to Bakan, 'corporate illegalities are rife throughout the economy. Many major corporations engage in unlawful behaviour, and some are habitual offenders with records that would be the envy of even the most prolific human criminals'.[40] General Electric, the world's largest corporation, was found guilty of 42 major legal breaches between 1990 and 2001, including repeated contamination of soil and water with highly toxic PCBs, defrauding government on defence contracts, violating worker safety rules, illegal sale of fighter jets to Israel, deceptive advertising, overcharges on mortgage insurance, safety violations at nuclear fuel plants and failure to properly test aircraft parts. Some of the fines were in the tens of millions of dollars, with one of US$2 billion.[41]

Bakan concludes:

> The corporation's unique structure is largely to blame for the fact that illegalities are endemic in the corporate world. By design, the corporate form generally protects the human beings who own and run corporations from legal liability, leaving the corporation, a 'person' with a psychopathic contempt for legal constraints, the main target of criminal prosecution. Shareholders cannot be held liable for the crimes committed by corporations because of limited liability ... Directors are traditionally protected by the fact that they have no direct involvement with decisions that may lead to a corporation's committing a crime. Executives are protected by the law's

unwillingness to find them liable for their companies' illegal actions unless they can be proven to have been 'directing minds' behind those actions. Such proof is difficult ... to produce in most cases, because corporate decisions normally result from numerous and diffuse individual inputs ...[42]

Even where directors have been found to have been the 'directing minds' for purposes of civil liability, this has typically rendered the corporation liable, rather than the directors themselves. And 'losses' in the form of compensation payouts have been readily passed on to insurers, the tax office and consumers. Furthermore, in recent times, in the area of the law of negligence, there has been an increasing push to restrict corporate liability, abolish punitive damages and radically limit payments to victims of injury and illness.

Everyone does not have equal access to legal resources. Corporate executives and other rich and privileged individuals can afford teams of skilled barristers, detectives and forensic scientists gathering and processing evidence, crowds of expert witnesses testifying for them, and access to the different quality of justice offered in the higher courts. Workers are now largely reliant on legal charity for the conduct of civil litigation. Members of the working class who fall foul of the criminal law are confined to brief chats with court-appointed solicitors and the summary justice of Magistrates Courts – without benefit of judge or jury.

To the extent that the law exists, essentially, to protect private property, its resources are disproportionately mobilised to protect the substantial property of the wealthy few, rather than the meagre property of the many poor. And it is law which defines property ownership (in terms of groups of rights of disposal, benefit and exclusion), identifying shareholders as owners of public corporations, for example, when it could conceivably identify the workers as owners of such corporations, and therefore responsible for appointing board members, or, as possessing equal rights to participate in such appointments along with shareholders – and perhaps local communities.

Competition policy

As noted in chapter 13, neo-liberal ideology supposedly supports legal enforcement of 'competition policy' aiming to try to correct what are seen as departures from 'perfect competition' and its 'inherent' efficiency. As Stillwell says, legislative restrictions and regulations have sought to preclude:

> ... anti-competitive agreements and exclusionary provisions, including primary and secondary boycotts; misuse of market power, such as charging excessively high prices; exclusive dealing, such as when a large firm insists that it's suppliers do not deal with other firms; resale price maintenance, whereby manufacturers insist on the price at which retailers sell their products; and mergers that have the effect of substantially lessening market competition.[43]

We saw how in Australia it was mainly the ACCC that was involved in enforcing such competition policy, including particularly prosecution of major price-fixing conspiracies. And we referred to recent success in the use of whistleblower evidence to mount prosecutions of power transformer and distribution transformer cartels, leading to record $35 million penalties against companies and senior executives.[44]

But such legal intervention has limitations, particularly in a relatively weak and dependent economy like Australia. When a handful of transnational corporations control 50% or more of world production and distribution in a range of important industries (oil-production and distribution, steel and aluminium production, car production, computer manufacture, food processing, laundry detergent manufacture, aircraft production and airline travel), they have great power to influence government policy.

In some countries this is a simple matter of 'buying' the politicians concerned with monetary bribes and other favours. In others it includes general media support – or withdrawal of such support – for particular parties and politicians, as well as more specific financial and media support for the election campaigns of such parties and politicians. Governments are dependent on such corporations to provide jobs and tax revenue. Members of government – or their associates – can be shareholders in such corporations and take up positions on their managing boards on retiring from politics.

Even if the will is there on the part of those formulating and enforcing legislation, it is seldom supported by anything like the resources necessary for effective action. There are substantial problems in acquiring legally acceptable 'evidence' of price fixing and misinformation and in mounting an effective prosecution when challenged at every step by the political, legal and media power of big corporations.[45]

At the same time, other neo-liberal policies work directly against any such law-driven return to 'perfect' free market competition. In particular, capital market deregulation around the world opens the way for takeover of all profitable local businesses, or effective competitors, by expanding multinational corporations. And privatisation of previously state-controlled monopolies can merely be a means to the creation of ruthless private monopolies.

International considerations

It's not difficult to see the problems with the orthodox neo-liberal ideology of international trade. As noted, in comparative advantage theory, mutual benefit depends on an appropriate exchange rate for the goods in question to allow for sharing of the productivity gains. In practice, power imbalances between nations and businesses allow big corporations and industrialised nations, as stronger parties, to appropriate the greater part of any productivity gains through control of such ratios.

The idea of a level playing field of international trade was always far from the reality. The industrialised nations have always had vastly superior infrastructure to sustain all kinds of production. They have had vastly larger capital markets to provide investment funds. And they have had much better access to advanced technology than any developing nations.

The original theoretical model involved capital mobility within a nation, to allow for investment to shift into goods of comparative advantage, maintaining jobs and wages in the territory concerned, but not mobility between nations, allowing capital to move wherever costs can be most effectively externalised.

Real world exchange depends on prices which don't necessarily reflect real cost as measured in expenditure of labour hours or any other inputs to production. Many developing countries have inherited from their colonial past economies built around raw materials production and export. This pattern has been re-enforced by IMF and World Bank pressure for numerous poor countries to maximise production of the same limited range of raw material exports in order to service debt, creating massive oversupply and competitive pressures that keep prices of such raw materials low in world markets.

The heavy dependence of such countries on industrially produced imports (including fertilisers, insecticides and medicines) puts further pressure on them to compete and to keep their own export prices low. Such industrially produced imports are typically the products of powerful oligopolies and monopolies in the developed world, restricting supply to keep prices high. To say that such a situation should continue in the name of comparative advantage is hardly acceptable.

Prices on world markets are also affected by radically different labour costs of different producers, determined in part by supply and demand conditions in local labour markets, rather than real productivity of labour. Agricultural revolution (including cash cropping and agribusiness based on the technology of the green revolution), population expansion and loss of farming land to big dam projects in the developing world, displacing subsistence farmers from the land have created huge reserves of excess labour, putting ongoing pressure on wages and conditions. This brings down the cost of production of goods by such labour without the requirement for high levels of real productivity.

Mobile capital now flows to these territories to take advantage of poor wages and working conditions. This is completely at odds with the idea of continued provision of jobs through the flow of investment within its 'home' territory.[46] And the bulk of what is called 'international trade' is now actually planned movement of goods within particular transnational corporate organisations – transfers between subsidiaries – with 'prices' determined as much by tax minimisation considerations (transfer pricing) as by productivity or real cost considerations.

Production 'cost' determined by prices of commodity inputs to the production process can radically misrepresent the real social costs of production to individuals, social groups and nation-states. The destruction of agricultural village life in the developing world to create cheap labour for industrial production and agribusiness typically has terrible social costs in terms of illness, destitution, crime and misery due to the breakdown of traditional social and material support systems. Addressing these issues – forcing purchasers of such labour to pay for compensatory health and welfare schemes as 'inputs' to production – would radically change market prices and 'comparative advantages'.

The concept of direct foreign investment (DFI) conjures up images of transfer of advanced technology from the developed world to create skills, jobs and new wealth in the developing world (so-called Greenfield investment). In fact, much DFI is simple purchase of profitable overseas businesses, followed by 'rationalisation' (including job loss) and subsequent repatriation of all profits to the investor's home territory, or purchase of valuable raw material assets which are simply pillaged at huge cost to local environments and ecosystems (public health, etc) without replacement or clean-up.

IMF and World Bank conditionalities, which can include devaluation of local currencies, supposedly to increase exports while reducing imports to stem the growth of debt and provide foreign currency for its repayment, make valuable local resources available to foreign purchasers at prices far below values, driving such looting and pillaging to still greater depths.

Decolonisation

We must remember that most of the poorest countries in the world today were until quite recently colonies of western imperial powers. Such colonial takeover meant destruction of indigenous industry to make way for manufactured imports from the colonial power, destruction of sustainable subsistence agriculture to make way for cash crops and mining operations to provide cheap raw materials to that power, and provision of infrastructure only for purposes of facilitating such import and export operations. Displaced indigenous people could then be forced to work in such plantations and mines in conditions close to slavery. Where feudal-style relations already existed, the westerners typically allied themselves with the landlord class. Elsewhere they built upon existing conflicts and antagonisms to create new local elites from particular tribal or ethnic groups in order to sustain divide-and-rule tactics, with other, disenfranchised groups focusing their hostility on the local elites rather than on the colonialists themselves.

At the end of World War II there were increasingly intense pressures for decolonisation. The United Nations provided an ideological foundation and forum for supporting such decolonisation. Western-educated elites within the occupied territories agitated for independence in anticipation that they would replace the foreign powers as ruling groups. In many areas the colonialists found themselves bogged down in increasingly costly and bitter struggles with guerrilla armies of national liberation. And colonial domination everywhere became increasingly less cost effective with pressures to improve the wages and conditions of indigenous populations.[47]

As we have seen, the favoured model in the west was one of sovereign states assisted by aid and loans to achieve a stable economic equilibrium with export of raw materials producing foreign exchange to allow for import of advanced producer goods to drive modernisation and industrialisation. Free trade, including increasing liberalisation of trade in such raw materials, was supposed to support the modernisation.

In fact, the newly independent territories in most cases lacked the infrastructure to support a modern sovereign state. They lacked any developed systems of roads, education, health, law and civil service. Inadequate pay for public officials encouraged widespread corruption. And there was no developed tax base to provide the funding to create any such infrastructure due to the low level of average wages and large proportion of economic activity carried on outside the organised economy. Because this left the territories massively dependent on overseas assistance, there are grounds for seeing decolonisation as simply a means of more cost-effective domination by the colonial powers, a way for such powers to continue to maintain their control in covert fashion, without the responsibilities associated with direct rule.[48]

The western ideology of free trade was belied by protection and subsidisation of both the agriculture and industry of the developed world, reducing markets for third-world exports and restricting the industrial development of the third world. Indeed, subsidised produce from the west was dumped in the developing nations to the massive detriment of indigenous producers. And protection of infant industries in the developing world was increasingly undermined by threats and bribes from the IMF and World Bank. As noted earlier, monopoly control of manufacturing industry in the west kept import prices high in the third world.

Valuable assets in the developing nations remained under the control of western corporations, with profits disappearing overseas. And wherever and whenever reforming regimes gained power in the third world with the aim of reclaiming such foreign-owned assets for the benefit of the people within the territories concerned, the United

States or other colonial powers would either invade the country or engineer a coup in the name of 'anti-communism' – through manipulation and support of local army units or other disaffected groups, killing the (often democratically elected) leaders and their supporters and establishing ruthless police-state dictatorships.

It is in this context that we must understand the interventions of the IMF, the World Bank and the WTO. All too often, ruthless and corrupt ruling groups utilised foreign aid and loans and pursued ongoing raw material exports, not to benefit their own populations but rather to acquire police-military technology to more effectively terrorise and repress such people, along with expensive foreign luxuries for their own consumption. And when these dictators were eventually removed or fled overseas, taking decades of aid and loan money with them, the burden of repayments fell on the very people who had suffered as their victims.

Neo-liberalism, monopoly power and externalities

Neo-liberals claim that decreasing regulation means increasing freedom of market relations where such freedom is seen as driver of efficiency. But, in fact, decreasing regulation actually fosters increasing monopoly and oligopoly power of big corporations, which undermines both free market operations and democratic politics. Indeed, there is substantial hypocrisy in neo-liberal lip service to free markets when neo-liberals in power have taken the lead in extending massive welfare payments (from tax revenues) to big corporations and extending tariff and quota protection for favoured national industries, particularly where such industries have backed their own political campaigns.

In the real world of twenty-first century capitalism, powerful monopolies and oligopolies control and restrict production so as to maximise their profits at the expense of consumers and workers denied employment by such restriction of output. Destruction of traditional employment and lack of investment in many areas create massive oversupply of labour, which, along with political restriction of workers' rights and powers of resistance, forces wages down below subsistence with no reference to real labour productivity.

Business leaders and orthodox economists try to justify US$1-a-day wages in their third-world operations, with six- and seven-day weeks of dawn-to-dusk labour, appalling working conditions and even child labour, on the grounds that any paid work is better than none. But it is they themselves who created the large-scale unemployment that they now exploit through their promotion of ill-conceived, debt-driven development programmes centred on export agribusiness, mining and big dam projects in the countries concerned, at the expense of traditional farmers thrown off their lands, and through their cheap and subsidised food exports to those countries, forcing small-scale farmers, who cannot compete, into bankruptcy. They refuse to consider the real alternatives of debt relief and land reform and small-scale sustainable technology in the interests of self-sufficiency, with the replacement of free trade by fair trade.

In this connection, the critics point to the much higher rates of growth, combined with low inflation, low unemployment and rising living standards of ordinary people achieved under a regime of regulated markets and substantial government intervention during the post-war boom period, compared to the achievements of the subsequent period of neo-liberal deregulation. As Susan George observes: 'Throughout the world, growth and development showed far greater gains between 1960 and 1980 than during the following twenty years from 1980 to 2000.'[49] And those developing countries which did continue to make significant progress both before and after 1980 (including Taiwan, South Korea and China) were characterised by well-constructed programmes of intervention and rejection of unregulated trade and investment.

The sort of outcomes which are actually achieved by unregulated markets – producing concentrated unaccountable corporate power, centralised decision-making without popular input, chronic unemployment, increasing casualisation and low and declining wages and conditions at the bottom, with rapidly growing executive salaries and unearned share income at the top – are directly antithetical to, rather than supportive of, democracy. Attempts to extend such market principles into public politics have disastrous consequences for democratic rights. And such unregulated markets are incapable, in the longer term, of achieving outcomes which are compatible with, or supportive of, a genuine or deep going democracy. On the contrary, the economic power of concentrated private wealth is inevitably used to subvert the democratic process.

Discussion topics

1. Are markets really efficient?
2. What is *the business cycle*?
3. Is monopoly inevitable?
4. Why did the post-war boom end?
5. What issues are raised by real-world corporate cost-benefit analysis?

Chapter 15

DISTRIBUTIVE JUSTICE AND ECONOMIC REFORM

Modern political and legal philosophy has followed Aristotle in seeing different theories of justice addressing different kinds of social practices. Theories of distributive justice concern the distribution of the benefits and burdens of social life across individuals and groups. Theories of retributive justice deal with the nature and justification of punishment. As political theorist Andrew Levine points out, the guiding idea for Aristotle, and for most subsequent researchers, has been that of 'treating like cases alike'. But there are many different ways in which such 'likeness' can be, and has been, understood.[1]

At first sight it might appear that it is the latter, retributive form of justice that is the main concern of law. But while criminal law is indeed concerned with issues of retribution, issues of distributive justice bear on virtually all areas of law. Corporations law, consumer law, employment law, tax law and tort law are built around ideas and assumptions concerning fair or just distribution of resources between individuals and social groups. And the day-to-day operation of these laws has profound implications for such distribution in contemporary society.

The actual distribution of benefits and burdens is particularly significant for criminal law, with higher levels of inequality significantly positively correlated with levels of violent crime around the world. Levels of social inequality also have profound implications for effective access to legal resources and influence on the law-making process.

Changes in dominant political ideology inevitably impact legislation, statutory interpretation and judicial decision-making. And a major change in such ideology in recent years with profound implications for law and society has been the increasing acceptance and attempted justification of increasing social inequality. This chapter explores, and refutes, the arguments offered in support of such increasing inequality.

Neo-liberalism and inequality

During the post-war boom, social liberal ideology identified significant inequality as a fundamental social problem which needed to be addressed by appropriate social policy intervention. Radical inequalities of social and political power, income, wealth and opportunity were seen as both unfair and unjust and as unacceptable in utilitarian terms, insofar as they contributed to (avoidable) mistrust and lack of social cohesion, to aggression, physical and mental illness, crime and conflict. It was also seen as possible to significantly reduce such inequality through social policies of redistribution and welfare, full employment and cheap housing.

As considered in earlier chapters, over the last thirty years, throughout the western world and beyond, the social democratic consensus has been replaced, as core ideology of major parties and directing force of government policies, by what has been called *economic rationalism*, neo-liberalism or the Washington Consensus. In the forefront of neo-liberal ideology is the prioritisation of individual freedom of choice, where such freedom is seen as maximised through the operation of free markets and business corporations, with a minimum of state intervention and regulation.

Rather than being identified as an ethical and practical problem, to be addressed by responsible social policy, significant inequality has come to be seen as an integral component of a just, efficient and prosperous society. Certain positions in society are seen as functionally more important than others. These more functionally significant social roles require special skills for their effective performance or are particularly demanding, difficult and stressful to perform, in part because of the great social responsibility associated with them.

In keeping with the centrality of free markets in neo-liberal ideology, such functional significance is understood primarily in terms of individual contribution to social wealth creation, measured by the market value of output. Greater wealth creation involves greater skill, training, effort, sacrifice, stress and responsibility, and needs to be rewarded accordingly. Only a limited number of individuals in any society have the innate talents that can be trained into the skills required – or the ambition, drive and commitment to undertake the appropriate training and responsibility.[2] Such training typically involves sacrifices on the part of those undergoing the training. And such positions involve greater responsibility and stress than is involved in less significant social roles.

In order to induce the talented persons to undergo these sacrifices, such positions must carry an inducement value in the form of disproportionate access to monetary payment, power and respect. At the other end of the scale, there will always be people who freely choose to renounce any such legitimate and socially useful striving in favour of sloth or crime. It is fair and socially functional that such individuals should reap the rewards of such free choices in terms of poverty, privation and punishment. As well as being 'just deserts' for those involved, so do such economic marginalisation and criminal retribution function to encourage others to do a better job.

Given that many talented or ambitious individuals work to give their children the best possible start in the world, it would be counterproductive to try to prevent them from bequeathing their own accumulated wealth to their families. Restriction of inheritance undermines the crucial functional role of differential reward. It is also unjust, insofar as 'genuine' ownership of such legitimate rewards integrally involves the owners' right to give them away to any other person of their choice.[3]

Free markets

Neoclassical welfare economics, as a central pillar of neo-liberal ideology, claims to show that, 'given competitive market conditions, utility-maximising consumers and profit-maximising entrepreneurs automatically act and interact so as to maximise social welfare'.[4] Free markets produce 'Pareto optimum' outcomes where 'no change in production and no additional amount of commodity exchange could make a single individual any better off without worsening the position of some other individual'.[5] Given any particular initial distribution of wealth, the free market ensures the achievement of the maximum possible level of welfare, as measured in terms of consumers' utilities, returns to capital and labour and rewards to entrepreneurs.

As outlined in chapter 13, market efficiency is understood in terms of firms combining the factors of production in the most cost effective ways, and consumers obtaining their products at the lowest possible costs, given existing technology. Competition promotes optimum entrepreneurial efficiency in organising the production process, innovation and specialisation supporting productivity increase, while keeping down prices to consumers.

New producers are attracted to areas of increasing demand where profits are higher than 'normal', thereby increasing output to meet such demand. But such increased output drives prices down, with excess profits eliminated, and lower efficiency firms forced out of the sector, to re-establish an equilibrium of supply and demand based on 'normal' equilibrium profits as minimum level of revenue above costs sufficient to motivate entrepreneurs to continue to conduct business.

Consumer purchasing decisions send signals to the producers as to which goods and services to continue supplying. Competition among such producers ensures that the prevailing market price is kept to a minimum.[6] It therefore generally makes sense, wherever possible, to shift provision of goods and services out of the regulated state sector and into the competitive private sector.

Assuming a fixed amount of capital for a firm in the short term, we can consider the consequences of varying the amount of labour employed and derive a schedule for the marginal product of labour – or the product added by an additional worker for each different level of employment. The assumption is that, beyond a point of maximum scale economies, such marginal product declines continuously as more labour is added. Given the money value of the marginal product of labour determined by labour productivity and market prices of goods, and the price of labour determined by the aggregate market for labour, an individual firm will maximise its profit by hiring labour up to the point where the marginal product of such labour is equal to the wage rate: where marginal revenue equals marginal costs. The same goes for capital. With a given amount of labour, we find a similarly declining marginal value product of capital, with profit maximisation where interest (as cost of capital) equals marginal value product of capital. This means that in a free market, in equilibrium, both workers and suppliers of capital are rewarded in proportion to their actual contribution to the value of the product.[7]

Greater value-creating-skills tend to be in limited supply because of the limited availability of relevant innate talents and the high levels of sacrifice and stress involved in acquiring or exercising them. Hence they will receive greater reward in a free market. Greater amounts of capital made available by particular individuals will receive greater rewards, reflecting the greater sacrifice involved in their provision, in terms of effort of acquisition and foregone consumption by the individuals concerned. So as well as being optimally efficient, free markets are also generally fair in their determination of returns to labour and capital.

The neo-liberal approach to human rights

Beyond core civil and political rights to life and property, to political participation and fair treatment in law, neo-liberals are generally hostile to the broad extension of human rights found in the Universal Declaration of Human Rights (UDHR).[8] They reject the idea of government responsibility for directly ensuring the realisation of economic, social and cultural rights to jobs, to education, to healthcare and to social security, insofar as these things are seen as most efficiently and most fairly acquired through free market transactions.[9] Government-financed provision of welfare services encourages sloth and wastefulness on the part of the recipients and can only be paid for by taxing effective wealth creation by others. This is seen as fundamentally unfair and unjust and as undermining property rights. Some work hard and see their legitimate rewards confiscated, some do nothing and receive expensive services for free.

Talented people are deterred from acquiring socially necessary skills or taking on necessary social responsibilities. Entrepreneurs are deterred from developing new technologies, new businesses and new jobs by high taxation of wealth, profits and income. Workers are deterred from hard work and thrift (providing savings to fund new investment) by access to free services. The end result is that the majority are worse off, since there are fewer jobs and less social wealth to pay for such education, healthcare and legal services.

Corporations

As also considered in chapter 13, neo-liberals generally see busi-ness corporations as appropriate organisations of control of major productive forces, with ownership of corporate assets vested in private shareholders. Such corporations are seen as efficient struc-tures of organisation by virtue of their effective mobilisation and integration of the work of professional experts, directed by a central authority.

Equality of opportunity, promotion through the hierarchy based on merit, and reward in proportion to social contribution, ensure efficiency and fairness. Higher positions involve greater skill, knowl-edge, experience, stress and responsibility. Greater material rewards to those higher up the pyramid motivate others to strive to join them by developing and applying socially valuable abilities. Higher profits are both the consequence of effective management and the means to ensure the rewards which drive such effective management.

It is fair and rational that shareholders who sacrifice immediate consumption and risk exposure in the stock-market to supply the physical capital for such corporations are legally empowered to select board members to manage such assets, and to receive a return which reflects both the extent of their sacrifice – and risk – and the social utility of their investment. Managers who successfully maximise returns to such shareholders continue to receive their support and a share of the profits.[10]

Issues in economic theory

Neo-liberal ideas are increasingly influential in shaping perceptions and policy. They are taught in universities around the world. But there are serious ethical, factual and practical problems with all aspects of the neo-liberal argument.

Considering first the economic underpinnings of neo-liberal ideas, we see that Pareto analysis uncritically accepts any initial pattern of wealth distribution and then supports changes which 'harm no-one and make some people better off – in their own estimation'. It therefore fails to challenge initial inequality or to consider the conse-quences of such inequality for subsequent developments.[11]

The Pareto analysis treats individual consumption and investment as completely rational, free and direct expressions of reliable utility calculations. In fact, decision-making in the market is shaped and manipulated by advertisers and marketers, and most consumers' funds, information and options are seriously restricted. The analysis ignores the many things of real value which have no market price. And it precludes objective assessments of genuine social improvement – in terms of universal, and equal, satisfaction of basic human needs, focusing instead on subjective individual assessments of utility in market acquisition.

It is easy to see why conservative economists shifted from objective to subjective measures of utility at an early stage of development of neoclassical theory. On any reasonable interpretation, beyond the satisfaction of basic needs the marginal utility of wealth falls away very rapidly. So a social system that fails to satisfy the basic needs of many while heaping up increasingly valueless wealth in the hands of a few demands radical redistribution for objective utility maximisation.

On a subjective interpretation of utility, by contrast, we cannot say that such excess wealth is worth less to its recipients than is the satisfaction of the basic needs of the poor. 'Progress' can be measured only in terms of at least one party's subjective judgment that the situation has improved, while no-one sees themself as worse off.

Orthodox theory sees the marginal revenue product of labour as dependent on the number of units of labour already employed 'and on the quantity and quality of other, complementary inputs'[12] rather than on 'the intrinsic quality' of the additional labour input itself. So the neoclassical analysis actually provides little support for the idea of 'reward in proportion to the value of individual contribution'. We know that workers are more productive if they can use better technology. But they have no control over provision of such technology. Why then should some suffer because of the inferior technology provided to them or the bad business decisions of their bosses?

As has frequently been pointed out, there is actually no way to measure the marginal productivity of capital because it cannot, typically, be broken down into homogenous minimal units which can be simply added together as can labour. Even if we could disentangle the value contribution of capital, there is no reason why such value creation should necessarily bear any particular relation to the process of provision of such capital by particular individuals. It doesn't matter whether such individuals have inherited such funds, or stolen them, they receive just the same returns as those who have acquired them through socially useful sacrifice, effort or stress.

Neoclassical theory notoriously neglects the true significance of negative 'externalities' – or deleterious consequences for third parties arising out of market exchanges. And 'free markets' are typically short lived as the scale economies of bigger operations allow them to crush or absorb their smaller competitors. And privatisation of public monopolies committed to public service and support of the welfare state all too often creates pernicious private monopolies committed only to profit maximisation.

In the previous chapter we considered the ways in which the trend towards competitive price and profit reduction encourages collusion and monopoly price fixing between different producers within a sector. This typically means restriction of output, leading to wastage of productive resources – including workers left without employment. Bigger profits for the monopoly sector mean smaller profits for the non-monopoly sectors that have to pay monopoly prices for their inputs.

We considered the ways in which monopolies and oligopolies 'use their power over economic resources to suppress socially beneficial innovation', to control consumption through extensive advertising and marketing, 'to limit the freedom of entry of new firms' and 'to influence government policy to serve their interests at the expense of other community concerns'.[13]

In the real world of twenty-first century global capitalism, powerful monopolies and oligopolies control and restrict production so as to maximise their profits at the expense of consumers and of workers denied employment. Destruction of traditional employment and lack of investment in many areas create oversupply of labour, which, along with political restriction of workers' rights and powers of resistance, forces wages down below subsistence with no reference to real labour productivity.[14]

At the upper end of the scale, wide dispersal of share ownership and the information gulf between owners and controllers of large corporations allows senior executives to determine their own salaries, again without reference to real productivity.

Conflict of rights

At the heart of the capitalist system is a fundamental conflict of rights between that of a business to negotiate a work contract with an individual worker, without 'outside interference', and the worker's right to job security, decent pay and conditions. The imbalance of power created by the limited availability of desirable jobs, and the worker's inability to live decently without employment, undermines any idea of free and fair negotiation.

Government steps towards ensuring employment for all who want to work and decent social security payments for those who can't, recognition and support for strong trade unions as agents of collective bargaining with management, support for legislative regulation of wages and conditions (including minimum wage and unfair dismissal laws) and arbitration by independent legal authorities can go some way towards redressing this imbalance. But neo-liberals in power have worked to undermine and dismantle all such protections, thereby rendering the wage contract increasingly unconscionable.

Inheritance involves conflict between the right of the property holder to dispose of their property as they wish, no matter how much of it they have amassed and how little others might have, and the right of members of the younger generation to equal economic opportunities. Most likely the offspring of the rich and the powerful will already enjoy the benefits of high-quality education, healthcare and 'contacts'. For them to also inherit vast wealth while the majority inherits little or nothing creates radically unequal opportunity between social class groups.[15]

Unrestricted inheritance also undermines the neo-liberal principle of reward for the value of social contribution. Even if talent is inherited, as the wealthy and powerful sometimes claim, talented inheritors don't need to use their talents for the social good in order to gain differential reward. Through inheritance they are already rewarded for nothing. And their inherited wealth concentration makes such wealth unavailable to reward other talented people. Inheritance is therefore a major threat to efficient social functioning on the neo-liberal 'special skills' model considered earlier.

Physical capital

Unrestricted inheritance of money or physical capital makes it possible for individuals to live a life of privilege without any 'real' social contribution whatsoever, merely consuming the income from such capital. They can pay for the best advice and assistance in safeguarding and extending their wealth.

Even if individuals have earned the money for their investment, through socially valuable effort and sacrifice, it is far from clear why they should get a lifetime of reward – in terms of regular dividend payments and capital appreciation – from a single contribution of capital. Such reward is actually paid for through the labour of generations of workers who typically have very little share in the surplus they are generating.

Investors' 'risk-taking' is significantly restricted by limited liability. Such investors benefit from the corporation's efforts to generate profits on their behalf in perpetuity, but are not personally responsible for any obligations which the corporation might incur or harms it might inflict in the process, beyond the value of their investment.

The greatest rewards of share ownership go to insiders, able to benefit at the expense of the majority of less-well-informed shareholders. The inherent 'asymmetry of information' between the majority of shareholders and managerial 'insiders' provides the basis for substantial gains through 'insider trading'.

In many cases rewards are achieved by speculation, rather than meaningful contribution to the long-term wellbeing of any particular productive operations. Speculation tends to destabilise share and currency markets and thereby cause major social disruption. Most of those who benefit from share ownership have not actually contributed anything to the funding of the corporations in question, since they have acquired their shares from other shareholders. And far more money flows out of corporations than flows into them as a result of operation of share markets, so that such markets actually constitute a huge drain on corporate resources of funds which could have been used for capital accumulation and job creation.

Risks

At best we can say that some shareholders take a risk by holding on to the shares of particular corporations for prolonged periods, thereby maintaining the share values of the corporations in question, and allowing such corporations to benefit from such stable or increasing values, in terms of access to further investment capital.

There are risks to individuals with limited resources investing in physical capital. Those who borrow money to start a small business are particularly vulnerable. They are typically undercapitalised and at the mercy of the monopoly prices of the big corporations without any of the benefits of economies of scale, political clout, large-scale advertising, or access to cheap labour overseas and tax minimisation through transfer pricing available to big transnationals. Many new small businesses collapse in debt at the first serious economic downturn or interest rate rise, despite the best efforts of those concerned.

Small investors are at serious risk of suffering as a consequence of the insider trading made possible by the information gulf between owners and controllers of corporate enterprise. So are they at the mercy of fraudulent and incompetent managers and accountants of particular corporate operations and investment funds and of periodic large-scale market adjustments that bring down the honest and efficient along with the inefficient and dishonest. With all their savings or retirement income bound up in such shares, they can indeed suffer badly from even short-term and limited falls in share prices.

But neo-liberals have been notoriously weak in addressing any of these issues, with some indeed arguing for decriminalisation of insider training. They have taken the lead in market deregulation which has facilitated and encouraged corporate fraud and criminality.

At the other end of the scale of wealth and power, large-scale share owners can protect themselves from downturns and fraud through access to inside information and ownership of large and diversified portfolios, through insurance and through the intervention of their allies in the political leadership. Their other assets and income allow them to weather the storm of even large-scale downturns, and benefit from the new period of growth and higher share values arising from such downturns. To try to justify the vast wealth of this latter group – of the less than 10% of wealthy families who own more than 50% of shares world wide, in terms of the obvious problems of the former, is misleading to say the least.[16]

Those on subsistence wages do make significant sacrifices in saving small sums to put into share markets. They could indeed be going without necessities to do so. But to suggest that the wealthy make any such sacrifices (through failing to convert all their wealth to immediate consumption) is not just misleading but also dangerously immoral. A crucial consideration here is the rapidly declining marginal utility of wealth; sacrificing your fifth – or fiftieth – house, counts for a lot less than the loss of your first and only one.

Executive salaries

Considering the increasingly inflated remuneration of corporate executives, we see further problems with ideas of reward for socially useful effort and sacrifice, stress and responsibility. Here again, positions are likely to be inherited rather than achieved (by special training or other sacrifice), as those at the top 'look after their own'. Even if special training is involved it's far from clear that it really is such a misery and a sacrifice. Many actually enjoy their university days, and such experiences are typically funded at least in part by taxpayers rather than directly by those undergoing the training in question.

Interesting and rewarding jobs provide significant recompense for onerous educational sacrifice, with little moral justification for a lifetime of extra salary as well. It could be argued that it should be those in less intrinsically rewarding work who should receive extra payment.

There is a paradox here, in terms of neo-liberal appeals to ideas of corporate efficiency to try to justify radical inequality. According to their own theory, such efficiency rests on long-term planning and control, rather than on free market chaos. But such planning inevitably favours and fosters bureaucratic hierarchy rather than individual initiative; monopoly and oligopoly rather than competitive price reduction. And neo-liberal ideology is implacably opposed to any such economic planning by state authorities.

A central emphasis on the role of collaboration and integration of work activities in order to maximise productivity in the modern corporation again makes it difficult and potentially counterproductive to try to apportion differential reward in proportion to the value of individual contributions. Empirical evidence refutes the claim that high levels of inequality support high levels of productivity. Kawachi and Kennedy refer to Matt Bloom's research involving major league baseball in the USA, where increasing disparities of reward for different players have developed since the late 1980s.[17]

Contrary to [neo-liberal] predictions, the wider the pay dispersion in
any given team, the worse was the performance of individual players. Unequal pay distribution had significantly negative effects on
player performance, over and above the effects of base pay, past
performance, age and experience. More tellingly, wider pay differentials translated into worse team performance. More unequal teams
won fewer games and they did worse financially in terms of fan
attendance.[18]

Kawachi and Kennedy suggest two possible explanations: that wider
pay differentials produce feelings of unfairness and resentment which
reduce individual performance, or that such differentials create disin-
centives to co-operation in a game reliant on effective teamwork.
Players concentrate on trying to improve their own performance to
increase their individual reward at the expense of effective co-operation with others. It's likely that both play a part.

The relevance of these considerations for 'wider segments of the
labour market' would seem to depend on the importance of effective
co-operation in the organisations concerned for quality and quantity
of output. But it is the effective integration of labour on a large scale
that is supposed to be the basis for efficiency and productive success
of the modern corporation. And Kawachi and Kennedy here refer to
the research of Cowherd and Levine, who found wider pay dispersion in US manufacturing firms in the 1990s resulted in lower-quality
products.[19]

Particularly significant here are the much higher growth rates
achieved by the major capitalist economies during the post-war boom,
with much lower levels of inequality than in the subsequent phase of
neo-liberal 'reform'. As Self observes, 'not long ago top earners in
Sweden paid over 90% (of their income) in taxes without any discern-
able adverse effects upon the good economic and export performance
of Sweden at the time'.[20] And the Japanese economy was particularly
successful during a period of restriction of top managerial salaries
to a small multiple of wages on the shop floor, when Japanese CEOs
were known to take voluntary pay cuts to preserve workers' jobs.

'For the largest 500 US companies the ratio of CEO pay to production worker earnings rose from 30 in 1970 to 570 in 2000, with most
of the increase taking the form of stock options. This contrasts with
ratios in the 10–25 range in Japan and Europe.'[21] Yet there is no
evidence to support claims of any better US CEO performance. On

the contrary, there was a close link between this massive inflation of executive compensation in the USA and 'the wave of corporate scandals (Enron, WorldCom, etc) that engulfed the USA after the stock market boom subsided in 2000'. As Krugman observed, 'a system that lavishly rewards executives for success tempts those executives, who control much of the information available to outsiders, to fabricate the appearance of success ... aggressive accounting, fictitious transactions that inflate sales, whatever it takes'.[22]

Stress

Far from corporate executives necessarily needing any particular unique skills or abilities, their position of power and privilege would seem to enable them to command the actions of others with every possible kind of special skill or ability that might be needed. And in relation to issues of rational efficiency, stress and responsibility, it is the ways in which reality departs from the neo-liberal ideal that are most significant.

Robert Jackall's empirical investigations of American corporations suggest that real structures are 'patrimonial' rather than rationally efficient. In other words, individuals are encouraged to ingratiate themselves with those above them in the hierarchy in the hope of protection and promotion, while they plot against those on the same level and exploit those below them. As Jackall says:

> It is characteristic of this authority system that details are pushed down and credit is pulled up. Superiors do not like to give detailed instructions to subordinates. The official reason for this is to maximise subordinates' autonomy. The underlying reason is, first to get rid of tedious details. Most hierarchically organised occupations follow this pattern; one of the privileges of authority is the divestment of humdrum intricacies. This also insulates higher bosses from the peculiar pressures that accompany managerial work at the middle levels and below: the lack of economy over one's time because of continual interruption from one's subordinates, telephone calls from customers and clients, and necessary meetings with colleagues; the piecemeal fragmentation of issues both because of the discontinuity of events and because of the way subordinates filter news; and the difficulty of minding the store while sorting out sometimes unpleasant personal details. Perhaps more important, pushing details down protects the privilege of authority to declare that a mistake has been made.[23]

Such a system functions to effectively push stress and responsibility down the corporate hierarchy, rather than concentrating them at the top. Far from CEOs 'deserving' their increasingly vast recompense by virtue of the great burden of stress and responsibility they bear, the whole system is actually constructed to relieve them of any such stress and responsibility.[24]

Legal issues

Corporations lack human minds and human bodies. But the legal fiction of corporate personhood, distinct from shareholders and corporate officers, is maintained by identifying some of the corporation's senior managers, 'those designated as directors, officers or executives', as if they were the 'mind' of the organisation. This might be thought to apportion responsibility for corporate wrongdoing to such individuals. But, generally, this is not the case.[25] As Glasbeek says:

> As the thoughts and acts of ... the directors and officers of the corporation are treated as if they were the thoughts and acts of the corporation, they are, legally speaking only, of course, not the thoughts and acts of the directors and officers as people. It follows that the corporation, and not the directors and officers, should be held legally responsible for those thoughts and acts. As a consequence, investors in the corporation are not the only ones blessed with limited liability for risks created by their wealth-seeking activities through the corporation. Directors and officers and executives have a form of limited liability as well.[26]

The complexity and cost of investigating and prosecuting corporate crimes to the cash-strapped and under-resourced public authorities entrusted with such tasks, and the very substantial resources available to corporate executives to deter and defend any such prosecutions, leaves such executives largely immune from genuine legal responsibility and the stresses associated with it.

Epidemiology

These observations – of decreasing stress up the social power hierarchy – receive strong support from the epidemiological studies of Marmot, Wilkinson, Kawachi, Kennedy and others. Marmot's classic studies of different employment grades in the occupational hierarchy of the British public service[27] demonstrated a direct relation between ranking, mortality and morbidity. As he says: 'The men at the bottom of the hierarchy have, at ages 40 to 64, four times the risk of death of the administrators at the top of the hierarchy.' Each occupational level was found to have higher mortality than the one above it in the hierarchy. The gradient got shallower at older ages, 'but even at the oldest age, the bottom group has twice the mortality of the top group'.[28] Those lower down the hierarchy had higher levels of lifestyle risk factors, in the areas of smoking, blood pressure, plasma cholesterol, and blood sugar ... which did contribute to higher mortality and morbidity. But adjusting for such factors made only a slight difference to the results.

Since the gradient applies to incidence of disease and since relatively high-quality public health services were, at the time, available to all British citizens, quality of healthcare does not explain the difference. Those lower in the hierarchy were found to have much more healthcare by virtue of higher levels of serious illness.[29]

Evidence from many different directions, particularly experimental manipulation of status hierarchies in monkey populations, as well as other large-scale epidemiological studies of human populations, point to work stress as the major cause of both the underlying health gradient and of the greater lifestyle risk factors down the hierarchy.[30]

As Marmot says, 'the nature of the hierarchy is the less control (and less reward for effort) the lower you go'.[31] A 'fight and flight' response, evolved to deal with brief emergencies, becomes increasingly chronically activated by increasing insecurity, powerlessness and fear as we move down the social hierarchy. Without the opportunity to relieve stress through fight or flight, the prolongation of the stress reaction of increased heart rate and blood pressure and rapid transmission of nutrients to muscles through the inhibition of insulin secretion undermines the bodily functions of tissue repair, growth, immune response and digestion, leading ultimately to illness and death.[32]

Lower-ranking public servants at the time of research had job security and living wages as well as access to comprehensive social welfare provision. Those in the lower reaches of corporate hierarchies in the contemporary world typically lack all of these things. They are in a situation where job loss will have a potentially disastrous impact on all aspects of their lives. This is in radical contrast to those at the top, who have the financial and social resources to see them through job loss without any such consequences.

Social issues

There is now plenty of evidence showing that high levels of inequality within and between countries is seriously bad for the health and wellbeing of those worse off. Absolute poverty in developing nations leads to millions dying of easily treatable and preventable infectious diseases and accidents. In the developed world, the extent of inequality within nations and regions is strongly correlated with lack of trust between people, with weakness of community life, higher homicide rates, higher levels of hostility and worse health outcomes, including higher infant mortality rates for the less well-off. The reduced life expectancy of poorer people in high inequality situations – five, ten or fifteen years less than that of the richer people – brings down the average life expectancy for more unequal societies.[33]

In leading to increased inequality, so do unregulated markets lead to objectively measurable declines in real social welfare, or to measurably lower levels of welfare than could be achieved under alternative possible arrangements. Pareto optimal outcomes, which increase wealth at the top without greater increase at the bottom, are objectively anti-welfare and anti-social wellbeing.

Ethical issues

Even if we could measure the market value of individual contribution, there is the question of whether this is a fair or rational basis for individual reward. The market fails to give any value to many different forms of obviously valuable social contribution of work and resources, from housework to provision of necessary social infrastructures, from mutual assistance in subsistence farming to provision of sustainable energy. At the same time it does value and reward production of many things of questionable or negative social value (including pollution and global warming).

Even if we accept market values as social values, and can measure individual value contributions, the question arises of whether it would not still be fairer to reward time and effort devoted to useful production rather than value produced. Neo-liberal theory itself suggests that some people are more productive simply because of inherited abilities –of strength and skill – which they have done nothing themselves to develop or improve, while others have made major efforts, but because of inherited limitations are still able to produce lesser amounts of social value. Is it really fair and just that the former receive more than the latter? Surely people should be rewarded for their actual useful – chosen amount of – socially valuable effort and sacrifice (including income lost or misery sustained during training), rather than for things over which they have no control.

The common law criminal justice system does not generally punish actions over which the actors concerned have no control, which they have not freely and intentionally (or recklessly) undertaken, such as harming others during epileptic fits. Why then should the economy punish individuals for things over which they have no control, by paying lower wages to those who, by chance, lack inherited physical and mental advantages?[34]

Even if it turns out that we could measure individual value contributions (as 'real' social values) and that such measures do indeed correspond to current wage and salary differentials, and that such differentials really do increase overall wealth production, there would still be very strong moral and practical arguments against maintaining such differentials.

It is morally unacceptable and unjust to deny any human beings satisfaction of basic needs while heaping up increasingly valueless rewards for the few. And we can see that the real 'wealth' of a society lies in the quality of life of the citizenry as measured in terms of health, lifespan, safety, security, trust, collaboration and realisation of the human potentials of all. The evidence shows that this is as much an issue of distribution and of the quality of output as of the actual quantity or market value of output. So even if it were true that overall quantity and market value of output could be increased by significant inequality of reward, it would still make basic utilitarian sense to sacrifice some such quantity and value in favour of reduced inequality.

Only if wealth production would necessarily fall so significantly – under a more egalitarian arrangement – as to push a first-world territory back into pre-industrial poverty, would there be ethical and practical reasons for maintaining significant differentials. And we have no reason to believe such a result to be necessary or even likely. On the contrary, available evidence suggests that increased equality would lead to significant productive gains, through greater mutual support, respect, trust, good health, collaboration and optimum real-isation of the potentials of all.[35]

Australian developments

In their recent study of *Who Gets What*, Frank Stillwell and Kirrily Jordan map out recent trends of increasing inequality in Australia, at least in part as a result of the policies of successive neo-liberal governments, both Labor and Liberal. In particular, they highlight the evidence suggesting 'a long-term redistribution of income away from labour and towards capital' in Australia since the mid 1970s, with wages as a share of total income falling from 62.5% in 1975 to 53% in 2005–06, and profits rising from 16% in 1975–76 to 26.9% in 2005–06.[36] As they say:

> The inegalitarian effects of the redistribution ... become more appar-ent when viewed in conjunction with figures on the concentration of ownership of capital. A recent study carried out by the ASX found that ... in 2004, ...only 10.6% of the population held more than $100 000 in direct share ownership, with 27.7% holding more than $10 000; 56% were holding none and therefore received no income from this form of capital.[37]

At the same time, the dividend imputation credit system has increased the proportion of income going to the wealthy minority of major shareholders.

> Ostensibly designed to alleviate double taxation of dividends, this imputation system allows tax paid by companies to be refunded to shareholders receiving franked tax-free dividends. The effect has been a massive redistribution of income to corporate shareholders.[38]

Wages have become increasingly uneven across occupations and within them, with a much greater proportion of managers and admin-istrators in the top income brackets. Stillwell and Jordan show that the ratio of CEO remuneration to average earnings has increased from 18:1 in 1989–90 to 63:1 in 2004–05, with one major bank's CEO, for example, receiving 'an annual pay of $21.2 million in 2005', equivalent to $400 000 per week.[39]

The federal Labor government started the process of dismantling centralised wage-fixing and collective bargaining in the 1980s. The Howard government's Work Choices legislation of 2005 radically reduced the range of safeguards and benefits provided by previous awards, further 'undermining the collective power of organised labour, making it possible for employers to offer contracts to individual workers on a take-it-or-leave-it basis', leading to 'further redistribution of income from labour to capital and further widening of wage disparities'.[40]

While the neo-liberal Howard government has 'significantly reduced welfare payments to some of the most disadvantaged groups in society', so too have they delivered substantially higher tax cuts to those on higher incomes, with 'the poorest 50% of taxpayers receiving just 19% of the cuts' in 2005–06.

> The unequalising effects of government policy have been further compounded by cuts in company tax rates, ... and reduction in the effective rate of capital gains tax ... Analysis of the official tax statistics shows that the annual revenue collected from [capital gains] tax fell from $5.3 billion to $3.3 billion over the three years immediately following the ... halving of the effective rate of [that] tax in 1999. In the very first year some 68 000 taxpayers earning over $100 000 – less than 1% of all taxpayers – received half of all the capital gains received by individuals during that year ... amounting to an average tax cut of $220 per week (ABC 2004).[41]

As Stillwell and Jordan emphasise, such tax cuts to the already wealthy:

> ... undermine the government's ... ability to spend on public goods, social services and social security provisions ... So the generosity to the owners of capital is matched by a corresponding austerity in respect of social infrastructure spending and payments to welfare recipients.[42]

Corruption of the political process

Increasing inequality of wealth is closely bound up with increasing inequality of political power insofar as private wealth – including corporate wealth – can be used to support particular political parties, programmes and causes in various different ways. And such political power can, in turn, be used to further increase private wealth. As

Stiglitz points out:

> In sophisticated economies such as the United States, outright bribery has been largely replaced by political campaign contributions ... Forty-one companies (including General Electric, Microsoft and Disney), which invested – 'contributed' – $150 million to political parties and campaigns for US federal candidates between 1991 and 2001, enjoyed $55 billion in tax breaks in three tax years alone. Pharmaceutical companies spent $759 million to influence 1400 congressional bills between 1998 and 2004 [and] the US government has made their interests paramount in international trade negotiations, and under the new Medicare drug benefit the government is proscribed from bargaining for lower prices – a provision worth billions of dollars just by itself.[43]

Things have not gone as far in Australia as in the US heartland of neo-liberalism. It remains to be seen how far they will go.

Justice and equality

We don't have to look too far to see the down sides of globalised 'free' trade and investment as currently practised, in terms of increasing inequality and injustice within and between nations, along with increasing environmental degradation and pollution primarily affecting poorer people and poorer nations. United Nations agencies have published numerous studies showing that inequalities both within and between countries have increased during the period of neo-liberal dominance.[44] In relation to increasing inequalities between nations, 'the International Labour Organisation calculates that half the world, or 3 billion people, live in poverty and that the income differential between the world's richest and poorest 20% has doubled over the past 40 years.'[45]

> According to the UN Development Programme's Report 2002, the top 5% of the world's population has an income 114 times greater than the bottom 5%. The richest 19% of Americans [some 27 million people, less than 1% of the world] has an income equivalent to the poorest 43% of the world population. At the rate we're going, according to the UNDP, it will take at least 130 years to rid the world of hunger. ... In 2003 less than 10% of the funds devoted worldwide to medical and biological research are available for poor countries' diseases of malaria, tuberculosis and AIDS, although [these] account for 90% of the global disease burden.[46]

In relation to increasing inequality within countries: 'Only Denmark and Canada are said by the UN to have reduced inequalities between 1979 and 1997 – through taxation and redistribution.' Everywhere else inequality increased. World authority on income inequality, Sir Anthony Atkinson of Oxford University, notes that the top 10% of earners in most OECD countries 'have been the biggest beneficiaries of globalisation, each year pulling further ahead of people on median earnings'.[47] He notes:

> They are able to live a life quite different from the rest of us in a way that was not the case in 1984 ... Gated communities have sprung up to separate the very rich from ordinary people, and the rise in the use of domestic servants, elite schools and private health insurance were signs of the wealthy being able to 'opt out of the community'.[48]

At the lower end of the distribution of wealth and income, many put in long hours of effort and sacrifice with very little reward. At the upper end, a minority benefit from inheritance and asset income with very little effort or sacrifice in the service of the community.

These radical failures of distributive justice are complemented by increasing lack of access to legal justice on the part of increasing numbers of less well-off people. While wages have stagnated, the costs of effective legal representation have massively increased. And neo-liberal regimes have cut back on the quality and quantity of legal aid available to the less well-off. Civil litigation is now effectively impossible for the great majority of the population, except through the charity of private law firms, or 'no win no fee' arrangements. So much for the threat of civil action to force negotiated settlement of externality issues.

While infamous corporate criminals who steal billions and slaughter thousands of workers and consumers (through exposure to asbestos, wood dust, pesticides and other carcinogens, through manufacture and construction in conditions with no legal protection of the workforce, etc) get away with fines and restrictions on their future directorial ambitions, or, more generally, no penalties at all, increasing numbers of poor and mentally ill people are thrown into dirty, dangerous, dehumanising prisons for frustration-driven drug use or isolated acts of violence, or poverty-driven minor drug dealing, petty theft and fine defaults. Here, indeed, the running down of social welfare provision in the neo-liberal era has been paralleled by a corresponding increase in prison populations, keeping the disempowered and disaffected off the streets.

Economic reforms

Detailed proposals for possible ethical reform, on a social liberal foundation, would address all of the critical points raised in the last three chapters. Here, we merely highlight the intrinsic instability of a system where inflated profits, produced by destruction of working-class organisation and power, coupled with monopoly restriction of output, put huge inflationary pressure on share markets, threatening major 'market adjustments'. At the same time the deepening debt crisis, both nationally and internationally, threatens to inflict upon first-world countries the sorts of consequences suffered by third-world countries since the 1980s.

As noted in chapter 14, the current pattern of the capitalist world economy is being maintained only through exponential growth of working-class consumer debt in first-world countries, along with continued massive subsidisation of US imports – and expansion of US deficits – by Asian central banks' purchase of US treasury bonds. Along with accelerated environmental degradation and continued reliance on unsustainable productive technologies, so do these developments threaten major debt-deflationary crisis.

The horrors of the Great Depression in the 1930s clearly demonstrated the instability and destructive potential of unregulated markets. This led to tight regulation of financial institutions and markets, with public ownership of key sectors of the economy. Since that time, the political and economic power of private wealth and big corporations has wound the clock back in the name of free market competition. Social democratic reform requires that such power must itself be wound back in the future.

A focus on free competition at all levels of society is immoral, insofar as it encourages greed, selfishness, exploitation and increasing inequality. It is wasteful, insofar as it implies duplication of productive resources, missing out on scale economies, and destruction of 'losing' enterprises, forced out of business with attendant damage to workers and communities. It is unachievable, insofar as private monopolies and oligopolies are the inevitable real world product of competition, crisis and economies of scale.

The focus in the future needs to be on constructive collaboration and mutual respect. And this involves ensuring effective legal protection of the human rights of all – as set out in the UDHR. It requires that the disadvantaged get enough to live in dignity and good health through transfers from the wealthy and the privileged.

As Robin Hahnel says, we need to emphasise values of solidarity – with equal reward for all socially responsible contributions, of diversity, allowing people to do things their own way, of self-management, giving everyone a voice, and of balanced job complexes, with equal sharing of both the rewarding and the drudge work.[49]

As Harry Shutt has eloquently argued, the current neo-liberal policy priority of competitive growth maximisation only exacerbates problems of inequality, debt, inadequate effective demand, poverty and environmental destruction. What is required is honest and transparent political intervention in pursuit of stability, equality and sustainability.[50]

Effective wealth, inheritance and capital gains taxes are necessary to support genuinely progressive income taxes in promoting equality of opportunity. And effective outlawing of private provision of education and health care would ensure the support of the wealthy for good quality public systems to further support such equality.

A guaranteed minimum income for all individuals could promote reward for effort and sacrifice by making abstention from paid employment a meaningful option, without stigma or destitution.

Effective state control of land and of the monopoly sector of production, including production of producer goods, could allow for control of pollution and resource depletion, with regulated prices for land and output to facilitate effective access of all to critical goods and services, while also generating profits sufficient to fund welfare and infrastructure development without recourse to taxation, thereby precluding tax avoidance.

In lieu of complete abolition of corporations in favour of a fully planned or participatory democracy, such corporations must themselves be radically democratised, with both central state and workers' representation and participation at the highest levels of management.

In this connection, Michael Albert highlights the need for 'balanced job complexes' in which both empowering management operations – of decision-making and agenda-setting – and relatively unrewarding routine 'rote tasks' are equally shared by all.

Each person has a job. Each job involves many tasks. Of course each job should be suited to the talents, capacities, and energies of the person doing it, But ... each job must also contain a mix of tasks and responsibilities such that the overall quality of life and especially the overall empowerment effects of work are comparable for all.[51]

Without genuine democratisation of share ownership, shareholders' limited liability must be abolished, insofar as it encourages fraud and other criminal activities by corporate controllers. Investment funding should shift away from intrinsically unstable, corrupt and wasteful share markets, with banks forced to lend in line with public priorities of equality and sustainability and more direct state control of enterprise. Profits must be restricted and restrained, rather than maximised, in order to reduce such fraud, reduce unsustainable growth and reduce the concentration of private wealth and power, with employees' wages and conditions and environmental sustainability as new policy priorities. Monopoly power must be balanced by central control of pricing and of the quality of goods, along with public access to all relevant financial records. Externalities must be meaningfully factored into corporate costs, with prioritisation of planned avoidance of their more destructive forms and consequences.

Current and future debt crisis can be overcome only through rational regulation and control of capital movement and credit creation. This means public rather than private control of the creation of money and credit. As Pettifor argues:

To function well, (and without usury or war) societies and the ecosystem need policies for debt-free government money; cheap commercial money and regulated credit creation. Policies for lending that will generate future income in line with the ecosystem's limits; investments that will yield sustainable results; and consumer borrowing that will not lead to over-consumption, debt, a slump and then unemployment.[52]

International flows of capital investment and currency buying must be restricted and controlled in the interests of effective local or regional economic regulation. Fair, rather than free, trade must predominate in world markets, with fair prices paid by the first world for third-world imports, and fair wages to third-world producers. Here too, accelerated transfer from the rich to the poor is required to rapidly accelerate sustainable third-world development.

There are currently promising signs on the fair trade front. As Litvinoff and Madeley point out:

> Fairtrade certification guarantees minimum prices for producer organisations. The minimum price is based on local economic conditions and covers production costs, plus provision for household members to enjoy a decent living standard, and the cost of farm improvements and compliance with fair trade standards, including the cost of belonging to a farmers' co-operative.[53] The International Fair Trade Association is [now] made up of 270 organisations in 60 countries[54] ... [with] global sales of Fairtrade-certified products reaching 758 UK pounds in 2005 – an increase of 37% over 2004. All the product lines are expanding ... Globally, the number of certified producer organisations has grown by 127% since 2001, to 580 groups in 58 countries, and the number of registered traders has increased by 132% in the same period ... All of this makes fair trade one of the fastest growing markets in the world.[55]

But there remains a very, very long way to go. Here is a simple choice to be made by first-world consumers with profound consequences for the rest of the world.

As considered in earlier chapters, political democracy must be protected from usurpation by private wealth through the breaking up of media monopolies, with public funding of diverse channels of communication and guaranteed effective outlets for minority opinions, through effectively insulating public officials from private sector bribery during and after their time in office, and through restriction of party funding by private business. The politicians must be made properly accountable through regular public scrutiny and sanctions against failures to comply with stated commitments and obligations. Again in lieu of abolition of existing agencies of international regulation and the creation of completely new ones, such democratisation must be meaningfully extended to the IMF, World Bank, WTO and United Nations.

Michael Albert proposes, instead of the IMF, World Bank and WTO, 'an International Asset Agency, a Global Investment Assistance Agency and a World Trade Agency'.[56]

> These three new institutions would work to attain equity, solidarity, diversity, self-management and ecological balance in international financial exchange, investment, development, trade and cultural exchange, they would try to ensure that the benefits of trade and investments accrue disproportionately to the weaker and poorer

parties involved, not to the already richer and more powerful. They would not prioritize commercial considerations over all other values, but would prioritize national aims, cultural identity, and equitable development ... Instead of downgrading international health, environmental and other standards to a low level through a process of downward harmonization, they would work to upgrade standards by means of a new upwards equalization ... Instead of bankers and bureaucrats carrying out policies of presidents to shape the lives of the very many without even a pretence at participation by the people affected, these new institutions would be open, democratic, transparent, participatory, and bottom up, with local, popular and democratic accountability. These new institutions would promote and organize international cooperation to restrain out-of-control global corporations, capital, and markets by regulating them so people in local communities could control their own economic lives.[57]

Discussion topics

1. What is *equality*?
2. Can inequality be justified?
3. Can inheritance be justified?
4. Can risk justify unearned income?
5. Can stress justify existing differences in material reward?
6. How might the current economic system be made more just or more able to fulfil the needs of all?

Law and contemporary social problems

Chapter 16

FREEDOM OF THE WILL AND CRIMINAL CULPABILITY*

Mens rea

In the common law, criminal culpability is understood primarily in terms of free individual decision and action. As Hart says, 'the principle of punishment should be restricted to those who have voluntarily broken the law'.[1]

From this perspective, the essential role of the criminal law is to protect the socially permissible free action of good citizens, centred upon 'enjoyment' of their life and property, through punitive redirection of the anti-social free choices of others. This emphasis upon free individual choice, as ground of culpability, finds expression in the requirement to establish that the accused's guilty mind, or mens rea, has caused a particular criminal action, or actus reus. Did they really intend to perform the action in question, and did their intention really cause them to perform the action?

The 'action' here refers to voluntary or intentional bodily movement – a physical movement that results from the operation of the will. Or, as Hart says, a bodily movement 'subordinated to the agent's conscious plan of action'.[2]

Mens rea has come to refer to a range of states of mind. But the underlying idea is that of a responsible agent who has chosen to break the rules. This includes a conscious – prior – decision to break the law, but can also include the intention to engage in action the subject knows involves a chance of causing a prohibited result, even though this is not the aim or purpose of the action.

Consciousness is therefore a necessary condition of criminal culpability. This is not merely consciousness in the broad sense in which animals, as well as humans, are 'aware' of their surroundings, and experience feelings of various kinds. Rather it is consciousness in the narrow – and possibly specifically human – sense of being able to stand back from our mental states and think about, appraise and evaluate them. As Richard Norman says:

> We need to do this in order to make rational decisions about our future states, by reviewing our various, perhaps conflicting desires, considering the reasons for and against acting on them and assessing the weight of these different reasons. [Because it allows us to plan and evaluate our actions, consciousness in this sense] is a precondition for our status as moral beings ... Because we are conscious beings ... we are not just prisoners of our immediate environment, but can [freely] choose our actions and thereby make them our own.[3]

The rationale of punishment as retribution is crucially dependent upon these ideas. The argument is that because the individual offender has freely chosen to break the law, so have they, therefore, in a sense, chosen to expose themselves to the possibility of state-inflicted pain and suffering as the cost of the suffering they have inflicted upon others. This idea of free decision is central to the rationale of punishment as specific and general deterrence. The infliction of suffering upon those found guilty of criminal offences aims to influence future free decisions by the individual concerned, and by others who might otherwise choose criminal, rather than legal, means, to encourage them to refrain from any such illegal choices.

Here we focus upon some major problems of the application of the idea of free individual decision-making within the criminal legal system, drawing particularly upon the work of the analytical philosopher John Searle. Searle's work is useful because of his clear picture of the nature of free will and free choice. But to understand this, it is necessary to first consider his analysis of certain aspects of the mind–body relation, centred upon the phenomenon of intentionality.

Intention

As Searle notes, intention in this sense refers to a mental state that is both a reason for action and a cause of action. Some intentions are formed prior to action, some are not. In the former case, we want to achieve X, we believe that we can achieve X by performing action Y. This desire and belief together provide at least part of the cause of our deciding, and hence intending, to perform action Y. We have the intention to perform action Y prior to the performance of the action itself. But such a prior intention then becomes part of the cause of our performing action Y – along with access to relevant means and opportunity. The appearance of opportune circumstances – which trigger us into action – might be called the 'proximate' cause of the action.

When the action is performed, what makes it an action (rather than a mere movement) is the involvement of a mental component or intention-in-action, as well as a physical component of body movement. The prior intention causes the action, which itself involves the intention-in-action causing particular muscular contractions. Bill had a prior intention to kill his uncle by shooting him, he decided to do so, and this prior intention was part of the cause of the intention-in-action of his shooting his uncle, when the uncle stepped out of his house. His intention-in-action (to shoot the uncle) caused his finger to pull the trigger.

Often the prior intention will be of quite high order (getting to work) and require a complex sequence of specific subsidiary actions for its achievement (opening the car door). In fact, intentions come in nested hierarchies, with some higher-order 'plans' possibly taking years to unfold, through innumerable more specific sub-plans and intentional actions.

At the other end of the scale, there may be no prior intention at all. 'Many of the actions we perform, we perform quite spontaneously, in response to the circumstances in which we find ourselves, without forming any prior intention to do these things.'[4] But such spontaneous actions still involve the causation of bodily movement by intentions-in-action. They involve pre-existing beliefs that shape and direct our perception of the situations in question, and hence also our responses to such situations. And they still result in part from previous prior intentions and actions that have brought us into particular situations.

Free will

In Searle's model 'free will' enters the picture in the space between reason and decision. I want X and can see that doing Y will get it for me. But is Y really the right thing to do? Will it hurt others? Is it legal? This gap, as Searle calls it, between reason and decision allows me to consider other possibilities, obligations or commitments that might conflict with, or override, the performance of Y to get X. They might more urgently command the resources necessary for accomplishing X – resources of time, effort, money or whatever. Y or X (means or end) might simply be morally or legally unacceptable.

This gap provides a space not just for adjudicating between conflicting reasons for action, but for rethinking the nature of our options, obligations and commitments in the light of new information and experience. Such rethinking need not just be a matter of internal thought processes. It can also involve discussion and debate with other people.

Just as the gap between desire and decision allows for the possibility of deliberation, including reference to moral and legal considerations, prior to decision, so do the gap between decision and action and possible gaps within ongoing sequences of actions allow for further reconsideration. We can sometimes still 'change our mind' even after we have embarked upon a particular 'course of action'.

Such gaps do not always exist. We do not always form intentions to perform actions prior to the performance of the actions themselves. Spontaneous responses are partly a result of external situations that might not allow for deliberation (for example, being attacked in the street or suddenly confronting a changed traffic light in the path of our car), and partly a result of internal situations: our tendency or propensity for (particular) spontaneous responses in situations of the type in question.

Our responses are determined by our perceptions of situations, as situations of a particular type; a situation of traffic-light change, for example. And our perceptions are shaped by our established patterns of belief, including, in this case, our beliefs about the operation of traffic lights and the consequences of ignoring their changes of colour. Our perceptions and actions can be affected by preceding trauma, or consumption of psychoactive substances.

Earlier 'free choices' might be relevant in causing such spontaneous responses. If we know that we are likely to respond in particular ways in particular situations, we might choose either to retain such propensities or to try to change them. We might pursue anger management strategies to change undesirable responses of spontaneous violence or aim to improve our driving skills. We might choose to avoid the sorts of situations likely to trigger undesirable responses. We might choose to avoid consumption of alcohol or other drugs because of the likely or possible consequences for our perceptions and spontaneous responses.

Action and omission

Criminal law-makers in the common law system have been anxious to distinguish 'action' – as a source of moral and legal responsibility – from 'inaction' – which incurs no such responsibility. From this perspective, everyone is responsible for looking after themselves alone. No-one should be bound to be 'their brother's keeper'. Thus, unlike continental civil law, the common law recognises no general duty to rescue others in distress, even where this can be accomplished with ease and little threat to the rescuer.

Traditionally, this distinction has been defended by the assertion that it is the law's business to 'arrest acts of positive harm' but not to 'encourage – or require – acts of positive good'. It is supported by the right-liberal idea of society as no more than an aggregate of competing human individuals, any one of whom is responsible to any other only to the extent that they have voluntarily entered into legally recognised contractual relations with the individual in question.

A closely related issue is that of medical personnel causing death by 'failing to administer' necessary medication or nutrition, at the request of the patient or their representative, to terminally ill adults or seriously handicapped newborn babies. This is treated as lawful, in contrast to 'active' administration of a lethal injection at the patients' or their representatives' request, for example, which is treated as unlawful. Here again, the causal efficacy of 'inaction' is denied, with death attributed rather to the 'natural course of the illness'.

But it is far from clear that such ideas make sense in practice. It has frequently been pointed out that failure to take action is a form of action since the individual actively restrains themselves from taking the apparently 'correct' action, or actively withdraws treatment, in the latter sort of case. As Norrie says:

> an omission can be described as a negative act, a description that indicates that omissions are in their essence similar to rather than different from acts. Omissions can be conscious decisions either not

to do something or to do something other than the thing that is not done ... Either way, to describe a failure to act is as much to describe a practical orientation to the world as is the description of an act.[5]

If the real moral and legal issue is 'free decision' to do 'the right thing' there is no moral distinction between the two sorts of cases. Definite causal consequences, including 'positive harms' and 'goods', flow from the decision not to take action, as much as from the decision to act. In Norrie's words:

> omissions can be as much the cause of an event as acts. An omission can serve just as well as an act as a necessary and sufficient condition for any particular outcome.[6]

This is particularly clear in the sort of medical case considered earlier. Here, abstaining from treatment has the same consequence as actively assisting suicide or engaging in voluntary euthanasia, in the form of the death of the patient. Furthermore, as acknowledged by the House of Lords in *Airdale NHS Trust v Bland*,[7] such legal abstention could also produce weeks of pain prior to death that could have been avoided by an illegal lethal injection.

In terms of Searle's analysis, 'inaction' in specific situations could be a result of a particular prior decision, producing a prior intention. We decide to refrain from action in some particular future situation, with a view to producing particular causal consequences of such inaction. Perhaps this involves 'actively restraining ourselves' from performing some action we might, otherwise, feel constrained to undertake.

Similarly, past decisions could contribute to 'spontaneous inaction', without any 'direct' prior intention. Failure to take steps to prepare ourselves to help others in need – as such occasions might arise – could contribute to our 'freezing up' when encountering situations in which we might otherwise have averted substantial harm to others, with minimum harm to ourselves, for example.

Reasons

As well as casting light upon the nature of 'freedom of the will', this analysis can illuminate the concept of 'reasons for actions'. The concept of a 'reason' implies some basis in rational deliberation. Prior intentions are products of deliberation concerning beliefs and desires. Such deliberation centres upon reasons why particular desires specify appropriate goals for action, why the individual concerned wants to do this, rather than something else; why this is seen as a priority, and/ or a just and right thing to do on this occasion. It involves reasons why particular actions are seen as appropriate means for achieving the goals in question, why they are the best or only way to achieve such goals at the time in question.

Some goals will be ends in themselves; some will be means to other ends. When we ask for the 'reason' or 'motive' behind a particular action we are really asking what ultimate goal the individual was attempting to achieve, why they were seeking to achieve such a goal, and why they believed the chosen means to be appropriate to achieving this goal.

This is the subjective side of the reason for the action in question. But we cannot properly understand any such subjective considerations without reference to their objective circumstances and determinants: the particular objective social facts or conditions that have caused the relevant perceptions, beliefs and desires and facilitated or triggered the relevant reasoning processes. And this applies whether or not such perceptions, beliefs and desires are based in fact, or such reasoning is sound or cogent.

With spontaneous actions, the nature of the subjective response will depend upon the way in which the external situation is perceived. An individual's belief system will classify situations in particular ways, and this will determine that individual's likely responses in the situations in question.

Here again, we must consider also the objective circumstances of formation of such beliefs. Are such beliefs factually based? And if not, why not? Did the individual have access to reliable information, or have they been misled? We must consider the extent to which the individual concerned has been able to make rational judgments about the appropriate behaviour in the situations in question, or to act, effectively, upon such judgments. Did they have access to appropriate counselling or training for example? Or did they lack the resources to access such assistance?

Autonomy and the limits of free will

In the literature of ethics and philosophy of mind practical preconditions for, and restrictions upon, free will and free action are traditionally discussed in terms of 'autonomy' or self governance. Moral philosophers typically distinguish three different ideas or dimensions of autonomy that go along with different sorts (and degrees) of possible obstacles and restrictions to free, conscious action.

1   *Liberty of action.* An individual is autonomous in this sense if their action results from their own conscious intention and is not the result of external coercion or duress. When autonomy is identified with liberty of action, the primary contrast drawn is between autonomy and coercion. Coercion involves the deliberate use of force or the threat of harm. The coercer's purpose is to get the person being coerced to do something he or she would not otherwise be willing to do.[8]

2   *Freedom of choice.* This refers to the range of real choices available to an individual, in terms of access to material means for the realisation of particular goals or desires. Thus, we noted earlier that intention was only ever a part of the causation of action. Such intentions only become 'operative' in effective causation of action if the individual concerned also has effective control of the necessary resources: of strength, skill, knowledge, tools, machines, assistance and opportunity.

3   *Effective deliberation.* This refers to internal, rather than external, resources available for, or restrictions upon, the exercise of individual autonomy, specifically to the individual's capacity for making rational and informed decisions. Such decision-making involves both rational choice of ends, in keeping with real need, for example, and rational choice of appropriate means for achieving independently chosen ends, in tune with what is logically, physically, and socially possible, and what is morally just and responsible.

Powers of effective deliberation can be limited in many ways ... some individuals may not have developed the necessary abilities or may even be incapable of sufficiently developing them ... even individuals who have the requisite abilities may be unable to exercise them on a particular occasion due to various internal factors ... emotions such as fear may make the impartial weighing of information impossible ... the presence of pain or the use of drugs may also affect the exercise of reasoning abilities ... Lies, deception, and a lack of appropriate information can all limit the effective exercise of the abilities required for rational deliberation.[9]

Defences

At first sight, this moral philosophical analysis of 'free will' seems quite compatible with the basic categories and procedures of contemporary criminal law.

First, the actus reus generally has to be an intentional action: a bodily movement that is the product of an intention-in-action.[10] The law does not generally hold individuals responsible for bodily movements that are seen as caused by anything other than such an intention-in-action on the part of the individual concerned.

The legal category of 'automatism' refers to non-intentional bodily movements that occur when an individuals' conscious awareness is seriously impaired in some way, in other words, 'when the ordinary link between mind and body is absent'. Where the automatism is caused by something other than an 'unsound mind' or serious mental illness, such as sleepwalking, diabetes, major stress or a blow to the head, it can be seen to render action involuntary and hence not criminally culpable.[11]

However, as with the preceding analysis of spontaneous actions and unintended movements (as consequences of prior choices), those who freely choose to put themselves in situations where it is possible or likely they will be drawn into involuntary movements with criminal consequences – unintentionally discharging firearms during armed robberies, for example – can be held liable for such consequences. (See *Ryan v R* (1967) 121 CLR 205.)

Further, the criminal law does not hold individuals responsible for criminal acts that are seen as products of duress, in other words, where an individual commits an offence under threat of physical harm to themselves or another person. Here, the prior intention is, indeed, to perform the forbidden act – of theft or whatever. And this 'criminal' prior intention is the cause of a 'criminal' intention-in-action. But the goal or purpose of the action is to avoid serious (and unjustified) harm to the individual concerned or to another, rather than, for example, gain unjustified personal enrichment.[12]

Duress involves a severe restriction of the options available to the individual concerned. They are forced to make a 'coerced choice from morally unacceptable options'.[13] Where circumstances other than the threat of serious violence or harm by another person similarly restrict the options available to a person, such that they can only avoid 'irreparable evil' through the commission of some criminal act (involving a lesser evil), they can apply the defence of 'necessity' (or duress of circumstances).

Self-defence is understood in a similar way. The decision and prior intention to use force is justified if the individual believes, on reasonable grounds, that such force is necessary to defend themselves against an unwelcome attack.

Where the individual's internal decision-making capacities have been radically compromised by a mental illness or by some 'abnormality of mind', the law allows defences of insanity and diminished responsibility or substantial impairment The former allows for excusing the individual of criminal liability in any offence. One or the other of latter is available in some jurisdictions in relation to murder.[14]

The defence of provocation relates to spontaneous action, triggered by acts or words of the victim that produced 'a sudden and temporary loss of self control'. Here the law excuses spontaneous responses that it is unreasonable to expect the individual to take prior action to avoid.

The criminal law's treatment of intoxication also appears to be in tune with the preceding analysis of individual responsibility in relation to spontaneous actions. Individuals are not criminally liable for actions committed in extreme states of intoxication – where their action ceases to be voluntary – if such intoxication does not result from their own free choice. If they have 'freely chosen' to become intoxicated, then they have chosen what they know to be possible criminal consequences.[15]

A black-and-white picture

But while the law is in line with the broad categories of the moral philosophical analysis, it departs from such analysis in its crudely black-and-white approach. Actions are regarded either as completely free – and hence culpable – or completely (or largely) determined by internal and/or external circumstances, and hence not culpable.

This is particularly evident in relation to insanity. Ideas of legally relevant insanity have been restricted to extreme states of mental illness where the defendant was, at the time of the crime, 'labouring under such defect of reason, from disease of the mind, as not to know the nature and quality of the act he was doing, or if he did know it, then he did not know that what he was doing was wrong'.[16] In effect, this test only covers those defendants who, in extreme cases of mental illness, are unaware of what they are doing or of the significance of their actions.'[17]

We might think that diminished responsibility – or substantial impairment – would cover lesser mental problems. But this defence is available only in relation to murder charges. It is not available at all in some jurisdictions. It merely reduces murder to manslaughter. And juries can return a verdict of murder even if there is medical evidence of the appropriate sort of mental abnormality or impairment.

In effect, the only sort of duress by the action of another, recognised by law, is 'the threat of immediate death or serious personal violence', where such immediate threat either 'overbears the ordinary power of human resistance' or provokes legitimate resistance in self-defence. The only sort of duress of circumstances – or of 'necessity' – recognised in law is a threat of immediate death or very serious injury by such natural disasters as fire or earthquake.

Provocation is a defence only in relation to murder, and only applies to actions of the deceased, immediately prior to the killing, 'of such a character as to cause an ordinary person to lose his self-control to such extent as to act as the killer has acted'. And though the NSW *Crimes Act* has recently been updated (in s 23) to include provocative actions of the deceased 'at any time before' the homicide, this is intended only to accommodate histories of ongoing domestic violence in relation to battered woman syndrome.

Beyond this point, the only idea of action by others 'pushing' individuals into criminal behaviour is that of unintentional and extreme intoxication by another's action.

But it is clear that, in reality, there are many different forms and degrees of freedom and determinism, autonomy and restriction, many sorts of ways in which the actions of some affect and constrain the decisions and spontaneous actions of others, increasing the likelihood of criminal behaviour. Not only does the black-and-white legal picture provide a false dichotomy, it also presents extremes that actually make little sense. There is no absolute and unconditional freedom, nor any pure determinism where human actions are concerned.

Motives

Most important, we cannot make sense of specific cases of choice as free choice without reference to the detailed processes of decision-making involved. This is, after all, the essence of 'free will', on the analysis developed so far. Free will exists where an individual is in a position to make a real choice between genuine alternatives on the basis of rational – and informed – deliberation. Such deliberation generates the reasons for their action. And only by examining the details and context of specific decision-making can we rationally access the extent and nature of restriction of the processes in question. Yet the criminal law steadfastly refuses to properly consider any such decision procedures.

As Norrie says:

> It is as firmly established in legal doctrine as any rule can be that motive is irrelevant to responsibility; a crime may be committed from the best of motives and yet remain a crime.[18]

'Motives' typically enter the discussion only at the level of prior intention, where such intention is part of the definition of the offence. Did the defendant really intend to permanently deprive the victim of their property? Was this their motive or reason for taking it? In other words, there is no consideration of the ultimate goal of the action, of the reasons why this goal was chosen or why these means were employed.

Sometimes, what Norrie has called a 'utilitarian psychology' of motive is seen as useful in establishing the relevant facts of the case. But this sort of analysis is very different from the earlier consideration of motive and reason, with its emphasis upon rational deliberation, belief and context. In this system of thought

> each individual is seen as a separate monad operating according to discrete personal motivating characteristics or emotions ... Individual psychic forces like 'jealousy' or 'greed' or 'anger' or 'love' are seen as the 'springs of action'. No thought is given to the social context within which 'jealousy' or 'greed' are stimulated or to the particular content they embody.[19]

As Norrie concludes, legal doctrine has become so structured that

> intention becomes crucial to liability and motive becomes irrelevant. Then, at the end of the trial, when justice has been done, and a crim-

inal has been properly convicted, the doctrine can be put to one side and motive allowed back into the courtroom, in the non-threatening guise of a factor in mitigation of sentence.[20]

The historical basis for this development is clear:

> Desperate social need and indignant claim to right were the motives of the poor in the seventeenth, eighteenth and early nineteenth centuries. These were hardly motives calculated to win favour or compassion from a social class determined to impose a property order on all regardless of the consequences.[21]

The only situations where the defendant's reasoning process and resulting goal or purpose (in performing the criminal action) is considered relevant to the issue of culpability are those involving duress and self-defence. As Mousourakis says, such cases involve 'a morally worthy motive; that is, self preservation'.[22] But these ideas are applied in such a narrow and restricted fashion as to be irrelevant in the great majority of criminal prosecutions.

In reality, reference to jealousy and greed, anger and love, 'desire for money and perverted lust', contributes little in the way of real explanation of criminal activity. Everyone experiences such thoughts and feelings more or less frequently. The real issue, as Norrie points out, is how and why such feelings come to take the particular forms they do and contribute to particular consequences, criminal or otherwise. And to understand this, we must consider the social context and psychological makeup of the individuals and the actions concerned.

Sociological issues

On the sociological side, we need focus only upon the broad reality of contemporary economic life. In a capitalist firm, the owners have ultimate authority. They are interested in profits and in maintaining the conditions that keep the profits rolling in. They cannot oversee every aspect of workplace activity to ensure that these conditions prevail so they hire special employees who are empowered to act on their behalf in the day-to-day organisation of such profit maximisation. Such co-ordinators oversee the day-to-day actions of the workers – the actual producers and wealth generators – whose jobs are, in consequence, hugely restricted, controlled and lacking in creative possibilities. They obey the co-ordinators out of fear of being punished or fired.

A hierarchical division of labour within larger and more complex corporate structures apportions tasks, empowerment, status, remuneration and quality of life in hierarchical order. A few at the top have excellent working conditions and substantial empowerment. They are autonomous in that they are largely free of day-to-day external duress, they have freedom of choice – in terms of real options in the organisation of their work and leisure time – and they have access to a wholly different quality and quantity of information for rational decision-making within the organisation, including access to substantial human and mechanical information processing resources.

The economic power of owners and higher co-ordinators gives them power to directly influence the political process, participating in the formulation of legislation and directing the day-to-day decision-making of the political leadership. They can exert huge social and political power via the control of mass communications.

Those who have acquired sufficient assets through inheritance or other means can live very comfortably with no need to work at all. They can leave the management of such assets to others. They can choose to do whatever work might appeal to them, or simply enjoy the benefits of consumption. They can study what they want, possess what they want, travel when and where they want.

Those in the middle ranks fall well below these levels of autonomy, in relation to both effective power and decision-making within the organisation and the power of money outside it. And the great majority, in the lower ranks, have effectively no power at all, within the structure or outside it. In the first world they probably do have access to basic necessities of food, clothing, accommodation and transport, though the increasing numbers employed on a casual or part-time basis find it more and more difficult to make ends meet.

Many of those at the bottom do not enjoy their jobs, or do not enjoy much of what they do at work. They work in order to get money to live. While they work they follow orders from others, with which they do not necessarily agree. Often they have no knowledge of the decisions underlying such orders, who has made them, how or why. And today, with high levels of chronic unemployment and underemployment, they must struggle all the harder – through appropriate deference and ever more unpaid overtime – in order to hold onto any kind of employment. In other words, the greater part of their working lives consists of coerced, rather than free, action. They operate under continuous duress. And their limited incomes similarly reduce the options available to them outside the working environment.

Beyond the corporate sector is the small business sector where owner-managers exercise some power over their day-to-day lives but struggle to keep their heads above water in an intensely competitive environment. They have to pay the monopoly prices of big corporate suppliers, and struggle to compete both with other small businesses and with the cartels, economies of scale and long-range planning of big corporate operators. And conditions for workers within such smaller enterprises are typically even worse than those in bigger operations because of much tighter profit margins, higher costs, negligible unionisation and weaker legal protections.

Beyond the small business sector is the world of the long-term unemployed and radically underemployed. Government social security payments fail to accommodate rents, food, clothes, etc to allow for even minimally decent living standards. Some do not even receive these payments and some are unable to make best use of them. In other words, their life options are severely restricted – so long as they stay within the legal economy. And powerful social forces of denigration and victimisation, by the police and social welfare authorities amongst others, work to undermine the self-esteem and psychological wellbeing of those in this group.

Advertisers and marketers make massive efforts to stimulate ever more wants for ever more consumer goods. New products can be presented as compensations for the general powerlessness, frustration, insecurity, domination and struggle of the majority of the population. But such potential consumers feel all the more inadequate and frustrated when they cannot – legally – access such proliferating 'compensations'. Here is another major source of duress for many people – the duress of thwarted desires, along with envy and resentment of those who apparently have everything while doing nothing to deserve it.

Supposedly, the advanced industrial democracies allow and encourage 'mobility', whereby, through appropriate effort, those born into the lower echelons of the social class structure can drag themselves up to higher levels. Anti-discrimination laws are supposed to safeguard and facilitate such mobility.

In reality, available positions rapidly decline up the hierarchy. No matter how much effort is expended by the lower orders, only a tiny percentage will be able to ascend and only at the expense of others moving in the opposite direction. Anti-discrimination legislation cannot compensate for the advantages of established wealth, influence and connections enjoyed by those born into the upper echelons.[23] Some individuals, through luck, as much as effort, through appeasing and pleasing those above them, are able to ascend a step up from the lower levels. Some choose not to try to do so, given the behaviour required of those in higher levels. Most remain in the social stratum into which they are born.

Class and crime

The hierarchy of the social class structure therefore corresponds to a hierarchy of degrees of liberty of action, freedom of choice and effective deliberation, with reduced free will and increased duress further down the system. And such a structure goes a long way towards explaining patterns of crime in contemporary society.

At the top, those who operate and benefit from such a fundamentally unequal and immoral system have the capacity to commit crime on a grand scale with effective impunity. The very scope of the freedom enjoyed by members of the ruling elite goes a long way toward explaining their proclivities for price fixing, collusive tendering, bribery, patent violation, false advertising, insider trading, trading while insolvent, paying below-award wages, tax and other fraud, manufacture and sale of dangerous products, environmental damage and provision of unsafe working conditions leading to industrial death, injury and disease. In their role as agents of the duress experienced by those below, they should also be held responsible as inciters of, and accessories to, the crimes of those below them.

In the lower ranks, it is restriction of the scope of free choice and action that explains predominant patterns of crime. The intense competitive pressures upon smaller businesses contribute to crimes in the interests of cutting costs, including employment offences, consumer offences, food offences, and environmental crime. 'Poor economic performance [can] make offending seem a rational choice to maximise profits or to ensure the survival of the business.'[24]

Within the working class a proportion of those who are continually reminded that they are without value in the legal economy may turn instead to the criminal economy. A proportion of those who are continuously victimised by the forces of law and order eventually lose respect for such a system, and become involved in street crime.

Some of the most frustrated, exploited and downtrodden members of society may turn to illegal drugs for solace, as well as to alcohol, cigarettes and legal anti-depressants and stimulants. Those who become addicted to such illegal drugs but cannot afford to pay for them through legal employment turn to crime to support their habits. Addiction is a potent form of duress, analogous to immediate threats of violence.

For some of those faced with the poverty and ignominy of long-term unemployment or a life of powerless drudgery with minimum respect and remuneration, a life of property crime or drug dealing can appear to offer a viable alternative, with mental challenge, excitement, financial reward, independence, empowerment and self-respect.

The two most common types of interaction identified as crimes of violence by the Australian criminal justice system are 'confrontational violence between males, typically young and of marginal socio-economic status', and 'violent interaction between family members and other intimates', both often involving alcohol.[25]

In the first case, we can trace a path of causal determination from income inequality and discrimination, through disrespect and powerlessness, to street violence associated with the defence of honour. The greater the scale of income and social power inequality, the more those at the bottom of the scale, experiencing comparatively greater poverty and powerlessness, and corresponding social disrespect, may feel that they have to defend the vestiges of self-respect they have left. Physical violence is sometimes seen as the only means at their disposal to do so. In the second case, as Hogg and Brown observe:

> it would be surprising if the material stresses generated by poverty, unemployment and social isolation did not seriously exacerbate the ordinary, day-to-day tensions that arise within family relationships and produce higher levels of conflict and violence.[26]

At the same time, it needs to be borne in mind that, as Wilkinson says, violence will always appear to

> [be] concentrated in poor areas and occur primarily amongst the poor themselves ... because what counts as violence are those forms of coercion not sanctioned by social institutions; making people

homeless by ending a tenancy is not an act of violence, whereas hitting the landlord is.[27]

The empirical evidence supports the idea that duress of social deprivation motivates a significant proportion of street crime. A prison survey in 1973 found that

> only 4% of prisoners had completed the HSC, compared to over 20% of the general male population aged 15 years or more. More than two-thirds belonged to the lowest occupational strata [unskilled], compared to just over two-fifths of the general adult population; a further 30% belonged to the second lowest stratum [clerical, trades skilled] and under 2% were from professional or middle management backgrounds compared to almost one-quarter of the general population.[28]

And a survey in 1996 found that

> 50% of male prisoners and more than 75% of females had not been employed in the six months prior to their imprisonment. More than 50% of males and almost 50% of females had not completed secondary schooling to school certificate level and fewer than 10% had experienced any post secondary education.[29]

Indigenous people are heavily overrepresented in the social underclass, with unemployment levels as much as 80–90% in some communities. As Hogg and Brown note:

> When at work, Aboriginal people earn on average about half of the income of non-Aboriginal Australians ... government payments [are] the main source of income for [over 50%] of Aboriginal people ... They are massively disproportionately over-represented amongst the homeless population and the educationally disadvantaged. Aboriginal communities continue to experience high levels of [substance abuse,] infant mortality and health problems.[30]

And, 'Indigenous people in Australia are incarcerated at massively disproportionate rates compared to the general population.'[31]

> As at the 2000 prison census, there were 4095 Indigenous prisoners in Australian prisons, constituting 19% of the prison population. The national rate of Indigenous imprisonment was ... almost 15 times the non-Indigenous imprisonment rate.[32]

Psychological issues

On the psychological side, individual life paths, including free decision-making, are profoundly shaped by personality structures established in early childhood. And different sorts of personalities impose different sorts of restrictions upon individual autonomy and free will.

Particularly significant are issues of self-esteem. Those who do not achieve a 'built-in sense of self-esteem' in childhood tend to develop depressive personality structures, leaving them vulnerable to self-blame and feelings of hopelessness and worthlessness in face of reverses and difficulties. Such individuals need repeated assurance in the form of others' good opinion in order to maintain their own psychic health.[33]

Given the potentially disastrous personal consequences of the negative judgments of peers and others for those prone to depression, such a need for recognition and reassurance can override both principled objections to criminal activity and fear of criminal penalty in motivating such individuals to participate in joint criminal operations, doing their part to retain the love or respect of other members of the gang or criminal 'community'.

Because depressive personalities tend to suppress their own opinions and defer to others in their attempts to win love and approval, they tend to accumulate an increasing amount of (repressed) resentment, anger and aggression. There is always the danger that such aggression will be turned away from themselves and onto others, particularly those they feel have let them down, or those who they feel they can safely abuse.

Hysterical personalities are similarly 'dominated by the urgent need to please others in order to master the fear of being unable to do so'. As a result of being disregarded in childhood, their needs not appreciated, they become demanding and attention-seeking as adults. 'This results in restless activity, dramatisation and exaggeration ... And unrealistic dependence upon others.'[34] 'People with hysterical personalities have high anxiety, high intensity and high reactivity.'[35] Their proneness to drama and risk, and to trying to master frightening possibilities by initiating them, can get them into criminal legal difficulties.

At the other end of the scale are those obsessional personalities driven to pursue their own priorities – of order, organisation and control – irrespective of what others might think, and sometimes at others' expense. Driven by their own conscience, rather than by the opinions of other people, it is quite possible for such individuals to fall foul of the criminal justice system, where its values do not happen to correspond with their own.

For some, the voice of conscience is the voice of God, commanding absolute obedience, even if this is at the expense of being seen – by some – as a criminal and a law-breaker. Direct sanction by divine authority can sometimes be seen to justify or demand horrific acts of violence.

A powerful, rigid and punitive conscience can be firmly established in early childhood on the model of parental authority, rewarding the individual concerned with feelings of pride for conforming to its dictates and punishing failure to do so with pangs of guilt. Its value system can be out of kilter with the more developed ideas and values of the adult. In such a situation the conscience itself is experienced as exerting powerful internal duress upon the individual concerned, forcing them to engage in – or avoid – particular actions 'against their better judgment'.

Schizoid personalities are still further removed from influence by group norms and values. By virtue of having lost a care-giver in early life, or having been treated as an appendage to the parents, or as someone whose needs are destructive of the person to whom they turn to fulfil them, they have withdrawn from intimate relations with other people (as too painful, dangerous or overwhelming). They have developed a complex fantasy world to compensate for their lack of fulfilment in the real world. And to the extent that fantasies of power and domination, including paranoid feelings and delusions, spill over into their actual relations with other people, such individuals can come into conflict with the criminal law.

Particularly serious problems of early childhood development and/or later social experiences lead to more extreme forms of such behavioural tendencies and greater likelihood of more serious psychopathology. And such psychopathology runs along a continuum from mild and temporary neurosis to serious long-term psychosis.[36]

Tangential to, but interacting with, such issues of personality are issues of intellectual development and disability. Here again, some individuals will be significantly disadvantaged by their heredity, or by developmental damage, and will not necessarily receive the special assistance they might need to realise their full potential.

Again, the empirical evidence confirms the significant involvement of psychopathology and intellectual disability in the causation of crime. The 1973 prison survey, referred to earlier, found that one-third of prisoners had received professional help or treatment for a nervous, emotional or mental problem. Nor does this mean that other prisoners were necessarily free of such problems. And studies by Hayes and McIlwain in 1988 and 1997 found 12.9% of the NSW prison population as having an intellectual disability.[37] Levy observes that

> the prevalence of mental illness among prisoners is higher than in the general community. In a submission to a recent NSW Parliamentary Select Committee Inquiry on the Increase in Prisoner Population, the Department of Corrective Services stated that 13% of female inmates in New South Wales have an intellectual disability, 21% had attempted suicide and 40% had a diagnosis of personality disorder.[38]

Interactions

Such psychological and sociological processes of disadvantage are intimately interconnected. Even relatively mild dispositions towards depression, compulsion, schizoid withdrawal or paranoia can lead to serious pathology under the pressure of social circumstances of discrimination, deprivation and powerlessness. And those suffering such deprivation are least likely to get effective assistance in coping with such pathology, or with intellectual disability.

The stresses of social powerlessness and anxiety in the parental generation can create major psychological problems for new generations, insofar as the latter become victims of parental mortality and morbidity, psychopathology, drug abuse, violence, disintegrating family structures, poor housing and nutrition.

Teenagers of all classes are driven by hormones and social dislocation into risk and challenge to established authority. But social and psychological disadvantage brings working-class youth into contact with the criminal justice system at an early age, whereas middle- and upper-class youth are protected. Significant numbers of such disadvantaged young people move from juvenile detention centres on to adult prisons. The appalling conditions of the latter, with inmates stripped of all human rights and human dignity, subjected to regular threats and assaults by staff and other inmates, exposed to dirty air, poor-quality food and rampant hepatitis C infection, with huge pressures towards hard drug use in dangerous, insanitary conditions, exacerbate social and psychological disadvantage.[39]

Inmates often emerge psychologically and physically damaged, with criminal reputations, which make them the objects of intensified police surveillance, harassment and victimisation, and make reward-ing employment – or any legal employment – all the more difficult to obtain. Hence the high recidivism rates, as victims become trapped in a cycle of ever diminishing real options and further reduced 'free will' and autonomy, with 56 per cent of prisoners known to have served a prison sentence on a previous occasion on prison census night in 2000.[40]

At the other end of the social scale, the wealthy and the power-ful have access to the best resources for coping with both mental illness and intellectual disability, including long-term humanistic and insight-based therapies, rather than debilitating and toxic drug treat-ments. At the same time, they are free to indulge the more anti-social tendencies of their psychopathologies without fear of criminal legal intervention.

Wealthy narcissists can command the uncritical approval and respect – indeed love and worship – of others, which they need to maintain self-esteem, or, at least, they can command the appearance of such love and respect, through appropriate positive and negative reinforcement procedures applied to those within their power.

Wealthy obsessives and compulsives can indulge their will to power, domination, control, discipline, order, and cleanliness through rigidly disciplining and controlling the lives of those subject to their author-ity, including workers driven to ever greater productive efforts, of harder work and longer hours.

Wealthy paranoids can indulge their need to oppose the forces of evil through seeking, and achieving, political office, or power within law-enforcement agencies. And serious psychopathology and intel-lectual disability seem to pose few problems for successful careers at this level of the social hierarchy.

Over a dozen research projects on corporate career mobility demonstrate that psychopathic or anti-social personality is an advan-tage when it comes to promotion to the 'top positions' of the corpo-rate hierarchy. As Box points out, such research shows that those who attain such positions are not so much intelligent as shrewd – their organisational sense enabled them to sniff out the golden chance and grasp it firmly ... they had the moral flexibility to meet shifting organisational demands and still enjoy the sleep of the just – their ability to relativise other moral imperatives while constantly prioritising the pursuit of organisational goals ... [facilitated] a moral flexibility others denied themselves.[41]

Croall notes that 'personality types ... associated with business success – including a propensity to take risks, recklessness, ambitiousness, drive, egocentricity and a hunger for power ... are [also] linked with white collar crime'. Such crime can be justified as 'being in the interests of the company'.[42]

Criminal minds versus class structures

In this context, we can see how generally meaningless and misleading is any idea of the 'criminal mind' as 'cause' of crime. Were those at the top to be exposed to the circumstances of those at the bottom, no doubt they would respond in similar fashion. Their minds are no different; it is their social circumstances that are different, leading to different behaviour or different treatment for the same behaviour.

Supposedly everyone is equally subject to the same laws in all common law jurisdictions. Judges and magistrates swear oaths to 'do right by all manner of people ... without fear or favour, affection or ill-will'.[43] And legal authorities have typically seen equal access to justice, including access to appropriate professional assistance, as an integral part of the 'rule of law'.

One might think that such equality implied treating those in similar situations in similar fashion. And, on the face of it, this is what the criminal law does. Supposedly, individuals are punished in proportion to the seriousness of their crime.

But 'seriousness' is ambiguous. It can mean the extent of actual harmful consequences. It can refer to something like the objective extent of risk of harm to which others are exposed by the action – how likely it is that such harm will eventuate and how great the possible harm is. Or it can refer to the extent of free will and autonomy – including the extent of restriction of such free will, on the part of individual perpetrators – along the lines considered so far. Extent of actual harmful consequences creates major problems in a class divided society. Stealing from the rich can cause far less suffering than stealing similar amounts or much lesser amounts from the poor.

At the moment, for the crimes of the working class, ideas of objective harmfulness are built into the definitions of the offences – as murder or manslaughter or theft or burglary or robbery – without any reference to such social contextual considerations. So those found guilty are supposedly punished for the extent of real harm caused, without any analysis of real harm, at least until sentencing.

Their employers, on the other hand, in the crucial areas of health and safety at work and pollution, are held responsible for the supposed extent of risk to which they have exposed others, through contravention of relevant regulations, without reference to actual harmful consequences up until the sentencing stage. With risk treated as inherently less 'serious' than actual harm, this de-emphasises the criminality of employers as against workers. Together, these operations effectively preclude any real utilitarian assessment of the extent of harm caused by either the rulers or the ruled – within the criminal legal process.

Such comparatively 'lenient' treatment of the crimes of the powerful can be seen as offset by strict and absolute liability, with no requirement to establish a subjective fault element, while such a subjective element does have to be proved in working-class property crimes and crimes of violence. This only serves to mask the extent of culpability of the employers, in terms of their generally greater scope of free action, compared to that of the workers. At the same time, the limited application of available defences, with no real consideration of the duress of social deprivation, radically restricts what actually has to be proved in this area of culpability for working-class crime.

If we really believe in punishment in proportion to culpability, where the latter is a function, not only of the seriousness of the crime, but also of the degree of real freedom of choice able to be exercised by the perpetrator, then we must take account of the disparities of autonomy and freedom of choice across the social class structure.

Action motivated by need or desperation, by enforced ignorance or lack of available alternatives, is different from action motivated by pursuit of wealth and power by the already wealthy and powerful, and chosen despite awareness of both its harmful consequences and of real non-criminal alternatives for achieving similar ends. Action, which is not only criminal but also betrays the special trust associated with social positions of power and privilege, would seem to carry greater moral culpability.

Beyond this point, it is unequal to impose punishments determined either by the seriousness of the crime or the extent of fault of the perpetrator, without reference to the circumstances of the individual punished. A fine can have quite different practical significance when imposed upon a rich person as against a poor person. A prison can have quite different consequences when imposed upon a vulnerable and attractive young man, likely to suffer rape in prison, or a hardened criminal psychopath likely to be the agent of such a prison rape.

Mandatory sentencing policies highlight, concretise and exacerbate the irrationality and immorality of the system. But past practices of judicial discretion in sentencing show little evidence of seriously addressing the issues raised here. Nor should the issues be left to the whims of such discretion.

As is suggested by the foregoing analysis, effective reduction of street crime (and, for that matter, corporate crime also) depends upon major social-structural change, addressing the inequalities of wealth and power that are the primary causes of such crime.

Discussion topics

1. Explain the role of free will in criminal liability. Include reference to omissions.
2. What is meant by a 'black-and-white picture' of free will and determinism?
3. How are issues of free will associated with issues of social class and or psychology?
4. Is there one law for the rich and another for the poor?

Additional resources

S. Box, Crime, *Power and Mystification*, Tavistock, London, 1983.

D. Brown and M. Wilkie (eds), *Prisoners As Citizens*, Federation Press, Sydney, 2002.

H. Croall, Understanding *White Collar Crime*, Open University Press, Buckingham, 2001.

R. Hogg and D. Brown, *Rethinking Law and Order*, Pluto Press, Sydney, 1998.

A. Norrie, *Crime, Reason and History*, Butterworths, London, 2001

Chapter 17

CRIME AND PUNISHMENT

In this chapter we focus upon some of the ways in which classical liberal and libertarian thinking have most profoundly influenced the common law criminal justice system. Specifically, we consider classical liberal and libertarian ideas of legitimate punishment for criminal wrongdoing, based upon ideas of 'just deserts'. Just as in the economic sphere, libertarians have traditionally favoured the idea of reward in proportion to valuable social contribution, so, in the sphere of law, have they favoured the idea of punishment proportional to the extent of harm inflicted.

As we have seen in earlier chapters, in the tradition of classical liberal and libertarian thinking, punitive state intervention is justified only in the case of violation of others' core 'natural' rights to life and property. This means that for consistent libertarians, victimless crimes should not be treated as crimes at all. On the other hand, we have also seen how libertarians subscribe to a generally negative and pessimistic view of human nature, as greedy and self-serving, implying that such violations are likely to be fairly frequent without sufficient deterrent measures put in place by the state.

At the same time, such selfish nature is (generally) not seen to override individual 'freedom of choice' of action as cause of criminal wrongdoing. Rather, such violations of basic rights are seen as (typically) produced by the free choice of individual violators, involving some sort of decision about the costs and benefits of such actions to themselves. Libertarians require that such individual rights violators be held fully responsible for their criminal choices, without any reference to social or biological determination of their actions. And all such wrongdoing should be treated in a consistent fashion, so as to allow rational decision-making, and effectively influence such individual cost benefit analysis, in the direction of crime reduction in the future.

First and foremost such responsibility and consistency are understood in terms of *retribution*, in the form of infliction of suffering commensurate with the seriousness of the wrong the perpetrator has inflicted upon others, along with possible compensation paid by the offenders to their victims. Such state-imposed suffering takes the form of deprivation of property (fines), of liberty (imprisonment) and, in some jurisdictions, of life (execution).

Such privation and suffering, seen as consequences of transgression, are also supposed to serve the function of both *individual and general deterrence*, dissuading the individual concerned from committing further offences (on the basis of a revised calculation of costs and benefits), and similarly dissuading others from committing any such offence for fear of similar punishment. Imprisonment can also serve to protect life and property through *incapacitation*, depriving the imprisoned individual of the opportunity for further crimes (in the wider community) through confining them to the precincts of the prison.

As White and Perrone point out, in line with general libertarian concerns to minimise state power:

> this approach also supports the idea that security, law enforcement and prisons should be private rather than public institutions. This reflects a broad ideological commitment to the so-called free market as the best and most efficient avenue for the provision of social services.[1]

More efficient private services will cost the public less in taxes. Ideally, ways should be found to enable such systems to pay for themselves, through the productive labour of the prisoners or through charging them for prison services.

Historical considerations

The legal system in the English-speaking world has been profoundly influenced by classical liberal/libertarian ideas since the first development of such ideas in the 17th century. As Norrie notes:

the revolution against absolutism came early in England, and the common law was instrumental in enshrining the rights and liberties of the subject against the sovereign and of establishing the role of judges as impartial interpreters of the law.[2]

In the 17th and 18th centuries, however, particularly draconian criminal penalties were imposed for any and every infringement upon the private property rights of the wealthy, with little consideration for the rights of offenders, or the justice or fairness of the punishments. Public displays of torture and execution were 'designed to manage the population at large, through fear and threat'. As White and Perrone observe, 'this approach to punishment [was] particularly concerned with the broader deterrent effect of exemplary sanctions, regardless of whether or not these [were] proportional to the crime'.[3]

But at the end of the 18th and in the course of the 19th centuries, under pressure from liberal, and particularly utilitarian, reformers, the focus increasingly shifted to the idea of 'doing justice to individuals' accused of law-breaking as well as to the victims or potential victims of crime.

This meant restricting culpability and punishment to those who had voluntarily broken the law, in the sense of freely choosing to do so, and consciously intending the criminal action in question, with knowledge of the likely harmful consequences of the action. In theory at least it meant applying the same principles, equally, to all offenders. And it meant applying punishments appropriate to the nature and extent of the harm caused.

Utilitarians, in particular, argued that only pain just sufficient to achieve effective deterrence should be inflicted, and no more. 'All punishments were pains and therefore evils in themselves, but they were justified because of their potential to deter the pain and evil of crime.'[4] As Norrie says:

> Translating [the classical] economic theory [of the free and rational utility maximiser] into the realm of social control, they argued that free individuals could work out for themselves that the costs of punishment must outweigh the benefits of crime and would, therefore, rationally desist from its commission ... Just as the market regulates individual economic actions, so the criminal law regulates social control as an adjunct to the market, The task of law, according to Bentham, was to secure the harmony of individual interests, to supplement the invisible hand of the market, by keeping egoism within acceptable bounds.[5]

It is easy to see problems here, not least the gap between the real social circumstances of those likely to be accused of criminal offences at the time – 'living in conditions that encouraged little respect for the social order and its laws'[6] – and the model of the 'freely choosing', rational calculator at the foundation of these ideas. Bentham himself recognised that, in fact, it is the conditions in which people live that determine their actions, particularly conditions of poverty, inequality and desperation, which determine the working class to do what they know is illegal despite harsh punishments (for example, stealing to live), so that crime reduction requires also substantial social-structural interventions by state power.

There are obvious parallels here with the problem of determining individual contribution to the value of productive output in the context of corporate structures and infrastructures, as the supposed basis for legitimate reward in the economic sphere, according to classical liberal ideas. Just as a complex constellation of interacting individuals is typically involved in the production of any particular finished good in an advanced industrial society, so is a similarly complex constellation of people involved in producing the harms classified as crimes.

As Box argues:

> conventionally defined crime is likely to rise amongst the poorest and most deprived sections of society, particularly in a time of recession. What is significant amongst those who are likely to turn to crime is the coupling of 'thwarted ambition' with 'relative deprivation' in a situation of marginalisation from institutionalised organisations of social change, and alienation from the forces of law and order.[7]

Therefore, all those who intentionally, recklessly or negligently contribute to such conditions of poverty, deprivation and alienation are, in part, responsible for the resulting criminal activity. This is likely to include politicians (particularly neo-liberal and libertarian politicians) and executives whose planning policies have directly contributed to increased unemployment, reduced access to social services, greater income inequality, and reduced social cohesion, trust and respect (including encouragement of racism and prejudice). It is likely to include police officers whose victimisation and persecution of particular social groups, such as working-class youth and ethnic and cultural minorities, has contributed to the alienation of such groups from established principles of law and order.

It is likely to include judges and prosecutors who send such victims of police discrimination to prisons where they become victims of further violence and abuse and acquire criminal reputations, connections and habits that increase the likelihood of further criminal involvements. And it includes those advertisers and marketers who contribute to the production of unlimited desires for expensive consumption items amongst those who cannot possibly legally acquire the means to purchase such items.

No doubt such individuals will respond by arguing that their contribution to crime was an unfortunate by-product of other useful activities whose social value outweighs the social costs of the crimes in question. Quite apart from the likely difficulties of establishing any such thing, libertarians have, anyway, strongly supported a general exclusion of considerations of motive from determination of criminal culpability. At best, such issues are to be addressed only at the sentencing stage.

There are also problems of appropriate matching of retributive punishment and crime, once we move beyond the old *lex talionis*, an eye for an eye and a tooth for a tooth. How do we compare the pain of losing a certain sum of money, for example, with that of a certain period of imprisonment? And from a utilitarian point of view, what if the extent of pain that needs to be inflicted to deter a particular sort of criminal activity is much greater than the pain inflicted by such an act? Presumably, no such penalty can be justified in such circumstances. It is fair enough to say that no-one should benefit at someone else's expense. But how much pain is permitted to avoid this?

There are issues here of how the extent of harm or pain to the victim is measured. Clearly, a theft of the same (small) sum of money from a very wealthy person will cause a lot less (objective) harm or (subjective) pain to that rich person than the theft of the same sum from a poor person will cause to that poor person. Indeed, stealing from the rich person to give to the poor person could cause very much more good (and happiness) than bad (and pain). Yet libertarians have been very reluctant to impose substantially lesser penalties on the perpetrators in the first – or third – sort of cases, as it would seem they logically should do. Perhaps the third case deserves reward.

There is plenty of evidence that by far the greatest harm to the greatest number of people is caused by politicians initiating wars of aggression with attacks on civilian targets, ruthlessly repressing dissi-

dents within their own states and pursuing economic policies (nationally and internationally) that produce increased unemployment,
inequality and poverty; by corporate executives killing their workers
through inadequate attention to health and safety at work, polluting
the world with longlasting poisons and carcinogens, and marketing
dangerous vehicles, drugs, foods, weapons and tools of torture and
repression on a huge scale. Yet these people are seldom, if ever, prosecuted by the criminal justice system. Nor are libertarians typically
very active or consistent in demanding any such prosecution.

On the other side of the coin, a small fine will cause much more
harm to a poor person than to a rich one. Thus, the utilitarian
Bentham argued for fines in proportion to the wealth of those fined,
as well as to the extent of their wrongdoing.

We can extend this idea to consider also the prison system. There is
reason to believe that some can survive and prosper in prison environments, largely at the expense of others, while those others can suffer
appallingly. Psychopathic thugs outside remain psychopathic thugs
inside, but inside there can be fewer obstacles to the exercise of their
selfish violence. In the barbaric 'state of nature' prevailing in many
prisons, the strongest and most unscrupulously violent (whether prisoners or warders) frequently rule, in the sense of effectively subjecting others to their will, in supplying money, drugs, labour and sexual
services. The suffering of such others can, of course, be unimaginably
terrible. But, again, libertarians have been reluctant to consider such
real issues of the extent of pain and suffering of specific perpetrators,
as, again, it would logically seem they should.

If we focus upon the utilitarian principle of pain just sufficient to
ensure effective deterrence, other problems arise. The evidenceindi-
cates

> no consistent deterrent effect from punishment in society, and that
> the use of the penal system, and in particular imprisonment ... is not
> an especially effective [individual] deterrent to crime. Recidivism
> rates remain high amongst those who receive custodial sentences
> [in one year, in England, approximately 50% of adults and 66%
> of juveniles were reconvicted within two years of a prior sentence].
> And there is no evidence that longer custodial sentences produce
> better results than shorter sentences.[8]

Similarly, in Australia, 'on prison census night 2000, 56% of prisoners
were known to have served a prison sentence on a previous occasion'.[9]

Of course, this does not tell us anything about all who might have avoided crime altogether through effective general deterrence by the prison system. But again, the evidence is that it is the 'subjective probability of being caught' as much as the nature of the punishment that is most significant in motivating those 'no longer fully anchored in the value system of society, but who still have sufficient to lose from being caught and imprisoned'.[10] And detection rates for many crimes are widely known to be very low.

As Norrie says, 'to increase them would involve substantial increase in police powers and numbers and levels of state surveillance in society ... with its own costs in terms of provoking other more serious kinds of crime',[11] including crimes of police corruption and public resistance. Certainly, libertarians and neo-liberals (generally) have problems in the increased tax costs and decreased individual freedom associated with such an expansion of state repressive powers.

Prisons

Libertarians have generally been strong supporters of maintaining and extending the prison system, without any major structural reform. Yet, as noted earlier, there are very serious problems with such a system.

Ever since the time of the reform movement (and before), prisons throughout the common law world have remained cultures of violence and disrespect, fostering and encouraging law-breaking rather than reducing it. As White and Perrone point out:

> An individual who enters the prison system undergoes a symbolic depersonalisation transition, stripped, probed, redressed and endowed with the status of a convict. As part of the process, the individual is required to take on the mores, customs and culture of the prison, all of which are premised upon conflict between inmates and guards.[12]

Even though the majority of prisoners have not been convicted of violent offences, prison officers perceive the prison situation as a battle for survival where they need to employ violent repression to control dangerous 'animals'. And 'the problems associated with an antagonistic prison environment and high levels of distrust and dishonesty make it very difficult for either side to change'.[13]

The prison environment is far removed from the realities of outside life and this is a central factor in prisoners' difficulties of reintegration. The prison leaves indelible marks on the inmates, both in personal antagonism and frustration, and in the official blot on their record which will dog them the rest of their lives and severely effect their chances of successfully re-entering the maintenance of social life ... The prison environment violates many of the known principles of social and psychological development. It promotes norms and practices which legitimate rather than reduce deviance.[14]

Cutting inmates off from friends and families, depriving them of heterosexual and caring relationships, depriving them of autonomy through subjection to a vast system of rigidly imposed rules, depriving them of all power over their own lives and circumstances – these are precisely the ways to undermine future coping and responsibility. Above all, throwing non-violent individuals together with others (including guards) with a history of violence in a situation effectively removed from all protection by the 'rule of law' is a way to create desperate, angry, bitter, physically and psychologically damaged people, rather than responsible, capable citizens. As Hogg points out, in Australia:

the national rate of recorded prisoner on prisoner assaults is about two and a half times the rate of assault in the general community. If the ratio of unreported to reported assaults in the prison system were the same as that in the general community [about 4:1] the difference ... would be about 11 times.[15]

At the same time, life within prisons 'is a judicial no-go area' with the courts deferring to executive authority in 'the management of the good order and discipline of the prison'.[16] Prisoners are subjected to continuous violence and unhealthy air and food, and forced to work for capitalist corporations with no proper payment, Workcover, occupational health or safety or workers' compensation coverage.[17] They have no protection from police authorities and effectively no legal rights to pursue any of these issues in the courts.

The criminal justice system in Australia systematically discriminates against particular social groups, with 50% of prisoners having failed to complete secondary schooling, 40% of females and 30% of males having long-term illnesses or disabilities, and one-third of males having been confined to juvenile institutions at some time. The unemployed are particularly likely to end up in gaol. And indigenous people are imprisoned at about 15 times the rate of non-indigenous people.[18]

With 25 per cent of young men in NSW gaols being raped, some on a daily basis, according to the research of NSW magistrate David Heilpern, with extensive use of hard drugs and rampant hepatitis C, with boys schooled in a life of crime and pleading with relatives to smuggle in drugs to stop them being bashed, there are very serious ethical questions of whether the existence of such institutions is not a much greater crime than the 'crimes' they are supposed to address, quite apart from their encouragement of further crimes in the wider society and the general failure of deterrence. Here, indeed, we can add judges and prosecutors who send young cannabis users and fine defaulters to prison to be raped and murdered, to become addicted to heroin and infected with hepatitis C and AIDS, to the list of most serious harm causers.

The social-liberal response

At the end of the 19th century, with the birth of welfare state interventionism (in the context of international imperialist rivalries and related concerns about the unhealthy state of the working class undermining national competitiveness), we see the development of alternative social-liberal ideologies of sentencing, as a response to the failure of classical libertarian models to 'control crime or legitimate punishment'.[19] As Norrie says, such social liberals 'added to the ideological brew of utilitarian deterrence and retributive justice new antithetical views of the nature and role of punishment', specifically 'ideas of social control that took the form of 'welfare', a 'welfare sanction'[20] based upon ideas of treatment and training. As Norrie explains:

> central to these developments was the growth of the positivist school of criminology which developed in this period. The essence of this new 'science' was its claim to knowledge of the nature, causes and treatment of criminality and delinquency, which held out the possibility of arresting its development in the social body. Like … doctors [at that time arguing for the absence of free will in psychologically disturbed individuals] the criminologists rejected the classical ideas of the penal reformers concerning the responsibility and freedom of the individual.[21]

The new criminologists saw criminal behaviour as the product of particular social or physiological circumstances influencing individual psychology. And criminality became, for them, 'the target of direct technologies of behaviour control, rather than the respectful response to a pre-existing rational moral act'.[22] In particular, they saw imprisonment as an opportunity for 'stimulating or awakening the higher susceptibilities of prisoners, [developing] their moral instincts, [training] them in orderly and industrial habits',[23] rather than 'a sanction essentially rooted in deterrence' and pain infliction.

At the same time, for those few wrongdoers who proved impossible to reform owing to their irremediable damage, and who posed a continuing serious danger to the community (as identified by the appropriate experts), prisons also provided a means of community protection through incapacitation. As White and Perrone point out:

> a quasi-military style of imprisonment adopted in the 1830s, with prisoners confined to small cells with strict rules of silence [supposedly maximising their opportunities to reflect upon past sins and thereby allowing their own consciences to contribute both to their punishment and spiritual healing], was replaced by the early 1900s with a more open sort of system, which allowed prisoners increased freedom of movement and interaction in exercise yards, and productive group work aiming to 'normalise' their behaviours and prepare their reintegration into society as productive and law-abiding citizens.[24]

However, it is again easy to see the problems with the new approach. Most obviously, there is the radical contradiction between continuing goals of retribution and deterrence (as previously understood), and new, humanitarian aims of moral reform and rehabilitative treatment through provision of an environment supportive of such 'positive' change in the offender. It is simply not possible (or, at least, extremely difficult) to seriously pursue the latter goals in the sort of environment generated and sustained by the former.

As White and Perrone note, the contradictions are further exacerbated when we factor in external pressures for 'cost effectiveness' as well, radically reducing the real material resources for effective rehabilitation, and contributing to overcrowding that itself further undermines such programmes.

As noted in the last section, despite rehabilitative ideas and interventions, prisons have generally remained cultures of violence, dishonesty and disrespect, which encourage crime, inside the prison itself and in the world outside. Such rehabilitative reforms as expanded education and skills training, drug treatment and group psychotherapy for prisoners have simply been grafted on to such a culture, without addressing the fundamental issues of conflict, brutality, dehumanisation and ill health considered earlier. And they have therefore never been given any real chance of general success.

Equally important, even an effective regime of genuine rehabilitation would fail to address major social-structural causes of crime. Effectively preparing offenders for constructive employment in the wider society counts for little if there are no jobs for them in that wider society. Treating them with care and respect while in confinement is of reduced significance if they are treated with a total lack of care and respect in the world outside, by employers, police and welfare services, for example.

Reaction

In this context we can understand the neo-liberal reaction against social-liberal, rehabilitative ideas in recent decades. On the one hand, this is merely part of the general shift away from social-liberal ideas arising out of the recession of the mid-70s and the subsequent rise to power of neo-liberal ideas, regimes and policies. But, at the same time, it has been possible for neo-liberals to point to the failure of previous regimes of rehabilitation in terms of continued high rates of recidivism and criminal activity.

So too have they focused upon criminological ideas of social causation of crime and social technologies of crime reduction, to argue that social-liberal reformers have treated criminals as mere objects of external manipulation, thus failing to respect their individual autonomy and powers of decision and choice. Genuine respect for such individuals requires treating them as free agents of their own actions, rather than mere 'puppets or 'effects' of external causes.

The truth of the matter is, as we have seen, that rehabilitation has seldom been given any real chance to succeed. In the few cases where genuinely rehabilitative policies have effectively replaced the culture of violence associated with retribution, as in the Dutch and Swedish prison systems, where there is no brutalisation of prisoners or stripping away of their rights and sentences are generally short, 'recidivism rates are no higher than in other countries with twice or three times the imprisonment rates'.[25]

There need be no necessary contradiction between ideas of social determinism and recognition of, and respect for, individual autonomy. As discussed in the last chapter, autonomy is a social creation: it depends upon social provision of material, psychological and emotional resources to enable individuals to make genuinely rational and responsible choices. Seen in this light, it is obvious that autonomy can be radically compromised by conditions that preclude or obstruct such rational and moral deliberation, choice and action.

Neither does rehabilitation need to treat offenders as mere objects of external manipulation and control. On the contrary, genuine 'rehabilitation' is a collaborative enterprise, integrally involving the understanding and active participation of the offender and aiming – precisely – to increase the scope of their effective 'choice' and rational decision-making (through offering, for example, new job opportunities).

Libertarian-inspired policies of mandatory sentencing and abolition of early-release schemes have increased prison overcrowding, leading to intensified conflict and violence within prisons and still further undermining limited rehabilitative efforts. Policies that have increased unemployment and/or inequality in the wider society have contributed to increased crime rates. More police and more prosecutions have further contributed to overcrowding, anger, frustration and violence.

This certainly looks like a general policy of neo-liberals in government to undermine social services, particularly through radical funding reductions with a view to creating chaos and scandal – which are built up by a sympathetic media. The regime then declares that such services are 'not working' and need to be abolished altogether.

In light of increasing corruption at all levels of public life in recent years, with politicians lying to the public on a daily basis and using their power to feather their own financial nests, and business people unconstrained by law or morality in their pursuit of ever greater personal wealth, rehabilitation as preparation for life outside of confinement does indeed become a problematic notion. Helping the generally poor and disadvantaged victims of the criminal justice system to function 'effectively' in this world would seem to require either helping them to prepare for reduced and miserable lives as docile drudge paupers in the service sector, or helping them to become more effective criminals on the other side of the fence – as 'managers'.

Socialist criminology

A socialist criminology focuses upon addressing what are seen as the real social causes of major suffering and privation. This means dismantling the structures of market relations and class power that (are seen to) produce greedy selfishness, inequality, poverty and discrimination and thereby contribute to those actions currently treated as crimes. It aims to achieve the abolition of criminal prosecution in a future communist society, through removing the social causes of crime.

During the process of social reconstruction, the approach of the transitional socialist state to selfish acts of social disruption would presumably be informed by social-liberal ideas of rehabilitative welfare, education and assistance, with therapeutic incapacitation of the small minority possibly unable to benefit from such assistance.

The typical libertarian and neo-liberal response to such ideas is to argue that it is human nature, rather than social relations, that is the major cause of criminal wrongdoing. Crime, in the sense of self-ish behaviour causing serious harm to others, will therefore continue to exist no matter what the form of prevailing social relations, and some sort of retributive punishment will still be required as both the morally respectful and the practically effective means of keeping criminal activity within acceptable bounds.

The argument of the chapter so far provides little support for any such – ultimately contradictory – libertarian ideas. Either social control (of harmful behaviour) is possible, in which case we must look to social insight, science and practical politics, rather than prejudice, to improve its effectiveness, or it is not, in which case there is even less excuse for gratuitous torture and cruelty. There is nothing remotely respectful about sending anyone into anything resembling the current (common law) prison system.

A wealth of everyday and historical experience tells us that treating people with (genuine) respect encourages them to treat others with respect. Giving them genuine non-criminal opportunities for exciting and rewarding and socially useful life activities, with fair and adequate recompense, is the best way to reduce criminal activity. And where they are unable to take advantage of such opportunities for one reason or another, comprehensive social welfare is crucial in protecting them from the need for criminal acts.

Human nature is a difficult and problematic concept. We have touched upon some of the difficulties in earlier chapters. At this stage, we merely note that human nature in the sense of hard-wired genetic propensities or predispositions or tendencies could, indeed, be a major cause of irresponsible and harmful behaviour in some sorts of social situation, where, for example, some innately programmed sequence of behaviour is triggered by some particular sort of environmental stimulus. But this in no way implies that such harm cannot be avoided by (a) removing such triggers or (b) rearranging circumstances such that the results of the behaviour in question are harmless, rather than harmful.

Discussion topics

1   What are said to be the purposes of punishment? Can these be justified?
2   Does the Australian prison system effectively fulfil these purposes? How might the situation be improved?
3   What should be the purposes of punishment? Could we do without it altogether?

Additional resources

D. Brown and M. Wilkie (eds), *Prisoners as Citizens: Human Rights in Australian Prisons*, Federation Press, Sydney, 2002.
R. White and S. Perrone, *Crime and Social Control: An Introduction*, Oxford University Press, Oxford, 1997.

Chapter 18

TERRORISM AND DEMOCRATIC RIGHTS

One of the most striking challenges for the 21st century is the protection of democratic rights. In the opening years of the new century, numbers of governments have used the threat of terrorism as a pretext to erode such vital principles as free speech, freedom of political association, prevention of arbitrary detention and the right to seek asylum.

In Australia (and there are parallels elsewhere, notably in the United States and Britain), the early years of the century have seen three fundamental shifts in the state machinery: legislation from 2000, to permit the calling out of the military against civilian unrest; from 2001, to authorise the forcible turning away of refugee boats; and from 2002, to grant unprecedented detention and proscription powers, as well as expanded surveillance powers, to the government and its security and intelligence agencies, notably the Australian Security Intelligence Organisation (ASIO). This chapter examines the military call-out and terrorism measures; chapter 19 reviews the anti-refugee provisions.

These measures have profound implications for civil liberties, as well as for the future of international covenants, such as the Refugee Convention and the International Covenant on Civil and Political Rights. These global human rights instruments have proved largely irrelevant in curbing such powers.

The Howard government in Australia followed the lead of the Bush administration in the United States and the Blair government in Britain by declaring that the 11 September 2001 terrorist attacks in the United States required an indefinite 'war' against terrorism abroad, accompanied by curtailment of legal rights at home.

Despite criticisms by civil liberties groups, both the British and American governments introduced severe anti-terrorism measures, including detention without trial and proscription of organisations.[1] Amnesty International condemned the Bush administration for breaching the International Covenant on Civil and Political Rights and other international protocols against arbitrary detention and inhuman treatment of prisoners.[2]

Significantly, the first two sets of Australian legislation pre-dated September 11, indicating that the anti-democratic trend is more fundamental than a response to the events in New York and Washington. Rather, these atrocities, and later the Bali bombing of 12 October 2002, were seized upon to retrospectively justify, as well as to introduce new, far-reaching alterations to the legal and consti-tutional framework.

These political and legal shifts, as this chapter will review, are profoundly anti-democratic. Despite the contrary impression created by the mass media, there is no evidence of strong popular demand for such measures; in fact, each legislative package aroused considerable public opposition. A careful review of the provisions and the circum-stances in which they were introduced suggests that the purpose for their introduction is to strengthen the repressive capacities of the state against the free movement of people and other perceived threats to the political establishment.

Striking a balance?

It may be helpful to begin by examining the official justifications for the new measures. In an address to the Sydney Institute, delivered in the Mallesons Conference Room on 20 April 2004, Attorney-General Philip Ruddock outlined what he termed a 'new framework' for considering terrorism and the rule of law:

> The war on terror is like no other war in living memory. This is a war which may have no obvious conclusion, no armistice and no treaty. Victory in this war will not necessarily be measured by terri-tory gained or regimes toppled. In this war victories will be meas-ured by disasters averted and democracy strengthened. This war's victories will be measured by citizens feeling safe in their homes.

> This war's victories will be measured in the steadfastness and resolve of Australians to be cognisant of, but not to fear, a potential terrorist threat ...
>
> Our Constitution, one of the world's oldest and most stable, provides us with a mechanism to protect our country and at the same time protect civil liberties through human security laws. In enacting such laws we are not only preserving traditional notions of civil liberties and the rule of law, but we are recognising that these operate in a different paradigm. If we are to preserve human rights then we must preserve the most fundamental right of all – the right to human security.[3]

While insisting that the government is upholding the Constitution, civil liberties and the rule of law, the minister asserted that these now operate in a new paradigm: the right to human security, which is said to be the most fundamental right of all. Citing remarks by UN Secretary-General Kofi Annan, Ruddock loosely defined 'human security' as encompassing human rights, good governance, access to education and healthcare and opportunities for individuals to fulfil their potential. All these, the minister asserted, depended on a secure environment. Thus, in the name of defending civil liberties and the rule of law, they are said to no longer have any independent or absolute existence. Instead, they have been subsumed under another concept, human security. Making 'citizens feel safe in their homes' has become the chief criterion for the unknown duration of the current 'state of war'.

Despite the sweeping breadth of such claims, much of the debate and analysis in academic publications concerning the 'anti-terrorism' legislation begins with the proposition that a balance must be struck between 'national security' and 'civil liberties'. According to this approach, the only disagreement concerns where the balance should lie. By this measure, some inroads into civil liberties must be accepted. There is good cause to question this assumption, however.

In the first place, it can be argued that for powerful historical reasons, fundamental democratic rights should be regarded as absolute. They embody centuries of deep-going political struggles. In Anglo-Saxon law, civil liberties – such as habeas corpus, the presumption of innocence, the requirement of proof beyond reasonable doubt for a criminal conviction, freedom of association and free speech – were substantially forged in the conflict against the absolutist monarchy from the Magna Carta of 1215 and culminating in the English Civil War of the 1640s and the so-called Glorious Revolution of 1688. Among these fundamental rights is freedom from detention without trial, as the US Supreme Court, by a 6–3 majority, commented in June 2004, in ruling that Guantanamo Bay detainees, including two Australians, David Hicks and Mamdouh Habib, could seek writs of habeas corpus in US courts. The majority judgment, delivered by Stevens J, suggested that at stake were democratic conceptions dating back nearly 800 years to the Magna Carta of 1215:

> Executive imprisonment has been considered oppressive and lawless since John, at Runnymede, pledged that no free man should be imprisoned, dispossessed, outlawed, or exiled save by the judgment of his peers or by the law of the land. The judges of England developed the writ of habeas corpus largely to preserve these immunities from executive restraint. [*Rasul v Bush*; *Al Odah v United States* (2004) 542 U.S. (Cases no. 03-343, 03-334) Quoting Jackson J in *Shaughnessy v. United States ex rel. Mezei*, 345 U.S. 206, 218—219 (1953) (dissenting opinion)].

Secondly, there is much evidence to suggest that the 'war on terror' has been declared for definite political purposes, both foreign and domestic, rather than to protect the security of ordinary people. It is now widely acknowledged that all the claims made to justify the central international operation of the 'war' – the United States-led invasion of Iraq (that is, the claims of 'weapons of mass destruction' and Saddam Hussein's links to terrorism) – have collapsed. Moreover, whether or not the Bush administration knew in advance of plans for some kind of terrorist atrocity on September 11 – and that question still has to be answered – the outrages in New York and Washington provided the opportunity for the implementation of plans prepared much earlier – during the 1990s – for the conquest of Afghanistan and Iraq. The Middle East and Central Asia, as is well known, contain the largest proven concentrations of oil and natural gas reserves in the world. The US-led interventions in the region, and the establishment of US military bases throughout Central Asia, have added weight to the evidence that Washington's underlying ambition is to secure hegemony over this entire vital expanse.

There is equal reason to doubt the domestic side of the war. Since the September 11 2001 attacks, the Howard government has eroded long-standing legal and democratic rights in the name of combating terrorism. Yet, on the face of it, none of ASIO's new powers were necessary to protect ordinary people against terrorism. Many submissions to parliamentary committees inquiring into the proposed legislation, including those of the Law Council of Australia and the Civil Liberties Councils of NSW and Victoria, questioned the need for the entire package. As pointed out by a parliamentary library report, any conceivable terrorist activity, such as murder, bombing, hijacking, kidnapping and arson, was already a serious crime under existing law.

ASIO hardly needed new powers to detect terrorists. It already had a vast array of powers to tap phones, install listening devices in offices and homes, intercept telecommunications, open people's mail, monitor on-line discussion, break into computer files and data-bases, seize computers and use personal tracking devices. The ASIO Director-General or his delegated officers could already issue emer-gency search-and-entry warrants, allowing officers wide scope to conduct operations against political activists and organisations, as well as to infiltrate them. Moreover, ASIO is part of an extensive security and intelligence network, which incorporates the external Australian Secret Intelligence Service (ASIS), the Office of National Assessments (ONA), special state police units (formerly called Special Branches), the military's Joint Intelligence Office (JIO), the Defence Intelligence Organisation (DIO), the Defence Imagery and Geospatial Organisation (DIGO) and an electronic eavesdropping agency, the Defence Signals Directorate (DSD).

The military call-out legislation

Since '9/11', the declaration of a 'war on terror' and the wars in Afghanistan and Iraq, Australian society has been increasingly milita-rised. This trend has grave implications for basic legal and democratic rights, not to speak of the political, social and ideological climate.

Over recent years, thousands of soldiers have been mobilised for major sporting events such as the Sydney 2000 Olympic Games, the Rugby World Cup 2003 and the Melbourne 2006 Commonwealth Games.[4] Naval vessels have been dispatched to repel refugees. Frequent anti-terrorism exercises have been conducted in urban environments, involving heavily armed troops alongside police and intelligence officers. Deployments have been conducted against civilian populations in Afghanistan, Iraq, the Solomon Islands and East Timor.[5] The armed forces have been used in highly publicised shows of strength, including air force jets and helicopters flying overhead during major political events such as the 2002 Commonwealth Heads of Government Meeting at Coolum, Queensland and US President Bush's visit to Australia in 2003.[6]

This trend is likely to accelerate. The *Defence Legislation Amendment (Aid to Civilian Authorities) Act* 2006 (Cth) considerably expanded the military call-out powers first enacted in 2000.[7] After a debate lasting only a total of about six hours in the Senate and House of Representatives, the amendments to the *Defence Act 1903* (Cth) were pushed through with little public discussion or media coverage, on the basis of essential agreement between the two main parties.

In 2006, the Howard government announced a major expansion in the Australian Defence Forces (ADF), citing the need to respond to 'regional challenges' and foreshadowing further military interventions in the South Pacific, including in Papua New Guinea, Fiji and Vanuatu.[8] During 2007, the government declared an 'emergency' in order to use the military across the Northern Territory, providing active support to police. In the same year, heavily armed SAS commandos, naval ships and air force planes were deployed at the Sydney APEC summit, in addition to the presence of huge contingents of police, ASIO agents and foreign security personnel.

This turn towards militarisation began before September 11, but has developed apace. It is now just seven years since the Sydney Olympic Games provided the initial rationale for call-out legislation that eroded the basic political and legal principle – dating back to the overthrow of the absolute monarchy in Britain in the seventeenth century – against using the armed forces to deal with civilian disturbances.[9]

The expanded military call-out powers

The original call-out legislation passed in 2000 limited deployments to where the government alleged that a danger of 'domestic violence' existed which required the protection of 'Commonwealth interests' or the protection of a state or territory where the state or territory could not, or was unlikely to be able to, protect itself.[10] Although 'domestic violence' – a term derived from section 119 of the Constitution – was nowhere defined legally, it was derived from American usage and meant 'to relate to intense political, industrial or social crises that imperilled the very existence of the state'.[11]

The amendments adopted in 2006, however, permit the air force and navy, as well as the army, to be mobilised more broadly and routinely to deal with lesser incidents, including any alleged act or danger of terrorism. According to the Explanatory Memorandum for the legislation, the amended Act would also apply to 'mobile terrorist incidents'[12], allowing for military mobilisations under the broad banner of combating terrorist acts.

Because the counter-terrorism legislation passed since 2001 defines terrorism so widely as to cover many traditional forms of political protest, such as mass demonstrations, blockades and picket lines[13], the armed forces could in theory be called out for political purposes. While s100.1 (3) of the *Criminal Code* (Cth) exempts 'advocacy, protest, dissent or industrial action' from the definition of terrorism, that exemption is substantially nullified by the proviso that the action must not be intended to cause physical harm to a person or 'create a serious risk to the health or safety of the public or a section of the public'. The 2006 amendments also authorise ADF operations against threats to physical property, judged by ministers to be 'critical infrastructure', rather than threats to people.[14]

Moreover, the procedures for calling out the ADF have been expedited so that in 'sudden and extraordinary emergency' situations the prime minister or two other 'authorising ministers' can give the order, which does not need to be in writing. The list of 'authorising ministers' includes the deputy prime minister, foreign affairs minister and treasurer, as well as the defence minister and attorney-general.[15] In addition, standing orders can be issued for the activation of the ADF whenever the chief of the armed forces deems it necessary.[16]

The government, backed by Labor, dismissed an amendment to require any ADF call-out to be followed by the recall of parliament with the power to disallow the decision.[17] This places great power in the hands of the executive, exercisable by the governor-general, prime minister, two cabinet ministers or the ADF chief. The 2006 amendments also permit the authorising ministers to dispense with a previous requirement under s51K to notify both houses of parliament (and the general public) within 24 hours of the declaration of a 'general security area'.[18]

One purpose of the 2006 amendments was to give ADF members explicit powers and legal immunities. Once deployed, the military will be legally authorised to shoot down aircraft, sink ships, use deadly force, demand answers to questions and require the production of documents. Potentially lethal force can be used where it is considered necessary to protect any infrastructure that the government designates as 'critical'.[19] These provisions raise the possibility of soldiers – who are, after all, specifically trained to shoot to kill – killing innocent civilians, in the manner that Jean Charles de Menezes was killed in the London Underground in 2005.[20]

Citizens have no right to refuse to answer questions or hand over material on the grounds of self-incrimination. Instead, they can be jailed for non-compliance.[21] Similar powers have been given to the intelligence and police agencies where people are detained without trial under the counter-terrorism laws passed since 2002[22], but their extension to the military raises even greater issues, given the lethal weaponry available to the armed forces, which may potentially be used to enforce compliance.

Under the 2006 amendments, all the ADF powers are now protected by a defence of 'superior orders', which exempt ADF members from criminal liability, except if the order they obeyed was 'manifestly unlawful'.[23] They no longer have to wear name tags during operations.[24] Furthermore, any criminal prosecutions will be handled by federal authorities under federal law, overriding state laws.[25]

Thomas v Mowbray:
a radical extension of the defence power

The constitutional scope for federal governments to use the military call-out provisions was extended in 2007 when the High Court upheld the validity of an interim 'control order' imposed on a Melbourne worker, Jack Thomas, sanctioning one of the central features inserted into the *Criminal Code* (Cth) by the *Anti-Terrorism Act 2005* (Cth).[26] In effect, by a 5 to 2 majority, the court legitimated the anti-terrorism legislation that the Howard government and its state Labor counterparts have introduced since 2002. In doing so, by a margin of 6 to 1 (Kirby J dissenting alone on this aspect) the court also condoned the extension of the Commonwealth Parliament's defence power under s51(vi) of the Constitution beyond war and external threats.

When *Thomas v Mowbray* was argued in the High Court, Commonwealth Solicitor-General David Bennett QC declared anyone who opposed an almost unlimited interpretation of the defence power was displaying 'September 10 thinking'. He insisted that the High Court had to take 'judicial notice' of the September 11 2001 attacks, and the growth of 'fanatical ideological movements which compass the destruction of Western civilisation'.[27]

The High Court essentially endorsed these assertions. Kirby and Hayne JJ dissented, but only Kirby J rejected the radical widening of the defence power. Led by Gleeson CJ, the majority gave the federal government enormous scope to use the power for 'military and naval defence' for domestic purposes. Although the judges used varying formulations, their language was sweeping. Callinan J said the defence power could apply whenever 'the Commonwealth or its people' were 'at risk of danger by the application of force' in situations where the Commonwealth military and naval forces could 'better respond, than state police and agencies alone'.[28]

In a joint judgment, Gummow and Crennan JJ spoke of 'the defence of the realm against threats posed internally as well as by invasion from abroad by force of arms'. These propositions are broad enough to sanction the use of the military to suppress political protests and civil unrest. Gummow and Crennan JJ cited a 1781 English case, *R v Lord George Gordon*[29] where Lord Mansfield denounced a mass demonstration outside parliament that had demanded the repeal of a statute. Mansfield and his fellow judges decided unanimously that 'an attempt, by intimidation and violence, to force the repeal of a law, was levying war against the King; and high treason'.[30] Gummow and Crennan JJ also relied on a 1532 English statute, *The Ecclesiastical Appeals Act*, which declared that the English people were bound to bear 'a natural and humble obedience' to the King, as well as God.[31] Such trawling back through the legal texts to the days of the absolute monarchy highlights the disturbing character of the High Court decision. It represents a reversion to absolutist conceptions of the state in relation to the 'war on terror'.

During the hearings, Solicitor-General Bennett argued that the 'war on terror' justified executive powers to detain not just individuals but thousands of people. Bennett said the federal government could potentially round up and detain anyone 'acting in any manner prejudicial to the public safety of the Commonwealth'. None of the majority judges opposed that proposition. Hayne J said it 'need not be decided' in the case at hand.[32]

The majority judgments declared that the court was obliged to accept as 'notorious facts' that the Commonwealth faced unparalleled dangers from terrorism. Ordinarily, courts require evidence to substantiate the claims made by litigants, including governments. In criminal cases, it is up to the prosecution to prove its charges 'beyond a reasonable doubt' and in cases involving deprivation of liberty it has been accepted, until now, that governments must prove their allegations. In *Thomas v Mowbray*, however, the judges broadened the concepts of 'constitutional facts' and 'judicial notice' to accept all the assertions made by the federal and state governments and their security and spy agencies, such as ASIO.

Callinan J, for example, declared it was 'blindingly obvious' that 'groups of zealots forming part of, or associated with Al Qa'ida' were 'making common cause of hatred against communities posing no threat to them' and 'planned to undertake violent, literally suicidal attacks upon even the institutions and persons of those communities'. Callinan J acknowledged that the evidence was 'hearsay' – not normally admissible in a court of law.[33] The judge also claimed it was a matter of public record that 'in Australia there have been persons convicted or charged of conspiring or planning to undertake terrorist activities in this country'.[34] As a matter of fact, only one person currently stands convicted of a terrorist offence in Australia, Sydney architect Faheem Khalid Lodhi, and he has appealed.[35]

The decision has torn asunder the half-century-old proposition, adopted by the High Court in the *Communist Party Case* of 1951, that the defence power cannot be used for domestic political purposes.[36] In that case, the court rejected the attempt of the Menzies government to ban the Communist Party during the Korean War. After winning the 1949 election in the wake of the coal miners' strike, Prime Minister Robert Menzies claimed a 'political mandate' to place Australia on a 'semi-war footing' against communism. Against a backdrop of global anti-communism, the Communist Party Dissolution Bill was the incoming government's first piece of legislation. The Bill's recitals claimed that its measures were required for the 'security and defence of Australia' in the face of a dire threat of violence, insurrection, treason, subversion, espionage and sabotage.

The High Court, however, rejected the use of these recitals to vali-
date the government's claim to be exercising the defence, incidental
and executive power of the Commonwealth. The judges warned of
the corrosive dangers of unfettered executive power. Dixon J stated:

> History, and not only ancient history, shows that in countries where
> democratic institutions have been unconstitutionally superseded, it
> has been done not seldom by those holding the executive power.
> Forms of government may need protection from dangers likely to
> arise from within the institutions to be protected.[37]

That stand was vindicated when Prime Minister Menzies called a
referendum to override the decision and was defeated, despite his
efforts to whip up a red-baiting campaign in the context of the Cold
War. None of today's judges mentioned the referendum, which gave a
clear public verdict against the unfettered use of the defence power.

In *Thomas v Mowbray*, Kirby J commented: 'I did not expect,
during my service, I would see the *Communist Party Case* sidelined,
minimised, doubted and even criticised and denigrated in this Court'.[38]
He said the majority view was 'further evidence of the unfortunate
surrender of the present court to demands for more and more governmental powers, federal and state, that exceed or offend the constitutional text and its abiding values'.[39] On the defence power, Kirby's
specific concerns were two-fold. Firstly, he expressed reservations
about the potential expansion of military power:

> Clearly, the defence power expressed in the Australian Constitution
> is to be read, limited by the conventionally narrow functions
> ascribed to defence forces in most polities that trace their consti-
> tutional tradition to that of Britain. The constitutional culture of
> such countries has long been properly suspicious of any notion that
> defence forces are available to be deployed at the government's will
> in civilian tasks and to safeguard the nation from itself. Not since
> Cromwell has our constitutional tradition seen the military taking a
> leading part in civilian affairs. The Australian Constitution keeps it
> that way. Although the law challenged in these proceedings does not
> contemplate the domestic deployment of the military, the interpreta-
> tion of the ambit of the defence power adopted in this case must be
> consistent with the foregoing principle.[40]

Secondly, he objected that the defence power could become a vehicle for Canberra to acquire general power over all aspects of law
enforcement, overriding the states:

As drafted, Div 104 [*Criminal Code* (Cth)] proceeds outside the proper concerns of s51(vi) and into areas of ordinary civil government. The plaintiff was correct to say that, if the Constitution were intended to empower the Commonwealth to make laws for the general safety and protection of the Australian public, irrespective of the source of danger and its targets, it could readily have said so. These being within the essential 'police powers' of the States, the rubric of 'naval and military defence' is a singularly inapt expression to use to attribute such powers to the Commonwealth.[41]

'Domestic violence': a core business?

The call-out legislation has significantly enhanced the federal government's unilateral power to mobilise troops internally and given the military unprecedented domestic powers, including to interrogate civilians and seize documents, and legally protected rights to use lethal force. There is no reason to trust any federal government with the use of such powers, and there are clear dangers of the powers being used to target social unrest and political dissent. It can be argued that the 'war on terror' is being utilised to condition public opinion to accept the internal deployment of the armed forces for broader political purposes.[42]

These concerns were further amplified by the 2006 publication of an Australian Strategic Policy Institute (ASPI) report advocating ten 'next steps' to establishing domestic security as a 'core business' of the ADF.[43] These steps include developing a 'defence domestic security strategy', strengthening 'special event security', reorienting military education, conducting 'no warning' exercises involving 'whole-city terrorism' and upgrading links and shared training with police and emergency services. Above all, the report called for a shift in what it called 'defence culture', complaining that the ADF had not yet 'embraced domestic security as core business':

> This reflects Australia's constitutional arrangements, but may not recognise the reality that, when the Australian people perceive themselves to be under attack, they will demand that governments bend every resource to their protection. Defence is a significant and highly visible government resource that will be expected to play its role in a domestic security crisis, not just trying to prevent an attack but also helping to restore some degree of normalcy after a major terrorist strike.[44]

ASPI specified that the ADF's role should extend far beyond a purely military function. The reference to 'restoring some degree of normalcy' envisaged a longer-term policing role, directed against any signs of political instability or popular unrest, perhaps in something akin to a martial law situation.

Furthermore, the report suggested ignoring or sweeping aside Australia's 'constitutional arrangements', which partly embody the centuries-old taboo on using the military on home soil. To some extent, this principle was enshrined in the Constitution at Federation in 1901, at least as it was interpreted prior to *Thomas v Mowbray*. The military power was handed to the Commonwealth under s51(vi), the colonial defence forces were transferred to the Commonwealth by s69, and under s114, the states were forbidden to raise military or naval forces without the consent of the Commonwealth Parliament. Residual authority over domestic law and order remained in the hands of the states and their police forces.

Over many years, the constitutional demarcation has become embedded in public consciousness. Domestic use of the armed forces has become widely regarded as conduct to be expected of a military or autocratic regime, not a democratic government. On the only occasion since federation that a Commonwealth government has called out the military in force in an urban situation – following a bomb blast outside a regional Commonwealth Heads of Government meeting at the Sydney Hilton Hotel in 1978 – the sight of armed soldiers patrolling highways and the streets of the New South Wales town of Bowral caused public consternation.[45] One local newspaper said the 'virtual siege conditions' were reminiscent of 'Franco's Spain'.[46]

The ASPI report canvassed overtly political calculations in advocating a further expansion and entrenchment of the ADF's internal role. It contended that the events of 11 September 2001 and the ensuing declaration of a 'war on terror' by the Bush administration and its allies have created a political climate in which the public will support – indeed, demand – the ADF's mobilisation for domestic purposes.

> Government is attracted to using the ADF because it projects strength. There is a high degree of public respect for the ADF. This image supports a public view that with Defence involved, security on the home front is in capable hands. Decisions on the employment of the ADF in domestic security post-9/11 have therefore been influenced by the political necessity of demonstrating effectiveness in the face of national security threats.[47]

Presumably, the ASPI report represents the views of senior figures in political and military circles, where their views are likely to carry considerable weight. Anthony Bergin is the Institute's research director, while co-author Brigadier Andrew Smith commands the army's 7th Brigade. Smith has served in the Iraq war and commanded the military task forces at the Sydney 2000 Olympics and the Melbourne 2006 Commonwealth Games. Bergin and Smith express contempt for civil liberties, dismissing such concerns as 'an elite debate':

> Unlike in other countries ... history has provided little reason for the Australian population to develop an aversion to the use of Defence in the homeland. Although civil liberty watchdogs have at times raised concerns about the dangers of excessive involvement by the armed forces in domestic security, especially where it involves the use of force, this appears to be an elite debate that does not resonate with the general public.[48]

As a matter of fact, Australian history has given plenty of cause for concern. There has been no recorded use of martial law in Australia since Federation in 1901 but it was invoked several times during the nineteenth century to suppress convicts, Aborigines and workers.[49] The great strikes of the 1890s saw troops mobilised against specific demonstrations and gatherings, with orders to shoot to kill. In one infamous incident, Colonel Tom Price ordered a Mounted Rifles unit to 'fire low and lay them out' during the extended Australian maritime strike of 1890.[50]

In the early years of the 20th century, Australian state governments requested military intervention on at least six occasions, to deal with such anticipated incidents as 'general strike, riot and bloodshed', 'disturbances', wharf strike 'violence', 'labour troubles' and the 1923 Victorian police strike. On each occasion, it seems, the Federal Government declined on the basis that the state police were capable of dealing with the threat (although troops were sent to guard federal buildings, including post offices, during the Victorian police strike). Only one of those requests – by Queensland in 1912 – was formally made under s119 of the Constitution.

Troops were mobilised to break strikes on several occasions during the twentieth century, mostly by Labor governments. The Chifley government sent in soldiers against the coal miners' strike of 1949; the Fraser government used the RAAF to ferry passengers during the 1981 Qantas strike; and the Hawke government mobilised the air force against striking pilots in 1989. These operations provoked bitter recriminations and questions as to their legality.[51] In a lesser known case, the Menzies Liberal government sent troops to break a wharf labourers' strike in Bowen, Queensland in 1953, but was forced to withdraw the soldiers after tensions involving strikers and state police, and a protest by the Queensland government.[52]

On several occasions, soldiers were deployed for political purposes. In 1970–71, the Gorton government called out troops to suppress secessionist agitation in Papua New Guinea, then an Australian protectorate[53] The gravest political crisis came in 1975, when the Governor-General Sir John Kerr reportedly placed the armed forces on alert after dismissing the Whitlam government.[54] No troops were seen on the streets, however. In 1983, the Hawke government authorised RAAF flights over Tasmania to photograph work being conducted by the Tasmanian government in breach of Commonwealth regulations and in 1989, the same government authorised the dispatch of troops to combat protesters at the Nurrungar joint Australian-United States military satellite base. Both deployments generated political controversy and legal uncertainty, particularly with regard to the potential use of soldiers to confront demonstrators outside the Nurrungar base perimeter.[55]

The 'anti-terrorism' legislation

The expanded military call-out legislation was among the measures agreed on by Prime Minister John Howard and the state and territory Labor leaders in their joint communiqué from the 27 September 2005 Council of Australian Governments (COAG) 'counter-terrorism' summit. As a result of that bipartisan communiqué, fresh anti-terrorism laws were introduced in the federal, state and territory parliaments in the final months of 2005.[56] At the federal level, the *Anti-Terrorism Acts* (Nos 1 and 2) 2005 were the latest of more than thirty pieces of counter-terrorism legislation introduced since 2001.[57]

Taken as a whole, the anti-terrorism legislation has four fundamental features. It:

• defines terrorism in vague terms
• permits the banning of political groups

- allows for detention without trial
- shrouds the operations of the intelligence and police agencies in secrecy and provides for semi-secret trials.[58]

All the measures have bipartisan support, and most are mirrored in matching state and territory legislation. In 2002 the leaders of the state and territory Labor governments agreed at a COAG summit to formally refer their constitutional powers over terrorism to the federal government. Their decision has the potential to give the Commonwealth substantially unfettered law-making and police enforcement power over politically-related crime for the first time since Federation in 1901.

A number of prominent legal and political commentators warned that the 2005 anti-terrorism legislation contained police-state features. The president of the Human Rights and Equal Opportunity Commission, John von Doussa, said:

> It might sound over-dramatic to say that the proposed laws are of the kind that may identify a police state, but let us reflect for a moment on that proposition. The defining characteristic of a police state is that the police exercise power on behalf of the executive, and the conduct of the police cannot be effectively challenged through the justice system. Regrettably, that is exactly what the laws which are currently under debate will achieve.[59]

A former prime minister, Malcolm Fraser, made a similar judgment in a lecture delivered at the State Library of Victoria in 2005:

> These are powers whose breadth and arbitrary nature, with lack of judicial oversight, should not exist in any democratic country. If one says, but they will not be abused, I do not agree. If arbitrary power exists, it will be abused.[60]

Fraser observed that the government was really saying, 'trust us'. His answer was as follows: '[N]o part of the Coalition's invasion and occupation of Iraq gives any member of that coalition the right to say on these issues: 'Trust us'.' The former prime minister referred to the lies about 'weapons of mass destruction' that could be dropped on London within 45 minutes. He also referred to the Australian government's false 'children overboard' allegations against a boat-load of asylum seekers in 2001, and the government's abandonment of David Hicks, an Australian citizen detained by the Bush administration in Guantanamo Bay, Cuba.

On the face of it, none of the anti-terrorism measures, including the military call-out laws, were necessary to protect ordinary people against terrorism. Specialist counter-terrorism and paramilitary units were established in federal, state and territory police forces during the 1970s, giving the authorities substantial and specialised resources to deal with any conceivable threat.[61] Every conceivable terrorist act was a serious crime – from murder to arson and hijacking – and the criminal law amply covered planning, preparing, conspiring, financing, supporting and attempting acts related to such activities.[62] Moreover, ASIO and the state and federal police possessed powers to infiltrate organisations, tap phones, bug premises, intercept mail, search homes and hack into computers.[63]

The legislation introduced in 2005 went further than the 2002–04 legislation, notably in allowing the police and intelligence agencies to charge people, or alternatively, detain them without trial, without evidence of involvement in specific terrorist activity or planning. The *Anti-Terrorism Act (No. 1) 2005 (*Cth*)* changed the wording of many terrorist offences from 'the' terrorist act to 'a' terrorist act. In effect, it means that people can be convicted of planning or preparing for terrorism without the police producing any evidence of a specific time, date, location or method of the supposed attack. The *Anti-Terrorism Act (No. 2) 2005 (*Cth*)* granted powers to intern 'suspects' without any charge or trial, either by way of 'preventative detention' or 'control orders'.[64]

The new provisions can be exploited to silence many types of political dissent. An organisation that 'advocates' a terrorist act can be outlawed. 'Advocating' includes 'praising' and could mean merely expressing sympathy for, or calling for an understanding of, the social and economic roots of terrorism.[65]

Moreover, the crime of sedition was extended to include urging conduct to assist an 'organisation or country engaged in armed hostilities' against the Australian military, whether or not a state of war has been declared.[66] These provisions allow for the criminalisation of expressions of support for resistance to the growing range of Australian military interventions, including the occupations of Afghanistan and Iraq or operations in the Asia-Pacific region, such as the dispatch of troops to the Solomon Islands.[67]

By expanding the range of 'terrorist' and related offences, the legislative package correspondingly enlarged the sphere of potential military deployment. More generally, it served to reinforce a climate of fear and insecurity that can be exploited to justify military measures. It should never be forgotten that Adolf Hitler cited the 1933 Reichstag Fire, which the Nazis falsely attributed to communists, as the reason for insisting that the parliament agree to rule by decree.[68] We are not suggesting that people in Australia currently face fascism or military rule. Nevertheless, whenever governments and security authorities cite 'national security' threats, especially of indefinite duration, as the justification for suspending or overturning constitutional norms and basic legal rights, the lessons of history – including Germany in 1933 – suggest a need for deep distrust.

Wide definitions

Of particular concern is the exceptional range of the definition of 'terrorist act' given by s100.1 of the *Criminal Code Act 1995* (Cth). It specifies that:

1   ... *terrorist act* means an action or threat of action where:

    (a)   the action falls within subsection (2) and does not fall within subsection (3); and

    (b)   the action is done or the threat is made with the intention of advancing a political, religious or ideological cause; and

    (c)   the action is done or the threat is made with the intention of:

        (i)   coercing, or influencing by intimidation, the government of the Commonwealth or a State, Territory or foreign country, or of part of a State, Territory or foreign country; or

        (ii)   intimidating the public or a section of the public.

2   Action falls within this subsection if it:

    (a)   causes serious harm that is physical harm to a person; or

    (b)   causes serious damage to property; or

    (c)   causes a person's death; or

    (d)   endangers a person's life, other than the life of the person taking the action; or

(e)   creates a serious risk to the health or safety of the public or a section of the public; or

(f)   seriously interferes with, seriously disrupts, or destroys, an electronic system including, but not limited to:

(i)   an information system; or

(ii)   a telecommunications system; or

(iii)   a financial system; or

(iv)   a system used for the delivery of essential govern- ment services; or

(v)   a system used for, or by, an essential public util- ity; or

(vi)   a system used for, or by, a transport system.

3   Action falls within this subsection if it:

(a)   is advocacy, protest, dissent or industrial action; and

(b)   is not intended:

(i)   to cause serious harm that is physical harm to a person; or

(ii)   to cause a person's death; or

(iii)   to endanger the life of a person, other than the person taking the action; or

(iv)   to create a serious risk to the health or safety of the public or a section of the public.

Thus, terrorism extends to acts or threats that advance 'a political, religious or ideological cause' for the purpose of 'coercing or influ- encing by intimidation' any government or section of the public. 'Advocacy, protest, dissent or industrial action' is exempted but not if it involves harm to a person, 'serious damage' to property, 'serious risk' to public health or safety, or 'serious interference' with an infor- mation, telecommunications, financial, essential services or transport system.[69]

This definition could cover any demonstration or strike action in which a person was injured or felt endangered. The 'coercion or intimidation' clause is practically meaningless, given that the purpose of many protests and strikes is to apply pressure to a government, employer or other authority. Nurses taking strike action that shuts down hospital wards in support of a political demand for greater health spending, for example, could be accused of endangering public health and thus the nurses could be charged as terrorists.

In some instances, terrorist intent is not necessary. The legislation imposes jail terms ranging from life to ten years for preparing, planning or training for 'terrorist acts' and for possessing documents or other objects used in the preparation of such acts. A person can be jailed for possessing such a 'thing' even if they did not know it was used for terrorist purposes, but were merely 'reckless' as to that fact.[70]

The various, related terrorist offences could apply to a wide range of political activity, such as planning a protest outside government buildings or facilities where damage may occur. Demonstrators who prepared to block roads or entrances to financial institutions, such as the stock exchange, could be charged as terrorists, as could computer hackers.

During questioning in a senate committee hearing, the Attorney-General's representatives admitted that someone who cut through a fence at the Easter 2002 protest at the Woomera refugee detention centre or who invaded the parliament building in Canberra during a 1996 trade union rally could have been charged with terrorism.[71] The officials acknowledged that a picketing striker who caused property damage or a person who possessed a mobile phone used to discuss a violent act could be prosecuted under the new provisions.[72]

The new laws grant unilateral powers to the federal and state police to intern 'suspects' without any charge or trial whatsoever. This can be done in two ways. First, anyone whom police allege may be involved in a future terrorist act, or may have information about such an act, can be seized for 'preventative detention' for up to 48 hours by federal police or 14 days by state police. (The second way is by 'control order', which we will discuss shortly.)

The grounds for obtaining a preventative detention order are extremely broad and effectively remove the burden of proof on the Crown to prove its case beyond a reasonable doubt. The *Criminal Code* s105.4 provides for an 'issuing authority' – a judge, former judge or magistrate operating in a 'personal capacity' (that is, not as a court, but as part of the executive) – to grant an order where:

(a)   there are reasonable grounds to suspect that the
        subject:

  (i)   will engage in a terrorist act; or

  (ii)   possesses a thing that is connected with the
          preparation for, or the engagement of a person
          in, a terrorist act; or

  (iii)   has done an act in preparation for, or planning,
          a terrorist act; and

(b)   making the order would substantially assist in
        preventing a terrorist act occurring; and

(c)   detaining the subject for the period for which the
        person is to be detained under the order is reason-
        ably necessary for the purpose referred to in para-
        graph (b).

Some questions can be asked. What are 'reasonable grounds'? How
can the police predict that someone 'will engage in a terrorist act'?
Does it mean reading their mind? How can the 'issuing authority'
conclude that a thing – which could be anything from a mobile phone
to a map – is connected to preparations for a terrorist act? If evidence
exists of an act in preparation for, or planning, a terrorist act, why
not charge the person and put them on trial? How long is 'reasonably
necessary'?

(These questions are all the more important because the power
under s189 of the *Migration Act* 1958 (Cth) to detain people that
an officer 'reasonably suspects' of being an unlawful non-citizen
has been used to wrongly detain more than 200 people, including
Cornelia Rau and Vivian Solon.[73])

An 'issuing authority' can approve the internment in an initial 'ex
parte' hearing, that is, without the 'suspect' being present. Suspects
will have limited rights to know why they are being detained. They
may be held incommunicado and any conversations they hold with a
lawyer can be monitored – removing any semblance of lawyer-client
privilege.

Anyone – including family members, lawyers and the media – who
reveals that the person has been detained can be jailed for five years.
Parents cannot even tell each other if their son or daughter is being
held. These extraordinary provisions are designed to ensure that no-
one knows how many people have been rounded up, or why, or in

what conditions they are being held. The Australian Press Council pointed out in its submission to the Senate Legal and Constitutional Legislation Committee:

> Even in circumstances where a person has been detained illegally or inappropriately, the media are unable to investigate or report upon the detention. If detainees have suffered torture or abuse during their detention, they cannot inform the media of this, and the media are prohibited from reporting the abuse.[74]

In the second form of detention, specially designated 'issuing courts' may grant 'control orders' – which can include house arrest, the fitting of personal tracking devices and bans on employment and all forms of communication – also without any initial notice or hearing. Like preventative detainees, those under house arrest can be barred from alerting anyone to their internment. The control orders can last 12 months and be renewed continuously. Detainees can only challenge them, possibly weeks or months later, in the same special courts.

The grounds for granting a control order are equally as vague as for preventative detention, and lower the burden of proof to the 'balance of probabilities'. The *Criminal Code* s104.4 states that a control order can be granted where:

<blockquote>

(c)   the court is satisfied on the balance of probabilities:

    (i)   that making the order would substantially assist in preventing a terrorist act; or

    (ii)   that the person has provided training to, or received training from, a listed terrorist organisation; and

(d)   the court is satisfied on the balance of probabilities that each of the obligations, prohibitions and restrictions to be imposed on the person by the order is reasonably necessary, and reasonably appropriate and adapted, for the purpose of protecting the public from a terrorist act.

</blockquote>

Again, this wording raises many crucial questions.

Like preventative detention, control orders can be granted ex parte, without the affected person being present, and access to judicial review is substantially circumscribed.

People placed under control orders can seek review by the court that made the order, but no time limit is set for the hearing of those applications, and they are only entitled to summaries of the grounds on which the orders have been made. Decisions by the Attorney-General to authorise an application for a control order are specifically protected from review under the *ADJR Act*.

Preventative detention orders are also exempt from the *ADJR Act* (s105.51), leaving a detainee only with the possibly expensive and lengthy option of seeking a writ or other common law form of review by a superior court. Such a remedy may be practically impossible to obtain within the 48-hour or 14-day time span of each detention.

In any case, Australian courts, from the High Court down, have shown great reluctance in recent decades to challenge the lawfulness of decisions made by the intelligence services on the basis of 'national security'.[75]

These laws can allow governments and their security agencies to lock someone away based solely on what they allege the 'suspect' might be intending to do in the future. How different is this from the 'thought crimes' envisaged in George Orwell's famous dystopian novel *Nineteen Eighty Four*? The legislation clears the way for practices commonly identified with totalitarian regimes. People can simply 'disappear' into police custody, without the media, or anyone else, being able to report it. Lengthy house arrest can be imposed on political opponents; secret evidence can be used; and security forces will have explicit 'shoot-to-kill' powers.

Another draconian aspect of the 2005 legislation is its far-reaching capacity to chill political dissent. In the first place, any organisation that 'advocates', 'praises' or 'counsels' a terrorist act can be outlawed, automatically exposing its members, supporters and financial donors to imprisonment as well. 'Praising' terrorism could mean merely justifying or expressing sympathy for a hypothetical terrorist act, or even calling for an understanding of terrorism's social and economic roots. For example, Kurt Vonnegut, author of the famous novel *Slaughterhouse Five*, on the fire-bombing of Dresden by the Allied forces in World War II, recently described suicide bombers as brave. He was not supporting their actions, merely pointing out that they required courage, and presumably strongly felt causes. Nevertheless, he could be accused of praising terrorism.

Section 102.1(1A)(c) of the *Criminal Code* proscribes 'indirectly' 'counselling' or 'urging' the doing of a terrorist act. In a March 2006 submission to an International Commission of Jurists Eminent Jurists

Panel, the Gilbert and Tobin Centre of Public Law commented:

> The effect of proscribing an organisation on this basis has seri-
> ous consequences under the accompanying criminal provisions.
> Individuals, be they either a member (Criminal Code, s 102.3) or
> an associate (Criminal Code, s 102.8), could be prosecuted merely
> because someone in their organisation praised terrorism – even if
> the organisation has no other involvement in terrorism; even if the
> praise did not result in a terrorist act; and even if the person praising
> terrorism did not intend to cause terrorism. This is an extraordi-
> nary extension of the power of proscription and of criminal liability,
> since it collectively punishes members of groups for the actions of
> their associates beyond their control. Conversely, it is likely to have
> a 'chilling' effect upon free speech.[76]

Moreover, the law of sedition has been radically extended. It now
includes 'urging disaffection' against the government, promoting
'feelings of ill-will or hostility between different groups' or urging
conduct to assist an 'organisation or country engaged in armed
hostilities' against the Australian military, whether or not a state of
war has been declared. Moreover, 'recklessness' has been added as
a seditious state of mind. That is, anyone can be guilty of sedition
even without intending their remarks to create disaffection, ill-will or
armed resistance.[77]

Those convicted will face up to seven years' jail. Organisations
that support such sentiments can be declared 'unlawful associations',
also exposing their property to seizure and their members, supporters
and donors to imprisonment.

Most notably, these laws allow for the criminalisation of any criticism of the government, or support for resistance to the growing
range of Australian military interventions, including the occupations
of Afghanistan and Iraq or operations in the Asia-Pacific region, such
as the dispatch of troops to the Solomon Islands, Papua New Guinea,
Indonesia or the Philippines.[78]

Lawyers warned the senate committee that the laws are so
wide that they could be used to prosecute supporters of Tamil and
Palestinian organisations, anti-Iraq war demonstrators and even
protesters chanting 'Bring Johnny [Howard] down!' Others said the
recent riots by youth across France could be defined as terrorism or
sedition under the Bill, along with statements such as '9/11 was a
hoax', 'America had it coming' or 'we must resist the occupiers'. The

same went for unions that urged disobedience to the industrial relations laws also due to be passed before the end of 2005. Summing up, Law Council of Australia president John North told the committee the sedition offences could catch 'legitimate protesters and even peace activists'.[79]

These sedition offences are currently under review, after a report by the Australian Law Reform Commission.

Power to outlaw organisations

The legislation contains wide-ranging powers for the federal government or a court to outlaw an organisation. Under s102.1 of the *Criminal Code*, 'terrorist organisation' means 'an organisation that is directly or indirectly engaged in, preparing, planning, assisting in or fostering the doing of a terrorist act (whether or not a terrorist act occurs)' or an organisation listed in regulations. To list organisation, the Attorney-General 'must be satisfied on reasonable grounds' that the organisation meets the above definition or 'advocates the doing of a terrorist act (whether or not a terrorist act has occurred or will occur)'.

Proscription orders may have far-reaching implications. Any person who directs or provides support to the activities of a terrorist organisation, knowing it to be terrorist, can be jailed for 25 years or, if they are 'reckless' as to whether the organisation is terrorist or not, for 15 years. A member of a group banned under a regulation faces up to ten years imprisonment. Membership is defined to include 'informal membership' or taking 'steps to become a member'. It is a defence to have taken 'reasonable steps' to cease membership 'as soon as practicable' after knowing the organisation was terrorist, but the burden of proof lies on the defendant.

The legislation also retains a backdoor method for banning organisations by freezing their funds, even if they have not been formally declared terrorist. The Attorney-General can freeze assets or proscribe groups if a UN Security Council freezing order has been issued. Either the minister can 'list' an organisation by Gazette notice or the Governor-General may make proscription regulations. Anyone collecting or providing donations for the organisation can be jailed for five years. If the funds are used for terrorist purposes, the penalty is life.

Detention without charge

At least four types of detention without charge or trial exist in the anti-terrorism laws. They are:

1   preventative detention
2   control orders
3   detention for investigation (*Crimes Act 1914* (Cth) s23CA)
4   ASIO interrogation and detention.

Division 3 of the *Australian Security Intelligence Organisation Act 1979* (Cth) gives ASIO the power to detain and question people. ASIO and federal police officers can raid anyone's home or office, at any hour of the day or night, and forcibly take them away, interrogate and strip-search them and hold them incommunicado, effectively indefinitely through the issuing of repeated warrants.[80]

Detainees do not need to be suspected of a terrorist offence, or any other criminal offence. The Attorney-General can certify that their interrogation would 'substantially assist the collection of intelligence that is important in relation to a terrorism offence', even if no act of terrorism has occurred. This power could be used to detain journalists and political activists, as well as the children, relatives or acquaintances of supposed terrorism suspects. Any detainee who refused to answer ASIO's questions would be liable to five years' imprisonment.

Those detained have no right to know why they are being hauled off for interrogation. If they resist, violent force, including lethal force, can be used against them. If they refuse to answer any question or hand over any material that ASIO alleges they possess, they face five years' jail. Detainees, including teenagers as young as 16, will be unable to contact their families, friends, political associates or the media. If they know the name of a lawyer, they can contact them for legal advice, but only if ASIO does not object to the lawyer.

Even if ASIO accepts a detainee's choice of lawyer, questioning can commence without the lawyer being present. In any case, the lawyer cannot object or intervene during questioning – if they do, they can be ejected for 'disrupting' ASIO. If they inform a detainee's family or the media about the detention, they too face up to five years in jail. A lawyer who is provided information by a client may also be detained for interrogation. The Act does not protect legal professional privilege in communications between the lawyer and the client.

Initial detention can last for up to seven days, including three eight-hour blocks of questioning over three days, but the Attorney-General can easily approve further seven-day periods. To justify serial extensions, ASIO and the government simply have to claim that 'additional to or materially different' information has come to light.

In a significant departure from established law, the Act effectively reverses the burden of proof, overturning a basic protection against police frame-up. If ASIO alleges a person has information or material, the onus is on the individual to prove otherwise.

Section 34V of the ASIO Act permits police officers to use 'such force as is necessary and reasonable' in breaking into premises and taking people into custody. This clause gives police the power to kill or cause 'grievous bodily harm', as long as they believe it necessary to protect themselves. In addition, officers may use 'reasonable and necessary' force to conduct strip-searches.

The legislation has radically extended ASIO's powers. The agency previously had no powers of arrest or interrogation. The state and federal police can detain people, but only on suspicion of committing a criminal offence and those suspects must be either charged or released within a short period of time, and generally cannot be detained for interrogation. Prisoners have the right to legal counsel, who can be present during questioning, and the right to remain silent. With the notable exception of the detention of asylum seekers, detention without trial is regarded as unconstitutional. A citizen is entitled to decline a request to attend a police station 'to assist police'.

The new powers are unparalleled. Not even during two world wars did an Australian government seek to overturn freedom from arbitrary detention (with the controversial exception of rounding up people of German, Japanese and Italian origin as 'enemy aliens') or abolish the centuries-old common law right to remain silent.

ASIO operations cloaked in secrecy

Amendments passed in December 2003 effectively gag all public protest against, or even reporting of, the use of the new powers. It is now a crime, punishable by up to five years' jail, to publicly mention any operation involving ASIO's powers. Even if ASIO itself breaks the law, for example by detaining someone for more than seven days without obtaining a new warrant, any journalist who reports the case could be imprisoned.[81]

In effect, these measures outlaw political campaigns against arbitrary or illegal detentions. If someone sees a person being hauled away by ASIO or federal police for questioning, they cannot disclose that fact to anyone – not even a family member, friend, civil liberties group, member of parliament or political party. If a detainee's family or associates somehow find out about the detention, they cannot publicly comment on it in any way.

The ASIO detention laws passed earlier already prohibited detainees or their lawyers from alerting their families, the media or anyone else that they had been detained. This gag has been broadened to cover all people, not just detainees and lawyers, and extended for the full 28-day period of a warrant.

A further two-year prohibition was imposed on the public disclosure by anyone of 'operational information' that was obtained, directly or indirectly, from the questioning process. 'Operational information' is defined in the widest possible terms. It covers all ASIO information, sources of ASIO information and any 'operational capability, method or plan' of ASIO.

The government insisted on pushing these provisions through parliament unamended, despite strong protests from civil liberties and media organisations. Amnesty International declared: 'The level of secrecy and lack of public scrutiny provided for by this Bill has the potential to allow human rights violations to go unnoticed and in a climate of impunity.'[82] Liberty Victoria stated: 'These secrecy offences pose a grave threat to Australia's democracy and could enable the government of the day to impose a 'war of terror' against its political opponents or vulnerable sections of the community.'[83]

Australia's main media proprietors' groups – Fairfax, News Ltd, SBS, the ABC, the Australian Press Council and Commercial Radio Australia – warned: 'This has the potential to completely remove from public scrutiny all discussion of ASIO's activities in relation to terrorism.'[84]

This legislation represents a grave erosion of political and press freedom. It is now possible for ASIO to cloak virtually all its operations in secrecy, simply by obtaining a questioning warrant from the Attorney-General. For that reason alone, the latest legislation increases the danger that ASIO's detention powers will be abused. ASIO has a long record in this regard. Since the Chifley Labor government established the intelligence service in 1949, it has been used by successive governments, Labor and conservative alike, to monitor, disrupt and harass a wide range of political opponents, including Labor Party members, trade unionists, anti-war activists, students and socialists.[85]

A case study: Mohammed Haneef

The potential for the anti-terrorism laws to be abused, in combination with migration legislation, was demonstrated in the 2007 case of a young Indian Muslim doctor, Mohamed Haneef. Australian Federal Police (AFP) officers arrested Haneef at Brisbane airport on July 2, as he was about to leave the country. Sensational media claims were made that Haneef was secretly fleeing Australia in the wake of failed bomb plots in London and Glasgow several days earlier. Yet Haneef had obtained emergency leave from the Gold Coast hospital where he worked to travel to India, where his newly born daughter was ill.

He was initially held for nearly two weeks without charge under the *Crimes Act 1914* (Cth) s23CA, which was introduced as part of a package of anti-terrorism laws in 2004. That section permits anyone to be arrested for the purpose of *investigating* whether they have committed a terrorist offence. Although a person can ordinarily be held for questioning for only four hours, the Act enables police to apply to a 'judicial officer' (a magistrate, justice of the peace or bail justice) for an extension of the 'investigation period' of up to 24 hours. The police can also ask for a suspension of the questioning time limit for a non-exhaustive list of reasons, including to allow other 'authorities', inside or outside Australia, 'time to collect information', and 'to collate and analyse information' from other sources. There is no time limit on how long the questioning clock can be stopped and no limit on the number of times a 'judicial officer' can approve such AFP requests. The provisions are broad enough to permit indefinite detention.

The doctor was eventually charged under s102.7 of the *Criminal Code* (Cth) with 'intentionally' providing support or resources to a terrorist organisation that 'would help' it engage in terrorist activity, while being 'reckless' as to whether the organisation is terrorist.

That offence carries 15 years in jail. Police alleged that, before he left the United Kingdom in May 2006 to work in the Gold Coast hospital, Haneef gave a mobile phone SIM card to his cousin, Sabeel Ahmed. The card was allegedly found in the jeep driven by Ahmed's brother Kafeel that was used in the attack on Glasgow airport. By this logic, anyone who sold petrol to the jeep driver, or 'recklessly' provided any other resources, could also be charged. And, for that matter, anyone who gave a SIM card to a friend or relative could be detained if that card were later connected to an alleged terrorist plot. Ultimately, police admitted that the SIM card was not in the jeep, and the Director of Public Prosecutions (DPP) dropped the charge.

In the meantime, Immigration Minister Kevin Andrews revoked Haneef's visa just after a magistrate had granted Haneef bail. The minister exercised a personal discretion vested in him by s501 of the *Migration Act 1958* (Cth) to cancel a visa if he considers a person fails the 'character test'. Attorney-General Philip Ruddock then issued a Criminal Justice Certificate under s145 of the *Migration Act*. The stated intended effect of the twin decisions was that Haneef would be held in immigration detention pending trial, rather than being released on bail. Haneef commenced an action in the Federal Court challenging the visa decision. Two weeks later, the minister announced that after seeking advice from the Commonwealth Solicitor-General, David Bennett, he did not propose to change his decision, even though the DPP had withdrawn the charge against Haneef.

Section 501 empowers the minister to personally cancel a visa if he 'reasonably suspects that the person does not pass the character test' and he 'is satisfied that the refusal or cancellation is in the national interest'. To cancel Haneef's visa, Andrews relied on a part of the character test which states that a person fails the character test if 'the person has or has had an association with someone else, or with a group or organisation, whom the minister reasonably suspects has been or is involved in criminal conduct'.

Decisions made by the minister personally under s501 can be supported by secret 'protected information' under s503A, which must not be divulged to the visa holder, and can even be withheld from the visa holder and his lawyers in court under s503B. Furthermore, s501 exempts ministerial decisions from the rules of natural justice, so no procedural fairness is required. Nor is there any right of review by the Administrative Appeals Tribunal (AAT).

The application for judicial review that Haneef lodged with the Federal Court argued that the decision was unlawful on several grounds, including that the minister had wrongly interpreted the word 'association' in s501. The *Migration Act* did not define 'association'. Haneef alleged that the minister had unlawfully considered that any association, even a purely family one, was sufficient to fail the character test.

In *Haneef v Minister for Immigration and Citizenship* [2007] FCA 1271, Federal Court Justice Spender agreed, saying that 'completely innocent' people could be stripped of visas simply because they had a relative, friend or even lawyer whom police suspected of criminal conduct.

Haneef also argued that the minister had misused a power intended for immigration purposes, for a different purpose – to hold a prisoner behind bars while awaiting trial. Instead of being detained until he could be removed from Australia, which is the purpose envisaged by the *Migration Act*, Haneef could not be removed because he was due to stand trial. Broad layers of the population, as well as many in the legal profession, had expressed shock at the use of executive power to block a court order. Australian Bar Association president Stephen Estcourt had condemned it as a 'threat to the rule of law'.

Nevertheless, despite noting that the visa was cancelled just two hours or so after the bail verdict, Spender J said this aspect of the case had not been proven. On the material before him, there was 'no proper basis' for any inference of improper purpose. Spender J declined to draw any adverse implication from the fact that the minister failed to appear in court to be questioned about his motives.

The Full Federal Court unanimously upheld Spender J's decision in *Minister for Immigration & Citizenship v Haneef* [2007] FCAFC 203. It agreed that the minister had misinterpreted the word 'association' and added that the view of 'association' set out in Ministerial Direction 21, adopted by the minister under the *Migration Act*, 'runs far too wide' by encompassing links or connections 'without any need to show sympathy, support for, or involvement in, criminal activity'. The court applied a traditional approach to statutory interpretation, which includes the principle that where words, such as 'association', can be read widely or narrowly, they should be construed 'so as not to encroach upon common law rights and freedoms'.

By the time that his case went to the Federal Court, Haneef had been released and returned to India. Some media commentators observed that his release was secured more by the 'court of public opinion' than the judicial process.

Discussion topics

1. What is *terrorism*? How has it been defined officially? What problems arise with that definition?
2. How does *terrorism* differ from *state terrorism*?
3. Is it possible, or appropriate, to strike a 'balance' between the 'war on terrorism' and basic democratic rights?
4. Should domestic security be a 'core business' of the military?

Additional resources

Amnesty International's concerns regarding post September 11 detentions in the USA, Amnesty International, March 2002.

A. Bacevich, *American Empire: The Realities and Consequences of US Diplomacy*, Harvard University Press, 2002.

Call Out the Troops: an examination of the legal basis for Australian Defence Force involvement in 'non-defence' matters, Australian Parliamentary Research Paper 8, Canberra, 1997–98.

B. Graham and J. Nussbaum, *Intelligence Matters: The CIA, the FBI, Saudi Arabia, and the Failure of America's War on Terror*, Random House, 2004.

N. Hancock, *Terrorism and the Law in Australia: Legislation, Commentary and Constraints*, Parliament of Australia, Department of Parliamentary Library, Research Paper 12, Canberra, 2001–02.

M. Head, *The Australian Military, 'Domestic Violence' and the War on Terror*, Federation Press, Sydney, 2008.

M. Head, '"Counter-terrorism" laws: a threat to political freedom, civil liberties and constitutional rights' 26 *Melbourne University Law Review* (2002) 266.

M. Head, 'A disturbing convergence? Civil liberties and the "war on terror"' 1 *Asia Pacific Yearbook of International Humanitarian Law* (2005) 63–92.

M. Head, 'The political uses and abuses of sedition: the trial of Brian Cooper' 11 *Legal History* (2007) 63–78.

J. Hocking, *Beyond Terrorism: The Development of the Australian Security State*, Allen & Unwin, Sydney, 1993.

H. Lee, P. Hanks and V. Morabito, *In the Name of National Security: The Legal Dimensions*, LBC, Sydney, 1995.

Royal Commission on Intelligence and Security (Commissioner Justice

Robert Hope), *Fourth Report: Volume 1*, Commonwealth Government Printer, Canberra, 1978.

Royal Commission on Australia's Security and Intelligence Agencies (Commissioner Justice Robert Hope), *Report on the Australian Security Intelligence Organisation*, AGPS, Canberra, 1985.

P. Ruddock, 'A New Framework: Counter Terrorism and the Rule of Law', Address to the Sydney Institute, 20 April 2004 <http://152.91.12/www/MinisterRuddockHome.nsf/Alldocs/RWPB046617DB0869> (accessed 29 June 2004).

V. Windeyer, 'Certain Questions Concerning the Position of Members of the Defence Force When Called Out to Aid the Civil Power' in R. Hope, *Protective Security Review Report*, AGPS, Canberra, 1979, Appendix 9.

Chapter 19

REFUGEES AND THE NATION-STATE

It has been apparent for some years that the global refugee system is in grave crisis. According to the available statistics, the flight of people from their countries of birth grew dramatically in the final decades of the 20th century and these mass movements are continuing in the 21st. Many of those fleeing are resorting to unauthorised methods of entry, often at great risk to their lives.

Western governments have increasingly shut their doors but are having considerable difficulties, logistically, diplomatically and politically, in removing those denied refugee status. Governments are spending mounting sums on detecting and detaining unwanted arrivals, deciding their fate and administering the outcomes, while giving decreasing funds to the UN High Commissioner for Refugees (UNHCR), which is responsible for most of the world's displaced persons. In 2000, a UNHCR-commissioned analysis of European governments' responses to the growth of 'people smuggling' concluded that official policy risks 'ending the right of asylum in Europe' and that the 'current status quo is practically and ethically bankrupt from all positions'.[1]

In Australia, governments have taken the policy of seeking to block and deter unwanted arrivals to the extent of detaining asylum seekers, usually in remote semi-desert locations, and, since the *Tampa* affair of August 2001, militarily barring entry to refugees.[2] Severe police and security methods, including the use of mass arrests, water cannon, tear gas and solitary confinement, led to hunger strikes, mass breakouts and determined protests.

This chapter reviews the development of the refugee debate, examines the basic contradictions and fundamental flaws of the 1951 Refugee Convention, considers the current debate over the Convention's future, and argues for a new paradigm that challenges the dichotomy between refugees and immigrants and recognises the essential democratic right to travel and live where one chooses.

The Refugee Convention

*Table 1: **Key provisions of the 1951 Refugee Convention***

Article 1: Definition of the term 'refugee'
Any person who, 'owing to well-founded fear of being persecuted for reasons of race, religion, nationality, membership of a particular social group or political opinion, is outside the country of his nationality and is unable, or owing to such fear, is unwilling to avail himself of the protection of that country; or who, not having a nationality and being outside the country of his former habitual residence as a result of such events, is unable or, owing to such fear, is unwilling to return to it'.

Article 31: Refugees unlawfully in the country of refuge

1   The Contracting States shall not impose penalties, on account of their illegal entry or presence, on refugees who, coming directly from a territory where their life or freedom was threatened in the sense of article 1, enter or are present in their territory without authorisation, provided they present themselves without delay to the authorities and show good cause for their illegal entry or presence.

2   The Contracting States shall not apply to the movements of such refugees restrictions other than those which are necessary and such restrictions shall only be applied until their status in the country is regularised or they obtain admission into another country. The Contracting States shall allow such refugees a reasonable period and all the necessary facilities to obtain admission into another country.

Article 32: Expulsion

1   The Contracting States shall not expel a refugee lawfully in their territory save on grounds of national security or public order.

2   The expulsion of such a refugee shall be only in pursuance of a decision reached in accordance with due process of law. Except where compelling reasons of national security otherwise require, the refugee shall be allowed to submit evidence to clear himself, and to appeal to and be represented for the purpose before competent authority or a person or persons specially designated by the competent authority.

3   The Contracting States shall allow such a refugee a reasonable period within which to seek legal admission into another country. The Contracting States reserve the right to apply during that period such internal measures as they may deem necessary.

Article 33: Prohibition of expulsion or return ('refoulement')

1   No Contracting State shall expel or return ('refouler') a refugee in any manner whatsoever to the frontiers of territories where his life or freedom would be threatened on account of his race, religion, nationality, membership of a particular social group or political opinion.

2   The benefit of the present provision may not, however, be claimed by a refugee whom there are reasonable grounds for regarding as a danger to the security of the country in which he is, or who, having been convicted by a final judgment of a particularly serious crime, constitutes a danger to the community of that country.

How the refugee numbers have grown

In 1951, when the UNHCR was established, there were an estimated 1.5 million refugees worldwide. On 1 January 2000, the UNHCR considered 22.3 million people to be 'of concern'. They included 11.7 million refugees, 1.2 million asylum seekers, 2.5 million repatriated refugees and 6.9 million internally displaced persons and others of concern. Another 13–18 million internally displaced persons were outside the UNHCR's jurisdiction, as were an estimated 3.5 million Palestinians. This gives a total of 43 million.

The number of people 'of concern' to the UNHCR nearly doubled during the 1990s, from 14.9 million in 1990, reaching an all-time high of 27 million in 1995 (in the wake of the first Gulf War against Iraq, the fomenting of communalism in Yugoslavia and the eruption of ethnic warfare in Rwanda and Africa's Great Lakes region).

Of the largest concentrations of refugees in 1999, 3.1 million came from Afghanistan and Iraq, about 2.7 million from sub-Saharan Africa and nearly 800 000 from Bosnia and Croatia. Most are living in camps in neighbouring countries – usually among the poorest in the world.[3]

According to the UNHCR, after slight reductions in the numbers of refugees, asylum seekers, internally displaced and stateless persons between 2002 and 2005, they began to rise again in 2006.[4] By the close of 2006, the global figure of persons of concern stood at 32.9 million, a rise of 56 per cent in 12 months. The number of refugees rose to 9.9 million, the first rise since 2002, while the number of internally displaced persons nearly doubled to 12.8 million, and the stateless persons total more than doubled to 5.8 million.

The biggest increase in the refugee population came as a result of 1.2 million Iraqis seeking refuge in Jordan. At the end of 2006, the largest number of refugees came from Afghanistan (2.1 million) and Iraq (1.5 million), which between them accounted for 36 per cent of the global total. Pakistan was the asylum country with the largest number of refugees, followed by Iran, with the two countries hosting 20 per cent of the world's refugees.

The rise in refugee numbers over the past two decades has been related to definite economic and political processes, particularly the collapse of the Stalinist-ruled states in Eastern Europe from the late 1980s, the US-led bombings of Iraq and Serbia, the US-led invasions of Afghanistan and Iraq, and the outbreak of regional conflicts in Eastern Europe, the Middle East, Asia and Africa. Millions of people fled war or sought refuge from severe social dislocation and civil and ethnic conflict. With the imposition of IMF restructuring measures in many countries, this global movement is likely to grow.

More fundamental driving forces are also at work. The increased demand for asylum has occurred amid an unprecedented globalisation of the world economy since the mid-1980s, creating massive flows of international capital, the rapid shift of production processes from country to country, and a worldwide labour market. At the same time, the ever-widening gulf between the capital-rich, techno-logically advanced and militarily powerful countries and the rest of the world has fuelled the demand for the right to escape poverty.

Moves to restrict the right to asylum

While embracing the global restructuring of economic life, western governments have generally sought to erect new barriers to the move-ment of ordinary working people. One British writer has suggested that 'for a growing list of governments the best interpretation of the Convention Relating to the Status of Refugees can only be to run it through the shredder'.[5]

Some of the arguments raised by those calling for the Convention's restriction cannot withstand careful scrutiny. There is official oppo-sition to the growth of 'human trafficking'. By this standard, those who sought to assist Jews escape the Nazis would have been damned as people smugglers. There is no doubt that so-called people smug-gling has become a big business. By one estimate, one million people were transported in illegal operations worth up to $US20 billion in 1999.

But if refugees are seeking assistance from private sources, and often facing life-threatening conditions as a consequence, this is largely due to the steady erosion of refugee protection over the past decade. As governments have restricted entry and intensified meas-ures to detect and exclude unwanted arrivals, refugees have made ever-more-risky efforts to gain a safe haven.

In Australia, temporary protection visas were introduced in 1999. Not only were refugees granted only short-term (usually three years) residence, making a secure, settled life impossible, but they lost the right to sponsor their families to join them and were no longer eligi-ble for a range of social security benefits. These restrictions forced a number of refugees' families to seek unauthorised entry in leaking boats, including some who perished aboard the *SIEV X*, which sank in international waters just north of Australia in 2001 with the loss of 353 lives. Many unanswered questions remain about the govern-ment's involvement in that terrible tragedy, which had the effect of deterring future boat arrivals, an outcome that Immigration Minister Ruddock welcomed at the time.[6]

Similarly, the official condemnation of 'queue jumping' is questionable. Far from being in an orderly waiting list, those seeking safe haven confront impossible situations and terrible delays. Those likely to be the most needy – refugees in Africa, Asia and the Middle East – are the least likely to be accepted. To take the case of Australia, out of the 7500 places for offshore applicants in 2000, 45 per cent were given to Europeans, leaving 2206 places for the entire Middle East and 1738 for all of Africa. On average, applications to Australia take 18 months to come up for consideration.

Moreover, the Australian government cuts its 12 000-a-year quota of humanitarian and protection visas for offshore applicants by the number of asylum seekers who reach Australia independently and are granted refugee status. This policy pits the two groups – both in urgent need of protection – against each other.

The charge that asylum seekers who arrive without permission are 'illegal' entrants is equally dubious. In most cases they have broken no laws and have not been convicted of any offence. In Australia, they are detained without trial. In any case, because refugees, by necessity, are often forced to escape from their countries and mislead authorities, Article 31 of the Convention stipulates that governments should not penalise applicants 'on account of illegal entry or presence'.

Another common argument is that a distortion of priorities is created when western governments spend far more on processing asylum applications than they donate to the world refugee effort. In 2000, Britain spent more on dealing with asylum seekers – US$2.2 billion – than the UNHCR budget of US$1.7 billion. Australia spends as much each year on the Refugee Review Tribunal (just one level of the determination process) as it allocates to the UNHCR. The distortion of priorities is primarily a product of the measures being taken to undermine the right to asylum. A leading UNHCR official summed up the situation:

> Broadly speaking, two parallel trends have emerged, both of which have impacted negatively on the accessibility of asylum and the quality of treatment received by refugees and asylum seekers. The first has been the growth in an overly restrictive application of the 1951 Refugee Convention and its 1967 Protocol, coupled with a formidable range of obstacles erected by states to prevent legal

and physical access to their territory. The second is the bewildering proliferation of alternative protection regimes of more limited duration and guaranteeing lesser rights than those contained in the 1951 Convention.[7]

The Migration Act

Table 2: **Key sections of the Migration Act 1958 (Cth)**

Section	Provisions
s36	incorporates Refugee Convention test as criteria for protection visa
ss91A–91W	include major exceptions, including narrowed definitions of 'persecution', 'particular social group' and 'serious crime', 'safe third country' and 'access to protection from third countries'
ss189, 196 and 245	provide for mandatory detention and removal

The Tampa case

Captain Arne Rinnan, the master of the *MV Tampa*, and Wallenius Wilhelmsen, the owners of the Norwegian freighter, displayed more concern for the survival, welfare and basic rights of the 433 Afghan refugees rescued by the *Tampa* on 26 August 2001 than the Australian government. In accordance with the norms of international humanitarian assistance, Rinnan, backed by the shipping line, responded to the refugees' distress calls and sought to ferry them to the nearest safe port.[8]

Led by Prime Minister John Howard and Immigration Minister Philip Ruddock, the Australian government deployed SAS troops to prevent the asylum seekers landing in a safe harbour (at Christmas Island), detain them on the deck of the container ship and ultimately transfer them to the *HMAS Manoora*, a naval troop carrier, for transportation to far-distant Nauru.

On 27 November 2001, the High Court brought the *Tampa* case to an abrupt halt. A panel of three justices refused to consider an appeal from a split decision of the Full Federal Court upholding the lawful-ness of the detention and expulsion of the *Tampa* refugees.[9] The deci-sion effectively sanctioned the federal government's continued use of military force to remove asylum seekers from territorial waters and transport them to detention camps on remote Pacific islands.

The verdict meant that hundreds of asylum seekers remained incarcerated, at the behest of the Australian government, in hellish conditions on the tiny island of Nauru. Within two days of the ruling, the government formally asked Nauru to take up to 500 more asylum seekers, on top of the 700 Afghan and Iraqi refugees already being held there against their will. In return for a further cash payment of $10 million from Canberra, the Nauru government agreed to detain up to 1200 people at a time.[10]

Seeking to act on behalf of the refugees, Melbourne solicitor Eric Vadarlis applied for a High Court appeal against a two-to-one ruling by the Full Federal Court, which declared that the government has vague executive or prerogative power under the Constitution to detain and remove 'aliens' and take any other action it considers necessary to protect 'national sovereignty'.[11]

Vadarlis asked the High Court to reinstate an original habeas corpus order by Federal Court Justice Tony North that the refugees had been illegally detained. North J ruled that the government had flouted its own migration legislation and had determined 'at the highest level' to 'use an unlawful process to detain and expel the rescuees'. He ordered the government to bring the *Tampa* refugees, then crammed aboard a military troop carrier, to the Australian main-land, where they would have the right to apply for asylum under the *Migration Act 1958* (Cth) and the 1951 Refugee Convention.[12]

By summarily dismissing Vadarlis' application, the High Court rubberstamped the military operation against the refugees rescued by the *Tampa*, in which government ministers deliberately flouted the law. When they sent 45 SAS soldiers to board the Norwegian freighter and detain the rescuees, members of the government were aware that they lacked any lawful power to do so. The government tried to rush retrospective legislation – the Border Protection Bill – through parliament to authorise its actions, but was initially defeated in the Senate.

Government ministers sought to evade the operation of the *Migration Act*, which requires government officers to detain all 'unlawful' arrivals. Under the 1999 'border protection' amendments to the Act, military officers who board refugee vessels – even on the high seas – are obliged to bring the people on board ashore, to be placed in detention.[13]

On the federal cabinet's instructions, various steps were taken to ensure that the people on board the *Tampa* could not contact lawyers to challenge the legality of the government's conduct or seek their release from the ship. Government leaders were determined to prevent the asylum seekers from applying for protection visas. According to the agreed facts:

> The ship has been forbidden by Australian authorities from proceeding any closer to Christmas Island and from entering the port ... The effect of the continuing presence of the SAS officers is that the captain and crew are unlikely to attempt to move the ship into the port. This is a consequence desired by the Australian government.

> None of the asylum seekers hold a visa entitling them to enter Australia. Therefore they would be unlawful non-citizens for the purposes of s14 of the *Migration Act* if they entered the 'migration zone' as that phrase is defined in s 5 of the *Migration Act*.

> The evidence justifies an inference that many of the rescuees would, if entitled, wish to apply for protection visas, and would wish to leave the ship and enter Australia. The rescuees have no access to communications with persons off the ship and persons off the ship are unable to communicate with them.[14]

Despite North J's ruling, the government continued on its course, having reached an agreement from the lawyers challenging its actions – Vadarlis and the Victorian Civil Liberties Council – that it would return the rescuees to Australia if it lost an appeal to the Full Federal Court. The refugees were shipped thousands of kilometres away to the remote Pacific island of Nauru. En route, the government crammed 237 more unwanted refugees – seized off Ashmore Reef – onto the *Manoora*. Upon arrival at Nauru, a desolate former Australian, New Zealand and British protectorate, military personnel forced the *Manoora*'s unwilling passengers into a detention camp of makeshift shelters and tents in the middle of the island's former phosphate mine.

Despite the historic significance of the case, the High Court judges summarily dispensed with it after a hearing that lasted less than two hours, followed by a bare 15-minute recess. In a one-page judgment, they declared that the claim for a writ of habeas corpus had been 'overtaken by events', namely the government's forced transfer of the *Tampa* refugees to Nauru. The three justices asserted that:

> If the persons concerned are now detained (a question about which there has been no trial) each would be detained in a foreign country subject to whatever is the law of that country.[15]

In doing so, the judges chose to disregard affidavits showing that the Australian government was paying all the costs of the Nauru detention camp and that Australian officers were 'overseeing' the 'arrangements' there. Whatever the precise legal situation in Nauru, the refugees were clearly being held on Australia's behalf. Moreover, Australian military personnel herded the refugees off a naval troopship onto Nauru, despite vigorous protests by the asylum seekers. This means that their imprisonment was the direct continuation of the detention that was ruled illegal by North J.

In any case, the government breached an undertaking to bring the refugees back to Australia should it lose the appeal. Instead, it presented the High Court with a fait accompli – Australia was no longer detaining the refugees, because they had been removed to Nauru. In effect, the three High Court judges rewarded the government for thumbing its nose at the legal process. Strangely, the court asserted that such an agreement between the parties would have required the court to determine a dispute that had become 'hypothetical'.

The three judges also refused to clarify the issue of standing for lawyers seeking to protect the rights of refugees who are militarily blocked from appealing to a court themselves and held incommunicado without access to legal advice. Apart from the asylum seekers transported to Nauru and Papua New Guinea, more than 1100 asylum seekers have been treated this way on the offshore Australian territories of the Cocos, Christmas, Cartier and Ashmore islands. These islands have been 'excised' from the Australian migration zone under legislation that was ultimately passed with Labor Party support to retrospectively authorise the expulsion of the *Tampa* and other refugees.

Likewise, the judges refused to rule on the dubious constitutional validity of the post-*Tampa* laws, which include provisions purporting to prevent any legal challenge to the forced removal of refugees and their boats from Australian waters. For example, one section of the legislation states: 'All action to which this Part applies is taken for all purposes to have been lawful when it occurred.' Another specifies that no legal proceedings can be commenced or continued against the Commonwealth in relation to such action.[16]

The legislation gives government or military officers wide-ranging authority to board, search, detain and turn around refugee boats, using whatever means are considered 'necessary and reasonable', including force.[17] These provisions could allow refugee boats to be sunk deliberately to prevent them landing on Australian soil. And this is not far-fetched. Shots were fired in the direction of at least one overcrowded and sinking boat, whose occupants government ministers then falsely accused of throwing children overboard.[18]

Basic contradictions

Governments have generally facilitated the globalisation of economic life, seeking to attract wealthy international investors while shutting their doors to the impoverished. They have deregulated their financial markets to enhance the movement of capital, but denied the same freedom to labour. These responses point to several basic contradictions, which can be summarised as follows:

* nation-state versus global economy
* mobility of capital versus border controls on people
* one law for the wealthy and another for the poor.

Nation-state versus global economy

The growing global mobility of people and commerce is increasingly in conflict with the efforts of governments to prevent the flow of unwanted arrivals. There is a worldwide movement of people, whether for employment, business, education, tourism, sport, entertainment, scientific and cultural exchange or social and political intercourse. More than ever, we live in a global village, linked electronically and by air travel. In large measure, this is the inexorable product of globalisation. National borders are becoming increasingly anachronistic.

The world economy today is characterised by the daily movement of vast quantities of capital across national borders, as international financial institutions scour stock and bond markets for the highest return on their investments. In the decade 1980–90, the volume of cross-border transactions in equities grew at a compound rate of 28 per cent a year, from US$120 billion to $1.4 trillion. Over the same period, international bank lending rose from $324 billion to $7.5 trillion and the international bond market increased in size from $295 billion to $1.6 trillion. These sums dwarf the capital at the disposal of any national government or central bank.

Mobility of capital versus border controls on people

While capital is free to roam the world, national governments deny its victims that right. In part, they maintain national barriers in order to better service the needs of transnational corporations, which require reliable supplies of skilled, as well as low-cost, labour. Governments internationally are competing to supply cheaper, better trained and more disciplined labour forces to investors. At the same time, they also retain national restrictions on labour movement in an attempt to shore up their own sovereignty and domestic political control, using 'illegal' migrants as scapegoats for mounting social problems.

One law for the wealthy and another for the poor

Both overtly and covertly, national governments discriminate against the poor and working people when deciding whom to admit as migrants, temporary residents, visitors and students. Those who have wealth, particularly money to invest, or sought-after skills – which usually require means to acquire – are far more likely to be granted entry. In some cases, they can literally buy their way in.

Australia provides an example. Officially, 'Australia has a non-discriminatory immigration policy, which means that anyone from any country can apply to migrate'.[19] In reality, a potential immigrant's personal and/or family wealth is among the most significant factors in the assessment of their application. Some classes of visa are reserved specifically for applicants who can pass wealth or income tests. For instance, Business Skills applicants obtain bonus points for having or bringing more money into the country. Thus, investors with $2 million obtain 80 of the points needed for a visa.

The poor and most workers can only dream of these sums. They are further blocked by visa application fees that exceed more than a year's earnings for the average person living in a third world country, as well as charges for skills assessment, English language tuition and medical testing. Health requirements are another barrier. Poorer people have less access to medical care and healthier lifestyles, and some diseases, such as tuberculosis, are inherently associated with poverty.

Echoes of 'White Australia'

As numerous commentators have observed, Australia, partly because of its remoteness, faces only a trickle of refugees arriving on its shores compared to the countries of Western Europe and North America. Even if the figures are adjusted for population, Australia ranks well behind countries such as Switzerland, Belgium, Austria and the Netherlands.

Yet the Australian government has been leading calls for harsher restrictions on asylum seekers, reviving memories of the 'White Australia' policy that prevailed at the turn of the last century. One of the first pieces of legislation passed by the Australian Parliament was the *Immigration Restriction Act 1901*, directed at preventing the entry of non-whites. It was soon followed by the *Pacific Islanders Labourers Act*, which required the deportation of some 8700 indentured South Pacific workers and their families. In the parliamentary debate, Labor Party MP and Australian Workers Union leader WG Spence summed up the programme of the Labor and trade union leaders:

> If we keep the race pure, and build up a national character, we shall become highly progressive people of whom the British government will be prouder the longer we live and the stronger we grow.[20]

The White Australia policy was only abandoned in the mid-1960s because of the growing dependence of Australian mining companies and graziers on Japan and other Asian markets. Right-wing populist politicians such as Pauline Hanson continue to advocate White Australia policies today. While the major parties – the Liberal-National Party Coalition and the Labor Party – formally eschew such policies, they maintain a considerable degree of bipartisan unity on the mandatory detention of asylum seekers, the restriction of detainees' legal rights and other measures designed to deter applicants for refugee status.

Under the banner of 'multiculturalism', they have sought to fashion a new national identity and international image but still within the framework of maintaining a relatively small population, insulated from the much larger populations of nearby Asia. This is a particular expression of a global divide. Despite the end of formal colonialism in most states, the world remains divided into oppressor and oppressed countries, with the advanced industrialised nations profiting at the expense of the so-called 'third world'.

To secure the means to finance investments, build infrastructure and operate basic facilities, the governments of the semi-colonial countries have to implement the 'structural adjustment' programmes of the IMF and the World Bank. These programmes usually require draconian cuts to social programmes, privatisation of state enterprises and tax concessions for international investors. Their effect is to transfer vast amounts of wealth into the coffers of the major banks and transnational corporations. In the words of one commentator:

> Not even at the height of its glory did the British Empire possess even
> a fraction of the power over its colonial subjects that the modern
> institutions of world imperialism such as the World Bank, the IMF,
> GATT and the EC routinely exercise over the supposedly independ-
> ent states of Latin America, Asia, Africa and the Middle East.[21]

Despite massive debt repayments, extracted at enormous social cost, the level of third world indebtedness continues to rise. In 1990, the total debt owed by developing countries was US$1.4 trillion; by 1997, it had risen to $2.17 trillion. In 1998, third world countries paid $717 million in debt service to the major banks and financial institutions every day. These glaring disparities will continue to cause catastrophic conditions in many parts of Africa, the Middle East, Asia and Latin America, adding to the demand for means of entry to the advanced industrialised countries. Debt forgiveness programmes adopted since 1996 by various creditor nations and international banks have had little impact in reducing the gap.[22]

Defending rights within the Convention

Asylum seekers and those who oppose the treatment meted out to them will naturally seek to defend their rights to the fullest extent possible within the existing framework of the Refugee Convention. Unfortunately, the Australian High Court has tended to restrictively interpret the scope of judicial review in the refugee context.

For example, there were strong grounds for the High Court to prevent the deportation of Kosovo and East Timorese asylum seekers, despite the provisions of the 2000 'Safe Haven' legislation, which denied them the right to apply for refugee status. However, in *Re The Minister for Immigration and Multicultural Affairs; Ex parte Fejzullahu* [2000] HCA 23, the court declined to hear the Kosovo refugees' cases.

Some commentators have argued that new uses can be found for the Refugee Convention in recognising international human rights claims on grounds of oppression related to gender and sexuality. Others have sought to find ways around the 'gaps' in the Convention by invoking other international instruments, including the Convention Against Torture and the International Covenant on Civil and Political Rights, to intervene on behalf of those needing protection.

Unfortunately, even in instances of extreme vulnerability, such as those being deported against their will, courts have failed to intercede, even though violent deportation methods can lead to death. In some cases, the individual actions of airline pilots or collective opposition in the form of trade union bans have saved deportees from disaster.

High Court sanctions indefinite detention

In three sets of judgments handed down simultaneously in 2004, the High Court declared that the federal government can detain rejected asylum seekers indefinitely – perhaps for life – regardless of their inability to be deported to any other country and irrespective of the intolerable conditions inside the government's immigration detention centres.

In the cases of *Al-Kateb*[23] and *Al Khafaji*[24], by a four-to-three majority, the court ruled that the government could use the 'aliens' power (s51(xix)) of the Constitution) to impose detention for as long as the government deemed it necessary. The judges held that, even if deportation were not possible, indefinite detention did not unconstitutionally impose punishment without trial. In the third case of *Behrooz*[25], by six to one, the court declared that the conditions of incarceration in the country's remote camps – no matter how harsh and inhumane – could not provide a defence to a charge of escaping from immigration detention.

The immediate impact of the decisions in *Al-Kateb* and *Al Khafaji* was to throw at least a dozen former detainees into a legal and political black hole.[26] Often after years of imprisonment, they had been released into the community, subject to certain reporting conditions, by the Federal Court, which ruled in several cases that it was unlawful to hold them for deportation when there was no prospect of any other country accepting them in the foreseeable future.[27]

While the cases concerned the imprisonment of asylum seekers, they have a broader significance for the relationship between state power and democratic rights and freedoms. They represent a departure from established Australian constitutional law concerning the ambit of executive power. They substantially broaden the scope for the Commonwealth government to impose detention without trial. Members of the minority in *Al-Kateb* and *Al Khafaji* warned that the logic of the decision could be extended to other federal powers, not just immigration. Kirby J said the majority view had 'grave implications for the liberty of the individual in this country which this court should not endorse'.[28] Gummow J noted that the government could potentially now lock up bankrupts, for example, supposedly to protect society.[29]

Ahmed Ali Al-Kateb, a stateless Palestinian, arrived in Australia without valid papers in December 2000. He sought asylum because he suffered persecution in Kuwait, where he had lived most of his life. Long-term residency or birth in Kuwait did not create a right of citizenship or permanent residence there. His application for a protection visa was rejected and, having exhausted his rights of appeal, he applied to be removed from Australia in August 2002. However, neither Kuwait nor Israel would allow him to enter (he sought to be removed to Gaza, but Israel refused this request). As a result, he had been incarcerated for four years by the time the High Court heard his case.

Al-Kateb challenged the legality of his continued detention, seeking a writ of habeas corpus. He argued that, as he could not be removed to another country, his incarceration had become punitive and was therefore beyond the scope and purpose of the *Migration Act 1958*, which requires, by ss189 and 196, that all refugee applicants be detained until they are either granted a visa or deported. In addition, he argued that his detention was unconstitutional, as a usurpation of judicial power, because only courts could order punitive imprisonment.

Similar arguments were mounted by Abbas Mohammad Hasan Al Khafaji, an Iraqi who was recognised as a refugee fleeing persecution in Iraq, but was refused a protection visa on the ground that he had a right to reside in Syria, where he once lived. However, that supposed right proved to be a chimera for Al Khafaji, because Syria refused to admit him, leaving him in a legal limbo.

Mahran Behrooz, an Iranian refugee, had been detained at the Woomera Detention Centre in the South Australian desert for nearly two years when he escaped, along with two others. After he was captured, he was charged with escaping from immigration detention, a criminal offence carrying a maximum sentence of five years. Behrooz justified his actions on the basis that the conditions of his incarceration were so gross, harsh and inhumane that they were an illegal form of imprisonment, under the Constitution and international law. In his trial, the government blocked the admission of evidence regarding conditions at Woomera, insisting it was irrelevant.

Nevertheless, the evidence placed on the record included a report by Professor Richard Harding, Inspector of Custodial Services in Western Australia, condemning the detention centres as an 'absolute disgrace'. Harding's report said the centres were 'in the middle of no-where' involving 'gross overcrowding, broken toilets, unprivate conditions, lack of medical and dental facilities'. He described Curtin Detention Centre as 'almost intolerable', adding that, 'such evidence as exists indicates things are little better at the other centres'.[30] Advice had been given to the immigration minister to close Woomera 'to help avert a human tragedy of unknowable proportions'. A psychiatric nurse stated in a report 'that the detainees felt that they were treated like animals, medication was fed through wire mesh to detainees and there was a pervasive belief that suicide was the only way out'.[31]

With only Kirby J dissenting, the High Court ruled 6–1 that the harshness of conditions was irrelevant to the validity of the deten-

458 SECTION THREE: LAW AND CONTEMPORARY SOCIAL PROBLEMS

tion, and therefore provided no defence. Kirby J held that the circumstances of the appellant's detention could be a form of punishment not sanctioned by a court of law and therefore unconstitutional. He also considered that the detention could be in breach of international law. If the appellant's detention was unlawful then he had a defence available to him in answer to the criminal charge of escaping. In rejecting this proposition, Gummow, McHugh and Heydon JJ cited with approval an opinion by Scalia J in *Wilson v Seiter*[32] in which the US Supreme Court overturned earlier decisions that a prison inmate was constitutionally entitled to medical treatment.

The potential for misuse or abuse of the detention power was demonstrated in 2005, when it was revealed that an Australian resident, Cornelia Rau, had been wrongly detained, and a citizen, Vivian Alvarez, had been unlawfully detained and deported. In 2005 and 2006, the federal government referred 247 unlawful immigration detention cases to the Ombudsman for investigation. His reports confirmed that the victims had been wrongly detained, but no changes were made to the *Migration Act*.[33]

The Convention's fundamental flaws

The Refugee Convention, even augmented by other treaties, does not assist the vast majority of the displaced persons. It is well established that the Convention is narrow and restrictive. As noted by Hathaway:

> Most third world refugees remain de facto excluded, as their flight is more often prompted by natural disaster, war, or broadly based political and economic turmoil than by 'persecution', at least as that term is understood in the western context.[34]

The Convention is deficient in at least four primary respects. First, it does not protect the starving, the destitute, those fleeing war and civil war, or even natural disaster, let alone those seeking to escape economic oppression. Its narrow focus on *individuals* who are *persecuted* does not allow for mass exoduses in the face of suffering, injustice or discrimination that is not considered serious enough to amount to persecution.

Its requirement that this persecution be on the *specific* grounds of race, nationality, religious belief, political opinion or membership of a particular social group does not apply to people seeking refuge from torture, cruel punishment or other infringements of democratic rights, no matter how serious, inflicted for other reasons, despite efforts to extend the interpretation of 'particular social group' to include gender, sexual preference and child-bearing.

Second, the Convention does not create a right to enter another state; only a limited obligation on a national state not to expel or return a refugee to a state where he or she faces persecution. In fact, the Convention does not recognise the individual's right to asylum, only the right of national states to decide who enters their territory. As stated in the Australian High Court:

> The right of asylum is a right of States, not of the individual: no individual, including those seeking asylum, may assert a right to enter the territory of a State of which that individual is not a national.[35]

Third, even those accepted as refugees have no right to permanent residence and hence can be consigned to a tenuous and insecure status. The principle of *non-refoulement* under the Convention's Article 33(1) allows them to be removed to a so-called 'safe third country' or to be forcibly repatriated to their home country once a government considers that the reasons for refugee status have ceased, as provided in Article 1C(5).

Fourth, the Convention only assists asylum seekers who manage, invariably by means designated as 'illegal', to arrive physically in the country where they seek refuge. It does not impose any obligation on a country to take offshore applicants, that is, the overwhelming majority of people languishing in refugee camps throughout the poorest parts of the world, whether in their own countries or neighbouring states.

Governments refer to unwanted arrivals as 'queue jumpers', 'illegals' and 'forum shoppers'. Yet, refugees can only obtain the limited protection available under the Convention by escaping and entering a 'safe' country without permission. (Moreover, as stated earlier, the Convention upholds their right to do so, implicitly forbidding discrimination on the grounds of illegal entry.)

These fundamental flaws reflect the Convention's Cold War origins. It was drawn up in the aftermath of World War II and the Nazi Holocaust, which had caused the displacement of more than 40 million people within Europe. The knowledge that the advanced capitalist countries had refused to open their borders to many fleeing fascist persecution led to a broadly held sentiment that never again should refugees be turned away.

These democratic aspirations were incorporated in the Convention, which set out that all asylum seekers – defined as those having a well-founded fear of persecution – were to be guaranteed certain inalienable rights, specifically that of refuge. Nevertheless, key governments only accepted the Convention on the basis that it did not create any duty to grant permanent residence and that they retained the sovereign right to decide which refugees were allowed entry to their countries.

Those who framed the Convention were also mindful of broader political considerations. In upholding the right to political asylum, the West sought to strengthen its democratic credentials against the Soviet Union and Eastern Bloc countries, and specifically to hold the door open for political dissidents from the Stalinist regimes. The very conception of 'persecution' was tailored to give western governments ideological kudos for providing sanctuary to 'defectors' to the 'free world'.

The need for an alternative perspective

Many writers in this field assert or assume a public opinion that is hostile to refugees and economic migrants. They tend to present governments as simply reacting to or appeasing this sentiment. Crock, for example, after noting that the UN Human Rights Committee had condemned as 'arbitrary' (under the International Covenant on Civil and Political Rights) the automatic and indefinite imprisonment of unlawful entrants in Australian detention centres, wrote:

> If Australia does not respond in real terms to the Committee's rulings, the case may stand in this country as a testament to an increasing mood of national introspection and even isolationism from the world community.[36]

This supposed 'mood' is, however, one that is aggressively cultivated by those who hold political office and by the media proprietors. Crock herself noted instances of poor reporting and blatant scaremongering in the media, such as early 1998 reports that refugee claimants ('tourists') were coming to Australia for a '$30 work visa'. During the *Tampa* case, Defence Minister Peter Reith insisted that if North

J's initial ruling stood, it would open the floodgates for terrorists to enter the country on refugee boats.[37] Without offering a skerrick of evidence, a junior minister, Peter Slipper, claimed there was 'an undeniable linkage between illegals and terrorists'.[38]

For public opinion on refugees to be genuinely tested, a viable alternative perspective must be advanced – one that corresponds to the requirements of global economic and social life and the needs and aspirations of the vast majority of people, rather than the vested interests of corporate and government elites.

A number of authors have suggested possible models for replacing the Refugee Convention with new international frameworks for protecting and assisting refugees. None of these models challenge the underlying assumption that nation-states and national borders will continue to exist throughout the 21st century. Instead, they seek ways to dilute the refugee obligations of nation-states according to what the authors consider politically palatable. Hathaway has argued specifically for tailoring proposals for change to meet the needs of national governments. 'In an international legal system based on the self-interest of states, it is critical that principled reform proceed in a manner which anticipates and responds to the needs of governments', he stated, calling for support for a 'broader (if shallower) level of protection for most of the world's refugees'.[39]

In general, these authors invoke notions such as limited safe havens, temporary protection, international, regional and bilateral co-operation, and burden sharing. They also seek to separate the refugee regime from migration programmes, suggesting that this will ease public concern over so-called asylum-driven migration and people smuggling.

This approach is based on maintaining the strict distinction between refugees and migrants. In a global world, and one increasingly dominated by social inequality, this is an artificial, inhumane and ultimately unreal perspective. The UN has estimated that 125 million people are, at any given time, outside their homeland in search of more secure political conditions or a better economic future. As a senior Canadian immigration official has observed:

> Almost all parts of the world are witnessing major migratory movements. While in 1965, 65 million people were living long term outside their countries of normal residence, by 1990 there were 130 million and in 2000 an estimated 150 million. Some are persons

with legal status in their adopted countries. Most are in an irregular situation and try by various means to regularise their status.[40]

This demand for a more decent life will only grow amid ever-wider disparities in wealth and life opportunities. According to the 1998 United Nations World Development Report, the three richest people in the world have assets exceeding the combined gross domestic product (GDP) of the 48 least developed countries; the 15 richest people have assets worth more than the total GDP of sub-Saharan Africa and the 32 richest have more assets than the GDP of South Asia. Of the 4.4 billion people in so-called developing countries, almost three-fifths lack basic sanitation, one third have no safe drinking water and one quarter have inadequate housing, while one fifth are under-nourished, and the same proportion have no access to decent health services. According to the UN, out of the 147 countries defined as 'developing', some 100 had experienced 'serious economic decline' over the past 30 years.

Moreover, the advent of new forms of mass information, information technology and greater accessibility to air travel will accelerate and facilitate the movement of large numbers of oppressed people.

Citizenship and democratic rights

There is a profound connection between democratic rights and the rights of the most vulnerable in society – those denied entry to, or citizenship of, a country where they feel secure and able to participate meaningfully in political life.

Without the right to live securely with full political and social rights, democracy itself is meaningless. As one study noted, in the 20th century:

> The possession of a nationality became a matter of crucial, practical importance to the individual. The stateless person has no right of residence in any territory, no right to apply for employment or establish a business in any particular place. In some countries, a stateless person has only limited access to the legal system and its protection. One needs a nationality in order to enjoy basic security of residence somewhere.[41]

In Australia, the High Court has drawn a sharp line between citizens and non-citizens. In the 1992 case of *Lim*, the court upheld the power of the government to detain non-citizens ('aliens') indefinitely without trial, a practice that breaches one of the most fundamental democratic rights – freedom from arbitrary detention – which is enshrined in the centuries-old common law doctrine of habeas corpus.

In the words of Brennan, Deane and Dawson JJ, Australian citizens enjoy a 'constitutional immunity from being imprisoned by Commonwealth authority except pursuant to an order by a court in the exercise of the judicial power of the Commonwealth'.[42]

However, the court found that this constitutional immunity did not extend to immigration detainees because they were not being incarcerated by way of criminal sanction but rather to protect the national interest. Remarkably, ignoring the reality of refugee persecution, the majority asserted that the detainees (Cambodian asylum seekers) were to some extent voluntary 'prisoners' who were free to return to their country of origin if they wished. In the final analysis, the High Court upheld the mandatory detention regime on the basis of the power to legislate with respect to aliens. The majority concluded that s51 (xix) of the Australian Constitution conferred on the executive the authority to detain an alien for the purposes of expulsion or deportation, with an incidental power of detention to investigate and determine an application for asylum.

Several commentators have observed that the High Court failed to protect basic human rights, acting under pressure to accommodate the vehement views of a government intent on having its way. Equally ominous was the readiness of the Court to acknowledge that similar regimes of administrative detention could be applied to citizens during times of war, under the defence power. Once a precedent is established for the denial of basic democratic rights, first for the most vulnerable members of society – refugees and others without citizenship status – it can more easily be extended to others whose commitment to the state is called into question.

Global citizenship

The existence of nation-states, partitioning the globe into a patchwork of larger and smaller entities, each with their own border controls and exclusion regimes, is not natural or of ancient origin. Modern nationalism and general restrictions on the movement of people emerged only in the late 19th and early 20th centuries. Dummett and Nicol note that:

> In earlier periods, restriction was by no means unknown but it was neither so general nor so systematic ... Before the 1914 war, it was possible to travel between a number of countries without a passport, and with no restriction on taking work after arrival. With the price of a passage, an individual could take a free decision to look abroad for a new life; even without it, one could 'run away to sea', work a passage and try one country after another.[43]

From the late 19th century, however, border restrictions began to limit these movements.

> Instead of being 'chained to the soil' of a feudal lord, the twentieth-century poor gradually became chained to the territory of their countries of origin because other countries' rules forbade them entry.[44]

Far from nation-states being rooted in primordial nationalist sentiments, or even geographical necessity, their relatively recent historical origins are bound up with the socio-economic requirements of emerging capitalism in the struggle against the old feudal order in Europe. The growth of industrial production and the accumulation of capital required the development of a national market and the breaking down of guild privileges, political restrictions, local customs barriers and tariffs, which hemmed in production on all sides.

In England, the United States of America and France, revolutions were necessary to overthrow monarchical rule and establish nation-states. By the early 20th century, however, the enormous development of production engendered by capitalism had already outgrown the nation-state framework, leading to two world wars between the major economic and military rivals. Just as the old feudal fiefdoms, principalities and kingdoms had to be swept aside to clear the way for economic development under capitalism, it is now necessary to replace the nation-state system to allow for the harmonious growth of world economy. That transformation is inseparable from establishing a new global conception of democracy and citizenship.

As currently instituted, citizenship is confined to a given nation-state and does not extend beyond its borders. Meaningful democracy in the 21st century demands the right of all people to move wherever they wish around the world; the right to live, work and study wherever they choose, enjoying the political, civil and social rights and benefits available to all. If the poor and the oppressed are to be given the same right to travel and live as the wealthy and if the right to immigrate as well as to emigrate is to be recognised, a new form of citizenship is needed – global citizenship.

Discussion topics

1. Who is a refugee? What problems arise with the official definition?
2. Assess current Australian policies towards asylum seekers.
3. Should the Refugee Convention be defended or should a new approach be adopted?

Additional resources

S. Castles and M.J. Miller, *The Age of Migration: International Population Movement in the Modern World*, Macmillan, London, 1993.

M. Crock, A. Dastyari and B. Saul, *Future Seekers II: Refugees and Irregular Migration in Australia*, Federation Press, Sydney, 2006.

R. Germov and F. Motta, *Refugee Law in Australia*, Oxford University Press, Oxford, 2003.

Globalization and the International Working Class: A Marxist Assessment, International Committee of the Fourth International, Mehring Books, Sydney, 1999.

M. Head, 'The High Court and the removal of Kosovar refugees' 4 *Macarthur Law Review* (2000) 197.

M. Head, 'The High Court and the Tampa refugees: a critical examination of Vadarlis v Minister for Immigration and Multicultural Affairs' 11 *Griffith Law Review* (2002) 23.

M. Head, 'Detention without trial – a threat to democratic rights' 9 *University of Western Sydney Law Review* (2005) 33–51.

E. Hobsbawm, *Nations and Nationalism since 1780*, Cambridge University Press, 1992.

The Immigration Kit, 7th edition, Federation Press, Sydney, 2005.

D. McMaster, *Asylum Seekers: Australia's Response to Refugees*, Melbourne University Press, Melbourne, 2001.

P. Mares, *Borderline: Australia's treatment of refugees and asylum seekers*, UNSW Press, Sydney, 2001.

The Problem with the 1951 Refugee Convention, Parliamentary Library Research Paper 5, 2000–01, Parliament of Australia, Canberra.

Chapter 20

JUST WARS AND CRIMINAL LAWS

The end of the Cold War did not bring the peace that many hoped for. Instead, the post-Cold War period has been characterised by continuous warfare around the world. Much of this warfare has included direct involvement or support from the leadership of the western nations, including the attacks on Afghanistan and Serbia, the first gulf war attack by Iraq on Iran, the two subsequent Gulf War attacks on Iraq and the 2006 Israeli attack on Lebanon.

Many people believe that these wars are, in important cases, far from just, either in terms of the causes pursued or the conduct involved. Intuition, logic and principle suggest that the supposed justifications offered by the authorities are unconvincing, unachievable or unjust, and that these wars have been – and continue to be – prosecuted in ways which directly involve large-scale killings of innocent people, which should be regarded as war crimes rather than legitimate acts of war. Or they have led to mass killings of innocent people which were reasonably foreseeable consequences of the military actions in question.

The other side of the issue is the failure of others to (promptly enough) institute legitimate defensive military action to protect the victims of illegitimate aggression. There is widespread recognition of such failure in the cases of Rwanda, the former Yugoslavia, East Timor and, more recently, Lebanon. To the extent that the allied attacks on Afghanistan and Iraq lacked moral or legal justification, so is there a case to be made that they too should have elicited appropriate action in defence of the victims of such unjustified aggression.

There are therefore also issues of the 'justice' of identifying foreign nationals participating in military action to defend such victims as 'terrorists'.

This chapter draws upon the work of moral philosophers Richard Norman and Peter Singer, criminologists Rob White and Santina Perrone, and social theorists Heikki Patomaki and Teivo Teivainen to clarify some of the issues involved here. In particular, it focuses on philosophical, legal and practical issues of 'just war' theory, and of enforcement of law based on such theory.

Morality

The major wars of recent times – along with genocide in Rwanda and the former Yugoslavia – raise the question of what circumstances (if any) can ever provide moral legitimation for killing in war. In recent years there has been increasing discussion of the tradition of 'just war' principles, originally developed by Christian thinkers and latterly influencing the development of international law. As moral philosopher Richard Norman notes, both leaders seeking to give moral legitimacy to wars in which they are involved and their critics 'often employ the same moral vocabulary' derived from this tradition of thought.[1]

This vocabulary includes ideas of just cause, right intention, legitimate authority, reasonable hope of success, last resort and proportionality of ends as necessary conditions for a just entry into warfare. Ideas of non-combatant immunity and proportionality of means are considered necessary conditions of just participation in warfare.

As Norman argues, criteria of 'rightful intention', 'reasonable hope of success', 'proportionality' of ends and 'last resort' are all closely tied to the issue of 'just cause'. Rightful intention requires the justice of the cause to be the real objective of the war, rather than a consideration satisfied incidentally. Reasonable hope of success can only mean 'a reasonable hope of succeeding in a just cause'.[2] Proportionality can only mean that military action is justified only so long as its harmful consequences don't outweigh 'the specific good which the war is intended to achieve'. And 'last resort' can only mean that all other, less harmful avenues have been found wanting in achieving the 'good' end in question.

As far as 'just cause' itself is concerned, as Norman notes, discussion has increasingly focused on the idea of 'defence against aggression'. Killing in war is justified only to defend victims from the aggressive acts of others. 'This is the version of 'just war' theory encapsulated in modern international law, and regularly invoked by politicians.'[3] In 2006 the Israeli leadership presented its attacks on Lebanon and the Gaza strip, with large-scale civilian casualties and destruction of essential infrastructure, as defence against aggression by Hizballah and Palestinian militants.

Ideas of self-defence in war, and of legitimate international legal regulation of killing in war, are typically grounded in considerations of individual self-defence, and its regulation by national criminal justice systems. But different theorists have different ideas of how to move from the individual to the social level. Particularly influential in recent years has been Michael Waltzer's analysis, focused on the idea of communal acts of killing in defence of territorial integrity and political sovereignty understood by analogy with individual acts of killing in defence of individual life and liberty (including bodily integrity).[4]

Self-defence and criminal law

Norman presents a clear moral analysis of issues of individual self-defence. Given the supreme value of human life and a universal individual right to life, an individual right to kill in self-defence exists only in situations of forced choice between lives, where the attacker is responsible for forcing the choice, and – due to the immediacy of the threat – there really is no other way for the person attacked to survive without killing their attacker. This right extends to third parties, intervening to save the lives of others under attack. Indeed, such third parties are probably under a moral obligation to intervene, so long as their own life is not seriously threatened through so doing.

Norman also argues that while 'someone might be entitled to kill an attacker who threatens to rape her, or kidnap her or enslave her', it is very doubtful that the justification would extend much further than this'. In particular, given the supreme value of human life, there can be no justification for killing in defence of property.[5]

People can, of course, be killed through destruction of property – crashing the plane, sinking the boat, destroying the heating in winter or subsistence food supplies during the famine. Destruction or theft of such necessary means of survival can therefore be regarded as an attack on human life, and loss of life in defence of such means can be justified.

These ideas are clearly reflected in the sorts of circumstances recognised by the criminal justice system of the common law world as justifying or excusing deliberate acts of homicide. For self-defence and the defence of others is central among the 'true' or 'complete' (as against 'partial') defences for such an otherwise criminal act. And this has to be defence of life, rather than merely of property.[6]

A key issue here is whether the accused believed – on reasonable grounds – that it was necessary to do what they did in order to save their own life or that of another innocent person from attack. Some authorities have argued also that the attack motivating the defensive action must be unjustified or illegal. If the belief in the necessity of the defence was not reasonable – if less than fatal force was needed, for example – then the defence fails. If the accused intended to kill, while knowing that less than fatal force was needed, or having no reasonable belief that it was, they are liable to be judged a murderer. If they were not aiming to kill but did so, the result would be manslaughter. Here, then, we see a clear focus on 'proportionality' of force and 'last resort'.[7]

The common law countries have generally rejected any legal requirement of duty to rescue others threatened by aggression. But legal theorists have periodically argued a strong case for recognising such a duty[8] and civil law jurisdictions have provided legal support for the kind of moral duty of rescue considered by Norman.

In some common law jurisdictions, provocation – sufficient to cause the ordinary person to 'lose self-control', to the point of intending to kill or injure – can reduce murder to voluntary manslaughter. In others, this partial defence has been abolished. In Victoria, concerns about the use of the defence by men, using issues of jealousy and alleged 'taunting' as excuses for killing female partners, has led to changes such that provocation can only be considered as an issue during sentencing.[9]

An individual whose mind has been found to have been substantially impaired by abnormality arising from an underlying condition of mental illness (at the time of the crime) can also be guilty of voluntary manslaughter in some jurisdictions. But duress, where a person commits a crime as a result of threats from another, has not been accepted as a defence to a murder allegation, where the accused is the actual killer.[10] The state of the law in relation to necessity – where the accused chooses, rather than is ordered – to commit a crime as the lesser of two evils is less clear, with conflicting ideas on whether it can be a defence to murder.[11]

From individuals to social structures

Waltzer's analogy focuses on threats to the life of a political community. Territorial integrity is associated with the 'life' of such a community, political sovereignty with its liberty – 'its right to control its own political life'. Just as a threat to the life or liberty of an individual can justify killing the aggressor, so can a military threat to the life or liberty of the community justify collective military defence involving the death of members of the invading army. And, just as other individuals have a responsibility to intervene to protect the life of another, and the right to kill in order to achieve this, 'so should a community's rights to territorial integrity and political sovereignty ... be defended by other states'.[12]

It is easy to see problems with the analogy. Why should actual killing of people be justified in defence of the merely analogical 'life' of the victim political system? As Norman points out, a consistent application of the analogy, with a corresponding analogical killing of the polity of the aggressor, makes no sense at all.

If we reject this analogy, we are left with collective application of the principles relating to individuals: collective killing justified only by imminent threat to the lives of individual members of the victim community, not to its culture, political institutions or territorial integrity. As Norman says, 'only something like a defensive war of resistance to genocide could be justified in this way'.[13]

As Norman argues, to justify killing in defence of a political community per se – a particular set of social institutions, relations and practices, rather than in defence of the lives of the members of such a community – requires us to show that that community (those institutions, relations, etc) is 'so valuable as to justify killing in its defence'.[14] We must also remember that lost social institutions and relations can be rebuilt in a way that lost human lives cannot. So that even destruction of good institutions may not necessarily be a disaster in the longer term.

Waltzer himself maintains that it is the right of self-determination – or rather the existence of institutions that derive from and continue to sustain such a right – that deserves to be defended, and he insists that this does not necessarily imply only liberal democracy. But he is less than clear in identifying what other sorts of regimes actually manifest or sustain such a right, or why contemporary liberal democracy should be thought to do so. Norman says that it would have to be a regime with widespread support and political structures grounded in popular culture.

Both Waltzer and Norman agree that non-military intervention is legitimate to attack repressive regimes (not allowing 'self-determination'). So do they argue that military intervention is another form of coercion, and coercion cannot create freedom. Foreigners can help in the self-organisation of groups struggling to achieve such self-determination, presumably including armed resistance to oppression, but they cannot 'impose' freedom on others through force of arms. As suggested earlier, such armed intervention is justified only in situations of imminent genocide, the threat of mass enslavement, undisciplined armies running amok, or political repression involving torture and murder.[15]

Recent developments in Iraq and Afghanistan seem to have provided significant verification of this latter point about the impossibility of coercive imposition of freedom. But the accounts of both of these theorists fail to clearly spell out the nature of the 'widespread support' which can supposedly justify killing in defence of particular sorts of political or economic institutions and practices. Massive central monopoly power over means of mass communication in the modern world contribute to the effective 'manufacture' of support for, or at least acceptance of, the policies of government and big business. And evidence of 'widespread support' for regimes engaged in brutal repression at home and abroad casts serious doubt upon the moral adequacy of such an idea.

The vagueness of these ideas of 'self-determination' and 'widespread support' is paralleled by Waltzer's idea of humanitarian intervention being justified 'as a response with reasonable expectations of success' – to acts 'that shock the moral conscience of mankind'.[16] As Peter Singer points out, 'conscience has, at various times and places, been shocked by such things as inter-racial sex, atheism and mixed bathing'.[17]

A more promising starting point for moral justification of intervention over and above an immediate threat of loss of life is the earlier consideration of slavery. Just as it may be legitimate (as a last resort) for individuals to kill to avoid enslavement, so might it be legitimate for organised groups of individuals to do the same. If there are reasonable grounds for seeing a forced choice as necessary under the circumstances, with no other recourse possible, to preserve or produce a condition of freedom from slavery – grounded in particular sorts of social and political institutional arrangements – then killing to preserve or achieve such freedom could be morally justified. But, at the same time, it is easy to see the potential for abuse of these ideas, with aggressors claiming their aim is to save the populations of the territories they attack from slavery, when in fact they have no such aim or interest.

Major problems also arise in relation to traditional interpretations of morally acceptable conduct within war – *jus in bello*. The idea of non-combatant immunity – 'the principle that it is wrong to attack or kill non-combatants' – is usually taken to derive from the supposed 'innocence' of civilians as individuals not directly involved in hostilities, as against soldiers actually engaging in the combat of the war. Civilians are supposedly innocent of direct involvement in warfare, rather than being innocent without qualification. But it seems clear, as Norman points out, that civilians involved in weapons production, for example, are more directly involved in the prosecution of the war than cooks or doctors in the military; that conscript soldiers, forced to fight on threat of court martial execution, are relatively non-culpable, while the politicians who direct the war, and big business leaders who supply the weaponry and reap the benefits of imperial conquest and who direct the politicians, are the most culpable, however far away they might appear to be from direct military action. Other civilian supporters of the war can hardly be regarded as innocent, but so are they likely to be victims of misrepresentations fed to them by the politicians and business leaders.[18]

It has been argued that soldiers have the power to defend themselves in ways that civilian populations do not. And this is certainly true in some cases. But soldiers can be much more vulnerable than civilians in other cases; certainly more vulnerable than leaders hidden in underground bunkers. And it is far from clear how this idea can sustain any clear moral principle on non-combatant immunity.

Justification of the mass killing of 25 000 conscript soldiers of dicta-
tor Saddam Hussein, shot down as they retreated from Kuwait on
Iraqi highways in the second Gulf War, provides a very clear example
of the inadequacy of the traditional ideas in practice.[19]

It seems that the combatant/non-combatant distinction is relevant
only in relation to earlier considerations of the right of self-defence.
To the extent that such self-defence is associated with an immediate threat to life and limb, it is more likely that soldiers will be the
objects of such legitimate defensive action. But, here again, it is quite
possible that self-protection on a large scale can most effectively be
achieved through the killing of political and business leaders, actually
directing the fighters.

From crime to warfare

Given the moral considerations which suggest that the core of just war
theory should be the defence of individuals from immanent threat of
aggression, it seems reasonable to explore the extension of the basic
categories of national criminal law from an individual to a collective
and international level. And here, certain issues and problems are
immediately apparent.

Both soldiers and other citizens involved in war efforts are
frequently subjected to systematic mental manipulation by political
authorities aimed at convincing them of the imminent threat to themselves and others, including innocent civilians at home, from foreign
armies. This creates problems for the idea of 'reasonable grounds'
for belief among such soldiers and civilians. On the other hand,
such manipulation itself indicates the complicity of such authorities
in assisting or encouraging the crimes of such soldiers and citizens,
where no real issue of self-defence exists. And criminal law allows for
the prosecution of such accessories before and after the fact as princi-
pals in the offence, whether or not the principal offenders themselves
have been tried.[20]

Political authorities themselves can be generally expected to have
access to more reliable information about the extent and imminence
of such a threat. The issue of such reasonable grounds loomed large
in relation to claims made about weapons of mass destruction allegedly developed by the Iraqi leadership in the period immediately
preceding the third Gulf War. It seems clear that no such reasonable

grounds existed in this case, making the justification of self-defence – or defence of another – inapplicable, and murder charges against the leaders of the 'coalition of the willing' might seem appropriate. Even if there were reasonable grounds for expecting some degree of threat, it seems clear that defensive action could have been taken short of large-scale attacks on soldiers and civilians with significant loss of life.

With revelations of the lack of real evidence for imminent mobilisation of weapons of mass destruction, such authorities fell back on what could be seen as variations on the 'freedom from slavery' theme. There are obvious doubts that this was the 'real' intention behind the attacks. Nor were there reasonable grounds for believing either that military intervention was the last resort for achieving significant improvements in the political-economic situation of the mass of the population or that such improvement would be the likely outcome of the sort of intervention intended.

Duress, provocation and substantial impairment could all be relevant to soldiers, forced into unlawful killing through threat of court martial execution, put through programmes of 'training' involving ruthless mental manipulation and seeing fellow soldiers killed by soldiers of an opposing army. Even more so, they would seem to be relevant in the case of desperate poor people, driven mad and/or provoked into aggression – including 'terrorist' acts – through illegal occupation of their land, destruction of their homes, arrest of their families and deprivation of basic human rights by a foreign power – as in Israel's Occupied Territories.

On the other hand, it's difficult to see how provocation or duress could provide any kind of a defence for powerful politicians and business leaders unleashing military attacks upon others. Indeed, the reasons for abolishing provocation as a defence in criminal law are closely paralleled by reasons for disallowing it at a political level: as an excuse born out of regular exercise of power and domination.

Issues of involuntary manslaughter, related in criminal law to causing death through criminal acts carrying appreciable risk of serious injury, without a specific intention to kill, seem clearly relevant to the behaviour of the political and military leaders ordering attacks upon 'strategic' sites in civilian population centres. Perhaps, indeed, they have no intention to kill innocent civilians, but their intentional actions can show a massive disregard for the life and safety of such civilians, making a charge of manslaughter by 'dangerous act' relevant.[21]

'Criminal negligence' is less relevant, insofar as this implies a failure to realise the probability of deaths as a consequence of the action in question.[22] Generally, we should expect such leaders to have a fairly clear idea of the dangerousness of their actions. Indeed, it will be difficult not to see them as intentionally killing civilians when they order intensive bombing of economic infrastructures, identified as 'military targets', such as has been a central feature of all recent wars involving the major capitalist powers. As Norman says, 'the bombing of such targets inevitably involves large numbers of civilian casualties', with longer-term effects of starvation and disease frequently 'even more catastrophic'.[23] This seems to be a clear case of killing people by destroying property, as considered earlier.

The foundations of international criminal law

As noted earlier, just war principles had their origins in the Christian church's acceptance of warfare in the Roman Empire. 'Force could be used provided it complied with the divine will.'[24] Later, with wars between competing Christian states, the idea became associated with a 'legal' requirement for 'serious attempts at a peaceful resolution ... before turning to force'.[25]

The League of Nations failed to prohibit war, but attempted to prevent it with arbitration or restrict its intensity and destructiveness.[26] Following World War II, however, the United Nations Charter decisively rejected any right of territorial conquest by military force, while supporting the goal of international security in a world ruled by law, with the promotion of equal rights and self-determination for all. In particular, Article 2(4) of the Charter committed all member nations to 'refraining from the threat or use of forces against the territorial integrity or political independence of any state ... .' And Article 2(6) requires that the UN 'shall ensure that states which are not members of the UN act in accordance ... with the maintenance of international peace and security'.

The 1970 Declaration on Principles of International Law interpreted Article 2(4) to mean that 'wars of aggression and acts of reprisal constitute a crime against peace under international law'. States 'must not use force to deprive peoples of the right of self-determination ... nor organise, institute, assist or participate in acts of civil strife or terrorist acts in another state'.[27]

Use of force is explicitly allowed under the Charter only in case of self-defence and Security Council decision. Article 51 of the Charter states that 'nothing ... shall impair the inherent right of individual or collective self-defence if an armed attack occurs against a member of the United Nations, until the Security Council has taken the measures necessary to maintain international peace'.

As Shaw explains, the *Caroline* case of 1837 has been taken to specify the circumstances of legitimate use of force in self-defence in customary international law. There has to exist 'a necessity of self-defence, instant, overwhelming, leaving no choice of means, and no moment for deliberation'. And the action taken must 'not be unreasonable or excessive ... since the act, justified by the necessity of self-defence, must be limited by that necessity, and kept clearly within it'.[28]

It might be thought that international law therefore runs closely parallel to the domestic criminal law of the common law nations, with protection from attack threatening immediate loss of human life seen as the only legitimate defence for intentional killing of other human beings through the use of military force, with reasonable grounds for believing that the level of force involved was necessary to save life under the circumstances.

The problem is the ambiguity of 'self'-defence as between the protection of human life (from death or enslavement) and Waltzer's metaphorical or analogical sense of defence of the territorial integrity and political sovereignty of a particular nation-state. Whereas human lives can be matched against one another in the former case in considering ideas of 'proportionality' and 'limitation', the second sort of idea leaves such 'proportionality' and 'limitation' totally unclear. How many lives can legitimately be sacrificed to 'save' particular political structures and institutions? How serious must be the threat to such institutions, or what extent of loss of territory (for example) justifies any use of force to take the lives of the invaders?

On the basis of earlier considerations, the answer seems to be that none of these things can, in themselves, justify any such use of force. The situation here is complicated by the fact that violations of territorial integrity typically also involve some loss of life in the territory in question. Nonetheless, it seems clear that it is 'protection' of territorial integrity rather than protection of human life that is the primary concern of international law in this context.

Here, we might expect that, as with individual human life in national law, it would only be a threat of imminent and total destruction of the institutions in question that would justify any corresponding loss of human life (on the part of the attackers or defenders) through the use of force against the invaders. But, again, this is not how the ideas in question have been interpreted.

Setting aside considerations of the legitimacy of the pre-existing regime in Kuwait (which was far from democratic), the Iraqi invasion of 1991 could be said to have constituted an imminent threat of destruction of that regime. On this basis, and following Iraqi refusal to withdraw, the UNSC support for the second Gulf War could be said to have been justified by the principle of 'defence' of 'sovereignty' and 'territorial integrity' (even if the principle itself cannot be justified). On the other hand, Shaw also uses the example of the British attack upon the Argentine forces occupying the Falkland Islands in 1982 as a classic example of defence of territorial integrity, fully legitimate in international law. And this despite the fact that the 'territory' in question was minimal and there was no question of any threat to the British regime itself.

It is true, as Norman points out, that 'the Argentine invasion was an act of aggression against British territory, [and] whatever the strength of the Argentine claim that the territory was wrongly taken from it in the past, British sovereignty in the islands was desired by the islanders and was internationally recognised'.[29] At the same time, the Argentine occupation itself involved minimal force and loss of human life; prior to the British attack a peace plan had been formulated that would have allowed the islanders to retain their culture and independence but the British refused to consider it, and the attack itself led to the loss of 255 British and 652 Argentine lives.[30]

Two closely related questions arise in respect of these ideas and events: the question of the legality of pre-emptive self-defence prior to actual armed attack, and the interpretation of the concepts of 'necessity' and 'proportionality' once such ideas are cut free of any reference to protection of specific human lives.

As Shaw argues, the general (legal) trend in relation to the first question has been to distinguish situations where a particular regime has good reason to believe that an armed attack is 'imminent and unavoidable', where pre-emption is justified, from those where such an attack is merely 'foreseeable', where pre-emption is not justified. This raises questions of the scale of the imminent attack (of stone throwing across a border or use of nuclear weapons, for example) and the corresponding scale of proportionality of legitimate pre-emptive attack.

The Bush regime in the United States has decisively rejected this interpretation in favour of their own conception of pre-emption, which apparently allows for the first use of force by the United States even when a possible future attack on the United States is not imminent, and could be avoided through use of non-military options. It also allows for the use of force against regimes said to be harbouring terrorists, as well as against those terrorists themselves.

As Shaw states, 'the concepts of necessity and proportionality are at the heart of self-defence in international law'.[31] He quotes the International Court in the Nicaragua case ([1986] *ICJ Reports* 14, involving US attacks on Nicaragua) as identifying a 'specific rule' of customary international law that warrants 'only measures [of self-defence] proportional to the armed attack and necessary to respond to it'.[32] But the precise interpretation of these terms remains radically uncertain and unclear.

It might be thought that the extent of legitimate response would be determined, not by the extent of the original attack, but by the extent of threatened future attack, and would specifically concern the extent of response needed to obviate such attack. Otherwise, the response looks much more like a reprisal than a defensive act. And reprisals, involving the use of force, are strictly illegal in international law. But there seems to be no such clear-cut interpretation of the concept of reprisal in this context.

Given the radical lack of clarity or principle in this area of law, we must apparently look to international humanitarian law for any hope of principled limitation of loss of life in attacks 'justified' as acts of legitimate 'self-defence'. Particularly significant here are the rules enacted by the Hague Peace Conferences of 1899 and 1907 relating to a range of *jus in bello* issues, including combatants regarded as lawful, permitted weapons and methods of combat and rules of neutrality.

Important for later developments, and for the issues under consideration here, were Articles 25 and 23(e) of the 1907 Hague

Regulations, outlawing direct attacks against non-military targets and prohibiting the use of weapons 'calculated to cause unnecessary suffering'. As Amichai Cohen says, there is an implicit idea of 'proportionality' involved here, with war declared illegal if the ends – in the form of military goals – cannot justify the means – in the form of human death and suffering.[33]

The Hague regulations focus on the requirement to 'protect civilians against the effects of the hostilities'.[34] Civilian populations and individual civilians 'shall not be objects of attack', and 'constant care' must be taken to spare and protect them.

Article 51(5) of the 1977 Protocol to the Geneva Convention attempted to clarify issues of proportionality. It prohibited 'attacks by bombardment' which treat clearly separated military objectives in areas of civilian population concentration as 'a single military objective', and attacks 'which may be expected to cause incidental loss of civilian life ... which would be excessive in relation to concrete and direct military advantage anticipated'.

As Cohen says:

> The principle of proportionality, as embodied in this and other similar articles in the first protocol, is based on two complementary ideas ... Measures have to be taken to limit the harm that efforts to attain military goals will cause to civilian populations ... the military target should be defined in the narrowest possible way ... the attacking power should consider whether there is a way to achieve the military objective with less or no damage to the civilian population.[35]

The attacking power is also required to 'make an audit of its proposed operation, comparing the foreseeable damage to the civilian population with the expected military advantage'. The attacking army is required 'to relinquish a military advantage if its attainment threatens to cause disproportionate harm to the civilian population'.[36] The problem is that the nature of the 'legitimate military advantage' to be balanced against the loss of innocent life remains unclear, by virtue, in part, of the earlier noted ambiguity in the idea of 'self defence'.

Article 8 of the Statute of the International Criminal Court of 2002 defines war crimes in such a way as to include:

> ... wilful killing, torture, wilfully causing great suffering or serious injury to body or health, or extensive destruction of property not justified by military necessity, forcing prisoners to serve in the armed

forces of the other side, depriving prisoners or civilians of a fair trial, unlawful deportation and taking hostages. And 8.2(b) lists 26 other indictable crimes including offences against civilians and civilian targets, various sexual crimes, conscripting children into armed forces and starvation of civilian populations.[37]

As far as proportionality is concerned, as Fletcher and Olin point out, the 'key provision' is Article 8(2)(b)(iv) of the Rome statute, prohibiting attacks 'when the collateral harm is excessive relative to the military objective'. 'Intentionally launching an attack in the knowledge that such attack will cause incidental loss of life or injury to civilians ... which would be clearly excessive in relation to the concrete and direct military advantage anticipated' is a war crime.[38]

Again, the issue of the nature of 'legitimate military advantage' remains unresolved. Recent discussions have focused on problems of terrorists taking refuge in civilian residences to prevent enemy attack – and whether this justifies 'greater' civilian casualties than were previously acceptable, and on the legitimacy of saving more of one's own soldiers at the expense of greater civilian casualties.

Many such discussions ultimately seem to come down to numbers of individual human lives likely to be lost with and without the intervention in question. Cohen refers to the 'cumulative effect of proportionality', where the sum total of civilian casualties 'caused by the overall campaign' is 'a clear boundary-marker'.[39] Fletcher and Ohlin note that 'you cannot kill 1000 people in order to save one person from assault'. Such considerations seem to be directly applicable to Israel's recent response to Hizballah attacks in Lebanon.

At the same time, Fletcher and Ohlin follow the Report of the UN Commission of Inquiry on Darfur in arguing that individuals should be convicted only in cases of 'extreme disproportion. It is not enough that the costs outweigh the benefits; the harm must be grossly and obviously excessive relative to the military purpose.'[40]

Humanitarian intervention

The United Nations' capacity for humanitarian intervention has in the past been taken to be significantly limited by Article 2(7) of the Charter which precludes UN intervention 'in matters which are essentially within the domestic jurisdiction of any state'.[41] Most importantly, as has frequently been pointed out, the UN lacks the institutional, financial and technical support needed to properly address these issues. In particular, it lacks any kind of international armed force, its own army or professional police force, capable of enforcing international criminal law. Its failure to act to prevent massive human rights violations in Rwanda and the former Yugoslavia starkly highlighted these limitations.

At the same time, the Charter specifies that 2(7) should not block 'enforcement measures decreed by the Security Council'.[42] And as Broinowski and Wilkinson observe, 'while article 2(7) worked for years to shield even the most repressive governments from outside intervention, over the last three decades the pendulum has swung slowly the other way and a vigorous debate continues on just where the new balance point should be'.[43]

In 2002 ethicist Peter Singer argued that the UN mandate should be understood in the context of international law relating to genocide and crimes against humanity. It should be accepted that 'the rights of domestic jurisdiction retained by the states in Article 2(7) [do] not extend ... to committing genocide or other crimes against humanity'.[44]

This is in keeping with the report of Kofi Annan's High Level Panel in 2004, setting out guidelines for justified military action at the behest of 'a more proactive' Security Council. The report makes specific reference to just war principles of 'seriousness of threat', 'purpose and proportionality of the response', the 'balance of consequences' and 'last resort assurance that other means have been exhausted'.[45]

At the high-level Plenary Meeting of the General Assembly in September 2005, world leaders affirmed a 'clear and unambiguous acceptance ... of the collective responsibility to protect populations from genocide, war crimes, ethnic cleansing and crimes against humanity'.[46] Not only does each individual state have the responsibility to protect its populations from these things, but the international community is 'prepared to take collective action, in a timely and decisive manner, through the Security Council, in accordance with the Charter ... should peaceful means be inadequate and national authorities manifestly fail to protect their populations ...'.[47]

In affirming also their 'strong and unambiguous commitment' to achieve the Millennium Development Goals – including eradication of poverty and hunger, provision of universal primary education, and

482 SECTION THREE: LAW AND CONTEMPORARY SOCIAL PROBLEMS

combating HIV/AIDS, malaria and other diseases of the less developed world by 2015 – so did the heads of state and government correctly recognise the role of poverty, inequality, disease and lack of education in contributing to the crimes in question, and the need to address causes as well as consequences.

With a recognised right and duty to intervene, both in cases of international aggression and intra-national crimes against humanity, the issue then becomes one of the UN being 'able to draw on sufficient military force to make intervention effective'. As Singer says, 'ideally, the United Nations would have sufficient revenue to have its own military forces available for that purpose to defend civilians anywhere in the world threatened with genocide or large-scale crimes against humanity'.[48]

Singer believes that while the spread of democracy, 'overcoming poverty, eliminating injustice and improving education may make genocide less likely, we cannot rely on these policies alone to prevent it'.[49] He argues that the human genetic inheritance renders 'a significant number of human males' potential perpetrators of genocide, and that in some cases this potential may be 'acted upon' without such precipitating factors as 'poverty, injustice, exploitation or lack of education'.[50] In light of this consideration 'we need to be able to do something that will make potential perpetrators of genocide fear the consequences of their actions'.[51] And this – apparently – means the likelihood of being brought to justice by an international police force and subjected to imprisonment in an international prison system.

Violence and law enforcement

No doubt our genetic inheritance does play some role in explaining violent behaviour. And it is probably true, as Michael Albert argues, that there will still be crimes in a good society, including violent crimes, 'and investigation and capture of criminals will [still] be serious matters requiring special skills'.[52] But this does not mean that we cannot very significantly reduce crimes, and particularly crimes of violence, by addressing issues of poverty, injustice, inequality and oppression.[53]

Most significantly, there are good reasons to believe that we cannot and should not try to address issues of law enforcement and punishment – at the national or the international level – without reference to a deeper understanding of the social causation of crimes of violence.

There is now very substantial evidence from around the world that a significant amount of crime in general, and violent crime in particular, is a product of relative inequality of income and power within particular societies. High levels of inequality within a society create increasing socio-psychological divisions between the relatively wealthy and powerful on one side and the relatively poor and power-less on the other.

The latter can be driven to violence through frustration and resent-ment, as a response to denigration and devaluation and as a means of attaining status or recognition for those with low social status and low self-esteem. They can be drawn into violence through subsist-ence-related property and drug crime, or by drug use born of frustra-tion and powerlessness.[54]

The relatively wealthy and powerful typically exercise their violence at a distance, subjecting the relatively poor and powerless to dangerous and unhealthy working conditions, products and environ-ment, to unemployment, homelessness and poverty. On the one hand, such actions are driven by the involvement of the rich and power-ful in the dynamics of corporate capitalist competition. As Albert says, 'capitalism imposes non-stop economic transactional requisites that convey invitations to lie, cheat and otherwise fleece one's fellow citizens through such means as price gouging, dumping pollutants, paying sub-minimum wages'[55] and economising on health and safety provisions in the workplace. On the other hand, their privilege insu-lates them from empathy with their victims and from any likelihood of prosecution or serious penalty.

In the USA in particular, the power of big capitalist corpora-tions has been mobilised to prevent any action to reduce accelerat-ing inequality, poverty and exploitation. It has produced 'poor and poorly educated people on one side, and rich and callous people on the other'. With 30 million people now 'worrying about falling into or already suffering socially defined poverty'[56], increasing numbers of the former have been pushed into circumstances where they are encouraged and required 'to seek means of sustenance outside the law'.[57] At the same time, the few million people who have so much wealth and power that they virtually own society and determine its course of development are obsessed with 'protecting themselves' from the former.

High levels of inequality of wealth and power in a society are reflected in, and exacerbated by, institutions and practices of criminal law enforcement. Here, in particular, are major problems of differential policing associated with the very substantial scope of discretion accorded to the police and other law enforcement agencies.

On the one hand, prejudice and stereotyping have sustained massive over-policing of those at the lower end of the hierarchy of wealth and power, including the long-term unemployed, indigenous people and migrants. In Australia, Aboriginal and Torres Strait Islander people are particularly vulnerable, with over-policing leading to 'over-representation at all levels of the justice system – initial contact, arrest, conviction and imprisonment'.[58] The constant surveillance and persecution of Aboriginal communities – and individuals – leads to mistrust, hostility and resistance on the part of such victims, which are then used to 'justify' intensified persecution. Similarly, police harassment of ethnic minority young people has contributed to mistrust, disrespect and, in some cases, anti-social behaviour and criminal activity by such young people.

On the other side of the coin, as White and Perrone maintain, police have 'historically failed' to provide protection for victims of domestic, homophobic and racist violence.[59] Patriarchal, homophobic and racist attitudes established within police forces have contributed to this failure to protect significant numbers of people at greatest risk. Most important, in terms of the scale of the associated harm, is the failure of the criminal justice system around the developed world to properly address the issues of work-related occupational health and safety (OHS) violations resulting in serious injuries and deaths as a result of the gross negligence of employers.

As White and Perrone point out:

> The law is seen to favour those who have the economic and social resources to both define the nature of social harm, and to defend themselves if prosecuted for criminal activity (for example, by hiring top legal defence teams). From the point of view of a Marxist interpretation, the law is structurally bound to reflect the broad class interests of the capitalist class. It does so ideologically through promulgation of the notion of 'equality before the law', and it does so practically through use of technical, procedural and administrative means that subvert the political and social meaning of particular kinds of social harm.[60]

Closely related to these considerations are issues of abuses of police power and the development of a police culture which obstructs democratic control and accountability. Abuses include the sorts of harassment of poor, indigenous and minority youth groups just considered – including 'processing' without customary safeguards, and the use of unwarranted violence and excessive force during arrest and interrogation. The latter are associated with coerced confessions and are supplemented by other fabrication of evidence. Police work provides ample opportunities for participation in crime, including collection of protection money from law-breakers and others, theft of money and drugs, with consumption and sale of the latter, acceptance of bribes, property and sexual favours. And numerous investigations around the world have revealed that such criminal activity is rife.

As White and Perrone say, the tight-knit character of police society, its isolation and marginalisation from mainstream society, the nature of police interaction with the public in situations of hostility and confrontation, and dissatisfaction with court procedures contribute to a siege mentality and code of silence, shielding police malpractice through systematic obstruction of application of criminal law to the police themselves. Along with 'inadequate instruction in public ethics', education by older police and persecution of non-conformists and whistleblowers, these factors contribute to situations of entrenched corruption and abuse.[61]

So too are there very significant problems associated with the theory and practice of punishment in the common law jurisdictions. We see a theoretical and practical clash of conflicting ideas and practices of deterrence, rehabilitation and reform incapacitation and community protection, denunciation and moral reprobation, retribution and just deserts as supposed guiding principles of the system. It is almost certainly impossible to design practices of punishment which simultaneously satisfy hard-liners' ideas of appropriate retribution while also delivering effective rehabilitation and reform. Nor does the evidence support the idea of draconian practices of retribution serving an effective deterrent or community protection function.

The prison system – particularly in the USA, but also increasingly in other common law jurisdictions – takes the place of a social welfare system, with increasing numbers of (costly, dangerous and dehumanising) prisons absorbing increasing numbers of people because of their ethnic and class position, rather than their criminal activity. These institutions foster hatred, prejudice, anger, crime, disease and drug addiction – rather than reducing them. Imprisonment undermines family ties and future prospects for legal employment. Prison slave labour undermines jobs and conditions in the rest of the community.[62]

As inequality and oppression increase, hostility between the forces of law and order and those most oppressed sections of the population likely to seriously challenge the status quo of capitalist class power becomes an increasingly important foundation and protection of such power. At the same time, big businesses benefit from prison construction, cheap prison labour and the pressure such labour puts on other wages.

Problems at the international level

These considerations at the level of the nation-state – including the most wealthy and supposedly democratic nation-states – must surely give us pause in considering the development of international police and prison systems. This is in addition to earlier raised concerns of the prioritisation of political institutions over human lives in the international law of war, about the failure to develop any clear principles of necessity and proportionality to limit the loss of human life in defence of such institutions, and the USA's apparent rejection of any principles.

Again, there are good reasons to see radical and increasing inequality within and between nations as a significant social cause of war crimes, genocide, crimes against humanity and other major human rights abuses. On one side poverty, frustration and powerlessness drive desperate people to violent acts. On the other, the requirements of capitalist profit maximisation motivate powerful corporations to push governments into aggressive imperialist wars to gain access to cheap or necessary raw materials, cheap labour, markets and investment opportunities. And the scale of such operations increases in proportion to the weakness of the effective opposition.

Without effectively addressing such underlying causes there are also reasons to believe that such structural inequality would radically undermine effective law enforcement at the international level – with international police and prisons – in the same sort of way it appears to have done at the national level. Certainly, the possibilities for abuse of police powers and enslavement of vast prison populations, promoting violent crime on a global scale, are matters of serious concern for would-be reformers of the international criminal justice system.

It is easy to sheet home some of these abuses to the radical inequality and lack of real or meaningful democracy in the highly conservative capitalist societies of the common law world. These are territories in which corporate power has been particularly effective in subverting democratic processes, through its capacity for economic bribery and blackmail, its funding of major political parties and their campaigns, its monopoly power over the mass media and its increasing control of education and research.

In other periods and other regions, corporate power has been more effectively kept in check, at least for limited periods, allowing for increased social welfare, reduced crime, reduced police corruption and reduced prison populations. The Scandinavian countries, in particular, have shown what can be achieved in these areas with state control of natural monopolies, genuinely redistributive taxation and developed social welfare programmes reducing crime through reduced inequality. The Dutch and the Swedes have also managed to keep prison populations down by decriminalisation of victimless crimes, by directing offenders into community correction programmes and imposing lower sentences than other countries. At the same time, they have reduced the oppression and dehumanisation of prison populations by respecting prisoners' human rights and encouraging genuine rehabilitation.

As noted earlier, there will probably still be some crimes even in highly democratic and egalitarian societies. And there seems no reason to assume that the creation of organisations and jobs involving special skills of criminal investigation, and capture of criminals, need necessarily lead to the sort of corruption and abuse considered earlier. In particular, removal of major pressures and incentives for corruption through reductions in inequality and crime and provision of appropriate training and safeguards can be expected to significantly reduce its likelihood or extent.[63]

But these considerations only highlight the dominance of regressive corporations, nations, ideas and institutions, and the lack of real and meaningful democracy, at the international level, within the United Nations itself, and particularly in the composition and operation of the Security Council. Here radical inequalities within nations are complemented by radical inequalities between nations, or between the powers of their political-economic leaders.

Proposals for reform

As Singer acknowledges, the democratic significance of the 'one nation, one vote' principle in the UN General Assembly is only as strong as the democracy actually prevailing within the nation-states in question. So too it crucially depends on the balance of power between such states influencing the voting in the General Assembly.[64]

It is clear that radical imbalances of economic and military power between richer and poorer nations have undermined any such international democracy from the start. A majority of poorer countries did organise together to push for UN support for greater international equality in the 1970s. But the effective takeover of poorer indebted nations by the World Bank and IMF from the 1980s marked a radical loss of autonomous decision-making power of such countries' representatives in the UN. As Patomaki and Teivainen point out, financial blackmail by the US power elite has ensured massive overrepresentation of US and UK citizens in top UN jobs, with an effective shift to a 'one dollar one vote' principle in 'agenda-setting power and decision-making criteria'.[65]

Real international law enforcement power resides in the Security Council rather than the General Assembly, with the US, UK, France, Russia and China as permanent members having a veto power on all decision-making. It is this thoroughly undemocratic body that can pass binding resolutions and enforce sanctions against any member states with a veto over all amendments and any review of the UN charter.[66] Following the end of the Cold War, the collaboration of Russian representatives allowed decisive action by the Security Council in pursuit of the neo-liberal agenda of the dominant economic powers, rather than in the interests of the UN majority or their citizens.[67]

The undemocratic dimensions of the Security Council are in conflict with the sovereign equality of all member states set out in Article 2, Paragraph 1 of the UN Charter. In particular, as Patomaki and Teivainen emphasise, the veto power and privileged position of the major powers stands in the way of any kind of 'impartial treatment of violent conflict' or repression anywhere in the world. This, in turn, undermines the effectiveness of the International Criminal Court (ICC), depriving it of any power of enforcement not endorsed by the major players, and the US in particular.[68]

The position of the ICC is further undermined by lack of jurisdiction over cases supposedly 'adequately processed' in national courts – in contrast to earlier ad hoc criminal tribunals in Rwanda and the former Yugoslavia. The US leadership has vigorously resisted any such compulsory jurisdiction over its own citizens – particularly soldiers and politicians. Rejection of Security Council veto over ICC policy led to US withdrawal of support. The US has subsequently pressured other nations to withdraw support for the ICC and/or to enter into binding agreements not to prosecute US citizens, and passed legislation to authorise US military intervention to free US citizens detained by the ICC.[69]

Here we must set beside such disproportionate US power within the UN and attacks upon the ICC also the rejection of basic principles of international law by the Bush administration as noted earlier, and recent revelations of the United States establishment of secret CIA-run prisons around the world for 'interrogation' of terror suspects, kidnapped and secretly transported by US agents.

Proposals for democratic reform of the Security Council include expanding its membership and/or reducing the veto power of the richer nations, giving the Assembly, as chief deliberative, policy-making and representative body, much greater power over Security Council decision-making, and International Court of Justice (ICJ) review of Security Council decision-making. Proposals for reform of the General Assembly itself include weighted voting rights in proportion to population (rather than financial contribution as favoured by the US) and direct involvement of 'authentic' political Non-Government Organisations (NGOs) (like Amnesty International and Greenpeace) rather than business-initiated NGOs, in the work of the General Assembly and its councils and organisations. Another proposal is for a new 'Peoples' Assembly' for debate and review, which might or might not have legislative power, to accompany (or replace) the General Assembly, with membership determined by direct global elections.[70]

Peter Singer describes such a democratically elected 'World Assembly' as 'an obvious solution' to problems of lack of democracy within the United Nations.[71] He suggests that:

... the United Nations could remain open to all governments, irrespective of their form of government or observance of human rights, but it could replace the present General Assembly with a World Assembly consisting of delegates allocated to its member-states in proportion to their population. The United Nations would then supervise democratic elections in every member country to elect this delegation. A country that refused to allow the United Nations to supervise the election of its delegation would have only one delegate, irrespective of its population. That system would provide experience in democracy for the citizens of most countries, but would retain the inclusiveness that is an important feature of the United Nations.[72]

Johan Galtung argues that such an Assembly should make laws, budgets and appointments, as a fully empowered world parliament.[73]

There are major ethical and practical problems with all such proposals. As Patomaki and Teivainen remind us, 'any amendment or review of the UN Charter would require a two-thirds support of the members of the General Assembly and the simultaneous backing of the permanent members of the Security Council'.[74] Any attempt to establish a Peoples' Assembly, particularly one with significant legislative power, would face massive opposition from the major world powers. And such powers would be able to exercise economic blackmail and bribery to sway the votes of the leaders of the weaker states.

As noted earlier, the powers of the ICC to enforce its laws are undermined by the lack of effective police powers to support it, and by the threat of US military action against any other nation's attempts to bring US citizens to justice. 'On the other hand, enforcement mechanisms controlled by the most powerful actors in world politics can easily have anti-democratic effects if these actors have the option to choose which Court decisions they want to enforce.'[75] Nor would the Court's decision-making itself remain immune from such influence.

Conclusion

As suggested earlier, the UN Millennium Development Goals of combating poverty, hunger and environmental damage, promoting equality of women, health and economic development do focus on some of the underlying causes of war crimes, crimes against humanity and genocide. And renewed commitment of world leaders at the

2005 Summit to achieving such goals by 2015 could be seen to be a step in the right direction.

However, as indicated in chapter 13 on economic efficiency, there are major problems with the formulation of the goals in question. And progress towards these goals has so far been very limited.[76] It remains to be seen whether things will really improve in the future. And, as Patomaki and Teivainen conclude, 'without other democratic reforms in world politics, judicial reforms [including the operation of the ICC] will remain limited in their democratic impact'.[77] All of the reforms considered so far fail to address the subversion of democracy by corporate power, both nationally and internationally. Without very significant change to the economic infrastructures that underlie such political-legal deliberations, without genuinely democratic account-ability of corporate power, such reforms are either unachievable or, if achieved, will fail to have significant impact on human rights abuses, warfare and the administration of criminal justice.[78]

Discussion topics

1 Can war ever be 'just'?
2 What is 'humanitarian intervention'?
3 Can the Security Council and the ICC be reformed in the interests of democracy and justice?

NOTES

Chapter 1

*   In organising this chapter, and in our later considerations of logical fallacies, we have been guided particularly by Patrick J Hurley's *Concise Introduction to Logic*, 5th edition, Wadsworth Publishing Co, Belmont California, 1994.

1   Hurley, p 1.

2   Ibid.

3   See J. Searle, *Mind, Language and Society*, Weidenfeld and Nicolson, London, 1999, pp 136–38.

4   Hurley, p 2.

5   Ibid, p 6.

6   Searle, p 5.

7   M. Kline, *Mathematics and the Physical World*, Dover, New York, 1959, p 76. Further facts can be established as deductive consequences of basic premises or axioms. And as deductive consequences of necessarily true premises, so are such conclusions themselves necessarily true, and can be used as the basis for further deductive reasoning processes. In mathematics and formal logic, such deductive consequences are called 'theorems'. On the basis of Euclid's axioms, it can be deduced that the sum of the angles of a triangle is 180 degrees. Further geometrical facts can then be deduced from this idea.

      Euclid's axioms are no longer taken to be true in all possible worlds. They are probably only true in limited regions of our world. But they are still assumed true for purposes of elementary geometry.

8   Hurley, p 101.

9   Sir E. Coke, *Institutes of the Laws of England*, 1797, vol 3, p 47.

10   A. MacAdam and J. Pyke, *Judicial Reasoning and the Doctrine of Precedent in Australia*, Butterworths, Sydney, 1989, p 41, quoting Cross.

11   [1967] 1 QB 443 at 502.

12   L. Waller, *Derham, Maher and Waller: An Introduction to Law*, 8th edition, LBC Information Services, Sydney, 2000.

13   R. Pine, *Essential Logic*, Harcourt Brace, Fort Worth, 1996, p 43.
14   Hurley, pp 14–21.
15   Hurley, p 19.
16   J.G. Fleming, *The Law of Torts*, 8th edition, The Lawbook Co, Sydney, 1992, p 194.
17   Pine, pp 233–34.
18   Hurley, pp 21–24.
19   J. Burbidge, *Within Reason*, Broadview Press, Peterborough, 1990, pp 99–100.
20   Hurley, p 31.
21   See for example C. Cook, R. Creyke, R. Geddes and D. Hamer, *Laying Down the Law*, Butterworths, Sydney, 2005, pp 56–57.
22   Hurley, p 41.
23   Ibid, p 42.
24   There are different levels of logical structure. At one level the arguments below have the invalid structure: A. B. Therefore C. This is why we must specify the 'most specific' level of structure in considering validity; that is, taking account of all 'logical words'.
25   A. Fisher, *The Logic of Real Arguments*, Cambridge University Press, 1988, p 142.
26   Ibid.
27   It is possible that premises and conclusion are true – depending on the particular content involved – as, for example, where A = you are human, B = you are warm-blooded and C = you are a mammal. But the argument remains invalid.
28   Hurley, pp 44–45.
29   Ibid, p 47.
30   Ibid, p 34.
31   Ibid, p 35.
32   Ibid, p 468.
33   Burbidge, p 18.
34   Ibid, p 18–19.
35   Hurley, p 524.
36   Ibid, p 468.
37   See A. Aczel, *Chance*, High Stakes, London, 2005, for a clear introduction.
38   Ibid, p 2.
39   Ibid, pp 5–6.
40   Ibid, pp 9–10.
41   Ibid, pp 11–16.
42   Ibid.
43   Ibid, pp 25–29.
44   Ibid, pp 17–24. See Aczel for the de Finetti Game.
45   Hurley, p 64.
46   J. Nolt and D. Rohatyn, *Logic*, McGraw-Hill, New York, 1988, p 18.
47   Ibid, p 26.
48   S. Barker, *The Elements of Logic*, McGraw-Hill, Boston, 2003, p 8.

Chapter 2

1   Of course, while the factual issues might be straightforward in theory, it

is not necessarily easy to provide definitive answers to such questions in practice. Chapter 4 considers some of the difficulties. And it could well be that the death penalty – or its abolition – has very significant unrecognised consequences that could profoundly influence ethical decision-making if they were recognised.

2   See for example S. George, *Another World Is Possible if...*, Verso, London, 2004, p 79.

3   R. Murugason and L. McNamara, *Outline of Criminal Law*, Butterworths, Sydney 1997, pp 170.

4   K. Hall, *Legislation*, Butterworths, Sydney, 2002, pp 73–4.

5   Ibid, p 78.

6   D. Khoury and Y. Yamouri, *Understanding Contract Law*, Butterworths, Sydney, 1995, p 89.

7   MacAdam and Pyke, p 267.

8   Ibid.

9   Ibid.

10   Ibid, pp 268–9.

11   Ibid, p 40.

12   Ibid.

13   Ibid, p 278.

14   Ibid, p 279.

15   See chapter 3.

16   See J. Conaghan and W. Mansell, *The Wrongs of Tort*, Pluto Press, London, 1993, pp 70–84.

17   Ibid, p 73.

Chapter 3

1   See R. Nader and W. Smith, *No Contest*, Random House, New York, 1996, pp 14–15.

2   Ibid, p 15.

3   Ibid.

4   Ibid, p 16.

5   Ibid, p 17.

6   Ibid, pp 17–18.

7   This example is drawn from a recent law textbook: P. Keyzer, *Legal Problem Solving*, Butterworths, Sydney, 2003, p 19. Unfortunately, Keyzer confuses validity with soundness, misrepresents the structure of *modus ponens* (confusing a conditional 'then' with a 'then' representing temporal sequence) and misrepresents *modus tollens* (confusing it with denying the antecedent).

8   P.J. Hurley pp 116–120.

9   Ibid, p 124.

10   S. McNicol and D. Mortimer, *Evidence*, Butterworths, Sydney, 1996, pp 103–4.

11   Hurley, p 127.

12   G. Gigerenzer, *Reckoning with Risk*, Penguin, London, 2002, pp 142–3. See also Appendix on probability.

13   Ibid, p 143.

14   Ibid, p 144.

15 Ibid, pp 144–5.
16 Ibid, p 154.
17 Gigerenzer, p 165.
18 Ibid. Claims of '1 in 10 million people with DNA base sequence X' actually derive from the multiplied frequencies of sub-sequences in many smaller sample groups. But there might be much less variability in particular – isolated – groups.
19 Ibid.
20 They also devised the playing card 'test' referred to earlier.
21 B.S. Everitt, *Chance Rules*, Springer-Verlag, New York, 1998, p 100.
22 Ibid, p 101.
23 Ibid, pp 108–9. In this case, the appropriate formula is as follows:
   1   Pr(innocent/DNA match) = Pr(DNA match/innocent) (= RMP) x Pr(innocent)/ Pr(match)
       Here, Pr(match), the unconditional probability of a match, is the difficult one. Here is where we need to take account of the population of possible perpetrators (for example, 1 million people).
   2   Pr(match) = Pr(match/innocent) x Pr(innocent) + Pr(match/guilty) x Pr(guilty); thus if
   3   Pr(match/innocent) = 0.000001 (1 in a million randomly sampled folk would match the sample); and
   4   Pr(innocent) = 0.999999 (out of 1 million possible perpetrators, only 1 actually did it); then
   5   Pr(guilty) = 0.000001 [1/M]; and
   6   Pr(innocent/match) = 0.000001 (Pr match/innocent) x 0.999999 (Pr innocent)/[(0.000001 x 0.999999) + (1 x 0.000001)] (Pr match) = 0.5 (approx.)
24 Moving on to the DNA case, we consider 1 000 000 men who could be responsible for the crime. 1 actually did it. 999 999 didn't do it. Assuming no false negatives, a DNA test given to that 1 will be positive. If DNA tests are given to all the other 999 999, 1 will be positive [1/M(RMP) x 999 999/1], the rest will be negative (assuming no false positives). So Pr(guilt/match) = 1/2.

Chapter 4

1 Hurley, pp 143–4.
2 J. Swanton, B. McDonald and R. Anderson, *Cases on Torts*, Federation Press, Sydney, 1992, p 136.
3 Ibid.
4 Ibid.
5 Ibid, p 137.
6 It is true that serial killers are frequently said to target their victims in random and unpredictable ways, often over large areas. But this does not mean that diligent investigation cannot effectively narrow the focus of investigation.
7 Hurley, p 138.
8 See for example A. Farrell, *Crime, Class and Corruption*, Bookmarks, London, 1992.
9 Hurley, p 139.

10   Ibid, p 142.

11   Cook et al, p 103.

12   MacAdam and Pyke, p 297.

13   Ibid, p 291.

14   Swanton et al, p 137.

15   Ibid.

16   In England in 1977 and 1978 the 'disappearance' of 28 sackfuls of captured cannabis and the adulteration of another major police drug haul with fingerprint powder received substantial publicity. See Farrell, p 40. The drug squad at Scotland Yard was disbanded in the early 1970s due to corruption and the Obscene Publications Squad was identified by Justice Jones as a 'vast protection racket' in 1977. Eighty-two officers were sacked and another 301 left during criminal or disciplinary enquiries between 1973 and 1976 under reforming Commissioner Robert Mark. By 1978 Operation Countryman had compiled evidence against 78 officers from Scotland Yard and 189 from the City of London police involved in armed robberies. In the early 1980s the Chief Constable of Cheshire was looking into allegations of misconduct on Humberside. Humberside was conducting investigations into South Yorkshire drug squad and this investigation itself was later looked at by Merseyside Police.

In 1989, the framing of innocent people, fabrication of evidence and lies on oath leading to the wrongful imprisonment of the Guildford Four were widely discussed in Britain. And the whole of the West Midlands Regional Crime Squad was disbanded amid accusations of forced confessions and tampering with evidence. That year there were 37 deaths in police custody in the Metropolitan Police area alone. As Farrell points out, 'Only 3 out of 17 coroners' inquests into such cases in 1989 found verdicts of "natural causes".' [And] there were 2372 complaints of assault carried out by the London police in 1989'. Farrell, p 19.

17   In Canada, in the case of *Jane Doe v Metropolitan Toronto [Municipality] Commissioners of Police* [1998] 160 DLR (4th) 697, the plaintiff was successful in establishing that the MTPF had conducted a negligent investigation and failed to warn women they knew to be potential targets of a rapist. '[A]s a result of such conduct, [the rapist] was not apprehended as early as he might have been and the plaintiff was denied the opportunity ... to take any specific measures to protect herself.' Similarly, in the German case of BGM LM S839[fg] BGB Nr 5, in 1953 the plaintiff successfully sued a police organisation for breach of official duty, involving failure to arrest known criminals and thereby prevent criminal acts. But this still contrasts starkly with English cases that have followed the Hill line even when the identity of the offender is known to the police. And as Surma notes:

> the reasoning of the German court in its entirety suggests that ... there is an official duty of the police to prevent criminal acts owed to possibly affected third parties whenever the police are in an obvious position to prevent serious crimes'. R. Surma, 'A Comparative Study of the English and German Judicial Approach to the Liability of Public Bodies in Negligence' (2000) *Oxford University Comparative Law Forum* 8.

18   A classic example here is the drug diethylstilbestrol widely prescribed to pregnant women to prevent miscarriage from 1940 to 1971.

19   R. Fogelin and W. Sinnot-Armstrong, *Understanding Arguments*, 5th edition, Harcourt Brace, Fort Worth, p 340.
20   McNicol and Mortimer, p 287.
21   Ibid, p 287.
22   Ibid, p 288.
23   We can here refer to the case of Fred Zain, a state serologist, who lied and systematically manufactured evidence in at least 133 rape and murder cases in West Virginia, leading to convictions of numerous innocent people. See D. Walton, *Appeal to Expert Opinion*, Pennsylvania State University Press, 1997, p 181.
24   Hurley, p 152.
25   J. Smith, *Misogynies: Reflections on Myth and Malice*, Faber and Faber, London, 1989, pp 118, 121–22.
26   Ibid, pp 123–4.
27   In 1998 the European Court of Human Rights (ECHR) rejected a decision by the British Court of Appeal in *Osman v Ferguson*, in which the Court of Appeal had relied upon Hill to reaffirm police immunity from liability in negligence in respect of their activities in the investigation and suppression of crime. The ECHR held that this decision was a violation of the plaintiff's civil rights to a fair and public hearing of her complaints. Despite this, Hill has continued to stand as 'good law' protecting the police in England and in Australia from any liability in negligence. On 29 March 2004, Hill was cited in *Cran v State of New South Wales* (2004) NSWCA 92. The appellant claimed to have suffered harm in gaol by way of chronic post traumatic stress disorder because the Police and the Director of Public Prosecutions neglected to secure prompt analysis of suspected prohibited drugs found in his possession. The Appeal Court supported an earlier judgment that since the omission in question 'occurred in course of police investigation, it was immune from civil action.
28   Hurley, p 155.
29   McNicol and Mortimer, p 88.
30   Ibid, p 87.
31   Ibid, p 95.
32   D. Brown, D. Farrier, S. Egger and L. McNamara, *Criminal Laws*, Federation Press, Sydney, 2001, p 232.
33   Hurley, p 157.

Chapter 5

*   This chapter draws significantly upon Ronald Giere's *Understanding Scientific Reasoning*, 1st (1979), 2nd (1984) and 4th (1997) editions respectively, Holt, Rinehart and Winston, Fort Worth.
1   T. Schick, Jr and L. Vaughn, *How To Think About Weird Things*, Mayfield, Mountain View, 1999, p 151.
2   Ibid.
3   A. Chalmers, *What Is This Thing Called Science?*, 2nd edition, Queensland University Press, St Lucia, 1982, pp 2–5.
4   Shick and Vaughn, p 162.
5   This terminology is owed to philosopher of science Rom Harre.
6   Isolation and control generally cannot be achieved in relation to large-

scale social phenomena. But sampling and surveying are still relevant here, including cross-cultural comparisons.

7   Giere, 2nd edition, p 177.

8   Ibid, p 180.

9   R. Hogg, in D. Brown and M. Wilkie (eds), *Prisoners as Citizens*, Federation Press, Sydney, 2002, p 11.

10   Ibid, p 14.

11   Ibid, p 15.

12   Ibid, p 10.

13   Here we are using a streamlined statistical procedure, and concrete examples, drawn from Ronald Giere's textbook on scientific reasoning, *Understanding Scientific Reasoning*, 4th edition, Harcourt Brace, Orlando, 1997.

14   Ibid, p 160.

15   J. Philips, *How To Think about Statistics*, 6th edition, W.H. Freeman and Co, New York, 2000, pp 150–1, p 193.

16   D. Rowntree, *Statistics without Tears*, Penguin, London, 1981, pp 156–7.

17   J.T. Dennis, *The Complete Idiot's Guide to Physics*, Alpha Books, Indianapolis, 2003, p 51.

18   Ibid, p 52.

19   L. Schultz, 'US Foreign Policy and Human Rights Violations in Latin America: A Comparative Analysis of Foreign Aid Distributions', *Comparative Politics*, Vol 13, No 2, January 1981, p 155; M. Stohl, D. Carleton and S. Johnson, 'Human Rights and US Foreign Assistance from Nixon to Carter', *Journal of Peace Research*, Vol 21, No 33, 1984, p 217; D. Carleton and M. Stohl, 'The Foreign Policy of Human Rights: Rhetoric and Reality from Jimmy Carter to Ronald Reagan', *Human Rights Quarterly*, Vol 7, 2, May 1985, p 215.

20   F. Gareau, *State Terrorism and the United States*, Zed Books, London, 2004, pp 220–1.

21   Ibid.

22   Ibid.

23   Ibid.

Chapter 6

1   Fleming, p 193.

2   Ibid, pp 193–4.

3   Ibid, p 203.

4   R. Martin, *Scientific Thinking*, Broadview Press, Peterborough, 1997, chs 18 and 19.

5   Ibid.

6   Ibid, pp 275–6.

7   Ibid.

8   Ibid.

9   Informed of the results of all previous tests; whether this drug is just a variation on a competitor's product with no real health benefits; provision of research funding by taxpayers; availability of the drug to those that need it.

10   Martin, chs 18, 19.

11　Giere, 4th edition, p 229.

12　Ibid.

13　Ibid, p 241. Given this sort of information, available for decades, obvious questions arise about the failure of criminal and civil law.

14　Ibid.

15　Ibid, p 233.

16　Ibid, p 237.

17　Ibid, p 238.

18　Hurley, p 524.

19　New Scientist, 6 March 2004, p 19.

20　R. Moynihan, *Too Much Medicine?*, ABC Books, Sydney, 1998, pp 54–5.

21　Ibid.

22　Gigerenzer, p 34.

23　Ibid.

24　Ibid, p 35.

25　D. Gee and M. Greenberg in P. Harremoes, D. Gee, M. McGarvin, A. Stirling, J. Keys, B. Wynne and S. Guedes Vaz, *The Precautionary Principle in the 20th Century*, Earthscan, London, 2002, pp 50–1.

26　Ibid, p 58.

27　A. Deville and R. Harding, *Applying the Precautionary Principle*, Federation Press, Sydney, 1997, p 19.

28　Harroemoes et al, p 51.

29　Ibid, pp 13–14.

30　Ibid.

31　Harremoes et al, p 191.

32　Deville and Harding, pp 71, 73.

33　Harremoes et al, p 189.

34　Ibid.

35　Ibid.

36　Ibid, p 192.

37　R.G. Wilkinson, *Unhealthy Societies*, Routledge, London, 1996, p 156.

38　Ibid, p 157.

39　E. Handsley, 'Market Share Liability and the Nature of Causation in Tort' (1994) *Torts Law Journal* 24 at pp 24–44.

Chapter 7

1　Schick and Vaughn, p 161.

2　See chapter 1.

3　Giere, 2nd edition, p 151.

4　Giere, 1st edition, p 137.

5　R. Norman, *On Humanism*, Routledge, London, 2004, p 43–4.

6　We see here a connection with some types of natural law theory discussed in later chapters. A womb is for bearing children, so abortion in unnatural and should be illegal.

7　Norman, p 36.

8　Ibid, p 37.

9　E. Mayr, *One Long Argument*, Penguin, 1992, p 22.

10　Norman, p 36.

11　Ibid, p 38.

12   D. Walton, *Appeal to Expert Testimony*, Pennsylvania State University Press, 1997, pp 182.
13   Ibid.
14   Ibid, p 184.
15   S. Odgers, *Uniform Evidence Law*, Federation Press, Sydney, 1995, pp 126–9.

Chapter 8

*   This chapter draws significantly upon Wilfred J Waluchow's recent book, *The Dimensions of Ethics*, Broadview Press, Peterborough, Ontario, 2003. So too does it draw upon the work of moral philosopher Richard Norman.
1   C. Parker and A. Evans, *Inside Lawyers' Ethics*, Cambridge University Press, Melbourne, 2007, p 4.
2   Ibid, p 6.
3   Ibid, p 23.
4   Ibid, pp 11–12.
5   See for example Waluchow, pp 35–37; 40–42.
6   See for example R. Harre and M. Krausz, *Varieties of Relativism*, Blackwell, Oxford, 1996, ch 5.
7   J.R. Searle, *Rationality in Action*, The MIT Press, Cambridge, 2001, p 224.
8   Ibid, pp 232–3.
9   See S. Freud, *The Standard Edition of the Complete Psychological Writings of Sigmund Freud*, J. Strachey et al (eds), 24 vols, Hogarth Press, London, 1953–74, 1930; *Civilization and Its Discontents* in *Standard Edition*, vol 21, pp 59–145.
10   See Waluchow, pp 58–59.
11   See for example R. Norman, *The Moral Philosophers*, Clarendon Press, Oxford, 1983, ch 2.
12   R. Norman, *Ethics, Killing and War*, CUP, 1995, p 7.
13   Ibid, p 8.
14   See Norman, ibid, p 10.
15   Waluchow, pp 96–97.
16   Ibid, p 101.
17   Ibid, p 102.
18   Ibid, pp 67–68.
19   Ibid, ch 3.
20   Ibid, pp 146–47.
21   Ibid, p 152.
22   Ibid, p 167.
23   R. Norman, *On Humanism*, Routledge, London, 2004, p 102.
24   Ibid, p 104.
25   Such interventions could be costly and ineffective in reducing the harmful behaviour in question; or the harm caused by enforcement of relevant penalties, particularly imprisonment, could outweigh the harm of the original behaviour, etc.
26   I Kant, *Groundwork of the Metaphysics of Morals*, H.J. Paton (trans), Harper and Row, New York, 1964, p 70.
27   R. Norman, *The Moral Philosophers*, p 52.
28   Ibid, p 52.

29   Ibid, p 54.
30   Waluchow, p 233.
31   Ibid, p 232.
32   Ibid, p 233.
33   Ibid.
34   C. Gilligan *In a Different Voice: Psychological Theory and Women's Development*, Harvard University Press, Cambridge, 1982.
35   R. Nader and W.J. Smith, *No Contest*, Random House, New York, 1996, pp 334–35.

Chapter 9

1   J.W. Nickel, *Making Sense of Human Rights*, 2nd edition, Blackwell, Malden, 2007, p 23.
2   Ibid.
3   See W. Hohfield, *Fundamental Legal Conceptions*, Yale University Press, New Haven, 1919.
4   A. Levine, *Engaging Political Philosophy*, Blackwell, Malden, 2002, p 16.
5   H. Fink, *Social Philosophy*, Methuen, London, 1981, p 16.
6   Levine, p 16.
7   See Fink, chapters 3, 4 and 6.
8   C.B. Macpherson, *The Real World of Democracy*, Oxford, New York, 1972, p 8.
9   D.J. O'Byrne, *Human Rights*, Pearson Education, Edinburgh, 2003, p 75.
10   Ibid.
11   B. Clark, *International Law*, Lawbook Co, Sydney, 2003, pp 132–33.
12   P. Self, *Rolling Back the Market*, Macmillan, Houndsmills, 2000, p 38.
13   Ibid.
14   J. McMurtry, *The Cancer Stage of Capitalism*, Pluto Press, London, 1999, p 105.
15   Ibid.
16   Ibid, p 152.
17   Ibid, p 153.
18   Ibid.
19   Ibid, pp 150–62.
20   See chapter 17 in this publication.
21   P. Sutch and J. Elias, *International Relations: the basics*, Routledge, London, 2007, p 85.
22   Clark, p 33.
23   R. Piotrowicz and S. Kaye, *Human Rights in International and Australian Law*, Butterworths, Sydney, 2000, p 4.
24   Nickel, p 8.
25   Ibid. p 15.
26   Ibid, p 9.
27   H. Shutt, *A New Democracy*, Zed Books, London, 2001, p 128.
28   Nickel, p 16.
29   Clark, chapter 11.
30   P. Singer, *One World*, Text Publishing, Melbourne, 2002, p 144.
31   Ibid, p 147. Universal jurisdiction gives any state a right to bring to trial individuals who infringe norms of international law recognised as binding

on all states. The case of the *Attorney General of Israel v Eichmann* [1961] 36 ILR 5 is a most famous case of the exercise of universal jurisdiction., with an ex-high-ranking Nazi abducted by Israeli agents in Argentina and brought to trial in Israel for war crimes and crimes against humanity.

32 Ibid.
33 Clark, p 49.
34 Ibid.
35 Singer, p 162.
36 H. Patomaki and T. Teivainen, *A Possible World*, Zed Books, London, 2004, p 18.
37 Ibid, p 19.
38 It is generally accepted that the US, and in particular the then US Ambassador to the UN, Madeleine Albright, sacked Boutros Ghali because of what was seen as his hostility to US foreign policy, including unconditional US support for Israeli aggression.
39 Patomaki and Teivainen, p 19.
40 Ibid, p 38.
41 Ibid, p 19.
42 Greenpeace International: Illegality of War, (accessed 16 July 2007) <http://www.greenpeace.org/international/campaigns/no-war/war-on-iraq/illegality-of>

Chapter 10

1 M. Freeman, *Lloyd's Introduction to Jurisprudence*, 6th edition, Sweet & Maxwell, London, 1994, p 90. *Lloyd's* (chapters 3, 4 & 6) is the main reference for this chapter, including the passages cited from legal theorists. The other main sources are M. Davies, *Asking the Law Question*, aw Book Co, Sydney, 1994; H. McCoubrey and N. White, *Textbook on Jurisprudence*, 3rd edition, Blackstone Press, London, 1999, Chapters 2, 3, 4 & 5; R. Wacks, *Swot Jurisprudence*, 5th edition, Blackstone Press, London, 1999, Chapters 3, 4 & 5.
2 McCoubrey & White, p 12.
3 Waluchow, p 107.
4 Ibid, pp 104–16.
5 *Lloyd's,* p 109.
6 Ibid, p 137.
7 Ibid, pp 114–15.
8 C.B. Macpherson, *The Political Theory of Possessive Individualism: Hobbes to Locke,* Clarendon Press, Oxford, 1962, pp 199–200.
9 (1765) 19 How. St. Tr. 1029.
10 *Lloyd's*, pp 116–17.
11 McCoubrey & White, p 81.
12 D. North, *Equality, the Rights of Man and the Birth of Socialism*, Mehring Books, Detroit, 1996, pp 10–11.
13 *Lloyd's*, pp 120–21.
14 Ibid, p 28.
15 Ibid, pp 122–23.
16 Ibid, p 250.
17 Ibid, p 224.

18   McCoubrey & White, p 26.
19   Ibid, p 32.
20   *Lloyd's*, p 343.
21   McCoubrey & White, pp 87–88.
22   *Lloyd's*, pp 157–61.
23   Ibid, p 171.
24   *Lloyd's*, pp 173 ff; McCoubrey & White, pp 96–97.
25   For a biting critique of Finnis, see Davies, *Asking the Law Question*, pp 67–72.

Chapter 11

1   C.B. Macpherson, *The Real World of Democracy*, Oxford University Press, New York, 1966, p 4.
2   Ibid.
3   S. Tansey, *Politics: the Basics*, 3rd edition, Routledge, London, 2004, p 189.
4   Ibid, p 190.
5   Ibid, p 179.
6   R. White and S. Perrone, *Crime and Social Control*, Oxford University Press, Melbourne, 2005, pp 19–20.
7   D. Solomon, *Pillars of Power*, Federation Press, Sydney, 2007, pp 114–17.
8   R. Swift, *The No-Nonsense Guide to Democracy*, Verso, Oxford, 2002, p 32.
9   Tansey, pp 193–95.
10   T. Honore, *About Law*, Clarendon Press, Oxford, 1995, pp 30–31.
11   Ibid, p 31.
12   H. Fink, *Social Philosophy*, Methuen, London, 1981, pp 41–42.
13   Ibid.
14   P. Self, *Rolling Back the Market*, Macmillan, London, 2000, p 38.
15   Ibid, p 39.
16   H. Stretton, *Economics: a New Introduction*, Pluto Press, London, 2000, p 407.
17   Ibid, pp 407–408.
18   Self, p 40.
19   E.K. Hunt, *History of Economic Thought*, updated 2nd edition, M.E. Sharpe, New York, 2002, p 467.
20   D. Harvey, *A Brief History of Neo-liberalism*, Oxford University Press, Oxford, 2005, p 22.
21   Ibid.
22   Ibid.
23   Ibid, p 23.
24   Ibid, p 25.
25   It's fair to say that there is some ambivalence among neo-liberals in this area.
26   A. Broinowski and J. Wilkinson, *The Third Try*, Scribe, Melbourne, 2005, p 197.
27   Macpherson, ch 1.
28   Neo-liberals are reluctant to accept that the right of public access to different political ideas and programmes should extend to any state

guarantee of such access. Instead, market forces are assumed to be able to sustain 'free speech', through private ownership and control of media of mass communication, and through private control of education and research. Indeed, free speech is equated with the freedom of individuals and corporations to acquire control of such means of communication via market transactions.

29   This was a central plank of Ronald Reagan's economic policy, cutting the top rate of income tax first from 70 to 50%, then to 28%. He argued that (a) reduced taxes for the rich would reduce their incentives to dodge taxation altogether and thereby increase government tax revenues; (b) reduced taxes would provide the rich with greater incentives to pursue effective wealth creation to the benefit of all; and (c) that 'trickle down' of such increased wealth – through the greater spending of the wealthy – would be one major means for the less well-off to benefit.

30   T. Cleaver, *Economics: the Basics*, Routledge, London, 2004, pp 122–25.

31   See H. Glasbeek, *Wealth by Stealth*, Between The Lines, Toronto, 2002.

32   S. Brown, *Myths of Free Trade*, The New Press, New York, 2006, p 103.

33   Ibid, p 102.

34   Quoted in R. Miliband, *Socialism for a Sceptical Age*, Polity Press, Cambridge, 1994, p 72.

35   Ibid.

36   Ibid, p 75.

37   Ibid, p 76.

38   I. Kawachi and B. Kennedy, *The Health of Nations*, The New Press, New York, 2006, p 171.

39   Ibid, p 175.

40   G. Stoker, *Why Politics Matters*, Palgrave, Macmillan, Basingstoke, 2006, p 33–34.

41   Ibid, p 34.

42   Ibid, p 36.

43   Ibid.

44   Ibid, p 40.

45   We are not saying that regression is either a necessary or sufficient condition for participation in dissident politics – or criminal gangs. We are saying that in some cases this is part of the explanation, and in such cases it can deeply affect the nature of such participation.

46   M. Sawer, Election 2004: How democratic are Australia's elections? at <www.australianreview.net/digest/2004/09/sawer.html>

47   R. Swift, *The No-Nonsense Guide to Democracy*, Verso, London, 2002, p 22.

48   Ibid.

49   Self, pp 102–107.

50   Ibid. The patrimonial principles of corporate bureaucracy have now permeated state bureaucracy. See ch 14.

51   R. Norman, *Free and Equal*, Oxford University Press, Oxford, 1987, p 160.

52   Miliband, p 73.

53   H. Shutt, *A New Democracy*, Zed Books, London, 2001, p 63.

54   Ibid.

55   Shutt, p 63.

56 Swift, pp 21–22.
57 Ibid, p 26.
58 Ibid, p 105. As Swift says, 'it is noteworthy that most of the systems of Eastern Europe and other societies like South Africa that have recently had the opportunity to shape new electoral systems have chosen some form of proportional representation rather than FPTP [first past the post] systems'.
59 Shutt, p 157.
60 Ibid.
61 Ibid, p 158.
62 Ibid, p 159.
63 Norman, p 157.
64 Ibid.
65 Ibid.
66 Shutt, p 158.
67 Ibid, p 165.
68 M. Albert, *Realising Hope*, Zed Books, London, 2006, p 26.
69 Ibid.
70 Norman, p 167.
71 Ibid.
72 Issues of statistical democracy are explored in depth by John Burnheim in his book; *Is Democracy Possible?*, Polity Press, Cambridge, 1985.

Chapter 12

1 *Marx-Engels Selected Works*, Progress Publishers, Moscow, 1969, vol 1, pp 98–137.
2 P. Foner (ed) *When Karl Marx Died: Comments in 1883*, International Publishers, New York, 1973, pp 39–40.
3 L. Trotsky, *In Defence of Marxism*, New Park Publications, London, 1971, pp 63–66.
4 V. Lenin, *Collected Works*, Progress Publishers, Moscow, 1977, vol 19, pp 21–28.
5 K. Marx, *Capital*, Progress Publishers, Moscow, 1977, vol 1, p 29.
6 *Marx-Engels Selected Works*, Progress Publishers, Moscow, 1969, vol 1, p 13.
7 *Marx-Engels Collected Works*, vol 4, International Publishers, New York, 1975, p 37 (emphasis in original).
8 C. Harman, *Explaining the Crisis*, Bookmarks, London, 1984, p 17.
9 'Nick Beams replies to a reader's question about the law of the falling rate of profit', *World Socialist Web Site*, 29 March 2000, <http://www.wsws.org/articles/2000/mar2000/nb-m29.shtml>
10 K. Marx, *The Grundrisse*, Random House, New York, 1973, p 340.
11 N. Beams, *The Significance and Implications of Globalisation*, Mehring Books, Sydney, 1998.
12 F. Fukuyama, *The End of History and the Last Man*, Penguin, London, 1992.
13 M. Head, *Evgeny Pashukanis: A Critical Reappraisal*, Routledge-Cavendish, London, 2007.
14 K. Marx, Preface to *A Contribution to the Critique of Political Economy*, in *Marx-Engels Selected Works*, vol 1, pp 503–4.

15   K. Marx, *The Civil War in France*, Progress Publishers, Moscow, 1948, p 17.

16   K. Marx, *Critique of the Gotha Program*, International Publishers, New York, 1970, p 10.

17   L. Trotsky, *The Revolution Betrayed. What is the Soviet Union and Where is it Going?*, Pathfinder Press, New York, 1972, pp 39–40. See also L. Trotsky, *Terrorism and Communism*, New Park Publications, London, 1975, ch 3, 'Democracy'.

18   F. Engels, Preface to Marx, *The Civil War in France*, p 16.

19   F. Engels, Letter to Conrad Schmidt, 27 October 1890, in *Marx-Engels Selected Correspondence*, Progress Publishers, Moscow, 1975, p 402.

20   F. Engels, Letter to J. Bloch, 21 September 1890, in ibid, pp 394–95.

21   F. Engels, Letter to Conrad Schmidt, in ibid, pp 399–402.

22   Ibid, p 482.

23   F. Engels, Letter to Mehring, in ibid.

24   K. Marx, *Capital*, Lawrence & Wishart, London, 1970, vol 1, p 80.

25   Trotsky, *Terrorism and Communism*, pp 60–61.

26   Ibid, p 9.

27   Trotsky, *The Revolution Betrayed*, p 54.

28   Ibid, p 58.

29   Ibid.

30   D. North, *Perestroika Versus Socialism, Stalinism and the Restoration of Capitalism in the USSR*, Labor Publication, Detroit, 1989.

31   N. Beams, 'UN report on Eastern Europe and the former USSR: The 'free market's' social catastrophe', *World Socialist Web Site*, 5 August 1999 <http://www.wsws.org/articles/1999/aug1999/un-a05.shtml>

32   A vivid portrayal of Stalin's fear of Trotsky is to be found in D. Volkogonov, *Stalin: Triumph and Tragedy*, Grove Weidenfeld, New York, 1988, pp 254–59.

33   See also M. Reiman, *The Birth of Stalinism: The USSR on the Eve of the Second Revolution*, Indiana University Press, Bloomington, 1987, pp 19–29.

Chapter 13

1   F. Stillwell, *Political Economy*, Oxford University Press, Melbourne, 2002, p 147.

2   R. Hahnel, *The ABC's of Political Economy*, Pluto Press, London, 2002, p 75.

3   They select the optimal commodity combination such that marginal utility of A/marginal utility of B = price of A/price of B. The marginal utility of a good is the additional utility the consumer gets from consuming one more unit of it. By consuming products so that their relative utilities at the margin are equal to their relative prices, the consumers maximise utility. Stillwell, ibid, p 158.

4   T. Cleaver, *Economics: the Basics*, Routledge, London, 2004, p 32.

5   Ibid, p 36.

6   Ibid, p 56. With many competing suppliers, and none big enough to individually influence market price, and effectively substitutable products, such price is determined by the overall world interaction of supply and

demand. Individual producers have to accept the sale price of a good as given. And given such a fixed sale price, the application of basic principles of calculus indicates that they will maximise their profits where marginal revenue equals marginal cost. Given that total profit equals total revenue minus total costs, then dTP/dq = dTR/dq – dTC/dq; that is, MP = MR – MC. Profit is maximised where the rate of increase of profit with increased output switches to a rate of decrease of profit; that is, where the MP curve gradient is 0.

High levels of profit attract intensified competition which pushes prices and hence also profits down – given fixed production costs. New price levels mean readjustment of output to maintain MR = MC and so on. The equilibrium position is that of what neoclassical theorists call normal profits – just sufficient to motivate entrepreneurs to continue to conduct business with what they see as sufficient reward for their effort and risk.

7   Stillwell, p 154.
8   Cleaver, p 25.
9   There is a problem here. If training has to be paid for, it's not clear how those without employment can pay for it.
10   Stillwell, pp 197–98.
11   Hahnel, p 30.
12   Hunt, p 381.
13   Stillwell, p 202.
14   For example, Hahnel, pp 88–91.
15   Hahnel, pp 84–96.
16   The logical conclusion of this approach is to make all the world's resources someone's private property.
17   R. Henson, *A Rough Guide to Climate Change*, Roughguides, London, 2006, pp 275–76. If such schemes offer emission credits to polluters in proportion to their then levels of pollution, they are, in effect, rewarding such pollution.
18   D. Whitman, *Economic Foundations of Law and Organization*, Cambridge University Press, New York, 2006, p 56.
19   Ibid, chapter 7.
20   Ibid, pp 42-–4.
21   Ibid, p 44.
22   Ibid, p 46.
23   Ibid.
24   Ibid.
25   Ibid, p 53.
26   See for example Stillwell, chapter 21.
27   See for example Whitman Part Ten. For an alternative perspective see Robert Jackall's study of *Moral Mazes*, Oxford University Press, New York, 1988.
28   Ibid.
29   Ibid.
30   In reality, most shareholders have acquired their shares from other shareholders rather than providing funds for corporations. And share markets actually drain away vastly more capital than they supply. See M. Kelly, *The Divine Right of Capital*, Berret-Koehler, San Francisco, 2003. It is the productive labour of their own workers, state subsidies, bank

loans, cost externalisation and monopoly pricing that are the real sources of ongoing corporate funding, and of shareholder dividends. And the 10% of families who own 50% of all shares world-wide are not generally renowned for abstinence or sacrifice.

31 The disastrous consequences of this policy were brought home to many by its role in driving the 'creative accounting' and major corporate collapses of the 1990s. See J. Stiglitz, *The Roaring Nineties*, Penguin, London, 2003, chapter 5.

32 D. Solomon, *Pillars of Power*, Federation Press, Sydney, 2007, p 135. See for example S. Mann, *Economics, Business Ethics and Law*, Lawbook Co, Sydney, 2003.

33 H. Glasbeek, *Wealth by Stealth*, Between the Lines, Toronto, 2002, p 74.

34 Ibid, pp 74–75.

35 <http://www.acc.gov.au/content/index.phtml/itemId/259608/fromItemId/6106> p 1.

36 <http://www.acc.gov.au/content/index.phtml/itemId/496100/fromItemId/142> p 1.

37 Solomon, p 139.

38 P. Lipton and A. Herzberg, *Understanding Company Law*, 13th edition, Lawbook Co, Sydney, 2006, p 550.

39 Ibid.

40 Whitman, pp 326–27.

41 Ibid, p 327.

42 Hahnel, p 175.

43 Stephen Pressman provides a numerical example. We suppose both Japan and the USA each produce cars and rice. 'In the US one worker can produce either 1 car or 1 ton of rice in any given year. In Japan, one agricultural worker can produce 2 tons of rice in a year and one manufacturing worker can produce 3 cars.' So Japanese workers are absolutely more productive in both areas. But they are relatively more efficient at producing cars, while US workers are relatively less inefficient at producing rice. If 200 US workers were divided equally between car and rice production they would produce 100 cars and 100 tons of rice. One hundred Japanese workers similarly divided would produce 150 cars and 100 tons of rice, making a total of 250 cars and 200 tons of rice. But with specialisation, 200 US workers produce 200 tons of rice and 100 Japanese workers produce 300 cars, an overall gain of 50 cars. So, potentially both countries can benefit from such specialisation and trade, sharing the extra output. See S. Pressman, *Fifty Major Economists*, Routledge, London, 1999, p 36.

44 Hahnel, p 191.

45 H. Patomaki and T. Teivainen, *A Possible World: Democratic Transformation of Global Institutions*, Zed Books, London, 2004, p 41.

46 S. George, *Another World Is Possible If ...*, Verso, London, 2004, p 54.

47 Ibid, p 25.

48 Ibid, p 26.

49 Ibid, pp 15–19.

50 Patomaki and Teivainen, p 59.

51 Ibid, p 58.

52 Ibid.

53   Ibid, p 63.
54   R. Peet, *Geography of Power*, Zed Books, London, 2007, p 123.

Chapter 14

1   Inadequate production for basic need satisfaction of all motivates conflict
      and monopolisation of resources by powerful minorities, at the expense
      of the rest, so that they, at least, can live decently. Where wastage and
      inefficiency leave people struggling throughout their waking hours to
      provide basic subsistence resources, there is little time or energy left for
      meaningful democratic participation..
      A substantial part of genuinely democratic decision-making concerns
      the best use of available resources for need satisfaction, and reduced
      output means restricted scope for such decision-making. More efficient
      use of human labour time can create the space for meaningful democratic
      participation. Increased output means new opportunities for genuine
      progress in the quality and quantity of need satisfaction, for moving
      beyond subsistence into science, art and culture, and exploration of the
      universe.
2   Neoclassicals point out that competition-driven price reductions in the
      innovating sector will encourage others who had not previously utilised
      their output to substitute such newly cheapened output for other factors of
      production. But this only displaces the imbalance to other sectors.
3   In this connection, economists refer to inflation produced by employers
      passing on increased wage costs to their customers as 'cost-push inflation'.
      There is a danger that such increased costs will drive further wage increases
      in a positive feedback.
4   F. Stillwell, *Political Economy*, Oxford University Press, Melbourne, 2002,
      p 180.
5   As Susan George points out, a firm producing raw materials in one country
      sells such materials to a manufacturing affiliate in another country and the
      finished product is marketed by a sales office of the same corporate group
      in a third country.
6   On a world scale, the norm is what is called *oligopoly*. As Stillwell says:
      'This is a market structure in which there are relatively few firms in the
      industry, and each usually produces differentiated [brand-named] goods
      or services, the prices of which are directly under the control of the firms
      themselves ... Typically ... non-price competition prevails. Rivalry over
      market shares, focused upon ... advertising ... may be intense, but ...
      collusion is a strong tendency ... firms may agree to a territorial division of
      the market ... [or] a system of tacit price leadership, whereby one firm sets
      the standard and the others follow, is commonly adopted.' Stillwell, ibid, p
      180, p 182.
7   Tony Cleaver, *Economics: The Basics*, Routledge, London, 2004, p 61.
8   Ibid, p 74.
9   Stillwell, p 184.
10   H. Shutt, *A New Democracy*, Zed Books, London, 2001, p 51.
11   Stillwell, p 186.
12   Whatever steps are taken in the short term to 'open up' competition,
      privatisation puts these resources into an open world market where they

become prey to takeover by multinational oligopolies. As Beder points out, foreign owners can then cut off crucial parts of the economic system of the countries in question for political reasons:
'In 1998 when Quebec was experiencing an electricity crisis ... a private US company shut down its plant until it could get the price it wanted for its electricity ... US companies also shut down supply in the Dominican Republic to force the government to pay its debt to them.' S. Beder, *Power Play*, Scribe Publications, Carlton North, 2003, p 19.

13   Real capitalist business enterprises are indeed driven by pursuit of profit in the sense of revenue in excess of actual costs of maintaining production, as neoclassical theory suggests. This is what funds innovation and expansion, services debt and pays the shareholders dividends. So does it sustain the inflated salaries of CEOs and other top executives and their contributions to political parties, which cannot be seen as necessary costs of production. But the real basis of such money profit, not considered in neoclassical theory, is the creation of surplus product, in the sense of output over and above that required in order to maintain the production process – with ongoing replacement and updating of the productive forces. It is only in this sense that profit can provide for the unproductive consumption of owners of productive assets or for accumulation and growth of productive capacity.

14   R. Hahnel, *The ABC's of Political Economy*, Pluto Press, London, 2002, p 129.

15   E.K. Hunt, *History of Economic Thought*, M.E. Sharpe, New York, 2002, chapter 15.

16   Ibid, pp 413–17.

17   Ibid.

18   Ibid.

19   F. Stillwell, *Political Economy*, Oxford University Press, Melbourne, 2002, p 294.

20   Hunt, pp 419–21.

21   A. Glyn, *Capitalism Unleashed: Finance, Globalisation and Welfare*, OUP, Oxford, 2006, p 24.

22   Hahnel, pp 149–50.

23   A. Pettifor, *The Coming First World Debt Crisis*, Palgrave Macmillan, Houndmills, 2006, pp 40–45.

24   S. Keen, *Debunking Economics*, Pluto Press, Sydney, 2001, pp 226–27.

25   J. Eatwell and L. Taylor, *Global Finance At Risk*, Polity Press, Cambridge, 2000, pp 12–13. Regulation aiming to damp down major fluctuations in share markets can be counterproductive insofar as it encourages risk taking which can drive overvaluation and eventual collapse.

26   Ibid.

27   D. Whitman, *Economic Foundations of Law and Organization*, Cambridge University Press, New York, 2006, p 326.

28   Ibid.

29   Many commentators highlighted the recent rise in the proportion of corporate equity owned by financial institutions as a significant step towards greater accountability and efficiency on the part of corporate management, insofar as 'big institutional shareholders have more resources and incentives to closely monitor company performance and bring pressure

to bear upon poor performers'. Whereas CEOs and directors might favour short-run profits, to maximise their bonuses and share values for a quick exit, such fund managers may be more concerned with 'the long-run fortunes of the company, better served by market share or maintaining good relations with customers, suppliers, banks and even the workforce'. Glyn, p 58.

However, as Glyn points out, such institutional shareholders were supporters of the proliferation of stock options plans which played a central role in the 'wave of corporate scandals [Enron, WorldCom, etc] that engulfed the USA after the stock market boom subsided in 2000'. Ibid.

30   Hunt, pp 393–94.
31   For the Coasian neoclassical line, see Whitman, ibid, Parts One and Two. For a straightforward critique see Hunt, ibid, chapter 14.
32   Hahnel, p 33.
33   Whitman, p 22.
34   J. Bakan, *The Corporation*, Free Press, New York, 2004, p 64.
35   Ibid, p 60.
36   Ibid.
37   Ibid, pp 62–63.
38   Ibid, p 63.
39   Ibid, p 64.
40   Ibid, p 75.
41   Ibid, pp 75–79.
42   Ibid, p 79.
43   Stillwell, p 186.
44   <http://www.acc.gov.au/content/index.phtml/itemId/496100/fromItemId/142> p 1.
45   In practice, collusion in fixing prices can be tacit, or passive collusion based on mutual understanding, while the law requires evidence of active collaboration.
46   Nor is there any guarantee that other investment will be available to take advantage of the more highly skilled and more productive labour available in the first world, as lower skilled jobs are exported to the developing world. Highly skilled labour is now available on-line at very low cost in India, China and elsewhere. And repatriated profits don't necessarily create jobs at home either – going instead into expensive imports, for example.
47   Shutt, chapter 1.
48   Ibid.
49   S. George, *Another World Is Possible If ...*, Verso, London, 2004, p 21.

Chapter 15

1   See A. Levine, *Engaging Political Philosophy*, Blackwell Publishers, Oxford, 2002, p 36.
2   This argument is particularly clearly formulated by sociologists K. Davis and W. Moore, 1945, 'Some principles of stratification', *American Sociological Review* 10: 242–49. This article is quoted and discussed in I. Kawachi and B. Kennedy, *The Health of Nations*, The New Press, New York, 2006, pp 86–87.
3   It is also argued that such death taxes involve double taxing of funds from

which income or profit taxes have already been extracted.

4   E.K. Hunt, *History of Economic Thought*, M.E. Sharpe, New York, 2002, p 379.

5   Ibid, p 381.

6   As Stilwell notes, according to this model, 'not only do consumers' choices signal what is to be produced, but consumers acquire their goods and services at the lowest prices consistent with sustaining the necessary levels of production'. F. Stillwell, *Political Economy*, OUP, Melbourne, 2002, p 174.

7   Given that such differential reward – in proportion to actual contribution – will inevitably lead to inequality of 'outcome', it could be said that such inequality is a necessary price to pay for market efficiency. And this would suggest an essentially functional justification of such inequality – in terms of the universal benefits of such free and efficient market relations, rather than in terms of reward for effort and sacrifice, as in the 'traditional' argument.

8   On the UDHR of 1948, also see chapter 9.

9   As implied by the International Covenant on Economic, Social and Cultural Rights of 1966.

10   Neo-liberals are long-time supporters of the idea of rewards in the form of stock options for such managers to ensure their ongoing diligence in maximising share values through maximising corporate wealth. The disastrous consequences of this policy were brought home to many by its role in driving the 'creative accounting' and major corporate collapses of the 1990s. See J. Stiglitz, *The Roaring Nineties*, Penguin, London, 2003, chapter 5.

11   As Hunt says, 'in a world of class conflicts, imperialism, exploitation, alienation, racism, sexism, and scores of other human conflicts, where are the changes that might make some better off without making others worse off? Improve the plight of the oppressed and you worsen the situation of the oppressor – as perceived by the oppressor, of course. Any important social, political and economic situations where improving the lot of one social unit is not opposed by naturally antagonistic social units are indeed rare. The domain of this theory would … seem to be so restrictive as to hardly warrant investigation. Hunt, p 385.

12   R. Hahnel, *The ABC's of Political Economy*, Pluto Press, London, 2002, p 29.

13   F. Stillwell, *Political Economy*, chapter 21.

14   See for example Hahnel, chapter 8.

15   The neo-liberal answer is to sacrifice equal opportunity to the rights of property. But there is no principled basis for such a move. And reference to the needs – and opportunities – of the majority leads to the alternative conclusion. As Hahnel says, 'while some freedom of consumption for the older generation is sacrificed by outlawing inheritance, this minor restriction of a right is necessary to protect a more fundamental right of the younger generation to equal economic opportunities'. R. Hahnel, *Economic Justice and Democracy*, Routledge, London, pp 23–24.
In a world where those who are not masters will inevitably be slaves, without adequate access to basic necessities, then it would seem that it is a parent's duty to do everything they can to ensure that their own children

are masters rather than slaves. But it is the duty of responsible government to ensure that this is not the situation confronting parents; that all members of the younger generation have the opportunity of a good life without the need for inherited wealth. With as much as 80% of personal wealth coming either from 'direct inheritance or the income of inherited wealth' [see Hahnel, ABC's, pp 27–28], such inheritance is a major contribution to the increasing inequality of wealth in contemporary society. Therefore so is it also a major contributor to the adverse social welfare consequences of such inequality, in terms of loss of social cohesion, crime, morbidity and mortality. Confronted with such realities, neo-liberals frequently fall back on appeal to the social benefits of inheritance to the less well-off. But to compare a little bit of inherited assistance for struggling families with inheritance of great business empires entirely misses the point. Here we need to ask why such families are struggling in the first place. And we need to recognise that it's perfectly possible to draw some legal lines somewhere between the two sorts of cases.

16   In the US, by 1989, 'the richest 1% of families held 45% of all non-residential real estate, 62% of all business assets, 49% of all publicly held stock, and 78% of all bonds'. Hahnel, *ABC's*, p 21. To suggest that these people sacrifice anything to buy or hold such shares is very misleading. They certainly don't go hungry to do so. Not buying shares with the sort of money available to these people would be the sacrifice – with bank interest rates less than dividend payouts; certainly they are not going to spend it all on immediate consumption – there is only so much a human can consume. We must remember that every dollar that actually contributes to investment in coal, uranium or genetically modified foods could have been invested in sustainable, healthy and non-polluting wind power and organics.

17   Bloom measured individual player performance using several well-established indicators. To gauge team performance, he used the winning percentage, fan attendance and the team's finishing position at the end of the season.

18   Kawachi and Kennedy, *The Health of Nations,* pp 89–90.

19   Ibid, p 91.

20   P. Self, *Rolling Back the Market*, Macmillan Press, Basingstoke, 2000, p 27.

21   A. Glyn, *Capitalism Unleashed: Finance, Globalisation and Welfare*, OUP, Oxford, 2006, p 58.

22   Ibid, p 59.

23   Jackall, p 20.

24   Ibid, p 20.

25   H. Glasbeek, *Wealth by Stealth*, Between the Lines, Toronto, 2002, pp 11–12.

26   Ibid, p 12. It's true that 'in recent times, as the public has become more conscious of the many unredressed harms done by, and through, corporations, legislators have felt themselves obliged to impose some responsibility for corporate behaviour on real people – on directors and officers'. A significant recent example here, arising out of the massive corporate frauds of the 1990s, is the Sarbanes-Oxley Act [passed in 2002] which requires CEOs to hand over 'any profits from bonuses or stock sales during the 12 months after a final report subsequently 'restated' because of 'misconduct'. [But generally] these attempts have met with a storm of

protest'. And remain limited in their application and significance.' Glyn, p 62.

27   Starting with Whitehall 1, involving a prospective study of 18 000 people over a 25-year period.

28   M. Marmot, *The Status Syndrome*, Bloomsbury Publishing, London, 2004, p 39.

29   Ibid, p 129.

30   Here stress is understood in terms of the lack of balance between demands made on an individual and the level of their control over resources and circumstances necessary to meet such demands, on the one hand, and the lack of balance between effort and reward on the other.

31   Relative mortality of lower grades to higher shifted from 1.8 (times that of the top grade) to 1.5 (over the 25 years of the study). And this raised the obvious question of why lifestyle risk factors became increasingly common lower down the social hierarchy. A second study found lower control in lower ranks 'whether we consider people's self-reports or managers' assessments of how much control each job entailed'. And 'this gradient in control over work appears to have strong implications for the gradient in heart disease and mental illness'. Marmot, p 29.

32   Ibid, p 129.

33   See for example R.G. Wilkinson, *The Impact of Inequality*, Routledge, London, 2005.

34   Hahnel, *Economic Justice*, pp 25–27.

35   Here indeed, we have good reason to believe that the alleged social benefits of high levels of inequality (of reward) are not really social benefits at all. See for example M. Tumin,1953, 'Some principles of stratification: A critical analysis', *American Sociological Review* 18: 387–94, discussed in Kawachi and Kennedy, pp 100–101.

36   F. Stilwell and K. Jordan, *Who Gets What*, Cambridge, 2007, pp 21–22.

37   Ibid, p 23.

38   Ibid, p 155.

39   Ibid, p 26.

40   Ibid, pp 158–159.

41   Ibid, p 155.

42   Ibid.

43   J. Stiglitz, *Making Globalisation Work*, Penguin, Camberwell, 2006, p 191.

44   S. George, *Another World Is Possible If ...*, Verso, London, 2004, p 20.

45   Ibid, p 23.

46   Ibid, p 21.

47   As reported in *The Sydney Morning Herald*, 20 August, 2006.

48   Ibid. In the developed world, inequalities have increased most of all in those English-speaking countries that have gone further down the neo-liberal path. Contributing to the phenomenon are individually negotiated employment contracts and performance-based bonuses, 'people being given more according to their [alleged] contribution', says Atkinson.

49   Hahnel, *Economic Justice*, p 384.

50   H. Shutt, *A New Democracy*, Zed Books, London, 2001, chapter 8.

51   M. Albert, *Realizing Hope*, Zed Books, London, 2006, p 13.

52   A. Pettifor, *The Coming First World Debt Crisis*, Palgrave Macmillan, Houndmills, 2006, p 82.

53 M. Litvinoff and J. Madeley, *50 Reasons to Buy Fair Trade*, Pluto Press, London, 2007, p 12.
54 Ibid, p 17.
55 Ibid, pp 46–47.
56 Albert, p 58.
57 Ibid, pp 58–59.

Chapter 16

* This chapter is written by Scott Mann and Mouaid Al-Qudah.
1 H. Hart, *Punishment and Responsibility*, Oxford University Press, Oxford, 1968, p 181.
2 Ibid.
3 Norman, *On Humanism*, pp 59–60.
4 See J.R. Searle, *Intentionality*, Cambridge University Press, 1983, p 84.
5 A. Norrie, *Crime, Reason and History*, Butterworths, London, 2001, p 121.
6 Ibid.
7 *Airedale National Health Services Trust v Bland* [1993] AC 789.
8 T.A. Mappes and D. DeGrazia, *Biomedical Ethics*, McGraw-Hill, New York, 1996, p 25.
9 Ibid, p 27.
10 Or a failure to perform a particular intentional action where there is a recognised duty to act.
11 Courts in England and Canada have associated 'sane automatism' with 'external causes' and 'insane' with 'internal causes'. But this distinction was rejected in the Australian case of *R v Falconer* (1990). Insane automatism can form the basis for a defence of insanity.
12 This is providing courts do not see the 'physically threatening situation' as a result of the action of the individual concerned. And duress is not available as a defence for the crime of murder.
13 C.M.V. Clarkson, *Understanding Criminal Law*, 2nd edition, Fontana Press, London, 1995, p 86.
14 In New South Wales, the defence of diminished responsibility was reformulated as 'substantial impairment' in 1997, with the latter understood as 'an abnormality of mind arising from an underlying condition', which was such as to 'substantially impair a person's 'capacity to understand events, or to judge whether their actions were right or wrong or to control himself or herself' at the times of acts or omissions causing death. This is supposed to exclude 'transitory disturbances of mind brought about by heightened emotions' and 'remove the requirement for a particular diagnosis of the accused's condition'. See D. Brown et al, Criminal Laws, p 660.
15 In the new Part 11A of the *NSW Crimes Act*, intoxication cannot be taken into account where crimes are not of specific intent.
16 Clarkson, pp 88–9.
17 Ibid, p 89.
18 Norrie, p 36.
19 Ibid, p 37.
20 Ibid, pp 38–9.

21   I. Grigg-Spall and P. Ireland, *The Critical Lawyers Handbook*, Pluto Press, 1992, p 79.

22   G. Mousourakis, *Criminal Responsibility and Partial Excuses*, Ashgate, Dartmouth, 1998, p 183.

23   Entry into the upper levels depends upon the sponsorship of those already there. And they are generally unwilling to sponsor anyone further than one level below them.

24   H. Croall, *Understanding White Collar Crime*, Open University Press, Buckingham, 2001, p 85.

25   R. Hogg and D. Brown, *Rethinking Law and Order*, Pluto Press, Sydney, 1998, pp 53–8.

26   In psychoanalytic terms, the poor and the powerless employ the defence of 'displacement' of their anger, away from those who really oppress them, who remain outside the scope of their effective action, and onto the closer targets offered by hostile peers and family members. Otherwise, the anger is turned against themselves.

27   R. Wilkinson, *Mind the Gap*, Wiedenfeld and Nicholson, London, 2000, p 24.

28   R. Hogg, 'Prisoners and the Penal Estate in Australia', in D. Brown and M. Wilkie (eds), *Prisoners As Citizens*, Federation Press, Sydney, 2002, p 14.

29   Suggesting a serious deterioration in the educational levels of prisoners since 1973. Ibid, p 15.

30   Hogg and Brown, p 69.

31   R. Hogg in Brown and Wilkie. pp 15–16.

32   Ibid, p 16.

33   A. Storr, *The Art of Psychotherapy*, Butterworth Heinemann, Oxford, 1990, p 100.

34   Ibid, p 85.

35   N. McWilliams, *Psychoanalytic Diagnosis*, Guilford, New York, 1994, p 302.

36   Ibid, pp 151–2.

37   Hayes' research in 1992 and 1995 suggested that 23.6% before the local courts in New South Wales had an IQ of less than 70, 'which placed them in ... the mildly intellectually disabled category', with 14.1% functioning 'within the borderline range'. Sjogren, 'Experiences of Inmates with an Intellectual Disability', in Brown and Wilkie, p 51.

38   Ibid, p 247.

39   The 1996 Inmate Health Survey by the NSW Corrections Health Service found one-third of male and two-thirds of female prisoners tested positive for Hepatitis C. One-third of males and one-quarter of females had been confined in a juvenile institution at some time. One-fifth of men and one-quarter of the women had used heroin in gaol. See R. Hogg, 'Prisoners and the Penal Estate in Australia', in Brown and Wilkie, pp 14–15.

40   Ibid, p 11.

41   S. Box, *Crime, Power and Mystification*, Tavistock, London, 1983, p 39.

42   Croall, p 89.

43   Chisholm and Nettheim, p 126.

Chapter 17

1   R. White and F. Haines, *Crime and Criminology*, Oxford University Press, Melbourne, 1996, p 142.
2   Norrie, p 25.
3   R. White and S. Perrone, *Crime and Social Control*, Oxford University Press, Melbourne, 1997, p 139.
4   Norrie, p 18.
5   Ibid, p 20.
6   Ibid, p 202.
7   Quoted in ibid, p 10.
8   Ibid, p 203.
9   Hogg in Brown and Wilkie, p 11.
10 Norrie, p 204.
11 Ibid, p 208.
12 White and Perrone, p 167.
13 Ibid, p 169.
14 Ibid.
15 Brown and Wilkie, p 18.
16 Ibid, p 6.
17 Ibid, p 197.
18 Norrie, p 214.
19 Ibid, p 125.
20 Ibid, p 215.
21 Ibid.
22 Ibid, p 216.
23 White and Perrone, p 140.
24 Ibid.
25 Ibid, p 171.

Chapter 18

1   For a comparison of the US and British legislation, see N. Hancock, *Terrorism and the Law in Australia: Supporting Materials*, Parliamentary Library, Research Paper 13, 2001–02, pp 2–8.
2   'Amnesty International's Concerns Regarding Post September 11 Detentions in the USA', Amnesty International, March 2002.
3   P. Ruddock, 'A New Framework: Counter Terrorism and the Rule of Law', Address to the Sydney Institute, 20 April 2004 <http://152.91.12/www/MinisterRuddockHome.nsf/Alldocs/RWPB046617DB0869> (accessed 29 June 2004).
4   A. Bergin and A. Smith, *Australian Domestic Security: The Role of Defence*, Australian Strategic Policy Institute, Canberra, 2006, p 10.
5   M. Head, 'Calling Out the Troops – Disturbing Trends and Unanswered Questions', 28 *University of New South Wales Law Journal* (2005) 484–92.
6   Bergin and Smith, p 10.
7   M. Head, 'The Military Call-Out Legislation – Some Legal and Constitutional Questions', 29 *Federal Law Review* (2001) 273; Head, 'Calling Out the Troops', 479.

8   J. Howard, 'A Stronger AFP: Responding to Regional Challenges', media release, 25 August 2006, <http://www.pm.gov.au/news/media_releases/media_Release2096.html>.

9   Head, 'The Military Call-Out Legislation', 278–84.

10 *Defence Act 1903* (Cth) ss51A, 51B, 51C.

11 Head, 'The Military Call-Out Legislation', 281.

12 Defence Legislation Amendment (Aid to Civilian Authorities) Bill 2005 (Cth), Explanatory Memorandum, 2, <http://parlinfoweb.aph.gov.au/piweb/view_document.aspx?ID=2144&TABLE=OLDEMS> (accessed 16 May 2006).

13 *Criminal Code 1995* (Cth) s100.1. See M. Head, 'Counter-Terrorism Laws: A Threat to Political Freedom, Civil Liberties and Constitutional Rights', 26 *Melbourne University Law Review* (2002) 666, 673.

14 *Defence Act* s51CB(2).

15 Ibid, s51CA(2).

16 bid, s51AB.

17 Senate, *Hansard*, Wednesday 8 February 2006, 23–24.

18 Section 51K requires a recall of both Houses of Parliament within six days of a declaration of a 'general security area', but provides that failure to do so 'does not make the declaration ineffective to any extent'. Under the 2006 amendments, s51K(2AA) permits the authorising ministers to avoid notifying parliament (and the public) of such a declaration, if they are satisfied that it 'would prejudice the exercise of powers'.

19 *Defence Act*, s51T(2A).

20 British Independent Police Complaint Commission (IPCC) reports on this killing have been submitted to the British government and the Crown Prosecution Service but not released to the public. See the IPCC media release: <http://www.ipcc.gov.uk/pr140306_stockwell.htm> (accessed 16 May 2006). In May 2007, the IPCC announced that the front-line firearms and surveillance officers involved in the shooting would not face a disciplinary tribunal: <http://www.ipcc.gov.uk/news/pr110507_stockwell.htm> (accessed 29 August 2007).

21 *Defence Act*, s51SO.

22 For example, *Australian Security Intelligence Organisation Act 1979* (Cth) s34G.

23 *Defence Act*, s51WB.

24 Ibid, s51S(1)(b).

25 Ibid, s51WA.

26 *Thomas v Mowbray* [2007] HCA 33.

27 [2007] HCATrans 76 and 78.

28 [2007] HCA 33, [588].

29 (1781) 2 Dougl 590 [99 ER 372].

30 [2007] HCA 33, [140].

31 Ibid, [142]

32 Ibid, [443–44].

33 Ibid, [543–44].

34 Ibid, [552].

35 *R v Lodhi* [2006] NSWSC 691.

36 *Australian Communist Party v The Commonwealth* [1951] HCA 51; 83 CLR 1.

37   83 CLR 1 at 187.
38   [2007] HCA 33, [386].
39   Ibid.
40   Ibid, [233].
41   Ibid, [264].
42   M. Head, 'Australia's Expanded Military Call-out Powers: Causes for Concern', 3 *University of New England Law Journal* (2006) 145–150.
43   Bergin and Smith, pp 13, 16–22.
44   Ibid, p 21.
45   See T. Molomby, *Spies, Bombs and the Path of Bliss*, Potoroo Press, Sydney, 1986 and J. Hocking, *Beyond Terrorism: The Development of the Australian Security State*, Allen & Unwin, Sydney, 1993.
46   *Southern Highland News*, 15 February 1978, p 1.
47   Bergin and Smith, p 15.
48   Ibid, p 21.
49   S.D. Lendrum, 'The "Corrong Massacre": Martial Law and the Aborigines at First Settlement' 6 *Adelaide Law Review* (1977) 26. Also V. Windeyer, 'Certain Questions Concerning the Position of Members of the Defence Force When Called Out to Aid the Civil Power' in R. Hope, *Protective Security Review Report*, Commonwealth Parliamentary Paper No. 397, 1979, Appendix 9.
50   Quoted in B. McKinlay, *A Documentary History of the Australian Labor Movement, 1850–1975*, Drummond, Richmond, 1979, p 377. Such instructions – to 'fire low and lay them out' – are still mirrored in the *Australian Military Regulations*. Regulation 421(6) specifies that: 'Care shall be taken to fire only upon those who can be seen to be implicated in the disturbance'. H.P. Lee, *Emergency Powers*, Law Book Co, Sydney, 1984, 242. Regulation 410 requires the commander of the forces to warn those present that, if the troops are ordered to fire, the fire will be effective. *Call Out the Troops: an examination of the legal basis for Australian Defence Force involvement in 'non-defence' matters*, Australian Parliamentary Research Paper 8, Canberra, 1997–98, p 5.
51   Ibid, *Call Out the Troops*, p 19.
52   Ibid.
53   Ibid, p 13. See also B.D. Beddie and S. Moss, 'Some Aspects of Aid to the Civil Power in Australia', *Occasional Monograph No 2 (University of New South Wales Dept of Government)*, 1982, 55.
54   See *The Canberra Coup*, Workers News, Sydney, 1976.
55   *Call Out the Troops*, pp 14–18.
56   M. Head, Editorial: 'Detention and the Anti-Terrorism Legislation' 9 *University of Western Sydney Law Review* (2005) 1–8.
57   National Security Australia web site, <http://www.nationalsecurity. gov.au/agd/www/nationalsecurityHome.nsf/headingpagesdisplay/ 9F291545F46DC7B9CA256E43000565D4?OpenDocument> (accessed 1 December 2005).
58   For full details see M. Head, '"Counter Terrorism Laws": A Threat to Political Freedom, Civil Liberties and Constitutional Rights' 26 *Melbourne University Law Review* (2002) 666 and M. Head, 'Another threat to democratic rights: ASIO detentions cloaked in secrecy' 29 *Alternative Law Journal* (2004) 127.

59   J. Von Doussa, 'Presentation at Forum on National Security Law and Human Rights', 31 October 2005, <http://www.hreoc.gov.au/about_the_commission/speeches_president/20051101_forum_on_national_security_laws_and_human_rights.htm> (accessed 2 December 2005).

60   M. Fraser, 'How Democracies Fight **Terrorism**', Stephen Murray-Smith Memorial Lecture delivered at the **State Library** of **Victoria** on 19 October 2005

61   J. McCulloch, *Blue Army: Paramilitary Policing in Australia*, MUP, Melbourne, 2001, p 1.

62   See also N. Hancock, *Terrorism and the Law in Australia: Legislation, Commentary and Constraints*, Parliament of Australia, Department of Parliamentary Library, Research Paper 12, 2001–02.

63   Head, 'Counter-Terrorism Laws', 666, 678-679.

64   For the Commonwealth provisions see *Criminal Code Act 1995* (Cth), Divisions 104 and 105. For an examination of these provisions and their human rights implications, see L. Lasry and K. Eastman, 'Memorandum of Advice: Anti-Terrorism Bill 2005 (Cth) and the Human Rights Act 2004 (ACT)' 9 *University of Western Sydney Law Review* (2005) 111.

65   See M. Walton, 'The Anti-Terrorism Bill (No. 2) 2005: An Overview' *Human Rights Defender* (2005) 3.

66   *Criminal Code Act 1995* (Cth) ss80.2(7) & (8).

67   The Senate, Legal and Constitutional Committee, *Provisions of the Anti-Terrorism Bill (No. 2) 2005*, Department of the Senate, Parliament House, November 2005, 77 <http://www.aph.gov.au/senate/committee/legcon_ctte/terrorism/report/index.htm> (accessed 1 December 2005). See also B. Saul, 'Speaking of Terror: Criminalising Incitement to Violence' 28 *University of New South Wales Law Journal* (2005) 868, 873.

68   I. Kershaw, *Hitler, 1889–1936 Hubris*, Penguin, London, 1998, pp 456–60.

69   *Criminal Code* s100.1.

70   Ibid, ss101.2, 101.4, 101.5, 101.6.

71   Evidence to Senate Legal and Constitutional Committee, Parliament of Australia, Sydney, Inquiry into the Security Legislation Amendment (Terrorism) Bill 2002 and Related Bills, Official Committee Hansard, 8 April 2002, 27 (Susan McIntosh, Principal Legal Officer, Attorney-General's Department).

72   Ibid, pp 14–15.

73   L. Crowley-Cyr, 'Mental Illness and Indefinite Detention at the Minister's Pleasure' 9 *University of Western Sydney Law Review* (2005) 53.

74   Australian Press Council, Submission, <http://www.aph.gov.au/senate/committee/legcon_ctte/terrorism/submissions/sub143.pdf> (accessed 2 December 2005).

75   M. Head, 'ASIO, Secrecy and Lack of Accountability' 11 Murdoch University Electronic Journal of Law (December 2004).

76   Submission to ICJ Eminent Jurists Panel, the Gilbert and Tobin Centre of Public Law, March 2006, <http://www.gtcentre.unsw.edu.au/publications/docs/pubs/submission_ICJPanel.pdf> (accessed 23 April 2008).

77   *Crimes Act* 1914 (Cth) s30A; *Criminal Code Act* 1995 (Cth) ss80.2–80.3.

78   The Senate, Legal and Constitutional Committee, *Provisions of the Anti-Terrorism Bill (No. 2) 2005*, Department of the Senate, Parliament House, November 2005, p 77 <http://www.aph.gov.au/senate/committee/legcon_

ctte/terrorism/report/index.htm> (accessed 1 December 2005).

79   Ibid.

80   Sections 34A–34Y of the *Australian Security Intelligence Organisation Act 1979* (Cth).

81   See Head, 'Another threat to democratic rights' 127 for references and further details.

82   Ibid, 129.

83   Ibid.

84   Ibid.

85   This record has been documented in several works and official inquiries. See, for example, D. McKnight, *Australia's Spies and their Secrets*, Allen & Unwin, Sydney, 1994; R. Hall, *The Secret State*, Cassell Australia, Sydney, 1978; F. Cain, *The Origins of Political Surveillance in Australia*, Angus & Robertson, Sydney, 1983; F Cain, *ASIO, an Unofficial History*, Spectrum, Melbourne, 1994; J. Hocking, *Beyond Terrorism: The Development of the Australian Security State*, Allen & Unwin, Sydney, 1993; Commonwealth of Australia, Royal Commission on Intelligence and Security: Fourth Report, volumes 1 and 2, AGPS, Canberra, 1977.

Chapter 19

1   J. Morrison, 'The Trafficking and Smuggling of Refugees: The End Game in European Asylum Policy?', UNHCR, Geneva, July 2000, <http://www.unhcr.ch/evaluate/reports/traffick.pdf>

2   M. Head, 'The High Court and the Tampa refugees: a critical examination of *Vadarlis v Minister for Immigration and Multicultural Affairs*' 11 *Griffith Law Review* (2002) 23.

3   The statistics in this section are sourced from M. Head, 'Refugees, Global Inequality and the Need for a New Concept of Global Citizenship' *Australian International Law Journal* (2002) 57.

4   UNHCR, *Global Trends: Refugees, Asylum-seekers, Returnees, Internally Displaced and Stateless Persons*, July 2007, pp 4–14, <http://www.unhcr.org/statistics/STATISTICS/4676a71d4.pdf> (accessed 17 January 2008).

5   J. Harding, *The Unwanted: Refugees at the Rich Man's Gate*, Profile Books, London, 2000.

6   T. Kevin, A certain maritime incident: the sinking of SIEV X, Scribe Publications, Carlton North, 2004.

7   E. Feller, 'The Convention at 50: The Way Ahead for Refugee Protection' 10 *Forced Migration Review* (2001) 6 at 7.

8   The Norwegian government awarded Rinnan the Order of St Olaf, First Class. See D. Marr, 'Arne Rinnan, a man who's not like us', *Sydney Morning Herald*, 22 December 2001, p 20.

9   *Vadarlis v MIMA and Ors* M93/2001 at <http://www.austlii.edu.au/au/other/hca/transcripts/2001/M93/2.html> (accessed 30 November 2001).

10   See M. Seccombe, 'Detainees for succour: Nauru to get $10 m more', *Sydney Morning Herald*, 12 December 2001, p 1.

11   *Ruddock v Vadarlis* [2001] FCA 1329 (18 September 2001).

12   *Victorian Civil Liberties Council Incorporated v Minister for Immigration and Multicultural Affairs* [2001] FCA 1297 (North J, 11 September 2001).

13   *Migration Act 1958* (Cth) ss189 and 245.

14   Judgment of North J at para 35.

15   *Vadarlis v MIMA & Ors* M93/2001.

16   *Border Protection (Validation and Enforcement Powers) Act 2001*, Part 2
ss6 and 7.

17   *Migration Amendment (Excision from Migration Zone) (Consequential
Provisions) Act 2001*, s198A(2).

18   Senate Select Committee, *A Certain Maritime Incident*, Parliament of
Australia, 2002, <http://www.aph.gov.au/Senate/Committee/maritime_
incident_ctte/report/index.htm>. See also M. Head, 'Australian election:
The Howard government's big lie unravels', *World Socialist Web Site*,
<http://www.wsws.org/articles/2001/nov2001/refu-n10.shtml>.

19   Department of Immigration and Multicultural Affairs, *Fact Sheet 1:
Immigration – The Background*, 23 June 2000, p 1.

20   Commonwealth Parliamentary Debates, House of Representatives, volume
1, p 5153, 25 September 1901, extracted in B. McKinlay, *A Documentary
History of the Australian Labor Movement, 1850–1975*, Drummond
Publishing, Melbourne, 1979, p 28.

21   D. North, *Capital, Labor and the Nation-State*, Labor Publications,
Detroit, 1992, p 1.

22   UICIFD Briefing No. 1: Debt Forgiveness, 20 January 2006, <http://www.
uiowa.edu/ifdebook/briefings/docs/forgiveness.shtml> (accessed 23 April
2008).

23   *Al-Kateb v Godwin* [2004] HCA 37 (6 August 2004).

24   *Minister for Immigration and Multicultural and Indigenous Affairs v Al
Khafaji* [2004] HCA 38 (6 August 2004).

25   *Behrooz v Secretary of the Department of Immigration and Multicultural
and Indigenous Affairs* [2004] HCA 36 (6 August 2004).

26   After a brief review, following the High Court decisions, the Immigration
Minister used her discretionary power under the *Migration Act* to grant
Mr Al-Kateb and Mr Al Khafaji bridging visas, giving them temporary
permission to live in Australia. However, the claims of 13 others, including
an asylum seeker who had been held in detention for six years, were
rejected. See M. Shaw, 'Stateless detainees get bridging visas in review', *The
Age*, 1 September 2004, p 7. See also Parliamentary Library, Research Brief
1, 2004–05, 'The High Court and indefinite detention: towards a national
bill of rights?' <http://www.aph.gov.au/library/pubs/RB/2004-05/05rb01.
htm> (accessed 14 January 2005).

27   In *Minister for Immigration and Multicultural Affairs and Indigenous
Affairs v Al Masri* (2003) 126 FCR 54, the Full Federal Court held that
the continued detention of an unlawful non-citizen was unlawful where
that person had requested removal from Australia, but there was no
real likelihood or prospect of that person's removal in the reasonably
foreseeable future.

28   [2004] HCA 37 at [148].

29   Ibid at [133].

30   Per Kirby J, [2004] HCA 36 at [96].

31   Ibid at [97].

32   501 U.S. 294 (1991).

33   *See media release, 2 July 2007, 'End of a chapter: Ombudsman releases
final immigration reports' <http://www.comb.gov.au/commonwealth/*

publish.nsf/Content/mediarelease_2007_07>.

34 J. Hathaway, *The Law of Refugee Status*, Butterworths, Toronto, 1991, pp 10–11.

35 Per Gummow J in *Minister for Immigration and Multicultural Affairs v Ibrahim* (2000) 175 ALR 585 at [137].

36 M. Crock, *Immigration and Refugee Law in Australia*, Federation Press, Sydney, 1998, p 32.

37 T. O'Loughlin and C. Skehan, 'Reith blasts court as new boat arrives', *Sydney Morning Herald*, 17 September 2001.

38 'Minister claims link between boatpeople and terrorists', *Sydney Morning Herald*, 18 September 2001.

39 J. Hathaway, 'Can International Refugee Law be Made Relevant Again?', in J. Hathaway (ed), *Reconceiving International Refugee Law*, Marinus Nijhoff Publishers, The Hague, 1997, p xxix.

40 G. Van Kessel, 'Global Migration and Asylum' 10 *Forced Migration Review* (2001) 10.

41 A. Dummett and A. Nicol, *Subjects, Citizens, Aliens and Others – Nationality and Immigration Law*, Weidenfeld and Nicholsen, London, 1990, p 13.

42 *Lim v Minister for Immigration, Local Government and Ethnic Affairs* (1992) 176 CLR 1.

43 Dummett and Nicol, pp 11–12.

44 Ibid, p 13.

Chapter 20

1 R. Norman, *Ethics, Killing and War*, Cambridge University Press, 1995, p 117.

2 Ibid, p 195.

3 Ibid, p 120.

4 M. Walzer, *Just and Unjust Wars*, Harmondsworth, 1980.

5 Norman, pp 128–29.

6 M. Eburn and R. Hayes, *Criminal Law And Procedure in New South Wales*, LexisNexis Butterworths, Sydney, 2002, p 354.

7 As explained by Mark Marien, in a summary of recent amendments to the NSW *Crimes Act*, prior to the enactment of the *Crimes Amendment (Self-Defence) Act* 2001 (NSW) (the Act), the law relating to self-defence in NSW was based on common law along with legislation relating to home invasions and workplace property damage, and centred on the right to repel an unlawful attack. The case of *Zecevic v DPP* (Vic) (1987) 162 CLR 645 was taken to have established the legitimacy of defensive action where the defendant believed on reasonable grounds that the resort to force was necessary to protect themselves and where the level of force the defendant believed was necessary was reasonable in the circumstances – as judged by the standards of a hypothetical reasonable person. As Marien notes, 'the common law ... under *Zecevic* insisted on some objective danger existing before self-defence could apply'. The new legislation applicable from February 2002 'removed the objective element of the test' such that 'a person who honestly thought they were in danger, even if they were wrong about that perception, may be able to rely upon self-defence for

their actions'. The person's actions are still required to be reasonable, but 'reasonable ... in the circumstances as he or she perceives them' rather than as a hypothetical reasonable person would be expected to perceive them. The Act still excludes self-defence where the defendant 'intentionally or recklessly inflicts death for the purpose of protecting property or preventing a criminal trespass', and it 'reduces murder to manslaughter in the case of excessive self-defence ... where the defendant uses force that inflicts death which is not a reasonable response in the circumstances, but where [they] believed the conduct was necessary to defend' themselves or another person 'or for preventing or terminating unlawful deprivation of liberty'. M. Marien, 'Recently Introduced Amendments to the *Crimes Act* and other reforms', 16 March 2002, Lawlink NSW, <_http://www.lawlink. nsw.gov.au/lawlink/clrd/ll_clrd.nsf/pages/CLRD_recently_intro_amend_ crimesact> (accessed 29 April 2008).

8   See A. Norrie, *Crime, Reason and History*, Butterworths, London, 2001.
9   R. White and S. Perrone, *Crime and Social Control*, 2nd edition, Oxford University Press, Melbourne, 2005, p 121.
10   Eburn and Hayes, pp 101–06.
11   Ibid, pp 322–41.
12   Norman, p 133.
13   Ibid, p 135.
14   Ibid, p 136.
15   Ibid, p 135.
16   P. Singer, *One World: The Ethics of Globalisation*, Text Publishing, Melbourne, 2002, p 135.
17   Ibid, p 137.
18   Norman, pp 159–63.
19   Ibid, p 202. In all, 200 000 Iraqis, civilians and soldiers, were killed in this war.
20   Eburn and Hayes, pp 399–416.
21   Ibid, pp 121–26.
22   Ibid, pp 126–27.
23   Norman, p 202.
24   M. Shaw, *International Law*, 5th edition, Cambridge University Press, Cambridge, 2003, p 1014.
25   Ibid.
26   Ibid, p 1017.
27   Ibid, p 1018.
28   Ibid, pp 1024–25.
29   Norman, p 158.
30   Ibid.
31   Shaw, p 1031.
32   Ibid.
33   A. Cohen, 'Proportionality in the Modern Law of War', BESA Centre, Perspectives Paper 20, 15 August 2006.
34   Shaw, p 1063.
35   Cohen, p 2.
36   Ibid.
37   See R. Piotrowicz and S. Kayr, *Human Rights in International and Australian Law*, Butterworths, Sydney, 2000, ch 9.

38 G.P. Fletcher and J.D. Ohlin, 'Reclaiming Fundamental Principles of Criminal Law in the Darfur Case', *Journal of International Criminal Justice*, 2005 3(3):539-561; doi:10.1093/jicj/mqi049, Oxford University Press, 2005, p 541.

39 Cohen, pp 4–5.

40 Fletcher and Ohlin, p 18.

41 Ibid, p 143.

42 A. Broinowski and J. Wilkinson, *The Third Try*, Scribe, Melbourne, 2005, pp 63–64.

43 Ibid, p 64.

44 Singer, p 147.

45 'A More Secure World: Our Shared Responsibility', Report of the Secretary-General's High-level Panel on Threats, Challenges and Change, < www.un.org/secureworld (accessed 30 April 2008). See also Broinowski and Wilkinson, ibid, p 230.

46 United Nations Fact Sheet, 2005 World Summit. High-level Plenary Meeting, 14–16 September 2005.

47 R2P Excerpt from Outcome Document of the High-level Plenary Meeting of the General Assembly in September 2005, sections 138–139.

48 Singer, p 159.

49 Ibid, p 124.

50 Ibid.

51 Ibid, p 125.

52 M. Albert, *Realizing Hope: Life Beyond Capitalism*, Zed Books, London, 2006, p 28.

53 Just because some basic categories of criminal offence and defence in the common law jurisdictions rest on a solid moral foundation, and have been appropriately extended to the international level, this does not mean that other institutions of the criminal justice system of the common law world – in particular its police and prison-based system of criminal law enforcement – have any such solid moral foundation, which would support the creation of similar institutions at the international level.

54 See for example R. Wilkinson, *The Impact of Inequality*, Routledge, London, 2005, chapter 5; I. Kawachi and B. Kennedy, *The Health of Nations*, The New Press, New York, 2006, chapter 6.

55 Albert, p 125.

56 Ibid.

57 Ibid, p 124.

58 White and Perrone, p 42.

59 Ibid.

60 Ibid, p 119

61 Ibid, pp 61–68.

62 See for example A. Davis, *Are Prisons Obsolete?*, Seven Stories Press, New York, 2003; D. Brown and M. Wilkie (eds), *Prisoners As Citizens*, Federation Press, Sydney, 2002.

63 Albert, p 28.

64 Singer, pp 159–160.

65 H. Patomaki and T. Teivainen, *A Possible World: Democratic Transformation of Global Institutions*, Zed Books, London, 2004, p 19.

66 Ibid, pp 20–21.

67   Ibid, p 18.
68   Ibid, p 21.
69   Ibid, p 103.
70   Ibid, pp 20–33.
71   Singer, p 162.
72   Ibid, p 163.
73   J. Galtung , 'Alternative Models for Global Democracy', in B. Holden (ed), *Global Democracy: Key Debates*, Routledge, London, 2000, p 156, quoted by Patomaki and Teivainen, p 32.
74   Ibid.
75   Ibid, p103.
76   See Broinowski and Wilkinson, pp 169–76.
77   Ibid.
78   There have been past attempts to try to come to grips with this issue of corporate regulation within the United Nations organisation. As Patomaki and Teivainen point out, the Economic and Social Council of the UN – consisting of fifty-four members elected for three terms by the General Assembly – was supposed to exercise democratic control of the IMF and World Bank. And in 1974 the ECOSOC established a Commission on Trans-National Corporations (TNC) to develop a code of practice for TNCs as a basis for international legal regulation, and to assist third world countries in their dealing with such TNCs. Ibid, p 33.

INDEX